ASSEMBLER LANGUAGE PROGRAMMING

The IBM System/370 Family

THIRD EDITION
ASSEMBLER LANGUAGE PROGRAMMING

The IBM System/370 Family

GEORGE STRUBLE
WILLAMETTE UNIVERSITY

ADDISON-WESLEY PUBLISHING COMPANY

Reading, Massachusetts ■ Menlo Park, California
London ■ Amsterdam ■ Don Mills, Ontario ■ Sydney

SPONSORING EDITOR
James. T. DeWolf

PRODUCTION MANAGER
Herbert Nolan

PRODUCTION EDITOR
William J. Yskamp

TEXT AND COVER DESIGNER
Maria Bergner Szmauz

COVER ILLUSTRATOR
Tom Norton

ART COORDINATOR
Loretta M. Bailey

MANUFACTURING SUPERVISOR
Hugh J. Crawford

This book is in the Addison-Wesley Series in Computer Science.

Michael A. Harrison
Consulting Editor

Library of Congress Cataloging in Publication Data

Struble, George, 1932–
    Assembler language programming.

    Includes bibliographies and index.
    1. Assembler language (Computer program language)
2. IBM 370 (Computer)—Programming.   I. Title.
QA76.73.A8S87   1984   001.64′24   83-17912
ISBN 0-201-07815-5

Assembler languages occupy a unique place in the computing world. Because most assembler language statements are symbolic of individual machine language instructions, assembler language programmers have the full power of the computer at their disposal in a way that users of other languages do not. Because of the direct relationship between assembler language and machine language, assembler language is used when high efficiency of programs is needed, and especially in areas of application that are so new and amorphous that existing problem-oriented languages are ill-suited for describing the procedures to be followed. Assembler language programming has particular advantages in character and bit-operation tasks.

This is one of the reasons for studying assembler language. Another is that assembler language is a great vehicle for learning the structure and organization of the computer. Beyond that, a study of how to program standard—and unusual—tasks in assembler language gives us new insight into how the computer must do its tasks when we write our programs in higher-level languages such as Pascal and FORTRAN. With that insight, we know what is quick and what is time-consuming, and can make very good guesses at the computer's behavior in somewhat unusual situations. This makes us much more effective as programmers in our higher-level languages.

This text couples the study of assembler language programming and programming techniques to the study of a particular family of computers, which we call the *IBM System/370 family*. This family includes not only the several models of IBM System/370, and their predecessors the IBM System/360 models, but the IBM 4300 series, the IBM 3030 series, and the IBM 3080 series. These computers are all compatible in executing user programs written in assembler language. There are a few differences; almost all of the differences are new features that can be used on newer models and we try to point these out. But we can take the programs written for the IBM System/360 fifteen years ago and run them without change on all of the newer models. This gives us some reason to expect that the assembler language (and machine language) features we learn to use now will still be applicable several years from now.

The structure and organization of the IBM System/370 have become an industry standard, and the same assembler language is also applicable to a number of "plug-compatible" computers produced by other companies, including Amdahl, Cambex, Control Data, IPL Systems, Magnuson, National Advanced Systems (NAS), and Trilogy. This text is therefore also applicable to the use of those computers, though there are some differences in the features used by the operating systems, which we explore in Chapter 17.

Study of assembler language *must,* by the nature of the language, be relative to *some* machine, and some particular machine, at that. The IBM System/370 series is a good choice for two principal reasons: (1) computers of the IBM System/370 family (including its plug-compatible competitors) are in use by the thousands, so thousands of computer users will find a study of the specifics of this computer immediately applicable; (2) the IBM System/370 exemplifies features of many other current computers, so concepts and techniques learned with respect to this computer will be applicable to other computer systems as well.

The aim of this text is therefore to introduce the detailed structure of the IBM System/370 and its instruction repertoire, programming in assembler language for this computer, and techniques useful in the applications of computers, especially those more easily programmed in assembler language than in higher-level languages.

It is assumed that you are already familiar to some extent with programming, probably in FORTRAN or Pascal. The particular language of your previous exposure is unimportant; what matters is experience in analyzing a problem, and in developing an algorithm for a computer solution. Many basic concepts are reviewed or presented in a framework that supports my development of further material, so with a basic background you should find this book suitable for individual study.

The book is intended primarily for use as a class text, in a "second" course in computing (though a teacher who wishes to use the book as an introductory text should be able to do so, with a reasonable amount of supplementary explanation). It may be used in a course in assembler language programming. It may also be used in conjunction with a more general or theoretical text on computer organization or information structures or as a stand-alone text. There is more than enough material for a semester, and sufficient opportunity for an instructor to omit or substitute other material. The text is also flexible in that the order of presentation of material after Chapter 11 can be rearranged at will, and parts of Chapter 12 can be introduced earlier without any difficulties.

The most frustrating problem for teachers—and students—of assembler language for IBM System/370 is that a student must learn a fairly large amount of information before submitting a first lab exercise to the computer. It is a problem inherent in teaching powerful and flexible systems. In this edition we introduce two facilities that make the job easier for the student. One is the ASSIST system, which is designed to be helpful to students with easy input, output, data conversion, linkage, and debugging facilities, and manages also to be significantly more efficient of computer time than the standard OS. Both OS and DOS versions of the ASSIST system are available to educational and commercial computer installations; for product and distribution information, write to

Program Librarian
214 Computer Building
Pennsylvania State University
University Park, Pa. 16802

The second facility new to this edition is CMS (Conversational Monitor System); CMS also is easier to use than the standard batch system, partly because it is interactive, but also because of some of its easy-to-use input, output, and debugging facilities.

Also available (but too new to include in this book) is ASSIST/I, an interactive system that interpretively runs IBM System/370 family programs on a variety of microcomputers and minicomputers. The ASSIST/I system is complete with full-screen editor and interactive debugging; it is available for IBM PC computers with MSDOS, UNIX systems, VAX VMS systems, and a number of other systems. ASSIST/I, or more information about it, is available from

Overbeek Enterprises
P.O. Box 726
Elgin, Ill. 60120

We are not comprehensive in our descriptions of either ASSIST or CMS, but in Chapter 5 we introduce enough information about each so that students can get started on their own programs. The second edition of this text mentioned READATA and PRINT subroutines, and had an appendix on linkage between assembler language and FORTRAN routines. Copies of READATA and PRINT and the appendix are still available from me to instructors.

Chapter 1 introduces the structure of a computer, especially the structures of the IBM System/370 and the ways information is represented in them.

Chapter 2 is an introduction to the machine language of the IBM System/370, and Chapter 3 follows immediately with the introduction of assembler language. Throughout the remainder of the book assembler language is used, though you should understand the machine language produced by the assembler language.

Chapter 4 begins the study of the characteristics and uses of individual IBM System/370 instructions, with the binary integer arithmetic and information move instructions.

Chapter 5 introduces a variety of topics—what they have in common is that they should be sufficient to get you started on the computer. Definition of constants and storage areas, assembler control statements, and register conventions are important here. Chapter 5 also shows how to use ASSIST and CMS.

Chapter 6 consolidates some of the Chapter 5 topics by discussing subroutine linkage in depth and introducing the machine language instructions that perform data conversions. Portions of Chapters 5 and 6 may be omitted or postponed, depending on what facilities are available to you.

Chapter 7 introduces control structures and their implementation in assembler language. Our approach to structured programming is to write Pascal-like pseudo-code structures in a standard form in remarks statements, and then follow the pseudo-code structures quite closely in the assembler language. We show easy and standard ways of implementing the structures through assembler language; the result is quite readable programs, with the added benefit that following the pseudo-code structures yields programs with fewer bugs. Chapter 8 continues with control structures but adds address modification as well.

Chapter 9 concentrates on debugging, showing debugging facilities of the standard system, ASSIST, and CMS. It also includes a discussion of debugging strategies, and some notes on programming methodology that may help minimize the need for debugging.

Chapters 10 and 11 deal with byte (character) and bit operations. In assembler language these functions are simple, direct, and efficient; this is one of the areas in which the power of assembler language, as compared to most other languages, is realized.

Chapter 12 introduces manipulation of data sets, both within a program by means of the input and output macros, and external to the program by means of job control statements. Basics of the OS operating systems are illustrated and explained.

Chapters 13 and 14 introduce two other modes of arithmetic available in the IBM System/370: floating point and decimal. These chapters should help you to understand what your programs written in higher-level languages do.

Chapter 15 describes five sophisticated and powerful instructions: Translate, Translate and Test, Edit, Edit and Mark, and Execute; these instructions are typical of efforts by computer manufacturers to extend the standard instruction repertoire.

Chapter 16 introduces the facility for defining macros in assembler language. This facility is really powerful, and probably the most intellectually exciting in the book.

Chapter 17 introduces virtual storage concepts, program status word formats and manipulation, input and output instructions and channel programming, interrupt handling and the storage protection system—the pieces of computer structure that are used by operating systems programmers, not applications programmers. The chapter is intended as an introductory survey to give the reader some understanding of a part of the computer structure used only implicitly by applications programs; even a little understanding can relieve anxiety and promote more efficient use of the facilities of the operating system.

An important feature of the book is that it discusses a number of common information processing problems, introduces significant computing techniques, and illustrates implementation of these techniques in assembler language. Thus while you are learning to handle certain features of the IBM System/370, you are also learning valuable techniques that are useful in many situations. Among the techniques discussed are generation of pseudo-random numbers, operations on linked lists, binary search, scatter storage and hashing methods, and a sort–merge algorithm.

This book, then, describes thoroughly the instruction repertoire usable by applications programmers of the IBM System/370. Functions reserved to the operating system are introduced, because an applications programmer needs some understanding of what lies behind supervisor functions, and because budding systems programmers must start somewhere too. However, the functions used only in supervisor state are treated in much less detail than the others, and some of the more specialized are not even mentioned. Assembler language is introduced and used extensively, but several advanced features of the assembler language are not mentioned. Instructions for use of facilities of the operating system are even less complete; users must learn more details from appropriate IBM manuals and must get information on the configuration in use at their own computing centers. I have tried to follow the terminology of IBM manuals to facilitate transition from this book to the manuals. It will be helpful if a good set of manuals is available to you for reference while you are studying this text.

I would like to express my deep appreciation to the many people who contributed to the development of both the original and this new edition. Most of the material, of course, is derived from various IBM manuals; the IBM Corporation has been generous in allowing me to use excerpts from the manuals listed in the bibliographies at the end of each chapter, and individuals within IBM have been encouraging and helpful in their explanations of further points. Robert Heilman, John MacDonald, Thom Lane, Michael

Harrison, Tim Hagen, Norman Beck, Sally Browning, Gordon Ashby, Kevin McCoy, Ed Rittenhouse, Jerzy Wilczinski, Darrell Jones, and Gary Bello made valuable suggestions and criticisms. Sharon Burrowes, Jenny Brown, Barbara Korando, and my daughters Jennifer and Laura did a masterful job of typing the manuscript in its several editions.

Finally, I wish to acknowledge the contributions of users of the book who have helped to debug and strengthen the ideas and presentation as they endeavored to learn about assembler language and the IBM System/360 and 370 from preliminary versions and the first edition of this book.

Salem, Oregon   G.W.S
March 1984

CONTENTS

CHAPTER 3

INTRODUCTION TO ASSEMBLER LANGUAGE

CHAPTER 4

INFORMATION MOVE AND BINARY INTEGER ARITHMETIC

CHAPTER 5

WRITING A COMPLETE PROGRAM

CHAPTER 6

CONVERSIONS AND SUBROUTINES

CHAPTER 7

ELEMENTARY CONTROL STRUCTURES

CHAPTER 8

LOOPING AND ADDRESS MODIFICATION

CHAPTER 9

DEBUGGING

CHAPTER 10

CHARACTER OR BYTE OPERATIONS

CHAPTER 11

BIT OPERATIONS

CHAPTER 15

TRANSLATE, EDIT, AND EXECUTE INSTRUCTIONS

CHAPTER 16

MACRO DEFINITION AND CONDITIONAL ASSEMBLY

CHAPTER 17

SYSTEM CONTROL FUNCTIONS

INTRODUCTION TO COMPUTER STRUCTURE: THE IBM SYSTEM/370

This chapter introduces the structure of a stored-program digital computer. Because this book is about programming, the structure is described as it appears to a programmer, not to an electronic engineer or a space layout designer. The first section introduces number systems, especially the binary system, used internally in many computers, and the hexadecimal system, used for description of contents of the IBM System/370. Section 1.2 contains a short analysis of the functional subsystems of a computer. Sections 1.1 and 1.2 will be review for many readers. They may be skimmed; their value lies mainly in the introduction of terms and an orientation to the approach taken in this text.

Section 1.3 is a survey of the structure of the IBM System/370; it attempts to show the overall pattern into which details will be fitted in the remainder of the book. Section 1.4 begins the actual detailed presentation of the IBM System/370 by discussing the representations of various types of information; this section should be read for content.

1.1 Decimal, Binary, and Hexadecimal Numbers

As a student of the IBM System/370, you must understand three number systems—the decimal, binary, and hexadecimal systems. You must know the nature and advantages of each, how to convert quantities from one representation to another, and how to do arithmetic in each. Skill comes slowly and is developed only through practice. But first must come understanding of the nature and processes of the systems. Fortunately, the three systems can be presented as three instances of a central idea, the idea of positional representation.

POSITIONAL REPRESENTATIONS

A *positional representation* of a number is a representation by which the position of each digit gives its value, or more precisely, gives the power of some *radix* by which it is multiplied. Our usual representation of numbers, which we call decimal, is a positional representation with radix 10. In the number 379, for example, the position of the three digits in the representation determines their value:

$$379 = 3 \times 10^2 + 7 \times 10^1 + 9 \times 10^0$$
$$= \quad 300 \quad + \quad 70 \quad + \quad 9$$

The same digits arranged differently represent a different number; we recognize the digit pattern 793 to represent a number different from 379.

By contrast, the roman system of number representation is *not* a positional representation. The numeral X means ten regardless of its position in the representation, though whether the ten is to be subtracted or added depends on whether or not the X precedes C or L.

The binary representation of numbers is a positional representation using 2 as a radix. We call numbers expressed in this form *binary numbers*. For example, the binary number 101011 has the meaning

$$101011 = 1 \times 2^5 + 0 \times 2^4 + 1 \times 2^3 + 0 \times 2^2 + 1 \times 2^1 + 1 \times 2^0$$
$$= \quad 32 \quad\quad\quad + \quad 8 \quad\quad\quad + \quad 2 \quad + \quad 1$$
$$= 43$$

In any positional representation system, the set of digits required runs from zero up to a digit representing the number that is one less than the radix. Therefore in the decimal system we need ten different digits 0–9. In the binary system only two different digits are required—0 and 1. It is natural for computers to use binary representations, because most of its components are two-state devices whose two states are easily associated with the digits 0 and 1.

ARITHMETIC

Addition of two numbers is performed according to the same rules, regardless of the radix of the representation. A pair of digits in corresponding positions of two numbers, and possibly a carry from the previous pair, are added, with the following results.

1. If the sum is less than the radix, it is expressed as a single digit, and there is a 0 carry.

2. If the sum is equal to or greater than the radix, it is reduced by the radix to yield a digit of the result, but a 1 is carried to be added with the next digit.

Put into this context, addition of the decimal numbers 273 and 465 is carried out from right to left as follows:

$$
\begin{array}{c}
3 \\
\underline{5,} \\
8
\end{array}
\quad \text{then}
\begin{array}{c}
7 \\
\underline{6} \\
3 \text{ with 1 carry,}
\end{array}
\qquad\qquad \text{then}
\begin{array}{c}
2 \\
4 \\
\underline{+\,1} \text{ carry,} \\
7
\end{array}
$$

which we normally write

$$
\begin{array}{c}
273 \\
\underline{465} \\
738
\end{array}
$$

With binary numbers, the addition table is especially simple:

$$
\begin{array}{cccc}
0 & 0 & 1 & 1 \\
\underline{+\,0} & \underline{+\,1} & \underline{+\,0} & \underline{+\,1} \\
0 & 1 & 1 & 0 \text{ with 1 carry}
\end{array}
$$

A carry, of course, adds another 1 to the sum. Addition of the binary numbers 10110 and 10011 is carried out, according to our rules, as follows:

$$
\begin{array}{cccc}
0 & 1 & 1 & 0 \\
\underline{+\,1} & \underline{+\,1} & \underline{+\,0} & \underline{+\,0} \\
1 & 0 \text{ with 1 carry} & \underline{+\,1} \text{ carry} & \underline{+\,1} \text{ carry} \\
& & 0 \text{ with 1 carry} & 1 \text{ no carry}
\end{array}
$$

$$
\begin{array}{cc}
1 & (0) \\
\underline{+\,1} & (0) \\
0 \text{ with 1 carry} & \underline{+\,1} \text{ carry} \\
& 1
\end{array}
$$

Collecting and writing in the usual way,

$$
\begin{array}{c}
10110 \\
\underline{10011} \\
101001
\end{array}
$$

Subtraction is the obvious converse process; if borrowing is necessary, a 1 borrowed from the next position has the value of the radix when used in the current position. For example, the difference of two binary numbers 101001 (decimal 41) and 1100 (decimal 12) is

$$
\begin{array}{c}
101001 \\
\underline{-\,1100} \\
11101 = \text{decimal 29}
\end{array}
$$

Multiplication of binary numbers is performed in essentially the same manner as multiplication of decimal numbers, but is much easier because the product of a digit by the multiplicand is either the multiplicand itself (1 × the multiplicand) or zero (0 × the multiplicand). For example, the product of 1101 (decimal 13) and 101 (decimal 5) is

$$
\begin{array}{r}
1101 \\
101 \\
\hline
1101 \\
0000 \\
1101 \\
\hline
1000001 = \text{decimal } 65
\end{array}
$$

Division of binary numbers is also easier than division of decimal numbers, because each digit of the quotient is either 1 or 0 and it is easy to tell which, by mere comparison. The quotient of 10011001 (decimal 153) divided by 1011 (decimal 11) is found to be

$$
\begin{array}{r}
1101 = \text{decimal } 13 \\
1011\overline{)10011001} \\
1011 \\
\hline
10000 \\
1011 \\
\hline
10101 \\
1011 \\
\hline
1010 = \text{decimal } 10
\end{array}
$$

These examples of binary arithmetic are provided for two reasons. The first is to show that arithmetic in any positional representation system is carried out according to the same rules that govern decimal arithmetic. Only the addition and multiplication tables are different, and different only in the digit symbols used and the carries generated. The second reason is that as a student of a binary computer such as the IBM System/370, you may need to do some binary arithmetic on occasion; because binary arithmetic is actually *easier* than decimal arithmetic, you should not panic at the prospect.

CONVERSIONS BETWEEN DECIMAL AND BINARY

The example showed how the definition of the positional representation of binary numbers can be used to help us find the decimal representation of a binary number. Each binary digit corresponds to a certain power of 2, depending on its position; these powers of 2, or rather, those corresponding to 1's in the binary number, are added to find the decimal equivalent. There are easier and more efficient conversion techniques, however. One can regard a number expressed in a positional representation as a polynomial in the radix, where the digits of the number are the coefficients of the polynomial. Then one can use the process called *nesting* for evaluation of a polynomial in evaluating, that is converting, the number. The technique of nesting consists of the following steps:

1. Start with the highest-order (leftmost) digit.
2. Multiply by the radix (2).
3. Add the next digit to the right.
4. If there are more digits, return to step 2 and continue; that is, multiply the result of each step by the radix 2, etc.

We illustrate with the binary number 101011,

$$
\begin{array}{ccccc}
① & 2 & 5 & 10 & 21 \\
\times 2 & \times 2 & \times 2 & \times 2 & \times 2 \\
\hline
2 & 4 & 10 & 20 & 42 \\
+⓪ & +① & +⓪ & +① & +① \\
\hline
2 & 5 & 10 & 21 & 43
\end{array}
$$

where the binary digits are circled and the decimal equivalent derived is 43, as shown earlier. This technique is a simple one to apply, and has the advantage that if there are n digits in the binary number, only $n - 1$ multiplications are required, each a multiplication by 2, and $n - 1$ additions. The technique assumes that the arithmetic is done in the number system *to which* the number is being converted—decimal arithmetic in this case.

The same technique is used by computers in converting numbers from decimal to binary. If, for example, each of the digits of the decimal number 347 is coded in binary (0011, 0100, 0111), the conversion of the number 347 to binary follows the scheme above but with 2's replaced by (decimal) 10's and all arithmetic done in binary:

$$
\begin{array}{ll}
\underline{(0011)} & (3) \\
\times\ 1010 & (10) \\
\hline
00110 & \\
0011 & \\
\hline
11110 & \\
{}+\underline{(0100)} & (4) \\
\hline
100010 & \\
\times\ 1010 & \\
\hline
1000100 & \\
100010 & \\
\hline
101010100 & \\
{}+\underline{(0111)} & (7) \\
\hline
101011011 & (347)
\end{array}
$$

In decimal arithmetic, conversion from decimal representation to binary is done by a division process. The decimal number is divided by 2, and the remainder is the units' digit of the number's binary representation. The quotient is divided by 2, and the new remainder is another digit of the binary representation. The process of dividing each new quotient by 2 continues; each remainder is another digit of the binary representation. The process terminates when the quotient is reduced to zero. We illustrate with the conversion of the decimal number 347 to binary:

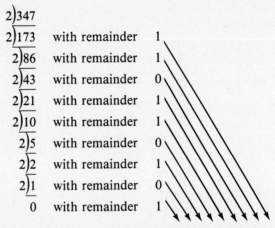

$$2)\overline{347}$$
$$2)\overline{173} \quad \text{with remainder} \quad 1$$
$$2)\overline{86} \quad \text{with remainder} \quad 1$$
$$2)\overline{43} \quad \text{with remainder} \quad 0$$
$$2)\overline{21} \quad \text{with remainder} \quad 1$$
$$2)\overline{10} \quad \text{with remainder} \quad 1$$
$$2)\overline{5} \quad \text{with remainder} \quad 0$$
$$2)\overline{2} \quad \text{with remainder} \quad 1$$
$$2)\overline{1} \quad \text{with remainder} \quad 0$$
$$0 \quad \text{with remainder} \quad 1$$

yielding 1 0 1 0 1 1 0 1 1

The same process, done in binary arithmetic and substituting 1010 (decimal 10) for 2, converts binary numbers to decimal. As an illustration, conversion of 110100111 proceeds as follows:

$$\overbrace{(101010)} \qquad \overbrace{(100)} \qquad \qquad 0$$
$$1010)\overline{110100111} \qquad 1010)\overline{101010} \qquad 1010)\overline{100}$$
$$\underline{1010} \qquad\qquad\quad \underline{1010} \qquad\qquad\qquad \underline{0}$$
$$1100 \qquad\qquad \text{Remainder: } 010 = \text{decimal 2} \quad \text{Remainder: } 100 = \text{decimal 4}$$
$$\underline{1010}$$
$$1011$$
$$\underline{1010}$$

Remainder: 11 = decimal 3

Because the digits are generated in low-to-high-order sequence, the decimal-number equivalent to 110100111 is 423.

HEXADECIMAL REPRESENTATION

It is natural for a computer to deal with numbers expressed in a binary representation, since the electronic elements used are two-state devices. One of the states of each device can be identified with the digit 0, and the other with the digit 1. Only these digits are needed for binary representations. A computer can easily deal with fairly long strings of binary digits, with each digit in the string represented by one electronic element.

It is not natural for us human beings, however, to write, recognize, work with, or remember long strings of digits. We prefer strings of fewer digits, and our minds more easily accept a variety of digits than do computer elements. We sometimes need to show, examine, and work with numbers *as the com-*

FIGURE 1.1 Hexadecimal digits

Hexadecimal digit	Binary equivalent	Decimal equivalent
0	0000	0
1	0001	1
2	0010	2
3	0011	3
4	0100	4
5	0101	5
6	0110	6
7	0111	7
8	1000	8
9	1001	9
A	1010	10
B	1011	11
C	1100	12
D	1101	13
E	1110	14
F	1111	15

puter does, and a shorter representation closely related to binary is helpful. For dealing with System/370 we choose a positional representation with radix 16, called the *hexadecimal representation.* The hexadecimal representation is chosen because 16 is 2^4, and therefore equivalent to combining binary digits in groups of four. There are 16 four-digit binary numbers; the characters we choose to represent them in a hexadecimal representation are 0, 1, . . . , 9, A, B, C, D, E, F, as shown in Fig. 1.1.

CONVERSIONS WITH HEXADECIMAL NUMBERS
Conversions between hexadecimal and binary are very easy; hexadecimal representations were chosen with this in mind. To convert a binary integer to hexadecimal one merely groups its digits into groups of four, starting from the right, and then converts each group to a hexadecimal digit according to Fig. 1.1. For example,

$$101100100011101$$
$$5 \quad 9 \quad 1 \quad D$$

shows that the hexadecimal equivalent of 101100100011101 is 591D. Conversion from hexadecimal to binary is even easier: one merely converts each hexadecimal digit to binary according to Fig. 1.1 and strings the binary digits together. The conversion of the hexadecimal number 6C08 illustrates the process:

6   C   0   8

0110110000001000

These conversion processes can be expressed in terms of the techniques just shown for binary-decimal conversions, and are equivalent to them.

Conversions between decimal and hexadecimal can be done by the techniques just developed for conversions with binary numbers. The number 16 replaces the number 2 where it appears in the descriptions of those techniques. For example, conversion of the hexadecimal number 6C08 to decimal is as follows:

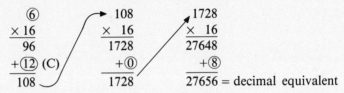

Conversion of the decimal number 17307 to hexadecimal proceeds as shown below:

$$
\begin{array}{r}
1081 \\
16\overline{)17307} \\
16 \\
\hline
130 \\
128 \\
\hline
27 \\
16 \\
\hline
11 = ⑧
\end{array}
\qquad
\begin{array}{r}
67 \\
16\overline{)1081} \\
96 \\
\hline
121 \\
112 \\
\hline
⑨
\end{array}
\qquad
\begin{array}{r}
4 \\
16\overline{)67} \\
64 \\
\hline
③
\end{array}
\qquad
\begin{array}{r}
0 \\
16\overline{)4} \\
0 \\
\hline
④
\end{array}
$$

The hexadecimal equivalent is 439B.

Arithmetic in hexadecimal is a strain on our decimal-oriented minds. We will have occasion to do addition and subtraction of hexadecimal numbers, but very rarely multiplication or division. One adds and subtracts by thinking of the decimal equivalents of each hexadecimal digit, adding or subtracting the decimal equivalents, then reconverting the results. Doing this, digit by digit, involves much less work than a full conversion of the numbers to decimal. The best way to multiply or divide hexadecimal numbers is to convert them to binary first and do the multiplication or division in binary.

Using hexadecimal arithmetic, hexadecimal-to-decimal conversion is done by division (by A = 10), and decimal-to-hexadecimal conversion by multiplication. However, these are recommended only as rather severe mental exercise.

1.2   Subsystems of a Stored-Program Digital Computer

A programmer deals with five major aspects of the modern stored-program digital computer which, for clarity, we will treat as discrete subsystems. They

FIGURE 1.2   Subsystems of a digital computer

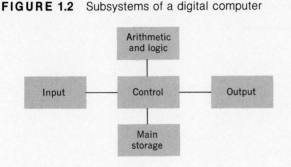

are the *main storage,* an *input subsystem,* an *output subsystem,* an *arithmetic and logic subsystem,* and a *control subsystem.* We can consider these subsystems to be connected as shown in Fig. 1.2. Although this description is a drastic oversimplification (for the actual connections are quite complex), it helps us to understand the function of each subsystem in the computer's structure.

MAIN STORAGE

The *main storage* of a computer, sometimes called its memory, holds information for the job (or jobs) being done by the computer at the moment. The information kept in storage may be of several kinds: programs in machine language that give directions to the computer, input data, constants used in the program, and intermediate and final results.

The main storage of modern computers is composed of elements that accept and hold a magnetic charge. Each element (ferrite core, spot on a chip, etc.) may accept a charge in either of two orientations. These two orientations or states can be interpreted as *on* and *off, yes* or *no, 0* and *1.* The information stored in one element as the choice between the two states is called a *bit,* which is a contraction of *binary digit.* The interpretation as 0 and 1 suggests naturally the representation of quantities as binary numbers, since in a binary representation every digit is 0 or 1. Practically all computers take advantage of this natural binary nature of the storage medium, although some superimpose a decimal structure.

We seldom have use for only one bit of storage, or for a number whose length is one bit. Instead we may wish to use a number equivalent to seven decimal digits, or four alphabetic characters, or an instruction to the computer. Therefore, the one-bit elements that make up the computer's storage are grouped into larger units. In some computers, such as the IBM System/370, the main unit is a *byte,* which is 8 bits. In other computers, the main unit is a *word,* which may be 16, 18, 24, 32, 36, 48, or more bits. In the IBM System/370, the bytes are further grouped into words, four bytes to a word.

FIGURE 1.3   Binary representation of decimal digits

Decimal digit	Binary representation
0	0000
1	0001
2	0010
3	0011
4	0100
5	0101
6	0110
7	0111
8	1000
9	1001

A *binary computer* is a computer in which each number is represented in binary form. In using a binary computer we input quantities in decimal form because we are accustomed to dealing with decimal numbers. The computer converts the input numbers into their binary representations. Similarly, before output the computer can convert binary quantities into decimal equivalents and output the results in decimal form.

In binary computers the words are usually of fixed size. The IBM System/370 is a binary computer, but it can also behave as a decimal computer. In a decimal computer, main storage elements are first grouped in some fashion—usually four bits to a digit (some call a four-bit group a *nibble,* so two nibbles make a byte). Each decimal digit is represented in binary, as shown in Fig. 1.3. Some decimal computers further group these decimal-digit groups into larger groups, again called *words,* of fixed length, for example, ten decimal digits plus sign. Other computers have the ability to handle groups of digits of varying length.

In any computer, units of storage must be identified, so that a program can store information in a particular storage location and retrieve it later from the same location. The locations are given *addresses;* a program retrieves a piece of information in storage by giving the address of the location of the information. The basic groups are numbered, ordinarily from an address of zero; hence the largest address would of course be one less than the number of storage groups in the computer. In a computer with a byte structure like the IBM System/370's, each byte in storage has its individual address; in other computers, with fixed word length, each word has an address.

INPUT

The input subsystem of the computer enables the computer to accept information from the outside world. The information, comprising data and instructions, is keyed in from terminals; read from diskettes, punched cards, magnetic tape, or from specialized input devices; and stored in the computer's main storage.

The device most used for initial introduction of programs and data into a computer is a *computer terminal.* There are many different terminals available; some are video terminals and some are printing terminals, as shown in Figs. 1.4 and 1.5. Some, called *dumb terminals,* merely transmit one character at a time from the terminal to the computer or back to the terminal, and some, called *intelligent terminals,* have processing capabilities in the terminal and can store a number of characters before sending them in a burst to the computer. Intelligent terminals are used most often in specialized data-gathering or transaction-processing applications.

All terminals code the characters to be sent to the computer into binary representations and send electrical impulses corresponding to the binary representation of each character over the transmission line to the computer. The computer uses these electrical impulses to magnetize some of the magnetic storage elements in the computer's main storage, and thus the representation of the characters sent is stored.

Microcomputers are becoming more used as terminals. Microcomputers, perhaps the ultimate in intelligent terminals, can do some of their own processing and store files on their own storage media as well as sending information to a larger computer.

Before the ascendency of terminals and microcomputers, the most widespread vehicle for the initial introduction of programs and data into the computer was the *punched card,* and punched cards still have advantages over other media in some situations. Figure 1.6 shows a punched card. The cards are punched by a person operating a *card punch.* Computers have card readers that sense the holes in the cards and send the information to the computer.

There is quite a variety of more specialized input media. *Magnetic Ink Character Recording* (MICR) is used primarily by banks in processing checks. The *universal bar codes* used primarily as product codes on items sold in grocery stores, are read by a scanner that can transmit the information to a computer. *Optical mark readers* are able to read the positions of pencil marks on forms; optical mark reader forms are handy because information can be recorded by many people with essentially no training and with no equipment other than a pencil. The forms can be gathered, from university preregistration or from exams, for example, and then read by the optical mark reader that is attached to the computer. A still newer technology is the *optical character reader,* which reads either information typed or printed in one of several special fonts, or information printed carefully by hand. Optical character scanners are used in point-of-sale systems in large department stores, in employee time cards systems, and for other applications where it is helpful for both a computer and people to be able to read the same information. All of these specialized input media and devices have their benefits in cutting the cost and increasing the accuracy and speed of data input. Because data input is the most

FIGURE 1.4   A Televideo 920C terminal. (Photograph courtesy of TeleVideo Systems, Inc.)

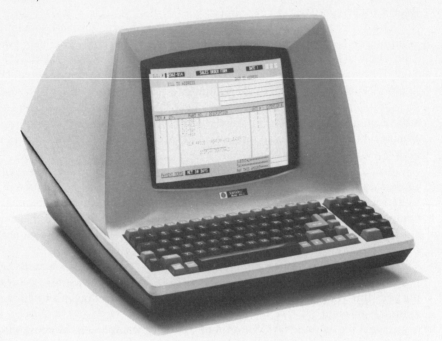

FIGURE 1.5   A DECwriter IV terminal. (Photograph courtesy of Digital Equipment Corporation)

FIGURE 1.6   A punched card

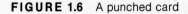

expensive phase of computer use, improvements in its cost-effectiveness are quite significant.

Magnetic tape is an efficient storage medium. The capacity of a reel of tape may be several million characters, and the tape can be written and read rapidly. The speed of tape drive units varies from 30,000 or less to 340,000 characters or more per second during actual information transfer. This speed is achieved partly by the high recording density: a density of 1600 characters per inch of tape is standard, though densities of 800 and 6250 characters per inch are also common. The high density, of course, is another factor contributing to the large capacity of a reel of tape.

Physically, information is recorded on magnetic tape, as shown in Fig. 1.7. The tape unit has sets of *writing heads* that record information by magnetizing spots on the ferrite coating of the tape. *Reading heads* sense the magnetic spots and construct electrical impulses representing the information from the magnetized spots; the impulses can be sent to the main storage subsystem of the computer. The information on a magnetic tape is written in discrete *records,* each consisting of several characters, with an *interrecord gap* between the records. Figure 1.8 shows a magnetic tape unit used by the IBM System/370.

The majority of the data processed by computers is organized sequentially. That is, the program starts at the beginning of the data and proceeds, item by item, to the end. Some computer data, however, possess a more elabo-

FIGURE 1.7   Information recorded on a magnetic tape

FIGURE 1.8 An IBM 3420 magnetic tape unit. (Courtesy of International Business Machines Corporation)

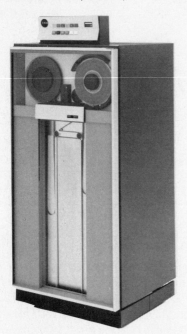

rate organization. If the nature of each record is known, as perhaps in an ordered table, the program may well need information from, say, the 27th record, then the 83rd record, then the 51st. An input device that will permit retrieval of these records without retrieving all records in between is called a *direct access* device.

By far the most extensively used direct access storage is *magnetic disk*. Magnetic disks are packaged in many sizes and have different speeds of access. Some disk storage units contain one or more disks that rotate but cannot be removed from the unit; these are called *fixed-disk* units. Other units accept *disk packs,* which typically consist of 11 disks, mounted on a spindle, with all surfaces except the very top and very bottom available for recording. The unit attached to the computer has magnetic heads aerodynamically suspended very close to the disk surfaces. Figure 1.9 shows a magnetic disk pack, and Fig. 1.10 shows a bank of storage units that uses disk packs. Still other units use *cartridges* that include not only the disks on their spindle but also the disk access arms and the read-write heads in the sealed cartridge. Disk packs and cartridges can hold up to 300 million characters or even more, with average access time to any piece of information about 75 milliseconds.

Smaller computers use smaller and less expensive versions of magnetic disk technology. Some use smaller versions of the cartridges just mentioned. Some use a single-disk cartridge that may hold up to 20 million characters. But

FIGURE 1.9 An IBM 3336 disk pack. (Courtesy of International Business Machines Corporation)

by far the most common are *diskettes,* often called *floppy disks,* or floppies. The diskettes are made in 8-inch and $5\frac{1}{2}$-inch sizes, and newer "microfloppies" are less than 4 inches in diameter. The diskettes themselves are inexpensive and do not need very strict environmental protection. Because the drives that read and write the diskettes are also inexpensive, diskettes are ideal for microcomputers. Some larger computers also have diskette units.

FIGURE 1.10 An IBM 3350 disk storage unit. (Courtesy of International Business Machines Corporation)

The recording technology used in magnetic disks is essentially the same as that used for magnetic tape. The disks are coated with a magnetic oxide, and spots on the disk can be magnetized just as they are on tape. One big advantage of a disk over a tape is that the heads can move to any desired track and be prepared to read or write information there in a fraction of a second, while it could easily take several *minutes* to read selected information from a tape. Magnetic tape once had large advantages of lower cost, greater compactness, and interchangeability among a larger variety of computers. Diskettes, which are even less expensive, more compact, and also interchangeable, are more convenient for relatively small jobs. Diskettes therefore have almost completely superseded cassette tapes for microcomputer use. Larger computers still use magnetic tapes for archival storage and interchange of data between computers, as well as disk storage.

A distinction should be made between devices for *primary input*—the input of data and programs on the first presentation to the computer from the outside world—and devices for what is called *backing store*. Backing store is storage, external to the main storage immediately addressable by the central processing unit of a computer, but yet accessible to and readable only by a computer. A computer writes into the backing store information for later reuse and stores this information (programs, data, intermediate and even final results) for relatively quick retrieval. Backing store is usually composed of direct access devices because retrieval may well be needed in a sequence different from that in which the information was originally written.

Magnetic disk units are good examples of backing store. They are used primarily for temporary storage or for programs or data to which frequent access is required. Magnetic tapes are often used as backing store, but where several kinds of backing store are available, they are used chiefly for storage of information to which frequent access is not necessary.

OUTPUT

The output subsystem enables the computer to give information to the outside world. The information coming from the computer's main storage is written onto output media such as the video screen of a computer terminal, paper, magnetic tape, or magnetic disk. We can distinguish logically the functions of input and output, but the devices are often not separate. The same magnetic tape drives read from and write onto the magnetic tapes, and the same disk drives read from or write onto the magnetic disk packs, cartridges, or diskettes.

Because a computer terminal is intended for interactive use, it must be an output device as well as an input device. Output displayed on a video screen can be transmitted and displayed at speeds up to 960 characters per second, though only 30 (maybe 120) characters per second can be transmitted over telephone lines. Printing terminals are slower because their mechanical functions are necessarily slower than the electronic functions of video screen display. In fact, when a terminal operates in *full duplex* mode, punching a key on the keyboard sends the character to the computer, which immediately returns it to be displayed or printed at the terminal. So the input function incorporates an output action, and the user has the assurance that the character keyed at the keyboard actually was received accurately by the computer.

For the magnetic media of tape and disk, the output data rates are the same as the input rates. Cards are punched by devices separate from card readers, and the output rates are much slower.

Printers attached to computers typically print a line at a time, and can print 1200 or more lines of 132 characters each per minute. Printers provide much of the output that is accessible to human understanding. Other forms of computer output serve primarily to prepare input for some later process in the computer.

Pen-and-ink plotters can be attached to computers to draw graphs and diagrams. It usually takes longer for a plotter to prepare a diagram than it takes a computer printer to print a thousand words; however, a complicated diagram may be well worth many thousand words (and especially numbers).

Special-purpose output devices convert computer output to analog form to control certain machines. These *digital-to-analog converters* are used in computers that control electric power grids, drive machine tools, and perform many other special functions. Such computers usually also accept input through analog-to-digital converters in order to implement feedback from the process being controlled.

ARITHMETIC AND LOGIC

The arithmetic and logic subsystem of the computer contains the circuitry that performs all arithmetic operations, comparisons, and other transformations of data. The operations available are addition, subtraction, multiplication, and division; multiplication is performed by repeated addition, and division by repeated subtraction. Operands can be compared and an indicator set to record the result of the comparison.

More sophisticated computers are capable of more than one kind of number representation, for example integer and *floating-point* (a floating-point number consists of some significant digits and an indicator of the placement of the decimal point), and can deal with various lengths of numbers of each type. The circuitry must be able to perform the arithmetic and comparison operations on numbers expressed in each representation.

Other manipulations that transform data are also performed by the arithmetic and logic section. Many computers have instructions that convert numbers from one representation to another. The circuitry to perform these instructions, as well as shifts and other logical operations described in Chapter 11, is located in the arithmetic and logic section.

Operands for all these operations are taken from the main storage of the computer, and results of the operations are stored again in the main storage.

CONTROL

In the center of Fig. 1.2 is the control subsystem, which controls the activities of each of the other sections. The sequence in which operations are performed is supervised by the control subsystem; this subsystem retrieves instructions from main storage and decodes them for execution. It also takes charge of getting operands needed by the arithmetic and logic or output subsystems from the appropriate locations in main storage, and storing arithmetic results or information from the input subsystem into main storage.

The unit of control in a computer is the *instruction;* a *program* is a set of instructions. An instruction is coded numerically and kept in the computer's main storage. The sequence of operations in retrieving, decoding, and executing instructions can be described as follows.

A computer has an *instruction address register,* which always holds in main storage the address of the next instruction to be executed. Execution of an instruction can be divided into two parts, an *instruction cycle* and an *execution cycle.* During the instruction cycle, the control subsystem retrieves the instruction from the location addressed by the instruction address register, and decodes the instruction preparatory to executing it. During the decoding process, the control subsystem identifies from the *operation code* in the instruction the type of operation to be performed. It decodes the rest of the instruction accordingly and sets up data paths for the execution of the instruction.

During the execution cycle, the operation, such as arithmetic, information move, or the start of an input operation, specified by the instruction is actually performed. The instruction address register is also updated during the execution cycle. Usually it is changed to refer to the instruction immediately following (in main storage) the instruction being executed; some instructions are *branch* instructions in which part of the execution of the instruction itself is to replace the contents of the instruction address register by one of the operands of the instruction.

Instruction and execution cycles alternate in the execution of a program. The instruction and execution cycles for one instruction are followed by instruction and execution cycles for the next instruction, and so on, until the whole program has been executed.

The control, arithmetic and logic, and main storage subsystems are usually housed in the same computer unit, called the *central processing unit,* or CPU; the distinctions made here between the functions are defined for pedagogical reasons, and do not represent a clear separation of circuitry elements.

1.3   Structure of the IBM System/370

Since the IBM System/360 was announced in 1964, there have been many different models. System/370 models had some improved capabilities, and some of these were the first IBM computers to implement virtual storage. Since then, the 3000 series and the 4300 series have continued the product line.

FIGURE 1.11   A configuration of the IBM 4341 system. (Courtesy of International Business Machines Corporation)

Though each model within each series is somewhat different in internal hardware from the others, all of these models are compatible at the user program level. Programs written in assembler language as well as in higher-level languages can be run on all models from smallest to largest, oldest to newest. There are a few exceptions, especially to the ability to run programs written for a newer model on an older one, because some instructions have been added to the repertoire in later models. There have also been a few models, most notably the 360/20, 370/25, and 360/44, that lie outside the compatible family of computers. Features that are not fully compatible will be highlighted as they are introduced; there are not many.

In recent years other computer manufacturers have introduced computers that are compatible with this family of IBM computer systems. Among them are Amdahl, Cambex, Control Data, Magnuson, and National Advanced Systems (NAS). Their models are not described here, but if you are using one of these computers, the information developed here should be applicable. In IBM and non-IBM models, the major differences in instructions are in the instructions that are reserved for the use of the operating systems ("privileged" instructions).

MAIN STORAGE AND ARITHMETIC

The main storage of the IBM System/370 is organized into *bytes,* each of which consists of eight bits. We will refer to either an eight-bit quantity or the storage required to hold it as a byte—the meaning in each case should be clear from the context. Each byte of storage has an address, and the capacity of main storage ranges from 8192 bytes in the smaller and older models to over 16 million bytes in some larger ones. For arithmetic and logical operations, the bytes in turn are grouped into *words* of four bytes each, *half-words* of two bytes each, and *double words* of eight bytes each. This grouping will be discussed in more detail in later sections.

In addition to the main storage, there is a set of 16 general-purpose *registers,* each one word (4 bytes or 32 bits) long. These registers are used in specifying addresses of operands and in performing binary integer arithmetic and most logical operations. Their addresses are 0 to 15. Still another set of four registers is used in floating-point arithmetic. These four registers, of 64 bits each, have addresses 0, 2, 4, and 6. The context of an address in an instruction determines whether the address refers to a floating-point register, a general register, or a location in main storage. Implicit in the operation code for each instruction are the addressing characteristics of each of its operands.

In models newer than System/360, there is a set of 16 *control registers* that hold parameters of the current program and status of the operating system. These registers are used almost exclusively by the operating system.

In the IBM System/370, arithmetic can be performed on numbers in three different representations. A set of instructions is provided for each of the three types, and the number representation assumed by each instruction is implicit in the operation code of the instruction. The first representation is *binary integer.* Numbers are represented in binary form, with lengths of 16 and 32 bits. Specific details of representation and the arithmetic instructions that operate on the numbers will be discussed in Section 1.4 and in Chapter 4. A second representation is called *floating point.* Exponents and fractions are both represented in binary, sharing 32-bit, 64-bit, or 128-bit storage areas. The use of floating-point numbers is familiar to FORTRAN, PL/1, BASIC, or Pascal programmers; more details about floating-point number representation and System/370 instructions for manipulating floating-point numbers are given in Chapter 13. The third number representation is *decimal.* Each decimal digit can be represented in four bits, so two decimal digits can be packed into one byte. Decimal arithmetic can be performed on numbers varying in length from 1 to 16 bytes, with one half-byte always reserved for the representation of the sign. This mode of arithmetic is discussed in greater detail in Chapter 14.

In addition to the three representations of data for which arithmetic instructions are furnished, there are other representations that permit nonarithmetic manipulations. Data in character form are represented one character to a byte; the characters can be tested, moved, and changed in main storage. Certain data are best represented by single bits, which can efficiently record yes or no, 1 or 0, present or absent, and so on. Logical and shift instructions (discussed in Chapter 11) operate on information in bit form.

Each IBM System/370 computer has one or more input and output *channels,* and several devices may be attached to each channel. A channel is the path between the processor and the devices; it transmits the input and output

FIGURE 1.12 An input–output configuration

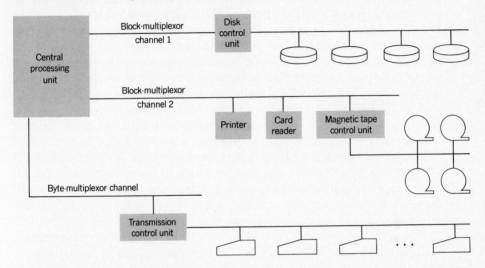

data; sends orders to the devices instructing them what to do, and reports the status of the devices and their operations to the processor. Each channel has some of the characteristics of a computer, as you will see in Chapter 17, in which we explore the functioning of channels and devices in more detail. There are two types of channels, *byte-multiplexor* and *block-multiplexor* channels. A byte-multiplexor channel permits several slow-speed devices to be active at the same time. The transmissions are mingled (multiplexed), and each byte to or from one device may be followed in the channel by a byte to or from one of the other devices. The block-multiplexor channel, on the other hand, is for higher-speed devices such as magnetic tape and disk units. In these devices the data transmission speed is higher and a physical block of data must be transmitted without interruption.

A computer may have one or more byte-multiplexor channels and may have several block-multiplexor channels. Older models of the family included *selector* channels instead of block-multiplexor channels; the selector channels were less capable of controlling several devices concurrently. A typical configuration of channels and devices is shown in Fig. 1.12.

OPERATING SYSTEM

The *operating system* of System/370 is a series of programs designed to aid and supervise both the internal activities of the computer and its input and output. Such an operating system has the twofold purpose of helping users utilize the complex and sophisticated features of the hardware and making such use efficient by means of careful planning and overlapping of activities. To ensure efficient computer use, the operating system provides for a high degree of concurrency: several input and output operations can be performed at the same time that instructions are being executed in the central processing unit.

For this concurrency to be possible, the computer must have some fairly sophisticated features, and the operating system makes use of these features in ways that individual programs would find terribly burdensome. Thus the operating system provides services in a comprehensive and consistent manner, relieving the individual programmer of many laborious chores.

Concurrency of operations occurs when several users' jobs are active at the same time. The jobs take turns at execution, but the operating system also enables a job to run when others are waiting for terminal input, waiting for completion of output to a terminal, waiting for completion of a disk input or output operation, etc. Further concurrency, of the operations for one user, is accomplished by *buffering* input and output, as will be described in Chapter 12. The operating system manages the sharing of resources, including CPU time, input and output devices, main storage space, and disk space. While doing so, it must protect the data and program of each job from destruction, intentional or inadvertent, by another job.

One of the hardware features that helps the *supervisor* (part of the operating system) perform its functions is the *privileged* nature of certain instructions. When the computer is running, it may be in one of two states: the problem state and the supervisor state. The computer is in the problem state when a user's program is running; it is in the supervisor state only when the supervisor is running. Input and output instructions, among others, are *privileged,* which means they can be executed only when the computer is in the supervisor state. Therefore, a user's program *must ask* the supervisor to do any input and output required.

The supervisor can also make use of the *interrupt* feature of System/370. Certain conditions, such as errors, requests from the user's program, and input or output terminations, can cause interruptions of the user's program and transfer of control to the supervisor. The supervisor may start new input or output transmission, honor requests for service by the user's program, analyze and correct errors—any or all of these—before returning control to the user's program. The interrupt feature thus allows the supervisor to operate input and output devices in a sophisticated and efficient manner and to retain firm control over the activities of the user's program.

An important part of the IBM System/370 computer is the *program status word,* PSW for short. The program status word is 64 bits long. It contains much important information about the status of the program currently being run, including the instruction address register. Also included are indicators for problem or supervisor state, bits specifying whether certain conditions should cause interrupt, a key designating which areas of main storage are available to the program, and other items of information. The supervisor can store a program status word and load a new one when the computer is in the supervisor state.

As you see, the supervisor is a ubiquitous part of the IBM System/370 computing system. You will be learning about various aspects of it throughout this book.

1.4   Representation of Information

STORAGE STRUCTURE

The IBM System/370 is basically a binary computer, in which numbers, including addresses, are represented in binary form. The *bit* is the smallest unit of information and represents a simple choice—0 or 1. Bits are grouped into bytes of eight bits each; in the IBM System/370 the byte is the smallest *addressable* unit of information—the smallest unit that has a distinct address. Because a byte is eight bits long, it can hold 2^8 or 256 different patterns of information or numbers—the binary forms run from 00000000 to 11111111. Because a byte is eight bits long, it holds exactly two hexadecimal digits. This is the reason for preferring the hexadecimal system for description of IBM System/370 contents.

Addresses in System/370 are usually 24-bit numbers, though in some modes in newer models 31-bit addresses can be used. We will stay with 24-bit addresses; the user is limited to these. Addresses may therefore be 0 to $2^{24} - 1$, or 16,777,215. These are *virtual addresses;* a program uses the portion of *virtual storage* (0 to 16,777,215) allocated to that program by the operating system, and the operating system manages the correspondence between the allocation given (*user's virtual space*) and the actual main storage space assigned. Actual main storage space available may be very much less than 2^{24} bytes; we will explore virtual storage hardware and management techniques in Chapter 17. Until then, we need not be concerned with virtual versus actual storage; we use the allocated storage and let the operating system juggle as necessary. Older models do not have virtual storage, but generally the way their users have treated their main storage is (at least for programs not requiring huge space allocation) exactly the way we now treat our virtual storage allocation.

The bytes are also grouped to form words, each of which is four bytes in length. A word in storage is addressed by its *highest-order* byte—that is, the byte holding the most significant part of a number, or the leftmost segment, as one would ordinarily picture the arrangement of storage. A word (sometimes called a *full word* to ensure clarity or to distinguish it from a half-word or a double word) normally begins on a word *boundary;* that is, its address must be divisible by 4. (To state the rule differently, the *lowest-order* two bits of its address expressed in binary must be 0's.) Figure 1.13 shows a full word in stor-

FIGURE 1.13   A full word in storage

Location	19423	19424	19425	19426	19427	19428
Contents	01101101	10011010	00100111	00111100	11010100	11110010

Full word

age, four bytes long, beginning with the byte addressed (decimal) 19424. Note that 19424, divisible by 4, is a word boundary.

Similarly, a *half-word* is a group of two bytes or 16 bits. In storage it is usually located at a half-word boundary; that is, its address must be divisible by 2. A *double word* is a group of eight bytes. In main storage it is normally located at a double-word boundary; that is, its address must be divisible by 8.

Privileged instructions require operands to be on their proper (half-word, full-word, or double-word) boundaries. Newer models have the *byte-oriented-operand* feature, which allows operands for ordinary (nonprivileged) instructions to disregard boundary requirements. Even in these models, alignment of operands to the proper boundaries is preferred because it permits slightly faster execution of instructions. The assembler naturally puts most operands on their preferred boundaries anyway, and we will follow good practice and show operands on the preferred boundaries.

In addition to the main storage, there are three sets of registers in the IBM System/370. There are 16 general registers, each a full word in length, with addresses 0 to 15, or 0000 to 1111 in binary. Registers are *not* part of the main core storage, but independent units with much faster access. There is no ambiguity as to whether a given address refers to a register or to a location in main storage because only certain portions of computer instructions contain register addresses, whereas other portions are used to define main storage locations of operands. The 16 general registers are used to hold operands and results of all binary integer arithmetic operations, to specify addresses in main storage, and for many other purposes.

The second set consists of four *floating-point registers*. Each is 64 bits long because floating-point numbers may be 32 or 64 bits long. The addresses of the registers are 0, 2, 4, and 6. Some instructions address floating-point registers, and others address general registers; the context of a register address determines whether a general or floating-point register will be used, and there can be no ambiguity. All floating-point computations are performed in the floating-point registers.

The third set of registers consists of 16 *control registers*. These contain parameters that control operation of the computer and are not used directly by a user's program. The instructions that work with control registers are almost all privileged instructions. (Further discussion of the control registers is deferred until Chapter 17.)

REPRESENTATION OF BINARY INTEGERS

A binary integer is usually represented in a full word of 32 bits. For purposes of specifying bits within a word, we number the bit positions from 0 through 31, left to right, as shown in Fig. 1.14. In binary integers, bit position 0 holds

FIGURE 1.14   The binary integer equivalent to 26 (decimal)

Bits   0 0 0 0 0 0 0 0 0 0 0 0 0 0 0 0 0 0 0 0 0 0 0 0 0 0 0 1 1 0 1 0
Bit positions   0 1 2 3 4 5 6 7 8 9 . . .   30 31

the sign of the number. If the sign bit is a 0, the number is positive; if it is a 1, the number is negative. For example, Fig. 1.14 shows the binary integer representation of the decimal number +26. (For the rest of this section we will show the 32-bit numbers just as strings of 1's and 0's, omitting the boxes representing bit positions.)

A negative number is represented in what is called *2's complement notation*. This means that if x is positive, $-x$ is represented by the 32-bit number $2^{32} - x$. The arithmetic is not difficult in binary. For example, to represent -26, we subtract 26 from 2^{32} in their binary forms as follows:

$$2^{32} = \quad 100000000000000000000000000000000$$
$$-26 = -\quad \underline{00000000000000000000000000011010}$$
$$11111111111111111111111111100110 = \text{representation of } -26$$

The 32-bit number shown as the difference is the binary representation of -26. Note that the sign bit is 1, denoting a negative number.

Another equivalent procedure for finding the 2's complement of a number is to form its *bit complement* (also called the *1's complement*); that is, we change every 1 to a 0 and every 0 to a 1, and then add the number 1. The representation of -26 by this procedure is as follows:

$$26 = 00000000000000000000000000011010$$
$$\text{Bit complement:} \quad 11111111111111111111111111100101$$
$$\text{Add 1:} \quad \underline{\qquad\qquad\qquad\qquad\qquad\qquad\qquad 1}$$
$$11111111111111111111111111100110$$

The two procedures are equivalent because the bit complement of a 32-bit number is in fact the result of subtracting the number from $2^{32} - 1$, which is a string of 32 1's.

Binary integers that are small enough are sometimes represented in half-words of 16 bits each. The representation is essentially the same: bit position 0 holds the sign and negative numbers are in 2's complement form. To find the 16-bit 2's complement of a number, one must of course subtract the number from 2^{16}, not 2^{32}. The 2's complement of 1111001101100111, for example, is found by subtracting as follows:

$$2^{16} = \quad 10000000000000000$$
$$-\quad \underline{1111001101100111}$$
$$0000110010011001.$$

Any number from $-32,768$ to $32,767$ can be represented by a half-word.

REPRESENTATION OF CHARACTERS

A *character* is represented in one byte of eight bits; some instructions allow processing of character strings up to 256 characters long; some allow longer operands. There are 256 different eight-bit numbers, and any of these could be used to represent characters. Of these, 88 numbers are actually assigned to characters for standard IBM use, including 26 for the uppercase alphabet, 26 for the lowercase alphabet, 10 for the digits 0–9, and the remainder for 25 spe-

FIGURE 1.15   A zoned decimal number

11110011	11111000	11000111
3	8	7+

cial characters,

$$\cent \quad . \quad < \quad (\quad + \quad | \quad \& \quad ! \quad \$ \quad * \quad) \quad ; \quad \neg \quad - \quad /$$
$$, \quad \% \quad > \quad ? \quad : \quad \# \quad @ \quad ' \quad = \quad ''$$

and a blank. The character representations generally used are called the EBCDIC (Extended Binary Coded Decimal Interchange Code); they are listed in Appendix A.

Some terminals that may be attached to IBM System/370 computers use the ASCII (American national Standard Code for Information Interchange) representations of characters. These codes are also shown in Appendix A. Normally, the operating system translates the characters from ASCII to EBCDIC as they are sent from the terminal, and from EBCDIC to ASCII before sending output to the terminal; thus we use the EBCDIC codes within our programs even if we are using ASCII terminals.

The character representation of decimal digits is also called *zoned decimal*. The first half of the byte, the first hexadecimal digit, represents a *zone* (+, − or blank); the second half of the byte contains the representation of one of the digits from 0 through 9. The word "zones" as used here derives from punched card descriptions, in which the +, −, and 0 punches are called zone punches, especially in the representation of letters and special characters. The zone punches are converted to four-bit codes in the EBCDIC representation as follows.†

Zone	Code
+	1100 or hexadecimal C
−	1101 or hexadecimal D
Blank	1111 or hexadecimal F

An example of a zoned decimal number is shown in Fig. 1.15. The three bytes represent the number +387, with the zones for blank in the first two bytes and the zone for + in the last byte.

DECIMAL NUMBERS: PACKED DECIMAL REPRESENTATION

A decimal digit can be represented in four bits; therefore, two decimal digits can be packed into one byte. The IBM System/370 can do arithmetic on numbers expressed in this form, which is called *packed decimal*. The sign of the number is represented in the *low-order* four bits of the low-order byte: usually

---

†These are the codes *produced* by the computer. It will recognize any digit A, B, C, D, E, or F as a sign.

FIGURE 1.16   A packed decimal number

Location	016130	016131
Bits	00011001	01101101
Decimal equivalent	1 9	6 —

1100 for plus, 1101 for minus. The low-order byte also holds the least significant digit of the number; other bytes hold two decimal digits each. Arithmetic may be performed on numbers whose lengths may vary from 1 to 16 bytes; numbers can therefore include from 1 to 31 decimal digits. Figure 1.16 shows a packed decimal field, two bytes long, holding the number −196.

The number is always *addressed* by its highest-order byte—location 016130 in Fig. 1.16, for example. Instructions that deal with packed decimal numbers include the lengths of the operands as arguments. Such instructions are described in Chapter 14.

FLOATING-POINT NUMBERS

Floating-point numbers are used for calculations with numbers of mixed and variable magnitudes when we wish that the computer retain as many significant digits as possible while keeping track of the magnitudes of the numbers. In a binary computer, this is accomplished by making one part of each number a *characteristic,* indicating a power (positive or negative) of 2, and the other part a *fraction,* a binary number considered to be less than 1. The number represented is the product of the power of 2 and the fraction.

In the IBM System/370, floating-point numbers can be of three sizes: 32 bits, called *short* (or *single precision*); 64 bits, called *long* (or *double precision*); and 128 bits, called *extended precision*. Older models do not include extended precision, and some were available with no floating point at all. In any of these representations, bit position 0 contains the sign, and bit positions 1–7 contain the characteristic. In IBM System/370, this characteristic indicates a power of 16; that is, adding 1 to the characteristic multiplies the number represented by 16. Values coded by the characteristic may range from −64 to 63, so the range of representable numbers is roughly from 16^{-64} to 16^{63}, or 10^{-78} to 10^{75}. Thus the IBM System/370 can be fairly called a hexadecimal computer with respect to floating point.

The fraction occupies bit positions 8–31 in short floating-point numbers, 8–63 in long floating-point numbers, and 8–63 and 72–127 (64–71 are unused) in extended-precision numbers. This allows the equivalent of about seven decimal digits of precision in short floating-point numbers, about 16 decimal digits in long floating-point numbers, and about 32 decimal digits in extended-precision numbers. Negative numbers are not complemented, but use what is called the *sign-magnitude* form; the sign bit of a negative number is set to 1, but both the characteristic and the fraction are shown as if the number is positive.

Figure 1.17 shows a short floating-point number representing the number 1.0. The fraction (binary) is .0001; the 1 in the fraction is in the position

FIGURE 1.17   Floating-point representation of 1.0

```
        Sign  Characteristic                        Fraction
        ⌒    ⌒⌒⌒⌒⌒⌒⌒                        ⌒⌒⌒⌒⌒⌒⌒⌒⌒⌒⌒⌒⌒⌒⌒⌒⌒⌒⌒⌒⌒⌒⌒⌒
  Bits  0│1│0│0│0│0│0│1│0│0│0│1│0│0│0│0│0│0│0│0│0│0│0│0│0│0│0│0│0│0│0│0│0
Bit positions  0  1  2  3  4  5  6  7  8  .  .  11  .  .  .                              31
```

representing 2^{-4}. The characteristic has a 1 in bit position 1; this represents a positive power of 16 and is sometimes called a *bias quantity*. The 1 in bit position 7 represents an exponent of 1, so the true number represented is 16^1 times the fraction:

$$16^1 \times 2^{-4} = 1.0.$$

Floating-point arithmetic and instructions are treated in Chapter 13.

m   a   i   n   i   d   e   a   s

- □ Binary numbers consist of 1's and 0's in a positional representation with radix 2. Hexadecimal numbers consist of digits 0–9 and A–F in a positional representation with radix 16. Conversion from binary to hexadecimal or from hexadecimal to binary is a matter only of compression of four-digit binary groups or expansion of single hexadecimal digits.

- □ The major logical subsystems of a computer are input, output, storage, arithmetic, and control.

- □ Storage is composed of groups of bits; each group has an address.

- □ Input and output subsystems allow communication between the computer and the outside world, through such media as magnetic tapes and disks, punched cards, printers, pen-and-ink plotters, and terminals.

- □ The control subsystem directs activities of the other subsystems by interpreting and executing instructions.

- □ Arithmetic in the IBM System/370 is performed on binary integers, floating-point numbers, and decimal numbers.

- □ Input and output in the IBM System/370 take place through channels: block-multiplexor channels handle high-speed devices; a byte-multiplexor channel can handle several slower devices simultaneously.

- □ The supervisor in the IBM System/370 maintains control of processing, especially input and output, with the help of interrupt facilities and privileged instructions.

- □ Main storage in the IBM System/370 is organized in eight-bit bytes, each of which is addressable. An address is usually 24 bits long. Bytes are grouped to form four-byte words, two-byte half-words, and eight-byte double words.

- □ The sixteen general registers, each 32 bits long, have addresses 0–15. The four floating-point registers, each 64 bits long, have addresses 0, 2, 4, 6.

- □ Binary integers in the IBM System/370 are expressed in 2's complement notation.

☐ A character has a representation (EBCDIC) in eight bits or one byte.

☐ Decimal numbers can be represented in the packed-decimal form, two digits per byte, with the sign represented in the lowest-order half-byte.

☐ Floating-point representation, including an exponent of 16 and a fraction, is used for numbers that vary greatly in magnitude.

■ PROBLEMS FOR REVIEW AND IMAGINATION

1.1 Learn the actual main storage size and input/output configuration of the computer you will be working with.

1.2 Make a list of other computers you know or can read about and their storage organizations and capacities.

1.3 Each byte of storage in the IBM System/370 contains eight bits of information and one parity bit. The parity bit is redundant; it is used only to guarantee that information bits are not lost. The parity bit is set to 1 or 0 so as to make the sum of 1's represented in the nine bits an odd number. For example, the character / is represented in eight bits (in EBCDIC) by 01100001. The parity bit to go with this character will be 0, because there are three 1's among the information-carrying bits. The character Q is represented by 11011000, and the parity bit is set to 1, so there will be five 1-bits among the nine. These representations with parity bit (we call this *odd parity*) are also used in magnetic tape and disk storage associated with the IBM System/370. Using the character representation table of Appendix A, code your name and telephone number in eight-bit EBCDIC representations, and add the correct parity bit to each character.

1.4 Computers used to be decimal or binary, but no one computer was both. Either kind was used for business data processing and scientific work. Only since the early 1960s have computers had *both* decimal and binary arithmetic capabilities. Given a computer with both, in what problems would you use decimal arithmetic? floating point? binary integers? Ignore considerations of storage and timing efficiency, and base your answers on such things as accuracy and naturalness.

1.5 By using the positional representation definition of binary numbers, convert the binary numbers 10101 and 1110111 to decimal.

1.6 By using the positional representation definition of hexadecimal numbers, convert the hexadecimal numbers A8 and 24D to decimal.

1.7 Write the hexadecimal number 24D in binary; the binary number 11011001110001 in hexadecimal.

1.8 Show the full-word 2's complement binary integer representation of the decimal number −18.

1.9 Express the number 7 as a full-word binary integer, and show how it would be added to the representation of −18.

1.10   There is a number expressible as a full-word binary integer in the IBM System/370, whose complement (negative) cannot be expressed in a full word. What is this number, and why can't it be expressed in a full word? Sometimes this number is used as the representation for "missing data" or "undefined quantity." Think of reasons for or against this convention.

1.11   Some computers represent negative numbers in what is called 1's complement notation, in which a complement is formed by changing every 1 to 0 and every 0 to 1. In this notation, are there numbers whose complement cannot be taken? What is the complement of the number 0, and how can it be interpreted? Addition and subtraction in a 1's complement machine require that a carry out of the high-order (sign) position be added to the units' position. Illustrate. Then think of advantages of 1's complement notation over 2's complement notation, and vice versa.

1.12   If a maximum of 64 different characters are to be represented in storage, six bits are enough to provide unique codes for the characters. Before the advent of the IBM System/360, most binary computers used six bits for storage of each character. The fact that words were multiples of six bits facilitated the handling of six-bit characters. The IBM System/370, with its eight-bit representations of characters, introduces an inefficiency of two bits per character. This is partly offset by the efficiency of storage of decimal numbers in the packed-decimal format: two digits into eight bits. Calculate the ratio of characters to decimal digits in storage for which the eight-bit character and two-digit byte are just as efficient as a six-bit system. With fewer characters than this break-even ratio, the eight-bit system is more efficient.

■ REFERENCES ▐▬▬▬▬▬▬▬▬▬▬▬▬▬▬▬▬▬▬

Amdahl, G. M., "The Structure of SYSTEM/360: Part III—Unit Design Consideration," *IBM Systems Journal* **3** (1964), pp. 144–64. An explanation of the rationale of the IBM System/360 structure.

IBM System/370 System Summary, GA 22-7001, IBM Corporation. An introductory description of the System/370, especially the input and output units.

IBM 4300 Processors Summary and Input/Output & Data Communications Configurator, GA 33-1523, IBM Corporation. An introductory description of the processors in the 4300 group.

IBM Input/Output Device Summary, GA 32-0039, IBM Corporation. A description of the devices and systems that can be attached to a channel.

Lewin, Morton H., *Logic Design and Computer Organization,* Addison-Wesley, Reading, Mass. 1983. A description in more depth of computer structure.

Lorin, Harold, *Introduction to Computer Architecture and Organization,* Wiley, New York, 1982. An alternate to Lewin, above.

INTRODUCTION TO IBM SYSTEM/370 MACHINE LANGUAGE

This chapter introduces in some detail the basic features of machine language of the IBM System/370, including the addressing of operands and the formats of the six types of instructions.

2.1 The Nature of Machine Language

Chapter 1 stated that the unit of control of a computer is an *instruction*. Instructions are coded numerically and kept in main storage during execution of the program. A set of instructions that are executed in sequence is a *program,* and the activity of programming is, strictly speaking, writing sequences of instructions. Each instruction contains an operation code, which designates the operation to be performed by the computer. Instructions also contain operand addresses, to instruct the computer which storage locations or registers to use in the operation. Some instructions also carry other information that helps to define the operation to be performed.

Instructions can be put into classes according to the computer subsystems they use. There are arithmetic instructions, which instruct, through the control subsystem of course, the arithmetic and logic subsystem to perform arithmetic or logical operations. Some instructions are classed as input/output instructions; they instruct the input and output subsystems to take action. Other instructions are information move instructions; they move information from one location to another in the storage subsystem, sometimes making simple transformations in the information as it is moved. Still other instructions are classed as control instructions. Control instructions do not cause arithmetic to be performed, information to be moved in main storage, or input or output to be accomplished; they affect the flow of control by changing the program status word in some way. The most common and important control instruction is the conditional branch, which makes a test, then depending on the result, either allows the computer to go on to the next instruction in main storage or, by replacing the contents of the instruction address register with the operand of the conditional branch instruction, starts execution of a different sequence of instructions. This kind of instruction is extremely important; it permits repetition of instructions and complexity of programs, as we will see in Chapters 7 and 8.

We will see examples of instructions in later sections of this chapter, and spend the rest of the book learning how to use them effectively. In the next section we examine the addressing structure of the IBM System/370; the ways in which instructions in System/370 address their operands are rather complex, so you are urged to pay special attention.

2.2   Operand Addressing in Machine Language

RULES FOR OPERAND ADDRESS REPRESENTATION

An operand in a register is addressed by the register number. This register address is a number from 0 to 15, and is expressed in four bits. We will show this number in examples as one hexadecimal digit, 0 to F, corresponding to the binary representations 0000 to 1111.

The address of an operand in main storage can be expressed in instructions in either of two ways. First is the sum of

contents of a register

and

a 12-bit number called a displacement.

The register used is called a *base register,* or more simply, a *base*. Second, and similar is the sum of

contents of a base register

and

contents of another (or the same) register, called an index,

and

a 12-bit displacement.

FIGURE 2.1 Forming an operand address (a) from base and displacement, and (b) from index, base, and displacement

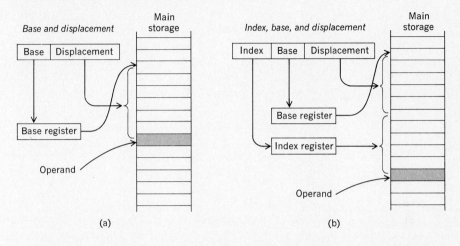

(a)   (b)

Figure 2.1 illustrates the forming of an operand address from base and displacement and from base, index, and displacement. Figure 2.1(a) shows how a pointer to a register used as a base and a displacement define the address of an operand. Figure 2.1(b) includes an index as well.

Some instructions use operands addressed by base and displacement; others use operands addressed by base, index, and displacement. In order to use the instructions correctly, we must know the addressing characteristics of each. The instructions in the IBM System/370 are organized and named, as you will see, to help us keep this information clearly in mind.

After the sum of base and displacement—or base, index, and displacement—has been formed, only the low-order 24 bits are used as an address. For compactness, register contents, displacements, and actual addresses will be shown in hexadecimal in the examples. Program listings and debugging information printed by the IBM System/370 also show addresses in hexadecimal, so familiarization with hexadecimal representations is necessary.

In storage address specifications, a base or index of 0 is a special case. By convention, it is taken to mean the *number* 0, *not* the contents of register 0. This allows for situations in which we want to specify an address by only base and displacement in instructions where addressing by base, index, and displacement is standard, and also for cases in which addresses are to be specified by displacement only.

As was mentioned in Chapter 1, in System/370 virtual storage systems, the addresses generated by base, index, and displacement are taken to be addresses in a virtual (almost imaginary!) storage. The virtual address is automatically translated by hardware into physical main storage addresses for access of actual operands and instructions. The system does the translation so consistently and thoroughly that the user's program operates entirely within its virtual stor-

FIGURE 2.2   The addressing of an operand

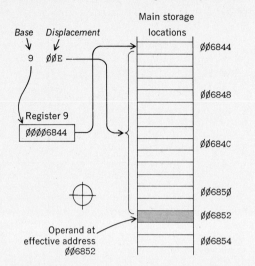

age, so you need not be aware of the translation system until you are doing quite advanced and complex manipulations. So far as your program knows, virtual storage is identical to main storage. Therefore we will ignore the address translation until Chapter 17.

STORAGE ADDRESSING EXAMPLES

a. Suppose that in an instruction addressing its operand in storage by base and displacement, the specification is a base of 9 and a displacement of ØØE (hexadecimal). Suppose further that register 9 contains (hexadecimal, as all numbers in this section) ØØØØ6844. The actual operand address—which is called the *effective address*—is formed as

$$
\begin{array}{lr}
\text{contents of register 9} & \text{ØØØØ6844} \\
+ \text{ displacement} & \underline{\text{ØØE}} \\
& \text{ØØ6852}
\end{array}
$$

The effective address is the low-order 24 bits of the sum, ØØ6852. The contents of register 9 are not altered; the addition is performed in a special nonaddressable register in the central processing unit. The addressing of the operand can be represented in diagram form such as that shown in Fig. 2.2.

b. Suppose register B (decimal 11) contains 5ØØ11C48. An instruction specifying base B and displacement 46A will address

$$
\begin{array}{lr}
\text{contents of register B} & \text{5ØØ11C48} \\
+ \text{ displacement} & \underline{\text{46A}} \\
& \text{Ø12ØB2}
\end{array}
$$

The effective address is Ø12ØB2.

c. An instruction using base, index, and displacement may call for base B, index 4, and displacement 46A. If register 4 contains 00001240, the effective address computation is

$$
\begin{array}{lr}
\text{contents of register B} & 500110\text{C}48 \\
+ \text{ contents of register 4} & 00001240 \\
+ \text{ displacement} & \underline{46\text{A}} \\
& 0132\text{F}2
\end{array}
$$

The effective address is 0132F2.

d. An instruction that normally uses base, index, and displacement may call for base B, index 0, and displacement 074. The effective address computation is

$$
\begin{array}{lr}
\text{contents of register B} & 50011\text{C}48 \\
+ (\textit{not} \text{ the contents of register 0}) & 0 \\
+ \text{ displacement} & \underline{074} \\
& 011\text{CBC}
\end{array}
$$

The effective address is 011CBC.

RATIONALE OF ADDRESSING STRUCTURE

Many computers are designed so that the actual address of an operand is in the instruction itself. This simple addressing structure is often enhanced by index registers and indirect addressing. With *indirect addressing,* the address in the instruction is not the address of the operand itself but that of a place in storage that contains the address of the operand. An addressing structure with indirect addressing and index registers is straightforward and reasonably powerful.

The addressing structure of System/370 is quite different from that of other computers, and compared to other addressing schemes it has both notable advantages and disadvantages. One disadvantage is that addressing in the IBM System/370 is difficult to learn. One principal advantage is economy of storage required for instructions. An IBM System/370 instruction requires only 16 bits for base and displacement specification; a full address, if placed in the instruction, would take 24 bits.

When a program is loaded into main storage for execution, the operating system must assign available space and load the program into this space. Because the storage locations may not be the same on different occasions, the program must be able to run properly no matter where it is loaded in main storage. This means that operand addresses in instructions must be adjusted to refer to the actual locations used. The process of loading the program and adjusting the address is called *relocation,* and the ability of a program to be relocated is called *relocatability.* In some computers, every operand address is modified as the program is loaded to make the address consistent with the address assigned currently to the program and its data areas. In System/370, relocatability is mostly accomplished by adjustment of the contents of base registers, and, as we shall see in Chapter 6, this is largely automatic. Thus another advantage of the System/370 addressing structure is the easy relocatability of programs and data blocks.

Often a loop in a program must address successive pieces of data in successive passes through the loop. The addresses in the instructions referring to these data must be modified so that successive executions of the instructions will in fact treat successive pieces of data. A programmer using an algebraic language such as FORTRAN or Pascal can refer to successive pieces of data by means of subscripted variables, but the programs translated into machine language must modify effective addresses of operands during execution. Another advantage of the addressing scheme of System/370 is the manner in which it facilitates address computation and modification. Doing arithmetic on the quantity in the index register is a most convenient way of modifying an effective address. Modification of a base register can also be a convenient and efficient means of address modification.

2.3   Machine Language Instruction Formats

Machine language instructions follow six different formats. The formats differ in the addressing characteristics—whether operands are in registers, in the instruction itself, or in main storage addressed by base and displacement or by base, index, and displacement. Because of the variation in space required for specification of storage operand addresses, register addresses, and data in the instruction, some instructions occupy two bytes of storage, others are four bytes long, and still others are six bytes long.

In all instructions the first one or two bytes are the *operation code,* which indicates the length of the instruction and the type of operation to be performed.

RR INSTRUCTIONS

The simplest of the five instruction forms is the *RR type.* Both operands of each of these instructions are in registers, giving the type the name RR, standing for register to register. Four bits hold each register address, so the address of the first operand is in bits 8–11 of the instruction, and the address of the second operand in bits 12–15. The instruction is therefore two bytes long, as shown in Fig. 2.3.

As an example, the instruction coded in hexadecimal as 1837 is an RR-type instruction. The operation code, 18, means load from a register. The operand addresses are 3 and 7; execution of the instruction causes the contents of register 7 to be loaded into register 3, replacing the previous contents of register 3. The contents of register 7 remain unchanged.

FIGURE 2.3   Format of an RR instruction

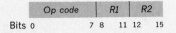

Bits 0   7 8   11 12   15

FIGURE 2.4 Format of an RX instruction

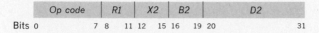

Bits 0   7 8   11 12   15 16   19 20   31

RX INSTRUCTIONS

An instruction of *RX type* has the form shown in Fig. 2.4. The first operand is a register operand, with address *R1* given in bits 8–11 of the instruction. The second operand is located in main storage; its address is specified by a base *B2* (register whose address is given in bits 16–19), index *X2* (a register whose address is given in bits 12–15) and a displacement given in bits 20–31 of the instruction.

As an example, the instruction coded in hexadecimal as 5B35C024 is an RX-type instruction. The operation code is 5B, meaning subtract (binary integer). The first operand is in register 3. The field *X2* is 5, the field *B2* is C, the displacement is 024; together they define the address of the second operand. Suppose register 5 contains 00000050 and register C (or 12) contains 00007404. Then the second operand address is generated as follows:

$$
\begin{array}{lll}
\text{contents of register 5} & 00000050 & (X2) \\
+ \text{ contents of register C} & 00007404 & (B2) \\
+ \text{ displacement} & \underline{024} & (D2) \\
& 007478 &
\end{array}
$$

The effective address is 007478.

This instruction will be executed as follows: The contents of location 007478 (actually the full word in locations 007478 to 00747B) will be subtracted from the contents of register 3. The result will be left in register 3; the contents of all storage locations are unchanged.

This is a good time to explain the notation and type fonts we will be using through the remainder of the text. Italics are used for three purposes. One, of course, is emphasis of particularly notable words. Second, the first and defining use of a term is italicized. In that context, *RX type* was italicized in its first mention at the beginning of this subsection, but is not in the text following. Third, italics are used to denote symbols that represent a possible range of actual values. In this context, *R1, X2, B2,* and *D2* are italicized because each represents a variety of possible values. Typewriter type, such as GSQ and 00747B, is used to denote actual values, codes, instructions, and statements as they might be submitted to the computer or be reported by the computer. These conventions are not followed to extremes; when no ambiguity should result, we stick to the regular text-type font to avoid the visual confusion of constantly changing fonts.

Programmers must be careful about the distinction between the letter O and the digit 0; in many contexts we can be ambiguous or even literally wrong. (If I say my telephone number is "six-eight-six, four-four-oh-eight," practically everyone will correctly get my number as 686-4408—all digits.) Computers are not as understanding, so we must be precise about distinctions between letters and digits. We need a good convention—especially for handwriting—to show the letter O as different from the digit 0. Many conventions have been used, and even more suggested. The convention most widely used in the computer field now is to put slashes through zeros—0—and leave the letter O plain. We used to follow the opposite convention of putting a slash through the

FIGURE 2.5   Format of an RS instruction

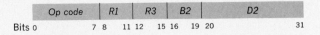

letter O instead, which is one of the reasons that slashing zeros is not a good solution. However, we will slash zeros wherever we are talking about computer contents (using typewriter type) or assembler or machine language instructions.

RS INSTRUCTIONS

An instruction of *RS type* has the form shown in Fig. 2.5. The first operand is a register operand, with address *R1* given in bits 8–11 of the instruction. The second operand is located in main storage, with address specified by a base *B2* (register whose address is given in bits 16–19 of the instruction) and a displacement *D2* given in bits 20–31 of the instruction. The RS-type instructions are the only ones that have three operands; the third operand is a register operand, whose address *R3* is given in bits 12–15 of the instruction.†

For example, the instruction coded in hexadecimal as 9868C024 is an RS-type instruction. The operation code is 98, meaning *load multiple*. The first operand is register 6, the third operand is register 8. The second operand is defined by the base C and displacement 024. If register C contains ØØØØ74Ø4, the second operand address is defined as follows:

$$
\begin{array}{lr}
\text{contents of register C} & \text{ØØØØ74Ø4} \\
+ \text{ displacement} & \underline{\text{Ø24}} \\
& \text{ØØ7428}
\end{array}
$$

The effective address is ØØ7428.

The execution of this instruction will be as follows. Registers from 6 (first operand) to 8 (third operand) will be loaded from consecutive locations of main storage, starting with location ØØ7428. Register 6 will be loaded therefore from locations ØØ7428 to ØØ742B, register 7 will be loaded from locations ØØ742C to ØØ742F, and register 8 will be loaded from locations ØØ743Ø to ØØ7433. Previous contents of registers 6, 7, and 8 are lost; contents of all storage locations are unchanged.

SI INSTRUCTIONS

An instruction of *SI type* is of the form shown in Fig. 2.6. The first operand is in main storage, with address specified by base *B1* and displacement *D1*. The second operand is the eight-bit quantity in bits 8–15 of the instruction itself. It is called *I2,* or the *immediate* operand.

For example, the instruction coded in hexadecimal as 92F3C231 is an SI-type instruction. The operation code is 92, meaning *move immediate*. The first operand is in main storage in a location defined by base register C and displacement 231. If register C contains ØØØØ74Ø4, the operand address is determined by

---

†There are some RS instructions, however, that do not have a third operand. In these, the *R3* portion of the instruction is ignored.

FIGURE 2.6   Format of an SI instruction

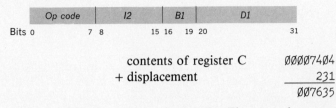

$$\begin{array}{r} \text{contents of register C} \quad \emptyset\emptyset\emptyset\emptyset 74\emptyset 4 \\ + \text{ displacement} \quad \underline{231} \\ \emptyset\emptyset 7635 \end{array}$$

Thus the effective address is $\emptyset\emptyset 7635$. The second operand is the eight bits coded in hexadecimal as F3, from the second byte of the instruction.

In the execution of this instruction, the byte of immediate data, the second operand F3, is stored at location $\emptyset\emptyset\emptyset\emptyset 7635$ of the main storage.

SS INSTRUCTIONS

An instruction of *SS type* is of the form shown in Fig. 2.7. It is the only type of instruction that is six bytes long. Both operands are in main storage: the address of the first is given by base *B1* and displacement *D1* from bits 20–31; the address of the second operand is given by a base *B2* (whose address is given in bits 32–35 of the instruction) and displacement *D2* from bits 36–47. Instructions of SS type are flexible in that the operands may be of various lengths, the actual lengths coded in bits 8–15 of the instructions. Numbers from 0 to 255 can be expressed in the length field of the instruction; they represent lengths of 1 to 256 bytes: $L = 0$ implies an operand length of 1 byte, $L = 1$ implies an operand length of 2 bytes, etc.

For example, the instruction coded in hexadecimal as $D2\emptyset 2C1\emptyset 6C735$ is an SS-type instruction. The operation code of D2 means *move character*. The first operand address is defined by base register C and displacement 106. Given that register C contains $\emptyset\emptyset\emptyset\emptyset 74\emptyset 4$, the address computation is

$$\begin{array}{r} \text{contents of register C} \quad \emptyset\emptyset\emptyset\emptyset 74\emptyset 4 \\ + \text{ displacement} \quad \underline{1\emptyset 6} \\ \emptyset\emptyset 75\emptyset A \end{array}$$

The effective address is $\emptyset\emptyset 75\emptyset A$. Similarly, the second operand address is

$$\begin{array}{r} \text{contents of register C} \quad \emptyset\emptyset\emptyset\emptyset 74\emptyset 4 \\ + \text{ displacement} \quad \underline{735} \\ \emptyset\emptyset 7B39 \end{array}$$

The length field contains 02, so each operand is three bytes long.

In the execution of this instruction, the three bytes beginning at location $\emptyset\emptyset 7B39$ (the second operand) are moved to three storage locations beginning at $\emptyset\emptyset 75\emptyset A$ (the first operand). That is, the byte from location $\emptyset\emptyset 7B39$ is moved to location $\emptyset\emptyset 75\emptyset A$, the byte from $\emptyset\emptyset 7B3A$ is moved to $\emptyset\emptyset 75\emptyset B$, and the byte from $\emptyset\emptyset 7B3B$ is moved to $\emptyset\emptyset 75\emptyset C$.

FIGURE 2.7   Format of an SS instruction

FIGURE 2.8   Format of an S instruction

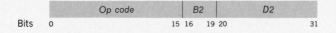

The execution of this instruction takes the five bytes from locations ØØ7E86–ØØ7E8A

In some SS instructions the two operands may be of different lengths. In these instructions the length field is broken into *L1,* a four-bit field in bit positions 8–11 giving the length of the first operand, and *L2,* a four-bit field in bit positions 12–15 giving the length of the second operand. The numbers in these four-bit fields may be 0 to 15, representing, by a transformation as above, actual operand lengths 1 to 16.

The instruction F224C248CA82 is this kind of SS instruction. The operation code of F2 means *pack*. The length field of the first operand contains a 2, so the first operand is three bytes long. The address of the first operand is

$$
\begin{array}{lr}
\text{contents of register C} & \text{ØØØØ74Ø4} \\
+ \text{ displacement} & \underline{\text{248}} \\
& \text{ØØ764C}
\end{array}
$$

The length field of the second operand contains 4, so the second operand is five bytes long. The address of the second operand is

$$
\begin{array}{lr}
\text{contents of register C} & \text{ØØØØ74Ø4} \\
+ \text{ displacement} & \underline{\text{A82}} \\
& \text{ØØ7E86}
\end{array}
$$

The execution of this instruction takes the five bytes from locations ØØ7E86–ØØ7E8A (second operand) assumed to be in the zoned decimal format and converts the characters to packed decimal form. The resulting packed decimal number is stored in the three-byte area ØØ764C–ØØ764E (the first operand).

One distinction made between single-length and two-length SS instructions is that those with only a single length process their operands from left (high-order byte) to right. Those that define a length for each operand process their operands from right (low-order) byte to left.

S INSTRUCTIONS
An instruction of *S type* is of the form shown in Fig. 2.8. This is the only type in which the operation code is two bytes long. The single operand (called the second operand in reference material!) is determined by base *B2* and displacement *D2* in the usual way. All S instructions are connected with advanced functions which we will not introduce until Chapter 17; almost all of them are reserved for use in supervisor state.

SUMMARY
The variety of instruction types is designed to give flexibility in length and location of operands. Figure 2.9 shows the operand configurations of the six instruction types. You will see, however, that a few instructions are exceptions.

In all instructions, the operation code occupies the first byte. A main storage reference is always given by base and displacement, except in RX-type in-

FIGURE 2.9 Operand configurations of instructions

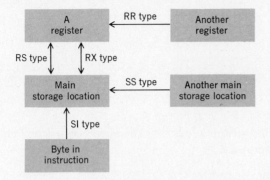

structions, where a register can also be used as index. A register address is given in four bits. Instructions of SS type involve variable-length fields in main storage, so a length (or two lengths) must be specified in the instruction. But when only one byte of data is to be processed, the SI instructions provide extra efficiency by eliminating a storage reference. The individual instructions and their use will be studied in the next several chapters.

2.4 An Example of a Program Segment

We can examine the structure of machine language more thoroughly and convey the flavor of System/370 processing by following even a trivial example. The following program segment illustrates program sequencing and the use of a few instructions.

Location	Instruction
ØØ8114	9824C3Ø4
ØØ8118	1A42
ØØ811A	5Ø4ØC31Ø
ØØ811E	92ØØC31Ø
ØØ8122	D2Ø7C438C3ØC
ØØ8128	

Instructions, as you have seen, are stored in two, four, or six bytes of main storage. They are executed sequentially, with the next instruction in storage being the next executed, except when a branch instruction causes a jump to an instruction sequence elsewhere, or an interrupt suspends execution of the current program and gives control to the supervisor. Each instruction must begin on a half-word boundary, that is, an even-numbered storage location.

Let us assume that before execution of the segment the contents of various registers and storage locations, expressed in hexadecimal, are as follows:

Registers	Contents	Storage locations	Contents
2	ØØØØ34Ø4	ØØ83ØC	ØØØØØ848
3	ØØ127CD8	ØØ831Ø	Ø336’21Ø3
4	FFF3ØE56	ØØ8314	1DCBA987
12 (C)	ØØØØ8ØØ8	ØØ8318	23FE5631

Execution begins with the instruction at ØØ8114. The operation is *load multiple*. The effective storage address is

$$
\begin{array}{lr}
\text{contents of register C} & \text{ØØØØ8ØØ8} \\
+ \text{ displacement} & \underline{\text{3Ø4}} \\
& \text{ØØ83ØC}
\end{array}
$$

The register operands are 2 and 4. This instruction causes register 2 to be loaded with ØØØØØ848, the contents from location ØØ83ØC; register 3 to be loaded with Ø336’21Ø3, from the next location, ØØ831Ø; and register 4 to be loaded with 1DCBA987, from location ØØ8314. The load multiple instruction is a four-byte instruction, so the next instruction is taken from location ØØ8118. The operation code is 1A; it stands for *add to register* and is recognized as a two-byte RR-type instruction. The contents of register 2 (second operand) are added to register 4 (first operand):

$$
\begin{array}{r}
\text{1DCBA987} \\
+ \text{ ØØØØØ848} \\
\hline
\text{1DCBB1CF}
\end{array}
$$

The result is left in register 4.

The next instruction is taken from location ØØ811A, since the add-to-register instruction was two bytes long. The instruction 5Ø4ØC31Ø is a *store* instruction, of RX type. The effective main storage address is

$$
\begin{array}{lr}
\text{contents of register C} & \text{ØØØØ8ØØ8} \\
+ 0 & \text{Ø} \\
+ \text{ displacement} & \underline{\text{31Ø}} \\
& \text{ØØ8318}
\end{array}
$$

The contents of register 4 (first operand), 1DCBB1CF, are stored at location ØØ8318 (meaning, as usual, the four bytes beginning at ØØ8318), replacing the previous contents. The fourth instruction, 92ØØC31Ø, is the SI-type instruction *move immediate*. It has the same effective address as the last instruction; the "immediate" byte, ØØ, is stored at location ØØ8318. The four bytes beginning at ØØ8318 are now ØØCBB1CF.

The last instruction, D2Ø7C438C3ØC, is an SS-type instruction *move character*. The length field contains 07, so eight bytes are moved. The second operand address is

$$\begin{array}{lr}
\text{contents of register C} & \text{Ø\!Ø\!Ø\!Ø8\!Ø\!Ø8} \\
+ \text{ displacement} & \underline{3\text{Ø}C} \\
& \text{Ø\!Ø8314}
\end{array}$$

The first operand address is

$$\begin{array}{lr}
\text{contents of register C} & \text{Ø\!Ø\!Ø\!Ø8\!Ø\!Ø8} \\
+ \text{ displacement} & \underline{438} \\
& \text{Ø\!Ø844\!Ø}
\end{array}$$

Eight bytes are moved from locations Ø\!Ø8314–Ø\!Ø831B to locations Ø\!Ø844\!Ø–Ø\!Ø8447. The eight bytes moved are 1DCBA987Ø\!ØCBB1CF; they replace previous contents of locations Ø\!Ø844\!Ø to Ø\!Ø8447. This instruction is recognized as a six-byte instruction, so the next instruction is taken from location Ø\!Ø8128.

m a i n   i d e a s

- A *program* in machine language is a sequence of instructions.

- The most important components of instructions are the *operation code* and *specification of operands.*

- Instructions can be classed by function as *arithmetic, input-output, information move,* and *control.*

- In the IBM System/370 the address of an operand in main storage is specified by a *base,* sometimes an *index,* and a *displacement.* The contents of the register(s) and the displacement are added to form the effective address.

- Six different instruction formats provide for different operand locations: register, main storage, immediate data. The types are RR, RX, RS, SI, SS, and S.

■ P R O B L E M S   F O R   R E V I E W   A N D   I M A G I N A T I O N

2.1 The IBM System/370 calculates addresses in a 24-bit register, adding together a displacement, the low-order 24 bits of a base register and, if applicable, the low-order 24 bits of an index register. Overflows are ignored. Convince yourself that the resulting address is the same as if the entire base and index registers and the displacement were added together in a 32-bit register, and the low-order 24 bits taken as the effective address.

2.2 Given contents of registers (in hexadecimal):

Register	Contents
0	Ø\!Ø\!Ø12345
1	Ø\!Ø\!Ø\!Ø6213
2	Ø\!Ø\!Ø\!Ø24A2
3	Ø\!Ø\!Ø\!Ø531\!Ø

What effective address will result from each of the following?

Base	Index	Displacement
2	–	1Ø4
3	–	ØØØ
Ø	–	ØCE
1	3	1Ø1
2	Ø	233
Ø	2	233
Ø	Ø	FFF
3	1	1Ø1

2.3 Given that register 10 contains the hexadecimal number ØØØØ9336, compute the displacement d such that d and base register 10 address the location ØØ958A.

2.4 A displacement is three hexadecimal digits. With fixed contents of a base register and varying displacements, how many main storage locations can be addressed? This number is often insufficient to hold all the program that needs to be addressed, let alone data areas. Several approaches to addressing more locations than can be addressed with fixed contents of one base register are possible in System/370, and some will be developed later in this volume. You are invited to think ahead and imagine what solutions to the problem you would set up in the hardware, in the operating system, or in the user's program.

2.5 An attempt was made in the design of the instruction set to let source operands of instructions be second operands, and destination operands, first operands. Thus MVC moves characters from the second operand address (and bytes following) to the first operand address. This is not possible with all instruction types; we need a STore instruction, which will store the contents of a register into main storage, and this is best defined as an RX instruction with second operand as destination. With what instruction types is it possible for the second operand always to be source and the first operand, destination?

■ **R E F E R E N C E** ▬▬▬▬▬▬▬▬▬▬▬▬▬▬▬▬▬▬▬▬

IBM System/370 Principles of Operation, G22-7000, IBM Corporation. For a reference description of instruction formats. *Principles of Operation* manuals for any of the computers in the System/370 family will do as well.

3

INTRODUCTION TO ASSEMBLER LANGUAGE

An assembler language is a symbolic form of machine language. While machine language is numeric, assembler language allows alphabetic names for operation codes and storage locations. A program called an *assembler* translates a program written in assembler language into machine language, which can be executed by the computer.

This chapter is an introduction to assembler language. We shall study the format of statements and forms for addressing operands in OS/VS Assembler Language.

The main assembler used in the IBM System/370 is the OS/VS–DOS/VSE–VM/370 assembler. It is used in computer systems operating under the OS/VS and DOS/VSE operating systems, and in the CMS (Conversational Monitor System) system operating under VM/370. Earlier assemblers included a DOS/360 assembler and an OS/360 (called F-level) assembler, which differ from the newer assembler in minor ways.

After this chapter descriptions of the individual instructions available in the IBM System/370 begin. Their use will not be shown in the context of a machine-language program, but in the context of assembler language, because programs are no longer written directly in machine language but in assembler language. You must bear in mind the formats of the machine language instruction types and should have a clear picture of the machine language instruction that would be produced by the assembler from the assembler language statement.

3.1 A First Look at Assembler Language

To write programs directly in machine language, you must perform several clerical activities. You must keep track of exactly what locations are used for which instructions, data areas, and constants, in order to be able to refer to these locations correctly later in the program and also so that your program does not erase data, instructions, or constants by inadvertently using the same space for another purpose. You must refer to tables in order to write the numerical operation codes required by the computer. Constants must be expressed in binary. You must make the conversions yourself with the help of tables.

Until the early 1950s all programming was done directly in machine language. It was tedious, and the performance of clerical jobs by programmers resulted in many clerical errors. Assembler languages evolved as symbolic ways of writing machine language. The clerical tasks are, as far as possible, delegated to the *assembler,* which is a program that translates programs written in assembler language into machine language. The assembler keeps track of the storage locations used. The programmer refers to them symbolically, using names suggestive of the actual meaning in the problem the program is being written for. The assembler language programmer is also allowed to write operation codes in symbolic form; STM, for instance, may be written for "STore Multiple" and the assembler will translate STM to the numerical operation code 90.

An assembler also allows the programmer to specify constants and data areas symbolically. The constant may be given in the form in which the programmer thinks of it, such as 1.0 for a floating-point constant, or SUM= for a representation of the characters SUM=. The length of the storage area to be assigned to the constant may be specified, as well as a symbolic name by which the programmer will refer to the constant. The assembler will do the necessary conversions of the constants to binary representations, allocate storage, and keep a table of names and corresponding addresses. The same storage allocation and symbol table procedures are used for data areas.

As an assembler language programmer, you can conveniently write calls on subroutines that are written by you, written by others and kept in a standard library, or included in the supervisor of the computer. The assembler generates the necessary linkages and prepares for the communication of parameters. The assembler also prepares a table of subroutine references with the assembled program. When the program is prepared for loading and execution, the operating system will retrieve the appropriate subroutines from a library if necessary. When all the programs and subroutines are loaded into main storage for execution, the table of subroutine references makes it possible for the actual addresses of entry points of subroutines to be filled in the subroutines where they are needed. These complex tasks of finding subroutines and filling in the proper linkages between calling and called subroutines are performed well in a standard fashion from the information generated by the assembler.

Modification of programs written in assembler language is much easier than modification of programs written directly in machine language. Insertion of instructions, for example, changes the allocation of all storage addresses after the point of insertion. In a program written directly in machine language, the programmer would have to change the addresses of all affected instructions and constants, *and all references to them,* with the strong likelihood of error. Changing the size of a data area has similar hazards. To change an assembler language program, however, it is usually necessary only to change or insert the directly affected assembler language; the assembler will reassign all addresses and references to instructions, constants, and data areas according to the current structure of the program. Thus the assembler helps us avoid many potential mistakes in the changing of a program.

The assembler produces a printed listing of the program, showing the assembler language, the corresponding machine language generated, and diagnostic error messages. Many programming errors are caught in the assembly process and do not have to be found, one by one, through debugging execution runs. The listing of the program, plus other tables printed, such as a cross-reference table listing all references to each symbol, help in the analysis and correction of logical errors uncovered during the debugging process.

Still another service performed by an assembler for the IBM System/370 is the automatic calculation of displacements and specification of base register for operands that are addressed symbolically. As you will see in more detail later, one or more registers are designated as *implied base registers,* and their contents made known to the assembler. A location addressed symbolically is then expressed by the assembler as the sum of the contents of one of the implied base registers and a displacement calculated by the assembler; the assembler fills in the base register address and displacement in the machine language instruction.

3.2 Format of an Assembler Language Program

In general, one *statement* of the assembler language program corresponds to and is translated into one machine language instruction. A statement is usually punched into one card or keyed into one line at the terminal for input to the assembler, though several cards or lines can be used for longer statements. A statement has four fields, which contain different aspects of the instruction to be coded. These fields are *name, operation, operands,* and *remarks,* each variable in length; the fields are separated by one or more blanks. Unless a statement is continued onto more than one card or line, it is not necessary for any field except the name field to begin in any particular card column or position. Some consistency, however, on the part of the programmer or keypuncher improves readability and is heartily recommended. A reasonable convention is that an operation code should begin in column 10 and the operands field in column 16. Greater leeway is given for remarks, but to begin most remarks in, say, column 30, helps.

When a statement cannot fit on one line or card, it may be continued onto a second line. Column 72 of the first line must contain a nonblank character (note that operands and remarks can extend only to column 71); the continued part of the statement must start in exactly column 16 of the second line. Similarly, a nonblank in column 72 of the second line can signal continuation to column 16 of a third line; two continuation lines for a statement is the maximum.

The first field of the assembler-language statement is reserved for the *name* or *location* symbol of the instruction, constant, data area, or other definition. The name field *must* begin in column 1. A symbol (to be defined later) may be entered in this field, or the field may be left blank. Use of the name is analogous to the use of a statement number in FORTRAN: the name is optional, and used only when the instruction, etc., is referred to elsewhere in the program.

After the name and at least one blank, or beginning in column 2 or later if no name is given, is the *operation* field. The operation is always given symbolically. Several kinds of operations can be specified:

- machine language instructions,
- constant or symbol definition,
- instructions to the assembler,
- macro instructions.

Generally, machine language instructions will predominate. After all, the program is meant to be a collection of machine language instructions; the other types of operations mentioned are merely given in support of the assembler in its job of generating machine language instructions. Symbols defining data areas or constants are specified in the name field of a statement; the operation field of such a statement specifies the type of definition. Some operations are used to give directions to the assembler about how to behave in assembling future statements. Some of these operations control options available in the listing or *object* (machine language) *program;* others give information to the assembler, such as which register to use in addressing symbolically specified operands. Finally, a *macro instruction* is a statement that will be translated into possibly several lines of assembler language according to some given macro pattern. Macros are used for commonly used sequences of instructions (and constants), such as subroutine calls and requests for supervisor services. A one-line macro instruction written by the assembler language programmer is expanded by the assembler into the full sequence, saving the programmer work.

The third field contains *operands* for the operation. The operands field is separated from the operation field by at least one blank. The operands within the operands field are separated by commas, but no blanks. Different operations have different numbers of operands, and of course the nature of the operands varies with different operations. To show what operands are appropriate to each operation and how to use them to advantage is one of the major concerns of this book.

The fourth field is the *remarks* field, separated from the operands field by one or more blanks. The remarks do not affect assembly; they are reproduced into the program listing where they help document and explain the program.

Observe that blanks are important. The name, operation, operands, and remarks fields are each separated by one or more blanks. Blanks are not allowed *inside* the name, operation, or operands fields, except in some operands inside quotation marks, where blanks are valid characters. Blanks are permitted in the remarks field.

A *symbol* used as a name may be from one to eight characters in length. The first character of the symbol must be a letter A–Z or the characters $, #, or @, which are called "national characters" in the IBM OS or OS/VS assembler language. Characters, if any, after the first character in a name may be letters, national characters, or digits 0–9, intermixed in any fashion. No special characters or blanks are permitted in symbols. Thus F, P81B, $3, #OZG38Q, and @ are valid names but for one reason or another 3$, Z*3, and ABCDE3456 are not valid symbols. Programmers should be warned, however, that some systems have adopted special conventions using $, @, and # as the first characters of symbols; to ensure compatibility with these systems, the student is urged to avoid beginning a symbol with $, @, or #.

A symbol is *defined* when it is used in the name field of an assembler language statement. Each symbol used in a program must be defined, and may be defined only once. In general, a symbol may be used in an operand before or after it is defined. There are uses of symbols, especially uses that affect the quantity of storage allocated, which require that the symbol be *previously defined,* that is, defined in a earlier statement; these uses will be noted specifically when they arise.

3.3   An Example

Let us now examine a segment of a program written in assembler language. We will follow this example through assembler language into machine language, loading into main storage, and execution.

Let us pay some attention to the general sequence of operations. First is the assembly process. The assembler is the program currently in execution in main storage. Input is the *source program,* a file—perhaps read from a card deck, perhaps typed at a terminal—containing assembler language statements. The assembler reads the source program and produces an equivalent machine language program, called the *object program* or *object module.* The object program is either punched into cards, which are then called an *object deck,* written onto a direct access device, or both. The program may have to be combined with subroutines required to support its functions; combining the routines, completion of references between them as required, and general molding into a consistent set of routines are often done by a *linkage editor,* though if the required tasks are appropriately restricted, they can be performed by the *loader.* The loader or the linkage editor combines modules as necessary, resolves references from each to others, and places the combined module into main storage ready for execution. Note that *all* instructions are loaded before they are executed; the complete program is loaded all at once (we ignore in this volume the concept of overlay). *Constants* are loaded as an integral part of the program.

After all the program and constants have been loaded into main storage, execution of the program begins. Instructions are executed in sequence except when a sequence is broken by a branch or an interrupt. Input data are read on command, and output produced. If new information is stored in areas in which constants were loaded, the constants are replaced and can be restored only by execution of subsequent machine language instructions.

A segment written in assembler language follows. When punched into cards or typed from a terminal, the E of the name EXPL in the first statement must be punched in column 1. Operation codes must follow at least one blank after the name field, so usually begin in column 10. The operands must follow at least one blank after the operation field, so usually begin in column 16.

```
EXPL    L      3,24(8,9)
        A      3,=F'29'
        LR     4,3
        S      4,B
        STM    3,4,B+4
        MVC    L(12),B
        MVI    L,X'ØE'
```

The example may look brutally incomprehensible to you at this point. Sorry about that. Explanations of the example follow, but what is important as you follow the example is not the computations performed by the individual instruction or by the segment, but the flavor of the assembly process and its relationship to actual execution of the instructions.

The intentions of the programmer in writing the segment are as follows. The first instruction will load register 3 from a location addressed by the sum of (decimal) 24 and the contents of registers 8 and 9. The (decimal) number 29 is added to the new contents of register 3. Register 4 is loaded with the contents of register 3, the result of the addition. The number at location B is subtracted from the contents of register 4. Contents of registers 3 and 4 are stored starting at a location four bytes beyond B. The next-to-last instruction moves 12 (decimal) characters starting at location B (up to and including B+11) to an area starting at location L. Finally, the byte whose hexadecimal contents are ØE is moved to location L.

ASSEMBLY

To understand what the assembler does with this segment, we must make some assumptions about affairs in the rest of the program. Let us suppose first that EXPL has been assigned to (relocatable) location ØØØØ86. Also, that B and L have been assigned to ØØØ218 and ØØØ344 respectively. Since storage is assigned sequentially, these assignments depend on statements not shown here. Last, we assume that register 12 has been declared the implied base register, with (relocatable) contents ØØØØ6.

The assembler listing of our segment is then as shown in Fig. 3.1. Machine language equivalents are shown opposite each assembler language statement. Locations are given in hexadecimal at the extreme left. Then follows the hexadecimal representation of the machine language instructions, arranged in two-byte groups. ADDR1 and ADDR2 fields show the relocatable locations addressed symbolically, or the displacement in cases like the first instruction, where contents of registers 8 and 9 are not known to the assembler. Statements are numbered consecutively by the assembler; in our example we see that (supposedly) the statement named EXPL is number 57 in the assembly. The numbers are followed by a reproduction of the statements themselves.

The first instruction begins, as we assumed, at location ØØØØ86. The operation code of 58 corresponds to L, for *Load*. The first operand of 3 is followed by 8, the index register designated; 9, the base register designated; and the displacement 018, which is the hexadecimal equivalent of 24.

Because the first instruction is four bytes long, the second begins at location ØØØØ86+4=ØØØØ8A. The noteworthy aspect of this instruction is the treatment of the second operand. A *self-defining term* can be a value, in single quotation marks, preceded by a single letter prefix giving the type of self-defining term. For example, F'29' specifies a full-word binary integer whose value is (decimal) 29. The operand =F'29' is called a *literal;* it causes a full word to be set aside at the end of the program—in the *literal pool*—which will contain the constant 29. The *address* of this constant is coded in this instruction. We will assume that the literal is assigned to location ØØØ518; its address is specified in the instruction by index 0, the implied base register C (with its assumed con-

FIGURE 3.1   Assembly listing of a program segment

LOC	OBJECT CODE		ADDR1	ADDR2	STMT	SOURCE STATEMENT		
000086	5838	9018		00018	57	EXPL	L	R3,24(R8,R9)
00008A	5A30	C512		00518	58		A	R3,=F'29'
00008E	1843				59		LR	R4,R3
000090	5B40	C212		00218	60		S	R4,B
000094	9034	C216		0021C	61		STM	R3,R4,B+4
000098	D20B	C33E C212	00344	00218	62		MVC	L(12),B
00009E	920E	C33E	00344		63		MVI	L,X'0E'

tents ØØØØØ6), and displacement ØØØ518−ØØØØØ6=ØØØ512, of which the last 12 bits are used.

Since the second instruction is also four bytes long, the third begins at location ØØØØ8A+4=ØØØØ8E. It is an RR-type instruction, so the only operand addresses are the register addresses 4 and 3.

The next instruction, subtract, begins at ØØØØ8E+2=ØØØØ9Ø. After the operation code, 5B, the register operand address 4 is followed by the specification of the second operand. The index register was unspecified, so it is 0; the base register is the implied C; and since B is at location ØØØ218, the displacement is ØØØ218−ØØØØØ6=212.

The fifth instruction is of RS type, so the second byte contains the register addresses 3 and 4 of the operands R1 and R3. Location B+4 is ØØØ218+4 =ØØØ21C, as shown in the ADDR2 column; this is the address of the next full word beyond B. Base and displacement are as in the previous instruction, but as might be expected, the displacement used in addressing B+4 is 4 greater than the displacement used in addressing B.

The sixth instruction, MVC (or MoVe Character), is of SS type. The second byte is a length specification; the actual length in decimal is 12, so the coded length is (decimal) 11 or hexadecimal ØB. The locations B and L are both in main storage, addressed by base and displacement. As before, the implied base register C is used, and the displacements are ØØØ344−ØØØØØ6=33E and ØØØ218−ØØØØØ6=212.

Since the MVC instruction is six bytes long, the last instruction, MVI, begins in location ØØØØ98+6=ØØØØ9E. The second operand, X'ØE', is a self-defining term standing for hexadecimal (X) value ØE. The MVI instruction includes the second operand in the second byte of the instruction, just after the operation code 92. The address L is specified as in the MVC instruction.

LOADING AND EXECUTION

Now let us suppose that the program, including this segment, is loaded into main storage preparatory to execution. Suppose the storage available for the program starts at location ØØ9Ø2Ø. Then the piece of the object program shown in the listing as beginning at location ØØØØØØ is actually loaded into locations starting at ØØ9Ø2Ø. All addresses are similarly relocated, or shifted, by ØØ9Ø2Ø, so the actual locations of our segment are as follows:

Relocatable location	Actual location	Contents		
ØØØØ86	ØØ9ØA6	5838	9Ø18	
ØØØØ8A	ØØ9ØAA	5A3Ø	C512	
ØØØØ8E	ØØ9ØAE	1843		
ØØØØ9Ø	ØØ9ØBØ	5B4Ø	C212	
ØØØØ94	ØØ9ØB4	9Ø34	C216	
ØØØØ98	ØØ9ØB8	D2ØB	C33E	C212
ØØØØ9E	ØØ9ØBE	92ØE	C33E	

Suppose B, which was assigned to relocatable location 000218 and now actual location 009238, contains (hexadecimal) 000004F9. Also suppose that the byte at L, actual location 000344+009020 = 009364, is a hexadecimal 80.

Here, as in Chapter 2, note that the user of a virtual storage system should consider "actual locations," as used in explanations here, to be locations in virtual storage. The translations to real storage are performed consistently so the user need not be aware of them. In Chapter 17 we explore the manner in which this is done.

Let us now simulate execution of the program segment. First, we must make some more assumptions, mostly about register contents. Register 12 was declared the implied base register, with relocatable contents 000006. Therefore we must assume that register 12 actually contains 00009026. Let us also assume that register 8 contains 00009834, and register 9 contains 00000014. All these register contents are presumably the results of previous segments of the program.

The first instruction in our segment loads register 3. The operand address is

$$
\begin{array}{lr}
\text{contents of register 8} & 00009834 \\
+ \text{ contents of register 9} & 00000014 \\
+ \text{ displacement} & \underline{018} \\
& 009860
\end{array}
$$

If we assume that the word at location 009860 is 000043E4, this number is loaded into register 3, replacing previous contents of register 3. The second instruction adds to register 3 the number from location 009026+512 = 009538. The contents of the word at location 009538 is a hexadecimal 0000001D, equivalent to the decimal number 29 specified in the literal in the assembler language instruction. This makes the contents of register 3

$$
\begin{array}{r}
000043E4 \\
+ 0000001D \\
\hline
00004401
\end{array}
$$

The third instruction, executed from location 0090AE, loads register 4 from register 3. After this instruction, both registers 3 and 4 contain 00004401. The fourth instruction subtracts from register 4 the number from location

$$
\begin{array}{lr}
\text{contents of register 12} & 00009026 \\
+ \text{ displacement} & \underline{212} \\
& 009238
\end{array}
$$

This is the location named B, so register 4 will contain

$$
\begin{array}{r}
00004401 \\
- 000004F9 \\
\hline
00003F08
\end{array}
$$

Note, however, that register 3 still contains 00004401. Also note how the addressing of relocatable operands is accomplished in the IBM System/370 by the proper setting of the base register, not by modification of the addresses in each actual instruction. The assembler language listing showed the address of the operand in this instruction as ØØ218, which would be relocated to ØØ9Ø2Ø+ØØ218=ØØ9238. The instruction was not changed during loading; proper setting of register 12 to ØØ9Ø2Ø+ØØØØØ6 takes care of the addressing of all of the operands in the segment that are addressed symbolically.

The fifth instruction has a main storage operand address of ØØ9Ø26+216=ØØ923C. The instruction stores registers 3 and 4 starting at this location, so locations ØØ923C through ØØ9243 will contain ØØØØ44Ø1ØØØØ3FØ8. The MVC instruction moves twelve bytes, from locations starting at ØØ9Ø26 +212=ØØ9238 to locations beginning at ØØ9Ø26+33E=ØØ9364. Therefore locations ØØ9364 through ØØ936F will contain

$$ØØØØØ4F9ØØØØ44Ø1ØØØØ3FØ8$$

Finally, the MVI instruction puts the byte ØE in location ØØ9364, thus changing the word in locations ØØ9364–ØØ9367 to ØEØØØ4F9.

3.4   Addressing of Operands in Assembler Language

This section will specify in some detail the components used in operands and operand addresses in assembler language. Try to assimilate the main points and get a good idea of what can be done before going on to the next chapter. After that you will do best to refer to this section for details of how to do what you find you want to do, and every now and then to refresh your memory of the options available.

Let us define the words that give structure to this section. First, an *operand* of an instruction is a piece of information that is operated with or upon by the instruction. Operands are defined by *expressions* or appropriately restricted *combinations of expressions*; an *expression* is a *term* or an *arithmetic combination of terms*; a *term* can be a *symbol*, a *self-defining term*, a *location-counter reference*, a *literal*, or a *symbol length-attribute reference*. The symbol length-attribute reference is mentioned only for completeness, and will henceforth be ignored until Chapter 16. The other types will be taken up in turn.

SYMBOLS
According to Section 3.2, a symbol is 1 to 8 characters long, is composed of letters, $, #, @, and digits, and begins with $, #, @, or a letter. A symbol is defined—that is, given a value during assembly—when it appears in the name field of an assembler language statement.

SELF-DEFINING TERMS
A value can be defined directly in what are called self-defining terms. The value may be expressed in several ways—decimal, hexadecimal, binary, and character, but in all cases the assembler converts the value to its binary equivalent for use by the assembler or for inclusion in the object program.

Decimal values should be and are the most natural to write; they are written in assembler language simply as unsigned decimal numbers, like 15 or 3729.

Values expressed in hexadecimal, binary, or character forms are enclosed in single quotes, and a prefix denotes the form used. Hexadecimal values are written with the prefix X, as in X'ØE' or X'F863'. Binary values are written with the prefix B, as in B'1Ø1' or B'ØØØØ111Ø' (note that the latter defines exactly the same value as X'ØE'). Character self-defining terms are written with the prefix C, as in C'AB9' or C'$'. Because the assembler uses the characters ' and & in a special way, if a single quote (apostrophe) or ampersand is wanted in a character self-defining term, *two* of them must be written. The string of characters &A' would be written C'&&A'''.

Self-defining terms are used throughout the assembler language, for specification of storage addresses, lengths, or displacements in instructions, immediate portions of SI-type instructions, and, as you will see later, in the definition of constants. We choose the form (decimal, hexadecimal, binary, or character) that seems most direct and natural at the moment. For example, if we wish to move the character / to an output area, the simplest way of expressing the term is C'/', though X'61', B'Ø11ØØØØ1', and 97 would all be equivalent. On the other hand, if we wish to construct a byte whose bit pattern is Ø1Ø1Ø1Ø1, the simplest and most direct form is B'Ø1Ø1Ø1Ø1', with perhaps X'55' as a close second.

LITERALS AND CONSTANTS

A literal is a constant preceded by an equals sign (=). The constant may be one of several types, such as decimal, binary, character, hexadecimal, floating-point, packed-decimal, and some special types of addresses. The value of the constant is usually enclosed in single quotes (apostrophes), with a prefix designating the type of constant, as in a self-defining term.

Definition of constants is treated in detail in Chapter 5. However, an introduction to some types is valuable at this point, so that they can be used from now until Chapter 5. Some types are

X Hexadecimal
B Binary
F Full-word fixed-point number
H Half-word fixed-point number
C Character

If a constant is specified as hexadecimal (X), the value given in apostrophes must be a string of hexadecimal characters whose binary equivalent will be the actual constant assembled. If a constant is specified as binary (B), the value given in assembler language must be a string of Ø's and 1's. If the constant is of F or H type, the value written in assembler language must be a decimal integer, with sign optional. The binary equivalent of the value of an F-type constant is assembled into four bytes, and will be located on a full-word boundary. The binary equivalent of the value of an H-type constant is assembled into two bytes, and will be located on a half-word boundary. The value of a character constant (C) is given as a string of characters whose EBCDIC representations are assembled into the object program, one character to a byte.

The definition of constants, therefore, is much like the definition of self-defining terms. However, as you will see in Chapter 5, there are many more options in the definition of constants than there are in the definition of self-defining terms.

When a literal appears in an assembler language program, the assembler takes the following action. The constant described is assigned space in an area called the *literal pool*, usually in storage following the rest of the program. The constant is assembled into this space, and its address is the term used in assembling the instruction in which the literal was encountered.

We saw an example of a literal in the last section, in the instruction

$$A \qquad 3,=F'29'$$

The prefix F designated the literal as a constant to be assembled as a full-word binary integer, whose value is expressed in the literal as a decimal number. The value itself was 29, so the assembled constant is the binary equivalent of 29, or

$$ØØØØØØØØ \quad ØØØØØØØØ \quad ØØØØØØØØ \quad ØØØ11101.$$

The address of this constant was the term used in assembling the instruction; the address was coded into base and displacement using the implied base register. This is the normal use of a literal; as the need for a constant in our program arises, we can insert the definition and reference to the constant into the instruction that needs it. The logic of the program is clear, and it is not necessary to make up a symbol that must be later defined and associated with a constant.

LOCATION-COUNTER REFERENCE

The assembler keeps many pointers, among them one called the *location counter*, which always contains the address of the next available location in storage for the instructions, data areas, and constants in the program. The location counter is increased during the assembly of each statement that requires allocation of storage, which includes the overwhelming majority of the statements written.

A programmer may refer to the current contents of the location counter by using an asterisk (*). The asterisk can be used as a term in a statement; the associated value is the location of the first byte of currently available storage. Some examples follow shortly.

During assembly of an instruction, the location counter refers to the address of the instruction, whether or not a name is given to the instruction. Therefore, if a name *is* given to an instruction, the location counter has the same value as the name (but only during the processing of that instruction).

ABSOLUTE AND RELOCATABLE TERMS

When a program is assembled, all addresses are assigned relative to some initial value of the location counter, usually ØØØØØØ. When a program is loaded prior to execution, it is loaded into main storage relative to some actual origin (which is *not* ØØØØØØ, because the lower portion of main storage must be reserved for the supervisor). The difference between the actual origin and the initial value of the location counter is called the *relocation factor*. For example, if the initial value of the location counter is ØØØØØØ but the program is actually loaded in main storage starting at location ØØ9Ø2Ø, the relocation factor is 9Ø2Ø.

An *absolute term* is a term whose value is independent of the relocation factor. Register addresses, most constants (but not *addresses* of constants), and values of some other symbols are absolute terms. A *relocatable term* is a term whose value must be adjusted by adding the relocation factor. Addresses of instructions, constants, and data areas in main storage are relocatable terms.

Let us be more specific about which terms are absolute and which are relocatable. A self-defining term is an absolute term; the value defined in a self-defining term does not change with relocation. The value of a literal is the address of a constant, so it is a relocatable term. The location-counter reference is clearly a relocatable term, since it represents an address of a statement in the program. A symbol may be either relocatable or absolute. If a symbol appears in the name field of a statement that defines a machine language instruction, data area, or constant (in all but supervisor programming), the symbol is relocatable. A symbol may be defined by an EQU (EQUivalence) statement, which equates the symbol to the value of some expression. If the defining expression is relocatable, the symbol is relocatable, but if the expression is absolute, the symbol is also absolute.

EXPRESSIONS

An operand entry in an assembler language statement may be an expression. Valid expressions include terms and, subject to some restrictions, arithmetic combinations of terms. Terms and expressions may be added, subtracted, multiplied, and divided to form new expressions. Addition, subtraction, multiplication, and division are represented by

$$+ \ - \ * \ /$$

respectively; parentheses may be used to enclose subexpressions.

The important rules are the following:

1. An expression may not start with an arithmetic operator or contain two consecutive operators or two consecutive terms.

2. An expression may not consist of more than 16 terms or have more than five levels of parentheses. There may be more than five pairs of parentheses, but any point inside the expression may not be enclosed by more than five.

3. An expression consisting of more than one term may not contain a literal.

4. No relocatable term or expression may enter a multiply or divide operation.

5. Expressions must be either relocatable or absolute. Relocatable terms may enter an absolute expression, but must be *paired*, meaning that for each relocatable term (or subexpression) added into the expression, one must be subtracted. Relocatable terms and subexpressions must also be paired in the definition of relocatable expressions: all but one of the relocatable terms and subexpressions must be paired, and the unpaired one must be added to the expression; it cannot be subtracted.

Suppose *rel* stands for any relocatable term or expression, and *abs* for any absolute term or expression. Then the pairing rule means that allowable operations are restricted to the following, with meanings as shown:

$$rel \pm abs \quad \text{Relocatable expression}$$
$$rel - rel \quad \text{Absolute expression}$$
$$abs \pm abs \quad \text{Absolute expression}$$
$$abs * abs \quad \text{Absolute expression}$$
$$abs / abs \quad \text{Absolute expression}$$

6. Except when parentheses specify otherwise, operations are performed from left to right, with addition and subtraction after multiplication and division.

7. Division always yields an integer result, with no rounding. For example, $2/3*10 = 0$. Division *by zero* is allowed, and yields a result of zero!

Suppose A, B, and C are relocatable symbols, and G and H are absolute symbols. The following are valid absolute expressions:

```
G
B-A+X'1C'
H+24
*-B+2*G
B'10111'
37
```

The following are valid relocatable expressions:

```
A
*-4
*+B'101'
=F'4095'
G*H+A-B+C
```

The following are invalid for the reasons indicated:

```
=F'4095'+4   Literal in a multiterm expression
2*A-B        Multiplication involving a relocatable term
A+B-G        Pairing rule violated
```

The programmer must keep in mind that the operations

$$+ \; - \; * \; /$$

discussed here are performed by the *assembler* on values which are addresses and constants. They result in values which are included in the object program. These operations *are not* performed during execution of the object program.

SPECIFYING OPERANDS IN INSTRUCTIONS

A register address in an instruction may be specified by any absolute expression whose value is in the range 0 to 15. Such an absolute expression can be used for *R1*, *R3*, *B1*, *B2*, and *X2*, as we name the register operands or portions of operands in the various instruction formats.

Many programmers adopt the convention of using a symbol to refer to a register. A good strategy is to use RØ to refer to register Ø, R1 for register 1, R2 for register 2,..., R15 for register 15. One reason for this convention is to make the program more readable by helping to distinguish register addresses from other uses of small numbers. Another reason is that the assembler can produce a cross-reference table listing each symbol defined in the program and all the statements that use the symbol. Using symbolic register addressing enables the assembler to give you a summary of your use of registers. In Chapter 5 you will see how to define the symbols RØ,..., R15 by equating them to the numbers Ø,..., 15, but in the meantime let's get used to using the symbols.

This convention should not be confused with the descriptions of operand formats, which use *R1*, *R2*, and *R3*, *always in italics*, to indicate a register used as first, second, and third operands.

Main-storage operand addresses in assembler language instructions are given by expressions combined with punctuation as shown in Fig. 3.2. Base registers are either explicit or implied, but if explicit, they are absolute expressions with values Ø to F. Note the three sets of forms for RX instructions: if no *X2* is specified, as in the second set of forms, *X2* = Ø is assumed, which will mean no indexing in that instruction. Similarly, if *B2* is left out, *B2* = Ø is assumed. Since base and index registers enter the address computations in the same way, we need not distinguish (until Chapter 15) between *D2(,B2)* and *D2(X2)*. For example, 4(R1) and 4(,R1) will indicate the same address.

An *I2* operand, the second operand in an SI-type instruction, must be given as an absolute expression with value less than or equal to 255 (decimal), which is sufficiently small to fit in one byte. Self-defining terms of one character or two hexadecimal digits are the usual self-defining terms given.

A value of *L1* or *L2* (in SS-type instructions with two lengths) must be in the range Ø through 16 (inclusive); a value of *L* (in SS-type instructions with a single length) must be in the range Ø to 256. The usual definition is a decimal integer.

FIGURE 3.2   Main storage address specification forms

Instruction type	Explicit address form	Implied address form
RX	D2(X2, B2)	S2(X2)
	D2(,B2)	S2
	D2(X2)	S2
RS	D2(B2)	S2
SI	D1(B1)	S1
SS (single length)	D1(L,B1)	S1(L) or S1
	D2(B2)	S2
SS (two-length)	D1(L1,B1)	S1(L1) or S1
	D2(L2,B2)	S2(L2) or S2

D1, D2, X2, B1, B2, L, L1, L2 are absolute expressions;
S1, S2 are relocatable expressions.

Some examples of entire assembler language instructions with operands follow. The L (Load) instruction is of RX type, LM (Load Multiple) of RS type, MVI (MoVe Immediate) of SI type, and MVC (MoVe Character) of SS type.

```
L     R0,4(R1)
L     R1,A+4(R8)
L     R2,A+4*N                N IS AN ABSOLUTE SYMBOL
L     R3,=F'4095'
L     R14,*+X(R10)
LM    R14,R2,SAV+12
LM    R14,R2,12(R13)
MVI   12(R13),X'FF'
MVI   LNG,G3                  G3 IS AN ABSOLUTE SYMBOL
MVC   OUT(10),CONV            10 IS THE LENGTH
MVC   *+8(12),4(R1)
MVC   30(LTH,R7),156(R7)      LTH IS AN ABSOLUTE SYMBOL USED AS LENGTH
MVC   0(17,R8),=C'STRING OF */+&&&&-'
```

SUMMARY

An address in main storage is specified by a relocatable expression or by absolute expressions for displacement and base. In addition, some instructions allow for specification of an index or a length, either of which is also an absolute expression.

Expressions are terms or arithmetic combinations of terms; they are relocatable if their values change with relocation of the program, absolute otherwise. The writing of expressions is subject to restrictive rules, but most things we would like to do are allowed. Terms studied here are symbols (relocatable and absolute), self-defining terms (absolute), literals (relocatable), and location-counter reference (relocatable).

m a i n   i d e a s

□ Assembler language permits the symbolic writing of machine language instructions, thus contributing to speed and accuracy of the programming and debugging processes.

□ An assembler language statement consists of a name (optional), an operation code, operands, and remarks. Blanks are used as delimiters between these fields.

□ Register operands in assembler language are specified by absolute expressions; main-storage operands are specified by relocatable expressions or by absolute expressions for base and displacement.

□ An expression is a literal or an arithmetic combination of terms, which may be symbols, self-defining terms, and location-counter references.

■ **PROBLEMS** ▐ **F O R   R E V I E W   A N D   I M A G I N A T I O N** ▌

3.1 Point out which of the following are valid assembler language symbols.

A3	(B9)	GIH2J3K4	#@$&
$3	7X	GIH2J3K4L5	#34$Q

3.2 Which of the following are valid assembler language expressions? Of the valid ones, which are absolute, which relocatable? Assume that G, H and K are absolute symbols, P, Q, R, and W are relocatable symbols.

G	*
P	*-7
X'123F'	*+X'123F'
=X'123F'	*+G
X'123F'+G	R+G+H
X'123F'+P	Q-(P-K)+B'10100'
=X'123F'+G	G-(P-K)
*-P	C'4578'-G-X'F4F23E4A'
P+4*X'CE'	P+Q+R-W-(*+4)

3.3 Which of the following are valid assembler language statements? Assume that G, H and K are absolute symbols, P, Q, R and W relocatable symbols.

L	R4,5(G)	L IS AN RX INSTRUCTION
L	19,19(H)	
L	G,W(H)	
L	G,5(H,K)	
L	R4,W(H,K)	
L	B'101',*+8	
L	10,P+Q-R-X'CE'(G-5+R-Q)	
L	W,4(R4)	
L	4(4),W	

```
          LR    R4,P                LR IS AN RR INSTRUCTION
          LR    R4,K
          LR    K,X'E'
          LM    K,W                 LM IS AN RS INSTRUCTION
          LM    3,R4,W+4
          LM    3,G,W-Q+K
          LM    3(R4),Q
          LM    3,R4,Q(5)
          MVI   R4,5                MVI IS AN SI INSTRUCTION
          MVI   R,5
          MVI   Q,X'CE'
          MVI   R,Q
          MVI   G(4),C'/'
          MVC   R(2),W              MVC IS AN SS INSTRUCTION
          MVC   X'24'(2,11),W
          MVC   G(8),W
          MVC   W(8),P(8)
          MVC   W(8,9),*+8
```

3.4 The machine language instruction generated from the following assembler language instruction is assigned to relocatable location ØØ9A4Ø. What is the second operand address?

$$L \qquad R15,*+8$$

3.5 During an assembly in which the implied base register is register 10, with assumed relocatable contents ØØØØØC, suppose the next available space in the literal pool is at relocatable location ØØØ3CC. How is the statement

$$L \qquad R6,=F'24'$$

assembled, and what actions must the assembler take with respect to the literal pool?

3.6 Simulate the assembler in assembling the operands of the following instructions in a program segment. Assume that the implied base register is declared to be register 9 and to contain relocatable ØØØØØ6. Assume that the symbol G is equated to absolute 10, and T and V are assigned relocatable addresses ØØØ458 and ØØØ82C, respectively.

```
          L     R4,T
          LM    R5,R6,V-4
          AR    R4,R5
          A     R6,T(G)
          MVI   V+4,X'FF'
          ST    R4,T+4(G)
          MVC   12(8,R9),V+5
```

3.7 An absolute term is one whose value is independent of relocation of the program; a relocatable term is one whose value must be adjusted upon relocation by addition of the relocation quantity. Absolute and relocatable expressions are defined similarly. Using arithmetic operations on relocatable terms, it is possible to write expressions that are, by our definitions, neither relocatable nor absolute. Illustrate. How are the rules for formation of valid expressions, especially the rules on pairing of relocatable symbols, related to the definitions of absolute and relocatable expressions?

■ **REFERENCES**

Calingaert, Peter, *Assemblers, Compilers, and Program Translation*, Computer Science Press, Potomac, Md., 1979. A good discussion of what an assembler is and what it does.

IBM OS/VS—DOS/VSE—VM/370 Assembler Language, GC33-4010, IBM Corporation. For reference and more advanced features, this is *the* manual.

Wirth, Niklaus, "PL360, a Programming Language for the 360 Computers," *Journal of the Association for Computing Machinery* **15** (1968), pp. 37–74. Another approach to realizing the power and directness of machine language, yet also some of the advantages of higher-level languages.

INFORMATION MOVE AND BINARY INTEGER ARITHMETIC

In any digital computer, the instruction repertoire must include instructions that move information from one place to another within the computer. These instructions are simple to describe, are used often, and for the IBM System/370 illustrate well the use of the various instruction types. Therefore detailed discussion of the instruction repertoire begins here with the information move instructions.

Any digital computer also needs instructions that do integer arithmetic. This chapter describes the binary integer arithmetic instructions of the IBM System/370, leaving the more complicated decimal arithmetic to Chapter 14. Information move and binary integer arithmetic instructions are used to illustrate real and significant program segments. With these instructions you will soon begin to comprehend and write meaningful program segments.

4.1 General Structure

Instructions must be provided for moving information to and from all parts of the IBM System/370 computer accessible to the programmer. In particular, a program must be able to move information from a register to another register, from a location in main storage to another location in main storage, and between a register and a location in main storage. Movement to and from floating-point registers must also be provided for, but this aspect will be discussed in Chapter 13. We can diagram the requirements as shown in Fig. 4.1.

FIGURE 4.1   Information move requirements

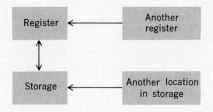

In contrast, binary integer arithmetic need only be provided for operands in registers. If it is possible to do arithmetic operations with all operands in registers, and to move numbers to and from registers, it is then possible to do arithmetic on numbers located anywhere and to place the result anywhere. All that is necessary is to move all operands to registers if they are not there already, do the arithmetic, then move the results wherever we please.

System/370 provides more than the minimum set of instructions. In every binary integer arithmetic operation the first operand is expected to be in a register, and the result will generally be left in the same register. Parallel sets of instructions permit the second operand to be either in a register or in main storage. Thus, if all operands and results are to reside eventually in main storage, a sequence of instructions like

1. place one operand in a register,
2. perform arithmetic with one register and one operand in main storage,
3. store result from a register into main storage

will be satisfactory.

SYMBOLIC NOTATION

Some symbolic notation is introduced here to help describe the working of instructions.† In specifications of instruction formats, the address of a register is denoted by $R1$, $R2$, or $R3$, depending on whether it is used as first, second, or third operand in an instruction. The *contents* of a register used as first, second, or third operand is denoted by $c(R1)$, $c(R2)$, or $c(R3)$. A location in main storage specified by base and displacement or by base, index, and displacement is denoted by $S1$ or $S2$, indicating first or second operand in the instruction. The contents of main storage location $S1$ or $S2$ will be denoted by $c(S1)$ or $c(S2)$. Such contents will be understood to be full words at locations beginning with $S1$ or $S2$, unless there is indication to the contrary.

---

†The notation used here is derived from that advanced in Kenneth Iverson, *A Programming Language*, Wiley, New York, 1962. The complete description of the IBM System/360 in Iverson notation is included in A. D. Falkoff, K. E. Iverson, and E. H. Sussenguth, "A Formal Description of SYSTEM/360," *IBM Systems Journal* **3**, 3 (1964).

When necessary, we will use subscripts to $R1$, $R2$, $R3$, $S1$, and $S2$ to indicate particular bit positions. Bits in a register are numbered 0 to 31, so the last 24 bits in register $R2$ will be denoted, for example, by $c(R2)_{8-31}$. Similarly, contents of a one-byte area in main storage can be denoted by $c(S1)_{0-7}$, which specifies bits numbered 0 to 7, starting from the leftmost bit of the main storage byte addressed by $S1$. We may also denote fields of destination operands as, for example, $R1_{8-31}$ and $S1_{0-7}$.

In the *Principles of Operation* manuals for the various models or subfamilies (3000s, 4300s, etc.) of the IBM System/370 family, which are the basic sources of information on the structure of the computer and details of its instruction repertoire, fields in instructions are sometimes abbreviated R_1, R_2, B_2, X_2, D_2, I_2, etc. We avoid this notation in order to use subscripts to show bit positions.

An arrow pointing to the left is used to indicate the act of placement. Thus $R1 \leftarrow c(R2)$ means that the contents of the register whose address is $R2$ are placed in the register whose address is $R1$.

The immediate byte of an SI-type instruction will be denoted by $I2$.

This notation and a few additions to it will be used in the remainder of this book in the definition of instructions. It is summarized in Appendix B.

The context should help you to distinguish between specification of instruction formats, in which $R1$, $R2$, and $R3$ denote any register used as first, second, and third operand, and actual instructions, in which RØ, R1, R2, ..., R15 are symbolic names for actual registers 0 to 15. The different type fonts should help too.

4.2   Information Move Instructions

REGISTER TO REGISTER

First, we will examine the information move instructions both of whose operands are in registers. These are RR-type instructions; each operand address is of course a register address. We will identify the instructions by the names or abbreviations used for them in assembler language, not by their numeric operation codes. A move instruction into a register is called a *load*, so the RR-type move instructions will all be called *load instructions*, and their names begin with the letter L. Every RR-type instruction name (with a few minor exceptions) ends with the letter R; this convention helps us to remember and recognize instructions. Four RR-type move instructions are

    LR   Load from Register
    LCR   Load Complement from Register
    LPR   Load Positive from Register (absolute value)
    LNR   Load Negative from Register (negative of absolute value)

In each of these, as in all RR-type instructions, the first operand address is the address of the register that is the destination of the move; the second operand address is the address of the register whose contents are to be moved to the destination. Therefore the

LR   *R1,R2*

instruction loads the *R1* register with contents of the *R2* register. The instruction

LR   R5,R8

for example, loads register 5 from register 8; the previous contents of register 5 are lost, and register 8 remains unchanged.

We follow closely the convention of using symbolic names for register addresses in actual instructions. Because R5, for example, is symbolic for actual register 5, we can discuss what the instruction does with register 5.

The

LCR   *R1,R2*

instruction loads the *R1* register with the complement of the contents of the *R2* register. The

LPR   *R1,R2*

instruction loads the *R1* register with the absolute value of the contents of the *R2* register. That is, if the contents of register *R2* is a positive number, it is loaded into register *R1*; if the contents of register *R2* is a negative number, its complement (a positive number) is loaded into register *R1*. The

LNR   *R1,R2*

instruction does the opposite in loading the negative (or complement) of the absolute value of the contents of register *R2* into register *R1*. That is, if the contents of register *R2* is a negative number, this number is loaded into register *R1*; if the contents of register *R2* is a positive number, the complement of this number is loaded into register *R1*.

Suppose registers 3 and 4 have as initial contents the binary numbers

Register 3:   ØØØØ1111 ØØØØØØØØ ØØØØ1111 1111ØØØØ
Register 4:   11111111 1111ØØØØ ØØØØØØØØ ØØØØ1111

Then the following instructions will have the indicated results.

Instruction		Register changed	New contents
LR	R5,R3	5	ØØØØ1111 ØØØØØØØØ ØØØØ1111 1111ØØØØ
LCR	R5,R3	5	1111ØØØØ 11111111 1111ØØØØ ØØØ1ØØØØ
LCR	R5,R4	5	ØØØØØØØØ ØØØØ1111 11111111 1111ØØØ1
LPR	R6,R3	6	ØØØØ1111 ØØØØØØØØ ØØØØ1111 1111ØØØØ
LPR	R6,R4	6	ØØØØØØØØ ØØØØ1111 11111111 1111ØØØ1
LNR	R7,R3	7	1111ØØØØ 11111111 1111ØØØØ ØØØ1ØØØØ
LNR	R7,R4	7	11111111 1111ØØØØ ØØØØØØØØ ØØØØ1111

In the notation of the last section, the general action performed by the RR-type move instructions is

$$LR: \quad R1 \leftarrow c(R2)$$
$$LCR: \quad R1 \leftarrow -c(R2)$$
$$LPR: \quad R1 \leftarrow |c(R2)|$$
$$LNR: \quad R1 \leftarrow -|c(R2)|$$

BETWEEN REGISTERS AND MAIN STORAGE

The second group of information move instructions includes those that load registers from locations in main storage, or store contents of registers into main storage. These instructions are of RX type; the first operand address is always the register, whether source of the information to be moved (as in a store instruction) or destination (as in a load instruction). Similarly, the second operand address is a main storage address given by base, index, and displacement, as described in Chapter 3. The four instructions in this group are as follows:

L	Load (from main storage):	$R1 \leftarrow c(S2)$
ST	STore (into main storage):	$S2 \leftarrow c(R1)$
LH	Load Half-word:	$R1_{16-31} \leftarrow c(S2)_{0-15}, R1_{0-15} \leftarrow c(S2)_0$
STH	STore Half-word:	$S2_{0-15} \leftarrow c(R1)_{16-31}$

In the

$$L \qquad R1,D2(X2,B2)$$

instruction the register $R1$ is loaded from the four bytes of main storage addressed by $B2$, $X2$, and $D2$. The second operand is a full word, and therefore its address (address of its first byte) should be on a full-word boundary, that is, divisible by 4. The contents of main storage are unchanged by this instruction; the previous contents of register $R1$ are lost.

The instruction

$$ST \qquad R1,D2(X2,B2)$$

is exactly the converse of the load instruction. The contents of register $R1$ are stored in the word addressed by $B2$, $X2$, and $D2$. The main storage address should be divisible by 4.

The instruction

$$LH \qquad R1,D2(X2,B2)$$

loads register $R1$ with the number found in the half-word in main storage addressed by $B2$, $X2$, and $D2$. The address of the half-word should be on a half-word boundary, that is, be divisible by 2. The high-order bit of the 16 bits in the half-word to be loaded is taken to be a sign bit. The half-word is loaded into the low-order (rightmost) half of the register $R1$, and 16 copies of the sign bit from the half-word are placed in the high-order 16 bits of $R1$. This preserves in the full word the value of the number expressed in the half-word as a sign and 15 bits. For example,

Ø1111111 11111111

is the largest positive number expressible in a half-word. If it is loaded into register 8 by the LH instruction, register 8 will contain

ØØØØØØØØ ØØØØØØØØ Ø1111111 11111111.

Similarly, the negative number in the half-word

1111111Ø ØØØØØØØØ

will be loaded into a register by the LH instruction as

11111111 11111111 1111111Ø ØØØØØØØØ

The

STH   *R1,D2(X2,B2)*

instruction stores the low-order 16 bits of register *R1* in the half-word addressed by *B2*, *X2*, and *D2*. The second operand should be on a half-word boundary. No check for sign or size of the number in register *R1* is made; the low-order 16 bits of the register are stored, regardless of the other bits in the register.

For example, suppose that the initial contents are as follows:

Register 2:	ØØØØØØØØ 1111ØØØØ 11111111 ØØØØ1111
Register 9:	ØØØØØØØØ ØØØØØØØØ 1ØØ1ØØØØ 1ØØØØØØØ
	(hexadecimal ØØØØ9Ø8Ø)
Locations ØØ9Ø94-7:	ØØØØ1111 11ØØ11ØØ 11111111 Ø1Ø1Ø1Ø1

Then the following instructions will have the indicated results.

Instruction		Register or locations changed	New contents
L	R4,2Ø(Ø,R9)	Register 4	ØØØØ1111 11ØØ11ØØ 11111111 Ø1Ø1Ø1Ø1
ST	R2,Ø(Ø,R9)	Locations ØØ9Ø8Ø-3	ØØØØØØØØ 1111ØØØØ 11111111 ØØØØ1111
LH	R5,2Ø(Ø,R9)	Register 5	ØØØØØØØØ ØØØØØØØØ ØØØØ1111 11ØØ11ØØ
LH	R6,22(Ø,R9)	Register 6	11111111 11111111 11111111 Ø1Ø1Ø1Ø1
STH	R2,4(Ø,R9)	Locations ØØ9Ø84-5	11111111 ØØØØ1111

Note that in the first instruction, the effective address is computed as follows:

base:	register	9:	hexadecimal	ØØØØ9Ø8Ø
index:		0:		Ø
displacement:	decimal 20 = hexadecimal			Ø14
				ØØ9Ø94

In the execution of the instruction

$$\text{LH} \qquad \text{R5,2Ø(Ø,R9)}$$

the two bytes loaded into the low-order half of register 5 have a high-order bit of Ø, so the high-order 16 bits of the register are set to Ø's. In the execution of the instruction

$$\text{LH} \qquad \text{R6,22(Ø,R9)}$$

the half-word loaded into the low-order half of register 6 has a high-order bit of 1, so the high-order bits of the register are set to 1's. Both ØØ9Ø94 and ØØ9Ø96 are addresses located on half-word boundaries; ØØ9Ø94 is also on a full-word boundary, as was required in the

$$\text{L} \qquad \text{R4,2Ø(Ø,R9)}$$

instruction.

STORAGE TO STORAGE

One instruction for moving information from one place to another in main storage is sufficient. The MVC (MoVe Character) instruction discussed briefly in the previous chapter has the flexibility of moving character or byte strings of length from 1 to 256 bytes, with no restrictions as to full-word boundaries and the like. Instructions that have both operands in main storage are all of SS-type and all have the destination or result as first operand and the source as second operand. Source and destination operands of the MVC instruction are naturally of the same length, so only one length is specified in the instruction. The MVC instruction is usually written with both operands expressed as symbols:

$$\text{MVC} \qquad \text{STORE(8),PLACE}$$

will cause eight bytes to be moved from PLACE to STORE. The length is coded in the second byte of the machine language instruction; in assembler language it is the first quantity enclosed in parentheses in the definition of the first operand. While looking at program listings, the programmer should bear in mind that in assembler language the actual length of the string to be moved is specified as the length, but in the assembled machine language instruction this number is decreased by one.† Thus

$$\text{MVC} \qquad \text{8(4,R9),24(R9)}$$

assembles into D2Ø39ØØ89Ø18. The actual length of the string to be moved is four bytes; the length coded in the machine language instruction is 03.

---

†Exception: The length of a one-byte field may be given in assembler language as either 0 or 1.

Another instruction which moves information to a location in main storage is the MVI (MoVe Immediate) instruction, which was also used as an example in the last chapter. As an SI-type instruction, MVI has a first operand, which is a location in main storage, and a second operand, which is a one-byte datum in the second byte of the instruction itself. The first operand is the destination; the second operand is the source of the information to be moved. The MVI instruction is used when a one-byte constant is to be moved to a location in main storage.

Suppose that registers and main storage locations have the following initial contents.

Register 9:	ØØØØØØØØ ØØØØØØØØ 1ØØ1ØØØØ 1ØØØØØØØ
	(hexadecimal ØØØØ9Ø8Ø)
Locations ØØ928Ø-83:	111ØØØØØ ØØØØ11ØØ 1ØØ11ØØ1 11111111
Locations ØØ9398-9B:	ØØØØØØØØ ØØ11ØØ11 11ØØØØ11 Ø111Ø111

Then the following instructions have the indicated results.

	Instruction	Locations changed	New contents
MVC	513(2,R9),792(R9)	ØØ9281-2	ØØØØØØØØ ØØ11ØØ11
MVC	64(1,R9),512(R9)	ØØ9ØCØ	111ØØØØØ
MVI	2Ø(R9),2Ø	ØØ9Ø94	ØØØ1Ø1ØØ
MVI	21(R9),C'E'	ØØ9Ø95	11ØØØ1Ø1
MVI	22(R9),X'ØE'	ØØ9Ø96	ØØØØ111Ø
MVI	23(R9),B'ØØØØ1111'	ØØ9Ø97	ØØØØ1111

Let us consider another set of examples, including use of symbolic addresses and showing in hexadecimal the contents of main storage and registers. Suppose that the following are initial contents:

Register 0:	FCAØ27Ø5
Register 1:	ØØØØ347C
Register 2:	DØØ342A3
Register 9:	ØØØØØØØ4
Register 10:	ØØØØ9Ø8Ø
Location Q (full word):	FFF432AD
Location Y (two words):	ØØ388[E4 ØØØØØØ14

Then the following instructions will have the indicated results.

Instruction		Action	
L	R3,Q	Register 3:	FFF432AD
L	R3,Y(R9)	Register 3:	00000014
LH	R3,Y+2	Register 3:	FFFF81E4
ST	R2,Y+8	Location Y + 8:	D00342A3
MVC	Q+3(7),Y+1	Location Q + 3:	3881E400000014
		(first byte:	38 replaces AD at Q+3)
MVI	Q+2,X'EE'	Location Q + 2:	EE

Let L indicate the length of an operand used in an SS instruction, in particular the coded length (0–255) as formed in the machine language instruction itself. Then, if we denote by BL the value $8L + 7$, the action of the MVC and MVI instructions can be summarized as

$$\text{MVC:} \qquad S1_{0-BL} \leftarrow c(S2)_{0-BL}$$
$$\text{MVI:} \qquad S1_{0-7} \leftarrow I2$$

4.3   Binary Integer Add and Subtract Instructions

Because binary integer addition and subtraction are performed in registers, the instructions performing the arithmetic are of RR and RX types. The register in which the arithmetic is performed is always the first operand of the instruction; one of the numbers taking part in the operation must already be in that register, and the result is left there. The second operand may be either in a register or in main storage.

The six instructions can be described symbolically as follows:

AR:	Add Register	$R1 \leftarrow c(R1) + c(R2)$
SR:	Subtract Register	$R1 \leftarrow c(R1) - c(R2)$
A:	Add	$R1 \leftarrow c(R1) + c(S2)$
S:	Subtract	$R1 \leftarrow c(R1) - c(S2)$
AH:	Add Half-word	$R1 \leftarrow c(R1) + c(S2)_{0-15}$
SH:	Subtract Half-word	$R1 \leftarrow c(R1) - c(S2)_{0-15}$

AR (Add Register) and A (Add) are simple: the two operands are added and the result left in $R1$. The SR (Subtract Register) and S (Subtract) are nearly as simple, but the programmer must remember that the instructions subtract the second operand from the first. Rules of signs prevail; for example, if we subtract a negative number, the number in $R1$ is increased.

In a half-word addition or subtraction, the half-word operand is aligned with the low-order portion of the register operand. The whole word in the register (first operand) participates. We may think of the half-word as expanded into a full word before addition or subtraction, with the sign bit of the half-word copied into the upper half of the full word, as in the LH instruction.

Suppose the following are initial contents of registers and storage locations.

Register 0:	ØØØØ123A
Register 1:	ØØØØØØ51
Register 2:	FFFFFFFE
Location Q:	Ø1CEBDEC
Location Y:	ØØØ1FFC2

Then the following instructions will have the indicated results. In each instruction, we assume that we deal with the initial conditions listed above—not, as in a program, with the results of the immediately preceding instruction.

Instruction		Register changed	New contents
AR	RØ,R1	0	ØØØØ128B
SR	RØ,R1	0	ØØØØ11E9
SR	R1,R2	1	ØØØØØØ53
A	R1,Q	1	Ø1CEBE3D
S	R2,Q	2	FE314212
AH	R1,Y	1	ØØØØØØ52
SH	RØ,Q	0	ØØØØ106C
SH	R2,Q+2	2	ØØØØ4212

Let us now examine some instruction sequences to see how the arithmetic and information move instructions can be used together on actual problems. Suppose that quantities named k, m, and j are stored at full-word storage locations named K, M, and J, and a quantity called jr is stored in register 4. Then the following instruction sequences perform the indicated computations.

Compute n as $k - m$:	L	R5,K
	S	R5,M
	ST	R5,N
Compute n as $k - jr$:	L	R5,K
	SR	R5,R4
	ST	R5,N
Compute n as $k - jr$:	LCR	R5,R4
(a second way)	A	R5,K
	ST	R5,N
Compute n as $m + k - 5000$:	L	R5,M
	A	R5,K
	S	R5,=F'5ØØØ'
	ST	R5,N

4.4 Binary Integer Multiplication

SPECIFICATIONS OF INSTRUCTIONS

Binary integer multiplication is performed in registers, and as in the binary integer add and subtract instructions, one operand is in a register at the beginning of the operation. Instructions of both RR and RX types are provided so that the second operand may be in either a register or main storage.

When two 32-bit numbers are multiplied, the product is 64 bits long. Therefore two registers are used in the operation. In System/370, whenever two registers are used as a connected pair, the first, holding the most significant part of the number, is a register with an even address; the second register is the one immediately following. Therefore instructions using register pairs must use registers 0 and 1, 2 and 3, 4 and 5, 6 and 7, 8 and 9, 10 and 11, 12 and 13, or 14 and 15. Conventions establish special uses for registers 0 and 1, 13, 14, and 15, so normally only 2–12 are available.

The full-word multiply instructions are

MR   Multiply Register: $[R1, R1 + 1] \leftarrow c(R1 + 1) * c(R2)$
M   Multiply: $[R1, R1 + 1] \leftarrow c(R1 + 1) * c(S2)$

The *first operand address*, $R1$, must be an *even* register address, the address of the first register of the register pair to be used. However, the *multiplier* is the contents of the following register, the one with *odd* address, $R1 + 1$. The product is left in the register pair $R1$ and $R1 + 1$; the brackets [ ] in the symbolic definition of the operation indicate the concatenation of the two registers.

For example, the instruction

MR   R2,R8

multiplies the numbers in registers 3 and 8, leaving the product in registers 2 and 3.

DETAILED LOGIC OF THE PROCESS

It is instructive to describe in some detail the multiplication process as implemented in the IBM System/370 computer; the description should remove some of the bewilderment caused by the instruction specifications. We will consider a multiplication in which both operands are positive, though the instructions handle negative operands perfectly well. Complementation of operands and, if necessary, recomplementation of results, take care of cases in which one or both operands are negative.

The first actions in multiplication are:

1. The multiplicand (second operand) is put in a special nonaddressable register.
2. Register $R1$ is cleared to 0.

Then come 32 repetitions of the following sequence:

3. The low-order bit of register $R1 + 1$ is examined. If this bit is 1, the multiplicand is added into register $R1$.

FIGURE 4.2   Multiplication in four-bit registers

Reg. 2   Reg. 3

1. Ø11Ø enters the special multiplicand register.
2. Register 2 is cleared to ØØØØ. For the remaining steps, we show registers 2 and 3.

ØØØØ	Ø1Ø1

3. Examine the low-order bit of register 3. It is 1, so add the multiplicand.

+Ø11Ø

Ø11Ø	Ø1Ø1

4. Shift both registers right one bit.

ØØ11	ØØ1Ø

5. Examine the lower-order bit of register 3. It is Ø so the multiplicand is *not* added.

ØØ11	ØØ1Ø

6. Shift.

ØØØ1	1ØØ1

7. Examine the low-order bit. It is 1, so add the multiplicand.

+Ø11Ø

Ø111	1ØØ1

8. Shift.

ØØ11	11ØØ

9. Examine the low-order bit. It is Ø, so no addition.

ØØ11	11ØØ

10. Shift.

ØØØ1	111Ø

4. Registers *R1* and *R1* + 1 are shifted right one bit. That is, the bit from bit position 63 (in the register pair) is lost, the bit from position 62 is moved into position 63, the bit from position 61 is moved to position 62, . . . , the bit from position 0 is moved to position 1, and a 0 is filled in position 0.

Thus the multiplier is gradually shifted away and lost, and the product is gradually shifted down until it fills the entire register pair.

For purposes of illustration, let us consider fictitious registers four bits long instead of 32. The process is the same, but an illustration using 32-bit registers would be more tedious. Consider four-bit register 3 containing Ø1Ø1, equivalent to the decimal number 5. Let us suppose that four-bit register 8 contains Ø11Ø, or decimal 6. The steps shown in Fig. 4.2 perform MR R2,R8.

The series of examine, add, and shift is carried out only four times because we are dealing with fictitious four-bit registers. The result is the binary number ØØØ111Ø, or decimal 30.

Note that this process is exactly equivalent and quite similar to our normal method of doing long multiplication. Compare the foregoing with a pencil-and-paper multiplication of Ø1Ø1 and Ø11Ø:

$$\frac{\begin{array}{r} 11\emptyset \\ 1\emptyset1 \\ \hline 11\emptyset \\ 11\emptyset \end{array}}{1111\emptyset}$$

USE IN A PROGRAM

When the result of a multiplication is left in a register pair, it is a 64-bit integer. The only arithmetic operation that can be performed by the IBM System/370 in a straightforward manner on 64-bit integers is division, as we shall see in the next section. Therefore some 32-bit segment of the 64 bits must usually be stored. In most cases the low-order 32 bits, the contents of register $R1 + 1$, will contain all the significant bits (that is, those not equal to the sign bit) of the result, and we can store the product merely by storing register $R1 + 1$. When this is not sufficient, some scaling analysis must be made, and a 32-bit segment of the product shifted into a register for storage. (Shift instructions will be considered in Chapter 11.) However, if quantities are expected to be generated which are larger than 2^{31} (about 2×10^9), floating-point arithmetic will usually be used.

Let us now show the results of binary integer multiply instructions in the actual 32-bit registers of the IBM System/370. Suppose the following are the intial contents expressed as hexadecimal numbers:

Register 2: ØØEA539F
Register 3: ØØØØØ2ØØ
Register 4: 5F349ABD
Register 5: FFFFDØØØ
Register 9: ØØ24ØC32
Storage location U: FFFFEEEF

Assuming that these are the initial conditions before *each* of the following instructions, the instructions have the indicated results.

Instruction		Register pair	New contents
MR	R2,R9	2, 3	ØØØØØØØØ 48186400
MR	R2,R5	2, 3	FFFFFFFF FFAØØØØØ
M	R4,U	4, 5	ØØØØØØØØ Ø3333ØØØ
M	R8,U	8, 9	FFFFFFFD 98CBDEAE

The following computations can be performed by program segments as shown.

1. Multiply contents of registers 7 and 8, storing the low-order bits of the result in BTF:

```
MR    R6,R8
ST    R7,BTF
```

2. Square the number in register 7, leave the contents of register 7 itself unchanged:

```
LR    R9,R7
MR    R8,R9
```

The result will then be in registers 8 and 9.

3. Perform (A+B)*Q, where A, B, and Q are all full-word integers in main storage, and store the low-order 32 bits of the result in Y:

```
L     R5,A
A     R5,B
M     R4,Q
ST    R5,Y
```

Our terminology becomes looser here. We say "Perform (A+B)*Q," meaning add and multiply certain quantities, full words A, B, and Q, in main storage. But A, B, and Q are really, for purposes of writing programs, *addresses* of locations containing the quantities to be added and multiplied. It is convenient to talk about the contents of the location named A as also being A, and we will often do so, when the meaning is clear. However, when we start doing much address arithmetic we must be clear whether B + 4, for example, means address B plus the number 4 or the number at location B plus the number 4.

THE HALF-WORD MULTIPLY INSTRUCTION

There is one other multiplication instruction of RX-type, which makes use of a full-word first operand in *any* register, multiplies it by a *half-word* in main storage, and leaves the low-order 32 bits of the product in the first operand register:

MH   Multiply Half-word: $R1 \leftarrow (c(R1)*c(S2)_{0-15})_{16-47}$

A 16-bit quantity times a 32-bit quantity will give a 48-bit product. The usual rule of signs will prevail. But of bits 0–47 of this product, only the last 32 are kept as a result by the computer. If the absolute value of the actual product is greater than 2^{31}, the sign bit of the result as left in the register does not necessarily agree with the actual sign of the product.

An example of the use of the MH instruction will conclude this section. Suppose that a half-word integer is stored at location G, and another half-word at K. Their product is to be stored at Z, as a full word.

```
LH   R2,G
MH   R2,K
ST   R2,Z
```

4.5   Binary Integer Division

SPECIFICATIONS OF THE INSTRUCTIONS

The dividend in a binary integer divide instruction in System/370 is in a register pair. As in any instruction using a register pair, the most significant part of the number must be in the register with even address, and the last 32 bits in the next register. The register pair is addressed by its first register, the one with even address. The address of the register pair containing the dividend is the first operand, *R1*, in the divide instructions.

Instructions are provided to allow for the divisor to be in a register or in a full word in main storage. The DR (Divide Register) instruction is of RR type; the D (Divide) instruction is of RX type. Both quotient and remainder are left as results of the division. The *quotient* is left in the *odd*-addressed register, and the *remainder* in the *even*-addressed register. The instructions are as follows:

DR   Divide Register: $R1 \leftarrow$ Remainder of $[c(R1),\ c(R1 + 1)]/c(R2)$
                         $R1 + 1 \leftarrow$ Quotient of $[c(R1),\ c(R1 + 1)]/c(R2)$
D   Divide: $R1 \leftarrow$ Remainder of $[c(R1),\ c(R1 + 1)]/c(S2)$
                         $R1 + 1 \leftarrow$ Quotient of $[c(R1),\ c(R1 + 1)]/c(S2)$

The sign of a nonzero remainder is always the same as the sign of the dividend. The sign of a nonzero quotient is determined by the rule of signs; that is, the quotient is positive if both dividend and divisor have the same sign; if dividend and divisor are of opposite sign, the quotient is negative.

DETAILED LOGIC OF DIVISION

As with the multiply instructions, a detailed explanation of the computer's process should help you understand how to use the divide instructions. Here too we will assume that both dividend and divisor are positive. The division process repeats 32 times the sequence of steps listed below.

1. The register pair *R1* and *R1* + 1 is shifted *left* one bit: the bit in position 0 is lost, the bit in position 1 is moved to position 0, the bit in position 2 is moved to position 1, . . . , the bit in position 63 is moved to position 62, and position 63 is filled with 0.

2. The divisor is subtracted from the contents of register *R1*, which must now be considered as a 32-bit unsigned number.

3. *If* the subtraction causes an overdraft—that is, if the divisor is greater than the quantity in register *R1*—the divisor is added back to restore the previous contents of register *R1*.

4. If there is no overdraft, the bit in position 63 is changed to a 1. Thus bit 63 is the new bit of the quotient; it is 1 if the divisor was successfully subtracted from ("goes into") the dividend, and 0 otherwise.

Each time this sequence is performed, another bit of the quotient is formed in bit 63. These bits, through shifting, ultimately fill the entire register *R1* + 1

FIGURE 4.3 Division in four-bit registers

1. Register pair 4–5 is shifted left one bit.	Ø1Ø1	Ø11Ø
2. The divisor Ø111 is subtracted from register 4.	Ø111	
	111Ø	Ø11Ø
3. The overdraft requires adding back.	Ø111	
	Ø1Ø1	Ø11Ø
4. Register pair 4–5 is shifted.	1Ø1Ø	11ØØ
5. The divisor is subtracted.	Ø111	
	ØØ11	11ØØ
6. No overdraft, so change last bit to 1.	ØØ11	11Ø1
7. Shift.	Ø111	1Ø1Ø
8. Subtract.	Ø111	
	ØØØØ	1Ø1Ø
9. No overdraft, so set quotient bit to 1.	ØØØØ	1Ø11
10. Shift.	ØØØ1	Ø11Ø
11. Subtract.	Ø111	
	1Ø1Ø	Ø11Ø
12. Overdraft, so add back.	Ø111	
	ØØØ1	Ø11Ø

with the quotient. The remainder, literally the number remaining after the division by repeated subtraction, is left in register *R1*.

Let us illustrate the process, again with four-bit registers to avoid tiresome repetition of the steps. Let us consider division of the eight-bit quantity ØØ1Ø1Ø11 (decimal 43) in four-bit registers 4 and 5 by Ø111 (decimal 7) in register 9. The steps outlined in Fig. 4.3 perform

$$DR \quad R4,R9$$

The quotient is Ø11Ø, or 6; the remainder is ØØØ1, or 1. Compare the sequence with the layout for pencil-and-paper long division of the same problem:

```
           0110
     111)101011
           111
           111
           111
          0001
```

If the relative sizes of dividend and divisor are such that the quotient cannot be expressed as a 32-bit word including sign, no division is performed, and a program interruption occurs. Program interruptions are described more fully in Chapter 9.

EXAMPLES

To illustrate further the action of the divide instructions, we will consider the results of several instructions on System/370 full 32-bit registers. The following are the initial contents:

$$
\begin{array}{lll}
\text{Register pair 4-5:} & \varnothing\varnothing\varnothing\varnothing\varnothing\varnothing\varnothing\varnothing\varnothing\varnothing\varnothing1\text{D}6 & \text{(decimal 470)} \\
\text{Register pair 6-7:} & \text{FFFFFFFFFFFFFF12} & \text{(decimal } -238) \\
\text{Register 9:} & \varnothing\varnothing\varnothing\varnothing\varnothing\varnothing28 & \text{(decimal 40)} \\
\text{Storage location P:} & \text{FFFFFFB6} & \text{(decimal } -74)
\end{array}
$$

Each of the following instructions, starting from these initial contents, will have the indicated results.

```
DR    R4,R9        Register 5   (quotient):  ØØØØØØØB (decimal 11)
                   Register 4 (remainder):   ØØØØØØ1E (decimal 30)
DR    R6,R9        Register 7   (quotient):  FFFFFFFB (decimal −5)
                   Register 6 (remainder):   FFFFFFDA (decimal −38)
D     R4,P         Register 5   (quotient):  FFFFFFFA (decimal − 6)
                   Register 4 (remainder):   ØØØØØØ1A (decimal 26)
D     R6,P         Register 7   (quotient):  ØØØØØØØ3 (decimal 3)
                   Register 6 (remainder):   FFFFFFFØ (decimal −16)
```

USE OF DIVISION IN PROGRAM SEGMENTS

When using a divide instruction, you must fill both registers of the register pair being used for the dividend. If the dividend is generated by a multiply instruction, it is automatically in the right form for division. If the dividend comes from a full word in storage, it should be loaded into the register with odd address. The register with even address, the first register of the pair, must then be filled with sign bits of the dividend: 0's if the dividend is positive, 1's if the dividend is negative. You will learn in later chapters how this can be done easily when the sign of the dividend is not known to you in advance.

The following instruction sequences perform the arithmetic indicated:

1. Compute E as $P*Q/Y$.

```
L     R5,P
M     R4,Q
D     R4,Y
ST    R5,E
```

2. Compute E as $P/3$ assuming P positive.

```
L     R5,P
L     R4,=F'Ø'
D     R4,=F'3'
ST    R5,E
```

3. Compute E as $Y/(Q+3)$ assuming Y negative.

```
L     R9,Q
A     R9,=F'3'
L     R5,Y
L     R4,=F'−1'
DR    R4,R9
ST    R5,E
```

4. Compute G as the remainder of $P/3$, assuming P positive.

```
L    R5,P
L    R4,=F'Ø'
D    R4,=F'3'
ST   R4,G
```

5. Compute G as $P/(Q+3)+Y/5$, assuming P positive, Y negative.

```
L    R9,Q
A    R9,=F'3'
L    R5,P
L    R4,=F'Ø'
DR   R4,R9
L    R7,Y
L    R6,=F'-1'
D    R6,=F'5'
AR   R5,R7
ST   R5,G
```

4.6 The LM and STM Instructions

The LM (Load Multiple) and STM (STore Multiple) instructions are information move instructions of RS type. They cause the movement of several words at a time between consecutive registers and consecutive main storage locations. The first and third operands (written first and second in the assembler language statement) are register addresses, defining a block of registers that take part in the move. If $R1$ is less than $R3$, all registers $R1$, $R1+1$, $R1+2$, . . . , $R3$ are loaded or stored. But if $R1$ is greater than $R3$, the registers $R1$, $R1+1$, . . . , 15, 0, . . . , $R3$ are loaded or stored. In other words the registers are considered as forming a loop, with register 0 following register 15, so that every register has a successor. The registers loaded or stored are in every case $R1$ and all succeeding registers in the loop up to and including $R3$. In main storage a consecutive block of full words is used, starting at the address given by the second operand.

We illustrate with some examples.

The instruction

```
LM    R3,R4,Q
```

loads register 3 from the full word at location Q, and register 4 from the next word, at location Q + 4.

The instruction

```
LM    R4,R3,Q
```

loads register 4 from the full word at location Q, register 5 from the word at Q + 4, register 6 from Q + 8, . . . , register 15 from Q + 44, register 0 from Q + 48, . . . , register 3 from Q + 60.

The instruction

```
LM    R4,R4,Q
```

loads register 4 from the word at Q, and therefore produces the same result as

$$L \quad R4,Q$$

Further examples are illustrated in Fig. 4.4.

The STM instruction operates with exactly the same pattern of registers, with the flow of information reversed: the contents of registers are stored in main storage. The instruction

$$STM \quad R14,R\emptyset,Y$$

would cause the contents of register 14 to be stored at the full word Y, contents of register 15 at Y + 4, and contents of register 0 at Y + 8.

The LM and STM instructions are used primarily in linkage to subroutines, as will be shown in the next chapter. They are also useful for loading and storing blocks of data.

For example, suppose that we wish to compute E as

$$3*Q/P + 3*Q/R + 3*Q/S.$$

FIGURE 4.4   Examples of LM instructions

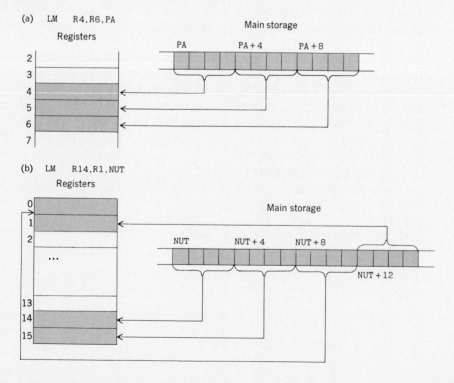

A program segment to accomplish this is the following.

```
L     R5,=F'3'
M     R4,Q
STM   R4,R5,DIVD      DIVD MUST BE DEFINED AS A TWO-WORD AREA
D     R4,P            COMPUTES 3*Q/P
LM    R6,R7,DIVD
D     R6,R            COMPUTES 3*Q/R
AR    R5,R7           SUM OF QUOTIENTS IN REGISTER 5
LM    R6,R7,DIVD
D     R6,S            COMPUTES 3*Q/S
AR    R5,R7           SUM OF THREE QUOTIENTS
ST    R5,E
```

4.7 The LA Instruction

The LA (Load Address) instruction is an important information move instruction of RX type, but is peculiar in that it does not access main storage. We can describe the instruction symbolically as

$$LA \quad \text{Load Address: } R1_{8-31} \leftarrow S2$$
$$R1_{0-7} \leftarrow 0$$

The address $S2$ is generated from base, index, and displacement as in any RX-type instruction. Since the normal address calculation circuitry is used, only the low-order 24 bits are kept. These 24 bits themselves are loaded into the low-order 24 bits of register $R1$, and the first 8 bits are cleared to 0's.

The instruction was designed to allow us to load actual addresses into registers; we will learn the usefulness of this possibility when we consider problems of address modification. The instruction is also useful for performing loads and additions with small numbers. Suppose, for example, that we wish to load the number 3 into register 5. Instead of requiring that a constant 3 be kept in storage for loading into register 5, we can issue an instruction

$$LA \quad R5,3$$

The second operand 3 is a self-defining term. The assembler will assemble the instruction with

$$R1 = 5 \text{ (EQUivalenced to R5)}$$
$$X2 = \emptyset$$
$$B2 = \emptyset$$
$$D2 = \emptyset\emptyset3$$

In execution of this instruction, the second operand address will be

$$
\begin{array}{lr}
B2: & \varnothing\varnothing\varnothing\varnothing\varnothing\varnothing \\
X2: & +\;\varnothing\varnothing\varnothing\varnothing\varnothing\varnothing \\
D2: & +\;\underline{\qquad\varnothing\varnothing3} \\
& \varnothing\varnothing\varnothing\varnothing\varnothing3
\end{array}
$$

Therefore, $\varnothing\varnothing\varnothing\varnothing\varnothing\varnothing\varnothing3$ will be loaded into register 5.

Furthermore, the LA instruction can be used as an efficient add instruction for small numbers whose sum is small and positive. One or two numbers in registers can be added to a positive constant up to (decimal) 4095. Consider the instruction

```
LA    R3,69(R6,R7)
```

The contents of register 6, the contents of register 7, and the (decimal) number 69 are added, and if the sum is positive and less than 24 bits in length, it is loaded correctly into register 3. While this example is slightly exotic, a very common use of the instruction is to add 1 to a register whose contents are known to be positive. For example,

```
LA    R4,1(,R4)
```

The following instruction sequences perform the arithmetic indicated:

1. Compute E as $(P + 3)/Q$ assuming P small and positive.

```
L     R5,P
LA    R5,3(,R5)
LA    R4,∅
D     R4,Q
ST    R5,E
```

2. Put the address of HPK plus the (small) number N found in register 4 into HPKN.

```
LA    R5,HPK
AR    R5,R4
ST    R5,HPKN

or

LA    R5,HPK(,R4)
ST    R5,HPKN
```

3. The address of the word in the first column and first row of an array of full words in main storage is ARBASE. The words in a column are stored sequentially, and the next column begins immediately after the 20th word of the preceding column. Given M as the row index of a particular word (that is, this

word is in the *M*th row) and *N* as the column index, load the word into register 6.

```
L    R5,N
S    R5,=F'1'          c(N) − 1 is the number of columns to be
                       skipped.
M    R4,=F'20'         20 words to a column.
A    R5,M              c(M) − 1 is the number of words to be
                       skipped in a column to get to the Mth
                       row.
S    R5,=F'1'
M    R4,=F'4'          Four bytes to a word.
LA   R5,ARBASE(R5)     Add base address.
L    R6,0(,R5)         Load word from computed address.
```

4.8   Generation of Pseudo-Random Numbers

One of the significant uses of computers is simulation of environments and activities in the real world, such as traffic flow patterns, drawing from and replacing inventory, flow of jobs through a digital computer, inheritance of genetic traits, or interaction of people in a group. In many of these simulations, actions occur at chance or random intervals or involve attributes whose values inside the computer must be assigned somewhat by chance. For example, in an inventory simulation the time at which the next customer makes a demand for an item should be considered to be determined at least partly by chance. Furthermore, the *number* of items the customer wishes to buy is a variable whose value should be determined by chance (under restrictions, of course). If a computer is performing the simulation, it must assign values to variables like "length of wait until next customer" and "size of transaction." A table of values carefully produced at random could be fed into the computer, but if the computer can produce its own random values easily, the program can be simpler and more efficient.

PSEUDO-RANDOM NUMBERS

If a computer starts producing truly random numbers—that is, numbers that cannot be adequately explained from knowledge of the machine's contents and input—we call for repair. If we attempted to build particular elements into a computer that would yield random values, we would have an extremely difficult time controlling the distribution of values produced. As it turns out, it is far better to produce *pseudo-random numbers*. Pseudo-random numbers are not random, but sequences of them have many of the properties that we desire sequences of random numbers to have. Two of these properties are the following.

1. *Controlled distribution.* We want to be able to designate the fraction of numbers in the sequence that attain a certain value or fall into a certain interval, but if the number sequence merely has some *known* distribution, we can transform its values to any desired distribution by programming.

2. *Independence of successive values.* The value of one number of the sequence should not affect the next value. We usually generate pseudo-random numbers *from their predecessors*, so this condition is clearly not met. But it can be met approximately, in the following sense: knowing only that a number in a pseudo-random sequence lies in some fairly small interval does not help one to predict the next number of the sequence; in other words, the distribution of numbers following numbers that may lie in the given interval is the same as the distribution of numbers following numbers in any other interval of similar size.

MULTIPLICATIVE CONGRUENCE METHOD
One widely used method for generating pseudo-random numbers is called the *multiplicative congruence method*.† This method is as follows:

1. A beginning value X is chosen, the first number of the pseudo-random sequence.

2. X is multiplied by some constant multiplier.

3. The product is divided by some constant (called the *modulus*) and the *remainder* taken as a new X, the next pseudo-random number.

4. Steps 2 and 3 are repeated for every successive pseudo-random number desired.

For binary computers, some theory has been developed about proper beginning values, multipliers, and moduli. First, if the modulus is chosen as a power of 2, no division need be performed at all; all that is necessary is to clear some of the *most significant* bits of the product. In System/370, for example, a word is 32 bits long; hence a convenient choice of modulus is 2^{32}, and instead of performing a division we need only *ignore* the first word of a product. Second, it can be shown that the last three bits of the multiplier should be 011 or 101, for if they are, the sequence of pseudo-random numbers can be made not to repeat until 2^{30} numbers have been generated (assuming the 2^{32} modulus).

---

†For a more formal description and further references, see Donald E. Knuth, *The Art of Computer Programming, Vol. 2: Seminumerical Algorithms,* 2nd ed., Addison-Wesley, Reading, Mass. 1981.

The only additional requirement for achieving a period of 2^{30} before repetition is that the last bit of the starting number X be 1. More conditions should be set on the multiplier, however. It should be close to the square root of the modulus in order to have maximum apparent independence of successive values, and to minimize the time required for the multiplication (on some computers) the number of 1-bits in the multiplier should be as small as possible! Therefore a good value for the multiplier in System/370 is $2^{16} + 5$ or 65,541.

The multiplicative congruence method yields a quite uniform distribution of numbers over the possible range of generation. For example, considering that there are 2^{32} possible 32-bit numbers, if the full sequence of 2^{30} different numbers were generated, each of the possible values of the high-order 29 bits of the numbers will occur exactly twice! The distribution of less than the full sequence of 2^{30} numbers would not be as even.

PROGRAMMING

Suppose that the current pseudo-random number, an integer in the range -2^{31} to $2^{31} - 1$, is always stored at RN. A program segment sufficient to generate the next pseudo-random number is

```
        L    R7,RN
        M    R6,=F'65541'
        ST   R7,RN
```

Suppose that in our *use* of pseudo-random numbers, what we really want is a digit randomly selected from 0 to 9, with each digit to be selected with equal likelihood. After the instruction sequence above, we can perform

```
        M    R6,=F'1Ø'
        LA   R6,5(,R6)
        ST   R6,RDIGIT
```

A number RN in register 7 is between -2^{31} to 2^{31} (noninclusive because it must end in 1). The

```
        M    R6,=F'1Ø'
```

instruction produces a number between -10×2^{31} and 10×2^{31} or -5×2^{32} and 5×2^{32}. Adding 5 to register 6 is equivalent to adding 5×2^{32} to the product; so after the

```
        LA   R6,5(,R6)
```

instruction the number in register pair 6–7 is between 0 and 10×2^{32}. If we take only the portion in register 6, we are in effect taking the *quotient* upon division by 2^{32}. Since 10×2^{32} is approached but not attained as a value, 10 is never generated in register 6; the values of RDIGIT will be uniformly distributed among the numbers 0 to 9.

m a i n   i d e a s

□ We describe the action of instructions symbolically, with notation as summarized in Fig. 4.5.

□ Information move instructions permit the moving of information from a register to another register, from a register to main storage, from main storage to a register, and from main storage to other main storage locations.

□ Binary integer arithmetic is always performed in registers. One operand is in a register; the second operand may be either in a register or in main storage, but the result is always put in a register.

□ Most binary integer arithmetic operations use full words, but some RX load, store, and arithmetic instructions allow for half-word operands from main storage.

□ The action of the instructions in this chapter is summarized in Fig. 4.6.

□ The usual instruction sequence for performing arithmetic is

Load an operand into a register from main storage.
Perform the arithmetic, possibly more than one operation.
Store the result.

□ Multiply (except half-word) and divide instructions use register pairs, beginning at a register with even address, for their processes of successive add and shift or subtract and shift.

□ Pseudo-random numbers are helpful in simulation programs; they are easily generated by the multiplicative congruence method.

FIGURE 4.5   Notation for symbolic description of instructions

$R1, R2, R3$	Register addresses given as operands.
$S1, S2$	Main storage addresses given as operands.
$I2$	"Immediate" byte of an SI instruction.
$c(R1)$	Contents of register $R1$.
$c(S2)$	Contents of full word at location $S2$.
$Quantity_{a-b}$	Bits numbered a to b of the $Quantity$.
$[Quantity\ 1, Quantity\ 2]$	Concatenation of $Quantity\ 1$ and $Quantity\ 2$.
$A \leftarrow Quantity$	The $Quantity$ is placed at location A.

FIGURE 4.6 Information move and binary integer arithmetic instructions

Mnemonic name	Type	Full name	Action
LR	RR	Load from Register	$R1 \leftarrow c(R2)$
LCR	RR	Load Complement from Register	$R1 \leftarrow -c(R2)$
LPR	RR	Load Positive from Register	$R1 \leftarrow |c(R2)|$
LNR	RR	Load Negative from Register	$R1 \leftarrow -|c(R2)|$
L	RX	Load	$R1 \leftarrow c(S2)$
ST	RX	STore	$S2 \leftarrow c(R1)$
LH	RX	Load Half-word	$R1_{16-31} \leftarrow c(S2)_{0-15}, R1_{0-15} \leftarrow c(S2)_0$
STH	RX	STore Half-word	$S2_{0-15} \leftarrow c(R1)_{16-31}$
MVC	SS	MoVe Character[1]	$S1_{0-BL} \leftarrow c(S2)_{0-BL}$
MVI	SI	MoVe Immediate	$S1_{0-7} \leftarrow I2$
LM	RS	Load Multiple	$[R1, \ldots, R3] \leftarrow c(S2)^{[2]}$
STM	RS	STore Multiple	$S2^{[2]} \leftarrow [c(R1), \ldots, c(R3)]$
LA	RX	Load Address	$R1_{8-31} \leftarrow S2, R1_{0-7} \leftarrow 0$
AR	RR	Add Register	$R1 \leftarrow c(R1) + c(R2)$
SR	RR	Subtract Register	$R1 \leftarrow c(R1) - c(R2)$
A	RX	Add	$R1 \leftarrow c(R1) + c(S2)$
S	RX	Subtract	$R1 \leftarrow c(R1) - c(S2)$
AH	RX	Add Half-word	$R1 \leftarrow c(R1) + c(S2)_{0-15}$
SH	RX	Subtract Half-word	$R1 \leftarrow c(R1) - c(S2)_{0-15}$
MR	RR	Multiply Register[3]	$[R1, R1 + 1] \leftarrow c(R1 + 1) * c(R2)$
M	RX	Multiply[3]	$[R1, R1 + 1] \leftarrow c(R1 + 1) * c(S2)$
MH	RX	Multiply Half-word	$R1 \leftarrow (c(R1) * c(S2)_{0-15})_{16-47}$
DR	RR	Divide Register[3]	$R1 \leftarrow$ remainder of $[c(R1), c(R1 + 1)]/c(R2)$ $R1 + 1 \leftarrow$ quotient of $[c(R1), c(R1 + 1)]/c(R2)$
D	RX	Divide[3]	$R1 \leftarrow$ remainder of $[c(R1), c(R1 + 1)]/c(S2)$ $R1 + 1 \leftarrow$ quotient of $[c(R1), c(R1 + 1)]/c(S2)$

Notes
1. $BL = 8L + 7$, where L is the length coded in the machine language instruction.
2. If $R1 \leq R3$, $4*(R3 - R1) + 4$ bytes of the main storage operand $S2$ participate.
   If $R1 > R3$, $4*(R3 + 16 - R1) + 4$ bytes of the main storage operand $S2$ participate.
3. $R1$ must be an even address; $R1 + 1$ is of course the address of the following register.

4.1 What sequence of two instructions, not including LPR, will have the same effect as

$$\text{LPR}\quad \text{R2,R7}$$

4.2 A quick way to set a register, say register 5, to zero is to perform

$$\text{SR}\quad \text{R5,R5}$$

List two other ways of setting a register to zero.

4.3 The LA instruction can be used to add a small positive constant to the contents of a register without requiring definition of the number as a constant in main storage. Why can it not subtract a small positive constant just as well?

4.4 Suppose that the initial (hexadecimal) contents of registers and storage locations are as given below.

Register 1:	ØØØØØØ2E	Location G (full word):	ØØØØØ1D6
Register 2:	FFFFFFCØ	Location K (full word):	FFFFFFF6
Register 3:	456789AB	Location Q (full word):	BA987654
Register 4:	CDEFØ123	Location Q + 4:	321ØFEDC

Assuming that these are the contents before *each* of the following instructions, show the result of each instruction.

LPR	R7,R2	A	R1,K	STM	R2,R4,Q
LNR	R8,R4	S	R1,K	LM	R5,R6,Q
AR	R1,R2	SH	R1,K	LH	R7,Q+6
AR	R2,R1	AH	R3,Q+2	STH	R3,K
SR	R1,R2	MVI	Q+5,17	LA	R8,2(R3,R4)
SR	R2,R1	MVC	K+1(5),Q+2	S	R2,Q

4.5 Distinguish among the effects of the instructions

$$\text{LR}\quad 5,4$$
$$\text{LA}\quad 5,4$$
$$\text{L}\quad 5,4$$
$$\text{L}\quad 5,Ø(4)$$
$$\text{LA}\quad 5,Ø(4)$$

4.6 Suppose that the initial contents in registers and main storage locations of the binary integer representations of the following decimal values are

Register 2:	Ø	Location U:	16
Register 3:	49	Location Y:	−5
Register 4:	−1		
Register 5:	−84		
Register 7:	12		
Register 9:	−3Ø		

Assuming that these are the contents before *each* of the following instructions, show the results of each instruction.

```
MR   R8,R9        DR   R2,R7
MR   R6,R9        DR   R4,R7
M    R8,U         DR   R4,R9
MH   R7,U+2       D    R2,Y
```

4.7 If a number is loaded into a register to become the dividend in a divide instruction, its sign must be extended into all bit positions of the even-numbered register of the register pair. If the sign of the number is unknown, one way to extend it is to multiply the number by 1. Illustrate this in a sequence which will divide the number at location K by the number in location Q, storing the result at location Z, even though signs of the numbers at K and Q are unknown.

4.8 The scheme for multiplication in System/370 involves starting with the multiplier in the lower half of the product area, adding the multiplicand at appropriate times into the upper half, and shifting right. Illustrate a valid scheme (at least for positive numbers), starting with the multiplier in the top half of the product area, adding the multiplicand to the lower half, and shifting left.

4.9 Can an equivalent scheme for division be devised that involves shifting right instead of left, similar to the alternative scheme just mentioned for multiplication? Illustrate such a scheme or explain why one cannot be constructed.

4.10 In general, if the dividend in a divide instruction fits completely in the odd-numbered register and the divisor is nonzero, there is no possibility of overflow in the divide instruction. There is one exceptional pair consisting of a dividend that is wholly in the odd-numbered register and a divisor that does produce an overflow (that is, the quotient cannot be expressed in 32 bits). What is this dividend and divisor pair?

4.11 Write program segments to perform the following:

Compute E as $K + 3$.

Compute E as $(K + 3)/Q$, K positive.

Compute E as $(K + U)*R$, where U is in register 6.

Compute E as $(K - T + R*P)/(Y - 5)$, where T is a half-word.

■ **REFERENCES** ▬▬▬▬▬▬▬▬▬▬▬▬▬▬▬▬▬▬▬

Falkoff, A. D., K. E. Iverson, and E. H. Sussenguth, "A Formal Description of SYSTEM/360," *IBM Systems Journal* **3** (1964), pp. 198–261. A comprehensive description of the structure and instruction repertoire of the IBM System/360, in the Iverson notation.

IBM System/370 Principles of Operation, GA 22-7000, IBM Corporation. This or any of the other IBM models' *Principles of Operation* manuals will include descriptions of the instructions introduced in this chapter.

Iverson, Kenneth, *A Programming Language,* Wiley, New York, 1962. Develops a symbolic language for description of computer processes, and discusses several data processing techniques expressed in the language. This study led to implementation of APL as a computer language.

Knuth, Donald E., *The Art of Computer Programming, Vol. 2: Seminumerical Algorithms,* 2nd ed., Addison-Wesley, Reading, Mass., 1981. Chapter 3 deals comprehensively with generation of pseudo-random numbers.

5

WRITING A COMPLETE PROGRAM

5.1 Introduction

The objective of this chapter is to complete the detail necessary for you to start writing and running complete programs. This is important; you need to start putting together the various pieces presented thus far, to consolidate your understanding, and to build a context for studying still more topics. First, the standard register conventions will be introduced, so you will know which registers have been assigned special purposes and which are available for you to use freely. The sections on definition of constants, storage areas, and symbols include a great amount of detail. You should not expect to remember all of it before you have used the material extensively. While studying these sections, you should try to remember the most important features, and prepare to retrieve additional details as you need them. The most important features at this point are the format and purpose of DC, DS, and EQU, the various types of constants, literals, and storage definitions, and the way values are specified in each. The most important types are C, X, F, and A; you should prepare to be able to use them immediately, while you note the others and agree to come back and read about them when you want them.

In the section on assembler control statements, CSECT and END are the important ones; TITLE, ORG, LTORG, and PRINT are useful but not immediately necessary.

There are several ways of running a program. The program may be entered either on punched cards or via the keyboard of a computer terminal. The commands to assemble and execute a program are very different. Both a set of job control statements that assemble and run a program in a batch environment (from cards or a disk) and a set of commands in IBM's CMS (Conversational Monitor System) system from a terminal are introduced. Similarly, during execution your program may take its input from cards (or a file on disk) and send its output to the system's printer, or accept input from the terminal and send its output to be displayed at the terminal. Both are in this chapter.

The standard batch-oriented operating systems of IBM and CMS are not the only software systems for using assembler language. Among other facilities is ASSIST, developed by the Pennsylvania State University Computation Center (and available from that center—see the preface). The ASSIST system was designed to be easy to use, efficient of computer time, and helpful in debugging. The use of the ASSIST system, or pieces of it, is illustrated in this chapter. The main advantage of ASSIST is that it takes care of many of the details of subroutine linkage, register management, input and output, and number conversions. This enables you to construct entire programs earlier than you otherwise could. There are three ways to use ASSIST facilities. You may use the entire system, in which your program is *executed interpretively* by the ASSIST system. This mode has a set of extra instructions defined by the system for input and output, data conversions, and dumps that simplifies matters enormously. A second mode is use of the standard batch system; the same input, output, conversion, and dump facilities are available to you in this mode as macro instructions, and are even written exactly the same in your program. The third mode is use of the ASSIST conversion macro instructions in the CMS system while using the CMS macro instructions for input and output. In all three modes you can use ASSIST instructions XSAVE, XRETURN, and EQUREGS for linkage and register management.

If you do not have access to the ASSIST system, you will have to supplement this chapter with sections from the next chapter on register usage and number conversions before you are ready to write a complete program. For batch-system input and output, your instructor can provide you with a skeleton to use until you learn details yourself in Chapter 12.†

In any case, you need not study *both* the section on using a batch system and the section using CMS. Studying the one that will be applicable to you is sufficient, though I would recommend at least skimming the other to see "how the other half lives."

5.2 Register Conventions

Every program or subroutine in an IBM System/370 computer uses the general registers; practically nothing can be done without them. Some of the uses are

- holding a base address for addressing operands and instructions,
- assisting in computing effective addresses of operands by indexing,

---

†In earlier editions of this book, I illustrated use of subroutines READATA and PRINT for this purpose; these are still available from me.

- holding operands,
- holding entry and return addresses for subroutines,
- holding addresses of parameters for subroutines,
- holding the address of an area in which to save register contents.

We will examine each of these uses in more detail. Because some of them involve communication between a program and a subroutine that it may call, it is very helpful to follow some conventions about the use of registers. This simplifies the task of all programmers because they can assume a standard interface with any routines provided by other programmers or the operating system. By convention, registers 0, 1, 13, 14, and 15 are reserved for special uses in subroutine communication, and therefore registers 2–12 are available for the internal use of any program or subroutine. Let us outline briefly the uses of registers 0, 1, 13, 14, and 15; we will explore each in more detail later in the next chapter.

Register 0 contains the single-word output of a subroutine. For example, the value of an integer function written in FORTRAN is left by the function in register 0, and from there retrieved by the calling routine. Contents of register 0 upon entry to the subroutine are lost.

Register 1 contains the address of an area of main storage that contains addresses of parameters, both input parameters to and output parameters from the subroutine. We will return to parameter passing and how a subroutine can access parameters in Chapter 6.

Register 14 contains the return address, the address in the calling routine to which a subroutine should return control when finished. Register 15 sometimes contains the address of the entry point in the subroutine, the address to which the calling routine branches to enter the subroutine. There are ways of branching to the subroutine, however, that do not involve register 15. The instructions used to enter the proper addresses into registers 14 and 15 and to transfer control to the subroutines and back will be discussed in Chapter 6; the present chapter will show how to accomplish the transfers of control through the ASSIST instructions XSAVE and XRETURN.

Register 13 contains the address of an area in which register contents can be stored by a subroutine. This is important; a calling program should be able to call a subroutine and upon return count on finding its registers intact. Therefore the calling program furnishes an area into which the contents of its registers can be stored temporarily; the subroutine stores those register contents, uses registers as it finds necessary, then restores the calling program's register contents just before returning control to the calling program. We illustrate this in detail in Chapter 6.

5.3 Definition of Constants in Assembler Language

The statement that defines a constant in IBM OS/VS assembler language is of the form

Label	Operation	Operands
Optional constant name	DC	One or more operands separated by commas

Each statement may define one or more constants, occupying consecutive locations in main storage. The label, if present, is a symbol that will be assigned the address of the first byte of the constant defined (the first constant if the DC statement defines more than one). Each operand may have the following operand subfields, *not* separated by commas or blanks:

- duplication factor, optional;
- type of constant, required;
- modifiers, optional;
- value of the constant or constants, required.

Each operand subfield will be described below. The most important subfields are the type and value of the constant. You may wish to skip or skim for now the discussions of duplication factor and modifiers because you can accomplish quite a bit before you need them.

THE DUPLICATION FACTOR
If a duplication factor is present in an operand defining a constant, the constant defined will be duplicated in successive locations as many times as this factor specifies. In a DC statement the duplication factor may be an unsigned decimal integer or, when the factor is enclosed in parentheses, another kind of absolute expression. Any symbol used in the expression must have been previously defined. Thus the operands

```
2F'19'
(X'E')F'19'
(G)F'19'
```

where G is a previously defined absolute symbol, are valid operands including duplication factors. A duplication factor of zero is permitted: *no* constant is assembled, but boundary alignment is performed according to the type of constant, as will be explained below. The absence of a duplication factor is equivalent to the presence of a duplication factor of 1.

MODIFIERS
The definition of constants may be modified by length modifiers, scale modifiers, and exponent modifiers. The modifiers are optional. We shall ignore the scale and exponent modifiers, and discuss only the length modifiers. The length modifier defines the length in bytes of the constant; it is written Ln, where n is given as either an unsigned decimal integer or an absolute expression in parentheses. Any symbol used in an expression defining length must have been previously defined. Thus in an operand of a DC statement, length modifi-

FIGURE 5.1   Summary of attributes of constants

Type	Alignment	Length range	Implied length	Specified by	Constants per operand	Truncation or padding
C	Byte	1–256	As in value	Characters	One	Right
X	Byte	1–256	As in value	Hexadecimal digits	Multiple	Left
B	Byte	1–256	As in value	Binary digits	Multiple	Left
F	Word	1–8	4	Decimal digits	Multiple	Left
H	Half-word	1–8	2	Decimal digits	Multiple	Left
E	Word	1–8	4	Decimal digits	Multiple	Right
D	Double-word	1–8	8	Decimal digits	Multiple	Right
P	Byte	1–16	As in value	Decimal digits	Multiple	Left
A	Word	3–4	4	Relocatable expression	Multiple	Left
A	Word	1–8	4	Absolute expression	Multiple	Left
V	Word	3–4	4	Relocatable symbol	Multiple	Left

ers L9 and L(G+4) where G is a previously defined symbol, are valid; in a literal, L(G+4) is not valid.

The *length attribute* of a named constant is kept by the assembler in a table. The length is either set by the length modifier in the constant definition or is set to a default value. Permitted length and default lengths for each type of constant are shown in Fig. 5.1. In SS-type instructions, the length of each symbolic operand may be left unspecified; in this case the assembler inserts the length attribute associated with the symbol. For example, the statement

```
        BSQ    DC    CL9'123456789'
```

defines BSQ to have a length attribute of 9. Therefore the assembler language statement

```
        PACK   GQ(5),BSQ
```

is equivalent to

```
        PACK   GQ(5),BSQ(9)
```

Similarly,

```
        MVC    BSQ,XH
```

is equivalent to

```
        MVC    BSQ(9),XH
```

but in the instruction

```
        MVC    GQC,BSQ
```

the length will be supplied according to the length attribute of GQC.

Lengths can also be stated in bits instead of in bytes, but we will not explore this possibility in this book.

Length modifiers are sometimes confused with duplication factors. The length modifier specifies the *length of one* constant, whereas the duplication factor specifies *how many copies* of the constant should be assembled.

TYPE AND VALUE OF CONSTANT

The type of each constant or set of constants is given as a single alphabetic character. We will discuss the following types:

C	character	E	floating point, single precision
X	hexadecimal	D	floating point, double precision
B	binary	P	packed decimal
F	fixed point (normally full word)	A	address
H	half-word	V	external symbol address

How values are given in assembler language operands and the representation of the constant as placed in main storage must be discussed for each type separately.

ALIGNMENT

Some types of constants are expected to be used by certain classes of instructions, and therefore the constants are aligned by the assembler on an appropriate boundary. The conventions are summarized in Fig. 5.1. H-type constants are expected to be used in half-word instructions such as LH, AH, SH, MH, and therefore each H-type constant is aligned to a half-word boundary. F-type constants are expected to be used in instructions like L, A, M, D, LM, so each F-type constant is aligned to a full-word boundary. E-type and D-type constants are expected to be used by single- and double-precision floating-point instructions, respectively, so they are aligned on full- and double-word boundaries. Address constants of A- and V-types are aligned on full-word boundaries, but constants of other types (X, B, C, and P) are begun at the first available byte of storage. However, *if a length modifier is specified* in the definition of *any* constant, boundary alignment is suppressed, and the constant begun at the first available byte of storage. Ways of forcing alignment are explained in Section 5.4.

The newer computers in the IBM System/370 family have the *byte-oriented operand* feature, which permits most instructions to work without requiring alignment of their operands. In recognition of this, the OS/VS assembler has a NOALIGN option that suppresses alignment of operands and thus saves the odd bytes of storage that would otherwise be left unused in order to align operands. Since nonaligned operands require slightly greater execution time, however, many installations prefer to continue to use the ALIGN option of the assembler in order to have the operands aligned.

PADDING AND TRUNCATION

In some constant definitions, such as character (C) and hexadecimal (X), if length is not specified, it is determined by the length of the constant value given. For example,

C'12345'   will define a constant whose length is 5,

X'123456'   will define a constant whose length is 3, and

X'0000123456'   will define a constant whose length is 5.

For other types a specific length is assumed if none is stated. For example, F'19' defines a constant whose length is 4.

If a specific length is assumed or if a length modifier for any constant is given, this length takes precedence over the length that may be implied by the length of the string of characters determining the constant. If, for example, we define CL5'123', we are defining a constant of length 5, whose first three characters are 123. Padding of two character blanks (hexadecimal 4040) is supplied by the assembler to fill the last two bytes of the five-byte constant. On the other hand, CL5'123456' also defines a five-byte constant. Not all the characters given can be stored, so the 6 is lost. The constant will contain the characters 12345. Padding or truncation, whichever is necessary, will take place at the same end of the constant. Character constants are padded or truncated on the right, almost all others on the left. However, special explanations are necessary for the floating-point constants. The types of constants will be presented one at a time.

CHARACTER CONSTANTS (C)

Any of the 256 eight-bit patterns may be entered into a character constant. Special arrangements must be made for apostrophes and ampersands desired within character constants: two apostrophes or two ampersands are written in the assembler language statement wherever one is desired in the character constant. For example, C'''&&' defines a character constant of length 2; the characters in the two bytes will be '&. As mentioned previously, the length of the constant is determined by the number of characters specified by its value unless a length modifier is given; in either case, 256 is the upper limit on the length of the constant. Each character is entered into one byte of main storage, exactly as written in the value portion of the constant definition. Padding with blanks or truncation is done at the right.

Only one character constant per operand may be defined, though a duplication factor may be used. For example,

```
        REPEAT   DC    3CL5'NOWIS'
```

will generate the constant NOWISNOWISNOWIS.

HEXADECIMAL CONSTANTS (X)

A hexadecimal constant is specified as a sequence of hexadecimal digits that are entered into main storage two digits per byte. If no length modifier is specified, the length of the constant is what is required to accommodate the digits. If, say, n digits are given, n even, the length of the constant is $n/2$ bytes. If n is odd, the length of the constant is $(n + 1)/2$ bytes, with 0's occupying the four high-order bit positions of the leftmost byte. If a length modifier is specified, padding with zeros or truncation takes place on the left. The length of a hexadecimal constant may be from 1 to 256 bytes. Several hexadecimal constants may be specified in an operand, and a duplication factor may be used.

It is often convenient to use a hexadecimal constant to set a pattern of particular bits in a word. In older systems without the byte-oriented operand feature, care must be taken, however, to ensure proper boundary alignment if the constant is to be used as an operand in instructions that require full-word, half-word, or double-word operands. Forcing alignment will be discussed in Section 5.4.

For example,

```
CPX        DC     X'A1245'
```

defines a three-byte constant whose hexadecimal digits are 0A1245.

```
PQR        DC     XL2'A1245'
```

defines a two-byte constant 1245.

```
STUV       DC     XL5'A1245'
```

defines a five-byte constant 00000A1245.

BINARY CONSTANTS

A binary constant is written as a string of 1's and 0's. The 1's and 0's are entered into main storage, eight to a byte, so that each 1 or 0 defines a bit in a binary number. If no length modifier is specified, the length is just sufficient to hold the number of bits written, and if the number of bits written is not a multiple of 8, the constant is padded with zeros on the left to make up full bytes. If a length modifier is specified, padding with zeros or truncation takes place on the left, to bring the constant to the number of bytes specified. The maximum length is 256 bytes. Several binary constants may be specified in an operand, and a duplication factor may be used.

For example,

```
BITTE      DC     B'10110'
```

defines BITTE as a one-byte constant whose bit pattern is 00010110.

```
BIT2       DC     BL2'10110'
```

defines BIT2 as a two-byte constant whose bit pattern is 0000000000010110.

FIGURE 5.2   Examples of F-type and H-type constants

Assembler language statement	Constants generated
NINETN DC F'19'	Full-word binary integer, representing 19 (00000000 00000000 00000000 00010011).
BIO DC FL1'513'	One-byte constant 00000001, formed by truncating the binary equivalent of 513 to eight bits.
G34 DC 2F'Ø'	Two full-word constants containing zeros.
PARAMS DC F'2Ø,-17,371'	Three full-word binary integers: binary equivalents of 20, −17 (2's complement), 371.
MAG DC FL3'1.234E2'	A three-byte binary integer: binary equivalent of $1.23 \times 10^2 = 123$ (00000000 00000000 01111011).

FIXED-POINT CONSTANTS (F AND H)

A fixed-point constant is written as a decimal number, which may be signed and may include a decimal point. It may also be followed by a decimal exponent of the form En where n is a decimal integer with or without sign. The number is adjusted by the power of 10 specified by the exponent, then converted to binary. The integer portion of the resulting binary number is the constant stored in main storage. The implied length is 4 for an F-type constant and 2 for an H-type constant; boundary alignment is made so that an F-type constant begins on a full-word boundary, an H-type constant on a half-word boundary. Either type may be declared by a length modifier to have a length of from one to eight bytes; if the length modifier is given, no boundary alignment is performed. Truncation and padding are made on the left. Multiple constants, separated by commas, can be defined with one operand; a duplication factor may also be used. Figure 5.2 shows some examples of F- and H-type constants.

FLOATING-POINT CONSTANTS (E AND D)

The value of a floating-point constant is written precisely the same as the value of a fixed-point (F or H) constant. The value is converted to binary and expressed in the standard floating-point form described briefly in Chapter 3 and in more detail in Chapter 13. If an E-type constant has no length modifier, it has an implied length of four bytes and is aligned on a full-word boundary. If a D-type constant has no length modifier, it has an implied length of eight bytes and is aligned on a double-word boundary. If either has a length modifier, the length must be from one to eight bytes; no boundary alignment is made.

Since the numbers in floating-point form are normalized, any extra zeros of padding are added on the right; similarly, any digits that must be lost because of lack of space are the less significant digits that are lost from the right. Multiple constants in one operand and duplication factors may be used. Examples are

```
FLONE     DC   E'1'
PI        DC   D'3.14159265'
FLLIST    DC   E'2.6E-4,7.94136,-1000.27E+5'
LISTONES  DC   6D'1.0'
```

PACKED DECIMAL CONSTANTS (P)

The value specified in a packed decimal constant is a decimal number; sign and decimal point are optional. No exponent is allowed. The decimal point does not affect the constant in any way and is permitted only as a possible help to reading and understanding the program. The number is put into the packed decimal form for placement in main storage.

If no length modifier is given, the length is determined as the minimum required to hold the digits given. If n digits are given, n odd, the constant will be $(n + 1)/2$ bytes long. If n is even, the constant will be $(n + 2)/2$ bytes long; the high-order four bits will be padded with zeros. If a length modifier is given, truncation or padding is on the left. In any case the length must be from 1 to 16 bytes. Multiple constants may be defined in one operand, and duplication factors may also be used. The following are valid packed decimal constant definitions, which cause definition and loading into storage of the corresponding constants, shown in hexadecimal.

```
PDQ       DC   P'-357'              357D
TAXRATE   DC   PL3'.26'            00026C
PERCENTS  DC   PL2'78.3,22,-.3'    783C022C003D
PHONE     DC   2PL3'0'             0000C00000C
DEPOSIT   DC   P'999999.99'        099999999C
```

ADDRESS CONSTANTS (A AND V)

An address constant is a main storage address contained in a constant. Unlike other constants, whose values are enclosed in apostrophes, address constants are enclosed in parentheses. Several addresses may be specified in one operand; they are separated by commas and the whole list is enclosed in parentheses.

An A-type constant may be specified as an absolute expression or as a relocatable expression (see definitions, Chapter 3). A V-type constant is the value of an *external symbol*—a relocatable symbol that is external to the current control section. The V-type address constants are used for branching to locations in other control sections, not for addressing data. A-type constants are also used in place of F-type constants: A(37) will generate the same constant as F'37'. The A-type constants have advantages; their values can be defined as expressions: A(32*NRTERMS) generates a valid constant if NRTERMS has been previously defined as an absolute symbol (usually through an EQU statement, as shown in the next section).

Implied length of an address constant is four bytes; the constant is aligned on a full-word boundary. A length modifier of 3 or 4 for a relocatable expression or 1 to 8 for an absolute expression may be given, in which case no boundary alignment takes place.

The following are valid address constants.

```
GSUBAD    DC    V(READATA)
AREAD     DC    A(AREA+4Ø)
BASEREG   DC    A(BEGIN+4Ø96,BEGIN+2*4Ø96)
```

LITERALS

Literals were mentioned briefly in Chapter 3; they provide us the facility to define constants in assembler language statements that translate into machine language instructions. The duplication factor, type, modifiers, and value are written as in definition of other constants, but they are preceded by an equals sign. They can be used where we would use a main-storage operand *but not* as a destination field of an instruction. The assembler understandably objects if we try to define a constant and store something else there at the same time! There are other minor restrictions on the use of literals:

1. A literal may have only one operand, unlike a DC statement, which may have several. The literal can define several constants, as in the instructions

```
MVC    B(2Ø),=5CL4'1234'
LM     R4,R5,=F'-1,-879'
```

but cannot define the equivalent of

```
G      DC    F'25',XL4'AC8'
```

2. A duplication factor of zero is not allowed.

All constants defined by literals are put by the assembler in a *literal pool,* usually at the very end of the program. The *address* of each literal is coded in base-and-displacement form in the machine-language instruction that refers to it.

Literals are arranged within the literal pool so as to respect as many boundary alignments as necessary. All eight-byte (and multiples thereof) literals are located first in the literal pool and aligned on a double-word boundary. Then come all four-byte (and odd multiples thereof) literals, which are aligned on word boundaries. Then all two-byte (and odd multiples thereof) literals, each aligned on a half-word boundary. Finally come all literals of an odd number of bytes, which presumably need no particular alignment. Therefore we can safely use an instruction like

```
L      R3,=X'FFFFØØØØ'
```

because the literal will be aligned on a word boundary as required.

5.4   The DS (Define Storage) and EQU (Equate Symbol) Statements

THE DS STATEMENT

The DS or Define Storage statement directs the assembler to allocate storage but not to put a constant in the space. By using DS statements, we can name and reserve work areas.

The format of the DS statement is identical to the format of the DC statement; the same operands and suboperands are used, with the same meanings. However, two differences must be noted. The maximum lengths for character (C) and hexadecimal (X) data types are 65,535 bytes in DS statements, rather than the 256-byte maximum in DC statements.

The second difference between the two statements is the central one. The DC statement assembles a constant that will be placed in main storage as the program is loaded, and thus DC initializes storage; the DS statement reserves space but does not initialize it. In the DC statement, the value of the constant or constants is therefore a required suboperand; in the DS statement the value *may* be included to specify the length of the storage space assigned, but this is not good practice, and we usually omit the value. If the value is omitted, the length of the storage space to be reserved is determined by the implied length or by a length modifier. The implied length of a C, X, B, or P field is one byte. However, if a constant-value suboperand is used, the length of the field is determined in exactly the same way as in a DC statement. No constant is assembled, but the constant specified governs the length assigned.

FORCING ALIGNMENT

Unless a length modifier is used, a DC or DS operand of types F, H, E, D, A, or V forces alignment of the constant or storage area to the beginning of the next half-word, full word, or double word. Storage space skipped over to align boundaries is not counted as part of the length of the constant or storage area, and this space is not set to anything in particular.

You the programmer define the constant or storage with desired boundaries in mind. Often you can choose the type of constant or storage area that will best meet your needs. Sometimes, however, you may wish to express a certain kind of constant but need a boundary alignment other than that provided automatically with your choice of constant type. You can then make effective use of the DS statement with a duplication factor of 0. Such a statement performs boundary alignment and may attach a name to a location, but does not reserve storage. For example, if you wish to use a full-word constant whose hexadecimal digits are FFFF0000, write

```
        DS    ØF
CONFO   DC    X'FFFFØØØØ'
```

The symbol CONFO will be aligned on a full-word boundary.

FIGURE 5.3   Constant and storage area definition

Assembler language statement			Location	Length attribute
	DS	ØH	ØØØ13Ø	
MULT	DS	X'4ØØ5'	ØØØ13Ø	2
SAV	DS	18F	ØØØ134	4
ENDCHAR	DC	C'END'	ØØØ17C	3
ASTER	DS	CL2'**'	ØØØ17F	2
ZEROAR	DC	2ØF'Ø'	ØØØ184	4
OUT	DC	132C' '	ØØØ1D4	1
OUT2	DC	CL133' '	ØØØ258	133
DBL	DS	D	ØØØ2EØ	8
GSUBAD	DC	V(READATA)	ØØØ2E8	4
PARAMAD	DC	A(G,W,K-4)	ØØØ2EC	4

Figure 5.3 shows the storage allocation of a series of constants and storage areas. Note that the length attribute of a constant or storage area is independent of the duplication factor. Storage is allocated, of course, for all duplicates made according to the duplication factor, but the length attribute as listed in the symbol table refers to just one copy. For example, the instruction using implied length

                    MVC   OUT,ASTER

is equivalent to

                    MVC   OUT(1),ASTER

Storage space is skipped for boundary alignment before SAV, ZEROAR, and DBL.

As explained in the previous section, the NOALIGN option will suppress the boundary alignment described here. But there is an exception:

                    DS   ØH

will still align the next instruction (instructions must be aligned on half-word boundaries anyway, and are, regardless of NOALIGN) or constant following to a half-word boundary; similarly,

                    DS   ØF
                    DS   ØD

will perform alignment to a full-word or double-word boundary, respectively.

THE EQU STATEMENT

The EQU statement is used to associate a fixed value with a symbol. The value is derived from an expression. EQU is used to name a constant that will be used during assembly or to name special objects (like registers!) or values. The general form is

Label	Operation	Operand
A symbol	EQU	An expression

The expression may be either relocatable or absolute; the symbol equated will be relocatable or absolute accordingly. All symbols in the expression must be previously defined. The symbol has the same length attribute and value as the expression; the length attribute of an expression is the length of its first term, with the convention that the location-counter symbol * and the self-defining terms each have a length attribute of 1.

For example,

$$R4 \qquad EQU \qquad 4$$

equates the symbol R4 to 4; R4 can be used as a register address in any instruction. Also

$$DRBACK \qquad EQU \qquad OUT+25$$

defines DRBACK as equivalent to the address OUT+25. The length attribute of DRBACK is the same as the length attribute of OUT. OUT must have been defined—that is, it must have appeared as the name in a statement, before the definition of DRBACK.

5.5   Assembler Control Statements

The statements described in this section are all pseudo-operations: they control the assembler but do not correspond to instructions or constants that are assembled into the object program.

The first one we discuss is the CSECT statement. It should be included in your program before any statements that affect the location counter. It attaches a name to the control section; the general form is

Label	Operation	Operand
Symbol	CSECT	None

Control sections will be discussed in more detail later.

We examine next the listing control statement, TITLE. The general form is

Label	Operation	Operand
Name or blank	TITLE	A string of up to 100 characters enclosed in apostrophes

The name, if entered, may be of from one to eight alphabetic and numeric characters in any combination. These characters will be punched in columns 73–80 of all cards of the object deck (if any) produced by the assembly. The string specified in the operand field is printed at the top of every page of the listing of the program. At any time in a program a new TITLE statement may give a new title for the pages that follow, but only the first TITLE statement may have an entry in the name field.

An ORG statement may reset the location counter at any time. The ORG statement must not have a name; its operand is a relocatable expression or blank. If a relocatable expression is given, the location counter is set to the value of the expression; all symbols in the expression must have been previously defined. The value in the location counter may be reduced by the ORG statement, but it must not be reduced to less than the initial value in the control section. If it has been reduced, say for the purpose of redefining an area, it can be restored to its highest previous value by an ORG without operand.

The LTORG statement causes all the literals used since the last LTORG to be assembled in a new literal pool. The LTORG statement has no operands; it may have a name, which is associated with the first byte of the literal pool. The beginning of the literal pool is aligned on a double-word boundary.

When two completely identical literals are used in the range of a LTORG, only one is assembled. For example, =X'FC' and =X'FC' used in two different statements are identical, and only the first is stored; however, =X'FC' and =B'11111100' are not considered identical although they define the same constant; hence both are stored. The literals =A(*–4) and =A(*–4) used in two different statements are not identical, since the value of * will be different in each statement. Therefore both literals must be stored.

The LTORG statement is not usually necessary in a program. If it is omitted, the literals are assembled automatically at the end of the program. However, if the length of the program and the definition of implied base registers are such that literals assembled at the end of the program cannot be addressed in the instructions in which they are used, a LTORG statement can force assembly of the literals at a location at which they can be addressed.

When a program includes macro instructions, the assembler listing of the program usually shows all of the statements that are generated by the macro instruction. Often this is not only instructive but also necessary—while debugging a program, for example. At other times the presence of these generated statements clutters up the listing and makes it hard to read. The statement

```
PRINT   NOGEN
```

tells the assembler not to list for us the statements generated by macro instructions. The NOGEN option is active from the point it is encountered until countermanded by

                                        PRINT GEN

The END statement is required as the last statement in an assembly; it signifies the end to the assembler. The END statement has no name, but may have an operand. The operand is a relocatable expression, identifying the location at which execution of the edited and loaded program should begin. The operand therefore should be specified only in main programs, never in subroutines.

One further kind of statement should be mentioned. A statement with an asterisk (*) in column 1 is a *remarks statement*; a remarks statement can be inserted in an assembler language program and not affect assembly. It is reproduced in the output listing for the edification of those reading the program. Remarks, either in remarks statements or in remarks fields of assembler language statements, should be sprinkled liberally throughout a program to help in its documentation.

5.6 Completing a Program with ASSIST Facilities

In addition to the elements of assembler language discussed to this point, a program needs a few others:

- a way to get input data,
- a way to print results,
- a way to convert data (usually input) from character representation to binary integer form,
- a way to convert data (usually output) from binary integer representation to character representation.

The ASSIST system provides these facilities conveniently. It also has facilities for helping a programmer analyze what a program has done. Some of the debugging aids will be introduced later; this section will introduce the facilities you need to complete a program.

The ASSIST facilities presented in this section are

XREAD	read input data (one card or record)
XPRNT	print a line
XDECI	convert a number from character representation to a binary integer
XDECO	convert a number from binary integer to character representation
XSAVE	initial linkage for a program
XRETURN	ending linkage for a program

In the full ASSIST system, XREAD, XPRNT, XDECI, and XDECO have the status of instructions, and you include them in your program just like LR, MVC, or the other instructions we have studied. In the standard system, these four are available as macro instructions. Your program is written the same either way; the only difference is in execution. In the full ASSIST system, *every* instruction is decoded, interpreted, and simulated by ASSIST, so execution of XREAD, XPRNT, XDECI, and XDECO need be no different. In the standard system, the assembler expands each macro instruction according to the directions given in a macro (these macros are kept in a macro library, but in Chapter 16 we will show you how you can write your own macros and incorporate them into a program) into several lines of assembler language that are then assembled and eventually executed as part of your program. Let us call these *ASSIST instructions*; you will understand what their status is in your own system. XSAVE and XRETURN are macro instructions in either case.

The ASSIST instruction to read input data is

$$\textit{label} \qquad \text{XREAD} \qquad \textit{area,length}$$

The label field may be a symbol (to which your program can branch) just as in an assembler language statement representing a machine language instruction, or may be left blank. The parameter *area* is the address of the area into which you want the input to be read. You may specify the *length* of the data record you want placed in your area, up to a maximum of 80 characters. Execution of XREAD will read one record (a punched card or the equivalent) and place the first *length* characters from the record into *area*. For example,

```
                XREAD CARDIN,6Ø
                ...
        CARDIN  DS    CL6Ø
```

will read the first 60 characters of an input record into the area CARDIN. A few other details about XREAD will be explained later; this will suffice to help you complete a simple program.

The ASSIST instruction to print data is similar:

$$\textit{label} \qquad \text{XPRNT} \qquad \textit{area,length}$$

The parameters to XPRNT parallel those of XREAD. Execution of XPRNT will print a line of *length* characters from *area*. However, the first character in the output area must be a vertical-spacing control (carriage control) character, and is not printed. For example,

```
                XPRNT OUTAREA-1,133
                ...
                DC    C' '
        OUTAREA DS    CL132
```

will print the 132 characters from OUTAREA: the space preceding OUTAREA specifies single spacing.

Numeric data are read in character form and must be converted to one of the numeric representations before any arithmetic can be done on them. The ASSIST instruction XDECI (DECimal Input) scans the characters in an area, bypassing leading spaces, and places the binary integer representation of the number found into a register. The form of the ASSIST instruction is

label   XDECI   *register,area*

The number can include one to nine digits; a plus or minus sign may immediately precede the first digit, or the sign may be omitted.

Because there may be several numbers in an area (e.g., read by one XREAD), XDECI places in register 1 the address of the first nondigit after the number scanned. Suppose we want a program to read a record that contains three numbers, then to convert those numbers into binary integer form in locations A, A+4, A+8. We can use the following ASSIST instructions:

```
        XREAD CARDIN,80
        BNZ   XRETURN
        XDECI R2,CARDIN
        ST    R2,A
        XDECI R2,Ø(,R1)
        ST    R2,A+4
        XDECI R2,Ø(,R1)
        ST    R2,A+8


CARDIN  DS    CL13Ø
A       DS    3F
```

The first XDECI finds the first number in the record, places its binary integer equivalent in register 2, and places in register 1 the address of the character just beyond the first number in the input record. The second XDECI starts its scan where the first finished; a main storage address in any of the ASSIST instructions may be specified in any of the forms that is legal for an address in a LA instruction. In this case the address is Ø(,R1), a displacement of zero and the contents of the base register R1.

Conversion of binary integers to character form is done by the ASSIST instruction XDECO (DECimal Output). The number in a register is converted; the character representation is right-justified in a twelve-byte area, prefixed by a minus sign if the number is negative; leading spaces are provided. The format of XDECO is very similar to XDECI:

label   XDECO   *register,area*

For example, we could print on one line the binary integers in register R6 and at location DISTRIB:

```
        MVC    OUTAREA(40),=CL40' '
        XDECO  R6,OUTAREA+4
        L      R5,DISTRIB
        XDECO  R5,OUTAREA+18
        XPRNT  OUTAREA-1,41


DISTRIB DS     1F
        DC     C' '
OUTAREA DS     CL40
```

One more pair of macro instructions is useful in completing a program: XSAVE and XRETURN manage the initial register manipulation required by the register conventions outlined in Section 5.2 and the final processing, which restores register contents and returns control from your program. Both of these macro instructions have several parameters; we will show simple forms that do what is necessary. The simple XSAVE with no parameters will

- save register contents at entry to your program,
- load register 13 with the address of a register save area,
- set and declare register 12 as a base register.

Chapter 6 will describe specifically the format and use of register save areas. Meanwhile, we appreciate XSAVE.

The macro instruction

```
        XRETURN   SA=*
```

restores registers to their status upon entry to your program and returns control from your program to the operating system (or the ASSIST system). It also allocates your register save area (SA) immediately after the instruction that returns control.

To close this section, a complete program using the ASSIST facilities is shown in Fig. 5.4. This very simple program reads one card, which must contain two numbers (there could be more data after the numbers, but it will be ignored), does a little arithmetic on the binary integer equivalents of the numbers, and prints the character equivalents of the results. The XSAVE and XRETURN macro instructions begin and end the executable portion of the program. XREAD reads the single input record, and XPRNT prints a line of headings and then the results, as shown in Fig. 5.5. The messages in the printed output about beginning and ending execution, however, are supplied as part of XSAVE and XRETURN. Input and output conversions are performed by XDECI and XDECO. As for the arithmetic, we draw your attention to the instruction

```
        MR        R2,R2
```

which multiplies the first operand *in register 3* by the second operand, which is in register 2. Do not misread the instruction as computing the square of the number in register 2!

FIGURE 5.4   A complete program

```
ELEM       CSECT
R1         EQU   1
R2         EQU   2
R3         EQU   3
R4         EQU   4
           XSAVE
           XREAD CARDIN,80
           XDECI R2,CARDIN              A
           XDECI R3,0(,R1)             B
           LR    R4,R2
           AR    R4,R3                  A + B
           XDECO R2,OUTAREA+6
           XDECO R3,OUTAREA+20
           XDECO R4,OUTAREA+34         STORE A + B
           LR    R4,R2
           SR    R4,R3
           XDECO R4,OUTAREA+48         STORE A - B
           MR    R2,R2
           XDECO R3,OUTAREA+62         STORE A * B
           XPRNT OUTHEAD,74
           XPRNT OUTAREA,74
           XRETURN SA=*
CARDIN     DS    CL80
OUTHEAD    DC    CL18'1           A '
           DC    CL14'      B '
           DC    CL14'    A + B'
           DC    CL14'    A - B'
           DC    CL14'    A * B'
OUTAREA    DC    CL74' '
           END   ELEM
```

FIGURE 5.5   Results of the program of Fig. 5.4

```
*** ELEM ENTERED ***
              A            B         A + B       A - B       A * B
             300          -65         235         365       -19500
*** ELEM EXITED ***
```

The next chapter presents the machine language instructions that convert numbers from character to binary form and back, and the subroutine linkage and register save area conventions; Chapter 7 explores how XREAD indicates there are no more records to be read and how XDECI indicates there are no more numbers in the input record to be converted. But you now have enough knowledge to write some complete programs, which is important.

5.7   Running a Complete Program: Batch Mode and Job Control Language

There are several ways of getting your program assembled and run. This section shows the use of the standard system, and the next section shows the interactive mode, using CMS, one of the interactive systems available on the IBM family of computers.

When you want your IBM computer to do work for you, you submit a *job*. A job is a series of interdependent steps; it is sealed off by the operating system from interaction with other jobs. The operating system is a set of programs and subroutines that controls the computer and the data and programs submitted to the computer. Some parts of the operating system remain in the computer's storage at all times, controlling all input and output (among other tasks).

The operating system deals with programs and data sets. A *data set* is a collection of related data treated as an entity by the operating system. The data set is composed of records. The individual records are read or written on command, but the data set is the unit made available to the user for processing of a program.

You the user submit in a job the program or programs you want run, the data sets you want used by your programs, and some *job control statements* that direct the operating system in the organization of processing. Of course, some of the programs and data sets may be already available to the operating system, often on direct-access devices; you need only request these programs and data sets by name in your job control statements.

The job control statements give the operating system directions about how to process a job: which programs to run, which data sets to make available to each program, and whom to charge for the run. The job control statements for a series of jobs are submitted in what is called a *job stream*; some data sets may also be submitted in a job stream.

The job control statements are punched into cards, which are then naturally called *job control cards*. They can also be keyed into a file from a terminal and the job then submitted through the terminal, but we will concentrate on punched cards and a strictly batch mode of operation. The job control statements are prepared in a special language called *Job Control Language*. There are only a few different kinds of statements in the job control language; we describe them briefly. On the IBM System/370, every job begins with a JOB *statement*, which names the job and identifies the user. An EXEC *statement* calls for execution of a *job step*, which may consist of execution of a program or of a catalogued procedure (catalogued procedures will soon be described in greater detail). Definition and assignment of a data set are accomplished by a DD (Dataset Definition) *statement*; the DD statement names and defines one data set.

In general, the format of job control cards is as follows: Columns 1 and 2 of a JOB, EXEC, or DD card contain slashes (//). The format of the rest of each job control card is much like the format of an assembler language statement. A name is usually required, and must begin in column 3. At least one blank must follow the name; the next field is called the *verb* field and contains one of the verbs JOB, EXEC, or DD. The verb is followed by at least one more blank, and then come the operands. As in assembler language, the operands are separated by commas but not by blanks.

Certain sequences of job control statements are standard. For example, execution of the assembler always requires the same data sets for temporary storage, a macro library, an output listing, and an object deck if desired. Each of these data sets requires definition in a job control statement. To save duplication of effort in the preparation of standard job control sequences for each user, the operating system keeps a library of *catalogued procedures*. A catalogued procedure can be called by an EXEC statement; the sequence of job control statements in the catalogued procedure will essentially be substituted for the EXEC statement that calls it. Thus the catalogued procedure is used like a macro. The job control statements in the catalogued procedure will in turn call for execution of programs and define data sets.

One of the standard catalogued procedures available in almost every installation using the operating system OS/370 or OS/VS is ASMFCLG, which calls for assembly and execution of a program written in assembler language. The ASMFCLG procedure has three steps—that is, calls for execution of three distinct programs. The first is the assembler. The assembler translates the assembler language program into machine language, creating what is called an *object module*, which contains the program assembled into machine language. The second step is called *link-edit*; in this step a program called the *linkage editor* combines the object module with any subroutines that are needed from a library, to form a complete program, ready to execute, which is called a *load module*. The third step loads your program (the load module) into main storage and runs it.

Now we describe the job control necessary to submit a job using the ASMFCLG procedure. The first two statements are

```
//TYPICAL   JOB    (279809,103),STRUBLE
//          EXEC   ASMFCLG,PARM.LKED=(XREF,LET,LIST),
//                 MAC1='USER.DA.TT279809.XMACRLIB'
```

A job always needs a name; TYPICAL is used in this example. Operands in the JOB statement include accounting identification and the programmer's name, but each installation has its own requirements for JOB statement operands, so you must learn those appropriate to your installation.

The second statement takes two lines; note that the first line ends with a comma to show that there are more operands to come, while the second line contains the mandatory // and more operands (which must begin somewhere between columns 4 and 16). The statement names the procedure to be executed, ASMFCLG. It also supplies some parameters (PARM) to the link-edit step (LKED) that tell the linkage editor what to report to us and how to treat certain linkage problems. The third operand specifies the name of a macro library to use; this library—whose name will certainly be different in your installation—contains the ASSIST macros.

The EXEC statements that perform the three steps, and most of the data set definitions they need are in the catalogued procedure ASMFCLG. The user need only provide data set definitions that modify or add to those defined in ASMFCLG.

For the first step of ASMFCLG, only the program to be assembled need be provided. The program is presented to the assembler as an input data set, most likely in the job stream with the job control statements. Just after the EXEC statement calling for execution of ASMFCLG, we include

```
//ASM.SYSIN DD *
```
Assembler language program (source program)

The DD card declares that the SYSIN data set for the ASM (assembler) step of the procedure follows immediately in the job stream (this is the meaning of *).

There is one job control statement for the link-edit step:

```
//LKED.SYSLIB DD DSN=USER.DA.TT279809.XMLOAD,DISP=SHR
```

FIGURE 5.6   A complete job to be run through OS

```
//DD103      JOB   (279809,103),STRUBLE.GEORGE,MSGCLASS=A
//           EXEC ASMFCLG,PARM.LKED='MAP,PRINT,CALL,LET',PRNTCLS=A,
//           MAC1='USER.DA.TT279809.XMACRLIB'
//ASM.SYSIN  DD    *
ELEM       CSECT
R1         EQU   1
R2         EQU   2
R3         EQU   3
R4         EQU   4
           XSAVE
           XREAD CARDIN,80
           XDECI R2,CARDIN            A
           XDECI R3,0(,R1)           B
           LR    R4,R2
           AR    R4,R3               A + B
           XDECO R2,OUTAREA+6
           XDECO R3,OUTAREA+20
           XDECO R4,OUTAREA+34        STORE A + B
           LR    R4,R2
           SR    R4,R3
           XDECO R4,OUTAREA+48        STORE A - B
           MR    R2,R2
           XDECO R3,OUTAREA+62        STORE A * B
           XPRNT OUTHEAD,74
           XPRNT OUTAREA,74
           XRETURN SA=*
CARDIN     DS    CL80
OUTHEAD    DC    CL18'l           A '
           DC    CL14'      B '
           DC    CL14'    A + B'
           DC    CL14'    A - B'
           DC    CL14'    A * B'
OUTAREA    DC    CL74' '
           END   ELEM
//LKED.SYSLIB   DD    DSN=USER.DA.TT279809.XMLOAD,DISP=SHR
//GO.XPRNT   DD    SYSOUT=A
//GO.SYSPRINT DD   SYSOUT=A
//GO.SYSIN   DD    *
300    -65
/*
```

FIGURE 5.7   Job deck for the full ASSIST system

```
$JOB     ASSIST   (project number)
*SYSLIB    XSAVE,XRETURN,EQUREGS
   (your program)
$ENTRY
   (your data)
```

This statement tells the linkage editor that if it needs any subroutines to complete your program (the ASSIST macros do call subroutines to accomplish input and output), it should look for them in the library USER.DA. TT279809.XMLOAD. The name in your system will surely be different.

Finally, in the GO step, which executes the assembled and link-edited program, no data set definitions are supplied by the catalogued procedure; all data set definitions must be supplied by the user. The simplest, defining input in the job stream and output to the printer, are

```
//GO.SYSPRINT    DD    SYSOUT=A
//GO.SYSIN       DD    *
Input data
```

The names SYSPRINT and SYSIN are standard names used by ASSIST for output (XPRNT) and input (XREAD). The operand SYSOUT=A directs output to the printer.

In summary, the full submission of a job, including the program you saw in Fig. 5.4 and the job control just described, are shown in Fig. 5.6.

If yours is a full ASSIST system, your job deck will be quite different, and rather simpler. The format is outlined in Fig. 5.7. The $ and * are in column 1 of their respective cards. The word ASSIST in the $JOB must begin in column 8, and the project number in column 15 or later. The project number (or account number) may be required by your installation, but is ignored by ASSIST. Your $JOB card may specify other options not covered here. The *SYSLIB card should list all the macro instructions (from the ASSIST macro library as well as the standard macro library) your program will use, so the ASSIST assembler can find them in the first of its two passes. The ASSIST *instructions*, such as XREAD and XDECI need *not* be listed on the *SYSLIB card. When you get to Chapter 16 and define your own macros, their definitions will go *between* the $JOB and *SYSLIB cards. The rest of the deck is self-explanatory; you need the $ENTRY card whether your program reads any data cards or not.

5.8   Running a Program under CMS

CMS is one of several systems that enables you to assemble and run an assembler language (or other language) program interactively from a computer terminal. The scope of this text does not permit a full description of CMS, its editor, commands, and macros, but we will examine a few of its macros and a minimal set of commands that can assemble and run an assembler language program.

One of the main features of CMS is interactive execution of your program. For this, you need output from the program to your terminal, and input from your terminal. The macro library CMSLIB includes the RDTERM macro for reading input from your terminal, and the WRTERM macro for writing (or perhaps call it "display") to your terminal. Let us look at WRTERM first.

The format of a WRTERM macro instruction is

Label	Operation	Operand
Symbol	WRTERM	area,length

The symbol is optional and would be included only if your program wanted to branch to the WRTERM macro instruction. The area is specified in one of three ways.

1. 'text'—the text included in quotes will be displayed.
2. symbolic name—names an area of main storage from which data will be displayed.
3. (reg)—the named register contains the address of the area from which data will be displayed.

If the area is given as text in quotes, the length need not be specified; otherwise, the length (in bytes) of the area to be displayed is necessary. One additional parameter is useful: EDIT=YES directs the operating system to remove trailing blanks from the data sent to the terminal and to do a carriage return to the beginning of the next line after the write is finished. This is the default if you do not specify EDIT=NO; the parameter EDIT=NO will direct the system *neither* to trim trailing blanks, *nor* to do a carriage return. We will see uses for both of these shortly. As an example,

```
WRTERM   'ENTER AN INTEGER ',EDIT=NO
```

will display the message ENTER AN INTEGER and will be ready to continue with the next input or output on the same line. As a second example,

```
WRTERM  OUTAREA,4Ø
```

will display the 40 characters from OUTAREA.

The RDTERM macro instruction has the form

Label	Operation	Operand
Symbol	RDTERM	area

As with WRTERM (and many other macro instructions) the symbol is optional, and would be specified only if your program wishes to branch to the macro instruction. The area is specified in either of two ways:

1. symbolic name—names a 130-byte area into which the input keyed in from the terminal will be read.
2. (reg)—the named register contains the address of the 130-byte area into which the input will be read.

Action of the macro instruction is a series of steps:

1. The computer prints a period at the terminal as a signal that input is expected. Execution of your program is then suspended, awaiting your action from the terminal.
2. You key in your input, and it is displayed for you to see as it is entered.
3. When you hit the RETURN key, this is the signal to the computer that you have finished your input, so it should resume execution of your program.
4. Your input is stored in the area you specified in your RDTERM macro instruction. Unless other parameters are included, your alphabetic input is converted to uppercase letters, and padded with spaces to the end of your 130-byte input area.
5. The actual number of characters keyed in is placed in register 0, and the program continues to the next instruction after RDTERM.

There are other parameters that may be included in a RDTERM macro instruction. For example, you may ask for different editing of your input. This form

FIGURE 5.8   A complete program to be executed under CMS

```
CMSREAL   CSECT
***   THIS PROGRAM ACCEPTS AN INTEGER FROM THE TERMINAL,
***   THEN DISPLAYS THE NUMBER AND ITS SQUARE
R2        EQU    2
R3        EQU    3
          XSAVE  TR=NO
          WRTERM 'ENTER A, FREE FORM ',EDIT=NO
          RDTERM KEYIN
          XDECI R3,KEYIN
          MR     R2,R3               SQUARE THE NUMBER IN REG. 3
          XDECO R3,OUTREA+32
          MVC    OUTAREA+9(10),KEYIN
          WRTERM OUTAREA,50
          XRETRUN SA=*,TR=NO
KEYIN     DS     CL130
OUTAREA   DC     CL50'NUMBER =            SQUARE = '
          END    CMSREAL
```

of the macro instruction is sufficient to get you going on a complete program, which is the main objective here.

Figure 5.8 shows a small program that can run interactively under CMS. Two more pieces of explanation are necessary. First, both XSAVE and XRETURN show a new parameter TR=NO. This parameter inhibits the printing of messages tracing entry to and exit from the program.

Note in Fig. 5.8 an important use for EDIT=NO in a WRTERM macro instruction. The user at the terminal should be prompted for the correct input. Therefore the RDTERM macro instruction is preceded by a WRTERM that instructs the user what input is wanted and in what form. It is common for this prompt message to appear on the same line at the terminal as the input, and this is the function of EDIT=NO in the WRTERM macro instruction.

In order to assemble this program, you must have access to the macro libraries CMSLIB and also the library perhaps named ASSTMAC MACLIB that holds the ASSIST macros. The GLOBAL command instructs the assembler to search the named libraries for any macros used in the program. Assuming that the disk that holds such libraries is available (which may take LINK and ACCESS commands), the program whose file name is CMS1 ASSEMBLE can be assembled by

```
GLOBAL    MACLIB    ASSTMAC    CMSLIB    OSMACRO
A         CMS1
```

The A command assembles the program, producing two files:

```
CMS1    TEXT
CMS1    LISTING
```

FIGURE 5.9   Transcript of assembly and execution of the program of Fig. 5.8

```
.GLOBAL MACLIB ASSTMAC CMSLIB OSMACRO
R;

.A CMS1

ASSEMBLER (XF) DONE
NO STATEMENTS FLAGGED IN THIS ASSEMBLY
R;

.GLOBAL TXTLIB ASSTSUB
R;

.LOAD CMS1
R;

.START
EXECUTION BEGINS...
ENTER A, FREE FORM . 401
NUMBER =   401          SQUARE =        160801
R(31072);
```

The first file contains the assembled program in a form ready to be loaded and executed; the LISTING file is the listing of the source program with the assembled machine language and any error messages.

To execute the program, load it into main storage, along with some subroutines required by the ASSIST macros. Assuming these subroutines are in the library ASSTSUB TXTLIB, you can load and execute the program with

```
GLOBAL   TXTLIB   ASSTSUB
LOAD     CMS1
START
```

Figure 5.9 shows the transcript of a piece of a terminal session in which the program of Fig. 5.8 is assembled and executed.

m a i n   i d e a s

□ By convention, registers 0, 1, 13, 14, and 15 each have a special use, as follows:

Register 0—single-word output of a subroutine

Register 1—address of area containing parameter addresses

Register 13—address of register save area

Register 14—return address from subroutine to calling program

Register 15—entry point address in a subroutine

□ DC and DS statements define constants and storage in assembler language. Literals are in general defined according to the same rules that govern the definition of constants. The subfields of a DC or DS instruction or literal definition are duplication factor, type, modifiers, and values.

□ Constant types C, X, B, F, H, E, D, P, A, and V allow for a variety of data representations, boundary alignment rules, and padding and truncation.

□ Assembler language statements CSECT, TITLE, ORG, LTORG, and END control the assembly of programs but are not translated directly to machine language.

□ Macro instructions are expanded by the assembler into one or more assembler language statements. They relieve programmers of burdens of knowing and writing standard sequences of statements. The ASSIST macros XSAVE and XRETURN and the ASSIST instructions XREAD, XPRNT, XDECI, and XDECO especially help in writing simple programs simply. The CMS macros RDTERM and WRTERM are similarly useful.

□ A user submits a batch job to the IBM System/370, with job control statements containing directions as to programs and data sets to be used.

□ Job control statements include JOB, EXEC, and DD statements; catalogued procedures provide job control for standard tasks.

□ Assembler language programs can be run in an interactive environment such as CMS. A set of commands takes the place of job control statements, and the macro instructions RDTERM and WRTERM enable interactive input and output via a user's terminal.

■ **PROBLEMS** F O R   R E V I E W   A N D   I M A G I N A T I O N

5.1 Show the bit patterns generated from the constant definitions

DC	C'Ø'	DC	PL4'Ø'
DC	CL4'Ø'	DC	C'A'
DC	X'Ø'	DC	X'A'
DC	XL4'Ø'	DC	F'19'
DC	F'Ø'	DC	XL4'19'
DC	E'Ø'	DC	HL4'19'
DC	P'Ø'		

5.2 Write DC statements for
   a) a list of three full words containing binary integer equivalents of (decimal) −11, +373, 0;
   b) a list of 10 full words containing zeros;
   c) a half-word whose binary bits are 1100100100100100;
   d) a double-word whose EBCDIC contents is EGC123*$;
   e) a three-byte field, each byte containing hexadecimal E4;
   f) four 120-byte areas, each containing the EBCDIC characters RESULT= followed by blanks.

5.3 Write statements that perform the following operations.
   a) Reset the location counter to 100 hexadecimal.
   b) Equate the symbol PORG with the value 256 decimal.
   c) Move the location counter to a full-word boundary if necessary and assign a full word to have the value 300 decimal. The location should be named DEC3ØØ.
   d) Create a symbol OUTBUF that represents a location whose contents are the address of OUTSTR.
   e) Create a 132-character storage area called OUTSTR.
   f) Stop the assembler from processing further statements.

5.4 One common way to set an entire field in main storage to zero, or blanks, or something, is to move one copy into the first byte, and then cascade its movement through the rest of the field with a MVC instruction. For example, we can store blanks in the 133-byte field PRTLINE by

```
MVI     PRTLINE,C' '
MVC     PRTLINE+1(132),PRTLINE
```

Trace how the blank is propagated through the entire field, and find examples previously given where this technique can be used to advantage. Overlap of fields in any manner is permitted the MVC instruction; explore other effects achieved by overlapping of fields.

5.5   What is the difference in effect among the instructions

```
LA    R4,=A(TENNIS)
LA    R4,TENNIS
L     R4,=A(TENNIS)
L     R4,TENNIS
```

5.6   State the difference between

a)   C1 DC FL2'19'   and   C2 DC H'19'

and that between

b)   C3 DC F'367'   and   C4 DC HL4'367'

5.7   Write an appropriate TITLE statement to be included in the program of Fig. 5.4.

5.8   Write a set of DS statements to make space for a name and address—up to 30 characters on each line. Then write a program segment using XREAD that will read records containing a name and address and putting them in the storage you have defined.

5.9   Adapt Problem 5.8 to an interactive environment: using RDTERM and WRTERM, get the name and address from the terminal.

5.10 Write an appropriate set of DS statements for a *Monopoly* deed: the name of the property, its price, and rents
a) undeveloped   b) with one house
c) with two houses   d) with three houses
e) with a hotel

Each of the dollar amounts should be expressed as a binary integer.

5.11 Write a program segment that will print the information about a *Monopoly* deed for which you allocated space in Problem 5.10. Include in your printed information the mortgage value, which is half the price. Use XDECO to convert the numbers to printable form.

5.12 Adapt Problem 5.11 to an interactive environment; identify each piece of data with appropriate text, and use the WRTERM macro instruction.

5.13 One main reason for using R2, R3, and so on for register addresses is that a cross-reference table will list all the statements where each symbol is used. Investigate how you would get a cross-reference table from your assembler.

■ REFERENCES

IBM OS/VS—DOS/VSE—VM/370 Assembler Language, GC 33-4010, IBM Corporation. For details of defining constants, storage, literals, and symbols in assembler language, and assembler control statements.

IBM OS/VS—VM/370 Assembler Programmer's Guide, GC 33-4021, IBM Corporation. Information on how to use the assembler: data sets and parameters.

IBM OS/VS1 Supervisor Services and Macro Instructions, GC 24-5103, IBM Corporation. A good description of the supervisor's role.

IBM System/370 and 4300 Processors Bibliography, GC 20-0001, IBM Corporation. Listing of IBM manuals by subject, system, and number, with abstracts. This is a good source for finding your way to the right manual.

IBM Virtual Machine Facility/370: CMS Command and Macro Reference, GC 20-1818, IBM Corporation. Reference on the commands and on the macros you can use in your assembler language programs.

IBM Virtual Machine Facility/370: CMS User's Guide, GC 20-1819, IBM Corporation. Overview of the CMS system and how to use it.

Presser, Leon, and John R. White, "Linkers and Loaders," *Computing Surveys* **4**, 3 (September 1972), pp. 149–67. A tutorial presentation on linking and loading programs in the IBM systems.

6

CONVERSIONS AND SUBROUTINES

6.1 Introduction

The concept of subroutines is very important, and so is the implementation, especially since a main reason for learning assembler language is to write asembler language subroutines to do tasks that would be more difficult in higher-level languages; these subroutines would then be called by programs written in higher-level languages. Control structures IF-THEN, WHILE, etc. are also vitally important. You may wish to skip all or most of Chapter 6 at this time and jump to Chapter 7 to work on control structures, then come back to Chapter 6 later. Your decision may depend on taste and your particular objectives in studying assembler language, and also on the type of system you are using.

A *subroutine* is a closed sequence of instructions (and perhaps data areas and constants) that is called by another program or subroutine. It usually returns control to the calling program. This is in distinction to a main program, which conceptually is in direct control, not subsidiary to or called by any other program. Actually, in the IBM System/370, a main program is regarded as a subroutine by the operating system supervisor; however, the concept of a main program as one not called by any other program or subroutine belonging to the user is still a useful one. A main program may or may not call subroutines, and subroutines may or may not call other subroutines. If we restrict our attention to a section that calls a subroutine, we see that it does not matter to the calling structure whether the section is a main program or a subroutine, so we use the blanket term *routine*, which applies to either.

Every program or subroutine in the IBM System/370 uses the general registers; practically nothing can be done without them. A routine (main program or subroutine) *A* that calls a subroutine *B* would be difficult indeed to write if the subroutine changed contents of all the registers. The subroutine *B* must use the registers, but writing the calling routine *A* will be much easier if its register contents are undisturbed, except for the registers explicitly used in communication with subroutine *B*. Fortunately it is possible to set up procedures and conventions so that a few designated registers have special uses in the subroutine communication. All registers can be used by the subroutine, but almost all are restored to the calling routine's contents before the subroutine returns control to the calling routine. This amounts to having our cake and eating it too: both the calling routine *A* and subroutine *B* have the use of registers; the cost of following certain register conventions is quite low. We introduced the conventions for use of registers 0, 1, 13, 14, and 15 at the beginning of the last chapter, and in this chapter we will show how we set up and use the registers according to these conventions.

We will relate the register save areas and register conventions to the XSAVE and XRETURN macros introduced in Section 5.7. We will show the conventions used in passing parameters to a subroutine and back to the calling routine. The problem of converting numbers between character representation and binary integers was treated with the XDECI and XDECO macros in Chapter 5, but this chapter introduces the machine language instructions that do the conversions. But first we must introduce the BR and BALR instructions and the setting and use of the implied base register.

6.2   The BR and BALR Instructions

A number of different branch instructions, conditional and unconditional, are needed in any digital computer. The instructions and their use are discussed at length in Chapter 7; here we only describe two unconditional branch instructions used in subroutine linkage.

The BR and BALR instructions are both RR-type instructions. In both, the second operand is the address to which control is transferred, called the *branch address*. That is, the register specified as *R2* contains the address of a main-storage location from which the next instruction is to be taken. Instructions are then taken from locations subsequent to the branch address until another branch is performed.

The BR operation code is a simplification of BCR 15, where 15 is the first operand. It will become clear in Chapter 7 why 15 is a first operand that makes a BCR (Branch Conditional to Register) instruction into an unconditional branch. The unconditional branch is important enough to warrant a separate alphabetic abbreviation and a simplification. Thus we write BR with only one operand, which in the normal RR-type pattern is the second operand. The instruction

                              BR   R14

causes a branch to the location whose address is in register 14 (as usual, we assume that R14 is EQUated to 14). If, for example, location ØØ9426 contains the BR R14 instruction and register 14 contains ØØØØ963Ø, the instruction executed after the BR R14 will be the instruction located (that is, beginning) at location ØØ963Ø.

A special convention attaches to a 0 as second operand in the BR and BALR instructions. The specification of 0 means that no branch takes place; the next instruction is taken from main storage directly following the BR or BALR instruction. Therefore BR Ø is a dummy instruction, the one used when a "no-operation" instruction is desired. The BALR instruction whose second operand is 0 does not reduce to a no-operation instruction; the action taken with respect to the first operand is explained below.

The BALR instruction performs a branch in exactly the same way as the BR instruction, but first loads the address of the instruction immediately after the BALR into the register whose address is given in the first operand. Suppose, for example, that location ØØ9472 (really ØØ9472 and ØØ9473) contains the instruction BALR R14,R15, and that register 15 contains ØØØØBC76. The BALR instruction causes two actions. The first is that ØØØØ9474, the address of the instruction immediately following the BALR instruction, is loaded into register 14, the first operand. The second action is the branch to location ØØBC76.

Actually, the BALR instruction loads some bits of the program status word into positions 0–7 of register *R1*, in addition to loading the address of the next instruction (actually bits 40–63 of the program status word) in positions 8–31 of register *R1*. Therefore the first two hexadecimal digits of register 14 in the preceding example may not be 00. The contents of register 14 usually serve only as a branch address, however, and so the eight high-order bits are irrelevant. The next sections will show the usefulness of these instructions.

6.3   An Implied Base Register; The USING Pseudo-operation

THE USING PSEUDO-OPERATION

In Chapter 3 we discussed the action of the assembler in converting the address of a symbol to base-and-displacement form. The assembler puts in the assembled machine language instruction the base register address that was declared previously to be used as an implied base register. The declaration of the implied base register also includes information about what relocatable address is assumed to be in that register, so the correct displacement can also be generated by the assembler. Now we show how the implied base register is declared.

An assembler language statement that is not translated into instructions or constants that become part of the machine language program is called a *pseudo-operation*. The pseudo-operation gives information or commands to the assembler, influencing the output of the assembler, either by specifying the form of the listing or object program or by instructing the assembler how to assemble subsequent instructions. The USING pseudo-operation instructs the assembler by giving it the information it needs in order to convert relocatable expressions to base-and-displacement form.

For this purpose, the most elementary form of the USING pseudo-operation is

$$\text{USING} \quad *,r$$

The second operand designates the register to be used as the implied base register; the asterisk used as first operand is the location-counter reference symbol. The statement informs the assembler that the register named in the second operand contains the relocatable address currently in the location-reference counter. This address is usually the address of the next instruction. For example, consider the following sequence of instructions with addresses assigned as indicated.

```
                          USING      *,R9
        000014            L          R8,G
                            .
                            .
                            .
        000156   G         DC         F'-1'
```

The implied base register is declared to be register 9, and it is declared to contain the relocatable address 000014. Therefore in assembly of the L R8,G instruction, the base designation *B2* inserted by the assembler is 9. The displacement *D2* is 000156 − 000014 = 142. The entire assembled instruction is 58809142.

THE BALR, USING **PAIR**

The USING pseudo-operation makes a promise to the assembler about the contents of a named register. The BALR instruction enables us to keep that promise. As discussed in the previous section, it loads the register named as first operand with the address of the next instruction. When a BALR instruction immediately precedes the USING statement, the USING becomes not a promise but a notice of action just taken. The BALR instruction is used to load the register, but there is usually no need to branch at the same time, so the second operand of the BALR instruction is 0.

For instance, we may have

```
              BALR  R9,0
              USING *,R9
              L     R8,G
                .
                .
                .
        G     DC    F'-1'
```

The BALR R9,∅ instruction loads register 9 with the address of the next instruction, but does not branch, since its second operand is 0. Therefore the next instruction to be executed is the next one in main storage, that is, L R8,G. The USING pseudo-operation has told the assembler how to construct base and displacement, so G will be loaded correctly into register 8.

RELOCATABILITY

The BALR instruction, used as we have just shown, permits a program to work properly independently of its placement in main storage. As long as the *differences* between addresses of various parts of the program are maintained and boundaries are where they were planned to be during assembly, displacements from the address placed by the BALR instruction in the implied base register will be correct.

Let us examine once more our example, showing assembler-assigned locations and actual core locations. Suppose that the program is relocated by (hexadecimal) 009020, so that every relocatable address is added to 009020. Then the program in main storage can be shown as

Actual location	Assembled location	Assembled instruction	Assembler language	
⋮	⋮	⋮	⋮	
009032	000012	∅59∅	BALR	R9,∅
			USING	*,R9
009034	000014	588∅9142	L	R8,G
⋮	⋮	⋮	⋮	
009176	000156	FFFFFFFF G	DC	F'−1'

The execution of the BALR instruction loads 00009034 into register 9. During the execution of the load instruction, the displacement 142 is added to the contents of register 9, 00009034, to yield an effective address of 00009176, which is the actual address of G: 009020 + 000156.

MORE ON USING

Several registers may be declared available for use as implied base registers by one USING pseudo-operation. The first operand of USING is any relocatable expression not involving a literal. This first operand is followed by from 1 to 16 absolute expressions whose values are register addresses. We can express the syntax of USING as

Label	Operation	Operands
Blank	USING	V,r1[,r2, . . . ,r16]

where the brackets around *r2, . . . ,r16* indicate that these are optional operands. Register *r1* is assumed to contain *V,* the value of the relocatable expression. If a third operand *r2* appears, register *r2* is assumed to contain the value
$V + 4096$. Similarly, if *r3, r4, . . .* are specified, registers *r3, r4, . . .* are assumed to contain values $V + 2*4096$, $V + 3*4096$, ... More than one implied base register must be declared if the length of program and data areas is
so great that some addresses exceed the address in the first base register by
more than 4095 (the largest possible displacement).

A location, or an expression specifying it, is said to be *addressable* if its
address is greater than the address declared to be in some implied base register
and less than 4096 greater than the address declared to be in that register. This
is a practical requirement that makes sure that the assembler will find one of
the declared implied base registers and construct a displacement to go with it to
address the desired location. No expression referring to a main-storage
location and involving a symbol or literal may be used as an operand in an instruction before the USING statement that makes it addressable. Register 0 can
be declared in a USING pseudo-operation, but special rules that we shall not
consider govern its use.

A base register may be redefined to have a different value in a subsequent
USING pseudo-operation. A register may be made unavailable for further use as
an implied base register by a DROP pseudo-operation. The form of this operation is as follows:

Label	Operation	Operands
Blank	DROP	From 1 to 16 absolute expressions referring to registers, of the form *r1[,r2,r3, . . . ,r16]*

An example of a more advanced usage of USING is the following:

Label	Operation	Operands
	BALR	R9,Ø
	USING	BASE,R9,R10,R11
BASE	LM	R10,R11,BADDR
⋮		
BADDR	DC	A(BASE+4Ø96,BASE+8192)

The BALR instruction and USING make 4096 bytes starting at BASE addressable.
After seeing USING BASE,R9,R1Ø,R11 the assembler believes that all addresses
up to BASE+12287 are addressable; we can see that locations BASE+4Ø96 to
BASE+12287 cannot in fact be correctly addressed until the LM R1Ø,R11,BADDR

instruction is executed, loading the proper values into registers 10 and 11. Note that for this procedure to work properly, BADDR must be located not more than 4094 bytes beyond BASE.

6.4 Subroutine Implementation

THE SUBROUTINE CONCEPT
A sequence of instructions that is to be executed at several different points in a computer program need not be included in its entirety at each such point. It can be enclosed and called a subroutine. Then at each point where execution of the sequence is desired, the right kind of branch to the subroutine is sufficient. Enough information must be given to the subroutine so that it knows what information to work with and where to return control when it is finished. The idea is to replace the storage and control structure of Fig. 6.1(a) with the structure shown in Fig. 6.1(b). The structure shown in Fig. 6.1(b), using the subroutine, requires less storage space than the other, since sequence A is loaded in main storage only once.

A subroutine structure has many advantages: It allows easy use of previously programmed solutions to subtasks of the programming problem. It facilitates debugging by allowing each small subroutine to be debugged separately when called by a minimal master program designed purely to test the given subroutine. It makes programming easier by breaking down the problem into pieces, each of which has only a minimal and explicit number of relationships with the others.

THE REGISTER SAVE AREA
It is a great convenience for a calling program to be able to set up registers 1, 13, 14, and 15 for a subroutine call, transfer control to the subroutine, and then expect all registers except register 0 to be unchanged when control is returned. Both calling and called routines need to use and change registers; a

FIGURE 6.1 Storage and control: (a) without a subroutine; (b) with sequence A as a subroutine

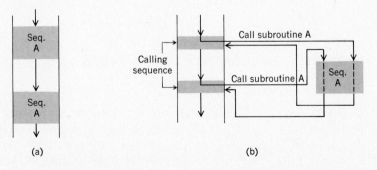

(a)   (b)

system for preserving the register contents left by the calling routine and restoring them just before return of control to the calling routine will allow both routines full use of registers.

The area used for storage of registers is 18 words long; it has the format shown in Fig. 6.2. The first and third words are not used in the more elementary linkage patterns. The called subroutine stores the contents of registers 14, 15, 0, 1, . . . , 12 in words 4 to 18 of the save area. Preservation of these register contents can be accomplished by the instruction

```
STM     R14,R12,12(R13)
```

at the beginning of the called subroutine, since register 13 contains the address of the save area. Similarly, the registers can be restored by the single instruction

```
LM      R14,R12,12(R13)
```

just before exit from the subroutine.

The calling program supplies the area (that is, puts the address of an area in register 13) in which the called subroutine stores the register contents as left by the calling program (read that again—carefully!). However, the called subroutine must make special arrangements for storing register 13. The called subroutine, subroutine B, usually stores the contents of register 13 in word 2 of the save area which *it* provides. The remainder of this area would be used by a subroutine C, called by subroutine B, to store the contents of registers as left by subroutine B. Alternatively, the called subroutine may store register 13 in an entirely separate location, or guarantee not to call any subroutines or change register 13.

To justify special treatment for register 13, let us draw an analogy. If we bury a treasure, we make a treasure map. It does no good to bury the map with the treasure; we must store the map elsewhere, so we can use it in finding the

FIGURE 6.2   A register save area

Word	Address	Contents
Word 1	SAV	
Word 2	SAV+4	Address of calling program's save area
Word 3	SAV+8	Address of called program's save area
Word 4	SAV+12	Contents of register 14
Word 5	SAV+16	Contents of register 15
Word 6	SAV+20	Contents of register 0
Word 7	SAV+24	Contents of register 1
⋮	⋮	⋮
Word 18	SAV+68	Contents of register 12

treasure again. So it is with register contents. We can bury the contents of registers 14, 15, and 0–12 at a location recorded in our treasure map, register 13, but we must keep the contents of register 13, namely the treasure map, elsewhere.

RESPONSIBILITIES OF THE CALLED SUBROUTINE

Immediately after gaining control, the subroutine should store the register contents as left by the calling routine. At the entry point of the subroutine, the instruction to accomplish this task is

```
STM    R14,R12,12(R13)
```

This instruction stores all registers except register 13 in the area provided by the calling program.

Usually the subroutine follows the STM instruction with

```
BALR  R12,Ø
USING *,R12
```

to define an implied base register. Some register other than 12 could, of course, be used. After these instructions have established the addressability of relocatable expressions in the subroutine, the subroutine may save the contents of register 13 by

```
ST    R13,SAVOWN+4
```

The last of the instructions in this minimal set of set-up instructions is

```
LA    R13,SAVOWN
```

which loads the address of the subroutine's own register save area into register 13.

The sequence of these instructions is important; a programmer varies them only at everyone's peril. Before register 13 can be stored, addressability of the subroutine's register save area must be established. Since establishing that addressability changes the contents of a register, at least that register must be stored in the calling routine's register save area. But all registers 14, 15, and 0–12 may be stored as easily as one with the STM instruction.

In fact, there are two other conventions that are normally followed as well. The first is that the subroutine stores the address of *its* register save area in the third word of the *calling program's* register save area. This is not necessary for the normal work of a subroutine and return to the calling program; the addresses in the third word of each save area establish a chain of register save areas, so that if the program crashes, the supervisor can print the contents of register save areas to help the programmer ascertain where things went wrong.

The second additional convention is storage of the name of the subroutine close to the beginning of the subroutine. This is useful if you have to examine a dump of storage; it is helpful to find the name of each subroutine embedded in the dump.

FIGURE 6.3   The equivalent of XSAVE TR=NO

```
        DS       0H                  ENSURE HALF-WORD BOUNDARY
        USING    *,R15               TEMPORARILY
        B        R14(,R15)           BRANCH AROUND THE CSECT NAME
        DC       AL1(9),CL9'CSECTNAME'
***  AL1 SPECIFIES A ONE-BYTE CONSTANT
        STM      R14,R12,12(R13)
        ST       R13,$PR#0001+4
        LR       R12,R13             HOLD ADDR. OF CALLING PROG.'S AREA
        LA       R13,$PR#0001        WHILE LOADING OUR OWN
        ST       R13,8(R12)          SAVE OUR OWN IN CALLING PROG'S AREA
        BALR     R12,0               NEW BASE REGISTER
        DROP     R15                 CLEAN UP TEMPORARY USING
        USING    *,R12
```

Figure 6.3 shows the statements generated as the expansion of the macro instruction

```
    XSAVE    TR=NO
```

which was used in the last chapter. I have changed the comments, and the name of register 12 to R12. Perhaps you now understand the advantage of having a nice simple-looking macro instruction like XSAVE! But it is worth your while to trace the execution of Fig. 6.3, so that you understand exactly how all the conventions are honored.

As a subroutine finishes its task and returns control, much less work is necessary. The subroutine must restore registers, then branch to the return address. This can be done by the sequence of three instructions

```
    L        R13,SAVOWN+4
    LM       R14,R12,12(R13)
    BR       R14
```

The first two of these are easily seen to reverse ST and STM instructions of the earlier sequence. Finally, with all registers restored to their contents upon entry, the branch instruction returns control to the address which the calling program loaded into register 14 for this purpose.

The expansion of

```
    XRETURN SA=*,TR=NO
```

generally follows this scheme, but with one important addition:

```
        L        R13,4(R13)         RESTORE PREVIOUS SAVE AREA POINT
        LM       R14,R12,12(R13)    STANDARD REGISTER RESTORATION
        BR       R14                RETURN NORMALLY TO CALLER
$PR#0001 DC      18F'0'             SAVE AREA
```

The parameter SA=* triggers the allocation of the register save area immediately after the executable instructions. The name $PR#0001 was generated during expansion of XSAVE, and must of course be used now. Perhaps you wondered earlier during the discussions of register conventions how the programs of Chapter 5 met the conventions by providing a register save area; now you know!

The standard macro library has macros SAVE and RETURN that are not as powerful as XSAVE and XRETURN, but can be used in a standard system that does not contain the ASSIST macros. The macro instruction

```
        SAVE    (R14,R12)
```

has the expansion

```
        STM     R14,R12,12(R13)
```

and therefore saves you the calculation of displacement in the STM instruction. With additional parameters, a SAVE macro instruction can store the CSECT name, but cannot set your base register or load register 13 for you the way XSAVE can.

Similarly,

```
        RETURN (R14,R12)
```

has the expansion

```
        LM      R14,R12,12(R13)
        BR      R14
```

It is your responsibility to reload register 13 before your RETURN macro instruction.

RESPONSIBILITIES OF THE CALLING PROGRAM

Not much is required of the calling program when it calls a subroutine. Parameters must be supplied, and the next section will show how that is done. Register 13 must contain the address of a register save area, but this was done in the initial sequence of the calling program, and the calling program leaves register 13 intact until it is ready to return control itself. Register 15 should be set to the beginning address of the subroutine; this can be done with

```
        L       R15,=V(SUBENTRY)
```

where SUBENTRY is the entry address (usually the CSECT name) of the subroutine. The V-type address literal is used if the subroutine is in a different CSECT from the calling program; if the subroutine entry address is in the same CSECT, it would be addressed by an A-type literal instead, as follows:

```
        L       R15,=A(SUBENTRY)
```

Finally, a BALR instruction stores the address of the next instruction in the calling program (to be executed after the subroutine returns control) into register 14 *and* transfers control to the subroutine:

```
        BALR    R14,R15
```

These two instructions are sufficient to call a subroutine.

6.5   Passing Parameters to a Subroutine

Most subroutines need data supplied by the programs that call them. Many
also produce more than one word of output to return to the calling program.
We prefer that all data supplied by the calling program that must be used by
the subroutine be defined explicitly as parameters and passed to the subroutine
according to clear conventions, and similarly the results to be returned to the
calling program. There are several advantages to defining formally the parameters:

- the interface between calling program and subroutine is made clear, which reduces confusion, misunderstandings, and nonworking programs;
- the subroutine is more flexible, in that it can be called with different parameters from different places in a program, or in different programs.

The standard interface requires that the *addresses* of parameters be placed in a
block of storage, and the address of this block be loaded into register 1 as the
subroutine is called. The subroutine can then access all of the parameters.
Both input and output parameters are treated the same way.

For example, suppose subroutine B has four parameters, two of which are
input parameters and two are output parameters. The routine A that calls on
subroutine B may wish to supply parameters T and U as input to subroutine B
and have the results of subroutine B placed at V and W. Routine A will therefore
put the *addresses* of T, U, V, and W in consecutive words, and place the address
of the first word of this area (the word containing the address of T) in register
1, as shown in Fig. 6.4. This may be done by defining a block of address
constants

```
              ADDS      DC      A(T)
                        DC      A(U)
                        DC      A(V)
                        DC      A(W)
```

among other constants and storage definitions, and loading the address of the
block

```
                        LA      R1,ADDS
```

FIGURE 6.4   The parameter address list

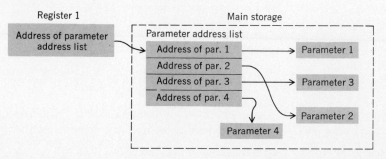

before entry to subroutine *B*.

Subroutine *B* may get the second parameter by

```
L      R3,4(,R1)
L      R8,Ø(,R3)
```

The first of these instructions loads register 3 with the word four bytes beyond the location whose address is in register 1; this word is the address of U as placed there by routine *A*. The second instruction, assuming that U is a full word, loads U into register 8. Addresses of all four parameters can be loaded into consecutive registers by, say

```
LM     R3,R6,Ø(,R1)
```

Let us explore several ways of following the parameter-passing conventions with some examples.

1. Suppose the fields named PSAT and NAME are to be passed to a subroutine. With other definitions of constants we can define the parameter address block:

```
ADBLOCK    DC     A(PSAT)
           DC     A(NAME)
```

Just before entry to the subroutine, we load register 1 with the address of the block:

```
LA     R1,ADBLOCK
```

2. Suppose we wish to call the same subroutine. The value of the first parameter is in register 3, and the address of the 108-byte area containing characters of the second parameter is in register 6. We must construct an address block as before. The parameter block may be defined

```
ADBK1      DC     A(FPARAM)
           DS     1F
```

The first parameter must be stored in main storage, perhaps by

```
ST     R3,FPARAM
```

The second parameter is already in main storage, but its address must be stored:

```
ST     R6,ADBK1+4
```

which places the address in the full word for which we defined the storage space with the DS 1F statement. Finally, the address of the parameter address-block is loaded:

```
LA     R1,ADBK1
```

3. Suppose we are preparing to enter another subroutine, whose single parameter is a binary integer. The subroutine could be written to accept the number itself

in register 1, but we presume it follows the standard conventions. If the number is in, say, register 5, we store it:

```
ST      R5,NUM
```

We need a parameter address block, even though it contains only one address; it could be defined

```
ADNUM   DC      A(NUM)
```

Finally, before entry to the subroutine, we load the address of the parameter address block:

```
LA      R1,ADNUM
```

4. One example of the use of a literal is the definition of a parameter address block. We saw earlier the definition of a block

```
ADDS    DC      A(T)
        DC      A(U)
        DC      A(V)
        DC      A(W)
```

We may note now that exactly the same definition could be made in the single statement

```
ADDS    DC      A(T,U,V,W)
```

However, the combination of this statement *and* the instruction that loads its address

```
LA      R1,ADDS
```

can be replaced by

```
LA      R1,=A(T,U,V,W)
```

A subroutine that produces one binary integer as its result and changes none of its input parameters can be classed as a *function* (as in FORTRAN or Pascal, for example), and a different convention can apply. The result may be left in register 0 instead of in a main storage location whose address is in a parameter address block. The calling program will expect to find the result in register 0, and of course may use it or store it in whatever way is desired.

If your function leaves its result in register 0, you must be careful not to restore register 0 from the register save area as you return control to the calling program. Your return sequence could be

```
L       R13,4(R13)
LM      R14,R15,12(R13)
LM      R1,R12,24(R13)
BR      R14
```

With the XRETURN macro instruction you can specify exactly which registers are to be restored; to restore all but register 0, you can use

```
XRETURN RGS=(R14-R15,R1-R12),SA=*
```

Note that the standard RETURN macro instruction restores only one contiguous set of registers, so in a standard system you would need

```
L             R13,4(R13)
LM            R14,R15,12(R13)
RETURN        (R1,R12)
```

If you have studied parameter passing by name, value, and by reference, you will recognize that the parameters passed using the conventions described here are passed *by reference*. This means that the subroutine refers to the actual values of the parameters in the calling program's area, and has full opportunity to change any of them. When you define a subroutine therefore, you should include in your documentation a very clear statement about exactly which parameters are changed by your subroutine.

How would we implement passing a parameter *by value*? With this type of parameter passing, the subroutine is to have its own copy of the parameter, so that anything done to the parameter in the subroutine does not affect its value in the calling routine. The preferred approach is for the calling routine to copy the parameter to a new location, and pass the address of that location to the subroutine. It is also possible to store the *value* of the parameter (at least, if it is a full word) in the parameter address block whose address is presented to the subroutine. Avoid doing this; the confusion caused by having some parameters themselves and addresses of other parameters passed to the subroutine is a problem you do not need!

6.6   Number Conversions

When numeric data are read by the IBM system from cards or from a terminal, the data are coded in the EBCDIC or zoned decimal code. We cannot perform arithmetic on data in this form; instead, we must convert the data to packed decimal or binary form and perform arithmetic on these representations. To send the results to a printer, card punch, or terminal, we must reverse the conversion process. In most computers, conversions must be done digit by digit; the IBM systems have powerful instructions that do a lot of the conversion task for us. We have illustrated the use of XDECI and XDECO macros, but now it is time to study the conversion instructions themselves.

We shall consider four instructions that convert

PACK:	EBCDIC to packed decimal
CVB:	packed decimal to binary
CVD:	binary to packed decimal
UNPK:	packed decimal to EBCDIC

The strategy of the use of the instructions is shown in Fig. 6.5.

FIGURE 6.5 The strategy of use of conversion instructions

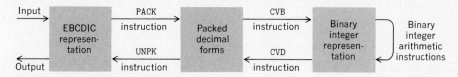

THE PACK INSTRUCTION

The PACK instruction converts a string of bytes, 1 to 16 bytes long, from the EBCDIC or zoned decimal format to a string, also 1 to 16 bytes long, in the packed decimal format. Both operands are in main storage, so the instruction is of SS type. The second operand specifies the source string, the bytes to be converted; the first operand specifies the destination, the location of the packed decimal representation. Each operand is of variable length, and the lengths need not be the same. Therefore the length suboperand portion of the instruction is divided into two parts: a four-bit *L1*, the length of the first operand string, and a four-bit *L2*, the length of the second operand string. As explained in Chapter 3, the number entered in each length field is one less than the actual length of the string. If the instruction contains an *L1* of 2 and an *L2* of 5, a six-byte EBCDIC string will be converted into a three-byte packed decimal string. In assembler language, however, we give the actual lengths. For example,

PACK   A(8),INP(6)

will cause a six-byte string starting at INP to be converted to packed decimal form; the packed decimal form will be stored in eight bytes, starting at A.

FIGURE 6.6 Execution of PACK instructions

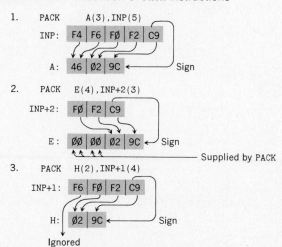

The PACK itself acts as follows. The operands are processed from right to left. The upper four bits of the rightmost byte of the second operand are assumed to contain a representation of the sign of the number and are moved to the low-order bit positions of the rightmost byte of the first operand. After that, the low-order four bits of each byte in the second operand string are packed into consecutive four-bit groups, made up of both lower and upper portions of bytes, in the first operand string. Zeros are filled or padded into the leftmost bytes of the first operand string if the second operand is too short to supply data to fill the first operand string. On the other hand, if the length of the first operand string is too small to accommodate all the digits from the second operand, the remaining digits are ignored. Figure 6.6 gives several examples illustrating how the PACK instruction is executed.

THE UNPK (UNPacK) INSTRUCTION

We next consider the UNPK instruction. The instruction UNPK (or UNPacK) is the converse of the PACK instruction. Also of SS type, it changes a string of packed decimal data specified in the *second* operand into a string of zoned decimal bytes, and stores them, starting at the location given in the first operand. Lengths of each operand are specified in the instruction.

During execution of the UNPK instruction, the strings are processed from right to left. Digits—that is, four-bit groups from the second operand—are expanded into full bytes. The upper four bits of each byte are filled with 1111 except for the rightmost byte, whose upper four bits are filled by the sign of the packed decimal string. If necessary, the packed decimal string is expanded (for purposes of conversion, but not altered in main storage) by adding zeros on the left before conversion. On the other hand, if the length of the first

FIGURE 6.7 Execution of UNPK instructions

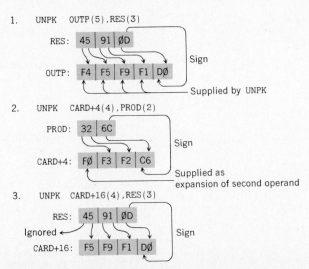

operand string is too small to accommodate all the digits from the packed decimal string, the high-order digits are ignored. Figure 6.7 illustrates the execution of the UNPK instruction.

THE CVB (ConVert to Binary) INSTRUCTION

The CVB (ConVert to Binary) instruction converts a number from the packed decimal to binary integer form. Since binary integer arithmetic is performed in registers, the binary integer result is left in a register. The packed decimal source operand is located in main storage, so the instruction is of RX type. The second operand is the packed decimal source, the first operand is the register to contain the result. The packed decimal source operand is assumed to be exactly eight bytes long and to begin on a double-word boundary. The low-order four bits of the packed decimal string are interpreted as a sign: 1010, 1100, 1110, and 1111 (A, C, E and F in hexadecimal) are recognized as plus, and 1011 and 1101 (B and D) as minus. If a minus sign is found, the result is, of course, in 2's complement form.

Some examples follow.

		Source	Result
CVB	R3,G	ØØØØØØØØ ØØØØØ25C	ØØØØØØ19

Both source and result are representations of the decimal number 25.

CVB	R4,H	ØØØØØØØØ ØØØØØ25D	FFFFFFE7

Both are representations of the decimal number −25.

THE CVD (ConVert to Decimal) INSTRUCTION

The CVD (ConVert to Decimal) instruction is the converse of the CVB instruction. Also of RX type, it converts a binary integer addressed by *R1* into a packed decimal number in a double word addressed by *B2*, *X2*, and *D2*.

With operands of R3,G and R4,H, the CVD instruction would exactly reverse the action performed by the CVB instructions above.

PROGRAMMING

Since the CVB and CVD instructions assume double-word operands in main storage, the PACK instruction will usually have a first operand whose length is 8 and whose address is defined to be on a double-word boundary, even if the number to be converted is known to be small. A typical sequence might be

```
PACK  DBLE(8),INP(6)
CVB   R4,DBLE
```

Conversely, when converting results to the EBCDIC form for output, a typical sequence might be

```
CVD   R7,DB
UNPK  OUTP+16(4),DB(8)
```

One further attribute of the UNPK instruction should be noted. The right-most byte of the converted string *will* have a sign. When the characters are printed, all digits except the rightmost one will print as ordinary digits. If the rightmost digit is 1–9, with a plus sign, one of the letters A–I will be printed. If the rightmost digit is 1–9 with a minus sign, one of the letters J–R will be printed. If the rightmost digit is 0 with either sign, a black will be printed. There are several ways of avoiding this; we shall mention some in Chapters 11 and 14.

6.7   Examples of Complete Subroutines; Pseudo-random Number Generation

Chapter 4 introduced the generation of pseudo-random numbers, and showed how the multiplicative congruence method could be incorporated into a program. Here these same statements will be shown in a complete subroutine. Then we construct a higher-level subroutine which uses this one, and follow the execution step by step.

RANDOM: A LOWEST-LEVEL SUBROUTINE

The subroutine RANDOM shown in Fig. 6.8 computes a pseudo-random number, an integer between -2^{31} and 2^{31}, and leaves the number in register 0. Every successive call on the subroutine yields a new number (at least, for the first 2^{30} calls). There are no input parameters, which is rare among subroutines. Note that registers 14 and 15 are in no way changed inside the subroutine, so they need not be restored.

FIGURE 6.8   The subroutine RANDOM

```
RANDOM    STM     R14,R12,12(R13)
          BALR    R12,0
          USING   *,R12
          L       R7,RN
          M       R6,=F'65541'
          ST      R7,RN
          LR      R0,R7
          LM      R1,R12,24(R13)
          BR      R14
RN        DC      F'8193'
```

FIGURE 6.9 The subroutine RDIGIT

```
RDIGIT   STM    R14,R12,12(R13)
         BALR   R12,0
         USING  *,R12
         ST     R13,SAV+4
         LA     R13,SAV
         L      R4,0(,R1)
         L      R5,0(,R4)
         L      R15,RANDAD
         BALR   R14,R15
         LPR    R7,R0
         M      R4,=F'2'
         MR     R4,R7
         LR     R0,R4
         L      R13,SAV+4
         LM     R14,R15,12(R13)
         LM     R1,R12,24(R13)
         BR     R14
SAV      DS     18F
RANDAD   DC     A(RANDOM)
```

RDIGIT: **A SUBROUTINE USING** RANDOM

The RDIGIT subroutine shown in Fig. 6.9 yields a random number in a more restricted range. Given a number N as an input parameter, RDIGIT returns a pseudo-random number in the range 0 to $N - 1$, with all these numbers more or less equally likely. The parameter N is to be a binary integer less than 2^{30}. The parameter N is in a main-storage location whose address is stored at a location we may call *param-addr*. The address of the location *param-addr* is in register 1, in accord with the normal subroutine linkage, when the subroutine begins execution. The subroutine RDIGIT must use two Load instructions in retrieving the value of N; the first Load instruction loads *param-addr*.

The two instructions

```
     L     R15,RANDAD
     BALR  R14,R15
```

are sufficient to call the subroutine RANDOM. When we define RANDAD as an A-type address we are assuming that RANDOM is in the same CSECT as RDIGIT. If RANDOM and RDIGIT are in different CSECTs, RANDAD must be defined as a V-type address.

When the statement after BALR R14,R15 is executed, control has been returned from the subroutine RANDOM, and the output of RANDOM is available in register 0. The scheme used to develop random numbers between 0 and 9 which we described in Chapter 4 is not applicable here, because N might be an odd number. Here we take the absolute value of the random number, yielding

FIGURE 6.10 Subroutines RANDOM and RDIGIT with addresses assigned

```
00EE22        000602        RANDOM    STM     R14,R12,12(R13)
00EE26        000606                  BALR    R12,0
                                      USING   *,R12
00EE28        000608                  L       R7,RN
00EE2C        00060C                  M       R6,=F'65541'
00EE30        000610                  ST      R7,RN
00EE34        000614                  LR      R0,R7
00EE36        000616                  LM      R1,R12,24(R13)
00EE3A        00061A                  BR      R14
00EE3C        00061C        RN        DC      F'8193'
00EE40        000620        RDIGIT    STM     R14,R12,12(R13)
00EE44        000624                  BALR    R12,0
                                      USING   *,R12
00EE46        000626                  ST      R13,SAV+4
00EE4A        00062A                  LA      R13,SAV
00EE4E        00062E                  L       R4,0(,R1)
00EE52        000632                  L       R5,0(,R4)
00EE56        000636                  L       R15,RANDAD
00EE5A        00063A                  BALR    R14,R15
00EE5C        00063C                  LPR     R7,R0
00EE5E        00063E                  M       R4,=F'2'
00EE62        000642                  MR      R4,R7
00EE64        000644                  LR      R0,R4
00EE66        000646                  L       R13,SAV+4
00EE6A        00064A                  LM      R14,R15,12(R13)
00EE6E        00064E                  LM      R1,R12,24(R13)
00EE72        000652                  BR      R14
00EE74        000654        SAV       DS      18F
00EEBC        00069C        RANDAD    DC      A(RANDOM)
```

a number between 0 and 2^{31}, and then multiply that number by $2*N$. The product is a number between 0 and $2^{32}*N$; the even register of the pair contains an integer between 0 and $N-1$ inclusive.

Now let us trace the execution of these subroutines. Before execution, we must simulate assembly and loading to the extent of assigning addresses. We assume that RANDOM and RDIGIT are being assembled as part of a larger assembly including perhaps a main program. Let us suppose that RANDOM comes first, and starts at relocatable location 000602 (most likely after some other subroutines), and that RDIGIT follows immediately. Let us further suppose that in the loading process the entire program is relocated by 00E820. Figure 6.10 shows the assembled and actual loading addresses of each instruction, constant and data area in this segment.

Now let us suppose that the subroutine RDIGIT is being called. At the moment of the call, the contents of relevant information are:

$$\begin{array}{ll}
\text{Register 1:} & \emptyset\emptyset\emptyset\emptyset\text{E890} \\
\text{Register 13:} & \emptyset\emptyset\emptyset\emptyset\text{E848} \\
\text{Register 14:} & \emptyset\emptyset\emptyset\emptyset\text{E838} \\
\text{Location 00E890:} & \emptyset\emptyset\emptyset\emptyset\text{E844} \\
\text{Location 00E844:} & \emptyset\emptyset\emptyset\emptyset\emptyset\emptyset\emptyset\text{B}
\end{array}$$

The parameter address area is at location 00E890; the parameter itself, at location 00E844, is 0000000B. This is the decimal number 11, so we infer that a random number between 0 and 10 (inclusive) is called for. The computer proceeds as follows.

Instruction		Location changed: new contents		Explanation
STM	R14,R12,12(R13)	Locations 00E854–00E88F: Contents of registers 14–12 For example, 00E854	: 0000E838	Store register contents as left by calling rou- tine, in locations pro- vided by calling routine.
BALR	R12,0	Register 12	: 0000EE46	
ST	R13,SAV+4	00EE78	: 0000E848	Store register 13 in
LA	R13,SAV	Register 13	: 0000EE74	RDIGIT's area.
L	R4,0(R1)	Register 4	: 0000E844	Address of parameter.
L	R5,0(R4)	Register 5	: 0000000B	Parameter.
L	R15,RANDAD	Register 15	: 0000EE22	Address of RANDOM.
BALR	R14,R15			Return address in RDIGIT
		Register 14	: 0000EE5C	Transfer control to location 00EE22.

Note that at this point the routine that called RDIGIT is suspended, waiting for return. Its register contents are all stored. Subroutine RDIGIT is now also suspended, while RANDOM begins to do its work.

STM	R14,R12,12(R13)	00EE80–00EEBB:		Contents of registers 14–12 as left by RDIGIT
BALR	R12,0	Register 12	: 0000EE28	
L	R7,RN	Register 7	: 00002001	Decimal 8193 = hexadecimal 00002001
M	R6,=F'65541'	Register 6	: 00000000	Decimal 65541 = hexadecimal 00010005
		Register 7	: 2001A005	= decimal 536977413
ST	R7,RN	00EE3C	: 2001A005	Replaces 00002001
LR	R0,R7	Register 0	: 2001A005	
LM	R1,R12,24(R13)	Registers 1–12	:	Restored to contents as they were when RANDOM was entered.
BR	R14			Transfer control to location 00EE5C, in subroutine RDIGIT.

Note that subroutine RDIGIT is in control again. The net result of subroutine RANDOM was that register 0 now contains 2001A005, as does location 00EE3C (RN).

LPR	R7,0	Register 7	: 2001A005	2001A005 is positive.
M	R4,=F'2'	Register 4	: 00000000	
		Register 5	: 00000016	
MR	R4,R7	Register 4	: 00000002	Product in hexadecimal
		Register 5	: C023C06E	is 2C023C06E.
LR	R0,R4	Register 0	: 00000002	Output of RDIGIT.
L	R13,SAV+4	Register 13	: 0000E848	
LM	R14,R15,12(R13)	Register 14	: 0000E838	
		Register 15	: Contents left by routine calling RDIGIT.	
LM	R1,R12,24(R13)	Registers 1–12	: Restored to condition as of entry to RDIGIT.	
BR	R14		Transfer to location 00E838, in calling routine.	

Both subroutines have done their work. The registers of the calling routine are intact, except that register 0 contains the pseudo-random number 2, the output of RDIGIT.

m a i n   i d e a s

- □ When a subroutine is called, the registers of the calling routine are stored; they are restored just before return from the subroutine. This gives both calling and called routines freedom to use registers without interference.

- □ When registers are stored at the beginning of a subroutine, contents of registers 14, 15, 0–12 are stored in the area supplied by the calling routine; register 13 is stored in the area supplied by the called routine.

- □ The BR instruction is an unconditional branch to a location whose address is in the register operand. It is used to return control from a subroutine.

- □ The BALR instruction stores the address of the next instruction before branching; if the second operand is 0, no branch takes place. It is used in branching to a subroutine.

☐ The combination of a USING pseudo-operation preceded by a BALR instruction establishes one or more implied base registers.

☐ When parameters are to be passed to subroutines, their addresses are placed in a block of main storage whose address is loaded into register 1 for use by the subroutine. This applies to parameters whose values are to be *changed* by a subroutine as well as those whose values are to be *used* by a subroutine.

☐ Conversions from EBCDIC to packed decimal to binary integer and back are performed by the instructions PACK, CVB, CVD, and UNPK. With these instructions, data can be read and printed in character form, while binary integer forms of the data are used in arithmetic operations.

■ **P R O B L E M S** F O R   R E V I E W   A N D   I M A G I N A T I O N

6.1 How would you expect the actions of the instructions

           BALR R12,Ø   and   BALR R12,R12

to differ, if at all?

6.2 There is a BAL (Branch and Link) instruction that has the same actions as BALR except that the branch address is given in base + index + displacement form according to the RX instruction format. The BAL instruction can be used to branch to a subroutine when it is convenient to express the entry point in base + index + displacement form, especially in symbolic form:

           BAL R11,SUBENTRY

What *two* subroutine linkage conventions does this instruction violate? In what circumstances is it even possible to use the BAL instruction? In what circumstances might it be desirable to use register 11 instead of register 14 to hold the return address?

6.3 Routine *A* may call three different subroutines, but may transmit via register 13 the same register save area for all three subroutines. How does this work?

6.4 Give reasons why it would be awkward for routine *A* to save all of its own register contents before branching to subroutine *B* and then restore the registers after return from *B*. Is it even possible? If so, how? If not, why not?

6.5 Would it be feasible for subroutine *B*, called by routine *A*, to store all of *A*'s register contents in an area provided by subroutine *B*?

6.6 Normally, subroutine *B* stores the contents of register 13 of the calling routine in word 2 of *B*'s register save area. What difficulties would be encountered if register 13 were saved instead at a location SAV13 defined by *B* apart from its register save area?

6.7 When the supervisor interrupts a program being executed, it must store the program's register contents. Is it safe for the supervisor to store them in the area addressed by the current contents of register 13? What must the supervisor do?

6.8 Suppose register 11 contains a base address. Show several ways of loading register 12 with an address 4096 greater than the address in register 11. Can it be done with one LA instruction?

6.9 Analyze the following, each of which purports to set up parameters to send to a subroutine, and determine which are correct, which are incorrect, and why.

a) There is one parameter, located at BBB:

```
                    L       R1,BADDR
                    :
        BADDR       DC      A(BBB)
```

b) There is one parameter, located at BBB:

```
                    L       R1,=A(BBB):
```

c) There is one parameter, located at BBB:

```
                    LA      R1,=A(BADDR)
                    :
        BADDR       DC      A(BBB)
```

d) There is one parameter, located at BBB:

```
                    L       R1,=A(BADDR)
                    :
        BADDR       DC      A(BBB)
```

e) There are three parameters, located at FF, GG, and HH:

```
                    L       R1,=A(FF,GG,HH)
```

f) There are three parameters, located at FF, GG, and in register 4:

```
                    ST      R4,TP
                    LA      R1,=A(FF,GG,TP)
```

g) There are three parameters, located at FF, GG, and a main storage location whose address is in register 7:

```
                    ST      R7,TP
                    LA      R1,BADDR
                    :
        BADDR       DC      A(FF,GG,TP)
```

h) There are three parameters, located at FF, GG, and a main storage location whose address is in register 7:

```
        ST    R7,BADDR+8
        LA    R1,BADDR
        ⋮
BADDR   DC    A(FF,GG)
        DS    1F
```

i) There are three parameters, located at FF, GG, and HH:

```
        BAL   R1,*+16
        DC    A(FF,GG,HH)
```

6.10 Under what conditions will the PACK instruction overflow? That is, under what conditions will the destination field be too small to hold properly the PACKed result? Under what conditions will UNPK, CVB, and CVD overflow?

6.11 If a field is PACKed and the result is UNPacKed, in what ways may the UNPacKed result be different from the original field?

6.12 Suppose a field N holds a packed decimal number. The field is three bytes long, and not aligned on any particular boundary. Write a sequence of instructions that will convert the contents of this field to a binary integer.

6.13 Trace execution of the instruction pair

```
        PACK  D(8),Q(1)
        CVB   R4,D
```

assuming that D is a double word and the byte at Q is 11000111 (C7 in hexadecimal).

6.14 Trace execution of the instruction pair

```
        CVD   R7,D
        UNPK  U(3),D(8)
```

assuming that register 7 contains the (hexadecimal) number 0000006B. What would be different if the UNPK instruction were changed to the following?

```
        UNPK  U(3),D+5(3)
```

6.15 Write a sequence of instructions that will take a field G of length five bytes containing a number in the EBCDIC form and construct a new field K of length seven containing the product 37*G in EBCDIC form.

6.16 A CVB instruction requires a double-word source operand. Suppose we know that a number to be converted is small (for example, if it is being

PACKed from only three bytes). We could save some time in the PACK instruction if its first operand (destination) were only two or three bytes instead of eight. We must then see that the two or three bytes are in the low-order portion of a double word whose upper portion is filled with zeros, before the CVB instruction is executed. Write DC or DS statements and a PACK instruction that will follow this suggestion.

6.17   In the example subroutine RANDOM, what are the base register, index register, and displacement assembled in the instruction below?

```
        L     R7,RN
```

6.18   In the traced execution of RANDOM shown in Section 6.7, just after the LR RØ,R7 instruction, what are the contents of register 4?

6.19   After the execution of RDIGIT shown in Section 6.7, the number RN is changed to 2ØØ1AØØ5. If RDIGIT is called a second time, what number will RANDOM return? What number will RDIGIT return?

6.20   Rewrite RANDOM, taking advantage of the fact that register 15 contains the entry point address of RANDOM.

6.21   In the subroutine RDIGIT, the address of RANDOM is defined as an A-type address, which can only be done if RANDOM and RDIGIT are assembled during the same CSECT. Could the address of RANDOM be loaded into register 15 in RDIGIT by the instruction given below?

```
        LA    R15,RANDOM
```

Does the order of assembly of RDIGIT and RANDOM make any difference?

6.22   If the instruction

```
        L     R13,SAV+4
```

near the end of subroutine RDIGIT were accidentally left out, what would be the consequences? To what address would the subroutine return? Then what?

6.23   If, in RDIGIT,

```
        USING *,R12 and BALR R12,Ø
```

appeared in this order instead of in the conventional order, how would you expect the error to show up?

6.24   Write a lowest-level subroutine which will return the cube of its binary integer argument. Assume that the result will not overflow one register.

6.25   Write a higher-level subroutine that will, given parameters A and B, return $A^3 + B^3$. Use the cube subroutine described in Problem 6.24.

6.26 Any register from 2 to 12 is available for use as a base register. It does
      not matter much which is used. One principle is that a number of in-
      structions, such as Multiply and Divide, use register pairs; so by using
      register 12 as base register, we preserve as many register pairs for use
      by the program as possible. Think of other considerations that might
      influence the choice of a base register.

6.27 During assembly of a program, the statement

$$A \qquad R4,G$$

is assembled into 5A4ØBCDE, at (relocatable) location ØØØDBC.
   a) What register is named in the USING statement in this program?
   b) At what relocatable address is the BALR instruction that loads the
       base register?
   c) At execution time, the program is loaded so that the BALR instruc-
       tion that loads the base register is at ØØ83A8. What address will be
       loaded into a register by the BALR instruction?
   d) What actual storage location will be referenced by the Add instruc-
       tion?

■ **REFERENCES** ▬▬▬▬▬▬▬▬▬▬▬▬▬▬▬▬

*IBM OS/VS—DOS/VSE—VM/370 As-
    sembler Language,* GC 33-4010, IBM
Corporation. Reference on USING and
DROP.

IBM System/370 Principles of Operation,
    GA 22-7000, IBM Corporation. Refer-
    ence on the conversion instructions.

ELEMENTARY CONTROL STRUCTURES

A computer program must be able to make tests and decisions, and follow alternative paths (that is, execute alternative sequences of instructions) as a result of those decisions. The idea is best expressed as a need for the control structures such as IF-THEN, IF-THEN-ELSE, WHILE, and REPEAT-UNTIL. In this chapter we show how we can implement such control structures in assembler language.

Assembler language and the underlying machine language are not nicely structured in a modern sense; you will look in vain for a WHILE instruction, for example. We will adopt the approach of expressing the control structures for our tasks first in a pseudo-code that uses IF-THEN, WHILE, etc. The pseudo-code can then be translated or implemented more or less mechanically into machine language. Our assembler language programs will show the pseudo-code in remarks statements, and our programs will therefore observe and document a structure that makes them easier to understand, debug, and maintain than if we did not impose this kind of discipline.

So in this chapter we will first introduce the tools: the program status word, the condition code, and the compare and conditional branch instructions. Then we will develop their use in implementing control structures. Chapter 8 will continue with address arithmetic and some special instructions that facilitate looping structures.

7.1 The Program Status Word and the Condition Code

The program status word (abbreviated PSW) has been mentioned earlier. It is a special 64-bit register containing information on the status of the computer and the program being run. Bits 40–63 of the PSW contain the instruction address, the address of the next instruction to be executed. During the instruction cycle for every instruction, the computer retrieves the instruction to be executed from main storage locations addressed by bits 40–63 of the PSW. Then the instruction address is increased by 2, 4, or 6, depending on the length of the current instruction; this enables the next instruction cycle to retrieve the next instruction from storage. The execution of a branch consists of storing a new value in the instruction address portion of the PSW; the value is specified by an operand of the branch instruction, and the effect of storing an address in the PSW is to force execution of the instructions starting at that new address.

Another important part of the program status word is the *condition code* (often abbreviated CC). The condition code is kept in bits 18 and 19 of the PSW and therefore can take on the binary values 00, 01, 10, 11, or the decimal values 0, 1, 2, and 3. The condition code is set by each of a number of instructions, including many arithmetic instructions. The value to which the condition code is set depends on the result of the instruction; for example, the condition code may be set to reflect whether the result of an arithmetic operation is negative, zero, or positive.

The condition code can be tested by a conditional branch instruction; the value of the condition code determines whether or not the branch will be taken. Thus the condition code is an extremely important intermediary between arithmetic instructions and conditional branch instructions. It is set by the arithmetic instructions and tested by the conditional branch instructions, and therefore allows a branch to be conditional on the result of an arithmetic instruction. The condition code can also be set by a compare instruction and therefore allow a branch to be conditional on the result of a comparison. Therefore the condition code is very important in implementing control structures.

7.2 Setting the Condition Code

Figure 7.1 shows the values to which the condition code is set as a result of each of the instructions you have so far encountered. Of all the instructions discussed, only some loads and the binary integer add and subtract instructions set condition codes. If the result of such an instruction is zero, the condition code is set to 0. If the result is negative, the condition code is set to 1; this outcome is possible for all except the LPR instruction. If the result is positive

FIGURE 7.1 Condition codes set by binary integer arithmetic instructions

	Instruction	Condition code set			
		0	1	2	3
LPR	Load Positive Register	Zero	—	> Zero	Overflow
LNR	Load Negative Register	Zero	< Zero	—	—
LCR	Load Complement Register	Zero	< Zero	> Zero	Overflow
LTR	Load and Test Register	Zero	< Zero	> Zero	—
AR	Add Register	Zero	< Zero	> Zero	Overflow
SR	Subtract Register	Zero	< Zero	> Zero	Overflow
A	Add	Zero	< Zero	> Zero	Overflow
S	Subtract	Zero	< Zero	> Zero	Overflow
AH	Add Half-word	Zero	< Zero	> Zero	Overflow
SH	Subtract Half-word	Zero	< Zero	> Zero	Overflow

and greater than zero (an outcome possible for all but the LNR instruction), the condition code is set to 2.

If the result is too large—positive or negative—to be expressed properly, that is, if the result is less than -2^{31} or greater than $2^{31} - 1$, we consider the result to have *overflowed* the register. When this happens as a result of a binary integer addition or subtraction, the overflow bit is lost, and the remaining contents of the result register are incorrect by exactly 2^{32}. In all overflow cases the condition code is set to 3, regardless of whether the actual result left in the result register is positive, negative, or zero. An overflow cannot occur as a

FIGURE 7.2 Instructions not affecting condition code

LR	Load Register	MVC	MoVe Character
L	Load	MVI	MoVe Immediate
ST	STore	LM	Load Multiple
LH	Load Half-word	STM	STore Multiple
STH	STore Half-word	LA	Load Address
MR	Multiply Register	BR	Branch to Register
M	Multiply	BALR	Branch And Link to Register
MH	Multiply Half-word	PACK	PACK
DR	Divide Register	UNPK	UNPacK
D	Divide	CVB	ConVert to Binary
		CVD	ConVert to Decimal

result of an LNR instruction; it can occur as a result of an LCR or LPR instruction only if the second operand is -2^{31} (hexadecimal 80000000).

Another load instruction, Load and Test Register (LTR), is exactly the same as the LR instruction, except that it sets the condition code. The condition code is set to 0 if the result (in register $R1$) is zero, to 1 if the result is negative, and to 2 if the result is greater than zero.

When a condition code is set by execution of one of the instructions listed in Fig. 7.1, the previous value of the condition code is lost. The condition code remains unchanged by instructions that do not set a condition code, even the instructions that *test* the condition code. The instructions we have discussed so far that do *not* affect the condition code are listed in Fig. 7.2.

As an example, consider the program segment

```
LCR    R4,R7
MR     R6,R4
ST     R7,MINUSASQ
A      R7,=F'4000'
```

Suppose that when the machine language translation of the assembler language segment has been executed, register 7 contains the binary equivalent of the decimal number 35. As a result of the LCR instruction, register 4 contains -35, so the condition code is set to 1. During the multiply instruction (yielding a result of -1225) and store instructions the condition code remains 1. As a result of the add instruction, however, the condition code is set to 2, since the addition yields 2775.

Let us return for a second look at the ASSIST instructions XREAD and XDECI. Each of these attempts a task that cannot be guaranteed to be completed successfully. An ASSIST instruction XREAD reads a record and makes it available, but what if there are no more records to be read? An ASSIST instruction XDECI converts a sequence of digits in character form to binary integer representation, but what if the characters presented are not spaces and digits? Each instruction needs a way to signal failure of its task. These instructions set the condition code. XREAD sets the condition code as

CC = 0:   a record has been read
CC = 1:   end of file—no record could be read

XDECI sets the condition code as

CC = 0:   the number converted = 0
CC = 1:   the number converted < 0
CC = 2:   the number converted > 0
CC = 3:   there is no number to convert

In Section 7.7 we shall see how these condition codes are used in a program.

7.3   The Compare Instructions

Three Compare instructions, whose sole result is the setting of the condition code, compare two operands; the only differences between the three instructions are the assumed locations and lengths of the operands. The CR (Compare Register) instruction is of RR type, and compares the contents of two registers. The C (Compare) instruction is of RX type and compares the contents of a register (first operand) with a full word in main storage (second operand). The CH (Compare Half-word) instruction is of RX type; it compares the contents of a register with the contents of a half-word in main storage. We may think of the half-word as expanded to a full word by propagation of the sign bit into the upper 16 bits of a full word (as in the LH instruction) before comparison.

The condition-code settings resulting from the compare instructions are

First operand = second operand: CC = 0
First operand < second operand: CC = 1
First operand > second operand: CC = 2

Since these instructions do not yield an arithmetic result, there is no possibility of overflow. Therefore the condition code is never set to 3 as a result of a compare instruction. In other respects the condition code is set exactly as if a subtract instruction with the same two operands were executed.

Suppose that the initial contents of registers and main storage locations are as follows:

Register 3:   ØØØØ46E9
Register 4:   FFBD238Ø
Location Q: 234689AC
Location W: FE3Ø46E9

The following compare instructions will set the condition code as indicated, but will not change the contents of registers or main storage locations.

Instruction		Condition code set
CR	R3,R4	2
CR	R4,R3	1
C	R3,Q	1
C	R4,W	2
C	R3,W	2
CH	R4,W	1
CH	R4,W+2	1
CH	R3,W+2	0
CH	R3,Q+2	2

7.4 The BC and BCR Instructions

The instructions that do or do not branch, depending on the value of the condition code, are BC (Branch on Condition) and BCR (Branch on Condition to Register); BC is of RX type, BCR of RR type.

The second operand designates the branch address. In execution of the BC instruction, the second operand, defined by *B2*, *X2*, and *D2* in the usual way, is the address which is stored in bit positions 40–63 of the PSW and is therefore the branch address. In the execution of the BCR instruction, the second operand *R2* designates a register *whose contents* (last 24 bits of the contents) is stored in bit positions 40–63 of the PSW. For example, if register 11 contains ØØØØA244, a BC instruction with *B2*, *X2*, and *D2* of 11,0,0 and a BCR instruction with *R2* = 11 both cause a branch to location ØØA244.

The first operand of either the BC or the BCR instruction is called a *mask* and designated as *M1*. The four-bit pattern *M1* and the condition code jointly determine whether the branch is taken or not—that is, whether the second operand is stored in bits 40–63 of the PSW. Each of the four bits of *M1* determines whether or not one of the four possible values of the condition code (CC) will cause a branch; *a branch is taken if $M1_{cc} = 1$, and not if $M1_{cc} = 0$.* For example, if the condition code is 2 and *M1* bit 2 (bit 10 of the instruction) is 1, a branch will take place; if CC = 2 and $M1_2 = 0$, no branch takes place and the next instruction in the normal sequence is executed.

Following the implications of this rule, the instruction

        BC   B'1ØØ1',BRPTA

will cause a branch to the instruction named BRPTA if at the time the instruction is executed the condition code is 0 or 3; if the condition code is 1 or 2 the branch will not be taken. As a second example, the instruction

        BCR   B'Ø1ØØ',R9

will cause a branch to the address held in register 9 if the condition code is 1, but no branch if the condition code is 0, 2, or 3.

Assembler language instructions usually do not state *M1* as a binary value but as its decimal equivalent. All 16 combinations of 1's and 0's in *M1* can be used to make branches occur under certain condition codes and not under others. The masks are summarized in Fig. 7.3. All possible values of *M1* are shown, both in binary and in their decimal equivalents, as well as the condition codes that would cause a branch with each value of *M1*. In the last two columns, we show which results of a compare instruction or of one of the binary integer arithmetic instructions listed in Fig. 7.1 will cause branching under each mask.

Several features of Fig. 7.3 are worthy of note.

FIGURE 7.3   Values of *M1* and branching control

Mask	Value of mask	Condition codes causing branch	Comparison results causing branch	Arithmetic results causing branch
1000	8	0	$Op_1 = Op_2$	= 0, no overflow
0100	4	1	$Op_1 < Op_2$	< 0, no overflow
0010	2	2	$Op_1 > Op_2$	> 0, no overflow
1100	12	0,1	$Op_1 \le Op_2$	≤ 0, no overflow
1010	10	0,2	$Op_1 \ge Op_2$	≥ 0, no overflow
0110	6	1,2	$Op_1 \ne Op_2$	≠ 0, no overflow
1110	14	0,1,2	All	No overflow
0000	0	None	None	None
0001	1	3	None	Overflow
1111	15	All	All	All
1001	9	0,3	$Op_1 = Op_2$	0 or overflow
0101	5	1,3	$Op_1 < Op_2$	< 0 or overflow
0011	3	2,3	$Op_1 > Op_2$	> 0 or overflow
1101	13	0,1,3	$Op_1 \le Op_2$	≤ 0 or overflow
1011	11	0,2,3	$Op_1 \ge Op_2$	≥ 0 or overflow
0111	7	1,2,3	$Op_1 \ne Op_2$	≠ 0 or overflow

1. Because a condition code of 3 cannot occur as the result of a compare instruction, bit 3 of the mask is irrelevant. This shows up in duplicate entries in the fourth column of the table; for example, after a compare instruction, a branch instruction with *M1* of 1001 or 1000 will cause branching under exactly the same conditions, namely, equality of the two operands.

2. The arithmetic results listed in the fifth column are the actual bit patterns left in the result register *R1*. It *is* possible to have a result of 0 *and* an overflow: consider addition of the hexadecimal numbers 80000000 and 80000000. The condition code will, of course, be set to 3.

3. If *M1* has the value 0, no branch will result, regardless of the condition code. The instruction

$$\text{BCR} \quad \emptyset,\emptyset$$

is therefore a no-operation instruction. It has its uses.

4. If *M1* has the value 15, a branch will always occur, regardless of the condition code. The instruction

$$\text{BCR} \quad 15,\text{R14}$$

therefore is an *unconditional* branch to the address held in register 14.

The following instruction sequences will perform the branches indicated.

a)   C   6,BSQ   Branch to BEQ if the contents of register 6 equals the
     BC   8,BEQ   word at BSQ.

b)   CR   6,9   Branch to PBA if the contents of register 6 is *not greater*
       BC   12,PBA   *than* (is less than or equal) the contents of register 9.
c)   S   5,=F'1'   Subtract 1 from the contents of register 5. Then branch
       BC   7,LOOPB   to LOOPB if the new contents of register 5 is not zero.

7.5   IF-THEN and IF-THEN-ELSE Structures

The IF-THEN control structure expresses an action to be taken only if some condition is true; the IF-THEN-ELSE structure expresses two actions to be taken, one if a given condition is true and the other if it is false. They are often expressed as

IF *condition*   IF *condition*
THEN *action*   THEN *action 1*
                    ELSE *action 2*

and can also be expressed in flowchart form as shown in Fig. 7.4.

As a first example, suppose we want to add the number at location TBY to the number in register 6, but only if the number at location RN is 7 or less. In pseudo-code, we can express the task as

IF c(RN) $\leq$ 7
THEN Add TBY to Register 6

In assembler language we must recognize that instructions are executed sequentially from their main storage locations unless we break the sequence by branching. Therefore our tactic must be

- compare,
- branch *around* the add instruction,
- add.

FIGURE 7.4   IF-THEN and IF-THEN-ELSE in flowchart form

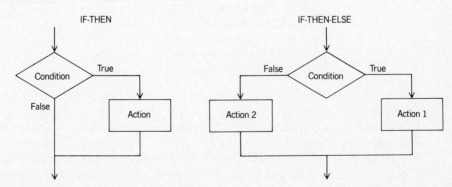

FIGURE 7.5   A segment implementing an IF structure

```
* IF C(RN) <= 7
STEP5     L      R3,RN
          C      R3,=F'7'
          BC     2,STEP6
* . THEN ADD TBY TO REG R6
          A      R6,TBY
* ENDIF
STEP6     DS     0H


RN        DS     1F
TBY       DS     1F
```

Figure 7.5 shows a program segment that follows this tactic. The load and compare instructions make the comparison between the contents of location RN and 7. The condition code is set by the compare instruction, and is tested by the BC instruction. With a mask of 2, the BC instruction will branch to STEP6 if the condition code is 2, which will be the case if the contents of RN is greater than 7. Restating it, the BC instruction will bypass the add instruction if the contents of RN is *not* less than or equal to 7, so the add instruction is executed only if the contents of RN *is* less than or equal to 7. Make sure you understand this example and its explanation, because this is a very common and very necessary kind of segment, and you must be able to write segments like these easily.

Let us now take an example of an IF-THEN-ELSE structure. Suppose we have an address in register 5. We want to compare the number at that address—let's call it *D*—with the number in a location named SRCHKEY. If *D* is larger than the contents of SRCHKEY, we are to add 4 to register 5 and store the result at LOWB. Otherwise, we are to subtract 4 from register 5 and store the result at UPPERB. We can express this task:

$$\text{IF } c(c(\text{register 5})) > c(\text{SRCHKEY})$$

    THEN   Add 4 to register 5
           Store register 5 in LOWB
    ELSE   Subtract 4 from register 5
           Store register 5 in UPPERB.

Figure 7.6 shows the program segment for the task. We load into register 6 the number at the address contained in register 5. After the compare instruction, the BC instruction branches around the THEN action; the mask of 12 provides a branch if the condition code is 0 or 1, therefore, if the number in register 6 is *not* greater than the number at SRCHKEY. Note that at the end of the THEN action we must branch around the ELSE action. *Beware*: It is easy to forget this

FIGURE 7.6   A segment implementing an IF-THEN-ELSE structure

```
* IF C(C(R5)) >= C(SRCHKEY)
STEP8      L      R6,0(,R5)
           C      R6,SRCHKEY
           BC     12,STEP8ELS
* . THEN ADD 4 TO R5, STORE R5 IN LOWB
           LA     R5,4(,R5)
           ST     R5,LOWB
           B      STEP9
* . ELSE SUBTRACT 4 FROM R5, STORE IN UPPERB
STEP8ELS   S      R5,=F'4'
           ST     R5,UPPERB
* ENDIF
STEP9      DS     0H
```

branch instruction; think out what the effect would be, so that when you make the mistake of leaving it out in some program you may recognize the symptoms!

Note that in both program segments, we include remarks statements that show the pseudo-code structure. The comment ENDIF at the end is also valuable in showing clearly the scope of the particular IF structure.

7.6   Extended Mnemonics

OS and OS/VS assembler language provides for the use of alphabetic operation codes that will be translated by the assembler into both the numeric operation code and the *M1* part of a branch instruction. For example,

BE   ADDPR

will be assembled into the same machine language instruction as

BC   8,ADDPR

The code BE stands for Branch on Equal, and is called an *extended mnemonic*. It includes the definition of not only the operation code 47 (for BC) but also the *M1* portion of the instruction, which is 8 in a test for equality. Since the first operand of the machine language instruction becomes in effect part of the operation code, only the second operand remains in the assembler language statement, and is written as a single operand. Use of the extended mnemonics simplifies the writing of programs in that the programmer need not think of or write the *M1* portion of a branch instruction.

Figure 7.7 lists extended mnemonics recognized by the assembler. The BR instruction introduced in Chapter 6 is merely an extended mnemonic for BCR 15. Extended mnemonics are provided for BCR instructions with *M1* codes

FIGURE 7.7 Extended mnemonics

Meaning	Extended code		Equivalent	
Unconditional Branch	B	*S2*	BC	15,*S2*
Unconditional Branch to Register	BR	*R2*	BCR	15,*R2*
No OPeration	NOP	*S2*	BC	0,*S2*
No OPeration (Register)	NOPR	*R2*	BCR	0,*R2*
For use after a compare instruction:				
Branch on Equal	BE	*S2*	BC	8,*S2*
Branch on Low	BL	*S2*	BC	4,*S2*
Branch on High	BH	*S2*	BC	2,*S2*
Branch on Not Equal	BNE	*S2*	BC	7,*S2*
Branch on Not Low	BNL	*S2*	BC	11,*S2*
Branch on Not High	BNH	*S2*	BC	13,*S2*
For use after an arithmetic instruction:				
Branch on Zero	BZ	*S2*	BC	8,*S2*
Branch on Minus	BM	*S2*	BC	4,*S2*
Branch on Plus	BP	*S2*	BC	2,*S2*
Branch on Not Zero	BNZ	*S2*	BC	7,*S2*
Branch on Not Minus	BNM	*S2*	BC	11,*S2*
Branch on Not Plus	BNP	*S2*	BC	13,*S2*
Branch on Overflow	BO	*S2*	BC	1,*S2*
Branch on Not Overflow	BNO	*S2*	BC	14,*S2*

Note:
S2 refers to an implied or explicit address appropriate as second operand in an RX-type instruction. *R2* refers to an expression appropriate to a register address.

other than 0 and 15; we do not list them here, since in practice almost all conditional branches are BC instructions.

Extended mnemonics are provided which are natural for use after a compare operation and others that are natural after an arithmetic operation. The codes are interchangeable, however; for example, BZ can be used after a compare instruction and BL after an arithmetic instruction.

Extended mnemonics could be used in the segments given in Figs. 7.5 and 7.6. The branch instructions used there and their extended mnemonic equivalents are

```
BC    2,STEP6        BH    STEP6
BC    12,STEP8ELS    BNH   STEP8ELS
```

Let us explore a more complex example using IF-THEN and IF-THEN-ELSE structures. Suppose we have full words A and B, each containing either

1, 2, or 3. Values 1 and 3 represent positive and negative attributes, 2 is a neutral value. If the attributes of A and B are both positive or both negative, we are directed to add 1 to a counter of *affinities*, named AFF. If one is positive and the other negative, we are directed to add 1 to a counter of *incompatibilities*, named INCOMPAT. If either is neutral, we are to add nothing. We can represent the logic by the pseudo-code

$$\text{IF } |A - B| = 2$$
$$\text{THEN Add 1 to INCOMPAT}$$
$$\text{ELSE IF } (A = B \text{ and } A \neq 2)$$
$$\text{THEN Add 1 to AFF}$$

The pseudo-code and the program segment in Fig. 7.8 that implements the pseudo-code assume that A and B indeed contain 1, 2, or 3. The assumption that data are correct and valid as represented is a dangerous one. In a real problem, data must be checked thoroughly, preferably when they first enter the computer. However, for simplicity we assume that the checking was done earlier and that we can count on clean data here.

In the pseudo-code and the comment statements that document the pseudo-code in the program segment, you may notice that I am using a notational shortcut. I write A and B to mean the *numbers* contained in the locations whose addresses are A and B (and similarly AFF and INCOMPAT). The longer and more accurate phrase is just too cumbersome to keep using, except that we must return to it where there might be ambiguity.

FIGURE 7.8   Counting affinities and incompatibilities

```
* IF ABS(A-B) = 2
STEP4      L      R4,A
           S      R4,B
           LPR    R4,R4
           C      R4,=F'2'
           BNE    STEP4ELS
* . THEN ADD 1 TO INCOMPAT
           L      R5,INCOMPAT
           LA     R5,1(,R5)
           ST     R5,INCOMPAT
           B      STEP5
* . ELSE IF (A = B AND A NOT = 2)
STEP4ELS L      R4,A
           C      R4,B
           BNE    STEP5           A NOT = B
           C      R4,=F'2'
           BE     STEP5           A = 2
* . . THEN ADD 1 TO AFF
           L      R5,AFF
           LA     R5,1(,R5)
           ST     R5,AFF
* . ENDIF (A = B AND A NOT = 2)
* ENDIF (ABS(A-B) = 2)
STEP5      DS     0H
```

The program segment in Fig. 7.8 follows the same schemes as Figs. 7.4 and 7.5. The first branch is taken if $|A - B| \neq 2$, i.e., if we should skip the THEN clause and execute the ELSE clause. The ELSE clause (beginning at STEP4ELS) contains an IF, and this contains a compound condition using the logical operator AND. The segment compares A and B, and if they are unequal, branches immediately to STEP5. If $A = B$, then A is compared to 2, and another branch to STEP5 completes the implementation of the IF test. We identify each of the ENDIF remarks to show which IF it is paired with; this helps to keep the pseudo-code readable. The segment assumes that both AFF and INCOMPAT are nonnegative integers less than 2^{24}; otherwise we could not use the LA instruction to add to them.

7.7   Looping Structures

Computer programs must have the ability to repeat execution of instruction sequences. We call it looping. The looping must be controlled in some way so that execution eventually leaves the loop. One of the common looping structures is the WHILE structure:

WHILE condition DO
action

The structure as we use it is borrowed from the language Pascal, but other computer languages have quite similar structures. The sequence of events is shown in Fig. 7.9(a). The condition is tested *first*; if it is *true*, the action is performed and the computer returns to test the condition again. As soon as the condition is found false, execution passes from the loop. Clearly, the action in the loop must be such as to make the condition become false eventually. But note that execution does not jump out of the loop immediately at the moment

FIGURE 7.9   Flowcharts of looping structures: (a) WHILE structure, (b) REPEAT-UNTIL structure

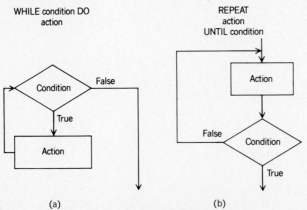

(a)   (b)

the condition becomes false; the entire loop action is completed and only then does the test of the condition prevent yet another execution of the loop action.

A second common structure is the REPEAT-UNTIL structure:

REPEAT
action
UNTIL condition

Figure 7.9(b) shows the sequence of events prescribed by this structure; it is quite similar to the WHILE, but the action is performed *first, then* the condition is tested. Looping in this structure continues as long as the condition is found to be *false*, and terminates when the condition is found to be *true*.

Let us show some of the standard uses of each of these structures. The WHILE structure is often used when processing records from a file:

WHILE there are still records to be read
Read a record
Process the record

In this example, the action of the loop is in fact *two* processing steps: read a record and process a record. The REPEAT-UNTIL structure is often used for performing some action a specific number of times. Suppose we want to perform Action A ten times.

Set counter to 0
REPEAT
Action A
Add 1 to counter
UNTIL counter = 10

FIGURE 7.10   Adding numbers, one from each record

```
        SR    R4,R4          SET TOTAL TO 0
* WHILE THERE ARE RECORDS TO BE READ
* . READ A RECORD
STEP2LP  XREAD CARDIN,80
         BNZ   STEP3
* . IF RECORD CONTAINS A NUMBER
         XDECI R3,CARDIN
         BO    STEP2LP
* . . THEN ADD IT TO TOTAL
         AR    R4,R3
* . ENDIF
         B     STEP2LP
* ENDWHILE (THERE ARE RECORDS TO BE READ)
STEP3    DS    0H


CARDIN   DS    CL80
```

It is time for an example of a program segment that implements a WHILE structure. Suppose we have a data set (deck of cards?). Each record (card?) in this data set is supposed to contain a number. Our task is to find the sum of the numbers. Figure 7.10 shows an assembler language program segment that performs the task. As in earlier segments we use remarks statements to show the structure. The WHILE test must *follow* the XREAD ASSIST instruction; XREAD is really a rather complex structure of its own:

> IF there is a record to be read
> THEN Read it
>   Set Condition Code = 0
> ELSE Set Condition Code = 1

The XDECI macro instruction is quite similar; we must attempt to convert the number before we know whether there is a number that can be converted. This is not at all uncommon in computing; we often find that the only reasonable way to find out whether some operation is possible is to try it. We can ask the segment or subroutine that attempts the task to indicate whether it was successful, and if the task was indeed possible, it was done.

Figure 7.11 illustrates use of the REPEAT-UNTIL structure. It prints each of the numbers 1 to 20 and the square of each of the numbers. In the next chapter we shall study some special instructions that facilitate REPEAT-UNTIL loop structures.

Note that in each of the structures we have studied in this chapter—IF-THEN, IF-THEN-ELSE, WHILE, and REPEAT-UNTIL the branch instruction that tests the condition branches on the *negative* of the condition. In Fig.

FIGURE 7.11   Generate a table of squares

```
          LA    R2,1              SET J = 1
* REPEAT
* . PRINT J AND J SQUARED (J*J)
STEP2LP  XDECO R2,OUTAREA+4
          LR    R5,R2
          MR    R4,R5             J SQUARED
          XDECO R5,OUTAREA+18
          XPRNT OUTAREA-1,41
* . ADD 1 TO J
          LA    R2,1(,R2)
* UNTIL J > 20
          C     R2,=F'20'
          BNH   STEP2LP
* ENDREPEAT


          DC    C' '
OUTAREA  DS    CL40
```

7.5, the condition is $c(\text{RN}) \le 7$, but the branch to STEP6 is taken if $c(\text{RN}) > 7$ ($c(\text{RN}) \le 7$ is false). In Fig. 7.6, the condition is $C(c(\text{R}5) > c(\text{SRCHKEY})$, but the branch to STEP8ELS is taken if the condition is false. In Fig. 7.10, the WHILE condition is "there are records to be read," and the branch to STEP3 is taken if there are *not* more records. Finally, in Fig. 7.11, the UNTIL condition is $J > 20$, but the branch back to STEP2LP is taken as long as J is *not* > 20. This little piece of consistency can help us to program our control structures correctly.

7.8   Example: Insertion in a Linked List

In a computer data items are often conveniently stored in list form. When the items in the list are to remain fixed or when insertions and deletions are to be made only at the bottom of the list, the data items can be efficiently stored in consecutive main storage locations. However, when insertions and deletions may be required anywhere in the list, storage in consecutive locations is not efficient. Room for an insertion would have to be made by moving all data items which are beyond the point at which the insertion is to be made. Deletions require either collapsing the list or substituting for the deleted item a value representing "vacant" space.

In situations requiring many insertions and deletions a *linked list* has advantages. In a linked list each data item is kept in what is called a *cell*. If we assume that a data item is one word long, a cell must be two words long. The first word of each cell contains the address of the next cell in the list; the second word of the cell contains the data item itself. Thus a segment of a list could be stored as follows.

> *First cell:*
> Location ØØA248: ØØØØA36Ø   (Link to second cell)
>   ØØA24C: C3D4F64Ø   (First data item)
>
> *Second cell:*
> Location ØØA36Ø: ØØØØA29Ø   (Link to third cell)
>   ØØA364: E7E4C9E2   (Second data item)
>
> *Third cell:*
> Location ØØA29Ø: ØØØØA128   (Link to fourth cell)
>   ØØA294: D4D14Ø4Ø   (Third data item)
> etc.

We may adopt as a convention that the *last cell* in the list has zero in its first word.

An insertion may easily be made at any point of a linked list. Suppose that given the list segment shown above, we wish to insert an item after the second cell. Suppose that the item F7F9E3E2 is in a cell whose address is, say, ØØA2Ø8. We need only change two link addresses to make the insertion:

> *Second cell:*
> Location ØØA36Ø: ØØØØA2Ø8   (Link to new cell)
>   ØØA364: E7E4C9E2   (Second data item)
>
> *New cell:*
> Location ØØA2Ø8: ØØØØA29Ø   (Link to former third cell)
>   ØØA2ØC: F7F9E3E2   (Inserted data item)

Figure 7.12 shows the change in the list structure; the broken line represents the connection replaced in the insertion process, and the changes are shown in boldface. Given the address of cell 2 in register 5 and the address of the new cell in register 6, the change of link addresses accomplishing the insertion can be done by

```
L    R7,Ø(R5)      ADDRESS OF NEXT CELL
ST   R7,Ø(R6)      STORE IN NEW CELL
ST   R6,Ø(R5)      STORE ADDRESS OF NEW CELL
```

To search for a given item in a linked list presents some problems. In terms of pseudo-code, we might write at first

> Search list for SRCHKEY
> IF found
>   THEN print "item found in list"
>   ELSE print "item not found"

This raises more questions. How is the search done? And how will the IF test whether the item is found? We can make the pseudo-code more specific:

FIGURE 7.12   Insertion in a linked list

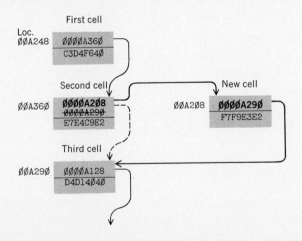

Set current cell address to beginning of list
Set found switch to false
WHILE current cell address ≠ 0 and found switch = false DO
    IF data item at current cell address = SRCHKEY
        THEN set found switch to true
        ELSE set current cell address to link from current cell
    IF found switch = true
        THEN print "item found in list"
        ELSE print "item not found"

The segment written from this pseudo-code is shown in Fig. 7.13. The segment shows all the essential steps in traversing a list; each cell of a list may contain more data, and the actions to be taken when the search succeeds or fails may be more complex, but the general-purpose framework is adaptable to many problems that differ in detail.

Now let us combine the ideas of inserting a cell in a linked list, the search strategy and a subroutine: we will ask for a subroutine that inserts a new cell in

FIGURE 7.13   Searching a linked list

```
*** SET R2 AS CURRENT CELL ADDRESS
          L      R2,CELLADDR
*** SET R3 AS FOUND SWITCH:  0 = NOT FOUND
***                          1 = FOUND
          SR     R3,R3
* WHILE CURRENT CELL ADDR. NOT = 0 AND NOT FOUND DO
SRCHLOOP  LTR    R2,R2
          BZ     SRCH2
          LTR    R3,R3
          BNZ    SRCH2
* . IF DATA ITEM FOUND, CURRENT CELL = SRCHKEY
          L      R4,4(,R2)
          C      R4,SRCHKEY
          BNE    SRCHLPA
* . . THEN SET FOUND SWITCH TO FOUND
          LA     R3,1
          B      SRCHLOOP
* . . ELSE GO TO NEXT CELL
SRCHLPA   L      R2,0(,R2)
          B      SRCHLOOP
* . ENDIF
* ENDWHILE (CURRENT CELL ADDR. NOT = 0 AND NOT FOUND)
* IF FOUND
SRCH2     LTR    R3,R3
          BZ     SRCH2ELS
* . THEN DISPLAY FOUND MESSAGE
          WRTERM ' ITEM FOUND IN LIST'
          B      NEXTSTEP
* . ELSE DISPLAY NOT FOUND MESSAGE
SRCH2ELS  WRTERM ' ITEM NOT FOUND'
* ENDIF
NEXTSTEP  DS     0H
```

a list just after the cell that contains a certain key, or at the bottom (tail end) of the list if the given key does not exist in the list. The subroutine needs three parameters:

1. the address of the first cell of a list,
2. the address of the key after which we are to insert the new cell,
3. the address of the new cell to be inserted.

The subroutine is shown in Fig. 7.14. The search strategy can be simpler than the one shown in Fig. 7.13; the action of inserting the new cell is exactly the same whether our search for the key is successful or not, so we do not need a "found" switch. The result is that the IF structure within the WHILE is mingled with the testing and exiting from the WHILE itself. This is a controversial kind of change to make: some programmers believe the mingled, shorter code is also clearer, and distinctly preferable, while others believe that

FIGURE 7.14   Subroutine to insert a cell into a linked list

```
**********************************************************************
*** SUBROUTINE INSERTS A CELL (THIRD PARAMETER)
*** INTO A LINKED LIST (FIRST PARAMETER)
*** AFTER THE CELL CONTAINING A GIVEN KEY (SECOND PARAMETER)
*** IF THE KEY IS NOT IN THE LIST, THE NEW CELL IS INSERTED
*** AT THE END, AND THE LIST MUST NOT BE EMPTY.
**********************************************************************
LSTINSRT XSAVE TR=NO
         LM      R2,R4,0(R1)
         SR      R6,R6            ZERO FOR COMPARISONS
* WHILE CURRENT CELL DOES NOT HAVE LINK = 0
LSTINLP  C       R6,0(,R2)
         BZ      LSTIN2
* . IF DATA ITEM FOUND, CURRENT CELL = KEY
         L       R5,4(,R2)
         C       R5,0(,R3)
         BNE     LSTINLPA
* . . THEN WHILE COND. (KEY NOT FOUND) IS FALSE, EXIT WHILE
         B       LSTIN2
* . . ELSE GO TO NEXT CELL
* . ENDIF
LSTINLPA L       R2,0(,R2)
         B       LSTINLP
*** INSERT THE NEW CELL
* ENDWHILE (CURRENT CELL DOES NOT HAVE LINK = 0)
LSTIN2   L       R7,0(,R2)        ADDR. OF NEXT CELL (OR ZERO)
         ST      R7,0(,R4)        STORE IN NEW CELL
         ST      R4,0(,R2)        STORE ADDR. OF NEW CELL
XRETURN  XRETURN SA=*,TR=NO
```

it is important for clarity and maintainability of programs to preserve the integrity of each control structure.

One other change had to be made: we must keep the address of the current cell in register 2, so we can put the address of the new cell in its link field. So the test for a link field of zero must be changed to look for a zero in the link field of the current cell, not wait for the contents of register 2 to become zero. This implies a requirement that the list we are to search is *not empty* when we begin! Try fixing the subroutine so it will properly insert a cell into an empty list.

7.9   Style and Control Structure Summary

In this chapter we have introduced the main control structures and their implementation in assembler language. In the examples shown, the control structures are documented by remarks statements in a sort of pidgin Pascal. For readability, it is worthwhile to adopt some uniformity of style in the use of these remarks statements. We follow here a set of style conventions:

1. The pseudo-code documenting the program is shown with *one* asterisk.

2. When one control structure is embedded in another, its pseudo-code is indented, and periods are inserted between the asterisk and the comment to show the depth of the structure. Indent two spaces for each level, and therefore use a space and a period to show the depth.

3. The end of each control structure is marked by a remark ENDIF, ENDWHILE, etc. If there has been another structure since the beginning of the one now ended, repeat the condition of the IF, WHILE, etc. to help document which structure is being ended. The ENDIF or ENDWHILE is at the same level of indentation as the corresponding IF or WHILE.

4. Other remarks are shown with *three* asterisks. Blocks of comments, showing perhaps the status of registers or the parameters to a subroutine, may be further set off by full lines of asterisks.

Figure 7.10 illustrates these conventions in a program segment; Figs. 7.13 and 7.14 illustrate them further, and in succeeding chapters some programs and segments become more complex so that the contributions made to readability by following style conventions become more important.

To conclude, see Fig. 7.15 for outlines of the implementation of the four control structures introduced in this chapter. There will of course be deviations from this outline; for example, not all conditions are evaluated and tested by one Compare followed by one Branch.

FIGURE 7.15 Outlines of control structure implementation: (a) IF-THEN, (b) IF-THEN-ELSE, (c) WHILE, (d) REPEAT-UNTIL

```
* IF   condition                              * WHILE      condition  DO
STEP      C   (evaluate the condition)        STEPLP       C  (evaluate the condition)
          B(not condition)  STEPNEXT                       B(not condition)  STEPNEXT
* . THEN   (describe action)                  * .  (describe action)
           action                                  action
* ENDIF                                            B STEPLP
STEPNEXT ...                                  * ENDWHILE
             (a)                              STEPNEXT . . .
                                                             (c)

* IF   condition                              * REPEAT
STEP      C   (evaluate the condition)        * .  (describe action
          B(not condition)  STEPELSE          STEPLP  action
* . THEN   (describe action)                  * . UNTIL   condition
           action  (THEN)                                 C  (evaluate the condition)
           B    STEPNEXT                                  B(not condition)  STEPLP
* . ELSE (describe action)                    * ENDREPEAT
           action  (ELSE)                     STEPNEXT ...
* ENDIF                                                     (d)
STEPNEXT ...
             (b)
```

m a i n   i d e a s

- Conditional branch instructions are essential to the use of the computer; they permit loops and logical complexity of programs.

- The program status word contains the instruction address register and the two-bit condition code. The condition code is set by compare, add, and subtract instructions, and serves as an indicator of the instructions' results.

- The conditional branch instructions are BC and BCR. The first operand, *M1*, indicates which condition codes would cause branching to occur; the second operand designates the branch address. These and the compare instructions are summarized in Fig. 7.16. Extended mnemonics in assembler language combine the operation code with *M1*, making the writing of branch instructions easier.

- The major control structures are IF-THEN and IF-THEN-ELSE for complex decision making, and WHILE and REPEAT-UNTIL for looping. The structures are implemented by compare and branch instructions as outlined in Fig. 7.15. Remarks statements document the structures.

- When data items are kept in a list and many insertions and deletions are required, a linked list is a time-saving device; searching, insertion, and deletion are fast.

FIGURE 7.16 Compare and branch instructions

Mnemonic name	Type	Full name	Action
CR	RR	Compare Register	$CC \leftarrow \begin{cases} 0 \text{ if } c(R1) = c(R2) \\ 1 \text{ if } c(R1) < c(R2) \\ 2 \text{ if } c(R1) > c(R2) \end{cases}$
C	RX	Compare	$CC \leftarrow \begin{cases} 0 \text{ if } c(R1) = c(S2) \\ 1 \text{ if } c(R1) < c(S2) \\ 2 \text{ if } c(R1) > c(S2) \end{cases}$
CH	RX	Compare Half-word[1]	$CC \leftarrow \begin{cases} 0 \text{ if } c(R1) = c(S2)_{0-15} \\ 1 \text{ if } c(R1) < c(S2)_{0-15} \\ 2 \text{ if } c(R1) > c(S2)_{0-15} \end{cases}$
BCR	RR	Branch on Condition to Register[2,3]	$\to c(R2)$ if $(M1)_{CC} = 1$
BC	RX	Branch on Condition[2,3]	$\to S2$ if $(M1)_{CC} = 1$

Notes

1. For purposes of comparison, the S2 operand is considered as expanded to a full word by propagation of the sign bit, bit 0 of the half-word, into the upper 16 bits of a full word.

2. We extend the notation introduced in Chapter 4. An arrow pointing to the right indicates a branch: $\to c(R2)$ specifies a branch to the address contained in R2. The arrow meaning branch is distinguished from that meaning store by its direction; storage of a quantity is always indicated by an arrow pointing to the left.

3. M1 represents the mask, bits 8–11 of the instruction. Whether a branch is taken depends on whether or not a particular bit of M1 is a 1.

■ **PROBLEMS** FOR REVIEW AND IMAGINATION

7.1 Write as many different instructions as you can, each setting the condition code to 0 if and only if the contents of register 4 is zero.

7.2 Why is an overflow possible with the LPR and LCR instructions, but not with LNR?

7.3 Given the following contents of registers and storage locations,

Register 2: ØØØØ697A
Register 3: 49564EDB
Register 4: 8ØØ39FFØ
Location Q: FFFFFCD4
Location Y: ØØØØØØØØ
Location W: FFFF9686

before *each* of the instructions listed below, determine the condition code set by each instruction.

```
SR   R3,R4        CR   R4,R3
S    R2,W         CR   R3,R4
SH   R2,W+2       C    R3,Y
```

```
                     A    R4,Q          LTR   R3,R3
                     C    R4,Q
```

7.4 What relationship must hold between contents of register 9 and storage location T for each of the following sequences to result in a branch to PROGPT2?

a)
```
    C    R9,T
    BC   12,PROGPT2
```

b)
```
    C    R9,T
    BC   5,PROGPT2
```

c)
```
    A    R9,T
    BC   5,PROGPT2
```

d)
```
    S    R9,T
    LPR  R9,R9
    S    R9,=F'30'
    BC   6,PROGPT2
```

7.5 AA, BB, and DD are main storage locations containing full-word binary integers. The 80-byte area CARDIN contains characters. Transcribe the following into assembler language:

a) IF $c(AA) < c(BB)$
      THEN store $c(BB) - c(AA)$ at BB.

b) IF $c(AA) = 15$
      THEN load $c(BB)$ into register 8
      ELSE load $c(DD)$ into register 8

c) IF $|c(AA)| < |c(BB)|$
      THEN store the remainder of $|c(BB)|/|c(AA)|$ at BB
      ELSE store the remainder of $|c(AA)|/|c(BB)|$ at AA

Can you fix up your segment so that if both numbers are zero, your segment will leave both locations intact but not attempt to divide by zero?

d) Store the minimum of $c(AA)$ and $c(BB)$ in DD.

e) Load the minimum of the three numbers into register 4.

f) IF the sum of each pair of numbers is greater than the third
      THEN print "VALID TRIANGLE"
      ELSE print "NOT SIDES OF A TRIANGLE"

g) Accumulate in register 7 the sum of the numbers in the area CARDIN. Assume that the set of numbers in CARDIN is followed by the character $, which will cause XDECI to set the condition code to 3.

h) Load the absolute value of $c(AA)$ into register 5. Write one segment using the LPR instruction, then write a segment that does the task *without* using LPR or LNR.

7.6 Modify the segment of Fig. 7.8 so that if either A or B is outside the range 1 to 3 neither AFF nor INCOMPAT will be incremented.

7.7 A certain neophyte programmer implemented

$$IF\ A = -B$$
THEN action 1
ELSE IF $A < -B$
THEN action 2
ELSE action 3

by the segment

```
        L      R4,A
        A      R4,B
        BM     ACT2
        BP     ACT3
        action 1
        B      NEXTSTEP
ACT2    action 2
        B      NEXTSTEP
ACT3    action 3
NEXTSTEP  . . .
```

The program worked well most of the time, but on a few occasions the segment performed action 1 when A and −B were decidedly not equal. Why? How would you correct the segment?

7.8 Modify the segment of Fig. 7.10 to use PACK and CVB instead of XDECI. Assume that the number is right-justified in bytes 1–7 of each record.

7.9 Further modify the segment of Problem 7.8 to print the total generated.

7.10 Write a full program that will read each 80-character record (card?) in a data set. Each record contains three numbers; for each record, print the three numbers and their sum. Try writing the program twice, once using XDECI and XDECO, and once using the PACK, CVB, CVD, and UNPK instructions.

7.11 Write a full program that will read each 80-character record in a data set. For each record, print the three numbers and, as in Problem 7.5(f), the message "VALID TRIANGLE" or "NOT SIDES OF A TRIANGLE".

7.12 Modify your program of Problem 7.10 to sum the *ten* numbers on each card, and to print only the sum for each record, not all the individual numbers. This should use a REPEAT-UNTIL structure to convert and add the ten numbers of each card.

7.13 Write a program segment that will print the data item in each cell of a linked list.

7.14 Deletion of a data item from a linked list is slightly more complicated than insertion of a data item if we know only the address of the cell containing the item to be deleted and not the address of its predecessor.

Considering only the case in which the item to be deleted is *not* in the last cell in the list, we proceed as follows: The data item *and link address* from the subsequent cell are put into the cell whose original data item is to be deleted; the subsequent cell is then considered to be empty and is deleted from the list. Diagram and program this process. What difficulties arise if the item to be deleted is in the last cell of a list? How might you avoid the difficulties?

7.15   During a process of insertions and deletions, the cells not in use will become scattered throughout the storage region used for list cells. The usual stratagem for keeping track of cells not in use is to string them onto a list of their own, called the available space list. So the complete process of adding a data item to a list is to delete a cell from the available space list, put the data item in the cell, then insert that cell into the desired list. To delete a data item from a list, we follow first the steps described in the previous problem, then add the deleted cell to the available space list. From where on the available space list is it most efficient to take a cell? Where should one be put back? Program the entire process of deleting a given data item from a list, including return of the deleted cell to the available space list.

7.16   In Fig. 7.14, there is a sequence of instructions

```
                     BNE    LSTINLPA
                     B      LSTIN2
        LSTINLPA  . . .
```

Show that this can be replaced by

```
                     BE     LSTIN2
        LSTINLPA  . . .
```

Can you make a general statement about sequences of branches like this?

7.17   The subroutine in Fig. 7.14 provides its own register save area (through the XRETURN macro instruction), but as a lowest-level subroutine, it does not need to. We can give parameters SA = NO to XSAVE and XRETURN to prevent provision and use of a register save area. Rewrite the subroutine, not using XSAVE and XRETURN.

7.18   Fix the subroutine of Fig. 7.14 so it inserts a cell into an empty list properly. *Hint:* When a subroutine leaves a result in register 0, it must restore registers *except* for register 0. We can specify which registers are to be restored by XRETURN; include a RGS parameter, something like RGS=(R1-R12) or RGS=(R14-R15,R1-R12).

7.19   There is a macro, CNOP, that inserts no-operation instructions into the object program in order to align the subsequent instruction at a particular boundary. There are two operands. The second operand should be 4 if alignment with respect to a full-word boundary is desired, 8 if

double-word boundary alignment is desired. The first operand specifies where within the full word or double word the subsequent instruction should start. For example,

```
              CNOP  Ø,4
       BP     L    R3,A
```

will cause assembly of one half-word no-operation instruction, or
nothing, so that BP will be located on a full-word boundary. If the
CNOP operands had been 2,8, BP would be two bytes after the beginning of a double word. CNOP is used within instruction sequences so
that execution of instructions can be unbroken, up to an instruction
for which boundary alignment is desired.

Another use is in assuring that relative addressing is carried out
properly. In the segment

```
              B    *+8
       A      DS   1F
              L    R3,A
```

the branch instruction may or may not go to the load instruction,
depending on whether the branch instruction is on a full-word boundary or not. Show how a CNOP instruction solves this problem. Then
think of other uses for CNOP.

7.20 Without flagging it as such, we introduced an example of a linked list
in Chapter 6. The chain of register save areas is a linked list; if we regard the area provided by the currently active subroutine as the cell at
the head of the list, word 2 is the link that points to the next cell. Section 6.5 explains how the register save areas also form a linked list
when viewed in the opposite direction, using the *third* word of each
register save area. Such a list is called a *doubly linked list*; try to think
of cases where it is useful to have links pointing in both directions.

7.21 Some subroutines should accept a variable number of parameters, and
the subroutine must therefore be able to recognize the length of a parameter list. The convention adopted in OS and OS/VS is that the first
byte of each four-byte parameter address is 0 except the last, whose
high-order bit is set to 1. For example, the parameter address block
could be set up

```
       PLIST     DC     A(T,U,V)
                 DC     X'8Ø'
                 DC     AL3(W)
```

This convention need not be followed where the number of parameters
is fixed and well understood. Write a program segment that will test a
parameter address block to determine whether the second parameter is
the last. Also, think of subroutines that should accept a variable-length
parameter list.

7.22   Write a subroutine that will use the convention described in Problem
       7.21, and find the maximum of two *or three* numbers given as parame-
       ters. Use the convention that the result should be returned in register 0.

■ REFERENCES

Aho, Alfred V., John E. Hopcroft, and
   Jeffrey D. Ullman, *Data Structures
   and Algorithms,* Addison-Wesley,
   Reading, Mass., 1983. A good description of linked lists and operations
   using them.

Computing Surveys **6,** 4 (December 1974).
   A special issue with several thought-
   provoking papers on structured programming.

Dahl, O. J., E. W. Dijkstra, and C. A. R.
   Hoare, *Structured Programming,* Academic Press, New York, 1972. An important book in the development of
   structured programming.

IBM System/370 Principles of Operation,
   GA 22–7000, IBM Corporation. Reference on the program status word and
   compare and branch instructions.

Kernighan, Brian W., and P. J. Plauger,
   Software Tools, Addison-Wesley,
   Reading, Mass., 1976. Techniques and
   style of structured programming.

Knuth, Donald E., *The Art of Computer
   Programming, Vol. 1: Fundamental
   Algorithms,* 2nd ed., Addison-Wesley,
   Reading, Mass., 1974. Chapter 2 includes a comprehensive presentation
   of the theory and principles of list processing.

Linger, Richard C., Harlan D. Mills, and
   Bernard I. Witt, *Structured Programming,* Addison-Wesley, Reading,
   Mass., 1979. A good, thorough discussion of structured programming.

8

LOOPING AND ADDRESS MODIFICATION

In Chapter 7 the looping control structures were introduced. Now we will consider the structure of a loop in more detail. We will examine the techniques of using tables in loops and systematically modifying the effective addresses of data used in the loop. These are the tasks that are handled as subscripted variables in higher-level languages, and they are quite important. We study the use of index registers, and also some special looping control instructions that help in the writing of looping structures.

This chapter also continues the discussion of searching that was started in the preceding chapter. We examine sequential searching of items in a block of storage and also the binary search technique. It will be shown that the general outline and therefore the control structure is the same for all of the searches in both chapters; only the structure of the data in main storage is different, but each storage representation requires a different implementation at the detailed level.

Address modification and searching are extremely common in programming tasks. Pay special attention to learning the techniques discussed in this chapter; you will have opportunities to use them in subsequent chapters as well.

8.1 The Anatomy of a Loop: Address Modification

Chapter 7 introduced the loop structures WHILE and REPEAT-UNTIL. Now we take a second look at what a loop structure is made of before we build

FIGURE 8.1   Two common loop structures (a) WHILE, (b) REPEAT-UNTIL

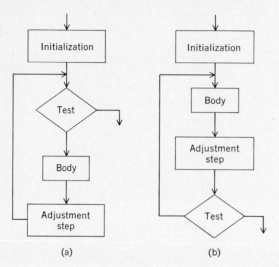

(a)   (b)

loops that modify addresses. A loop structure has four components: initialization, the body of the loop, an adjustment step, and a test for exit. Figure 8.1 shows these components in the WHILE and the REPEAT-UNTIL structure in flowchart form. Sometimes two of the steps are included in the same instruction. On some occasions no instructions are required to perform the functions of one of the steps. In any event division into these four steps is useful for some of the discussion in this chapter. Let us examine the steps one by one.

THE BODY
The *body* of the loop is the segment containing the instructions that are the principal business of the loop—the real work we want the computer to do. The body includes input, output, arithmetic computations, information move, tests, and branches within the loop—whatever we want done repetitively. The other three steps have only one purpose: to ensure that the body will be performed the right number of times on the right data.

THE ADJUSTMENT STEP
The *adjustment step* of the loop is often a set of instructions that adds to a count of the number of repetitions of the loop that have already been performed, or subtracts from a count of the number of times the loop has yet to be performed. A count is, of course, kept in a register or storage location that we treat as a counter with ordinary arithmetic instructions. As we shall see in more detail later, the adjustment step may also include adding to or subtracting from a register that specifies the address of the data items to be used in the next repetition of the loop. The adjustment step may also include moving some information around so that it will be in the correct place for the

next repetition of the loop. Thus the adjustment step has the functions of updating a quantity to be used in the test for exit and of ensuring that the right data are available to the next repetition of the loop.

EXIT FROM THE LOOP

Obviously, in all but the most trivial problems the computer needs an *exit* from the loop as well as an entry to it. The exit must be some sort of conditional branch that is not always taken; otherwise there would be no loop at all! So a test for exit is a branch point involving a test: if certain conditions occur, control leaves the loop; if other conditions occur, the loop is continued. Often a test for exit is a test of whether the body has been repeated a given number of times, specifically, a comparison of the count of repetitions of the loop with some predetermined limit, and a branch on the condition code resulting from the comparison. But any possible test that can be made by a computer may be a possible test for exit from some loop.

INITIALIZATION

The body, adjustment step, and test for exit are repeated over and over again inside the loop. The *initialization step* takes place outside the loop, before execution of the loop begins. In the initialization step, all counters, addresses of first data items, and other conditions necessary to the proper functioning of the loop itself are set. A location to be used as a counter of the number of times the body of the loop has been executed will be filled with zero; a location used to address the data items in a list as the body of the loop is executed will be set to address the first item on the list, and so on.

It is important that the initialization be performed by instructions executed before entry to the loop. To understand this point, let us examine two inferior alternatives. The first alternative is initialization of the counters by constant definitions. Definitions can be made so that at first entry, the loop proceeds properly. However, if after exit from the loop we wish to enter the loop from the beginning a second time, the counters and other items that have changed during execution of the loop will not be properly set. The second alternative is an improvement on the first: reset the counters after exit from the loop. The difficulties with this approach are subtler. In the first place there may be several possible paths after the loop, with perhaps different actions needed to reset the appropriate quantities in each path. So the coding of the reinitialization becomes longer and more complex than if initialization were done before entry in the first place. Second, reinitialization after exit from the loop complicates the logic of the program and confuses the programmer, thereby creating a greater danger of programming errors. Third, the programmer may see from the total logic of the program that shortcuts can indeed be taken in reinitialization, or that certain loops can be left without reinitialization because they will not be entered again. However, if it is necessary to modify the program at a later date—and any worthwhile program is often modified to fit slightly different circumstances—then the shortcuts taken will likely increase the work of making and debugging the modifications out of proportion to the time saved by the shortcuts in the first place. Therefore the initialization comes before execution of the loop itself, as shown in Fig. 8.1.

EXAMPLES OF LOOP STRUCTURES

Now let us illustrate loop structure with some simple examples. The first example is the addition of 20 numbers, which will be called $A_0, A_1, \ldots, A_{19}$. Figure 8.2 shows the pseudo-code and a flowchart for the addition. Each of the four steps is represented by one box in the flowchart. The body is the addition of A_i to the sum; the other steps serve to execute the body exactly 20 times, adding the proper numbers to a register holding the appropriate initial contents. The quantity i is used both as an indicator of which A is to be added next and as a counter of how many times the loop has been executed; incrementing i is the only action needed in the adjustment step. The test for exit is a comparison of i with a limit of 20; when i has reached 20, we leave the loop. We state the test as i greater than or equal to 20 as a guard against programming errors that might creep in and cause an infinite loop in some later modification of the segment. The only quantities changed during the loop are *Sum* and i, so they are the only quantities that need to be initialized.

As a more complex example, let us consider polynomial evaluation. Suppose we have quantities $A_0, A_1, \ldots, A_n$ which are coefficients of a polynomial of degree n: $A_0 x^n + A_1 x^{n-1} + \cdots + A_{n-1} x + A_n$. The polynomial can be rewritten for efficiency of computation as

$$((\cdots((A_0 x + A_1)x + A_2)x + \cdots)x + A_{n-1})x + A_n,$$

which can be evaluated as

$$A_0 x + A_1,$$

then

$$(A_0 x + A_1)x + A_2,$$

then

$$((A_0 x + A_1)x + A_2)x + A_3,$$
$$\vdots$$
$$(\cdots((A_0 x + A_1)x + A_2)x + A_3)\cdots)x + A_{n-1},$$
$$((\cdots((A_0 x + A_1)x + A_2)x + A_3)\cdots)x + A_{n-1})x + A_n.$$

This technique, called *Horner's method* and also sometimes called *nesting*, was introduced in the discussion of number conversions in Chapter 1. It requires only n multiplications and n additions, and can easily be programmed in a loop as shown in Fig. 8.3. We assume that X, the value at which the polynomial is to be evaluated, is available. *Sum* and i are the only quantities changed during execution of the loop, so they are the only ones that need to be

FIGURE 8.2   Addition of 20 numbers

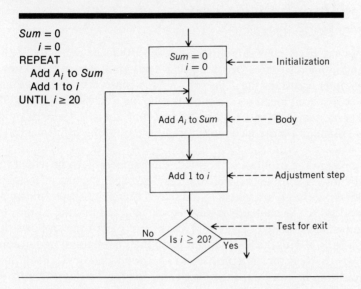

initialized. By making the test for exit first, we have made our loop able to evaluate polynomials of 0 degree, namely, constants. The body and adjustment step are straightforward.

FIGURE 8.3   Evaluation of a polynomial by Horner's method

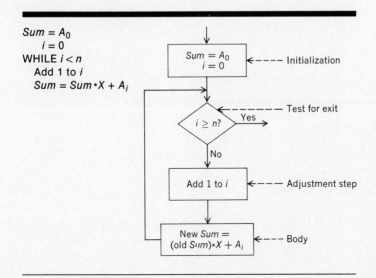

8.2   Address Modification: Changing and Testing Contents of a Base Register

In many loops the data items to be treated in repetitions of the body of the loop are found in main storage. Often the data items are stored in consecutive locations. On other occasions the items, while not in consecutive locations, are at least in evenly spaced locations. In such a situation, you can derive the address of each data item after the first by adding a constant to the address of its predecessor. This addition can be done naturally as part of the adjustment step of a loop.

For example, in the problem of Fig. 8.2, the numbers A_i to be added together may be in consecutive full words in main storage, starting at location AA. If the address of the A_i just added to the sum is kept in a register, the number 4 can be added to the contents of that register; the result is the address of the next number to be added. Figure 8.4 shows a program that follows the flowchart of Fig. 8.2, with the added assumption that the A_i are stored in consecutive full words. Register 7 is initialized to AA, the address of A_0. Each time the adjustment step is executed, the quantity in register 7 is increased by 4. Thus the second time the instruction

$$A \qquad R8,\emptyset(,R7)$$

is executed, the address in register 7 is 4 greater than the address of A_0; therefore it is the address of A_1. The third time the body of the loop is executed, the address in register 7 has been increased again, so A_2 is added to the growing *Sum*. The process of adding an A_i and adjusting the address continues until execution of the loop is terminated.

Note that for addressing the A's we use the implied base register specified (earlier) in the USING statement only for loading the address AA into register 7.

FIGURE 8.4   A segment to add 20 numbers

```
*** INITIALIZATION
          SR     R8,R8         SUM = 0
          LR     R9,R8         I = 0
          LA     R7,AA         ADDRESS OF FIRST A
* REPEAT
* . ADD A(I) TO SUM
LOOP      A      R8,0(,R7)
* . ADD 1 TO I
          LA     R9,1(,R9)     INCREASE I
          LA     R7,4(,R7)     GET ADDR OF NEXT A
* UNTIL I >= 20
          C      R9,=F'20'
          BL     LOOP
* ENDREPEAT
```

Then register 7 holds the address of the *A* to be used next. If we had tried to use the implied base register for addressing all the *A*'s, incrementing it by 4 each time through the loop, the *A*'s could have been correctly addressed, but everything else, like the address LOOP and the address of the literal =F'2Ø', would be incorrect.

The counter *i,* which is kept in register 9, is incremented in a regular pattern, attaining the values 0, 1, 2, . . . , 20. The contents of register 7 are also incremented in a regular pattern, attaining the values

$$AA, \qquad AA+4, \qquad AA+8, \qquad . . . , \qquad AA+8\emptyset$$

We exit from the loop when the contents of register 9 is 20, and when the contents of register 7 is AA+8Ø. *We could test for exit from the loop with a test of register 7 just as well as by a test of register 9;* the compare instruction would be changed to

$$C \qquad R7,=A(AA+8\emptyset)$$

and the branch instruction is unchanged. The program is equivalent to the original: it will produce exactly the same results. But with the change, it is no longer necessary to use register 9 at all; we can eliminate it from the program. The resulting, more efficient program is shown in Fig. 8.5. Several important points are illustrated by the problem of adding 20 numbers:

1. A sequence of data items arranged in a regular pattern in main storage can be addressed easily in successive repetitions of the body of a loop.
2. The adjustment step of a loop obtains the address of the next data item by incrementing the address of the last one.
3. Since these addresses are advanced in a regular pattern, they can be tested and used to cause exit from the loop at the appropriate time. The register containing the addresses is thus essentially a counter of times through the loop.

These points will be illustrated by further examples.

FIGURE 8.5   A shorter segment to add 20 numbers

```
*** INITIALIZATION
          SR      R8,R8          SUM = 0
          LA      R7,AA          ADDRESS OF FIRST A
* REPEAT
* . ADD A(I) TO SUM
LOOP      A       R8,0(,R7)
* . ADD 1 TO I
          LA      R7,4(,R7)
* UNTIL I >= 20
          C       R7,=A(AA+80)
          BL      LOOP
* ENDREPEAT
```

PROGRAM SEGMENT FOR A POLYNOMIAL EVALUATION LOOP

Next, let us consider polynomial evaluation, following Fig. 8.3. Again assume that the coefficients are in consecutive full words in main storage, but that they start at location COEF. Assume further that N, the degree of the polynomial, is in register 2 and that X is a binary integer in register 3. A program segment following the flowchart in Fig. 8.3 is shown in Fig. 8.6. Assume that the sums and products will not overflow one register.

Note that the branch out of the loop is taken on the condition that I is equal to *or greater than N*. We expect N to be nonnegative, and if N is nonnegative, I will reach N by coming up from underneath. However, if by some mischance N is negative, I will never be equal to N. The test suggested here, which costs no more in time or space than the plain test for equality, will cause a quick exit from the loop anyway. It is always good practice to make programs secure against mischances in the data. Any time you can do it with no extra effort, you certainly should; however, the security may sometimes cost more than it is worth.

In this example we could have the program calculate the limiting address, COEF+4*N, the value that register 7 should attain before exit from the loop, and then have it test register 7 for exit. If we did, we could abolish all references to I and register 9 as we did in Fig. 8.5. This conversion of the segment is left as an exercise for you. You will find that

- the segment is expanded by one instruction,
- the loop is one instruction shorter, so it will run faster, and
- the logic of the segment is somewhat more obscure.

FIGURE 8.6 Evaluation of a polynomial

```
**********************************************************************
***      EVALUATION OF A POLYNOMIAL BY HORNER'S METHOD
***      COEFFICIENTS A(0),A(1),...,A(N) ARE STORED IN CONSECUTIVE
***      FULL WORDS STARTING AT COEF, COEFFICIENT OF X**N FIRST
***      N IS IN REG R2, X IN REG R3
**********************************************************************
*** INITIALIZATION
         LA    R7,COEF
         L     R5,0(,R7)      SUM = A(0)
         SR    R9,R9          I = 0
* WHILE I < N
LOOP     CR    R9,R2
         BNL   NEXTSTEP
* . ADD 1 TO I
         LA    R9,1(,R9)
         LA    R7,4(,R7)
* . SUM = SUM * X + A(I)
         MR    R4,R3
         A     R5,0(,R7)
         B     LOOP
* ENDWHILE
NEXTSTEP DS    0H
```

Either segment may be preferable, under different circumstances. Real programming problems are usually accompanied by considerations that help the programmer make the choice between segments such as these.

8.3 Address Modification: Use of Index Registers

An effective address in the IBM System/370 is generated either as the sum of a displacement and contents of a base register or as the sum of displacement and contents of base and index registers. The effective address specified in a particular repeated instruction can therefore be modified by changing the displacement, changing the contents of a register used as a base, or changing the contents of a register used as an index. Section 8.2 illustrated techniques associated with change in the base register. Address modification by change in the displacement in an actual instruction is possible but awkward; it is not illustrated here but is left to you as a challenging exercise. Comparable techniques are necessary in the use of some computers.

FIGURE 8.7   Adding 20 numbers, using an index register (a) using an explicit base register (b) using an implied base register

```
*** INITIALIZATION
        SR    R8,R8         SUM = 0
        LA    R7,AA         BASE ADDRESS = AA
        SR    R10,R10       INDEX = 0
* REPEAT
* . ADD A(I) TO SUM
LOOP    A     R8,0(R10,R7)
* . ADD 1 TO I
        LA    R10,4(,R10)
* UNTIL I >= 20
        C     R10,=F'80'
        BL    LOOP
* ENDREPEAT
                    (a)
```

```
*** INITIALIZATION
        SR    R8,R8         SUM = 0
        SR    R10,R10       INDEX = 0
* REPEAT
* . ADD A(I) TO SUM
LOOP    A     R8,AA(R10)
* . ADD 1 TO I
        LA    R10,4(,R10)
* UNTIL I >= 20
        C     R10,=F'80'
        BL    LOOP
* ENDREPEAT
                    (b)
```

This section introduces the use of an index register in modification of an effective address. Of course, this technique can be used only when the instructions addressing the items with varying addresses are RX-type instructions. The index register specification was included in RX-type instructions especially to make address modification easy, and since many instructions are of RX type, index register techniques can be widely used.

The use of an index register will first be illustrated by twice changing the segment of Fig. 8.5, which adds 20 numbers from main storage. The first changed segment is shown in Fig. 8.7(a). The logic of the segment has not been changed at all. One extra instruction sets the initial contents of the index register. The instruction at LOOP addresses by base and index registers one of the numbers to be added; the contents of the base register is left fixed, and the index register (10) is incremented and tested for exit. We have not improved the program segment with our use of an index register; we have in fact made it longer!

If *all* the modification of effective addresses is done by changing the value of an index register, it becomes possible to use the implied base register. The second change to the same program, shown in Fig. 8.7(b), makes use of the implied base register and again shortens the segment. The specification AA(R1Ø) is the only change from the segment of Fig. 8.7(a). Register 7 is no longer used, so the segment is shortened by deleting the instruction that loaded it. In constructing a machine language instruction corresponding to

LOOP   A   R8,AA(R1Ø)

the assembler inserts the address of an implied base register as the base register *B2* of the second operand. The assembler also calculates and inserts the proper

FIGURE 8.8   Addressing successive operands by AA(R1Ø)

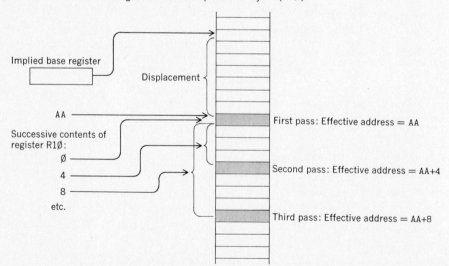

displacement *D2* so that *D2* and *B2* together address AA. The assembler includes *X2* = 10 (presuming R1Ø is equated to 10), but without knowledge or thought of the contents of register 10. During repeated execution of the instruction, the base and displacement together always address AA, and the contents of register 10 is also added, yielding effective addresses

$$AA, \qquad AA+4, \qquad AA+8, \qquad \ldots$$

In diagram form, the addressing of successive operands by AA(R1Ø) can be represented as shown in Fig. 8.8. The change in the contents of register 10 changes the effective address.

Now that you have seen how an index register can be used in a simple situation, let us observe another in which the use of the index register is clearly advantageous. Consider a problem in which there are 20 numbers, $A_0, A_1, \ldots,$ A_{19}, stored in consecutive words in main storage starting at AA, and 20 numbers, $B_0, B_1, \ldots, B_{19}$, stored in consecutive words in main storage starting at BB. We wish to calculate 20 numbers: $C_0 = A_0 + B_0$, $C_1 = A_1 + B_1, \ldots,$ $C_{19} = A_{19} + B_{19}$, and store the 20 *C*'s in consecutive words beginning at location CC. In a loop, effective addresses of an *A,* a *B,* and a *C* must be used and modified. Using the base-register modification techniques of Section 8.2, we would need a program segment like that shown in Fig. 8.9. There are eleven instructions, including eight that are executed each repetition of the loop. However, using index register techniques, we can have a shorter and faster segment, as shown in Fig. 8.10. Only one register needs to be initialized and modified; the same register serves to vary the effective addresses in three instructions, giving a clear reduction in storage space and time required and making a more readable program segment.

FIGURE 8.9 Computation of $C_i = A_i + B_i$, ($i = 0, 1, \ldots, 19$) by modifying the base registers

```
          LA    R7,AA        I = 0
          LA    R8,BB
          LA    R9,CC
* REPEAT
* . C(I) = A(I) + B(I)
LOOP      L     R4,0(,R7)
          A     R4,0(,R8)
          ST    R4,0(,R9)
* . ADD 1 TO I
          LA    R7,4(,R7)
          LA    R8,4(,R8)
          LA    R9,4(,R9)
* UNTIL I >= 20
          C     R7,=A(AA+80)
          BL    LOOP
* ENDREPEAT
```

FIGURE 8.10 Computation of $C_i = A_i + B_i$, $(i = 0, 1, \ldots, 19)$ by modifying an index register

```
         SR      R10,R10            I = 0
* REPEAT
* . C(I)  = A(I) + B(I)
LOOP     L       R4,AA(R10)
         A       R4,BB(R10)
         ST      R4,CC(R10)
* . ADD 1 TO I
         LA      R10,4(,R10)
* UNTIL I >= 20
         C       R10,=F'80'
         BL      LOOP
* ENDREPEAT
```

You will see more examples of the modification of contents of base registers and index registers in later sections and chapters.

8.4 The BXH and BXLE Instructions

In many of the examples of loops presented in this chapter, the adjustment step and test for exit have followed the pattern

```
         LA      REG1,INCR(REG1)
         C       REG1,LIMIT
         BL      LOOP
```

This three-instruction loop control sequence and slight variants of it are indeed standard in many computers. In the design of the IBM System/370, thought was given to facilitation of the looping process, and the instructions BXLE and BXH were provided. Either of these instructions, in different situations, can be substituted for the three-instruction loop control sequence. To prepare for BXLE or BXH usually requires additional initialization instructions, but the reduction in instructions repeated in the loop gives a net saving of time.

The BXH and BXLE instructions are of RS type; there are two register operands, *R1* and *R3*, and a main-storage operand. The operands for the two instructions are the same; only the branching criterion is different. The first operand *R1* is the register that will be incremented and then tested. The second operand *D2(B2)* is the address to which control will branch if the branch criterion is met.

Examining the three-instruction loop control sequence, we see that the increment and the limit to be compared against must still be specified. Because it is impossible to specify four operands in any IBM System/370 instruction, we are driven to the use of an even-odd pair of registers, so that one operand address can specify two operands, one in the even register, the other in the odd register. The operand address $R3$ can therefore be the address of a register pair. Register $R3$ contains the increment that is added to register $R1$. The addition performed is ordinary binary integer addition; note that either or both registers could contain negative numbers. The odd register, register $R3 + 1$, contains the limit that is compared with register $R1$ after $R1$ has been incremented. Branching depends on the result of the comparison. The BXH instruction (BXH stands for Branch on indeX High) will cause a branch to operand 2 if the contents of $R1$, as incremented, is greater than the contents of register $R3 + 1$. The BXLE instruction (BXLE stands for Branch on indeX Less than or Equal) will cause a branch if the contents of register $R1$, as incremented, is less than or equal to the contents of register $R3 + 1$. There is one further wrinkle to the BXH and BXLE instructions: register $R3$ can be specified as an odd register. If it is, the contents of register $R3$ is used as *both* increment and limit.

The BXLE and BXH instructions can therefore be summarized as follows:

BXLE   *R1,R3,S2*: $R1 \leftarrow c(R1) + c(R3)$;
If $R3$ even:
$\rightarrow S2$ if $c(R1) \leq c(R3 + 1)$
If $R3$ odd:
$\rightarrow S2$ if $c(R1) \leq c(R3)$

BXH   *R1,R3,S2*: $R1 \leftarrow c(R1) + c(R3)$;
If $R3$ even:
$\rightarrow S2$ if $c(R1) > c(R3 + 1)$
If $R3$ odd:
$\rightarrow S2$ if $c(R1) > c(R3)$.

Neither instruction affects the setting of the condition code.

Let us illustrate the action of these instructions before we use them in program segments. Suppose that the initial contents of the registers are

Register 2:	ØØØØØØØ1	Register 6:	ØØØØØØ26
Register 3:	ØØØØØØ4A	Register 7:	ØØØØØØ6E
Register 4:	FFFFFFFF	Register 9:	FFFFFFFC
Register 5:	ØØØØØØØØ	Register 12:	ØØØØ9434

The following instructions, each starting from these initial contents, will have the results indicated:

BXLE   R6,R2,Ø(R12)   Contents of register 6 are incremented by the contents of register 2, to ØØØØØØ27. The number ØØØØØØ27 *is* less than ØØØØØØ4A, so branch to location ØØ9434.

BXH   R6,R2,Ø(R12)   Similarly, contents of register 6 are increased to
                        ØØØØØØ27. The number ØØØØØØ27 is *not* higher than
                        ØØØØØØ4A, so no branch.

BXLE R7,R2,Ø(R12)   Contents of register 7 are increased to ØØØØØØ6F,
                        which is *not* less than or equal to ØØØØØØ4A, so no
                        branch.

BXH   R6,R4,Ø(R12)   Contents of register 6 are incremented (but
                        decreased) to ØØØØØØ25, which *is* higher than
                        ØØØØØØØØ, so branch to ØØ9434.

BXH   R3,R9,Ø(R12)   Contents of register 3 are incremented (by −4) to
                        ØØØØØØ46, which *is* higher than FFFFFFFC, so branch
                        to ØØ9434.

EXAMPLES OF USE OF BXLE AND BXH INSTRUCTIONS

Now that the instructions have been explained, their use will be illustrated. The
first example will be the last problem presented in Section 8.3: computation of
$C_i = A_i + B_i$ ($i = 0, 1, \ldots, 19$). Modifying the program segment shown in
Fig. 8.10, we are able to replace the last three instructions by a BXLE instruction, as shown in Fig. 8.11. In the execution of the BXLE instruction, register 10
is first incremented by the 4 contained in register 8, then compared with the 76
in register 9. The first 19 times the instruction is executed (when register 10
contains 4, 8, 12, . . . , 72, 76 after incrementing) control branches back to
LOOP. The twentieth time the BXLE instruction is executed, the contents of register 10 is raised to 80, which is *not* less than or equal to 76, so no branch takes
place, and control passes from the loop. Note that the limit in register 9 is the
number 76, the last contents of register 10 with which the body of the loop
should be executed. Two extra instructions had to be added to the loop
initialization, so the total segment shown in Fig. 8.11 is the same length as the
segment shown in Fig. 8.10. The advantage of the segment in Fig. 8.11 is in the
smaller number of instructions to be executed repeatedly.

FIGURE 8.11 Computation of $C_i = A_i + B_i$, ($i = 0, 1, \ldots, 19$) using the BXLE
instruction

```
* DO FOR INDEX = 0 TO 19
        SR    R10,R10        INDEX = 0
        LA    R8,4           INCREMENT = 1
        LA    R9,76          LIMIT = 19
* . C(I) = A(I) + B(I)
LOOP    L     R4,AA(R10)
        A     R4,BB(R10)
        ST    R4,CC(R10)
        BXLE  R10,R8,LOOP
* ENDFOR
```

Note that not only have the instructions in the loop been streamlined, but the pseudo-code shown in the remarks statements has been streamlined too. The pseudo-code phrase DO FOR is used here to represent a structure that is essentially REPEAT-UNTIL. The next example is essentially a WHILE, in that the test for exit from the loop *precedes* the first execution of the loop action, and the word DO is placed at the end rather than the beginning of the pseudo-code remark. This convention is recommended because the old-style FORTRAN DO statement is really a REPEAT-UNTIL and because the BASIC and Pascal FOR statements are really WHILE structures. You may have better reasons for using some other convention.

For a second example, we return to the problem of polynomial evaluation. We retain the logic of Fig. 8.3 except that in the single instruction BXH the adjustment step comes before the test for exit. Figure 8.12 is a modification of Fig. 8.6, using the BXH instruction to exit from the loop at the appropriate time. Again you see that the number of instructions repeated in the loop is reduced by two, but two instructions must be added to the initialization step. However, note that if *N* were made available in register 11 in the first place instead of in register 2, the instruction

```
        LR      R11,R2
```

would be unnecessary. You are invited to simulate execution of the segment, to convince yourself that the change of the branch test from Branch if Not Low to Branch on High, coupled with the incrementing of register 9 before the test instead of afterward, makes the segment execute properly.

Note that although the names of the instructions BXH and BXLE suggest that a register *used as an index* is incremented and tested, there is no requirement that the incremented and tested register be used for anything in particular. In Fig. 8.11, register 10, incremented and tested by the BXLE instruction, was in fact used as an index. In Fig. 8.12 however, register 9, incremented and tested by the BXH instruction, was used as a

FIGURE 8.12   Evaluation of a polynomial, using a BXH instruction

```
            LA      R7,COEF        INITIALIZATION
            L       R5,0(,R7)      SUM = A(0)
    * FOR I = 1 TO N DO
            SR      R9,R9          START AT 0. BXH INCREMENTS.
            LA      R10,1          INCREMENT = 1
            LR      R11,R2         LIMIT = N, FROM REG R2
    LOOP    BXH     R9,R10,NEXTSTEP ADD 1, COMPARE WITH N
            LA      R7,4(,R7)
    * . SUM = SUM * X + A(I)
            MR      R4,R3
            A       R5,0(,R7)
            B       LOOP
    * ENDFOR
    NEXTSTEP DS     0H
```

base register, not as an index. In still another example, the incremented and tested register might be used only as a counter, and not at all in the forming of an address. Each instruction operates by itself, without knowledge in the computer of what else its operands may be used for.

Consider a third example. The contents of 20 cards are to be read into the computer and stored backward in a block from locations TABLE to TABLE+1599. That is, the first card is to be stored at locations TABLE+1520 to TABLE+1599, with the characters from the card columns stored in normal order: column 1 at TABLE+1520, column 2 at TABLE+1521, . . . , column 80 at TABLE+1599. The second card read is to be stored at locations TABLE+1440 to TABLE+1519, etc. The last card is to be stored at locations TABLE to TABLE+79. We use a register as an index in the area address in the XREAD ASSIST instruction. The contents of the register used as index must decrease in steps of 80; and the last time used, it must contain 0. The BXH instruction, with suitable register contents, can handle looping control by testing the contents of the register used as index.

The program segment to perform this task is shown in Fig. 8.13. Looping control is prepared by initialization of register 8 to 1520 and register 9 to a number that turns out to be usable as *both* increment and limit: −80. In successive repetitions of XREAD, the effective addresses, generated as the sum of the address TABLE and the contents of register 8, are

TABLE+1520,   TABLE+1440,   TABLE+1360,   etc.

After the card is read, the single looping control instruction

BXH   R8,R9,LOOP

completes the loop. On first execution the contents of register 8 is reduced to 1440, and because it is higher than −80, the branch back to LOOP closes the loop. Similarly, the second execution reduces the contents of register 8 to 1360 and branches back. Finally, after executing XREAD with register 8 containing 0 and therefore reading the 20th card into TABLE, the contents of register 8 is reduced to −80, which is *not* higher than −80, so the branch does not take place and the loop concludes.

FIGURE 8.13   Reading 20 cards into a table

```
* DO FOR INDEX = 1520 TO 0, INCR = -80
         L     R9,=F'-80'
         LA    R8,1520
* . READ CARD INTO TABLE + INDEX
LOOP     XREAD TABLE(R8),80
         BXH   R8,R9,LOOP
* ENDFOR
```

8.5   The Programming Process: A Sequential Search

Let us briefly examine the programming process. Using whatever outline or pseudo-code helps you think about the steps of your problem, you can break your program into blocks or sections. Each block or section can be broken into smaller ones until you have a rather detailed structure of your entire program, in terms of the control structures IF-THEN, IF-THEN-ELSE, WHILE, REPEAT-UNTIL, and FOR. If you have not made decisions about your information structures yet, you should do it at this point. Lay out your blocks of main storage and the data representations to be used in each. Then you are in a good position to make precise the task of each of your program blocks—what information should be in each storage area before each block of program, and what each piece of information is supposed to mean, and precisely what the program block is supposed to do and therefore what information is expected at the end of the program block.

When it comes time then to write the actual assembler language, some of the programming can be quite mechanical, but some is not. The programming of IF-THEN and IF-THEN-ELSE structures, as laid out in Chapter 7, is rather straightforward, though compound conditions (with *and* and *or*) can challenge your ingenuity. Address modification and looping offer us some range of techniques: modification of base and index registers, looping control using compare and branch instructions or the special instructions BXLE, BXH, or BCT (BCT is described in the next section). You can choose an implementation that is efficient but understandable. You will want to choose an implementation that is easily understood, so you can have a good chance of writing it correctly and an even better chance of fixing it easily if your first effort turns out to contain a bug. Often you will find it convenient to design the body of the loop first, then the adjustment step and test for exit, and finally the initialization of the loop.

You may also find that after a program segment containing two or more control structures has been written from the pseudo-code, you can find ways to simplify and streamline the segment.

Let us take an example. Suppose we have an area TABLE containing 20 records of 80 bytes each. The first word in each record is an identification number for the record. The next 12 bytes contain a description. At a location named SRCHKEY we have an identification number, presumably matching one of the 20 in the table. We want to search the table for the record whose identification number matches the number at SRCHKEY, and put the description from the record found at PRTAREA+18. If no matching identification number is found, put spaces at PRTAREA+18. This is a very ordinary kind of search problem. It is very similar to the problem of searching a linked list (Section 7.8), but this problem requires address modification techniques not necessary there. Figure 8.14 shows a program segment for the task. In fact the logic of the search, as shown in the pseudo-code, is almost identical to that in Fig. 7.13, which searches the linked list. The segment follows the pseudo-code faithfully. Figure 8.15 is a revision that does away with the use of register 3 as a FOUND switch and instead uses the comparison of identification numbers directly to branch to SRCHFOUN.

FIGURE 8.14   Searching 20 records for a search key

```
*** INITIALIZE
          SR      R10,R10        INDEX = 0
          SR      R3,R3          FOUND SWITCH = 0 (NOT FOUND)
          L       R4,SRCHKEY     KEEP KEY IN REG R4 FOR COMPARISONS
* WHILE INDEX <= 1600 AND NOT FOUND DO
SRCHLOOP  C       R10,=F'1600'
          BH      SRCH2
          LTR     R3,R3
          BNZ     SRCH2
* . IF DATA ITEM IN RECORD = SRCHKEY
          C       R4,TABLE(R10)
          BNE     SRCHLPA
* . . THEN SET SWITCH TO FOUND
          LA      R3,1
          B       SRCHLOOP
* . . ELSE GO TO NEXT RECORD
SRCHLPA   LA      R10,80(,R10)
          B       SRCHLOOP
* . ENDIF
* ENDWHILE (INDEX <= 1600 AND NOT FOUND)
* IF FOUND
SRCH2     LTR     R3,R3
          BZ      SRCH2ELS
* . THEN PUT DESCRIPTION FROM RECORD INTO PRINT AREA
          LA      R5,TABLE+4(R10)
          MVC     PRTAREA+18(12),0(R5)
          B       NEXTSTEP
* . ELSE PUT SPACES IN PRINT AREA
SRCH2ELS  MVC     PRTAREA+18(12),=CL12' '
* ENDIF
NEXTSTEP  DS      0H
```

The segment is reduced from 19 instructions to 12, and the loop itself is shortened from 10 instructions to 6. We preserve the pseudo-code to help the readability of the segment.

Is this kind of change worth making? Saving a few microseconds of computer time is generally not worth the effort that novice programmers delight in, especially if it results in programs that are harder to correct and maintain. In some situations, especially where instructions in a loop are to be executed very many times, shortening is worthwhile. Searching is such a common activity that it is worthwhile to adopt the structure of Fig. 8.15 as a chunk and use it essentially as a structure in its own right.

8.6   The BCT and BCTR Instructions

The BCT and BCTR instructions, Branch on CounT and Branch on CounT to Register, are special looping control instructions that are easier to use than BXLE and BXH but are less flexible and less generally applicable.

FIGURE 8.15 A shortened search segment

```
*** INITIALIZE
        SR    R10,R10
        L     R4,SRCHKEY
* WHILE INDEX <= 1600 AND NOT FOUND DO
SRCHLOOP C    R10,=F'1600'
        BH    SRCHNOTF
* . IF DATA ITEM IN RECORD NOT = SRCHKEY
        C     R4,TABLE(R10)
        BE    SRCHFOUN       *SEARCH SUCCESSFUL
* . . THEN GO TO NEXT RECORD
        LA    R10,80(,R10)
        B     SRCHLOOP
* . ENDIF
* ENDWHILE (INDEX <= 1600 AND NOT FOUND)
* IF FOUND (BRANCH FROM WHILE LOOP)
* . THEN PUT DESCRIPTION FROM RECORD INTO PRINT AREA
SRCHFOUN LA   R5,TABLE+4(R10)
        MVC   PRTAREA+18(12),0(R5)
        B     NEXTSTEP
* . ELSE PUT SPACES IN PRINT AREA
SRCHNOTF MVC  PRTAREA+18(12),=CL12' '
* ENDIF
NEXTSTEP DS   0H
```

The BCT and BCTR instructions are of RX and RR type, respectively. The second operand of each instruction defines a branch address: the second operand of the BCT instruction is the sum of *D2* and contents of registers *X2* and *B2*. If the second operand *(R2)* of the BCTR instruction is zero, no branching will occur, regardless; otherwise, a branch if taken will be to the address given in register *R2*.

The first event in the execution of BCT or BCTR is that the contents of register *R1* is decreased by 1. Then the branch occurs if the result in register *R1* is not zero. A result either greater or less than zero will cause a branch; only in case the result is exactly zero will there not be a branch. The condition code is not affected by either the BCT or BCTR instruction.

The action of the BCT and BCTR instructions can be described formally as

$$\text{BCT} \quad R1,S2\text{:} \quad R1 \leftarrow c(R1) - 1;$$
$$\rightarrow S2 \text{ if } c(R1) \neq 0$$
$$\text{BCTR} \quad R1,R2\text{:} \quad R1 \leftarrow c(R1) - 1;$$
$$\rightarrow c(R2) \quad \text{if} \quad \begin{cases} c(R1) \neq 0 \text{ and} \\ R2 \neq 0. \end{cases}$$

Thus the BCT instruction is similar to the BXH and BXLE instructions. Register *R1* is incremented, but by a constant -1 instead of the contents of an operand register; it is compared to a limit, but a constant limit 0 instead of the contents of an operand register. Branching takes place or not as a result of the comparison, but on a criterion of not equal.

As examples, let us detail the effects of the following instructions.

1. Suppose that register 6 contains ØØØØØØF4. The instruction

```
          BCT   R6,BRCHAA
```

will reduce the contents of register 6 to ØØØØØØF3, and because this result is not zero, control will branch to BRCHAA.

2. Suppose that register 7 contains FFFFFFEA and register 10 contains ØØØØA344. The instruction

```
          BCTR  R7,R1Ø
```

will reduce the contents of register 7 to FFFFFFE9, and because the result is not zero, control will branch to ØØA344.

3. Suppose register 3 contains ØØØØØØØ1. The instruction

```
          BCT   R3,LOOP
```

causes the contents of register 3 to be reduced to ØØØØØØØØ; because the result is zero, no branch takes place.

The BCT instruction is most often used when the branching control needed is a simple count of the number of times the loop should still be executed. The structure is

```
          L       REG1,LIMIT
LOOP              BODY OF LOOP
          ⋮
          BCT     REG1,LOOP
```

The number of repetitions desired is entered into a register as part of the initialization step. The BCT instruction at the end of the loop decreases the contents of that register by 1 every time it is executed, in effect making the register keep the number of times the loop is yet to be executed. Until the number reaches zero, there are still more repetitions desired; the BCT instruction causes

FIGURE 8.16   Read 20 cards, using a BCT instruction

```
*** INITIALIZE
          SR      R8,R8           SUM = 0
          LA      R9,20           CARDS YET TO READ = 20
* FOR COUNT = 20 TO 0, INCR = -1, DO
* . READ A CARD
LOOP      XREAD   CARDIN,80
* . CONVERT A NUMBER AND ADD TO SUM
          XDECI   R7,CARDIN
          AR      R8,R7
          BCT     R9,LOOP
* ENDFOR
```

a branch back to LOOP. The register is reduced to zero immediately after the last desired repetition of the loop body; the BCT instruction does *not* cause a branch, and control exits from the loop.

As an example program segment, consider the problem of reading exactly 20 records and forming a sum by taking the first number from each of the 20 records. No address modification is required; we need only a looping structure that repeats the body of a loop 20 times. The program segment for this problem is in Fig. 8.16. The BCT instruction essentially takes the place of an instruction that reduces the count by 1, another that compares the resulting count, and one that branches back. We can write loops simply and reliably using BCT.

8.7 Ordered Lists and Binary Search

In Section 7.8 and again in Section 8.5 we examined some sequential search procedures. In this section we shall consider more deeply the subject of list organization, and finally a procedure called *binary search* will be presented that is quite efficient in some search situations.

A list is made up of data items that we may call *records*. Records may all be of some fixed size or of different sizes. Usually, if records have varying lengths, a list of pointers is created, each record of which is of fixed size and serves mostly to point to the locations of the variable-length records. So we will restrict our attention in the following discussion to lists of fixed-length records.

Each record in the list is identified with a *key*; the key is a data item in the record. To obtain information from a record, we use a data item called a *search key*, which bears some relation to the key of a record in the list; the search problem is that of finding the record with the right key. The data item is said to "bear some relation" to the key in the right record; the relationship could be any simple or complex relationship that can be tested for by program. We shall restrict our attention to matching the data item with the key because no conceptual problems of the search attend other relationships.

Assuming that consecutive keys are stored in locations whose addresses differ by some constant amount, we can search for the key associated with the record we desire. We also assume that the record is located in constant relation to the key, so that once the key is found, we can easily calculate the address of the information in the desired record from the address of the key.

Let us describe two lists for illustrative purposes. First is the functional table of chemical elements shown in Fig. 8.17. The atomic numbers, which we would normally call the arguments in the table, are the keys in the list. The arrangement in the computer might be that all the keys are stored in consecutive words beginning at ATOMNO and all the atomic weights are stored (in packed decimal or floating-point form) in consecutive words starting at ATOMWT. If the address of a particular atomic number (key) is generated in, say, register 6, the address of the corresponding atomic weight can be derived simply by

```
        A    R6,=A(ATOMWT-ATOMNO)
```

FIGURE 8.17   Atomic numbers and weights of chemical elements

Atomic number	Atomic weight
1	1.008
2	4.003
3	6.940
4	9.013
5	10.820
6	12.011
7	14.008
8	16.000
9	19.000
10	20.183
18	39.944
36	83.8
54	131.3
86	222.

A second example of a list is a payroll information file, in which the information on each employee is held in an 80-byte record. Each employee may have an employee number, which can act as key to the list. The employee number may be stored in the 80-character record, as perhaps the first word. The records may be stored in consecutive 80-byte blocks of storage. A search for the employee with some particular employee number could be as shown in Fig. 8.14 or Fig. 8.15. For example, suppose that the employee number is in the first four bytes of the record and the year's earnings to date is stored in the 9th through 12th bytes. Once the address of the employee number of the desired employee is found through a search, the address of his year's earnings to date can be derived by adding 8 to the address of the employee number.

LIST DENSITY
We shall suppose that consecutive blocks are set aside in the computer's main storage for the items (keys and records) of a list. There may not be a list item in each block. If there are gaps in the storage of list items, the storage not used will usually have to contain some indicator which, by convention, is taken to mean absence of a list item. If there are gaps, we call the list *loose*. If there are no gaps, we call the list *dense*. For efficient storage, and often for efficient retrieval, a dense list is best.

We can also talk about a *key-dense* list, in which there is a common fixed increment between consecutive keys. The first 10 keys in the list of chemical elements given in Fig. 8.17 are consecutive integers; therefore this portion of the list is key-dense. The entire list as given is not key-dense, because the 11th to 14th keys do not follow the same pattern of consecutive integers.

For retrieval of information from a key-dense list it is not necessary to search for a key. The address of the desired key can be *calculated* from the key itself. Therefore in the following discussions about searches, we shall assume a list which is dense (sometimes called *item-dense* for extra clarity) but not key-dense.

ORDERED LISTS

If the keys of consecutive records are in some order, either ascending or descending, the list is said to be *ordered*. A key-dense list is a special case of an ordered list. If the list is not ordered, there is, in general, no search strategy that is more efficient than the *sequential search* (search of consecutive records) illustrated earlier in the chapter. On the average, we would expect to search half the list before finding the desired record. If the list is ordered, we can still use sequential search, with the same expectation of a search of half the list before finding the desired item. With an ordered list, however, a different strategy called *binary search* is more efficient.

BINARY SEARCH

In a binary search of an ordered list, the principal idea is that each comparison of a data item against a key is made on the key in the middle of the segment of the list to which the desired record might belong. The result of a comparison is either that the desired record is found or that one of the two pieces is rejected as not containing the desired record. Thus with each comparison the segment remaining to be searched is cut in half.

To describe the binary search procedure in more detail, let us adopt some notation. Let L be the ordered list to be searched for a search key x. Let the length of the list L be $N + 1$ items, and the keys be denoted by $L_0, L_1, \ldots, L_N$. We can denote largest integer not greater than a quantity q by int(q): int(16.5) = 16, int(17) = 17, and so forth. Figure 8.18 describes the search strategy in pure pseudo-code form. The pseudo-code follows the general strategy of Fig. 8.14, the sequential search. The differences are consideration of

FIGURE 8.18   Pseudo-code for binary search

```
Set i = 0
    k = N
    found = false
WHILE i ≤ k and not found DO
    j = int((i + k)/2)
    IF Lj = x
      THEN found = true
      ELSE IF Lj < x
              THEN k = j − 1
              ELSE i  = j + 1
```

which list element to look at next, and the criterion for search failure. The variables i and k always define the bounds of the list segment in which the desired record must lie (if in fact it is in the list at all). The variable j defines the midpoint of the segment; after the comparison of L_j and x, the list segment remaining to be searched is cut in half by a revision of one of its limits. As long as there remains a segment to search, the loop continues. If i becomes bigger than k, *no* segment remains to be searched; the search has failed.

Figure 8.19 shows a program segment that implements a binary search. The segment uses the streamlining adopted in Fig. 8.15, and otherwise follows the pseudo-code of Fig. 8.18. The variables i, j, and k (in registers 4, 5, and 7) change during the loop. These control the ultimate exit from the loop and the

FIGURE 8.19   A binary search, implementing the pseudo-code of Fig. 8.18

```
*** INITIALIZE
          SR      R4,R4            I = 0 (LOWER BOUND)
          L       R5,N             K = N (UPPER BOUND)
********************************************************************
***     M CONTAINS LENGTH OF EACH RECORD (CONSTANT)
***     TABLE IS ADDRESS OF FIRST RECORD
***     THERE ARE N + 1 RECORDS IN THE TABLE
***     REGISTER R2 CONTAINS SEARCH KEY
********************************************************************
* WHILE I <= K AND NOT FOUND DO
SRCHLOOP  CR      R4,R5
          BH      SRCHNOTF
* . FIND MIDDLE RECORD
          LA      R7,0(R4,R5)     I + K
          D       R6,=F'2'        J = MIDDLE (REG R7)
          LR      R3,R7           SAVE J
          M       R6,M            J * M = DISPLACEMENT FROM TABLE
* . IF DATA ITEM IN RECORD NOT = SEARCHKEY
          C       R2,TABLE(R7)
          BE      SRCHFOUN        SEARCH SUCCESSFUL
* . . THEN GO TO NEXT RECORD..
* . . IF DATA ITEM (J) < SEARCH KEY
          BNL     SRCHLPEL
* . . . THEN K = J - 1 (ELIMINATE CURRENT TOP HALF)
          S       R3,=F'1'
          LR      R5,R3
          B       SRCHLOOP
* . . . ELSE I = J + 1 (ELIMINATE CURRENT BOTTOM HALF)
SRCHLPEL  LA      R4,1(,R3)
          B       SRCHLOOP
* . . ENDIF (DATA ITEM(J) < SEARCH KEY)
* . ENDIF (DATA ITEM IN RECORD NOT = SEARCH KEY)
* ENDWHILE (I <= K AND NOT FOUND)
* IF FOUND
* . THEN ...
SRCHFOUN  ...
          B       NEXTSTEP
* . ELSE ...
SRCHNOTF  ...
* ENDIF (FOUND)
```

address calculations within the loop. The address of the jth key is $j \cdot m$ greater than the address of the first (actually, zeroth) key.

Let us illustrate execution of a binary search with the table of atomic numbers and weights, Fig. 8.17. Suppose each record is eight bytes ($m = 8$): the four-byte atomic number followed by the four-byte atomic weight. The records are stored starting at location Ø09840 (TABLE). There are 14 records in the table, so $N = 13$. Suppose the search key happens to be 10. In the initialization phase, $i = 0$, $k = 13$. In the first execution of the loop, $j = 6$, and $j \cdot m = 48$ or hexadecimal 00000030. The search key, 10, is compared with the key at location Ø09840+Ø00030=Ø09870; the key at that location is 7, so the search key is larger, and i is set to $j + 1 = 7$. The list segment containing (possibly) the search key is now known to contain records 7 through 13. The second time through the loop, $j = 10$, $j \cdot m = $ hexadecimal 00000050, and the comparison of the search key with the key(18) at location Ø09890 shows the search key smaller. This time k is set to 9, and we loop again. In the third execution of the loop, $j = 8$, and the key 9 is found to be too small, so i is set to $j + 1 = 9$. The remaining list segment now consists of only one record. In the fourth execution, that record is found to be the correct one.

Because the segment remaining to be searched is approximately halved during each execution of the loop, the loop must be executed approximately $\log_2 N$ times. This number is close to the *expected and maximum* numbers of iterations required. For example, if the list contains 256 items, eight executions of the loop will suffice. This compares to an expected number of 128 executions of a sequential search loop and shows the binary-search technique to be more efficient. Each execution of the body in a binary-search loop takes longer than an execution of the sequential-search loop, so the binary search is more efficient only for lists of perhaps 16 items or more. You might like to try to calculate a more precise estimate of the break-even point.

m a i n   i d e a s

□ The general loop structure includes initialization before the loop, and a body, adjustment step, and test for exit inside the loop.

□ When a list of data items is used in a loop, the effective addresses of the items can be conveniently modified in the adjustment step of the loop by incrementing a register used as base or index in addressing the data items. A register used as index can serve as modifier for several lists at once.

□ The test for exit may be made on the register used in modifying effective addresses. The BXH, BXLE, and BCT instructions are specially designed for looping control; they can perform adjustment and test for exit in one instruction.

□ When a list of records is searched for the record with a certain key, and the list is ordered (by key), a binary search can be much more efficient than a sequential search.

■ **P R O B L E M S** ` F O R    R E V I E W    A N D    I M A G I N A T I O N `

8.1 Suppose that we have a list of numbers $A_0, A_1, \ldots, A_{19}$ in consecutive full words of main storage starting at AA. We wish to compute $B_0, B_1, \ldots, B_{18}$, as $B_i = A_i - A_{i+1}(i = 0, 1, \ldots, 18)$ and to store the results in consecutive full words starting at location BB. The body of the loop is the sequence

```
        L     R5,AA(R3)
        S     R5,AA+4(R3)
        ST    R5,BB(R3)
```

Design the adjustment step and the test for exit to follow the body, and determine the initialization necessary to complete a segment to do the problem. Try to do the problem twice, once using, and once not using, the BXLE instruction. Be sure to include remarks statements showing your control structure in pseudo-code.

8.2 Suppose that in evaluation of a polynomial by Horner's method we try to keep the intermediate sums. The initialization step (in Fig. 8.3)

$$Sum = A_0$$

would be replaced by

$$B_0 = A_0$$

and the step in the loop

$$Sum = Sum \cdot X + A_i$$

replaced by

$$B_{i+1} = B_i \cdot X + A_i.$$

The procedure, as modified, is known as *synthetic division*, and it is used in a change of variable, computation of the derivative, and other mathematical operations. Modify Fig. 8.6 or 8.12 so that the coefficients B_i are stored at consecutive full-word locations starting at BB. You may want to revise your segment to use an index register.

8.3 Examine and simulate the following program segment that is designed to store 80-byte blank areas in a block of main storage. From where to where in main storage are blanks actually stored by execution of this segment? How would you describe the control structure in pseudo-code?

```
              LA    R7,PRTAREA
              LA    R8,80
              LA    R9,PRTAREA+1920
LOOP          MVC   0(80,R7),BLANKS
              BXLE  R7,R8,LOOP
              ⋮
BLANKS        DC    CL80'   '
```

Note that a register cannot be used as an index in this problem because MVC is not an RX-type instruction.

8.4 The following segment is designed to store copies of the contents of register 4 in a block of consecutive words in main storage. Assume that C is located on a full-word boundary. Will the store instruction always have a second operand address that is a full-word boundary? If so, how many times will the store instruction be executed? In exactly what block of main storage is the contents of register 4 stored?

```
              LA    R7,48
       LOOP   ST    R4,C(R7)
              S     R7,=F'3'
              BCT   R7,LOOP
```

8.5 The following segment is intended to add the ten full-word numbers starting at location BB, and to store the sum at SUM. The effective address of the second operand of the add instruction is modified by the process of modification of the displacement in the instruction. Make suitable assumptions, then simulate execution of the segment. *Beware*: The half-word at location LP+2 is used as part of an instruction, but it is also composed of numbers in main storage, so it can be, and is, changed by execution of the program. What are the contents of the half-word at LP+2 when the program segment is completed? Is the initialization complete; that is, if the segment were entered a second time, would it form the sum of the numbers in the same ten locations? If not, how can you complete the initialization?

```
              SR    R6,R6
              LA    R8,1Ø
       LP     A     R6,BB
              LH    R5,LP+2
              LA    R5,4(,R5)
              STH   R5,LP+2
              BCT   R8,LP
              ST    R6,SUM
```

8.6 Suppose that we have a list of 29 numbers stored in consecutive full words starting at FF, and that we wish to store the list *in reverse order* in consecutive full words starting at BB. Each of the following segments can perform correctly the body, adjustment step, and test for exit of this problem. Supply the proper initialization for each segment to make each segment work.

```
   a)         LOOP   L     R3,Ø(R6)
                     ST    R3,Ø(R7)
                     S     R6,=F'4'
                     BXLE  R7,R8,LOOP
```

```
b)                          LOOP     L      R3,FF(R8)
                                     ST     R3,BB(R9)
                                     LA     R8,4(,R8)
                                     BXH    R9,R7,LOOP
```

8.7   There is a list of 17 consecutive full words in main storage, starting at
      location GG. Every word in the list whose contents is 4 should be
      replaced by a zero. Write first a pseudo-code control structure. Then
      write a program segment to accomplish the task, following the logic of
      your pseudo-code.

8.8   There is a list of 17 consecutive full words in main storage, starting at
      location GG. Write pseudo-code and program segment for the task of
      finding the address of the largest number in the list. If there are ties,
      take the first of the equal numbers.

8.9   Adapt one of the program segments for evaluation of a polynomial by
      Horner's method into a subroutine. Have as parameters the address of
      the beginning of the coefficient list, the order N of the polynomial, and
      the value X at which the polynomial is to be evaluated. The output, the
      value of the polynomial, should be left in register 0.

8.10 Adapt one of the program segments in Fig. 8.9, 8.10, or 8.11 to form
      $C_i = A_i + B_i$ for a list of indefinite length, the length (in words) being
      stored at location N.

8.11 Try to make some general statements concerning the exact proper situ-
      ation under which to use a BXLE instruction, a BXH instruction, or a BCT
      instruction, and cite the exact initialization steps (instructions and
      operands) that must be written in preparation.

8.12 The loop in Fig. 8.15 can still be shortened by one instruction. Find a
      way.

8.13 Figure 7.10 shows a loop that reads records until the data set is
      exhausted. Figure 8.16 shows a segment that attempts to read exactly
      20 records. What would you expect to happen in Fig. 8.16 if there were
      only 17 records in the data set? Modify the segment and its pseudo-
      code so it will read up to 20 cards but not attempt to read any more
      when the data set is exhausted and will not try to convert and add any
      numbers that are not there.

8.14 Make the program segment shown in Fig. 8.15 into a subroutine. Have
      as parameters the address of the first record in the list, the length of
      each record, the number of records in the list, and the search key. Out-
      put should be the address of the key found, or 0 if the search ends in
      failure; the output should be left in register 0. Do the same with Fig.
      8.19.

8.15 Using the subroutine constructed in Problem 8.14 from Fig. 8.19, write
      a program segment for the following problem.

A student information record is 80 bytes long, and there are NN records in the list at the moment. The list is stored as consecutive 80-byte records starting at STUDINF. In the record the first word contains a student number, and the fifth word contains the total number of credits the student has earned. The list is ordered, and the student number is the key.

A particular student, whose student number is stored at CURRNO, has earned additional credits in transfer work; the number of additional credits is stored in CREDUP. Update the student's record by adding the additional credits to her total. Remember that the output from the subroutine is an address in register 0, but register 0 cannot be used directly in addressing main storage.

8.16 One way to store and access a table in main storage is to define a vector (list) of addresses that point to rows of the table. (Assume that the table is stored row-wise—that is, all entries of the first row, then all of the second row, etc.) Declare storage for a table of ten rows, each row containing ten full words. Also create a vector of addresses, starting at a location called ROW, which point to the rows of the table. Show how the vector addresses help in accessing
   a) all entries in a given row in succession,
   b) all entries in a given column in succession,
   c) a single entry, given row and column indexes.

8.17 If a subroutine may have a variable number of parameters, the last word in the parameter address block contains 1 as its highest-order bit (Problem 7.21). Write a subroutine that will find the largest number among its parameters. The subroutine may have one or more parameters and should return the largest number in register 0. Your subroutine is essentially the *max* function often found in subroutine libraries.

■ **R E F E R E N C E S** ▬▬▬▬▬▬▬▬▬▬▬▬▬▬▬▬▬▬▬▬▬

IBM System/370 Principles of Operation, GA 22-7000, IBM Corporation. Reference on the looping control instructions.

Knuth, Donald E., *The Art of Computer Programming, Vol. 3: Sorting and Searching*, Addison-Wesley, Reading, Mass., 1973. Chapter 6 is a detailed discussion of search techniques over various data structures, including ordered lists.

Price, C.D., "Table Lookup Techniques," *Computing Surveys* 3, 2 (June 1971), pp. 49–65. A tutorial article on search techniques.

The references on structured programming at the end of Chapter 7 apply to this chapter too.

DEBUGGING

Writing correct programs is always a goal of programmers. Yet even with the best efforts, programs inevitably contain errors. What happens in case of error, how to diagnose errors, and how to try to prevent errors in the first place are the subjects of this chapter. First we shall explore what happens when we break the rules for use of individual instructions—the interrupts, error messages, and dumps we get. You will learn how to read the messages and dumps and pinpoint the actual errors. You will also learn what advance preparation you can make for debugging, and the partial dumps and other information you can get to help you track down the errors. Also explored in this chapter are the interactive debugging environment and the possibilities it presents for monitoring *and controlling* the progress of a program. Finally, the programming process and its relationship to the quality of programs produced are discussed.

9.1 Exceptions and Interrupts

When instructions were introduced and described in earlier chapters, restrictions on the operands were given—restrictions like proper boundaries, coding of signs in a CVB instruction, and so on. You may have wondered what would happen if the restrictions were not met. Breaking one of the rules is what is called an *exception,* and the usual effect is an interruption of the program. The program can be designed to control whether or not some exception conditions cause interrupts, but most of the interrupts are automatic.

As was mentioned in Chapter 1, the effect of an interrupt is that execution of the current program is suspended. The entire program status word is stored at a special main storage location. A new program status word is loaded from a fixed location in the portion of storage controlled by the supervisor, and this starts execution of the appropriate interrupt-handling routine. It is possible for the user's program, working through the supervisor, to send control to a user-written interrupt routine for any particular kind of interrupt. For program exceptions, however, the usual action is the supervisor's default option of terminating the program and the job step, outputting diagnostic information as directed. We will examine later in this chapter the various kinds of diagnostic information that can be obtained, and when and how to call for and get information from it.

Let us now consider some of the exceptions that might be encountered.

INTERRUPTION CODE 1: OPERATION

The operation code in the instruction currently being executed is illegal. That is, there does not exist any such operation, at least not on that particular model of computer. The operation is suppressed before interrupt.

INTERRUPTION CODE 2: PRIVILEGED OPERATION

The operation code is of an existing operation, but one that can be executed only in the supervisor mode. Such an operation is called *privileged*; if execution of a privileged operation is attempted while in the problem (opposite of supervisor) state, this kind of interrupt occurs. The operation is suppressed. Privileged operations are mainly those that change the more sensitive parts of the program status word or control registers, or directly affect input or output operations. None of the operations introduced thus far is privileged.

INTERRUPTION CODE 4: PROTECTION

There is a four-bit storage key associated with each 2048-byte block of main storage. Many blocks may have the same key; the keys are stored in a special area that is inaccessible to a program operating in the problem state. The keys designate which areas of main storage are to be available to a program. Four bits of the program status word contain a protection code that is matched with the storage key for a main storage location that the program is attempting to access. When the protection code and storage key match or when the protection code is zero (used by the supervisor) the access is allowed. A mismatch is a protection exception.

In some IBM System/370 models, there is no storage protection; any part of main storage may be used in any way without generating a protection exception. In some, protection is furnished for store operands only: the storage and protection key comparisons are invoked only on instructions that store results into main storage. Of the instructions we have studied, the following could generate protection exceptions:

CVD ConVert to Decimal (first operand)

MVI MoVe Immediate

MVC MoVe Character (first operand)

PACK PACK (first operand)

ST   STore

STH STore Half-word

STM STore Multiple

UNPK UNPacK (first operand)

In still other models of System/360 and 370 (including all of the newer models) protection is furnished on the store operations noted above and also on *fetches,* instructions that use information from main storage. Fetching an instruction outside your main storage area is also recognized as a fetch protection violation.

If a protection exception is generated by the first reference to main storage used by the instruction, the operation is suppressed. But sometimes some of the operation is carried out—for example, movement of several characters by an MVC instruction—before an address is generated that causes a protection key mismatch. In such cases the operation is terminated as soon as the violation is sensed.

For example, if a program is running with a protection code in the program status word of (binary) 0001, it has access to all blocks of storage whose storage key is 0001. When the program attempts to store information in a block whose storage key is 0010, an interrupt occurs. The storage keys are set by the supervisor before the program begins execution.

INTERRUPTION CODE 5: ADDRESSING

If an address of a specified instruction or data (to store or fetch) is outside the limits of available storage on the particular computer, an addressing exception is generated. The operation is terminated before interrupt. Any instruction that accesses main storage in any way can generate an addressing exception.

In a virtual-storage System/370, the protection and addressing exceptions result from faults discovered in the *real* main storage addresses, not the virtual addresses. The virtual address and dynamic address translation system will be studied in more detail in Chapter 17.

INTERRUPTION CODE 6: SPECIFICATION

A specification exception occurs when there is something wrong with the way in which an operand is specified in an instruction. (When something is wrong with an operand itself, other exceptions result.)

There are some instructions that require a register operand address to be even. Those we have encountered are

D   Divide

DR   Divide Register (first operand)

M   Multiply

MR   Multiply Register (first operand)

If a first operand address is odd in any of these instructions, a specification exception results.

Floating-point register addresses are 0, 2, 4, 6; floating-point register operand addresses 1, 3, 5, or 7 through 15 will cause specification exceptions.

If the *byte-oriented-operand* feature is installed, the system allows main storage operands of nonprivileged instructions to begin at any address, not necessarily at half-word, full-word, or double-word boundaries. This cuts down the conditions that cause specification exceptions. We continue to recommend alignment, however, not only for systems that require it but because instruction execution using nonaligned operands is somewhat slowed by use of the byte-oriented-operand feature.

In computers that do not have the byte-oriented-operand feature, specification exceptions are generated by main storage operand addresses that do not conform to required boundary alignment. Some instructions require half-word alignment, some full-word alignment, and some double-word alignment. All of these instructions are of RX or RS type; the ones we have seen are

A	Add	full word
AH	Add Half-word	half-word
C	Compare	full word
CH	Compare Half-word	half-word
CVB	ConVert to Binary	double word
CVD	ConVert to Decimal	double word
D	Divide	full word
L	Load	full word
LH	Load Half-word	half-word
LM	Load Multiple	full word
M	Multiply	full word
MH	Multiply Half-word	half-word
ST	STore	full word
STH	STore Half-word	half-word
STM	STore Multiple	full word
S	Subtract	full word
SH	Subtract Half-word	half-word

For example, if a program attempts to execute an LH instruction whose second operand address (as defined by base, index, and displacement) is Ø09340, the operand specification is legal (Ø09340 is a half-word, full-word, and double-word boundary), but an operand address of Ø09341 is illegal and will cause a specification exception.

A branch instruction may also generate a specification exception by attempting to branch to an odd address. All instructions must begin on even half-words, even where the byte-oriented-operand feature is installed.

INTERRUPTION CODE 7: DATA
The ConVert to Binary (CVB) instruction assumes that the operand is in the packed decimal format. If the codes in the operand are not the expected valid digit and sign codes, a data exception results. The instruction is terminated after an invalid code is discovered. The data exception can also result from other instructions having to do with packed decimal data, as you will learn in Chapter 14.

INTERRUPTION CODE 8: FIXED-POINT OVERFLOW
A fixed-point overflow results from the binary integer load, add, and subtract instructions when they yield results too large to be expressed in 32 bits in the 2's complement form. These instructions are

A	Add
AH	Add Half-word
AR	Add Register
LCR	Load Complement Register
LPR	Load Positive Register
S	Subtract
SH	Subtract Half-word
SR	Subtract Register

A fixed-point overflow by these instructions sets the condition code to 3, as we learned in Chapter 7. The overflow is also recognized as a fixed-point overflow exception. A fixed-point overflow exception may cause an interrupt. The option can be controlled by the program itself; if the first bit (bit 0) of the *program mask* in the program status word is 1, a fixed-point overflow exception causes an interrupt, but if that bit of the PSW is 0, a fixed-point overflow exception does not cause an interrupt.

The *program mask* is one of the fields of the program status word. The bits of the program mask enable *masking* (controlling) of the interrupts resulting from 4 of the 15 different causes. We shall learn in Chapter 17 how the program may change the program mask; it is one of the few pieces of the program status word that can be accessed and changed by a program in the problem state.

In the case of a fixed-point overflow interruption, the operation is completed, and the result left in the register is too large or too small by 2^{32}.

INTERRUPTION CODE 9: FIXED-POINT DIVIDE

A fixed-point divide exception can result from either of two conditions. First is binary integer division by zero or the development of a quotient too large to be expressed in 32 bits in the 2's complement form. Either D (Divide) or DR (Divide Register) can produce these results. The second condition leading to a fixed-point divide interruption is that the result of a CVB (ConVert to Binary) instruction is too large to be expressed in 32 bits in the 2's complement form.

Division is suppressed if a fixed-point divide exception arises; a CVB instruction is completed, but the portion of the result that would fall outside the register is ignored. Interruption of the program is automatic in either case.

OTHER INTERRUPTION CODES

Other conditions also cause interrupts. Interrupts that result directly from attempts at invalid program execution are called *program* or *program-check interrupts*; they are identified by codes, eight of which have already been described. Seven more result from execution of the instructions shown in Fig. 9.1. Each of these will be explained when the instructions producing it are discussed. Decimal overflow, exponent underflow, and significance are the three conditions besides fixed-point overflow that can be (independently) masked on or off by the program mask.

Besides program-check interrupts, there are four other classes of interrupts. *Input and output* conditions can cause interrupts, as will be described in Chapter 17. There are *ex-*

FIGURE 9.1 Additional interruption codes

Code number	Code name	Causes
3	Execute	Invalid use of the EXECUTE instruction.
10	Decimal overflow	Overflow in addition or subtraction of packed decimal numbers.
11	Decimal divide	Quotient in a packed decimal division is too large.
12	Exponent overflow	The result of a floating-point operation is 16^{64} or greater.
13	Exponent underflow	The result of a floating-point operation is smaller than 16^{-64}.
14	Significance	The result of a floating-point operation is an all-zero fraction.
15	Floating-point divide	Floating-point division by zero.

ternal interrupts, resulting from signals from external lines or the console interrupt key or from overflow of the interval timer. *Supervisor call* interrupts take place when a program executes the SVC (SuperVisor Call) instruction to request some action by the supervisor. *Machine check* interrupts occur when the computer discovers that some part of its circuitry has failed. The interrupt system as a whole will be discussed more thoroughly in Chapter 17.

9.2   Indicative Dumps

You may furnish your own routine to handle various kinds of interrupts; the supervisor gives control to this routine if and when the appropriate kind of interrupt occurs. Usually, however, you do not supply any interrupt-handling routines, and in case of a program check interrupt, the supervisor terminates the job step. As the job step is terminated, an *indicative dump* is printed, with information about the program and the cause of the interrupt.

The indicative dump is of variable length, but is usually about 8–12 printed lines long. As a programmer you should learn to read indicative dumps and deduce most of your errors from them. The completion code, on the first line, is a code furnished by the operating system to designate the reason for termination of the step. Completion codes and their meanings are listed in the IBM manuals *OS/VS Message Library: VS1 System Codes,* GC 38-1003; *OS/VS1Debugging Guide,* GC 24-5093, *OS/VS2 Debugging Guide,* GC 28-0632, and various other OS/VS system manuals. In case of program-check interruption, the first two digits of the completion code are 0C, and the third is (in hexadecimal) the interrupt code number: 1 for operation, 6 for specification, and so on. If your completion code begins with 0C, you can use the rest of the indicative dump, and we will explore how. Otherwise, the explanations in the manuals will tell you what kind of supervisor service or input/output operation the system was trying to perform for you and give some explanation of why the task could not be done; these explanations should give you enough of a clue so that you can fix job control, parameters to input/output requests, and so on. If these are not sufficient, you will need to rerun the job, getting a more extensive dump of some kind. (The more extensive dumps are discussed later in the chapter.)

If your program had a program-check interrupt (0Cx), the ACTIVE RBS can be useful to you. An RB is a request block; each supervisor service is represented by a request block. Initiation of your program creates the first RB, and its most important component is the USE/EP, which is the entry point of your program. When your program caused the program-check interrupt, a second RB was created; what is important in this one is the register contents, the contents *at the point of interruption.* Because the second line of the dump tells the interrupt address, you have some real information about what your program was doing. Actually, the instruction that caused the interrupt is usually the one just before the interrupt address given.

FIGURE 9.2 A program and its indicative dump

```
COMPLETION CODE - SYSTEM=0C1  USER=0000

INTERRUPT AT 330010

FL.PT.REGS 0-6      42.630000 00000000      4E.000000 00000002      41.200000 00000000      FB.172EBA D6DDC73C

ACTIVE RBS

PRB   42F9F0  NM GO           SZ/STAB 000400C2  USE/EP 00330000  PSW 077D1000 00330010     Q          42FB48 WT/LNK 00011278
SVRB  42F840  NM SVC-801C  SZ/STAB 0016D062  USE/EP 00AF4000  PSW 070C0000  00A998C0  C09ECE66  Q  00C273 WT/LNK 0042F9F0
              RG 0-7    00000040    0042F708      00011278      00A998C0    00033D5C  0042F780     0042F6F0    00000058
              RG 8-15   0042F560    00011278      0042F608      0042F708    50330006  00330010     00011CC0    C0330000

                                                                                                          PAGE   2

LOC     OBJECT CODE       ADDR1 ADDR2   STMT   SOURCE STATEMENT                                    ASM 0201 15.54 07/27/83
000000                                    1  EXAMPLE2 CSECT
                                          2           PRINT NOGEN
                                          3           EQUREGS
                                         20           SAVE  (14,12)
000004  05C0                             23           BALR  R12,0
                                00006    24           USING *,R12
000006  50D0 C00E             00014      25           ST    R13,SAV+4
00000A  41D0 C00A             00010      26           LA    R13,SAV
000010  1B88                             27  SAV      DS    18F
00058                                    28           SR    R8,R8       SUM = 0
                                         29  * DO FOR COUNT = 20 TO 0 INCR -1
00005A  4190 0014             00014      30           LA    R9,20
                                         31  * . READ CARD
                                         32  LOOP     XREAD CARD,80
                                         42  * . CONVERT NUMBER, ADD TO SUM
                                         43           XDECI R7,CARD
0000B8  1887                             55           LR    R8,R7
0000BA  4690 C058             0005E      56           BCT   R9,LOOP
                                         57  * ENDDO
                                         58           XDECO R8,OUTAREA+6
                                         68           XPRNT OUTAREA,60
00010E  58D0 C00E             00014      78           L     R13,SAV+4
                                         79           RETURN (14,12)
000118                                   82  CARD     DS    CL80
000168  404040E2E4D4407E                 83  OUTAREA  DC    CL61' SUM = '
000000                                   84           END   EXAMPLE2
```

The *relocation quantity* can be computed as the entry point to your program minus the relocatable entry point shown in the program listing produced by the assembler. For example, if the entry point in the first RB is 150000 and your relocatable entry point is 000000, which is common, the relocation quantity is

$$150000-000000=150000$$

The relocation quantity is added to each relocatable address in the program listing to give the corresponding actual address.

Figure 9.2 is an example of a program and the indicative dump produced by execution of the program. The program was designed to be entered at relocatable location 000000, so the entry point reported by the RB, 330000, is the relocation quantity. The error noted is an operation exception, the kind we often get if we are executing instructions where there are no instructions. By subtracting the relocation quantity from the reported interruption address of 330010, we find the offending instruction is at relocatable address 000010. We see from the program listing that this instruction is the address of our SAV area, where we do not intend to be executing instructions at all. What is there is not a valid instruction, so program execution is terminated. The error in the program is placing the SAV area directly after the instruction

```
        LA      R13,SAV
```

Either the definition of the SAV area must be moved, or else a branch instruction should be supplied to branch around the area and prevent use of the garbage left in the area as instructions.

9.3   Error Messages

Often the computer, through whatever system is in control, will discover an error before affairs degenerate to the point of invalid instruction and interrupt. The FORTRAN compiler, the assembler, and COBOL and PL/1 translators all catch syntax errors and print messages pointing out the errors. Warning messages are given for conditions that are not necessarily errors but that are often symptomatic of an error somewhere. During execution, error messages are given on discovery of errors in input data validity, data set format, and other things that can be caught by the operating system. Each error message is short, but a longer explanation of the errors and often of how to correct them is given in the manual *OS/VS Message Library: VS1 System Messages,* GC 38-1001.

You must remember that the error messages and their explanations reflect the error as seen by the system. The *cause* of the error may be something quite different from the cause suggested by the message; you must try to find not necessarily what error the message said you made, but instead what error you made that would *look* to the system like the error the system said you made.

For example, you may have in your program

```
MR    R6,LFACTOR(R2)
```

which generates an error message

```
IFO032   LFACTOR(R2) APPEARS IMPROPERLY IN THE OPERAND
         OF THIS STATEMENT
```

The assembler is correct in giving this kind of message. However, the error is not in the operand; the error was in using the operation MR when M was intended.

One of the strong reasons for using the full ASSIST system is that it gives you good error messages, especially during execution of your program, when almost anything could be more directly helpful than an indicative dump!

9.4   Fuller Dumps

Sometimes the information given in an indicative dump is not sufficient to enable a programmer to find the program error. The clues needed may be in main storage instead of in registers, so a dump of at least a portion of main storage is necessary. If you include in your job control the statement

```
//GO.SYSUDUMP   DD   SYSOUT=A
```

an *abend dump* will automatically be provided instead of an indicative dump. Some of the information provided in an abend dump is outlined here; full details must be found in one of the manuals on debugging mentioned in Section 9.3, perhaps supplemented by information on options taken in your local installation. There is a lot of information in an abend dump that you do not want to know, so you should *not* ask for an abend dump unless you need it.

The abend dump is identified by computer, job, step, time, and date. The completion code is given, as well as a short message about the cause of the termination. The location of the instruction causing the interrupt is important; the PSW at entry to abend gives a little more information, but the PSW fields in addition to instruction address are not often essential to a debugging task.

Skipping the TCB, the ACTIVE RBS are important, and are exactly as produced as part of the indicative dump (see Section 9.2), but registers at the time of abend are also given clearly just before the main storage areas. The LOAD LIST and several tables that relate to virtual storage management can be skipped. The SAVE AREA TRACE can be useful in showing what routines have been called, and what were the register contents upon entry to each. The address in word 3 of each register save area points to the SAVE AREA of the subroutine called by the routine that provided the SAVE AREA. Thus, the SAVE AREAs make a chain, and the chain is printed. Similarly, word 2 contains the address of the area provided by the calling routine; the chain of SAVE AREAs linked by word 2 addresses is also printed.

The important part of the abend dump is the contents of main storage. There is probably a lot of main storage laid out for you; what you want is in the portion named P/P STORAGE (P/P means problem program). The address of storage dumped on each line is indicated; the contents are given both in hexadecimal and in character format; the name of each routine stored at the beginning of the routine can help you to find the beginning of the routine in the dump. However, the kind of relocation quantity calculations shown in Section 9.2 are also available to help make the correspondence between your assembler listing and the dump.

In virtual storage systems, it is the user's virtual storage area, not fragments of real storage, that appear in the dump. This is as it should be; the virtual storage addresses are the ones meaningful to the programmer, and the operating system takes complete care of the correspondence with real storage.

The use of an abend dump might be as follows. You first examine the completion code to discover the immediate cause of program termination. With a puzzled look, you ask, "How did that happen?" You next examine register contents, the program status word, and the listed entry point of your program, to find what portion of your program was being executed when the termination occurred. Still puzzled, you ask what data were being used. To determine which data were being used, you must look at your main-storage dump, calculating addresses of data areas by adding the relocation quantity to the data area addresses in your listing and independently calculating them from register contents and displacements that you can see from the dump. By looking carefully at the input data and intermediate results in main storage, you can deduce a great deal about what your program did. The SAVE AREA TRACE helps you to follow the path your program took in arriving in the current subroutine. However, the SAVE AREA TRACE follows only the direct chain and does not contain information about subroutines whose executions have been completed.

Let us follow an example of the use of an abend dump. Suppose that you need a program that will read 20 cards into a block of main storage and then go on to manipulation of the data from the cards. A difficulty in this particular application is that the cards are not to be stored in the order they are read; each of the 20 cards contains a number between −10 and 9 (inclusive) in columns 79–80, and its place in the block of storage is to be computed from this number. The card containing −10 is to be placed first in the block, the card containing −9 is to be placed second, and so on, regardless of the order in which the cards are presented to the program.

Following good programming practice, you check the program you have written section by section. The first section you write and check merely reads in the 20 cards, places them in their block in the proper order, then prints the contents of the block. Figure 9.3 shows this program. After each card is read into CARD, the address in the block WORK for storing the contents of the card is

FIGURE 9.3 A program that produces an abend dump

```
LOC     OBJECT CODE       ADDR1  ADDR2   STMT   SOURCE STATEMENT
000000                                    1     WSORT  CSECT
                                          2            PRINT NOGEN
                                          3            EQUREGS
                                         20            XSAVE
                                         47     * DO FOR R9 = 20 TO 0 INCR -1
000062  4190 0014           00014        48            LA    R9,20
                                         49     * . READ CARD, STORE IN PLACE
                                         50     RDLOOP XREAD CARD,80
00008A  F271 C10E C164      00170  001C6  60            PACK  D(8),CARD+78(2)
000090  4F50 C10E           00170         61            CVB   R5,D
000094  5C40 C7A6           00808         62            M     R4,=F'80'
000098  4150 500A           0000A         63            LA    R5,10(,R5)
00009C  4155 C166           001C8         64            LA    R5,WORK(R5)
0000A0  D24F 5000 C116      00000  00178  65            MVC   0(80,R5),CARD
0000A6  4690 C004           00066         66            BCT   R9,RDLOOP
                                         67     * ENDFOR
                                         68     *** NOW PRINT THE CARDS IN ORDER
                                         69     * DO FOR R7 = WORK TO WORK + 19*80 INCR 80
0000AA  4170 C166           001C8        70            LA    R7,WORK
0000AE  4180 0050           00050        71            LA    R8,80
0000B2  4190 C756           007B8        72            LA    R9,WORK+19*80
                                         73     * . PRINT CARD ADDRESSED BY R7
                                         74     PRTLOOP XPRNT (R7),80
0000DA  8778 C054           000B6        84            BXLE  R7,R8,PRTLOOP
                                         85     * ENDFOR
                                         86            XRETURN SA=*
000170                                  105     D      DS    1D
000178                                  106     CARD   DS    CL80
0001C8                                  107     WORK   DS    20CL80
000000                                  108            END   WSORT
000808  00000050                        109                  =F'80'
```

```
                                                                LAST 2 COLUMNS
                                                                SHOULD BE -10 TO 9
                                                                NR * 80
                                                                ADD 10
```

FIGURE 9.4 Portions of the first four pages of an abend dump

```
* ABDUMP REQUESTED *

CPUID   VERSION = FF   SERIAL = 010718   MODEL = 4341                                          PAGE 0001
JOB CH9F3              STEP GO                        DATE 83208
COMPLETION CODE        SYSTEM = 0C4                   TIME 161105
PROGRAM INTERRUPTION (PROTECTION)
INTERRUPT AT 8300AA
PSW AT ENTRY TO ABEND  072D0000 008300AA

...

ACTIVE RBS
PRB   92F9F0   NM GO       SZ/STAB 000400C2   USE/EP 00830000   PSW 072D0000   008300AA   Q      92FB18   WT/LNK 000108F0
SVRB  92F808   NM SVC-601C SZ/STAB 0016D062   USE/EP 00AF4000   PSW 040C0000   C0AF427C   Q      00C273   WT/LNK 0092F9F0
               RG 0-7   00000040   0092F708   000108F0   00A998C0   FFFFFFFF   00830092   0092F6F0   0000006C
               RG 8-15  0092F560   00000012   0092F608   0092F708   50830062   00830128   00011CC0   00830000
               EXTSA    000021BE   0092F650   000108F0   C9C7C3F0   00830F10   0092F808   000108F0   00000000
                        22000000   7F0108F0   00000000   C1C2D5C4   000C4000   00000000   00000000   00000000
                        00000000   00000000   0092F808   00000000

...

REGS AT ENTRY TO ABEND
FL.PT.REGS 0-6   41.400000   00000000   00.000000   00000000   41.100000   00000000   4E.000000   0000000B
REGS 0-7   00000040   0092F708   000108F0   00A998C0   FFFFFFFF   00830092   0092F6F0   0000006C
REGS 8-15  0092F560   00000012   0092F608   0092F708   50830062   00830128   00011CC0   00830000
P/P STORAGE
   REAL ADDRESS=830000
   STORAGE KEY FOR THIS BLOCK=2E
830000 2E  47F0F00C  076E2D6  D9E34040  47F0F028   F05C5C5C  40E6E2D6  D9E340C5  D5E3C5D9   *.00..WSORT  ....WSORT ENTER*
830020 2E  C5C4405C  5C5C4040  90E0F03C  4100F010   58F0F038  070000EF  00830810  00011CC0   *ED....  ..0...0...........*
830040 2E  00830000  00000040  001899E0  E00490EC   D00C50D0  F12C18CD  41D0F128  50DC0008   *......  .......1.........*
830060 2E  0SC04190  00149080  C0164100  C1165BF0   C0120SEF  00830AC0  00011CC0  00830000   *....  A..0.......*
830080 2E  00000040  005098E0  E004F271  C10EC164   4F50D4C1  C3C8C9D5  C5E240C1  D9C54D05   *...2.A.A....MACHINES ARE N*
8300A0 2E  C5C9E3C8  C5D940C1  E240C9D5  E3C5D9C5   E2E3C5C4  40D5D6D9  40C1E240  C9D5E3C5   *EITHER AS INTERESTED NOR AS INTE*
8300C0 2E  D9C5E2E3  C9D5C740  C1E240D7  C5D6D7D3   C5404040  40404040  40404040  40404040   *RESTING AS PEOPLE               *
8300E0 2E  F0D4C6D9  D6D440E3  C8C540E2  E3C1D5C4   D7D6C9D5  E340D6C6  40D5C5E6  40D5C5E6   *OMFROM THE STANDPOINT OF THE NEW*
830100 2E  40D4D6D9  C1D340C1  E3D6D4C9  C340E3C8   C5D6D9E8  6B40C9E3  40C9E240  C1D3D340   *MORAL ATOMIC THEORY. IT IS ALL  *
830120 2E  D9C5D3C1  E3C9E5C5  40404040  40404040   F0D30000  00000000  40C9E240  C1D3D340   *RELATIVE   OI...........      *
830140 2E  00000000  00000000  00000000  00000000   00000000  00000000  00000000  00000000   *..............MACHINES  *
830160 2E  00000000  00000000  00000000  00000000   0000004D  D4C1C3C8  C9D5C5E2  C9D5C5E2   *.......MACHINES *
830180 2E  40C1D9C5  40D5C5C9  E3C8C5D9  40C1E240   C9D5E3C5  D9C5E2E3  C5C440D5  D6D940C1   *ARE NEITHER AS INTERESTED NOR A*
8301A0 2E  E240C9D5  E3C5D9C5  E2E3C9D5  C740C1E2   40D7C5D6  D7D3C540  40404040  40404040   *S INTERESTING AS PEOPLE       *
8301C0 2E  40404040  4040F0D4  00000000  00000000   00000000  00000000  00000000  00000000   *   OM...........*
8301E0 2E  40404040  40404040  00000000  00000000   00000000  00000000  00000000  00000000   *                                *
LINE   830200      SAME AS ABOVE
830220 2E  000C09D4  D7D9D6E5  C9D5C740  E3C8C540   D8E4C1D3  C9E3E840  D6C640C2  D6E3C840   *..IMPROVING THE QUALITY OF BOTH *
830240 2E  C9D5E2E3  C9E3E4E3  C9D6D5E2  40C1E240   C8C540E6  C5D5E340  40404040  40404040   *INSTITUTIONS AS HE WENT         *
830260 2E  40404040  40404040  40404040  40404040   F0F10000  00000000  00000000  00000000   *  01............*
```

computed, and the contents of the card are moved to the proper place. After all 20 cards are read, another section of the program prints the block.

When the program is executed, it does not work. The first time you get an indicative dump. You cannot find the cause of the trouble from the indicative dump (maybe you should be able to, but that would spoil the example), so on the next run you call for a SYSUDUMP by inserting a card

```
//GO.SYSUDUMP    DD    SYSOUT=A
```

Portions of the first four pages of the dump are shown in Fig. 9.4. The entry point is 83ØØØØ, which we find as USE/EP in the first RB. The relocation quantity is therefore 83ØØØØ; the interruption occurred at 83ØØAA, so the instruction causing the interruption was at relocatable location 83ØØAA−83ØØØØ = ØØØØAA. From the listing, you see that the instruction just before that location is supposed to be

```
BCT    R9,RDLOOP
```

You find in the listing also that the machine language instruction is 469Ø CØØ4, and that is what you should find on the dump at location 83ØØA6. Instead, you find 4ØC1 E24Ø. A hint on the origin of this garbage is provided by the character part on the right of the dump, where this general area seems to contain NEITHER AS INTERESTED. More investigation, including a peek at the area CARD (locations 83ØØØØ+ØØØ178=83Ø178 on) and the data deck, shows that these characters come from a data card.

You have made progress; the problem now is to find how the contents of the data card strayed into the instruction area. The instruction presumably executed just before the interruption was

```
MVC    Ø(8Ø,R5),CARD
```

which was supposed to move the contents of the card to an appropriate place. A glance at register 5 shows ØØ83ØØ92, the address of a most inappropriate place. Now you examine the instructions that computed such an address, and the light dawns: after multiplying the number from the card by 80, you must correct for the lowest card number −10 by adding 800, not 10. With this correction made, the program segment runs properly.

If your program terminates abnormally in the full ASSIST system, you get much less of the mystifying stuff that a regular abend dump gives you. However, in addition to the PSW, your register contents and the contents of your main storage, you get two very helpful features:

- a list of the last ten instructions performed by your program,
- a list of the last ten branches taken by your program.

These two lists give you a rather clear picture of what your program did that led up to the fatal instruction.

9.5   Advance Preparation

While programming, you should bear in mind the necessity for debugging, and plan ahead for the debugging. Of course no one plans to make errors that need debugging, but testing at least is necessary, and odds are very heavy that there *will* be errors to be corrected. Computing folklore includes the "theorem" that every program contains at least one more bug.

One of the most important debugging aids is good documentation of the program. It is difficult to read a program and understand its intent. This is why it is important to use clear and simple control structures and to document them through pseudo-code in remarks statements. Besides the control structures, document the use of each storage area; this is done best by using meaningful names for the areas and constants. Also document what the registers are used for and any special techniques that are out of the ordinary. Inserting remarks in the program as documentation not only will help you to understand the program after it has been tried and found to be bug-infested but also gives you an extra perspective and understanding during the programming. This helps to prevent bugs in the first place or to exterminate them even before you try the program in the computer for the first time. Preventing a bug or fixing it during the writing stage has been estimated to take only about one-tenth the time it takes to find and fix it later!

A program is said to be "robust" if it is not easily killed or wounded by poisonous data. Many of the program segments shown in this chapter are not robust; to keep simple the examples of particular concepts and techniques, it was necessary to assume that the data would be very well-behaved: yes, there *are* 20 cards to be read; yes, each *does* contain a number that can be converted by XDECI; and so forth. An especially nonrobust example is the program of Fig. 9.3. The program *assumes* that each of the 20 cards will contain one of the numbers −10 to 9. The program died because of a program bug, but after that is fixed, and the program is "correct," it will be killed by a data card containing, say, the number −15. A weak program like this should be strengthened. If a test for valid data takes the form of checking the address into which this card should be stored—checking that the address is not less than WORK and not greater than WORK + 19 ∗ 80, say—this will not only keep the program alive when attacked by its data, but will signal certain types of program bugs, such as the one in the program given. So good data checking can actually help in the debugging.

An initial test of any program must be carried out with carefully prepared test data. The test data should be the simplest possible that still afford a significant test of the program's features. The data should be simple enough so that you can check the results for *correctness*. Don't be satisfied that the results "look reasonable." You may make the correctness check by carrying out yourself the operations to be done by the computer. This is called a *desk check*; if done carefully, it can catch most of the remaining bugs, again *before* your program gets near the computer itself. The desk check seems tedious, but it can be a much more efficient way to find bugs than waiting for a computer run to show the symptoms of a bug.

For complex problems it is worthwhile to think about what intermediate results would help you to see what progress the program had made during each major section. You can insert extra XPRNT statements to report intermediate results, or use special facilities like SNAP dumps (discussed in the next section). Somehow or other, you should plan how you will know what your program does when you try to run it.

9.6 Partial Dumps

The SYSUDUMP and indicative dumps are taken only at the point of termination of the program. Among these types the completeness of the information provided varies. There are many debugging situations in which a dump at the time of termination is not the best information to have. At times it is much more helpful to have dumps, not necessarily of everything, at intervals throughout execution of the program. With such a dump you can analyze the program's actions by sections. Ask yourself the question "Up to this point in the program such-and-such should have been done: was it?" If not, the problems are localized to the particular section of program; if so, look at the dump after another section to see the results of its actions. Because some errors compound themselves and their effects sometimes even wipe out the evidence of their causes, periodic dumps can be very valuable indeed.

Partial dumps can be implemented in several ways. First, of course, is to call in the regular fashion (e.g., XPRNT) for the output of a line of intermediate results, with format, conversions, and identification all handled in the program itself. This is the most flexible but also the most difficult method of obtaining intermediate dumps. Any desired output can be accomplished by programming, but at the risk of introducing additional errors! Not only is there the possibility of creating errors through the writing of the instructions that provide intermediate output but also there is the possibility that the removal of the instructions after the debugging process is "completed" will introduce further errors.

There are special facilities for producing limited dumps during execution of a program. One of these is a pair of ASSIST instructions that are simple to use. First, an ASSIST instruction

```
XDUMP
```

will have printed for you the current contents of your registers, identified by a serial number of the dump and the location in your program from which the dump was called. The ASSIST instruction XDUMP can dump a storage area instead of registers, if you give as parameters the beginning address and the length of the storage you would like to see. For example,

```
XDUMP CARD,1680
```

will dump the 1680 bytes starting at CARD, but not dump your registers. The contents of your storage area will be shown both in hexadecimal and in character form (anything but letters, digits, and spaces shows as a period).

The ASSIST macro instruction XSNAP is more powerful, but therefore there are more operands to learn. There are four operands; we will only highlight some of the options here. The first operand specifies what is to be done with registers:

T=PRINT	dumps the general registers (the default)
T=NOREGS	does not dump the general registers
T=FLOAT	dumps general and floating point registers

The second operand allows you to provide a text label that will identify your dump; for example,

```
LABEL='CARD STORAGE AFTER READING'
```

The third operand permits specification of one or more areas of main storage to be dumped; unlike XDUMP, the XSNAP macro instruction wants you to specify beginning *and ending addresses* of each area.

```
STORAGE=(RDLOOP,PRTLOOP-1,CARD,WORK+1599)
```

asks for two areas; the first is from RDLOOP to PRTLOOP-1, and the second is from CARD to WORK+1599.

The fourth operand is the most powerful because it enables you to specify a condition upon which the XSNAP is to be performed.

```
IF=((R5),L,=A(WORK))
```

specifies that this dump is to be made *only* if the contents of register 5 are less than the address WORK. The first and third parameters are compared, by an appropriate compare instruction, and the second operand is attached to B to make the extended mnemonic instruction to branch to the instruction that will provide the dump. By convention, a first or third operand in parentheses is expected to be a register address. The IF operand will generate code something like

C	R5,=A(WORK)
BL	location to do the dump
B	instruction just after XSNAP, so bypass dump

Any of the operands may be omitted; the defaults are

T=	omitted: print general registers
LABEL=	omitted: the system manufactures a short label
STORAGE=	omitted: no storage areas dumped
IF=	omitted: the dump is always provided

Operands are separated by commas:

```
XSNAP   T=PRINT,LABEL='AFTER READING',STORAGE=(CARD,WORK+1599),
        IF=((R5),L,=A(WORK))
```

One other requirement: in the standard systems XSNAP or XDUMP expect a data set named XSNAPOUT. So if your catalogued procedure does not already supply a DD statement, you should supply one like the following:

```
//GO.XSNAPOUT   DD  SYSOUT=A
```

You may find more detailed explanations of options for XDUMP and XSNAP in the ASSIST system documentation if the system is installed in your computing center.

Another way to get a partial dump during execution of a program is to call on the SNAP feature of the operating system. The SNAP macro instruction permits you to obtain a dump in the abend dump format, then continue execution of your program. Of course, this provides a very comprehensive dump, almost always containing much more information than you need. Requirements for preparation of the SNAP data set will not be discussed at length here; one of the manuals on debugging listed in Section 9.3 contains full details, but information on the input and output macro instructions (which we shall study in Chapter 12) is prerequisite.

Still another way to get partial dumps is to use special dump subroutines that are available at most installations. The subroutine PDUMP, written for use in FORTRAN but also usable with assembler language, is an example. Parameters to PDUMP come in groups of three: the first two parameters of each group are addresses of locations between which storage contents are to be printed. The third parameter of each group defines the representation in which the storage contents are to be printed: hexadecimal, decimal equivalent of a binary integer, or decimal floating-point equivalent of the IBM System/370 floating-point format, either single or double precision. Several areas can be dumped with one call on PDUMP. Since PDUMP is written for use with FORTRAN, it assumes an output on a data set with ddname FT03F001, so a job control statement

```
//GO.FT03F001   DD   SYSOUT=A
```

must be provided even though another data set may already be assigned to the printer.

9.7   Trace Features

A trace of a program can be regarded as a special case of a partial dump. A full trace reports each instruction executed and its results; a flow trace reports each branch instruction and the direction of branch. Either one gives information about the flow of execution of instructions. A trace is useful especially in situations where the programmer cannot follow the flow of control from partial dumps and the program listing.

A trace involves a full interpretive execution of at least the portion of the program being traced; that is, a program examines and interprets each instruction, retrieves operands, and stores results; in short, it simulates the operation of the computer. This obviously takes time and storage space for the trace program as well as the user's program, and it can produce a whale of a lot of paper. Therefore any trace feature allows the trace to be turned on and off at various times according to various criteria.

Since the full ASSIST system *is* interpretive, it is amenable to several kinds of debugging aids. We will not go into detail here, but just hint at the variety of features. The ASSIST instruction XOPC (Options Call) has a number of different parameters. With these parameters, you can, among other actions:

- define an area of your program in which each instruction is to be traced;
- prescribe storage modification checking: a message is sent whenever a location within a specified range is modified;
- set an interrupt (and further actions) after a certain number of instructions have been executed;
- get statistics on how many times *each instruction* in your program has been executed.

With facilities like these, you can really fine-tune your debugging approach.

Some computer installations may have other trace features of their own. Many computing centers discourage tracing, feeling that with dumps and careful thought the alert programmer can find the errors, and therefore traces, with their invitation to overdependence, are unnecessary. Nonetheless the object of this section, like others in the chapter, is to introduce you to facilities about which you may wish to learn to help you cope with future debugging situations. Tracing is helpful when you cannot follow and understand the flow of control through your program; partial dumps are helpful when intermediate results in main storage that lead to erroneous output must be examined. Dumps obtained upon termination are usually sufficient to help you find the error in an invalid instruction. You are urged to remember the basic debugging tools and to develop sophistication and skill at using these tools to the degree of sophistication required by your programs (and errors).

9.8   Interactive Debugging in CMS

Debugging is an activity that is assisted tremendously by appropriate interactive facilities. CMS has a good comprehensive facility. Because it is interactive, there is no need to ask for the comprehensive information available from abend dumps or even SNAP dumps. Instead you derive information from what the program is doing and ask only for what you specifically want to know.

FIGURE 9.5 Three CMS environments

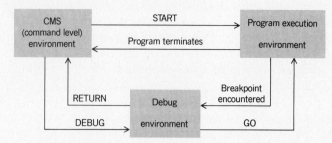

Several modes or environments must be distinguished within CMS. One is the CMS environment, in which the system is ready to accept and execute CMS commands, such as L (List file names), A (assemble), X (enter the editor), GLOBAL (identify libraries), and ERASE (delete a file). One is the program execution environment, in which a program is being run. You get into this environment by giving the CMS command START after loading your program. If the program pauses to wait for your input from the terminal, you are still in the program execution environment. You leave this environment when program execution stops, normally or abnormally. Third is the debug environment. It can be entered from the CMS environment by using the DEBUG command, either just before you START your program, or just after an abnormal termination. It can also be entered from the program execution environment, when execution reaches a location at which you have set a *breakpoint*. If you enter the debug environment by the DEBUG command, you can return to the CMS environment by the RETURN command. The GO command can resume (or begin) execution of your program from the debug environment. Figure 9.5 shows the three environments and the transitions among them.

Any time we are in the debug environment, we can set a breakpoint. But prerequisite is an ORIGIN debug command; without parameters, it sets the origin at 0 for all debug commands that specify main storage locations. With an origin of 0, your debug addresses will correspond to the addresses in your assembly listing.

Up to 16 breakpoints can be set. Debug commands of

```
BREAK     1      0002E
BREAK     2      00054
```

will set breakpoints at (hexadecimal) locations 0002E and 00054. When execution reaches the instruction at location 0002E, execution is suspended with a message

```
DMSDBG728I  DEBUG   ENTERED   BREAKPOINT   01   AT   00002E
```

and you are in the debug environment. Each address given as a breakpoint *must* be the address of the operation code byte of an instruction. As the breakpoint is encountered, the breakpoint is cleared, so that unless it is reset, the second time execution reaches the address will not cause a break in execution.

In the debug environment, the contents of all registers, the PSW, and all storage locations are available for you to display *and change.* To display the program status word, use the simple debug command

PSW

To display contents of registers, you must specify a register or a range of registers; for example,

GPR   2   12

will display the contents of registers 2 to 12. Unlike most other places where a range of registers is specified, you cannot wrap around register 0, by specifying 14 12 for example. To display (eXamine) a portion of main storage, specify the beginning location for the display (relative to the ORIGIN, of course) and a (decimal) length of 1 to 56 bytes. The command

X   ØØØ2A8   5Ø

will display 50 bytes, in hexadecimal, starting from location ØØØ2A8. For the occasions when you want to see contents of lots of storage or specifically want them printed, there is a DUMP command that permits you to specify the beginning and ending addresses of a block of storage to be printed. You may also specify up to eight characters of identification to help you to distinguish one dump from another. The debug command

DUMP   ØØØ2A8   ØØB1FØ   WORK1

will dump the contents of locations ØØØ2A8 to ØØB1FØ to the system printer, and identify the dump as WORK1.

The ability to *change* the status of registers and main storage is very powerful.

SET   GPR   4   ØØØØØ6A7

will set the contents of register 4 to ØØØØØ6A7. We can change two registers if we wish. For example,

SET   GPR   5   8   E4

sets the contents of registers 5 *and* 6 to ØØØØØØØ8 and ØØØØØØE4. When fewer than eight hexadecimal digits are specified, they are right-justified. The STORE debug command will store 1 to 12 bytes at an address in main storage:

STORE   ØØØ3F4   C6C1D5C3   E8

will store C6C1D5C3E8 (the hexadecimal equivalent of the characters FANCY) in the five bytes starting at ØØØ3F4.

FIGURE 9.6   Short summary of debug commands under CMS

BREAK	ident hexloc		Sets breakpoint at hexloc, identified by ident.
DUMP	hexloc hexloc ident-8		Prints dump of main storage between two hexlocs, identified by up to eight characters ident-8.
GO			Resume execution of program from the location where it stopped.
GO	hexloc		Execute program starting at hexloc.
GPR	reg		Displays contents of register.
GPR	reg1 reg2		Displays contents of reg1 to reg2. Requires that reg1 < reg2.
ORIGIN			Sets origin for hexloc main-storage locations to 0.
RETURN			RETURN from debug to CMS environment (Only if debug environment entered by DEBUG command.)
SET GPR	reg hexinfo		Sets register reg to hexinfo.
SET GPR	reg hexinfo1 hexinfo2		Sets registers reg and reg+1 to hexinfo1 and hexinfo2.
STORE	hexloc hexinfo		Stores hexinfo (1 to 12 bytes, in groups of up to eight hex digits) in main-storage locations hexloc.
X	hexloc n		Displays n (1 to 56) bytes from hexloc.

There is one other capability that is quite useful; the GO command permits us to specify the location at which program execution should resume (or start):

$$GO \quad \emptyset\emptyset\emptyset14E$$

The debug commands are summarized in Fig. 9.6. There are more commands and more options; fuller descriptions are found in *IBM Virtual Machine Facility/370: CMS User's Guide,* GC 20-1819, and *IBM Virtual Machine Facility/370: CMS Command and Macro Reference,* GC 20-1818.

A typical use of CMS DEBUG would go as follows: First, assemble, load, and run a program. It abends. You can enter the debug environment at this point with the DEBUG command, and set an origin, display register contents and storage contents to try to determine what happened. Often, this will be enough to reveal the error.

If this is not enough, you may need to check the status of the machine at various points. Reload the program (reassemble if you did not generate and keep the module); then go into the debug environment to set a few breakpoints:

```
DEBUG
BREAK     1        ØØØ2E
BREAK     2        ØØØ54
RETURN
START
```

The first breakpoint may be set at a point nearly at the end of the first loop. When that point is reached, the debug environment is entered and you can display registers and storage locations to satisfy yourself that the body of the loop is doing its job properly. The GO command (without parameters) will resume execution where it was suspended. The second breakpoint may be set just after the end of the first loop; at that point, you can check whether the entire loop did what it should. You will probably set more breakpoints now, if you had not earlier. If you are concerned about an IF-THEN-ELSE structure, you may want to set a breakpoint near the end of the THEN action and another near the end of the ELSE action. You can continue to set breakpoints and check the progress of the program until you have the information you need about what went wrong.

The SET and STORE commands are very useful for testing a program. You can use them to generate special conditions and execute small sections of the program under these conditions; this can give a much more direct and comprehensive test than if you had to generate original input data that would produce each special case far into the program. This is especially useful for testing the program's behavior under pathological conditions that you *hope* your program could never duplicate with honest data!

When you are using CMS DEBUG, you will *need* a copy of your program listing on paper. To try to jot down a few key addresses while displaying your assembly listing on your video screen will *not* be satisfactory. Furthermore, it is important to have a *current* listing of your program. Many novice programmers have trouble finding errors because they debug from listings of what they *intended* to submit and therefore do not see the "corrections" they made incorrectly!

9.9   A Last Few Hints on Programming and Debugging

Maturity in programming shows, like maturity in automobile driving. Maturity is not synonymous with skill or experience, though it is related; maturity is the use of good judgment on problems and consideration for others.

Learn not to be hasty in correcting an apparent error and rushing your program back to the computer. Examine your output carefully, and try to ensure that you know exactly what caused your erroneous results. Only then can you truly correct the error. The best programmers are not satisfied to find and correct one error after a run; they examine their results to try to find and correct all errors possible. The effort spent in this kind of thorough examination is amply repaid in fewer debug runs and shorter total debugging time.

In order to be an effective programmer, you must learn the detailed specifications of at least the features and instructions you are trying to use. One of the requirements of almost-error-free programming is that you know what you *know* and what you do not. What you do not know or are unsure of you must look up and then use correctly, because what you don't know *can* hurt you. You lose much time if you must look up everything, but it is the mark of a professional to know where to look for information and to refer to it when necessary.

Not only will you, as a mature programmer, test your program with a variety of data; you will collect and maintain carefully a comprehensive set of test data. Whenever the program needs to be changed by the addition of some new feature, for example, a run with the set of test data can verify that the program still works properly in the circumstances originally planned for. The addition of a new feature will usually necessitate the generation of more test data to test the new feature, perhaps in connection with a variety of other features.

In recent years there has been significant study of the nature of the programming process, and there have been developments that enable us to write programs with fewer bugs in the first place and later to *prove* that the programs work properly. A primary thrust is that simplification of the control structures used in programming aids in more error-free program development. This is why we emphasize the control structures as we do in Chapters 7 and 8. Some installations have macros to implement control structures, and they can help in representing intended control structures accurately and in enforcing their use.

Meanwhile we should strive for honesty and straightforwardness in programming. There is enough room for ingenuity and efficiency in the intended capabilities of almost any system that a programmer should avoid usage contrary to advertised features. You should also avoid involved and complex structures when possible. This aspect of mature programming style has two benefits. First, the debugging process is much simplified, not only because the program to debug is simpler, but also because there are likely to be fewer errors. Besides, a correction is less likely to cause new errors. Second, good programs have a life in which they grow, change, and are transplanted. New features are added; old ones are modified; the program may be transcribed to run on a different computer. These changes are facilitated by straightforward programming and prevented by the tricky use of special features. A novice's programs, even if they work, often cannot be understood; programs written by responsible professional programmers can be understood and adapted readily to new demands.

m a i n   i d e a s

☐ Each instruction in IBM computer systems has its requirements of operand validity. When these requirements are not met, the condition is called a program-check *exception.* Most exceptions will always cause an interrupt and termination of the program. The most important types of exceptions are operation, privileged operation, protection, addressing, specification, data, fixed-point overflow, and fixed-point divide.

☐ In the absence of other requests, an exception and interrupt will cause an *indicative dump*, which prints for the programmer some information on register contents, program status word fields, and the instruction currently attempted.

☐ Error messages are printed by the operating system when it detects requests that cannot be satisfied by the operating system components or by assemblers, etc.

☐ If you wish, you can ask for a full dump of the status of your program upon abnormal termination. You can also ask for partial dumps to be produced at various points during execution of the program. Trace features can also help in following the path of program execution.

☐ Interactive systems can offer interactive debugging; they enable the programmer to call for particular information at particular points in the execution, and even change the contents of registers and storage and control the path of execution of the program.

☐ Planning and discipline in programming, debugging, and testing result in working programs sooner, and in programs that are understandable and maintainable.

■ **PROBLEMS** F O R   R E V I E W   A N D   I M A G I N A T I O N

9.1 Suppose that instead of the error found in the program of Fig. 9.3, the statement on line 71 had extra spaces included, as follows:

```
        LA    R9,WORK + 19 * 8Ø
```

First, what is the error? Second, how would you expect it to show up in execution of the program? Third, devise a debugging strategy, presuming of course that you see the symptoms but do not know the actual error in advance.

9.2 Add to the program of Fig. 9.3 a test on the number read from the card to make sure it *is* between −10 and 9. Second, as an alternative version, test the address computed to make sure it falls within the area WORK. Which test is preferable, and why?

9.3 How many statements must be changed in the program of Fig. 9.3 if instead of 20 cards containing −10 to 9, there are 24, numbered −12 to 11? A professional programmer would have seen this kind of change and written the program so that only two or three statements need be changed to make the modification. Can you rewrite the program to meet that objective? The program is longer, and a trifle more complex, but it helps a programmer to sleep through the night without phone calls like "Hey! We're trying to run that old program you wrote. Pat had to make a minor change in it today but didn't find all the places where modifications were needed. You'd better come down and fix it; the run has to be done tonight."

9.4 Return to your program segment for one of the end-of-chapter problems for Chapter 8—Problem 8.8, 8.9, or 8.10, for example. Write a main program around your segment that does nothing more than permit testing of your segment. What errors in the resulting complete program might be found by studying an indicative dump? How might XDUMP and XSNAP help in tracking down still other errors?

9.5 Redo Problem 9.4 presuming a CMS environment; your program will be run under CMS. Think again of various kinds of errors your program might contain, and design CMS DEBUG strategies that would help track down the errors.

9.6 Design a set of test data for your program of Problem 9.4 or 9.5—a set that will be a sufficient test of correctness of your program segment. And what is the difference between debugging and testing, anyway? (Debugging is the process of finding and removing bugs. Testing enables you to conclude (finally) that there are no more bugs.)

■ REFERENCES

Beizer, Boris, *Software Testing Techniques*, Van Nostrand, New York, 1983. A good discussion of a difficult subject.

Computing Surveys **14**, 2 (June 1982). Several papers on testing, validation, and verification of programs.

IBM OS/VS and VM/370 Assembler Programmer's Guide, GC 33-4021, IBM Corporation. The assembler's error messages, among other things.

IBM OS/VS1 Debugging Guide, GC 24-5093, IBM Corporation. How to call for various dumps, and formats of the dumps.

IBM OS/VS1 System Messages, GC 38-1001, or *OS/VS Message Library*, VS2 System Messages (*Current Release*), GC 38-1002, IBM Corporation. Error messages: their meanings and possible corrective action.

IBM OS/VS System Codes, GC 38-1003, or *OS/VS Message Library: VS2 System Codes* (*Current Release*), GC 38-1008, IBM Corporation. Completion codes and their meanings and possible corrective action.

IBM System/370 Principles of Operation, GA 22-7000, IBM Corporation. This and *Principles of Operation* manuals for other models describe the exceptions and interrupts.

CHARACTER OR BYTE OPERATIONS

The byte is a basic unit of information in the IBM System/370, chiefly because it holds the coding of one character. Many of today's problems and more of tomorrow's will be problems of processing text, i.e., characters. The IBM System/370 has a good set of instructions that facilitate byte manipulation. Those instructions that are exclusively byte processors are discussed in this chapter. The next chapter discusses manipulation of bits and groups of bits; the bit manipulation facilities also help in processing bytes, which are, after all, just groups of eight bits.

10.1 Byte Transfer or Move Instructions

In the computers of the IBM System/370 family single bytes can be moved from one main-storage location to another or to a register, from a register to a main-storage location, and directly from an instruction to a main-storage location, as can be seen pictorially in Fig. 10.1. In addition, a string of several bytes can be moved from one main-storage location to another.

The MVC and MVI instructions were discussed in Chapter 4; we will further illustrate their use here.

The IC (Insert Character) instruction is of RX type. It inserts a character from the byte addressed as the second operand to the low-order bit positions, 24–31, of the register R1. Bit positions 0–23 of register R1 are unchanged by the instruction. Thus the IC instruction is different from the LH (Load Half-

FIGURE 10.1   Byte move instructions

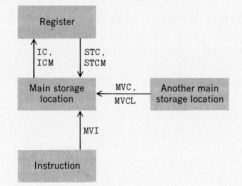

word) instruction, which loads a half-word from main storage into a register but changes the contents of the whole register.

The STC (STore Character) instruction is the converse of IC. Also of RX type, it stores the low-order eight bits of the register $R1$ into a main-storage location addressed as the second operand.

The two instructions can be described as

$$IC: \quad \text{Insert Character:} \quad R1_{24-31} \leftarrow c(S2)_{0-7}$$
$$STC: \quad \text{STore Character:} \quad S2_{0-7} \leftarrow c(R1)_{24-31}$$

The main-storage operands are only one byte long so do not have to begin on any word or half-word boundary. Thus a specification exception cannot occur in the execution of these instructions; the only exceptions possible are access exceptions. The condition code is not affected by either instruction.

Consider the following examples. The instruction

```
IC    R6,INAREA
```

inserts the byte from location INAREA into the low-order eight bits of register 6. So if INAREA contains (hexadecimal) F7 and register 6 contains F3C2D540 before the instruction, execution of the instruction will change contents of register 6 to F3C2D5F7. Similarly, the instruction

```
STC   R5,OUT+14
```

will store the low-order eight bits of register 5 into the main storage byte at location OUT+14.

MOVE CHARACTER LONG

A programmer often wishes to move a block of information from one place in main storage to another. The MVC instruction does that, but programmers find it annoying that MVC can move at most 256 characters; sometimes they want to move much longer strings. The instruction MVCL (MoVe Character Long) moves arbitrarily long strings. MVCL is an RR-type instruction; each register address is the address of an even-odd pair of registers. The first pair defines the address and length of the destination field: $c(R1)$ designates the beginning (leftmost) address of the destination field, and $c(R1 + 1)$ designates the length of the field to be filled. The second pair similarly defines the address and length of the source field. However, bits 0–7 of register $R2 + 1$ are a *padding character*; if the destination field is longer than the source field, the padding character is copied into the remainder of the destination field after the source field is exhausted. (If the source field is longer, only enough of it is moved to fill the destination field.)

Unlike MVC, the number of characters moved is not one more than is specified by the length codes. One result is that if a length of 0 is coded in register $R1 + 1$, *no* characters are moved.

Some examples will illustrate the action.

a. Suppose the address P has been loaded into register 2, the address Q into register 4. The hexadecimal contents of register 3 is 000004E0, and contents of register 5 is 400001B4. The instruction

                         MVCL   R2,R4

will move
    i)   1B4 characters starting at location Q to a field starting at location P;
    ii) 32C(4E0–1B4) copies of the padding character 40 into locations starting at P+1B4, which is immediately after the last character from Q.

b. With the same original contents, the instruction

                         MVCL   R4,R2

will move 1B4 characters from location P to location Q.

The registers $R1$ and $R2$ are incremented by 1 each time a character is moved, and $R1 + 1$ and $R2 + 1$ are each decremented by 1. Therefore the final results in the registers will be

Register $R1$ is incremented by the original contents of $R1 + 1$.

Register $R1 + 1$ is set to 0.

Register $R2$ is incremented by the smaller of the original contents of $R1 + 1$ and $R2 + 1$ (ignoring the padding character).

Register $R2 + 1$ is decremented by the same amount that $R2$ was incremented.

The condition code is set by MVCL to

0 if the field counts are equal,

1 if the first operand count is lower,

2 if the second operand count is lower,

3 if no movement is performed because of destructive overlap.

The destructive overlap condition is recognized if a byte is used as a source after it is used as a destination.

Use of the fill character makes MVCL a useful instruction for clearing a section of storage to zeros, or storing blanks in it, or filling it with copies of any single character. For example,

```
LA    R2,Y
LA    R3,8ØØ
L     R4,*
L     R5,=F'Ø'
MVCL  R2,R4
```

will set the 800 bytes beginning at Y to zeros. The address in register 4 can be any valid address not causing destructive overlap, because no characters are moved from the second operand field; all are copied from the padding character.

The instructions MVCL and CLCL (described in the next section) are *interruptible*; that is, execution can be interrupted before completion. Because the instructions can take a long time (at least in comparison with other instructions), the interruptibility is essential in preserving the system's timely response to interrupts, such as some input/output and clock-generated interrupts that impose a time pressure for prompt action. No other instructions are interruptible (except, of course, for interrupts generated by conditions arising in execution of the instructions themselves); interruptions are held until after execution of an instruction is completed. One reason so much information used by MVCL and CLCL is kept in registers is that the information will therefore be available for restart of the instruction after interruption. The interruptibility of the instructions is of concern to you as a programmer in that you should avoid letting the destination (first) operand area of MVCL contain the MVCL instruction itself; it might be gone when needed for resumption!

THE INSTRUCTIONS ICM, STCM

The three instructions ICM (Insert Characters under Mask), STCM (STore Characters under Mask), and CLM (Compare Logical under Mask—described in the next section) form a family. All are RS-type instructions. In each, *R1* designates a register operand, *S2* an operand in main storage. In each, the third operand, *M3*, is not another register operand but a mask that designates which bytes of the register *R1* participate in the instruction. Each of the four bits of the mask determines whether a corresponding byte of the register is used in the instruction. The assignments are as follows:

Mask bit	Mask value	Register byte	Register bit positions
1	8	1	0–7
2	4	2	8–15
3	2	3	16–23
4	1	4	24–31

For example, a mask of 4 selects the second byte of the register; a mask value of 6 (= 4 + 2) selects the middle two bytes of the register. In each case, the same number of bytes in main storage, starting at the location *S2*, participate.

The actions of the instructions can be guessed: ICM inserts characters from main storage into the selected byte positions in the register, leaving the nonselected bytes unchanged. STCM stores selected bytes from the register into main storage.

These instructions are more flexible extensions of other insert, load, and store instructions. For example,

```
ICM    R7,1,Y
```

is equivalent in action to

```
IC     R7,Y
```

Similarly,

```
STCM   R7,3,HLF
```

is equivalent to

```
STH    R7,HLF
```

except that STCM does not require HLF to be on a half-word boundary. The point is that any subset of bytes in a register can be stored in a contiguous main-storage field, or can be replaced by the contents of a main-storage field. The selected bytes in a register operand need not be contiguous, but the corresponding main-storage field will always be contiguous bytes. For example,

```
STCM   R7,1Ø,Y
```

stores the first byte of register 7 (bits 0–7) at Y and the third (bits 16–23) at Y+1.

ICM sets the condition code:

0   all inserted bits are 0, or mask = 0

1   first bit of inserted field is 1

2   first bit of inserted field is 0, but
     not all inserted bits are 0

10.2   Character Compare Operations

THE MEANING OF "LOGICAL" IN IBM SYSTEM/370

Certain instructions work with data in a "logical" fashion. Some of these correspond to logic functions of *or* and *and*, and are discussed in Chapter 11. Others deal with data as numeric quantities, but without sign. This latter is the use of the word "logical" that concerns us in this section; it has nothing to do with logic or reasonableness, and is really only a synonym for *unsigned*.

All bits in the quantity, including the highest-order, are considered as numeric bits, so all logical quantities are nonnegative. If we have quantities

$$A: \quad 11111111 \quad 00000000 \quad 11110000 \quad 00001111$$

and

$$B: \quad 00000000 \quad 11111111 \quad 11111111 \quad 00001111,$$

the relationship depends on whether they are considered as arithmetic or logical. As an arithmetic quantity, A is negative and therefore less than B. However, as a logical quantity, A is positive and greater than B. The IBM System/370 allows comparisons in either arithmetic or logical mode. Logical instructions are discussed further in the next chapter, but because the character compare instructions are logical instructions, they are the next topic.

THE CLC AND CLI INSTRUCTIONS

The CLC (Compare Logical Character) and CLI (Compare Logical Immediate) instructions are designed to permit comparison of characters and strings of characters. Both perform logical, that is, unsigned, comparisons, setting the condition code to

0   if the two operands are equal,

1   if the first operand is less than the second operand,

2   if the first operand is greater than the second operand.

The CLC instruction is of SS type; it permits comparison of strings of characters from 1 to 256 bytes long in main storage. Only one length, which describes both operands, is specified. The CLI instruction is of SI type; it performs a comparison of a first operand, which is one byte in main storage, with a second operand, which is a byte in the instruction itself.

Neither instruction requires any particular boundary alignment of its operands; only protection and addressing exceptions can occur. For example,

$$\text{CLI} \quad \text{INAREA+4,C'\%'}$$

compares the character in main storage at INAREA+4 with the character %, setting the condition code accordingly. The instruction

$$\text{CLC} \quad \text{NAME(24),INAREA+10}$$

compares the 24-byte string starting at NAME with the 24-byte string starting at INAREA+10.

The instructions can be described symbolically as

CLI	Compare Logical Immediate	$CC \leftarrow \begin{cases} 0 \text{ if } c(S1) = I2 \\ 1 \text{ if } c(S1) < I2 \\ 2 \text{ if } c(S1) > I2 \end{cases}$
CLC	Compare Logical Character	$CC \leftarrow \begin{cases} 0 \text{ if } c(S1)_{0-BL} = c(S2)_{0-BL} \\ 1 \text{ if } c(S1)_{0-BL} < c(S2)_{0-BL} \\ 2 \text{ if } c(S1)_{0-BL} > c(S2)_{0-BL} \end{cases}$

where if L is the length operand coded in the machine language instruction, $BL = 8L + 7$ so $L + 1$ bytes of each operand are tested. It must be understood that the quantities are compared as unsigned integers.

COMPARE LOGICAL CHARACTER LONG

The instruction CLCL (Compare Logical Character Long) is very similar to MVCL. CLCL is an RR-type instruction, and the registers define fields and a padding character in exactly the same way as MVCL. The difference, of course, is that instead of moving contents of one field to another, the two fields are compared. The result of the comparison is expressed in the condition code, which is set to

  0   if the operands are equal or if both fields have zero length,
  1   if the first operand is low,
  2   if the first operand is high.

The comparison treats the fields as unsigned binary integers, and it continues until either a mismatch is found or the *longer* field is exhausted. If either field is shorter than the other, the shorter field (note: *either* field if shorter) is considered to be extended by the padding character.

If the operation ends because of a mismatch, the contents of the registers identify the byte of mismatch. The contents of registers $R1 + 1$ and $R2 + 1$ are decremented by the number of bytes that match, except that they stop at 0 when the comparison is continued by use of the padding character. Registers $R1$ and $R2$ are incremented by the same quantities that the count fields are decremented.

THE CLM INSTRUCTION

The RS-type instruction CLM is like ICM and STCM in its configuration of operands: $R1$ designates a register operand, $S2$ an operand in main storage, and $M3$ a mask that selects bytes of the first operand that will be compared with bytes in main storage. For example,

                    CLM   R7,11,SPLT

compares the first, third, and fourth bytes of register 7 with the three bytes at SPLT. The comparison, like the other logical compares, treats the operands as unsigned. CLM sets the condition code as other compare instructions do:

          CC = 0:   selected bytes are equal, or mask = 0.
          CC = 1:   selected field of the first operand is low.
          CC = 2:   selected field of the first operand is high.

In the remainder of the chapter we shall explore character manipulation techniques and give examples of the use of these instructions.

10.3 An Example: Searching for a Name

Consider the following problem: A file consists of records, each 120 bytes long. Considering the first byte of each as byte 0, each record contains a person's name in bytes 10–33 and his street address in bytes 34–93. The file is in main storage, starting at location PEOPLE. The name of one of the people in the file is at location NAME; the problem is to find from the file his address and place it at ADDR. Let us suppose that the records are ordered on some key other than name, so the names are not ordered. We must therefore make a sequential search. Suppose the number of records in the file is in register 7.

A program segment to accomplish this task is shown in Fig. 10.2. Register 9 holds the address of the record currently being considered. It is therefore incremented by 120 in each execution of the body of the loop. The specification 10(R9) addresses the first byte of the name in the current record, and 34(R9) specifies the corresponding street address. The CLC instruction is used to compare the names; all 24 bytes are compared by the single instruction. Note that an index register method of address modification cannot be used in

FIGURE 10.2 Program segment to search for a street address corresponding to a name

```
***********************************************************************
***      SEARCH A BLOCK OF 120-BYTE RECORDS FOR THE STREET ADDRESS
***      CORRESPONDING TO A NAME, AND STORE THE STREET ADDRESS IN ADDR
***      IF NAME NOT FOUND, STORE SPACES IN ADDR
***      NAME IN EACH RECORD IS IN BYTES 10 - 23
***      ADDRESS IN BYTES 34 - 93
***      REG R7 CONTAINS LENGTH (IN RECORDS) OF THE BLOCK
***********************************************************************
*** INITIALIZE R9 TO FIRST RECORD
         LA      R9,PEOPLE
* WHILE (THERE ARE MORE RECORDS TO SEARCH) AND (NOT FOUND) DO
SRCHLOOP LTR     R7,R7
         BNH     SRCHNOTF
* . IF NAME IN RECORD NOT = KEY
         CLC     NAME(24),10(R9)
         BE      SRCHFOUN
* . . THEN GO TO NEXT RECORD
         BCTR    R7,0            SUBTRACT 1
         LA      R9,120(,R9)
         B       SRCHLOOP
* . ENDIF
* ENDWHILE (THERE ARE MORE RECORDS) AND (NOT FOUND)
* IF FOUND
* . THEN PUT ADDRESS FROM RECORD IN ADDR
SRCHFOUN MVC     ADDR(60),34(R9)
         B       NEXTSTEP
* . ELSE PUT SPACES IN ADDR
SRCHNOTF MVC     ADDR(60),=CL60' '
* ENDIF
NEXTSTEP DS      0H
```

this problem, since CLC and MVC are of SS type and therefore do not include index specification in their operand addressing.

Some remarks on the reality of this example are in order. In the first place, searching for an (exact) name is a perilous business. Everyone knows that names are written in many ways, with full middle name, middle initial, no middle name, wife's first name or Mrs. and her husband's name, etc., not to mention the never-ending misspellings. If the name to be found comes from, say a credit card charge plate, consistency with the name in the file can be assumed. In other cases failure to find an exact match in the file should cause a much more sophisticated search for a name that is most likely to be the correct one. The more sophisticated search would perhaps include first a search for all records with the last name correct (the last name is all the characters up to the first blank, and we can find *that*), then a survey of first and middle names and initials. The program would still suffer from both errors of omission and commission.

In the second place, a reasonable file to be searched would not likely be kept in main storage. A disk pack or something else of large capacity would hold the file, and only small portions of it would be brought into main storage. The program segment given could be a search through a portion of the file, with SRCHNOTF introducing the program segment that brings a new portion of the file into main storage. Furthermore, if possible in the application, names whose street addresses are needed would be grouped, so that one pass through the file would search for, say 15 names.

10.4   Control Sections

In Chapter 5 the CSECT statement was introduced, and in Chapter 6 the implementation of subroutines. Now it is time to learn more about control sections.

A *source module* is all of the assembler language assembled by one execution of the assembler. An *object module* is the machine language result of assembling a source module. Until now we have included only one control section in a source module, but there may be more than one control section in a source module, and there can be advantages.

In Chapter 6, where two subroutines and a main program made up one control section, A-type address constants were used in their linkage. It was noted that a subroutine assembled elsewhere would be linked with a V-type address constant. We can be more uniform if each subroutine has its own control section; then we use V-type address constants (or literals) when the control sections are assembled together in the same source module or assembled separately and then linked by the linkage editor or loader.

A *control section* is the smallest unit that can be relocated independently of other units. Each control section is initiated by a CSECT statement, and ended by another CSECT or the END statement. Each control section should include its own USING, and have a LTORG at the end to make sure that each control section contains the literals it needs (even though this may result in some duplication).

We can also make use of *dummy control sections*, which are descriptions or formats of data areas in main storage. Dummy control sections do not themselves allocate storage, however. They are initiated by DSECT statements,

and are ended by other DSECT or CSECT statement or the END statement. A
DSECT can also end a CSECT. As an example, we could define a dummy control
section,

```
PARMLIST    DSECT
AREAADDR    DS      A
SRCHARG     DS      A
AREALEN     DS      A
```

In a CSECT defining a subroutine, we could include

```
            USING   PARMLIST,R1
            . . .
            L       R2,AREAADDR
            L       R5,AREALEN
```

which would have the same effect as

```
            L       R2,Ø(,R1)
            L       R5,8(,R1)
```

but is considerably more readable.

A DSECT may be used to describe any area of main storage. It can be, as
shown before, a way of naming relative positions of fields within a block. Let
us use as a second example the program of Fig. 10.2. There is a block of
120-character records, and the segment uses displacements of 10 and 34 (with
base register 9) to designate name and address fields, respectively. The program can read more clearly if we describe a 120-byte record in a DSECT:

```
NAREC       DSECT
NASSN       DS      CL9
NASEX       DS      C
NANAME      DS      CL24
NAADDR      DS      CL6Ø
NAOTHER     DS      CL26
```

In the program segment itself, we include

```
            USING   NAREC,R9
```

just before or after we load the address of PEOPLE into register 9. The instructions that use fields in the records become

```
            CLC     NAME(24),NANAME
```

and

```
SRCHFOUN    MVC     ADDR(6Ø),NAADDR
```

This has the added advantage that if the format of the record changes, it is
much easier to modify the program correctly; all that may be necessary is to
update the DSECT. Note that the instruction

```
            LA      R9,12Ø(,R9)
```

FIGURE 10.3   A program segment that searches a table, using a DSECT

```
***********************************************************************
***     SEARCH A BLOCK OF 120-BYTE RECORDS FOR THE STREET ADDRESS
***     CORRESPONDING TO A NAME, AND STORE THE STREET ADDRESS IN ADDR
***     IF THE NAME IS NOT FOUND, STORE SPACES IN ADDR
***     REGISTER R7 CONTAINS LENGTH (IN RECORDS) OF THE BLOCK
***********************************************************************
*** INITIALIZE R9 TO FIRST RECORD
         LA     R9,PEOPLE
         USING  NAREC,R9
* WHILE (THERE ARE MORE RECORDS TO SEARCH) AND (NOT FOUND) DO
SRCHLOOP LTR    R7,R7
         BNH    SRCHNOTF
* . IF NAME IN RECORD NOT = KEY
         CLC    NAME(24),NANAME
         BE     SRCHFOUN
* . . THEN GO TO NEXT RECORD
         BCTR   R7,0          SUBTRACT 1 FROM COUNT OF
         LA     R9,120(,R9)   REMAINING RECORDS
         B      SRCHLOOP
* . ENDIF
* ENDWHILE (MORE RECORDS TO SEARCH) AND (NOT FOUND)
* IF FOUND
* . THEN PUT STREET ADDRESS FROM RECORD IN ADDR
SRCHFOUN MVC    ADDR(60),NAADDR
         B      NEXTSTEP
* . ELSE PUT SPACES IN ADDR
SRCHNOTF MVC    ADDR(60),=CL60' '
* ENDIF
NEXTSTEP DS     0H


NAREC      DSECT
*** DESCRIBES A RECORD IN THE TABLE 'PEOPLE'
NASSN      DS     CL9
NASEX      DS     C
NANAME     DS     CL24
NAADDR     DS     CL60
NAOTHER    DS     CL26
```

is still necessary; it moves the "window" described by NAREC to the next record in the table. The revised segment is shown in Fig. 10.3.

The sequence of CSECTs and DSECTs in a source module usually does not matter. For example, the DSECT describing NAREC could be placed either before or after the CSECT of the main program.

We will find places later where CSECTs and DSECTs are helpful, and you can use them in end-of-chapter problems as well.

10.5   An Example: Character Set Conversion

Character set conversion is a not uncommon problem. You may have to send characters to a terminal or printer in which a few of the special characters have different representations from the computer's regular character set. Or you

FIGURE 10.4   Converting lowercase to uppercase letters

```
LCTOUPC  CSECT
*******************************************************************
***      SUBROUTINE TO REPLACE LOWERCASE LETTERS WITH UPPERCASE
***      INPUT PARAMETERS ARE ADDRESS OF STRING AND LENGTH
***      THE STRING IS CHANGED IN PLACE
*******************************************************************
         XSAVE SA=NO,TR=NO
         LM    R4,R5,0(R1)    ADDR OF STRING IN R4
         L     R5,0(,R5)      LENGTH IN R5
* DO FOR R4 = ADDR OF FIRST BYTE TO ADDR OF LAST BYTE
         LA    R6,1
         LA    R7,0(R4,R5)
         SR    R7,R6          R7 = ADDR OF LAST BYTE IN STRING
* . IF CHAR IS LOWERCASE LETTER
LCTLOOP  CLI   0(R4),X'80'
         BNH   NOTLC          BELOW LC RANGE
         CLI   0(R4),X'A9'
         BH    NOTLC          ABOVE LC RANGE
         CLI   0(R4),X'A1'
         BE    NOTLC          X'A1' IS NOT A LETTER
* . . THEN ADD X'40' TO CONVERT TO UPPERCASE
         IC    R8,0(,R4)
         LA    R8,X'40'(,R8)
         STC   R8,0(,R4)
* . ENDIF
NOTLC    BXLE  R4,R6,LCTLOOP
* ENDFOR (R4 = ADDR OF FIRST BYTE TO ADDR OF LAST BYTE)
         XRETURN SA=NO,TR=NO
         EQUREGS
```

---

may have to accept data from such a terminal and convert its nonstandard character representations to the regular set. Or a particular language translator will accept only uppercase letters, so you must convert any lowercase characters you may have accepted from a terminal to uppercase. Let's consider the lowercase to uppercase problem.

In the EBCDIC code, the lowercase letters have representations in the range (hexadecimal) 81–A9; the uppercase letters have representations C1–E9; each uppercase letter is exactly 40 greater than its lowercase counterpart. There is one code in the 81–A9 range that does not represent a letter: A1 is the character ~ . There are also codes that have no meaning. So our procedure is that every character code between 81 and A9 (inclusive) except A1 is to be increased by 40.

Figure 10.4 shows a subroutine that will do the conversion for every byte in a string. The address of the string and the length of the string are the only parameters to the subroutine; the string is to be converted in place. The subroutine uses the CLI instruction when testing each character to see whether it should be changed. The CLI instruction is ideal for this because it compares a main storage byte with a constant byte, which might as well be in the instruction. To change a character, you must do the addition in a register, so use IC and STC to bring the byte into a register and put it back (a shorter way is shown in Chapter 11). Note that register 8 is not initialized before the character is inserted into it; what is in the other 24 bits of register 8? Convince yourself that it does not matter at all.

In Chapter 15 you will learn how to do the conversion for an entire string in just one instruction!

10.6   An Example: Counting Digits

A common use of a computer is to tabulate various sorts of things. In the following example, which constructs a table of the frequencies of digits occurring in a particular position of a record and the frequencies counted over a group of records, you will see how the character manipulation instructions facilitate the task.

Suppose that a record is read or somehow generated in main storage starting at REC. The position within the record is in register 9; for example, if we are to tabulate position (byte) 23 of the record (assuming the first byte to be position 0), the number 23—hexadecimal 00000017—is in register 9. Any of the digits 0–9 are expected to be in that position of the record, represented as EBCDIC characters, and we wish to count, over a group of records, just how many 0's, how many 1's, . . . , how many 9's, occur. It is likely that we may be asked to generate several tables from a group of records, so storage space may be at a premium. Let us suppose, then, that no count will exceed 255, so we can keep each counter in one byte. To keep ten counters, one for counting each of the digits 0–9, we need 10 bytes of main storage; we assume that the address of the first byte of this area is in register 10.

Figure 10.5 shows a program segment that adds 1 to the appropriate counter, depending on the digit found in the current record. The IC instruction is used in two ways. First, it brings into register 6 the digit to be counted. The IC instruction is of RX type, so indexing is possible and used to advantage here. The character is brought into a register so arithmetic can be done on it. The EBCDIC codes for the digits 0–9 are hexadecimal F0–F9, or decimal 240–249. Therefore if 240 is subtracted from the EBCDIC representation, a number 0–9 results, and the second IC instruction uses the digit as an index to grab the right counter to update!

If each of the counters had been two bytes long, the number 0–9 remaining after the subtraction of 240 would have been multiplied by 2, and the result would have been used to obtain a counter in the same way; however, the instruction to bring a counter into a register would then have been

```
LH   R6,∅(R1∅,R5)
```

The segment of Fig. 10.5 would likely be the body of a loop entered for each record of a group of records. Perhaps there would be an intermediate loop, counting several positions (into several counter areas) in each record.

FIGURE 10.5 Counting digits

```
************************************************************************
***     UPDATE CONTERS OF DIGITS
***     BY COUNTING DIGIT IN CURRENT RECORD
***     R9 CONTAINS THE INDICATOR OF WHICH POSITION
***        IN THE RECORD NAMED REC CONTAINS THE DIGIT
***     ADDRESS OF 10-BYTE COUNTER AREA IS IN R10
************************************************************************
         SR    R6,R6
         SR    R5,R5
* IF CHAR IS A DIGIT AND RESULTING COUNT <= 255
         IC    R5,REC(R9)     CHARACTER TO BE COUNTED
         S     R5,=F'240'     CODE FOR DIGIT 0
         BM    NEXTSTEP
         C     R5,=F'10'
         BNL   NEXTSTEP
* . THEN ADD 1 TO APPROPRIATE COUNT
         IC    R6,0(R10,R5)
         LA    R6,1(,R6)
         C     R6,=F'255'
         BH    NEXTSTEP
         STC   R6,0(R10,R5)
* ENDIF
NEXTSTEP DS    0H
```

The two instructions

```
         SR    R6,R6
         SR    R5,R5
```

could be placed outside the loop if the high-order 24 bits of registers 5 and 6 were not changed during the loop. The instructions are necessary *somewhere* since the IC instruction changes only the low-order eight bits of a register.

When the counters are finally to be printed, the IC instruction can again be used to bring each counter into a register for conversion to decimal and unpacking.

10.7 An Example: Generating a Symbol Table

One of the tasks for any computer language translator—assembler, compiler, or whatever—is the generation and use of a symbol table. All the names of storage areas must be kept in a table, along with information about the nature of the symbol and addresses and lengths assigned by the translator. The problem is not unique to language translators; many diverse applications require generation of tables of similar sorts of information. The symbol table for the IBM System/370 assembler serves as an example because you are already familiar with the language and thus definition of the problem is not difficult.

In the IBM System/370 assembler systems, a symbol or name is from one to eight characters long. The table must store all characters of each symbol. It is most convenient to allow space for eight characters for each symbol in the table, filling in blanks on the right if necessary. Several other pieces of information are necessary:

- the length attribute of the symbol, a half-word;
- the address assigned to the symbol, three bytes;
- an indicator whether relocatable or absolute, one bit;
- an indicator whether or not yet defined, one bit;

and a few other small pieces of information. To hold all of this, let us allocate four words, or 16 bytes, to each symbol entry. We may call each four-word space a cell in the table.

Several different operations must be performed on the symbol table. First is insertion of a symbol in the table, which must be performed once for each symbol. Second is search and retrieval of information, which may be required several times for each symbol, but this "several" is more likely to be four times than 400.

Depending on the organization of the assembler, a third operation of search, followed by insertion of further definition, may be required. For example, if a symbol is entered into the symbol table when first encountered, either as name or operand, each subsequent encounter will require a search, but a subsequent encounter in the name field will at last cause definition of the symbol.

THE SYMBOL TABLE AS A LIST; DERIVED KEYS

The symbol table is a list, according to the definition of list given in Chapter 8; the key in the list is the symbol itself. Since the IBM System/370 assembler language allows over 10^{10} different symbols, a key-dense list is out of the question. The list could be ordered, which would minimize search time in the list. However, the cost in time spent in sorting the list could be great. Insertion time can be minimized by putting the entries in the list in consecutive cells as they are encountered, but a significant amount of time would thereafter be spent in searching. So both the completely ordered list and the unordered, easy-to-generate list have their disadvantages.

Other alternatives are available. From the eight-byte key, the symbol itself, the computer can derive a new key by division or other manipulation of the symbol. The *derived key* can then be a pointer to a particular cell in the list. Search and insertion can be a matter of deriving a key from the symbol and then looking in the space pointed to by the derived key. The process is not this simple, however, because many original keys can correspond to one derived key. This raises a *collision* problem. For example, a first symbol may generate the derived key 8, and it can be inserted into cell 8 in the list. A second symbol may also generate derived key 8, so it must be put elsewhere. The collision problem can be minimized by deriving keys to be as uniformly distributed as possible, so any key derivation strategy should attempt to do that.

COLLISION MANAGEMENT

There are several ways of handling collisions. One is to put the new entry into the next available cell. The organization of the list is simple; to retrieve any particular entry, start a sequential search at the cell corresponding to the derived key. The search ends upon either finding the right entry or finding a blank cell. The efficiency of this solution decreases as the list gets full and overflow entries have to be stored farther away from the cell corresponding to their derived keys. Main storage is used efficiently, however.

This treatment can be improved. Given that there is a collision of an element whose derived key is $k_0^{(0)}$ with another element already at cell $k_0^{(0)}$, let us denote the cells searched by $k_0^{(1)}$, $k_0^{(2)}$, $k_0^{(3)}$, . . . Each index is reduced by an appropriate multiple of N, the table size, so that the residue used to address a cell is in the range 0 to $N - 1$, inclusive. If cells are taken in sequence, so that $k_0^{(1)} = k_0^{(0)} + 1$, $k_0^{(2)} = k_0^{(0)} + 2$, etc., clusters tend to develop, because a search starting from $k_1^{(0)} = k_0^{(0)} + 1$ covers the same cells $k_0^{(2)}$, $k_0^{(3)}$, . . . in the same order. Deriving a scheme by which a search starting at $k_1^{(0)} = k_0^{(1)}$ does *not* cover cells $k_0^{(2)}$, $k_0^{(3)}$, . . . , in this order will shorten searches. One such scheme is called *quadratic probing*†; according to this scheme, the sequence of cells searched is k_0, $k_0 + a + b$, $k_0 + 2a + 2^2 b$, $k_0 + 3a + 3^2 b$, . . . with appropriate choices of a and b. For example, we can generate a sequence by

$$k_0^{(i)} = k_0^{(i-1)} + i, \qquad i = 1, 2, \ldots ,$$

or by

$$k_0^{(i)} = k_0^{(i-1)} + (N+1)/2 - i, \qquad i = 1, 2, \ldots$$

The table size N is required to be a prime number, and a search sequence will cover $(N + 1)/2$ cells before repeating. The result that the table is declared full if a cell is not available among the $(N + 1)/2$ cells searched is usually acceptable, especially since the $(N + 1)/2$ cells searched for one derived key are not precisely the same as those for another derived key.

Another collision management technique is the provision of a separate overflow area, where only overflow entries are stored. The overflow area can be filled sequentially; if the derived keys are well assigned, only a small fraction of the entries will be in the overflow area.

Links can be appended to each cell, so that in case of collision a particular next cell to search is indicated. Thus if entries have been made for derived keys 8 and 9, and a new entry is encountered with derived key 8, it could be stored in cell 10, and the link in cell 8 would point to cell 10. Thus cell 9 would not be searched for an entry with derived key 8. If an entry with derived key 10 were encountered next, it could be stored in cell 11, and that fact recorded in cell 10. Still other entries encountered with derived keys 8 or 10 would be mixed in what is essentially the same linked list. The link technique can

---

†W. D. Maurer, "An Improved Hash Code for Scatter Storage," *Communications of the Association for Computing Machinery* **11,** No. 1 (January 1968), pp. 35–38.

also be used in connection with an overflow area, to minimize still further the burdens of search.

Another technique is called *bucketing*. Keys are derived in such a way that there are fewer different derived keys, and each derived key points to, say, a group of 10 cells, which is called a bucket. Entries associated with the same derived key are placed in the bucket in the order they are encountered. Insertion and searching are reasonably fast since only one bucket of 10 cells will usually have to be searched. Most of the overflows are averaged out, so there will be many fewer overflows from the buckets than from individual cells associated with individual keys. Overflow areas will not usually be buckets associated with other keys, but more likely separate areas. The programming required for bucketing is more complicated than for other techniques, but not prohibitive.

A search using any of these techniques is in most cases actually much faster than a binary search of a completely sorted list, since only a very few tests are required even in a large table until the table is 80 or 90 percent full.

IMPLEMENTATION: AN EXAMPLE

Let us now examine one of the simpler techniques as it might be implemented in the IBM System/370. The procedure will derive keys that will be associated with individual cells, perhaps allowing for 509 cells in the table. The first task is to derive the keys in such a way as to minimize the chance of collision. There is no known solution to the problem, but there are considerations that will at least assure a distribution that is more uniform than a completely random distribution would be.

Programmers use symbols that are similar; that is, many of the symbols used in a program differ in only one character out of eight. Our procedure then should assign different derived keys to symbols that differ in only one character. We should also derive keys in such a manner that if two symbols are different merely by the transposition of two characters, we obtain different keys. Many different procedures will conform to these requirements. You can think of more requirements, but for the purposes of this book we will be satisfied with these. The procedure is first to divide the last half of the symbol by 253. A new dividend is formed as the remainder from the the first division (say in register 4), followed by the first half of the symbol (in register 5), and the derived key is the remainder after this dividend is divided by 509. We thus derive keys that may take on 509 different values; each will point to a cell. If

FIGURE 10.6   Deriving a key from a symbol

```
S2         L    R5,SYMBOL+4
           SR   R4,R4
           D    R4,=F'253'      DIVIDE SECOND HALF
           L    R5,SYMBOL
*** FORM NEW DIVIDEND FROM REMAINDER AND FIRST HALF
           D    R4,=F'509'      DERIVED KEY IS REMAINDER IN R4
```

FIGURE 10.7   Pseudo-code for finding a symbol

```
Set ERIND to 0
Set SYMBOL to spaces
Set i to 0
WHILE stmt (i) not = spaces and i < 8   DO
   Move stmt (i) to SYMBOL (i)
   Increase i by 1
IF stmt (i) not = space
   THEN set ERIND to 1
```

---

the symbol is stored in a double word called SYMBOL, the program segment shown in Fig. 10.6 would derive a key from it.

FINDING A SYMBOL

Let us examine more phases of our problem. The first thing to be done, of course, is to find a symbol. For our example, we shall restrict ourselves to looking for a symbol in the name field, which vastly simplifies the job we undertake. We remember that a name is optional, but if one is present, it begins in position 1 of the statement and is terminated by the first blank encountered. Supposing that a statement has just been read, and that it is stored at STMT, our procedure might be as shown in Fig. 10.7.

A program segment for finding the symbol is shown in Fig. 10.8. We use IC and STC for moving characters of the symbol because these are RX-type instructions and can therefore be indexed. There are two results of the segment: the eight-byte SYMBOL and the one-byte ERIND. In the next step, our program can most efficiently test ERIND by using the CLI instruction.

SEARCHING FOR A SYMBOL

After a symbol is found, a key can be derived from it; the segment of Fig. 10.6 thus follows logically after that of Fig. 10.8. Next we can try to find the symbol in our table. The search may have any of three possible outcomes:

1. The symbol is found, and the address of the cell containing it is presented.

2. The symbol is not in the table, but the address of an empty cell appropriate for entering the symbol in the table is presented.

3. The symbol is not in the table, and there is no appropriate cell for it.

As often, we set an indicator to identify which of the three outcomes is the result.

Figure 10.9 shows a procedure for the search. The main control structure is a WHILE loop that essentially says to keep searching until something happens. Inside the loop, there are two IFs that distinguish among the three possibilities (symbol found in a cell, empty cell found, or neither, so keep searching). We need one more IF to bring the cell address back into the table if

FIGURE 10.8   Program segment for finding a symbol

```
            MVI    ERIND,X'0'
            MVC    SYMBOL(8),=CL8' '
            SR     R4,R4          I = 0
            SR     R5,R5
* WHILE STMT(I) NOT = SPACES AND I < 8 DO
FINDSLP     IC     R5,STMT(R4)
            C      R5,=F'64'      64 IS DEC. EQUIV OF SPACE
            BE     FINDS2
            C      R4,=F'8'
            BNL    FINDS2
* . MOVE STMT(I) TO SYMBOL(I)
            STC    R5,SYMBOL(R4)
* . INCREASE I BY 1
            LA     R4,1(,R4)
            B      FINDSLP
* ENDWHILE
* IF STMT(I) NOT = SPACE
FINDS2      C      R5,=F'64'
            BE     NEXTSTEP
* . THEN SET ERIND TO 1
            MVI    ERIND,X'1'
* ENDIF
NEXTSTEP DS         0H
```

the increment has pushed the cell address beyond the table.

Figure 10.10 shows a program segment that follows the strategy of Fig. 10.9. Assume that the empty table is initialized by storing a space in at least the first byte of every cell in the table; the segment makes use of this assumption in the CLI instruction, which tests whether a cell is empty. The segment is useful both for entering and for retrieving information about a symbol.

FIGURE 10.9   Procedure for searching a table for a symbol

```
Set Incr = (N − 1)/2*(cell length)
Set K = index to table:(derived key)*(cell length)
Set ERIND = 2
WHILE Incr ≥ 0 and ERIND = 2   DO
   IF SYMBOL is at cell K
     THEN Set ERIND = 0
     ELSE IF cell K is empty
        THEN  Set ERIND = 1
        ELSE  Add Incr to K
              Subtract cell length from Incr
              If K is beyond table
                    THEN decrease K by table size (in bytes)
```

FIGURE 10.10   Program segment for searching a table for a symbol

```
***********************************************************************
***      FIND ADDRESS OF CELL IN TABLE CONTAINING SYMBOL
***         IN R4, WITH ERIND = 0
***      OR IF TABLE TOO FULL FOR THIS SYMBOL, ERIND = 2
***      DURING WHILE LOOP, ERIND = 2 MEANS
***         HAVE NOT YET FOUND SYMBOL IN TABLE
***         OR AN EMPTY CELL TO STORE SYMBOL IN
***      ASSUME INITIALIZATION:
***         R5 = TABLE SIZE (NUMBER OF CELLS)
***         R6 = CELL LENGTH
***         R3 = DERIVED KEY FROM SYMBOL
***      USE QUADRATIC PROBING METHOD
***********************************************************************
          MR    R4,R6
          LR    R7,R5           TABLE SIZE IN BYTES
          LA    R9,TABLE(R7)    TOP OF TABLE
          SR    R5,R6
          D     R4,=F'2'
          LR    R8,R5           R8 CONTAINS INCREMENT
          MR    R2,R6           DERIVED KEY * CELL LENGTH
          LA    R4,TABLE(R3)
          MVI   ERIND,X'2'
* WHILE INCR >= 0 AND ERIND = 2 DO
SRCHTBL   LTR   R8,R8
          BM    NEXTSTEP
          CLI   ERIND,X'2'
          BNE   NEXTSTEP
* . IF SYMBOL IS AT CELL K (ADDRESS R4)
          CLC   SYMBOL(8),0(R4)
          BNE   SRCHELS1
* . . THEN SET ERIND = 0
          MVI   ERIND,X'0'
          B     SRCHTBL
* . . ELSE IF CELL K IS EMPTY
SRCHELS1  CLI   0(R4),C' '
          BNE   SRCHELS2
* . . . THEN SET ERIND = 1
          MVI   ERIND,X'1'
          B     SRCHTBL
* . . . ELSE K = K + INCR, INCR = INCR - CELL LENGTH
SRCHELS2  AR    R4,R8
          SR    R8,R6
* . . . IF CELL ADDRESS IS BEYOND TABLE
          CR    R4,R9
          BL    SRCHTBL
* . . . . THEN REDUCE ADDRESS BY TABLE SIZE
          SR    R4,R7
          B     SRCHTBL
* . . . ENDIF (CELL ADDRESS BEYOND TABLE)
* . . ENDIF (CELL K EMPTY)
* . ENDIF (SYMBOL IS AT CELL K)
* ENDWHILE (INCR >= 0 AND ERIND = 2)
NEXTSTEP  DS    0H
```

As an illustration, suppose that the symbols START, STARSTAR, GMTC, A, NLEC, SASOT, and ENUF are encountered in this order and placed in a table of size 509 according to the procedures described. The first four symbols generate no collisions, and so are placed in the table in cells

START	cell	84
STARSTAR	cell	243
GMTC	cell	309
A	cell	471

The symbol NLEC generates a derived key 309, which creates a collision; NLEC must be stored at cell $309 + 254 - 509 = 54$. The symbol SASOT generates a derived key of 54; although 54 is not the derived key of another symbol encountered, it generates a collision nevertheless, with NLEC, which was just stored at cell 54. Cell $54 + 254 = 308$ is used for SASOT. Finally, ENUF has a derived key of 309, so must be stored at $54 + 253 = 307$. In summary, the symbols are associated with keys and cells as follows:

Symbol	Derived key	Cell
START	84	84
STARSTAR	243	243
GMTC	309	309
A	471	471
NLEC	309	54
SASOT	54	308
ENUF	309	307

m a i n   i d e a s

- ☐ Instructions are available for moving one or more characters between main-storage locations and for moving single characters between main storage and a register or from an immediate byte in an instruction to a main storage location.

- ☐ Character compare operations CLI, CLC, and CLCL permit comparison of one or more characters without bringing the characters into registers. The comparisons are made on byte strings considered as unsigned integers.

- ☐ When a list is to be generated, but relatively few retrievals are to be made from the list later, the labor of ordering the list is uneconomical. Derived keys can be used to minimize total search and insertion time.

■ **PROBLEMS** FOR REVIEW AND IMAGINATION

10.1 Write a sequence of instructions that do not include IC that will have the same result as

```
IC    R4,AB
```

Do the same for

```
STC   R6,G
```

10.2 The program segment of Fig. 10.2 can be shortened by making the search loop into a REPEAT-UNTIL instead of a WHILE structure, and then making use of a BCT. Make the change.

10.3 Some models include an instruction MVCIN; it is just like MVC except that the second operand address is the address of the *rightmost* byte, and the sequence of bytes is reversed during the move. For example, if storage location GN contains GEORGE STRUBLE, the instruction

```
MVCIN GNREV(14),GN+13
```

will put ELBURTS EGROEG in the area GNREV. This instruction is useful in preparing output for certain printers that print one line left to right, then the next line right to left, thus saving the time required for a carriage return. Think of other uses for MVCIN.

10.4 Write two program segments that will each move the eight characters stored starting at SOURCE to a field at RESULT, reversing the order of the characters. In one segment, use the MVCIN instruction, in the other, do not use MVCIN.

10.5 Rewrite the segment of Fig. 10.4 so that you do *not* convert characters that are inside a pair of quotes. Actually, to make it easier, do not convert lowercase characters that are after an *odd number* of quote characters. This kind of modification might be needed if we were converting characters in an assembler language program but preserving lowercase characters in constants and literals.

10.6 Rewrite the program segment shown in Fig. 10.5 to keep count regions of a half-word per count.

10.7 Making suitable assumptions, write loops around the segment shown in Fig. 10.5 that will read a number of records (find the number at location NREC), and count all positions 0 through 39 of the record.

10.8 You are writing a small part of the System/370 assembler. The assembler has already figured out that the current statement is a DC statement of character type (C) *without* an explicit length specification (like L17). The address of the opening quote of the constant itself is in register 2. Your segment is to put the constant itself in an area named CON, and its length in register 3. Assume that the constant terminates with a quote (') in the same line. Remember that if the writer of the statement needed a character ' or &, *two* of them are included in the statement, so your segment must check for and decode such occurrences.

10.9   What additional character-handling instructions would you like to see in computers? Explain advantages with respect to particular problems.

10.10   The arguments made in Section 10.7 about the time spent in insertion and search of items in a list are rather sketchy. Outline how you would evaluate each proposed organization and choose one for a class of uses.

10.11   Devise and program a procedure for deriving keys to be used given that each of 50 derived keys is to be associated with a bucket of, say, 10 cells.

10.12   Program the insertion of an item in a list using one of the organizations mentioned but not illustrated in Section 10.7—an overflow area used sequentially, links to overflow cells, or bucketing techniques.

10.13   Why can we not divide both halves of our symbol by 509 in the segment below (replacing Fig. 10.6) in order to derive a key?

```
        L       R5,SYMBOL
        SR      R4,R4
        D       R4,=F'509'
        L       R5,SYMBOL+4
        D       R4,=F'509'
```

10.14   Rewrite the segment of Fig. 10.8 to use MVC instead of IC and STC instructions to move the characters into the SYMBOL area.

10.15   Rewrite Fig. 10.8, using a BXH instruction (as well as a comparison with a space) to implement the WHILE structure.

10.16   Write a program segment for System/360 that will have the same effect as a given CLCL instruction; the older models did not include MVCL, CLCL, ICM, STCM, CLM.

10.17   Write a program segment that will spread the 40 characters from HEAD into every second byte of the area DHEAD, namely DHEAD, DHEAD+2, DHEAD+4, etc. Have blanks put in the intervening bytes of DHEAD.

10.18   The last six instructions of Fig. 10.10 are

```
        AR      R4,R8
        SR      R8,R6
        CR      R4,R9
        BL      SRCHTBL
        SR      R4,R7
        B       SRCHTBL
```

These instructions can be replaced by

```
SR      R8,R6
BXLE    R4,R8,SRCHTBL
SR      R4,R7
B       SRCHTBL
```

What must be the contents of register 9 for this to work properly? Because the increment (register 8) is now incremented *before* instead of *after* use, what else must be done to fix the entire segment?
Compare the two versions stylistically.

10.19 The segment of Fig. 10.10 was written with some generality: the length of the table and the length of each cell are given in registers, and if they change, the segment need not be changed; only the values in the registers must be initialized to different values. However, the length of a symbol is included as exactly eight bytes; no generality here. Since this quantity is used as a *length* in a CLC instruction, it is hard to use it as a register value (until you learn the EX instruction in Chapter 15). However, the CLCL instruction *does* want the length of a comparison to be in a register. Rewrite Fig. 10.10 to use the length of a symbol as presented in a register; use the CLCL instruction in place of the CLC instruction.

■ **REFERENCES** ▬▬▬▬▬▬▬▬▬▬▬▬▬▬▬▬▬

Calingaert, Peter, *Assemblers, Compilers, and Program Translation,* Computer Science Press, Potomac, Md., 1979. Discussion of the organization of symbol tables.

Dodds, D. J., "Reducing Dictionary Size by Using a Hashing Technique," *Communications of the Association for Computing Machinery* **25**, 6 (June 1982), pp. 368–70. An application of hashing.

IBM System/370 Principles of Operation, GA 22-7000, IBM Corporation. Reference for the byte operations instructions.

Knuth, Donald E., *The Art of Computer Programming, Vol. 3: Sorting and Searching,* Addison-Wesley, Reading, Mass., 1973. An analysis of hashing and collision resolution.

Maurer, W. D., and T. G. Lewis, "Hash Table Methods," *Computing Surveys* **7**, 1 (March 1975), pp. 5–20. A good tutorial discussion of hashing.

11

BIT OPERATIONS

The previous chapters showed how to do manipulations of an arithmetic nature and movement of character data. Not all data are numerical or character in form, so some must be manipulated in still different ways. This chapter presents logical operations and operations that can set or change any preselected pattern of bits in a word or character string. Also presented are the shift instructions that move bits from right to left or left to right in a register. All these instructions are useful and necessary for performing a number of processes, as you will see in examples.

11.1 Logical Instructions: Arithmetic on Unsigned Numbers

In Chapter 10 the nature of logical instructions in the IBM System/370 was introduced; these instructions treat data as unsigned integers. In Chapter 10 only the logical instructions CLI, CLC, and CLCL were discussed, since that chapter was concerned with character manipulation. There are also logical instructions that deal specifically with full words; we introduce them now. There are six, including the RR and RX forms, which perform the functions add, subtract, and compare.

The add and subtract operations leave the same results in the first operand register as do the normal add and subtract operations. The difference is in the setting of the condition code and the exceptions that can possibly cause interrupts. The add and subtract instructions can be described as

Instruction	Type	Full Name	Action
AL	RX	Add Logical	$R1 \leftarrow c(R1) + c(S2)$
ALR	RR	Add Logical Register	$R1 \leftarrow c(R1) + c(R2)$
SL	RX	Subtract Logical	$R1 \leftarrow c(R1) - c(S2)$
SLR	RR	Subtract Logical Register	$R1 \leftarrow c(R1) - c(R2)$

The condition code records whether the result is zero or nonzero and also whether or not there is a carry out of the high-order (sign) position. The carry represents overflow of the addition of the two unsigned numbers, which is not at all the same as overflow of the addition of the same words considered as signed numbers. Subtraction is performed by adding the 2's complement of the second operand to the first operand, so a carry must be interpreted in that light. For example, if both operands of an SL instruction are hexadecimal *33333333*, the result in the first operand register will be zero, but a carry is generated since the operation is really addition of *33333333* and *CCCCCCCD*. The first bit of the condition code is set to zero if the operation (AL, ALR, SL, SLR) results in no carry and 1 if a carry is generated. The second bit of the condition code is set to zero if the result of the instruction is zero and to 1 if the result is not zero. We can summarize condition code settings of the four instructions as

$$CC \leftarrow \begin{cases} 0, \text{ if result is zero, no carry;} \\ 1, \text{ if result is not zero, no carry;} \\ 2, \text{ if result is zero, carry;} \\ 3, \text{ if result is not zero, carry.} \end{cases}$$

The logical compare instructions that apply to registers are equivalent to the character-oriented compare logical instructions studied in Chapter 10. The comparisons are made assuming that both operands are unsigned 32-bit integers; the results are

CL   Compare Logical $CC \leftarrow \begin{cases} 0, \text{ if } c(R1) = c(S2); \\ 1, \text{ if } c(R1) < c(S2); \\ 2, \text{ if } c(R1) > c(S2). \end{cases}$

CLR   Compare Logical Register $CC \leftarrow \begin{cases} 0, \text{ if } c(R1) = c(R2); \\ 1, \text{ if } c(R1) < c(R2); \\ 2, \text{ if } c(R1) > c(R2). \end{cases}$

Since none of the six instructions recognizes such a thing as an overflow, there is no possibility of a fixed-point overflow exception. The only exceptions possible as a result of AL, SL, or CL are access and specification. No exception can result from an ALR, SLR, or CLR instruction.

An efficient means of setting the contents of a register to zero is to subtract the contents from itself with an SLR instruction. The instruction

```
        SLR    R5,R5
```

sets register 5 to zero, just as does

```
        SR     R5,R5
```

FIGURE 11.1 Addition of 64-bit integers

```
*** A AND B ARE DOUBLE WORDS HOLDING INTEGERS
*** IN 2'S COMPLEMENT FORM.
*** THIS SEGMENT PUTS THEIR SUM AT LOCATION C.
        LM    R4,R5,A
        AL    R5,B+4          ADD LOWER HALVES
* IF CARRY FROM ADDITION OF LOWER HALVES,
        BC    12,ADDBST2
* . THEN ADD CARRY TO UPPER HALF
        AL    R4,=F'1'
* ENDIF
ADDBST2 AL    R4,B            ADD UPPER HALVES
        STM   R4,R5,C         STORE RESULT
```

As an example of the use of these instructions, let us consider the problem of multiple-precision integer arithmetic, in which a number is represented in several words. As the most trivial case, let us add two integers A and B, each occupying double words in main storage, leaving the result in a double word at location C. Each integer has a sign in the high-order bit in the first of the two words; the numbers are in 2's complement form, but the high-order bit in the second word is an ordinary information-carrying bit. The sum of A and B can be derived and put in C by the segment shown in Fig. 11.1.

The segment shown in Fig. 11.1 ignores the possibility of overflow in the total process. The condition for overflow is that the sign bits of A and B be alike but different from the sign bit of the result. After studying the logical instructions introduced in Section 11.4 you can test the sign bits and set an overflow indicator of your own; this is suggested as Problem 11.2.

11.2 Shift Instructions

Shift instructions move data "sideways" within registers. The movement from right to left is in one sense equivalent to a multiplication by a power of 2, and movement from left to right is equivalent to a division by a power of 2. A shift of any distance is possible; the second operand of each instruction specifies the distance desired.

GENERAL DESCRIPTION OF THE INSTRUCTIONS

There are eight shift instructions; they differ in three ways. First, there are left shifts (bits move right to left) and right shifts (left to right). Second, there are single and double shifts. In single shifts, contents of one register are shifted, but in a double shift, contents of a register pair are shifted, with contents of one register flowing into the other just as though they formed a single register 64 bits long. Third, there are arithmetic shifts and logical shifts. In a logical

FIGURE 11.2   The shift instructions

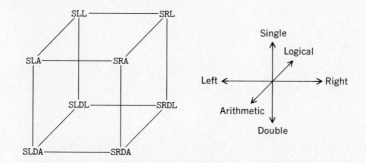

shift all 32 or 64 bits are shifted uniformly, and no considerations of sign are made. In an arithmetic shift the high-order bit of the 32 or 64 is considered to be a sign and is not moved. Each of these characteristics of the shift instructions will be described in more detail in the next few pages. The eight instructions are

SLA   Shift Left single Arithmetic,

SRA   Shift Right single Arithmetic,

SLDA   Shift Left Double Arithmetic,

SRDA   Shift Right Double Arithmetic,

SLL   Shift Left single Logical,

SRL   Shift Right single Logical,

SLDL   Shift Left Double Logical,

SRDL   Shift Right Double Logical.

The three dimensions of difference can be seen in the three-dimensional diagram shown in Fig. 11.2.

All shift instructions are of RS type, but the $R3$ field of the instruction is ignored. The first operand specification $R1$ designates the register or register pair to be shifted; in shift double instructions this must be an even register address, specifying an even register and the odd register following. The second operand, specified by $B2$ and $D2$ as usual, gives the number of bit positions by which the contents of register $R1$ are to be shifted. However, only the low-order six bits of the sum of $B2$ and $D2$ are used, so the maximum shift that can be specified is 63. Since the maximum length of a field to be shifted is 64, a shift of 64 or more bit positions is unnecessary.

LOGICAL SHIFTS

Let us now examine the logical shift instructions, which are simpler in operation than the arithmetic shifts. The SLL (Shift Left Logical) instruction shifts the contents of one register to the left. Bits are lost from the left end of the register (we say they fall into the "bit-bucket"), and zeros are filled on the right in

FIGURE 11.3 Action of the SLL instruction

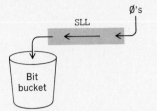

the bit positions vacated in the shift. Figure 11.3 shows the movement of bits through the register. For example, if register 4 contains

$$10011001111111111100110010000001,$$

an instruction

$$\text{SLL} \quad \text{R4,6}$$

will change the contents of register 4 to

$$01111111111100110010000001000000.$$

The six leftmost bits of the original contents, 100110, are lost; the remaining 26 bits are moved to the left six bit positions, and 000000 is filled in the rightmost positions.

Similarly, SRL (Shift Right Logical) shifts a single register's contents to the right, losing bits from the right end and filling in with zeros on the left end. Figure 11.4 shows movement of bits performed by SRL.

FIGURE 11.4 Action of the SRL instruction

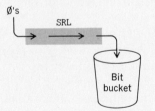

FIGURE 11.5 Action of the SLDL instruction

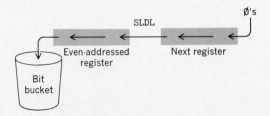

The double-register logical shifts are performed similarly on what is essentially a 64-bit register. In a SLDL (Shift Left Double Logical) instruction the leftmost bits of the even-addressed register are lost, and other bits are moved left. The leftmost bits of the odd-addressed register are moved to the rightmost portion of the even-addressed register; other bits are moved left in the odd-addressed register, and zeros are filled in the rightmost bit positions of the odd-addressed register. Figure 11.5 shows the movement of bits in the two registers. For example, suppose registers 4 and 5 contain

Register 4   Register 5
10011001111111111100110010000001   00001111000000001111111101010101.

Execution of the instruction

SLDL R4,6

will change the contents of registers 4 and 5 to

Register 4   Register 5
01111111111100110010000001000011   11000000001111111101010101000000.

The six bits 100110 are lost from register 4; the remaining 26 bits are moved left. The low-order six-bit positions of register 4 are filled with 000011, the high-order bits from register 5. The low-order 26 bits of register 5 are moved left six positions, and six zeros are filled in the rightmost end of register 5.

Similarly, a SRDL (Shift Right Double Logical) instruction shifts the contents of an even-addressed register into the following odd-addressed register. The entire register pair acts as a 64-bit register with bits moving to the right, some bits being lost from the right end, and zeros being filled in at the left end, as shown in Fig. 11.6.

None of the four logical shift instructions, SLL, SRL, SLDL, or SRDL, affects the condition code.

The only possible program check exception to occur on a logical shift instruction is a specification exception; this occurs if *R1* is given as an odd register address in a double-register shift instruction, SLDL or SRDL.

The logical shift instructions are often used to pack data. For example, suppose that there is a two-bit quantity IND in register 4 in the low-order bit positions, a 15-bit quantity P in the low-order positions of register 5, and a 15-bit

FIGURE 11.6 Action of the SRDL instruction

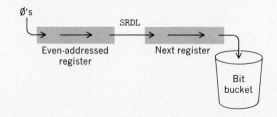

quantity Q in the low-order positions of register 6 that are to be stored in one word W in the order IND, P, Q. Multiplications and additions could be performed, but shifts are simpler and faster, and do not require assumptions about the contents of the high-order bit positions in the registers containing IND, P, and Q. The packing can be done by

```
SLL    R5,17    P TO UPPER PART OF R5
SLDL   R4,15    IND,P IN R4
LR     R5,R6    Q TO R5
SLL    R5,17    Q TO UPPER PART OF R5
SLDL   R4,15    IND,P,Q IN R4
ST     R4,W     STORE AT W.
```

You are urged to diagram the exact placement of IND, P, and Q after each instruction, and to convince yourself that contents of upper-order bit positions of registers 4, 5, and 6 are irrelevant to this sequence.

Similar shift instructions can be used to break a word down again into its component parts. Such packing and unpacking are often quite necessary to reduce the space required for data and intermediate results and to permit them to be kept in main storage, where the alternative is to store some of the data on external devices such as magnetic disk, drum, or tape, and to recall the data when needed. The savings in time spent writing and retrieving the data far outweigh the cost in time of packing and unpacking data kept in main storage.

In Section 11.4 you will see how any one particular field may be retrieved more efficiently by logic and shift instructions than by shift instructions alone.

ARITHMETIC SHIFTS

The four arithmetic shift instructions, SRA, SLA, SRDA, and SLDA, follow the same patterns as the logical shift instructions. There are right shifts (SRA, SRDA) which move bits to the right in registers, and left shifts (SLA, SLDA) which move bits to the left. There are single-register shifts (SRA, SLA) and double-register shifts (SRDA, SLDA), which couple a register pair just as is done for the logical double shifts. The arithmetic shift instructions differ from the logical shifts only in their treatment of signs and fill bits and in the setting of condition code.

The bit in position 0, the sign bit, does not participate in an arithmetic shift; only the low-order 31 bits (or 63 bits in a double-register shift) are shifted. Thus the sign of the original number is always preserved. During a left shift, bits filled at the right of the register or register pair are zeros. This is consistent with treating the arithmetic shift as a multiplication by 2, regardless of the sign of the original number. A shift of a bit *unlike the sign bit* out of the high-order portion during a left arithmetic shift constitutes an overflow. The overflow is recorded in the condition code, which is discussed later.

In a right arithmetic shift, bits filled on the left of the register or register pair are *copies of the sign bit*. This is necessary if the result of the shift is to be considered as a division of the original number by 2. Actually, the right shift is

FIGURE 11.7   Action of the arithmetic shift instructions

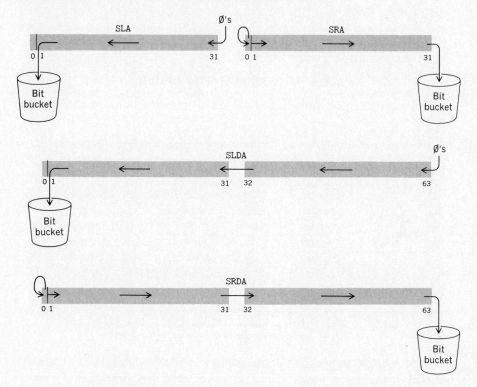

equivalent to a division by 2 or a power of 2 *with rounding down*. For example, the result of shifting a number 7 right one position is the number 3, but the result of shifting −7 right is the number −4. This is in distinction to the action of the divide instructions; a division of −7 by 2 would give a quotient of −3 and a remainder of −1. Among other things, the rounding down implies that if all "significant" bits of a negative number are shifted right and lost, as, for example, in a SRA R5,34 instruction, the result will be a string of 32 1's in the register, which is equivalent to the number −1. Similarly, if all significant bits of a negative number are shifted out and lost in a left shift, the sign bit of 1 will remain and the result will be -2^{31}.

The arithmetic shifts can be represented pictorially as shown in Fig. 11.7.

An arithmetic shift instruction sets the condition code. The condition code is set to

> 0, if the result = 0;
>
> 1, if the result < 0;
>
> 2, if the result > 0;
>
> 3, if there is an overflow on a left shift.

Let us consider some examples of arithmetic shifts. Assume the contents of register 4 to be

100110011111111111100110010000001

and the contents of register 5 to be

00001111000000001111111101010101.

With these contents before *each* of the following instructions, results will be as follows:

SRA	R4,1	Register 4:	11ØØ11ØØ111111111ØØ11ØØ1ØØØØØØ	CC:1
SLA	R4,1	Register 4:	1Ø11ØØ11111111111ØØ11ØØ1ØØØØØØ1Ø	CC:3
SRA	R4,31	Register 4:	11111111111111111111111111111111	CC:1
SLA	R4,31	Register 4:	1ØØØØØØØØØØØØØØØØØØØØØØØØØØØØØØØØ	CC:3
SRA	R5,1	Register 5:	ØØØØ1111ØØØØØØØØØ11111111Ø1Ø1Ø1Ø	CC:2
SRA	R5,28	Register 5:	ØØØØØØØØØØØØØØØØØØØØØØØØØØØØØØØØØ	CC:0
SLA	R5,3	Register 5:	Ø1111ØØØØØØØØØ11111111Ø1Ø1Ø1Ø1ØØØ	CC:2
SLA	R5,4	Register 5:	Ø1111ØØØØØØØØ11111111Ø1Ø1Ø1Ø1ØØØØ	CC:3
SLA	R5,31	Register 5:	ØØØØØØØØØØØØØØØØØØØØØØØØØØØØØØØØØ	CC:3
SLDA	R4,8	Register 4:	111111111ØØ11ØØ1ØØØØØØ1ØØØØ1111	
		Register 5:	ØØØØØØØØ11111111Ø1Ø1Ø1Ø1ØØØØØØØØ	CC:3
SRDA	R4,8	Register 4:	111111111ØØ11ØØ11111111111ØØ11ØØ	
		Register 5:	1ØØØØØØ1ØØØØ1111ØØØØØØØØØ11111111	CC:1

Two program-check exceptions may occur on arithmetic shift instructions. On the double-register instructions SLDA and SRDA a specification exception occurs if *R1* specifies an odd address for a register pair. In case of overflow, the left shifts generate a fixed-point overflow exception, which causes interrupt if the fixed-point-overflow bit in the program mask is set to 1.

Because of their treatment of signs and possibilities of overflow, the arithmetic shift instructions are less well suited to packing of fields than are the logical shift instructions. The arithmetic shift instructions, however, are better suited to performing what should amount to multiplication and division by powers of 2. You can find in program segments and problems of earlier chapters several instances in which an arithmetic shift is more convenient than the multiply or divide instruction actually shown. Other examples cannot be improved by the use of shift instructions, given the statement of the problem, but if some length or other parameter is given as a power of 2, a shift instruction can replace a multiply and simplify the segment.

COUNTING BITS IN A WORD

Let us examine another short example of the use of a shift instruction. Figure 11.8 shows a program segment that counts the 1-bits in the word AFFW. Each bit is moved into the low-order bit position of register 2 from where it is added to register 5. Thus each 1-bit is added, forming the count. The 0-bits are added

FIGURE 11.8 Counting the 1-bits in a word

```
*** COUNT THE 1'S IN A WORD AT AFFW
*** STORE THE COUNT IN AFF
          L      R3,AFFW
          SLR    R5,R5           COUNT IN R5
* DO FOR R6 = 32 TO 1, INCR -1
          LA     R6,32
LP        SLR    R2,R2           CLEAR R2
* . MOVE A BIT INTO R2, ADD IT TO COUNT IN R5
          SLDL   R2,1            MOVE A BIT INTO R2
          AR     R5,R2           ADD BIT TO COUNT
          BCT    R6,LP
* ENDFOR
          ST     R5,AFF          STORE COUNT
```

too, but of course they do not affect the sum, and it is easier to add them than to decide not to. Note that the instruction SLR R2,R2 must be inside the loop so that 1-bits once found do not have a chance to be shifted over and add 2, 4, 8, etc. to register 5.

11.3   An Example: Hexadecimal Conversion

At times you will want the hexadecimal contents of a register printed. Each of the hexadecimal digits must be converted to printable characters; the shift instructions can help in the conversion.

The procedure illustrated in the program segment of Fig. 11.9 is to move the hexadecimal digits one at a time into a register, add a factor to each to generate the appropriate printable character, and store it in a character string. The segment uses a double-length shift instruction to move a hexadecimal digit into register 2; the result of a logical or arithmetic instruction would be the same, since the entire register 2 contains zeros before the shift.

There are two cases in the conversion of a hexadecimal digit to its character form. It is necessary to know something about the character representations. The segment does *not* require that you know the exact representation of each hexadecimal digit, but it does assume that the digits 0–9 have consecutive character representations and that the digits A–F also have consecutive character representations. These cases are distinguished in an IF-THEN-ELSE structure, and some unusual absolute expressions, C'Ø' and C'A'-1Ø, are used for displacements in LA instructions. Perhaps you should take this occasion to review (in Chapter 3) the definitions of absolute and relocatable expressions and where they can be used. Also, with a few examples, follow the IF-THEN-ELSE structure and trace how hexadecimal digits are converted to the proper character form.

FIGURE 11.9   Conversion from hexadecimal to character

```
*** CONVERT 8 HEXADECIMAL DIGITS
*** FROM WORD ADDRESSED BY R1
*** TO CHAR FORM, IN AREA ADDRESSED BY R5
           L      R3,0(,R1)
           SLR    R4,R4
* DO FOR R4 = 0 TO 7
           LA     R6,1
           LA     R7,7
* . MOVE HEX DIGIT TO R2
LP         SLR    R2,R2
           SLDL   R2,4
*** CONVERT TO CHARACTER; STORE IT
* . IF DIGIT < 10
           C      R2,=F'10'
           BNL    LPELSE
* . . THEN CONVERT TO '0' - '9'
           LA     R2,C'0'(,R2)
           B      LPSTORE
* . . ELSE CONVERT TO 'A' - 'F'
LPELSE     LA     R2,C'A'-10(,R2)
* . ENDIF
LPSTORE    STC    R2,0(R4,R5)
           BXLE   R4,R6,LP
* ENDFOR (R4 = 0 TO 7)
```

11.4   Taking a Square Root

Perhaps you remember learning several years ago a technique for taking square roots that resembles long division. The technique can be described.

■ Mark off the number into pairs of digits, both directions from the decimal point

■ Set root and remainder to zeros

■ REPEAT
Append the leftmost pair of digits not yet used to the remainder (on the right)
Multiply root by 20 to get a divisor
Find the largest digit so that the digit times (divisor plus digit) is not greater than the remainder
Subtract the product just computed from the remainder
Append the digit to the root
UNTIL you have developed all the digits that you want of the root

The computation of the square root of 69169 can serve as an example.

```
                    2   6   3.
             2 | 6  91  69.
             2 | 4
            46 | 2  91
             6 | 2  76
           523 | 15  69
             3 | 15  69
                        0
```

The successive remainders are 0, 2, 15, and finally 0. The numbers designated as *divisor* are 0, 40, and 520. The digits of the square root are developed as 2, 6, and 3.

This process is even easier to carry out in binary because the choice of each digit for the square root is merely a choice between 1 and 0. Take as an example the problem of computing the square root of 121, which is binary 1111001. The same process described by the pseudo-code above applies; where the process prescribes multiplication by 20, we multiply by 4 when working in binary; this is simply a shift of 2 bits.

```
                      1   0   1   1
             1 | 1   11  10  01
             1 | 1
           100 | 11
             0 | 0
          1001 | 11  10
             1 | 10  01
         10101 | 1  01  01
             1 | 1  01  01
                          0
```

The resulting square root is 1011, or decimal 11.

In implementing this algorithm on a computer, the shift instructions are found to be very useful. The step of appending two more bits to the remainder is accomplished nicely by a shift of a register pair. Construction of the proper divisor at each stage uses shifts, and a shift also moves over the bits in the root to make room for a new bit. Figure 11.10 implements this algorithm for taking square roots; you can trace execution on a small number like 121. The shift instructions used could be arithmetic shifts just as well as logical shifts.

11.5   Logical Instructions: AND and OR

This section introduces a class of logical instructions that are quite different from those discussed in Chapter 10 and in Section 11.1. The logical instructions now to be defined perform manipulations on individual bits, manipula-

FIGURE 11.10 Taking a square root

```
*** TAKE SQUARE ROOT OF A POSITIVE NUMBER IN REG. 5
*** LEAVES SQUARE ROOT IN REG. 3
          SLR    R3,R3
          SLR    R4,R4
          LA     R6,16
* DO FOR REG. 6 FROM 16 DOWN TO 1
GENDIGIT SLL     R3,1              MAKE ROOM FOR NEXT DIGIT OF ROOT
*** GENERATE PORTION TO SUBTRACT
          LR     R2,R3
          SLL    R2,1
          A      R2,=F'1'          4 * (CURRENT PORTION OF ROOT) + 1
          SLDL   R4,2
* . IF C(R2) <= C(R4)
          CR     R2,R4
          BH     LOOPCTRL
* . . THEN SUBTRACT FROM REG. 4, ADD 1 TO ROOT
          SR     R4,R2
          A      R3,=F'1'
* . ENDIF
LOOPCTRL BCT     R6,GENDIGIT
* ENDWHILE
```

tions related to the functions used in logic, instead of arithmetic on unsigned numbers.

DEFINITION OF THE FUNCTIONS

This section defines four logical functions before discussing their implementation in a computer. Suppose that we have two operands, each with a value 0 or 1. We can define the AND function as a function of two operands; the value of the function is 1 if *both operands* have the value 1, and 0 otherwise. We can illustrate or define the function as

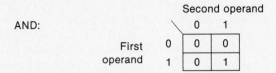

where the numbers in the boxes show the value of the function in each of the four possible cases.

There are two varieties of OR functions; they differ in their treatment of the case in which both operands are 1. First, the EXCLUSIVE OR function has a value 1 if either of the two operands, *but not both*, has the value 1; the value is 0 if both operands are 0 or if both are 1. In tabular form, the function can be described as

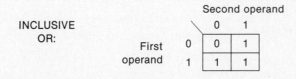

EXCLUSIVE
OR:

The third function is OR, or for emphasis, INCLUSIVE OR. The value of the OR function is 1 if *either or both* of the operands is 1, and 0 only if both operands are 0. In tabular form we have

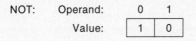

INCLUSIVE
OR:

The fourth function is the NOT function, which is a function of one operand. Its value is what the operand is not; that is, the value is the opposite of the operand. The value is 1 if the operand is 0, and 0 if the operand is 1. In tabular form we have

NOT:	Operand:	0	1
	Value:	1	0

USE OF THE LOGICAL FUNCTIONS IN SYMBOLIC LOGIC

The logical functions get their names from their original use in the representation of symbolic logic. Let the value 1 represent the truth of a proposition (a proposition, roughly speaking, is a statement), and 0 that the proposition is false. Then we can talk about truth or falsity of various new propositions made from other propositions with the aid of connectives AND, OR, and NOT.

A compound proposition, (proposition 1) AND (proposition 2), is true if both proposition 1 and proposition 2 are true, false if either or both are false. If t_1 is a value 1 or 0 representing the truth or falsity of proposition 1, and t_2 acts similarly for proposition 2, then t_1 AND t_2, where AND is the logical function defined above, yields a value 1 or 0 correctly representing the truth or falsity of (proposition 1) AND (proposition 2). The OR, EXCLUSIVE OR, and NOT functions similarly help in assigning values to represent truth or falsity of compound propositions or statements formed using OR and NOT connectives. Mathematicians and logicians always use OR to mean the *inclusive* OR (either or both), and the definition of logical functions here follows this usage. The EXCLUSIVE OR is a useful function, however.

As an example, suppose that proposition 1 is "This book is lousy," and proposition 2 is "So is the IBM System/370." We can form a compound proposition "This book is lousy AND NOT so is the IBM System/370," which in better English is "This book is lousy but the IBM System/370 is not.'' Suppose that proposition 1 is true; the variable t_1 has the value 1. Suppose also that proposition 2 is false, so $t_2 = 0$. The truth of the compound proposition is represented by t_1 AND NOT t_2 ,which has the value

$$1 \text{ AND } (\text{NOT } 0) = 1 \text{ AND } (1) = 1$$

so the compound proposition is true.

USE OF THE LOGICAL FUNCTIONS IN BOOLEAN ALGEBRA

In the 19th century, George Boole developed the algebra that bears his name. In Boolean algebra all quantities have values 0 or 1, and arithmetic is defined by

$$
\begin{array}{ll}
0 + 0 = 0, & 0 \times 0 = 0, \\
0 + 1 = 1 + 0 = 1, & 0 \times 1 = 1 \times 0 = 0, \\
1 + 1 = 1, & 1 \times 1 = 1.
\end{array}
$$

The only abnormal relationship is that $1 + 1 = 1$. Subtraction and division are not usually used. Boolean algebra is used in circuit design and analysis and in many other instances of manipulation of binary-choice data.

The AND logical function is equivalent to Boolean multiplication; if X and Y are Boolean variables (having values 0 or 1), the Boolean product $X \times Y$ is the same as the logical function X AND Y. Either has the value 1 if and only if both X and Y are 1.

The INCLUSIVE OR function is equivalent to Boolean addition. The Boolean sum $X + Y$ has the same value as the logical function X OR Y: either is 1 if at least one of the variables X and Y has the value 1, and zero only if both X and Y are zero.

IMPLEMENTATION IN THE IBM SYSTEM/370

There are twelve instructions in the IBM System/370 that perform the logical functions AND, OR, and EXCLUSIVE OR on a number of bits in parallel. For each of the three logical functions there are four instructions of different types, allowing for operands in various places and of various lengths. The mnemonic operation codes of the 12 instructions can be shown in a table as follows:

Type	AND	OR	EXCL. OR
RR:	NR	OR	XR
RX:	N	O	X
SI:	NI	OI	XI
SS:	NC	OC	XC

In the RR instructions, for example, two full-word operands are in registers. Each logical function is performed on 32 bit pairs in parallel: on the bit in position 0 in the first operand and on the bit in position 0 of the second operand to yield a result in bit position 0 of the first operand, and so on for each of the other 31 bit positions. These logical instructions are distinguished by the fact that the function, AND, OR, or EXCLUSIVE OR, is performed on each of the 32 pairs of bits in corresponding positions independently of the action on other bit positions; there are no carries or other interactions.

The RR-type instructions NR, OR, and XR perform the corresponding logical instructions on contents of two registers. The RX-type instructions N,O, and X perform the logical functions on contents of two full words, one in a register and one in main storage; the result is placed in the register named as first operand. The SI-type instructions NI, OI, and XI perform logical functions on the contents of one byte in main storage and a byte *I2* in the instruction. The SS-type instructions NC, OC, and XC perform the logical functions on two strings of bytes in main storage. The lengths of the two strings are equal, so only one length is specified; strings from 1 to 256 bytes long can be accommodated.

The condition code is set by each of the 12 logical instructions. It is set to 0 if the result of the instruction is 0, that is, if every bit is 0; and to 1 if at least one bit of the result is 1. Condition codes 2 and 3 are not used by these instructions.

Let us examine some examples of the instructions. Suppose that the initial contents of registers and main storage are

Register 5:	00001111000011110000111100001111
Register 6:	00110011001100110011001100110011
Word at main storage location Q:	01010101010101010101010101010101
Three bytes at main storage location P:	000000001111111100111100

If these contents are assumed before *each* of the following instructions, the results will be as indicated in Fig. 11.11.

Program-check exceptions are possible in most of the logical instructions. Access exceptions are possible in all but the RR-type instructions, since these instructions can make reference to nonexistent main storage or to storage protected for other use. Specification exceptions can be generated by the N, O, and X instructions if your computer does not have the byte-oriented-operand feature. No other program checks are possible.

There is no instruction specifically for the NOT logical function, but it can be performed by any of several instructions. An EXCLUSIVE OR operation, with 1 as its second operand, has the same result as a NOT operation on its first operand; that is: (*a* EXCLUSIVE OR 1) is the same as (NOT *a*). You can use this fact to implement NOT in the IBM System/370:

```
        XI      G,X'FF'
```

FIGURE 11.11 Results of logical instructions

Instruction		Result		Cond. code
NR	R5,R6	00000011000000110000001100000011	in R5	1
OR	R5,R6	00111111001111110011111100111111	in R5	1
XR	R6,R5	00111000011110000111100001111000	in R6	1
N	R5,Q	00000101000001010000010100000101	in R5	1
O	R6,Q	01110111011101110111011101110111	in R6	1
XI	Q,B'11000011'	10010110	at Q	1
NI	P+2,X'F0'	00110000	at P+2	1
OC	Q(3),P	010101011111111101111101	at Q	1
XC	P+1(2),Q+2	1010101001101001	at P+1	1
NC	Q(1),P	00000000	at Q	0
XI	Q+1,B'01010101'	00000000	at Q+1	0

performs a NOT function on each of the bits of G. The four types of EXCLUSIVE OR instructions make it easy enough to perform a NOT function on any number of bytes in main storage or on the contents of a register. Besides the EXCLUSIVE OR, there are other ways to perform the NOT function. For example,

```
L    R4,=F'-1'
S    R4,WRONG
```

places NOT WRONG in register 4. You can verify this, and also the claim that there is no possibility of overflow on the subtraction!

USE OF THE LOGICAL INSTRUCTIONS IN BIT MANIPULATION
Interpret the logical instructions as selectively changing bits in an operand. The bits to be changed are in the first operand; which bits are eligible for change are determined by the bits in the second operand, which thus acts as a mask, covering and protecting some bits while leaving other bits exposed and eligible for change.

The AND instructions NR, N, NI, and NC selectively set bits in the first operand to 0, in bit positions where the second operand has 0's. Thus in the mask a 1-bit protects the bit in the corresponding position of the first operand from change; a 0-bit in the mask directs that the bit in the corresponding position of the first operand be set to 0 regardless of its previous value. For example,

```
NI    G,B'00001111'
```

directs that the first four bits of the byte at location G be set to 0's while the last four bits remain unchanged.

The condition code can be thought of as recording whether there are any 1's left in the first operand (CC = 1) or whether all bits are now 0's (CC = 0).

The INCLUSIVE OR instructions OR, O, OI, and OC selectively set bits in the first operand to 1, in positions where the corresponding bits of the second operand are 1's. In positions where the bits of the second operand are 0, the bits in corresponding positions of the first operand are left unchanged. As an example,

```
OC    R(2),=B'1111ØØØØ1111ØØØØ'
```

directs that the four high-order bits of each of the two bytes at R and R+1 are to be set to 1's; the four lower-order bits of each byte are to remain unchanged. There is thus a kind of symmetry to the masks used by AND and OR functions in selectively setting bits: if bits are selectively to be set at 0's, 0's appear in corresponding positions in the mask used by an AND instruction; if bits are to be set to 1's, then 1's appear in corresponding positions of the mask used by an OR instruction.

The EXCLUSIVE OR instructions XR, X, XI, and XC selectively change or complement bits in the first operand in positions where the bits in the second operand are 1's but leave unchanged bits in positions where the corresponding bits in the second operand are 0's. For example,

```
XI    SWITCH,X'Ø1'
```

will change the last bit of the byte SWITCH from 1 to 0 or from 0 to 1, whichever it finds, and leave the other seven bits unchanged. Note that execution of this instruction a second time will change the contents of SWITCH back to what it was before the first XI instruction. Thus location SWITCH can act as a switch, causing certain actions on alternate passes through a segment. For example,

```
        MVI  SWITCH,X'ØØ'
        ...
LOOP    XI   SWITCH,X'Ø1'
        BZ   ON
OFF     ...
```

will cause a branch to ON on the second, fourth, sixth,... time control is passed to LOOP; the segment beginning at OFF will be executed the first, third, fifth,... time control is passed to LOOP.

AN EXAMPLE: RESOLVING THE SIGN OF AN UNPACKED NUMBER

When a number is unpacked, perhaps by the instruction

```
UNPK  CHAR(8),PAKD(8)
```

FIGURE 11.12   Separation of sign from units digit

```
*** PLACE THE SIGN OF AN UNPACKED NUMBER (CHAR TO CHAR+7)
*** AT CHAR-1, BEFORE THE DIGITS, AS A PRINTABLE CHARACTER
*** AND CHANGE DIGIT TO PLAIN PRINTABLE DIGIT
* IF SIGN IS MINUS (HEX D)
             MVI    TW,X'F0'
             NC     TW(1),CHAR+7   ISOLATE SIGN
             CLI    TW,X'D0'
             BNE    ST3ELSE
* . THEN STORE MINUS
             MVI    CHAR-1,C'-'
             B      ST4
* . ELSE STORE PLUS
ST3ELSE      MVI    CHAR-1,C'+'
* ENDIF
ST4          OI     CHAR+7,X'F0'
```

its sign is placed in the upper four bits of the last (units) digit. For printing, it is preferable to have the upper four bits all 1's so that the digit will be printed like other digits. First, assuming the number to be positive, we can set the bits to 1's by

$$\text{OI} \qquad \text{CHAR+7,X'F0'}$$

which, as noted above, sets the four upper-order bits to 1's while leaving the lower-order bits intact.

Second, if the sign is unknown, you may wish to store the sign as a printable character at CHAR-1, as well as changing the coding of the units digit as before. You must use the information that a minus sign is coded as 1101 (hexadecimal D) over the units digit. Figure 11.12 shows a segment that performs the entire task.

AN EXAMPLE: RETRIEVING A FIELD FROM A WORD

Section 11.2 discussed the task of packing several fields into a word and indicated that the fields could be separated again by the converse of the same process. This technique is quite satisfactory if you wish to separate all the fields, but if you wish to retrieve or change just one field, you can use the logical instructions to advantage.

For example, suppose a word W is composed of three fields: a 2-bit field IND, a 15-bit field P, and a 15-bit field Q, in that order. Suppose also that you wish to retrieve field P, that is, put it in a register by itself. This can be done with the sequence

```
L      R3,MASKP
N      R3,W        FIELD P ONLY LOADED INTO R3
SRL    R3,15       RIGHT-JUSTIFY
```

where the constant MASKP is defined by

```
     MASKP        DC     BL4'ØØ111111111111111ØØØØØØØØØØØØØØØØ'
```

The AND function performed by the instruction N R3,W sets to 0 in register 3 all bits outside the P field, and loads P in register 3 in its corresponding positions. The shift instruction moves the field to the right of the register.

In older computer models without the byte-oriented-operand feature, precede the definition of MASKP with

```
     DS     ØF
```

to align the constant on a full-word boundary because B-type constants do not force alignment.

Again, suppose that a new 15-bit quantity has been generated that is to replace the P field in the word W, but IND and Q are to remain unchanged. This can be accomplished by the segment (assuming that the upper-order 17 bits of register 3 containing the new P are 0's):

```
     L      R4,W
     N      R4,MASKNOTP     ERASE P
     SLL    R3,15           MOVE NEW P INTO POSITION
     OR     R4,R3           INSERT NEW P
     ST     R4,W
```

where MASKNOTP is defined by

```
     MASKNOTP     DC     BL4'11ØØØØØØØØØØØØØØØØØ111111111111111'
```

AN EXAMPLE: MATCHING AND OPPOSING CONFIGURATIONS

Suppose that you wish to describe a set of objects and have a list of 32 aspects; each object may be represented by whether it is a positive example, a negative example, or a neutral example of each aspect. You may describe an object then in two full words in main storage of a System/370 computer; each bit position of a word holds information about one of the aspects. In the first of the two words a 1-bit represents a positive instance of the aspect, a 0 represents a neutral or negative instance. In the second word, a 1 represents a negative instance and a 0 represents a neutral or positive instance. Thus a positive instance would be recorded as 1 in the first word and 0 in the corresponding position of the second word, a neutral instance would be recorded as 0's in both words, and a negative instance would be recorded as 0 in the first word and 1 in the second word.

Now suppose that two objects so described are to be compared as to the aspects in which they match (either both positive or both negative) and the aspects in which they are opposed (one positive and the other negative). The objects might be boys and girls being paired for dates, and the aspects such important things as "like Chinese food?" "squeeze toothpaste from the top of the tube?" and "root for the New York Yankees?" Or the objects may be subgoals and initial positions in a problem-solving situation, and the aspects be properties that allow one to decide which of several subgoals is closest to the

FIGURE 11.13   Finding matches and oppositions

```
**********************************************************************
*** OBJECTS ARE DESCRIBED IN 32 ASPECTS BY A WORD
***     SHOWING POSITIVE INSTANCES FOLLOWED BY A WORD
***     SHOWING NEGATIVE INSTANCES.
*** THE ADDRESS OF THE FIRST (POSITIVE) WORD OF ONE
***     OBJECT IS IN R8. THE ADDRESS OF A SECOND
***     OBJECT IS IN R9.
*** THIS SEGMENT CONSTRUCTS WORDS MATCH AND OPPOSE
***     SHOWING INCIDENCE OF MATCHES AND OF OPPOSITIONS.
**********************************************************************
        L    R3,0(,R8)     POS. WORD, OBJ. 1
        N    R3,0(,R9)     BOTH POS.
        L    R4,4(,R8)     NEG. WORD, OBJ. 1
        N    R4,4(,R9)     BOTH NEG.
        OR   R3,R4         COMBINE MATCHES
        ST   R3,MATCH
        L    R3,0(,R8)     POS. WORD, OBJ. 1
        N    R3,4(,R9)       AND NEG. WORD, OBJ. 2
        L    R4,4(,R8)     NEG. WORD, OBJ. 1
        N    R4,0(,R9)       AND POS. WORD, OBJ. 2
        OR   R3,R4         COMBINE OPPOSITIONS
        ST   R3,OPPOSE
```

initial conditions and therefore the one with most promise for further work. In any case, we are to construct a word MATCH in which a 1 represents a match of an aspect and 0 represents either opposition or at least one object neutral, and another word OPPOSE in which a 1 represents opposition of the two objects with respect to the aspect and 0 represents either match or at least one object being neutral.

Figure 11.13 shows a program segment that constructs the words MATCH and OPPOSE. AND instructions are used to generate coincidences of 1's in all four relevant pairs of words. The both-positive coincidences and the both-negative coincidences are combined by means of an OR instruction (XR should yield the same result) to form the word to be stored in MATCH, and the positive-negative coincidences are combined similarly to form the word to be stored in OPPOSE.

11.6   Generating Moves in Checkers

As an example in which bits in a word have no arithmetic or character significance but only meanings as individual bits to be manipulated, we show a small part of a checker-playing program. This example shows the use of the bit manipulation facilities provided by logical and shift instructions.

DESCRIBING THE BOARD

The squares on a checkerboard are usually numbered from 1 to 32, which would seem to be nicely suited to use of the 32-bit word of the IBM System/370. However, a much more convenient numbering for our purposes is

FIGURE 11.14 Numbering squares on a checkerboard

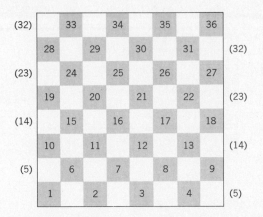

that given in Fig. 11.14. The advantage to this numbering is that a move from a square x forward and to the right is always a move to square $x + 5$, and a move from square x forward and to the left is always a move to square $x + 4$. This numbering was first used by Arthur Samuel in his computer checker-playing experiments in the mid 1950's;† the numbering was especially happy for him since the computer he was working with, the IBM 704, had a 36-bit word length. In the IBM System/370 we can commit the first 36 bits of a double word to a board picture and still realize significant execution-time efficiencies. The contents of square 1 will be recorded in bit position 0, square 2 in bit position 1, and so on.

Still following Samuel's scheme, we allocate four 36-bit sequences (in the IBM System/370, four double words) to the complete description of a board position. We assume that the bottom row (squares 1–4) is the home position for black; that is, black moves up the board, while red moves down. We will record in the first of the four double words describing a board position a 1 in the bit position corresponding to each square on which there is any black *forward-active* piece, that is, a checker or king. In the second of the four double words we record a 1 corresponding to black *backward-active* pieces, that is, kings. Thus at the beginning of a game, bits 0–3, 5–8, and 9–12, representing "squares" 1–4, 6–9, and 10–13 of the first double word, would contain 1's, with all other bits in that double word set to 0's. All the bits in the second double word would be 0 because there are no black kings. The third word contains the configuration of red forward-active pieces, forward-active meaning up the board from black's viewpoint, actually backward for red. Thus the third word records the positions of red kings. The fourth word records the positions of red backward-active pieces, that is, checkers and kings. In none of these double words will there be a 1 in positions corresponding to "squares" 5, 14, 23,

---

† A. L. Samuel, "Some Studies in Machine Learning Using the Game of Checkers," *IBM Journal of Research and Development* **3**, pp. 210–229 (1959).

FIGURE 11.15   Generating black's forward right moves

```
*** GENERATE POSSIBLE FORWARD MOVES TO THE RIGHT FOR BLACK
        LM    R4,R5,0(R1)    LOAD BLACK FORWARD-ACTIVE (BFA)
        SLDL  R4,5           MOVE BACK 5 SQUARES
        LM    R6,R7,24(R1)   LOAD RED MEN AND KINGS (RBA)
        SLDL  R6,5           MOVE BACK 5 SQUARES
        OR    R4,R6          COMBINE
        O     R4,MM5         COMBINE WITH BITS FOR SQ. 14, 23, 32
*** REGISTER R4 NOW CONTAINS 1 IN EVERY SQUARE THAT IS NOT ELIGIBLE
*** FOR MOVING INTO, EITHER BECAUSE OCCUPIED OR BECAUSE NONEXISTENT
        X     R4,=F'-1'      CHANGE SO 1 REPRESENTS ELIGIBLE SQUARE
        N     R4,0(,R1)      BLACK FORWARD-ACTIVE AND ELIGIBLE SQ.
        ST    R4,FORDRGHT


MM5     DC    BL4'00000000100000000100000000100000'
```

and 32, and we must see to it that we never try to move a checker into one of these "squares."

We shall assume that the four double words describing a board position are consecutive, and that the address of the first is given in register 1.

GENERATING MOVES

The small parts of the checker-playing problem that will be illustrated are the generation of possible moves and the manipulations required to make a move or jump. Illustrated first is the way all possible right forward moves (not jumps) can be generated *at once* by use of logical and shift instructions. This is the advantage of the square numbering we have adopted.

Figure 11.15 shows a short program segment that accomplishes this task. A word is generated showing which squares are not eligible for moving into by performing OR functions on the squares occupied by black and by red and on

FIGURE 11.16   A sample checkerboard position

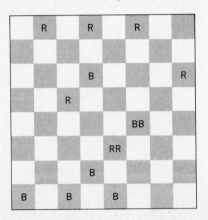

the fictitious squares 14, 23, and 32. Everything is shifted left 5, first so that a single word can hold the relevant information (black cannot move *forward* into squares 1–4) and second so that the bits will correspond with squares from which black checkers or kings might move. After the word of ineligible squares is generated, the configuration of eligible squares is generated by a NOT, actually an EXCLUSIVE OR with an operand full of 1's. The AND instruction N R4,Ø(,R1) is almost anticlimactic; it matches black pieces with positions that are free to be moved into, leaving a word in which each 1 indicates the position of a black piece that can move forward to the right.

To illustrate the processes shown in this segment, let us follow its execution with respect to the board configuration shown in Fig. 11.16. A red checker is shown by the letter R, a red king by RR; similarly, black checkers and kings are shown by B and BB. The first 36 bits of each of the double words representing this board position are as follows.

Black forward active (BFA):

$$111ØØØ1ØØØØØØØØØ1ØØØØØØØ1ØØØØØØØØØØØ$$

Black backward active (BBA):

$$ØØØØØØØØØØØØØØØØ1ØØØØØØØØØØØØØØØØØØØ$$

Red forward active (RFA):

$$ØØØØØØØØØØØ1ØØØØØØØØØØØØØØØØØØØØØØØØ$$

Red backward active (RBA):

$$ØØØØØØØØØØØ1ØØØØØØØ1ØØØØØØ1ØØØØØ111Ø$$

Black checkers are shown in squares 1, 2, 3, 7, and 25, and a black king in square 17. Red checkers are shown in squares 20, 27, 33, 34, and 35, and a red king in square 12. Execution of the segment shown in Fig. 11.15 will have the following result.

Instruction		Register	New contents
LM	R4,R5,Ø(R1)	4	111ØØØ1ØØØØØØØØØ1ØØØØØØØ1ØØØØØØØ
		5	ØØØØØØØØØØØØØØØØØØØØØØØØØØØØØØØØ
SLDL	R4,5	4	Ø1ØØØØØØØØØ1ØØØØØØØ1ØØØØØØØØØØØØ
LM	R6,R7,24(R1)	6	ØØØØØØØØØØØ1ØØØØØØØ1ØØØØØØ1ØØØØØ
		7	111ØØØØØØØØØØØØØØØØØØØØØØØØØØØØØ
SLDL	R6,5	6	ØØØØØØ1ØØØØØØØ1ØØØØØØ1ØØØØØ111ØØ
		7	ØØØØØØØØØØØØØØØØØØØØØØØØØØØØØØØØ
OR	R4,R6	4	Ø1ØØØØ1ØØØØ1ØØ1ØØØØØ1Ø1ØØØØØ111ØØ
O	R4,MM5	4	Ø1ØØØØ1Ø1ØØ1ØØ1ØØ1Ø1Ø1Ø1ØØØØ111ØØ
X	R4,=F'-1'	4	1Ø1111Ø1Ø11Ø11Ø11Ø1Ø1Ø1111ØØØ11
N	R4,Ø(,R1)	4	1Ø1ØØØØØØØØØØØØØ1ØØØØØØØ1ØØØØØØØ
ST	R4,FORDRGHT		

The result records that the checkers (or kings) in squares 1, 3, 17, and 25 can move forward and to the right.

SEPARATING THE POSSIBILITIES

For an analysis of the moves, it is necessary to separate them so that they can be considered one at a time. Figure 11.17 shows a program segment that will separate the 1-bits of a word like FORDRGHT. The WHILE structure finds and isolates each 1-bit, representing one possible move, and calls the informal subroutine ANAL, which will analyze that particular possible move. Inside the WHILE structure, the segment moves each bit in turn into register 4 to test whether it is 1, and if it is not, moves the next bit. During all this, we must keep track of how many times we have shifted the word, so that when we find a 1-bit we can shift it back to its original position (but in a word in which it is the only 1-bit). Note the use, which is fairly rare, of a register holding the count by which another register is shifted.

The subroutine ANAL is presumed to be in our own program (CSECT), and takes its parameter from register 9. It must leave unchanged (or restore) registers 5 and 6. We can use this kind of relaxation of the normal subroutine linkage conventions (see Chapter 6, Problem 6.2) when we want to use a subroutine for top-down program design but do not need the other advantages of modularity that a subroutine can bring.

FIGURE 11.17   Separating possible moves

```
*** GENERATE A WORD FOR EACH POSSIBLE MOVE
*** WHEN ONE IS FOUND, IT IS LEFT IN R9,
*** WITH A CALL TO SUBROUTINE ANAL

* WHILE THERE ARE POSSIBLE MOVES YET TO ANALYZE
GENFRMLA LTR    R5,R5
         BZ     NOMORE
* . REPEAT
* . . SHIFT A BIT, COUNT THE SHIFT
GENFRMLB SLR    R4,R4
         SLDL   R4,1
         LA     R6,1(,R6)
* . UNTIL 1-BIT MOVES INTO R4
         LTR    R4,R4
         BZ     GENFRMLB
* ENDREPEAT
* . MOVE BIT BACK TO ORIGINAL POSITION, IN R9, CALL ANAL
         LR     R8,R4
         SLR    R9,R9
         SRDL   R8,0(R6)
         BAL    R11,ANAL
         B      GENFRMLA
* ENDWHILE (POSSIBLE MOVES YET TO ANALYZE)
NOMORE   DS     0H
```

With the board position given as shown in Fig. 11.16, the segment of Fig. 11.17 will generate, in turn, the words

```
1ØØØØØØØØØØØØØØØØØØØØØØØØØØØØØØØØ
ØØ1ØØØØØØØØØØØØØØØØØØØØØØØØØØØØØØ
ØØØØØØØØØØØØØØØØ1ØØØØØØØØØØØØØØØØ
ØØØØØØØØØØØØØØØØØØØØØØØØ1ØØØØØØØØ
```

and after generating each one, will call ANAL.

MAKING A MOVE

One of the first steps in the analysis of any move is to generate the board position that would result from it. Ignore for now the requirement that contents of registers 5 and 6 must be saved for use after the return from ANAL; you will see how the logical instructions may be used to generate a new board position. Assume that register 1 still contains the address of the eight-word description of the current board position, and that register 2 contains the address of an eight-word block into which to put the description of the new board position.

Figure 11.18 shows a program segment that generates a new board position. The entire old board position is moved to the new area; the red configuration remains unchanged, and the black configuration can most easily be changed in place. The complement of the position of the piece to be moved is found, preparatory to an NC instruction that sets that one particular position to

FIGURE 11.18   Making a forward right move

```
***    MAKE A FORWARD RIGHT MOVE, AND
***    GENERATE A NEW BOARD POSITION IN AN AREA ADDRESSED BY R2
***    THE PIECE TO BE MOVED IS IN R9
          LR      R8,R9           COPY THE MOVE
          X       R8,=F'-1'       COMPLEMENT
          ST      R8,TEMP
          MVC     0(32,R2),0(R1)  MOVE THE COMPLETE BOARD CONFIGURATION
          NC      0(4,R2),TEMP    REMOVE PIECE FROM OLD BFA POSITION
          LR      R6,R9
          SLR     R7,R7
          SRDL    R6,5            MOVE BIT TO NEW SQUARE (FORWARD RIGHT)
          STM     R6,R7,TEMP+4
          OC      0(5,R2),TEMP+4  PUT PIECE IN BFA
*  IF PIECE MOVED IS A KING
          N       R9,8(,R2)
          BZ      NEXTSTEP
*  . THEN REMOVE FROM OLD AREA, INSERT IN NEW POSITION IN BBA
          NC      8(4,R2),TEMP
          OC      8(5,R2),TEMP+4
*  ENDIF
NEXTSTEP  DS      0H
```

0. The original bit is next moved five bit positions to the right to represent moving the piece forward to the right. The piece is stored in the configuration in its new position with an OC instruction. Note that the OC is performed on five bytes, since any of the five might contain the new position. A test is necessary to ascertain whether the piece moved is a king; the test is an AND function of the piece with the black backward active (BBA) word, which yields 0 if the piece is not a king. If the piece is a king, it is expunged from its old square and entered into the new square of BBA in the same manner it was moved in BFA.

You are urged to simulate execution of the segment as we did for Fig. 11.15.

GENERATING JUMPS

As one more piece of a checker-playing program a segment is exhibited in Fig. 11.19 that generates all possible jumps for black forward to the left. The strategy is first to generate the eligible squares that might be jumped into, in the same way that the segment in Fig. 11.15 found blank squares. Then we find positions in which a red piece has a blank square forward and to the left; this is done by an AND function whose operands are the red pieces and the blank squares shifted 4. Finally, the red pieces followed by blank squares are matched against black pieces, after the red pieces are shifted 4. Note that the fictitious squares preclude the possibility of generating a jump around the left edge of the board to the right edge.

Making an actual jump involves the same kind of manipulation that was shown in the segment in Fig. 11.18, but a little more of it, since the red piece that is jumped must be removed from the board.

FIGURE 11.19 Generating all possible jumps for black forward to the left

```
***    GENERATE BLACK'S FORWARD JUMPS TO THE LEFT, AND
***    STORE IN FORDLFJP
***    FIRST, GENERATE ELIGIBLE OPEN SPACES
          LM      R4,R5,0(R1)      BFA
          SLDL    R4,4
          LM      R6,R7,24(R1)     RBA
          SLDL    R6,4
          OR      R4,R6            1'S TO REPRESENT ALL OCCUPIED SQUARES
          O       R4,MM4
          X       R4,=F'-1'    ALL OPEN SQUARES REPRESENTED BY 1'S
***    FIND RED PIECES IN FRONT OF OPEN SPACE
          N       R4,24(R1)
***    MATCH WITH BLACK PIECES
          SLL     R4,4
          N       R4,0(,R1)
          ST      R4,FORDLFJP



MM4       DC      BL4'10000000010000000010000000010000'
```

m a i n   i d e a s

☐ Logical arithmetic instructions AL, ALR, SL, and SLR allow arithmetic operations to be carried out on full-word quantities as unsigned integers; the condition code records a result of zero or nonzero, carry or no carry. Logical full-word compare instructions CL and CLR set condition codes showing whether the first operand is equal to, less than, or greater than the second operand, each considered as a full-word unsigned integer.

☐ Shift instructions provide left and right, single- and double-register, logical and arithmetic shift capabilities. Logical shift instructions consider quantities to be bit strings, moving the entire contents of one or two registers and filling in with zeros at one end; they do not set a condition code. Arithmetic shift instructions move all bits but the sign bit; on a left shift zeros are filled in at the right, and overflows may result, but on a right shift copies of the sign bit are filled. The condition code is set, and an overflow exception may result.

☐ Logical functions AND and OR have many uses, including interpretations in symbolic logic and Boolean algebra. Instructions in the IBM System/370 implement the AND, EXCLUSIVE OR, and INCLUSIVE OR, each in instruction types RR, RX, SI, and SS. These instructions are exceedingly useful in bit manipulation problems, and can selectively set any configuration of bits to 0's or to 1's, change them, or leave them alone. They are especially powerful in combination with the shift instructions.

■ **PROBLEMS** FOR REVIEW AND IMAGINATION

11.1 The process followed in execution of SL or SLR is addition of the 1's complement of the second operand and of a low-order 1 to the first operand. Show that this process does, in fact, the logical subtraction of the second operand. Show also that a zero result is not possible without a carry (even when 0 is subtracted from 0!) and that therefore a condition code of 0 can never result from SL or SLR.

11.2 Write an extension to the program segment shown in Fig. 11.1 that will solve the problem of overflow, that is, store an indicator somewhere if and only if the sum C is incorrect because of overflow.

11.3 Write a program segment to simulate a "logical multiply" instruction, that is, one that finds the product of two operands considered as unsigned 32-bit numbers. The arithmetic multiply may be used, but adjustments must be made. Considering each logical operand as

signed operand + 2^{32}*(high-order bit of operand)

will help in making clear what adjustments are needed.

11.4 Write a program segment to form the 4-word product of two 2-word signed integers. This entails some of the difficulties of Problem 11.3.

11.5 The first operand in a division instruction must be placed in a register pair. A one-word operand is usually loaded into the odd-numbered register, with the sign bit extended to the preceding register. Show how the SRDA instruction helps make this easy.

11.6　In some computers a left shift is a circular shift; that is, bits lost from the left end of a register are inserted on the right end. This kind of shift is especially appropriate if negative numbers are represented in 1's complement form (subtracted from 1111...1 instead of from 10000...0). Why? Write an IBM System/370 assembler language segment to perform a left circular shift of seven bits on the contents of register 5. It can be done in two or three instructions.

11.7　Write a program segment that will reverse the order of bits in the word at FORWARD, placing the result at BACKWARD. That is, place the bit from bit position 0 of FORWARD in bit position 31 of BACKWARD, the bit from position 1 of FORWARD in position 30 of BACKWARD, ..., the bit from position 31 of FORWARD in position 0 of BACKWARD. A four-instruction loop, plus a few instructions outside the loop, can do the task.

11.8　Write program segments to simulate the arithmetic shift instructions by others. You can try two approaches, using either multiply and divide instructions or using logical shift instructions. If you are exceedingly brave, try to simulate the setting of the condition code too.

11.9　In Section 11.2, fields IND, P, and Q were packed into a word using left logical shifts. Can the packing be done using only right shifts? If so, how and under what conditions? If not, why not, and under what different conditions would right shifts be more useful in packing data into words?

11.10　Show how data fields that were once packed into a word can be unpacked and returned to separate registers.

11.11　Exhibit improvements that can be made in segments of previous chapters, or in segments you have previously written, through use of arithmetic shift instructions.

11.12　Write a program segment analogous to that in Fig. 11.9, which will construct a string of 32 printable characters 0 and 1, representing the binary number in register 5. This is a simpler problem than hexadecimal conversion, but employs the same principles.

11.13　The program segment shown in Fig. 11.8 for counting the 1-bits in a word can be written using an NR instruction instead of a shift instruction. If the word to be tested is in register 3, the count can be generated in register 5 by

```
        LA    R5,∅
P       LTR   R6,R3
        BZ    NEXTSTEP
        SL    R3,=F'1'
        NR    R3,R6
        LA    R5,1(,R5)
        B     P
```

Simulate execution of the segment to see how it works. How many repetitions of the body of the loop are required?

11.14 Write a sequence of instructions that sets bits 8–11 of the contents of register 4 to 1100, complements the bits in positions 16–21, and leaves the others unchanged.

11.15 The contents of registers 4 and 5 can be interchanged, *without* the use of a temporary storage location, by

```
XR      R4,R5
XR      R5,R4
XR      R4,R5
```

Show how this segment does the job.

11.16 Is it true that any two of the logical functions AND, INCLUSIVE OR, EXCLUSIVE OR, or NOT can be simulated by combinations of the other two? Try to do it. If it can be done, it would be sufficient to provide for only two of the functions in a computer instruction repertoire; we would assume that direct provision of more than two is for convenience and programming ease.

11.17 Show the difference between a NOT function on the bits of a word in register 6 and the operation of

```
LCR     R6,R6
```

11.18 Think of a bit manipulation function which is not implemented directly on the IBM System/370. What would be the uses of your function, and how can it be simulated on the IBM System/370?

11.19 The logical functions and their IBM System/370 implementation can be useful in set arithmetic. Suppose the 32-bit positions of a word represent 32 points or disjoint subsets of a space. The contents of any word can represent a set of the space; if a bit is 1, it indicates that the point or subset corresponding to that bit position is in the set, a 0-bit indicates that the corresponding point or subset is not in the set. If two words X and Y represent sets P and Q, respectively, then X AND Y represents the intersection $P \cap Q$. Similarly, X OR Y represents the set union $P \cup Q$. Continue and expand the interpretation: what represents the complement of a set? What does the EXCLUSIVE OR represent? What other set operations should be defined, and how can they be implemented?

11.20 Using the storage scheme described in Section 11.6, write a program segment to generate all the possible backward moves to the right for black kings. Also generate the possible jumps backward and to the right, and make one if you can.

11.21 It is convenient to store a board position in four double words, in order to be able to use Load and Load Multiple instructions. However, 14 of the 32 bytes used are empty. Show how one could store each 36-bit string in 5 bytes, keep the whole board position in 20 bytes, and then expand the position into a 32-byte area for actual manipulation. The savings in main storage space are perhaps worth the extra instructions. How might one store a board position in the minimum space of 18 bytes and expand the configuration to double words for convenient analysis?

11.22 Write a program segment that will simulate the instruction

```
              CVD    R1,DBW
```

without using a CVD instruction. *Hint*: (a) Determine the sign of the number in register 1, and store the sign. Then work with the absolute value of the number. (b) Develop digits of the resulting packed decimal number as remainders upon division by 10. The digits can be gathered and shifted in a register pair and finally stored in DBW.

11.23 The word MULTJP contains at least one 1-bit. Write a program segment that will replace all but the first (highest-order) 1-bit with zeros. For example, ØØEC8927 would be changed to ØØ8ØØØØØ.

11.24 An interpreter is to execute IBM System/370 machine language programs. The interpreter keeps contents of simulated general registers 0–15 at SIMREG; that is, register 0 at SIMREG, register 1 at SIMREG+4, etc. The current instruction is at INSTR, and it is already known to be of RX type. Write a program segment that will compute and place in the full word EFFAD the *effective address* of the main storage operand of the current instruction.

11.25 A word at W contains character representations of four octal digits (e.g., '3' = X'F3'). Form and leave in register 4 the full-word binary equivalent of the 4-digit octal number. The upper 20 bits of the word should be zeros. Use a loop; the whole segment may be as short as six instructions.

11.26 There is an instruction TM (Test under Mask), of SI type, which tests bits of a 1-byte first operand and sets a condition code. The second operand, the *I2* field of the instruction, controls which bits of the first operand are tested. Only the first operand bits in positions where the second operand bits are 1 are tested, and the condition code is set to

0 if all tested bits are 0's or if all of the mask (second operand)
  is zero,

1 if the tested bits are mixed 0's and 1's,

3 if all tested bits are 1's.

For example, if the byte at IND8 contains 11ØØØØØ1, the instruction

```
      TM     IND8,B'11ØØØØØØ'
```

will cause only the first two bits of IND8 to be tested and, because they are 1's, the condition code will be set to 3. Similarly,

$$\text{TM} \quad \text{IND8,B'0000110'}$$

will set the condition code to 0, and

$$\text{TM} \quad \text{IND8,B'11110000'}$$

will set the condition code to 1. This instruction is useful because it is the easiest way to test a single bit in storage. Show how several 1-bit indicators can be packed into a byte, and tested singly or in various combinations using the TM instruction.

■ **REFERENCES** ▓▓▓▓▓▓▓▓▓▓▓▓▓▓▓▓▓▓▓▓▓▓▓▓▓▓

IBM System/370 Principles of Operation, GA 22-7000, IBM Corporation. References on logical and shift instructions.

Preparata, Franco, and Raymond Yeh, *Introduction to Discrete Structures*, Addison-Wesley, Reading, Mass., 1973. Boolean algebra and applications.

Samuel, A. L., "Some Studies in Machine Learning Using the Game of Checkers," *IBM Journal of Research and Development* **3** (1959), pp. 210–229. Samuel's original paper.

———,"Programming Computers to Play Games," in *Advances in Computers*, Vol. 1, edited by Franz Alt, Academic Press, New York, 1960, pp. 165–192. A more accessible survey including analysis of the checker-playing experiments.

INPUT AND OUTPUT THROUGH
THE OPERATING SYSTEM

In earlier chapters the functions of input and output were treated very lightly. It was noted that these functions are performed by the supervisor on request from the user's program, but the nature of the requests was not examined, nor the variety of forms of requests available. The examples either concentrated entirely on processing within the computer, completely without reference to input or output, or used the simplified facilities provided by ASSIST. It is now time to take up the subject of input and output and explain just exactly how one makes requests of the operating system. This chapter, then, discusses the various options available and the principles guiding selection among them, in various situations. The discussion will include a foray into job control language, where various options and parameters are also specified.

You must realize that the material here is a small representative subset of all the facilities and options available. It is quite specific, and usable in several systems, especially OS/VS1 and MVS (OS/VS2). The details are specific to these systems and do not necessarily apply to other operating systems. As new versions of even these systems are released, some of the material here may become obsolete. Furthermore, each installation chooses parameters and options when it generates the operating system it will use, and many installations further modify or add to the systems provided by the IBM Corporation. Only the most standard features and methods of use are described, so that the explanations will have as wide and long applicability as possible. The material in this chapter will indeed be almost completely trustworthy.

12.1 Basic Structure of Input and Output Processing

During execution of a user's program, input and output actions are done by the supervisor on request from the user's program. The requests may be of several sorts, and each has a variety of forms, parameters, and implications, as will be shown. Some of the requests are as follows:

1. Open a data set, which means prepare it for processing: make sure the device is available and ready, read or write the data set label, and generally set up or complete the communication patterns needed for further processing.

2. Retrieve a record from the data set and make it available to the user's program.

3. Wait until a particular event, such as retrieval of a record, is completed; this request is made when the user's program cannot proceed further until the event is completed, and the supervisor suspends operation of that program until control can be returned with the event completed.

4. Check on *correct* completion, without errors, of an event, which implies waiting for completion as well as examining possible error return codes.

5. Output a record (or block) onto a data set.

6. Position the reading or writing heads of the input or output device (magnetic tape or a direct access device) so that they are ready to read or write a certain record or block of a data set.

7. Control the device on which a data set resides, in some way that is particular to the device, such as backspacing on a magnetic tape.

8. Close a data set: write a trailer label on an output data set, and generally break the communication patterns established for use of the data set.

WHAT IS A DATA SET?

It would be helpful if we could define data set at this point, in terms of concepts already established. We are unable to do this. A data set must be defined operationally in the discussions that follow, as a set of data that we and the operating system treat in some sense as a whole. The data set is made up of records and blocks, which we will define shortly. A data set is both a conceptual entity and a physical one; the operating system helps to adjust the physical to our conceptions.

For example, a disk pack may contain several short data sets if we choose, and the operating system will help us to retrieve data from the data set we choose at any moment. On the other hand, a long data set may occupy several reels of magnetic tape, and the operating system makes the transition from one reel to the other during processing. By writing and keeping track of records containing housekeeping information, the operating system is able to overcome some of the physical limitations, such as reels of magnetic tape of particular lengths, and thus allow a data set to conform to our concept rather than to some physical necessity.

Some conceptual examples of data sets are introduced here and we shall explore some possible physical representations of them. We shall explore the processing of each of these data sets in the course of the remainder of this chapter.

The first data set is meant to be a data set used as input in a program. It contains results obtained from questionnaires, and can reasonably be thought of as a deck of punched cards. Questionnaire results are somewhat likely to be punched into cards, so the data set may still *be* a deck of punched cards. There may be more than 80 characters of information for one subject, and so more than one card per subject. There may be almost any number of subjects, though most likely somewhere between 50 and 5000. The data set would be used as input by programs making tabulations of results or various statistical analyses. You the user may submit the data set on cards the first time you want to use it but may want the data set written on a magnetic tape or direct access storage device so that further uses will not require reading cards and will therefore be more efficient. A program to make tabulations, for example, should be able to process the data set from *either* cards or a magnetic tape or a direct-access device, and you will see that the operating systems for the IBM System/370 easily allow this kind of flexibility.

The second data set to consider is purely an output data set, perhaps the tabulations developed by a program working on the first data set. The data set will certainly appear on the printer and may be quite long. You will most likely want to control the page format and cause a skip to the top of a new page here and a double or triple space there. For the sake of efficiency in use of the printer, the data set will probably be first written to a direct-access device, then later printed if several copies must be produced or if the printing can be done on a cheaper computer.

The third example data set is a file of reference data. It may be a table of physical characteristics of a number of chemicals, of meanings and grammatical properties of English words, or of costs and ordering characteristics of a number of airplane parts. But whatever the application, we have in mind an ordered file of data, any record of which may be required at any point in a user's program. This can be called a "random-access" application, because so far as the operating system knows, the demands for the next record are random, and decidedly not in the same order as the file itself. However, the file is for reference use only; it is never changed.

The fourth example of a data set is a file of information, perhaps inventory information, which is to be updated by the user's program. Quantities on hand are to be modified as a result of the day's or week's transactions, so this data set has both input and output aspects. It is an ordered file, most likely ordered on something like part number, and if the data set of reports of transactions is sorted into the same order, our data set can be processed sequentially. The data set may be kept on one or more magnetic tapes, or on a direct-access device, especially if a sophisticated online information system wants access to the inventory information. But that is beyond the scope of our current discussions.

Therefore, in summary, a data set is defined by what we can do with it; we try to define our data sets as naturally as possible for each application, and the operating system helps us to treat the conceptual unit as a programming unit.

THE DATA CONTROL BLOCK

The physical connections necessary between the various parts of the computer system are reasonably evident, and more detail about channels and the commands given to accomplish physical input and output will be given in Chapter 17. The programming connections embodied in a chain of communication between data set, job control statements, the supervisor, and the user's program are far from obvious, and must be sketched at this point.

The operating system maintains a *data control block* for each data set in use by a user's program. The data control block is kept in the user's own main storage area, and the user has opportunities to modify parameters and addresses in the data control block during execution of the program. However, this is not really common or desirable; most of the time the user is content to set parameters through the assembler and the operating system and let the supervisor maintain the data control block. The user must include in the program a DCB macro instruction, including several parameters for the data control block. The DCB macro instruction defines the skeleton of the data control block. It is expanded by the assembler into a sequence of constants and addresses, but it contains no executable instructions itself. Therefore it has the status of, and is usually placed with, constant and symbol definitions in the user's program. The user gives each data control block a name (which the assembler of course translates into an address) through the DCB macro instruction and uses this name when making requests to the operating system for action regarding the data control block and the data set to which it corresponds.

The supervisor completes the data control block with information from several sources. One source is the DD (Data Definition) statement included in the job control statements for the job. Every data set needs a DD statement, which may contain a number of items of information about the data set. The main advantage to having some data set definitions and parameters specified in a DCB macro instruction and others in a DD statement is flexibility; certain parameters can be fixed (in the DCB macro instruction) for all executions of a given program while others (in the DD statement) can vary from one execution of the program to the next. Items like the name of a data set, the device on which a data set resides, or the amount of space to be reserved on a direct access device, *should* be variable between executions.

A *ddname* must be included as one of the parameters of the DCB macro instruction. The same ddname must appear on the DD statement, which is to correspond to and supplement the particular DCB macro instruction. The oper-

FIGURE 12.1   Construction of the data control block

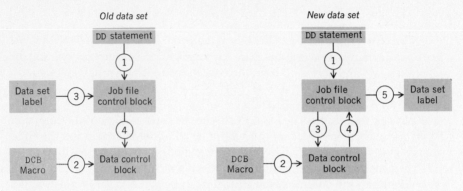

ating system uses the ddname to make the correspondence and to take information from the DD statement to help complete the data control block.

The third source used in completing the data control block is the label from the data set itself, if the data set already exists before execution of the program begins. Such information as record length and format can be included in the label, which every data set on a direct-access device or magnetic tape should have, and this information will be used in completing the data control block if the information has not been provided by the DCB macro instruction or the DD statement.

The operating system must be told how to find the right data set to go with a particular data control block and DD statement. The operating system keeps a *catalogue* of the data sets under its control. A user may have any direct-access data set or magnetic tape data set catalogued, and the operating system will remember where it is (it cannot tell, of course, whether a particular reel of magnetic tape is in Pasadena or Madrid, but it knows the serial number of the tape, and if it is not mounted on a tape unit it can ask the operator to mount it). So if a data set is catalogued, the user may give the data-set name (dsname) in a DD statement, and the operating system will find it by using the information in the catalogue. If the data set is not catalogued, the user directs the operating system to it by designating an input or output unit, such as a card reader, direct-access device, or magnetic tape drive. In the case of magnetic tape or direct-access device, it will also be necessary, perhaps, to give the serial number of the tape or direct-access device to ensure that the correct one is used.

The sequence of operations followed in setting up the data control block is roughly as follows and is summarized in Fig. 12.1. While the job scheduler is in control, at the beginning of a job or between job steps, the job control statements are read, and a *job file control block* is set up with the information from each DD statement. Each job file control block is identified by a ddname and contains at least a unit specification or a dsname. Second, while the program is loaded into main storage for execution, the expansion of the DCB macro instruction made by the assembler becomes the skeleton of the data control block. The data control block is identified by an address (which in the

FIGURE 12.2 The chain of data set identification

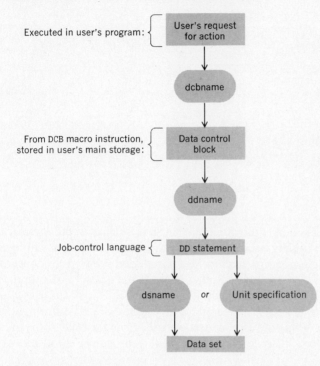

assembler language program was the *dcbname*), and it contains at least a ddname. Third, the user's program, during execution, "opens" the data set and causes completion of the data control block. The program requests the opening of the data control block by giving the supervisor the address of the data control block (dcbname). The supervisor finds the job file control block whose ddname matches that in the to-be-completed data control block. If the data set already exists, it is located through use of the dsname or unit specifications, and any uncompleted entries in the job file control block are filled in with information from the data set itself. Finally any uncompleted items in the data control block are filled in from the job file control block. For new data sets, the job file control block is completed by information from the data control block and in most cases a label is written for the new data set. The chain of identification that is followed is shown in Fig. 12.2.

12.2 Organization of a Data Set

BLOCKING
First we make a distinction between *logical records*, which we shall hereafter call just plain *records*, and *physical records*, which will henceforth be called *blocks*. A logical record is the quantity of data (input or output) that the user

FIGURE 12.3   Blocked and unblocked records

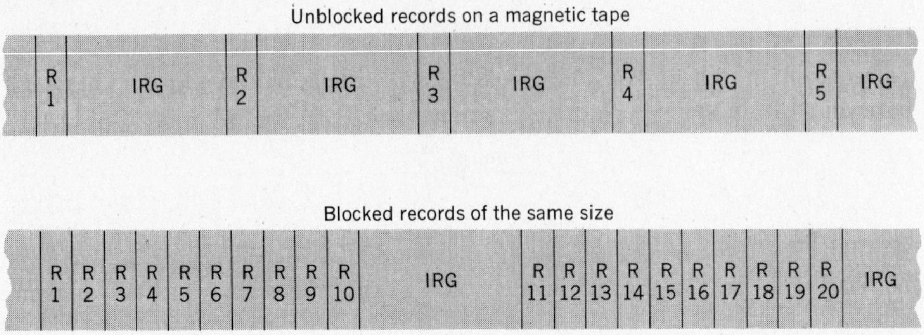

Unblocked records on a magnetic tape

Blocked records of the same size

wishes to process as a unit, the quantity that makes sense to the *logic* of the program. The user usually issues a request to the supervisor in terms of logical records, and in the processing sections of the program need not be concerned with anything else. A block, on the other hand, is the quantity of data that is physically read or written by the computing system. The block consists of one or more records, which are grouped into a block for more efficient input and output processing. While the user requests records from the supervisor, the supervisor reads a block, then doles out the logical records from the block one at a time.

The economy of blocking records is best understood from a discussion of data sets on magnetic tape. On magnetic tape a block is the quantity of information physically read or written in one operation, i.e., the data (we called it a record in Chapter 1) between interrecord gaps. If we consider logical records to be, for example, 80 characters long, a record occupies 0.05 in., at 1600 bpi density. If each record is a block, it is followed by a 0.5 in. (approximately) interrecord gap, and a series of a hundred logical records will occupy 55 in. of tape. On the other hand, if the tape is blocked with 10 logical records to a block, each block (0.5 in.) is followed by a 0.5-in. interrecord gap, and a hundred logical records occupy only 10 in. of tape. Thus the blocking cuts the length of tape necessary by a factor of 5. The comparison is shown graphically in Fig. 12.3. The elapsed time required to read the tape is cut by at least a factor of 5 and most likely much more, since usually the tape comes to a halt at the center of each interrecord gap and thus its average speed in passing interrecord gaps is less than half of its reading or writing speed.

For devices other than magnetic tape, the blocking advantages are less pronounced, but the convenience of the concept is still very much present. On direct-access devices such as magnetic disks, blocking can save time by permitting a larger segment to be read continuously before waiting for the disk to rotate to the appropriate spot for beginning the next record. As to a data set on punched cards, a block is a card and that is that.

SEQUENTIAL, PARTITIONED, AND VSAM DATA SETS

There are a number of different ways in which a data set can be organized, and we shall explore some of them now. These organizations correspond directly to concepts implemented under the IBM operating systems, and indirectly to options available with other computing systems.

The first and simplest type to discuss is the *sequential* organization. Under a sequential organization each record follows the preceding one, and the records must be processed in that order. It may sometimes be possible to back up one record, or to go back to the beginning of the data set, but not to jump around otherwise. This type of organization is that necessarily followed physically on a magnetic tape: the actions possible are to read the next record, to backspace a record, to rewind, and no others. A data set being read by a card reader is the same except there is no going back at all. A data set being printed must also be sequential, with the addition of a few options as to line spacing. A data set on a direct-access device may be treated sequentially, and *can* even be created so that the beginning of the next record is known only after the previous one is read, so that the data set *must* be read sequentially.

A second organization type is called *partitioned*. A *partitioned* data set is divided into several *members*, each of which can be referred to as a sequential data set in its own right. A *name* is associated with each member, but the names of members, unlike the keys of records in an indexed sequential or VSAM data set, are not ordered. A *directory* allows the operating system to find any member of the data set; this obviously requires that the data set be kept on a direct access device. Once a member is selected, it is processed like an ordinary sequential data set, although some extra handles are provided for use by the sophisticated user.

A third organization type is *virtual storage access method*, abbreviated VSAM. This is a rather complex type, which includes three major subtypes. The first is *entry-sequenced,* which is essentially a sequential organization. A second is *key-sequenced*; in this organization the records are stored in ascending sequence on a field in each record designated as the *key*. There is an index hierarchy, so that the system can find any record when its key is given. The system also permits additions and deletions of records anywhere in the sequence, and the index will be adjusted automatically. The third option in VSAM is a *relative record* data set, in which each record is stored by a record serial number; this is essentially an array of records, with the record serial numbers acting very much like subscripts in an array.

Preceding the development of VSAM, the *indexed sequential* organization was widely used. Its major idea was the same as key-sequenced VSAM data sets, but the index and data organizations were less efficient, especially after numerous additions and deletions.

The data set of questionnaire responses and the data set of program output, which were introduced in the previous section, would both be examples of data sets organized sequentially. The third example, the table of reference information, should be organized as a key-sequenced VSAM data set, so that the indexes kept by the operating system will facilitate rapid direct access to any item in the table. The fourth example, the file of inventory data, is again a sequential data set; because the processing we envision can treat the data set sequentially, there is no advantage, and considerable overhead, to organizing it any other way.

All three of these organizations—sequential, VSAM, and partitioned—are recognized and handled by OS/VS. The *access methods*, sets of routines for processing the data sets, are identified with one or more of these types (or a few others, such as *direct*, which leaves almost everything to the user). The simplest one, the sequential organization, will be investigated in greater detail. Many of the points discussed will be relevant to VSAM and partitioned data sets, but the details will be with particular reference to the sequential data sets recognized by OS/VS.

RECORD AND BLOCK FORMATS

Records and blocks may be of almost any size. Small blocks are uneconomic; there are also practical limits to the maximum length of a block. Since an entire block must be read into main storage at once, areas called *buffers* must be provided to hold entire blocks. Thus long blocks cut down on the main storage available for other purposes. Second, but less important, no records from a block can be made available to the user until the entire block is read, so a very long block delays the beginning of a user's processing. Third, an input/output hardware error will cost more time in correction procedures if blocks are long, and if the error cannot be corrected, the data loss is larger. A balance must be reached; the balance depends mostly on how restricted main storage will be *in all programs and on all occasions* in which the data set is to be used. In practice, reasonable lengths of blocks are from 400 to 4000 characters.

It may not be convenient for all (logical) records to be the same length. Certain records may need to contain more information than others. For example, in a dictionary some words have more meanings and a greater variety of syntactic uses than others. Access methods under OS/VS allow for data sets with fixed-length records and for data sets with variable-length records.

If records are of fixed length, all the blocks will be of the same length (except perhaps the last which may be shorter). If the supervisor is informed, either by the DCB macro, the DD statement, or the data set label, of the length of a record and of a block, the block need contain only the records themselves, without any other control information.

On the other hand, if the length of a record is variable, the length must be written just prior to the record.

For data sets destined for printing on the line printer, we control vertical spacing by appending a spacing control character at the beginning of each record. The common codes and their actions:

space   normal single spacing

0   double space to the next line

      –   triple space to the next line

      +   suppress spacing before printing the next line

      1   skip to the top of the next page before printing the next line

The spacing control (also called *carriage control*) character is not itself printed, but is used merely to give spacing control commands to the printer. However, if we are using a spacing control character, we must include it when counting record length and block size.

Variable-length records may be blocked or unblocked; if they are blocked, the length of a block is variable too, and that length must be written at the beginning of a block. The supervisor will handle the blocking and furnish the block and record descriptor words, and the programmer need only work with logical records. Requirements, formats, and procedures are more fully explained in the IBM manuals listed at the end of the chapter. Provision is made for blocks which the supervisor considers to have "undefined" format, but for these blocks the programmer must do his own blocking and unblocking.

12.3   Buffering and Exit Options

In Section 12.2 we investigated various options for the organization of a data set: blocking of fixed- and variable-length records, in sequential, indexed sequential, and partitioned data sets. Now we examine some of the more important techniques and options used during the processing of a data set.

BUFFERING

The supervisor's input and output routines read blocks into and write blocks from areas called buffers. The areas are called buffers because they are intermediate between the user's own areas and the input and output devices themselves, protecting, in a way, each from the other. The idea is that the supervisor can be processing input and output through the buffers while the user's program is working in its own areas, which are not affected by the simultaneous reading and writing. This simultaneity would not be possible without buffers.

Usually the supervisor has more than one buffer assigned to each data set. For sequential data sets, this affords still more economies by enabling simultaneity of operations more of the time. For example, when an input data set is opened, two buffers are usually assigned to it, and immediately the supervisor starts reading a block into the first one. As soon as the first block is read, the user's program may be given the first record from the first block. But immediately the supervisor also starts reading the second block into the second buffer. Thus one buffer is being filled, character by character, from the data set, while the other is being emptied, record by record, by the user's program. When all records of the first block have been taken by the user's program and the second block is read, the buffers interchange roles, and the third block is read into the first buffer while records are doled out to the user's program from the

FIGURE 12.4 Buffering action: (a) during request for first record, and (b) during request for fourth record

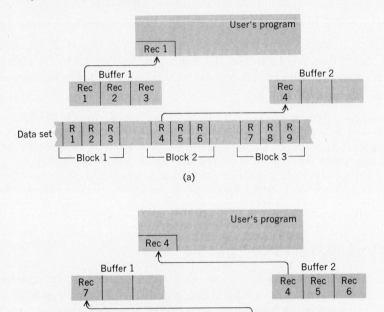

(a)

(b)

second buffer. Figure 12.4 illustrates the simultaneous uses of the two buffers and their interchange of roles. Assuming three records to a block, for simplicity, we first see the status at the time the user's program requests the first record (part a). The first block is in buffer 1, waiting to be given to the user's program, and the second block is being read into buffer 2. Figure 12.4(b) shows the action when the fourth record is being given to the user's program; the third block is already being read into buffer 1, whose first contents—records 1, 2, and 3—are no longer needed there.

During output the process is more or less reversed. As the user delivers each output record to the supervisor with a request to write it, the supervisor puts the record in the first output buffer. When the first buffer is filled, physical output of the block is begun, and while it proceeds, the user's program can deliver other records to the second buffer. When the second buffer is full and output of the first buffer is completed, the roles of the buffers are interchanged: the second block is written from the second buffer while more records are delivered to the first buffer.

There are many possibilities for variation in the implementation of this elementary but important concept of buffering. The options provided, such as the number of buffers associated with each data set and the method of managing buffers, can give the user a very flexible system.

Buffers associated with a data set are organized into a *buffer pool*. Each buffer in the pool is as long as the longest block in the data set; the buffers are normally provided automatically by the supervisor, though it is possible for a user to build a pool directly. Two buffers are usually provided, but in some circumstances it is desirable to request more buffers either in the DCB macro instruction or in the DD statement.

Access methods under OS/VS are generally provided in two forms; there are "basic" access methods, in which a great deal is left to the user, and "queued" access methods, in which many more things, especially buffering, are done automatically for the user. Under the *queued sequential access method* (QSAM), for example, reading ahead and filling buffers is done automatically, but under the *basic sequential access method* (BSAM) such functions must be performed by the user's program, using macro instructions that allow much more control by the user but require more careful work. We shall restrict our attention now to facilities available under QSAM; these are the most often used, and most easily used by beginners. After you have become reasonably conversant with the concepts and facilities embodied in QSAM and with the channel structure and commands, which are explored in Chapter 17, you will be in a good position to learn about BSAM and other access methods from the appropriate IBM manuals when you need them.

Control of buffering under QSAM is done by the supervisor, but there are several options the user may choose. First, there is a decision between *simple buffering* and *exchange buffering*. Under simple buffering each buffer is associated with only one data set. Under exchange buffering, on the other hand, a record may be read into a buffer while it is associated with one data set, and the supervisor gives the record to a user's program by exchanging the buffer for an area of the same size belonging to the user's program. The first buffer now belongs to the user's program, and can be exchanged again, this time becoming the property of an output data set. The advantage of exchange buffering is that a record that is read, used, and then written again need not be physically moved. It can stay where it is while only possession of the buffer containing it changes hands.

MOVE AND SUBSTITUTE MODES
There are several *modes*, which indicate how the record is given to (or from) the user's program. Under simple buffering, *move mode* is the most used; an input record, when requested, is physically moved by the supervisor from its input buffer to an area designated by the user's program. The buffer is then immediately available for further use by the input routines. With output under move mode, a record that is ready to be output is physically moved by the supervisor from the area in which the user's program prepared it to a buffer. If no buffer is available—that is, if all are full of other records waiting to be out-

put—execution of the user's program is suspended until an output buffer can accept the current record.

Under exchange buffering, we use a *substitute mode*. Upon an input or output request in substitute mode, a work area belonging to the user's program is substituted for a buffer segment. In processing an inventory file, for example, we read a record, perhaps update it with a new transaction, and write it in a new data set.

EXIT OPTIONS

The user has options as to what should be done in a few special situations. If an error is encountered during input or output processing, the system automatically follows procedures that attempt to correct the error. If the error proves uncorrectable, the supervisor will, upon orders from the user's program, either accept the record anyway, skip the erroneous record, terminate the job abnormally, or give control to a routine specified by the user.

Similarly, when the end of an input data set is encountered and a request for an input record is made after there is no more input, the supervisor will branch to a routine specified by the user. This allows the user to build a loop for normal processing of records, with exit from the loop provided automatically to a location of the user's choice upon end of the data set.

The options mentioned in this section for the processing of data sets are mostly exercised in the macro instructions of the user's program and in the DD statement. The next section shows how the options in macro instructions are specified, and in Section 12.6 we shall examine in more detail the parameters of the DD statement.

12.4   Using QSAM Macros in a Program

Most of the ideas, options, and structures of input and output processing that we shall consider have already been introduced. It remains to describe exactly how they are used and specified, and to illustrate their uses with examples. In this section we attempt to do that with the use of QSAM macros, and later sections will show their relationship to job control language.

Under the QSAM access method, requests to the supervisor for input and output actions are made through the use of macro instructions. There are only a few, and all but the DCB macro are simple to use. Briefly, the macros are

OPEN	prepare the data set and complete the data control block,
GET	get a logical record for the user's program,
PUT	present a logical record for output,
CLOSE	terminate processing of a data set, and
DCB	organize the data control block.

All except the DCB macro instruction are translated into executable statements and thus need entries in the name field only if the programmer wishes to branch to one. The DCB macro instruction sets up the skeleton of the data control block and is not executable. It *must* have a name (called the *dcbname*), and all other macro instructions refer to a particular data set by giving the dcbname associated with the data set.

The input and output macros are expanded into calls on subroutines, the subroutines residing in the supervisor. Therefore a routine that does not call subroutines of its own must still save registers 13, 14, 15, 0, and 1, and must provide a register save area if it uses the input or output macros. Registers 14, 15, 0, and 1 will not, in general, have the same contents after one of the macros as before, since these registers are changed by the calling sequence built into the user's own routine.

OPEN AND CLOSE MACROS
The first macro instruction to be executed, with respect to any data set, must be the OPEN. The supervisor prepares the data set for processing: it completes the data control block and either analyzes the label of an input data set or writes the label of an output data set. The syntax is

Name	Operation	Operands
[label]	OPEN	(dcbname[,(options)])

where dcbname may be given in any form allowable in an A-type constant.

Under QSAM, one or two options are specified for each data set opened. The first must be one of the words INPUT or OUTPUT. The default option is INPUT, so the first option need not be explicitly stated for an input data set. The second option controls positioning of the data set, but if you want to start reading or writing the data set at the beginning, you need not specify this parameter. If only the first option is specified in the macro instruction, the option need not be enclosed in parentheses, although the entire operand list must be. For example,

```
OPEN    (CARDIN,INPUT)
```

opens an input data set whose dcbname is CARDIN, and

```
OPEN    (INVFILO,OUTPUT)
```

opens an output data set whose dcbname is INVFILO. Several data sets can be opened with one OPEN:

```
OPEN    (CARDIN,INPUT,INVFILO,OUTPUT)
```

or

```
OPEN  (CARDIN,,INVFILO,OUTPUT)
```

are equivalent to the sequence of two OPENs. When there is only one operand for a macro instruction, it need not be put in parentheses.

```
OPEN  CARDIN
```

will correctly open the input (by default) data set whose dcbname is CARDIN.

The CLOSE macro instruction is the converse of the OPEN. It causes records remaining in output buffers and a data-set trailer label to be written, repositions the device, and, in general, disconnects the data set from the program. The syntax is

Name	Operation	Operands
[label]	CLOSE	(dcbname[,option])

Again, dcbname may be given in any form that could be used in an A-type constant. One option may be specified REREAD, LEAVE, or DISP. This option controls the positioning of the data set after it is closed: REREAD positions it for rereading, LEAVE positions it at the end, and DISP passes the buck to the DISP parameter of the DD statement. It is possible, with a magnetic tape or direct access data set, to process a data set, close it with REREAD, then open it again and reprocess it from the beginning. Under QSAM this is the only way to perform a rewind operation on a magnetic tape.

GET AND PUT MACROS

The GET macro instruction retrieves for the user's program a record from an input data set. If the data set is exhausted, control is returned to the location given in the EODAD parameter of the DCB (see below), and if there was a persistent error in the reading, return of control depends on the EROPT parameter of the DCB (also see below); otherwise control is returned to the instruction immediately following the GET macro instruction as soon as a record is available. The syntax of the GET macro instruction is

Name	Operation	Operands
[label]	GET	dcbname[,area address]

The mode (move or substitute) of the GET is determined by a parameter in the DCB macro instruction for all GETs referring to a data set. If the move mode is specified, the area address must be included in the GET statement; the record is placed by the supervisor in the area beginning at the given address. If the substitute mode is specified, the address of the record returned is placed by the supervisor in register 1. In substitute mode the area-address parameter must be included, but it is the address of the area given to the supervisor as a substitute for the area containing the current record. For example, in the move mode

$$\text{GET} \quad \text{CARDIN,INAREA}$$

will retrieve a record from the data set associated with CARDIN; the supervisor will store the record starting at INAREA. In the substitute mode

$$\text{GET} \quad \text{INVFILI,(3)}$$

will retrieve a record from the data set associated with INVFILI; the address of the new record will be in register 1. The second parameter (3) indicates that the address of the area to be substituted for the buffer containing the new record is in register 3. This form is common in macro instructions; where an address is required but the address to be given is in a register and cannot be given symbolically, the register address in parentheses can be used. It is particularly appropriate here; the address of the area to be substituted is most likely the address of the most recent record *received* in exchange, and therefore not an address known symbolically to the programmer.

The PUT macro instruction is quite similar to the GET. It presents a record to the supervisor, with orders to output the record when convenient. The syntax is

Name	Operation	Operands
[label]	PUT	dcbname[,area address]

The operands have precisely the same meaning as the corresponding operands of the GET macro instruction. In GET and PUT macros the dcbname and area address may be given in any form allowable in an RX-type instruction.

THE DCB MACRO INSTRUCTION

The general form of the DCB macro instruction is

Name	Operation	Operands
dcbname	DCB	operands, separated by commas

The DCB macro instruction is nonexecutable, so it is placed with the constant and symbol definitions in one's program. The operands in a DCB macro instruction are all *keyword parameters*, which means that each is specified as

$$\text{keyword} = \text{option}.$$

For example, one of the keywords is DSORG; the operand specifying it may be written DSORG = PS, where PS is the option taken. Keyword parameters can be written in a list in any order, and if one is omitted, no extra comma or other adjustment need be made. The data control block is built in the space reserved by the DCB macro instruction, and much of the control information is supplied from the DCB operands, which we now take up one at a time. The list will not be exhaustive, but for each operand the discussion must make clear whether the information is required or optional and whether it can be supplied in the DD statement or data-set label instead of the DCB macro instruction. You should remember the order in which information is taken to complete the data control block. It is taken first from the DCB macro instruction. If certain items are omitted from the DCB macro instruction, they are filled in from the DD statement, if the DD statement includes the items. If any remain unfilled, they may be filled from the data-set label. If an item is specified in both DCB macro and the DD statement, the DCB parameter takes precedence. The DCB operands of interest are as follows:

DSORG stands for Data-Set ORGanization and must be specified in the DCB. For sequential data sets one specifies DSORG=PS or DSORG=PSU, the PS standing for Physical Sequential. The U, meaning Unmovable, is included only if the data set contains location-dependent information that would prevent its being moved; this is unlikely for sequential data sets.

RECFM specifies the ForM of data RECords: fixed or variable length, blocked or unblocked. This information is essential, but it may be given in the DD statement or in the data-set label instead of the DCB macro instruction. If given in the DCB macro instruction, it is given as

RECFM=V	Variable, unblocked;
RECFM=VB	Variable, Blocked;
RECFM=F	Fixed, unblocked; and
RECFM=FB	Fixed, Blocked.

To each of the codes V, VB, F, FB, add the code A if you are using printer spacing control characters as explained in Section 12.2, thus making four additional allowable codes, VA, VBA, FA, and FBA. Other letters S, T, and M are sometimes included in defining record form but are ignored here.

BFTEK stands for BuFfer TECHnique (be careful not to spell it with a U). The options are simple buffering (coded S) and exchange buffering (coded E), as introduced in the preceding section. Buffering technique may be specified in the DD statement instead of the DCB macro instruction, or it can be omitted from both, in which case simple buffering is assumed. So in the DCB macro instruction we have

BFTEK=S   or   BFTEK=E

or neither.

MACRF, MACRo Form, is the fourth and last of the major parameters. In this parameter you specify which macros you are going to use with the data set and in which mode they are to be used. This parameter is required in the DCB macro instruction. The letters used to code the information for this parameter are

G   GET macro will be used;

P   PUT macro will be used;

M   move mode; and

T   (watch this one) substitute mode.

As we have learned, GET or PUT can be used in either mode. The parameter can be coded

GM   GET used in Move mode

GT   GET used in Substitute mode

PM   PUT used in Move mode

PT   PUT used in Substitute mode

If the same data set is opened for both input and output, specify which modes of both GET and PUT are to be used; the possibilities therefore are

(GM,PM)   (GT,PM)

(GM,PT)   (GT,PT)

BLKSIZE is the BLocK-SIZE parameter, which is specified as the length of the largest block to be processed in the data set. For fixed-length-record data sets, the block size must be an integral multiple of the record length; for variable-length-record data sets, BLKSIZE is the length of the largest block that may have to be processed. For a data set being created, BLKSIZE must be specified in either the DCB macro instruction or the DD statement. For already existing data sets, the data-set label is another possible source. Absolute maximum block size is 32,760.

LRECL is the Logical RECord Length. This parameter is required and can be provided from the same sources as BLKSIZE. There must be a relationship between BLKSIZE and LRECL:

■ For fixed-length unblocked data sets, BLKSIZE = LRECL.

■ For variable-length unblocked data sets, BLKSIZE = LRECL + 4. This is in recognition of the block descriptor word the operating system furnishes at the beginning of a variable-length record.

■ For fixed-length records blocked, BLKSIZE must be a multiple of LRECL.

■ If a printer spacing control character is included, it must be included as the first character of every record, and it must be counted along with other characters in calculating LRECL; other of the foregoing rules then apply.

For example, if fixed-length 80-character records are blocked into 800-byte blocks, the DCB statement would include

RECFM=FB,BLKSIZE=8ØØ,LRECL=8Ø

Unblocked records, each of 80 characters, would be specified as

RECFM=F,BLKSIZE=8Ø,LRECL=8Ø

Variable-length records to be printed would normally have a maximum of 132 characters to be printed because there are 132 print positions on the most standard printers. Adding the space control character results in LRECL=133. If the records are to be blocked, the DCB could contain

RECFM=VBA,BLKSIZE=1100,LRECL=133

BUFNO is the Number of BUFfers assigned. This operand is optional: it may be specified in the DCB macro instruction or in the DD statement, or it may be omitted, in which case two buffers are supplied.

DDNAME is the name that must be included as the ddname in the corresponding DD statement. Any name up to eight characters long, composed of letters and digits, and beginning with a letter is acceptable, but you will soon discover that using certain standard names saves trouble. For example, SYSIN is usually used for the standard input data set, SYSPRINT for the output to be printed, and SYSPUNCH for any output to be punched into cards. You may discover other more-or-less standard names used in your installation, but you may still use your own names if you wish. The DDNAME operand is mandatory in the DCB macro instruction.

DEVD stands for DEVice Description and it allows you to specify the type of device to be used for the data set. This operand is optional. There are subparameters that allow you to specify certain options within the device class, such as the density used on a magnetic tape or character codes used in paper tape. To preserve maximum flexibility, this kind of specification should be left to the DD statement if possible. The possible parameters for this operand will not be listed here; refer to the manuals *OS/VS2 Data Management Macro Instructions*, GC 26-3873, or *OS/VS Data Management Macro Instructions*, GC 26-3793.

EODAD stands for End-Of-Data ADdress and is an optional operand. Specify by any relocatable expression the address of the segment of your program that is to be executed when the end of an input data set is encountered. The supervisor transfers control to this address when a record is requested by a GET statement after the data set is exhausted. If EODAD is not specified, a GET statement appearing after exhaustion of the data set causes abnormal termination of the program.

EROPT, ERror OPTion, specifies the action to be taken upon an uncorrectable input or output error. Any one of the following options may be chosen:

ACC   accept the record anyway,

SKP   skip the record and proceed to the next, or

ABE   abnormally terminate the program.

On output, however, SKP cannot be chosen, and ACC can be chosen only for printer output. If EROPT is not specified in the DCB macro instruction, a default option of ABE is assumed.

The preceding DCB parameters include the important ones. Figure 12.5 summarizes the methods of specifying their information. This table may be

FIGURE 12.5 DCB operands

Operand	Required in DCB	Optional sources of information	May be entirely omitted
DSORG		DD statement, data-set label	
RECFM		DD statement, data-set label	
BFTEK		DD statement	x
MACRF	x		
BLKSIZE		DD statement, data-set label	
LRECL		DD statement, data-set label	
BUFNO		DD statement	x
DDNAME	x		
DEVD		DD statement	x
EODAD			x
EROPT			x

used as a checklist to ensure that you do not forget any of the parameters. Remember that the list, if exhausting, is not exhaustive even for QSAM; if you intend to become a sophisticated input/output programmer, you still have many hours of manual reading ahead of you.

EXAMPLES
This section closes by showing how a program may actually use the QSAM macros. First, consider a simple program that reads an unblocked data set of 80-byte records (perhaps from punched cards) and creates a blocked data set. There are only two data sets, one input and one output. Figure 12.6 shows the complete program for this job. The processing loop is a WHILE structure, running until the input file is exhausted. The WHILE test does not appear explicitly; the GET action is essentially

> IF there is a record to give to the user
>   THEN supply the record
>   ELSE transfer control to the EODAD address

This is exactly what the WHILE structure needs; it combines the test for end of the loop and the first action inside the loop into the use of GET. So the WHILE test is implicitly provided in the EODAD parameter of the DCB macro instruction. Opening and closing sequences are standard, and the entire program is almost too easy after the long discussions in this chapter.

The first DCB, for the input data set, includes almost all of the necessary parameters, leaving almost nothing to the corresponding DD statement. Default options are accepted for EROPT, BUFNO, and BFTEK. The second DCB, for the output data set, specifies the data set as blocked, but leaves block size to the DD statement.

FIGURE 12.6   Complete program to create a blocked data set

```
BLOCK     CSECT
          XSAVE TR=NO
          OPEN  (FILE1,INPUT,FILE2,OUTPUT)
* WHILE THERE ARE FILE1 RECORDS
* . READ FROM FILE1, WRITE TO FILE2
READLOOP GET   FILE1,AREA      EXIT FROM WHILE THROUGH EODAD
          PUT   FILE2,AREA
          B     READLOOP
* ENDWHILE
FINISH    CLOSE (FILE1,,FILE2)
          XRETURN SA=*,TR=NO
AREA      DS    CL80
FILE1     DCB   DSORG=PS,RECFM=F,MACRF=GM,BLKSIZE=80,
                LRECL=80,DDNAME=SYSIN,EODAD=FINISH
FILE2     DCB   DSORG=PS,RECFM=FB,MACRF=PM,LRECL=80,
                DDNAME=BLKFILE
          END   BLOCK
```

Actually, the program as written can be improved in a number of ways. This is a classic case where exchange buffering can increase efficiency. Using substitute mode with both data sets, one would insert the instruction

```
          LA    R2,AREA
```

before the loop. The loop itself would be changed to

```
READLOOP GET   FILE1,(R2)
          LR    R3,R1
          PUT   FILE2,(R3)
          LR    R2,R1
          B     READLOOP
```

Of course, you must insert the EQUREGS macro instruction into the program and change a few parameters of the DCBs. Also, BFTEK=E must be added to both DCBs. If the initial buffers assigned to FILE1 are denoted as 1A and 1B, and those assigned to FILE2 as 2A and 2B, action of the buffering and the exchange of buffers will change the buffer ownerships as follows:

	Belong to FILE1	Belong to user	Belong to FILE2
After the OPEN	1A, 1B	AREA	2A, 2B
After 1st GET	AREA, 1B	1A	2A, 2B
After 1st PUT	AREA, 1B	2A	1A, 2B
After 2nd GET	AREA, 2A	1B	1A, 2B
After 2nd PUT	AREA, 2A	2B	1A, 1B
After 3rd GET	2B, 2A	AREA	1A, 1B
After 3rd PUT	2B, 2A	1A	AREA, 1B

etc.

After each GET, the address of the buffer segment containing the record is left in register 1; it is then moved to register 3 to be given to the output processors in exchange for another area.

Another improvement that can be made in the existing program is the loosening of the input restrictions. The DCB parameters could easily state that the input is blocked, and if BLKSIZE is left for the DD statement to specify, the program could thus serve as a more general data-set move program.

Next, consider a questionnaire analysis program. Since this is a simple but somewhat general program, there will be three data sets: the data, control records specifying in detail the analysis desired, and printed output. The DCBs for the three data sets may be as follows:

```
DATA        DCB     DSORG=PS,RECFM=FB,MACRF=GM,                    X
                    DDNAME=INDATA,EODAD=FIN
CONTROLC    DCB     DSORG=PS,RECFM=F,MACRF=GM,                     X
                    BLKSIZE=8Ø,LRECL=8Ø,DDNAME=SYSIN,EODAD=D
OUT         DCB     DSORG=PS,RECFM=FBA,MACRF=PM,LRECL=133,         X
                    DDNAME=SYSPRINT
```

In the DATA DCB, both LRECL and BLKSIZE are left unspecified; they can be supplied by the data-set label. The parameter BUFNO may be given in the DD statement if the default option of 2 is not acceptable. In the OUT DCB, LRECL is specified to be 133 (to include a carriage-control character and 132 print positions) but BLKSIZE is left to be fixed in the DD statement.

The structure of the processing would be something like the following:

1. After standard beginnings, OPEN the CONTROLC data set.
2. Read control records and set up the analysis areas and procedures accordingly. The data reading is accomplished by statements like

```
GET     CONTROLC,CONT4
```

3. After all control records are read, the segment at D is given control; it concludes the set-up phase, closes CONTROLC, and OPENs the DATA:

```
D           CLOSE CONTROLC
            OPEN  DATA
```

4. Data records are read and analyzed, one at a time, through the instruction

```
GET     DATA,DATAREA
```

5. The reading and analyzing continues until there are no more records, at which time the operating system gives control to the segment starting at FIN. Here DATA is closed and the output data set opened, and the final analysis performed and results printed. At FIN, then, we have

```
FIN         CLOSE DATA
            OPEN  (OUT,OUTPUT)
```

and during output we have statements like

```
        PUT    OUT,RESULT
```

Finally, the OUT data set is closed and the program terminated.

A number of things can be done differently. All data sets could be opened at the beginning of the program and left open until the end, but it is best not to tie up the devices longer than necessary. In some operating environments this permits gains in efficiency. Second, it may be that main storage space will not permit generation of all the desired tables with one pass through the data; further passes are needed. If the data are assumed to reside on a magnetic tape or on a direct-access data set, this is possible; at FIN perform

```
        FIN        CLOSE (DATA,REREAD)
```

and reopen DATA again when ready to make another pass.

The job control, especially the DD statements, for these two example programs will be introduced in the next several sections.

12.5   Survey of Job Control Language

Section 5.6 gave a lick and a promise to job control language in order to prepare you to submit jobs of the simplest kind. This section expands on that treatment and treats the syntax and use of job control statements in more detail. The treatment will still neither be exhaustive nor extremely sophisticated. The emphasis is on manipulation of data sets. Comprehensive information can be found in the *OS/VS Job Control Language Reference Manual*, GC 28-0618, or *OS/VS2 MVS Job Control Language,* GC 28-0692.

STRUCTURE OF JOB CONTROL

The largest unit of work a user is concerned with is a job. The user submits a job to the computer as a request for execution of one or more programs. The execution of an individual program is a *job step*, and within the job there can be a certain amount of interdependence between steps. Between jobs there is none, except that, of course, different jobs may use the same data sets. A user may call for execution in a step of either a single program or a sequence of programs defined by a catalogued procedure. The catalogued procedures are introduced in order to enable users to request in a very simple way any of a number of standard sequences of programs, operating on a more-or-less standard series of data sets. A catalogued procedure is, in turn, composed of steps, each step being the execution of a single program; procedures do not call on other procedures.

You the user submit, along with programs and data sets, a series of job control statements that define your requests. Job control statements for a job always begin with a JOB statement. Following this statement are one or more EXEC (for EXECute) statements, each defining a step, each calling for execution of a program or a catalogued procedure. Following each EXEC statement are the DD (Data Definition) statements necessary to the step. The standard DD statements supplied by a catalogued procedure can be replaced or supplemented by the user to fit the requirements of the job you are submitting.

The format of job control cards, containing the job control statements, will be defined next. Each of the three kinds of job control statements begins with two slashes (//) in columns 1 and 2 of the card. Most statements need labels or names, and the names begin in column 3. A name is composed of from one to eight letters and digits but begins with a letter. After the name and at least one blank comes the *verb* field; the allowed verbs are JOB, EXEC, and DD. After the verb and at least one blank are operands, which are separated from each other by commas but no blanks. Finally, following at least one blank after the operands may appear comments. The syntax requirements are summarized as

//[name] $\begin{Bmatrix} \text{JOB} \\ \text{EXEC} \\ \text{DD} \end{Bmatrix}$ operands, separated by commas   [comments]

        one or   one or   one or
     more blanks   more blanks   more blanks

A job control statement can be continued onto a second and subsequent cards. Columns 1 to 71 are available for slashes, names, verbs, operands, and comments; operands may be interrupted after a parameter or subparameter and its succeeding comma (*don't* forget that comma!) at or before column 71. A character in column 72 is optional. The next card must have // in columns 1 and 2 (and *woe* if you forget those slashes!); operands must resume with any column from 4 to 16, and they can continue to column 71 and be followed by more continuation cards similarly if necessary.

There is one more job control statement, the *delimiter statement*. It has /* in columns 1 and 2, with only comments thereafter. The delimiter statement is used to signal the end of a data set in the main job stream.

SYNTAX OF THE JOB STATEMENT

A JOB statement must have a name, which is called a *jobname*. Try to make your name different from other users in the batch, to avoid possibility of confusion in the operations staff, but it is not worth checking other jobs to make sure of not duplicating their names. Operands requirements are somewhat dictated by the particular installation, but the general structure can be laid out.

The first operand, in parentheses, is accounting information, and what that should include is really up to the individual installation. The second operand is the programmer name. This can be coded with, say, a period or hyphen between first or last names, as GEORGE.STRUBLE or GEORGE-STRUBLE, or it may be enclosed in apostrophes, in which blanks are permitted: 'GEORGE STRUBLE'. The forms of both the accounting information and the programmer name may be prescribed by the installation.

The other operands are all keyword parameters and are all optional. One is MSGLEVEL; an operand of MSGLEVEL=1 directs the operating system to print in the system output the job control statements used by the job. MSGLEVEL=∅ directs that printing of the job control be suppressed. Each installation chooses which case is the default option in its system.

A parameter commonly required to help the job scheduler in a system that does multiprogramming is the CLASS parameter. It is coded CLASS= *a letter*; classes are assigned to types of jobs with similar attributes to help the scheduler balance the load on the system or respond appropriately to priorities. Each installation develops its own definition of job classes.

The last operand of the JOB statement we shall discuss is the COND parameter, which allows the user to give conditions for terminating the job. Each program, when terminated, returns a value called the *return code* to the job scheduler. The return codes can be used, as they are by the assembler, linkage editor, FORTRAN compilers, and elsewhere, to indicate the success of execution: a low number may mean no errors and a high number may mean grave errors that render the result useless. The return code can be compared with values given in the COND parameter to determine whether the remainder of the job should be canceled. The syntax is

$$\text{COND} = ((code, operator), \ldots, (code, operator))$$

with up to eight (*code,operator*) pairs. The value *code* is compared against the return code given by each program; *operator* can be any of

GT	greater than,
GE	greater than or equal to,
EQ	equal to,
LT	less than,
LE	less than or equal to,
NE	not equal to.

If a comparison

code   operator   return code

makes a true statement, the job is terminated. For example,

$$\text{COND} = ((12, LE), (7, EQ))$$

means that the job is to be terminated after any step that returns a return code such that 12 is less than or equal to the return code or 7 equals the return code.

Sample JOB statements would be

```
//GTRY    JOB    (321414),GEORGE.STRUBLE,MSGLEVEL=1,CLASS=B
//MWILKR   JOB    (4∅∅261),'A. LINCOLN',COND=((12,LE),(7,EQ))
```

SYNTAX OF THE EXEC STATEMENT

The name of an EXEC statement, called the *stepname*, is optional, but it must be used if the step or a data set in the step is referred to from another step.

The important and only required operand in the EXEC statement is the one designating the program or procedure to be executed. A program is kept as a data set; its execution is requested by data-set name. The data set may be catalogued and always known to the job scheduler, or it may be known temporarily as the result of a previous step in the same job. These two cases are recognized in the two optional forms:

$$\left\{ \begin{array}{l} \text{PGM=program name} \\ \text{PGM=*.stepname.ddname} \end{array} \right\},$$

where * stands for "this job" and is further qualified by the name of the step in which the data set was defined and the name of the DD statement within that step. The third possible case is the request for execution of a catalogued procedure:

$$\left\{ \begin{array}{l} \text{PROC=procedure name} \\ \text{procedure name} \end{array} \right\},$$

where PROC= is optional.

Other operands are COND and PARM. The COND parameter is like that described under the JOB statement, but it enables the user to specify conditions for bypassing each step individually. The syntax of the COND parameter in the EXEC statement is

COND=((*code,operator,stepname*), . . . , (*code,operator,stepname*)),

where up to eight triples, enclosed in parentheses, specify conditions for bypassing the current step. *Code* and *operator* have the same meanings given above, but the name of a particular step must be supplied for each, and the return code from that step is the one tested. For example,

```
//STEP3    EXEC   PGM=*.STEP2.DD2,COND=((12,LE,STEP2),(7,EQ,STEP1))
```

asks for execution of the program in the data set defined under the name DD2 in STEP2, unless either 12 is less than or equal to the return code issued by STEP2 or 7 is equal to the return code issued by STEP1.

Up to 40 characters of control information may be passed to a program from the PARM operand of an EXEC statement. The information is enclosed in apostrophes, for example,

```
PARM='LIST,NODECK'
```

Control information can be passed to a step of a procedure when calling for the procedure by naming the step:

```
//        EXEC   ASMFCLG,PARM.ASM='LIST,NODECK'
```

passes the control information to the program named in the ASM step of the ASMFCLG procedure.

A catalogued procedure may use a *symbolic parameter* in one or more operands. The parameter actually to be used in these operands is specified in the EXEC statement that calls the procedure. One symbolic parameter often used in catalogued procedures is &PRNTCLS; how it is used will be shown presently. It can be given a value of A by the statement

>>   //   EXEC   ASMFCLG,PRNTCLS=A

The value A is in effect only during this execution of the catalogued procedure ASMFCLG.

SYNTAX OF THE DD STATEMENT

There are more rules for the syntax of the DD statement than for the JOB or EXEC statements, because there are more different options and parameters to be specified. OS/VS provides a very flexible and powerful facility for allowing various data sets to be used with any given program. We shall not exhaustively examine all options but shall consider several of the most important.

Almost every DD statement has a name, which is called the *ddname*. When a data set is used in a step of a catalogued procedure, the user must qualify the ddname by the name of the procedure step: procstep.ddname. For example, ASM.SYSIN specifies a ddname of SYSIN for a data set to be used in the ASM step of a catalogued procedure.

When a data set is entered in the main job stream with the job control statements, the single operand * on the defining DD statement will inform the job scheduler that the data set immediately follows the DD statement. The delimiter statement (/*) must then follow the data set. For example,

>>   //ASM.SYSIN   DD   *
>>   records containing the data set
>>   /*

is the complete definition for a data set whose ddname is SYSIN for use in the ASM step of a catalogued procedure.

Another simple variety of statement is the one assigning an output data set to be printed. The simple operand SYSOUT=A defines the data set to have a printer as its ultimate destination; the operating system, for the sake of efficiency, usually writes the data set to magnetic disk first and prints it later, but this should not bother the user. In more sophisticated systems or for data sets with special requirements (special forms, exceptional length), more operands may be required in addition to SYSOUT=A; you must learn such things in your own installation. For example,

>>   //GO.RESULT   DD   SYSOUT=A

can direct toward the printer the data set whose ddname is RESULT in the GO step of a catalogued procedure.

Installations that have several printers or want to distinguish among categories of printer use (for example, postponing longer print runs) may establish several print classes; A is a common print class in many installations. The class V usually means (e.g., in a job submitted through CMS) return the output to the "CMS reader" for potential display at the user's terminal. An installation

may give its users easy control of the print class by using the symbolic parameter &PRNTCLS in each SYSOUT parameter in its catalogued procedures. For
example,

```
//SYSOUT DD    SYSOUT=&PRNTCLS
```

If the catalogued procedure is called with the parameter PRNTCLS=A (note that
the ampersand is omitted here) in the EXEC statement, A will be the print class
used.

If the data set to be defined is not one of these simple kinds, a minor host
of operands may be needed in the DD statement. A brief outline of them is
presented next, followed by a more detailed description of each. In the next
section a number of complete DD statements are used in a variety of situations.

The location of a data set must be specified; it can be named with a
dsname in a DSNAME operand if it is already known to the operating system, or a
UNIT can specify a specific device or device class to be used. For magnetic tapes
or magnetic disk packs which are demountable, a VOL specification identifies a
particular reel, disk pack, or whatever to be used. In any case a DISP operand
will usually be needed to tell the job scheduler whether the data set is new or already exists, and what to do with it after the current job step or procedure
step. If the data set is to be created on a direct-access device, the job scheduler
needs direction as to the SPACE to be allocated. Finally, a DCB operand may
specify parameters, such as block size, to be included in the data control block
for the data set.

The DISP operand has three subparameters. The first gives the previous
status of the data set, and the others the disposition to be made of the data set
at the end of the step. Possible entries for the first subparameter are NEW, OLD,
SHR, and MOD. NEW indicates that the data set does not yet exist and is to be created; the other three possibilities are all used for an already existing data set. If
the data set is to be read, and especially if there may be other jobs in the job
stream also wanting to read the data set, the first subparameter should be
coded as SHR, since it permits shared use. On the other hand, OLD insists on exclusive use, and if one job is using the data set, all other jobs that want it are
shut out, thus slowing system operation and giving fits to the computer operators. The entry MOD is used for an existing sequential data set which is to have
new information tacked on at the end. When opened, the data set is positioned
at the end of the existing information, ready for writing.

The MOD subparameter introduces a very dangerous mode of operation. When an
existing data set is modified, either on magnetic tape or on a direct-access device, there
is always the possibility that if the job step is abnormally terminated or writes the wrong
information (both of which happen more often than we programmers care to admit),
the data set is left in a state from which it is difficult to recover even the previous status.
It is far better practice to make a new data set by copying the information from the old
and then adding on the new; this preserves the original data set in case something goes
wrong. It is always good practice anyway to keep backup copies of data sets, so that if
one is accidentally destroyed or lost through some mishap, it can be reconstructed from
a recent copy or version.

There are five possible dispositions of the data set after the step is completed: DELETE, KEEP, PASS, CATLG, and UNCATLG. Let us consider first the system catalogue. In this catalogue, the operating system keeps a list of data sets, by dsname and exact location—that is, the serial number of magnetic tape reel, magnetic disk pack, etc., and the location on a disk pack. The operating system tries to ensure that the data sets listed in the catalogue are protected from accidental destruction, and it locates the data sets automatically for use in a job.

A data set, new or old, may be catalogued after successful completion of a step if CATLG is specified. A previously catalogued data set can be removed from the catalogue, but its space still not be made available for other use, if UNCATLG is specified. KEEP is specified for a data set, new or old, which is to be kept but not catalogued. A disposition of PASS directs that the data set be kept temporarily—either until the end of the job or until it is used in a subsequent step, whichever is sooner. Another disposition may be specified in a subsequent step. If no further disposition is specified in any subsequent step, the data set is deleted at the end of the job. Finally, a disposition of DELETE directs that the data set immediately be deleted, and its space be made available for other data sets.

The second subparameter directs the disposition to be made of the data set if the job step is completed successfully, the third if the step ends abnormally. If the first subparameter is left unspecified, NEW is assumed; if the second is omitted, the default is its disposition before the beginning of the step: DELETE for new data sets, KEEP for old, but DELETE for PASSed data sets. If the third subparameter is omitted, the second is taken to cover both normal and abnormal termination.

As examples, say you have an old data set that is to be read and to keep its original status after the step, whatever the outcome:

$$DISP=(OLD,KEEP)$$

On the other hand, you may be able to delete a data set at the end of the current step if it was successful, but otherwise keep it for a rerun:

$$DISP=(OLD,DELETE,KEEP)$$

A temporary data set perhaps has no further use if the step runs satisfactorily, but must be kept to aid in the diagnosis of trouble otherwise:

$$DISP=(NEW,DELETE,CATLG)$$

Conversely, a new data set is created for future use, but if the step was not successful, it must be rerun and this copy is useless:

$$DISP=(NEW,CATLG,DELETE)$$

Because direct access space required for the catalogue is usually at a premium and because the number of magnetic tapes being saved seems to grow without bound, many installations prefer that data sets on magnetic tape not be catalogued. They can be protected in other ways and identified by serial number. Data sets on magnetic tape are usually given dsnames, however.

A data set to be entered in the catalogue, or retrieved by reference to the catalogue, must have a dsname. The name is specified in the DD statement as DSNAME=dsname, or if the data set desired is a member of a partitioned data set, DSNAME=dsname (member name). We can shorten DSNAME to DSN if we wish. If a temporary data set is to be used in a subsequent step of the same job, however, it need not be given a dsname when first created, and DD statements in subsequent steps may refer to it by the DD statement creating it: DSN=*.stepname.ddname. However, when the defining DD statement was used in a step of a catalogued procedure, both the step calling the procedure and the step within the procedure must be referred to, as follows:

DSN=*.stepname.procstepname.ddname

For example, DSNAME=*.STEP2.SYSLIN is a valid reference to the data set with ddname SYSLIN, used in STEP2, but if STEP2 were a call on a catalogued procedure which had a step LKED, then DSNAME=*.STEP2.LKED.GODATA refers to a data set GODATA defined in that step.

The UNIT parameter is required unless

1. the data set is retrieved by reference to its dsname and no volume (see below) information is given, or

2. the data set is passed from a previous step and no volume or unit information is given in the preceding definition.

The UNIT may be indicated as a particular unit or class of units. There are two major kinds of unit specification:

■ UNIT=model, where model stands for a model number of input or output units; UNIT=3330, for example, requests that the data set be created by a model 3330 disk storage drive, but any 3330 drive in the system is acceptable. A user will know, or must learn, the model numbers of devices he is likely to use, so we do not attempt a list here.

■ UNIT=group, where group is an alphabetic designation of a class of units, for example, SYSDA for *all* direct-access devices, SYSSQ for all direct-access devices and magnetic tape units, which can handle sequential files, TAPE16 for all 1600-bpi tape units, etc. The classes and names are set up by each installation, so the user must learn them locally.

The specification of a unit group or class is preferable to the model because it allows the job scheduler the widest latitude in employing devices for maximum efficiency.

When a data set is not catalogued, it can be requested by

UNIT=class,VOL=SER=serial number

A volume is an integral unit of peripheral storage capacity, such as a magnetic tape reel or a disk pack. A labeled magnetic tape has a serial number as part of its label, and a disk pack or any other demountable storage unit also has a serial number. Uncatalogued data sets on such volumes are usually requested by volume serial number. The keyword can be written VOLUME or VOL.

When a data set is to be created and a possible location for it is a direct-access device, an allocation of space must be requested. The space can be requested in terms of average block size or, more device-dependent, tracks or cylinders. A quantity of the units chosen is requested by SPACE=(unit, quantity); for example, SPACE=(8ØØ,5Ø) requests 50 blocks each of length 800, SPACE=(TRK,12) requests 12 tracks, and SPACE=(CYL,4) requests four cylinders. To request tracks or cylinders, you must have some understanding of the structure and capacities of devices. For example, on disk packs for model 3330 disk storage units, a track holds 13,030 bytes and a cylinder consists of 19 tracks. If you request space in terms of a block size, this block size is only for purposes of computing space required, and need not be the same as the length of actual blocks of data in the data set.

You need not request *exactly* the space your data set will need. The quantity of units requested may be only an initial quantity and an *increment* specified—the number of units to be assigned when the already allocated space is exhausted. This kind of request is phrased as SPACE=(unit,(quantity,increment)). For example, SPACE=(8ØØ,(5Ø,1Ø)) requests an initial allocation of space for 50 blocks of 800 characters each. If that space is used up during the execution of the program, an increment of space for ten 800-character blocks is allocated. If *that* is used up, an additional increment of ten 800-character blocks is allocated. If necessary, this process continues until either 15 increments have been allocated or the space available on the volume is exhausted. Wonderful though this facility is, there is significant overhead, in both time and space, required for the additional increments, which are called *extents*, so you are well advised to estimate your needs as well as possible, but not to make the increments too small. On the other hand, be sure to release the space allocated but unused after creation of the data set is completed. The third subparameter of SPACE directs the operating system to release the unused space; for example,

SPACE=(8ØØ,(5Ø,1Ø),RLSE)

The last of the DD operands to be presented here is the DCB operand. It is written DCB=(parameter list), where the parameter list is a list of keywords and corresponding values, coded exactly as they would be in a DCB macro instruction in assembler language. All parameters not supplied by the corresponding DCB macro instruction, by the data-set label, or by default, must be supplied in the DCB operand of the DD statement. Such an operand might be

DCB=(BLKSIZE=8ØØ,LRECL=16Ø,RECFM=FB)

In summary, the DD statement can include as operands

*	data set follows directly,
SYSOUT=A	direct toward printer,

or any combination of

DISP=(status,disposition)	previous and future status,
DSNAME=dsname	name is used in catalogue references,
UNIT=ident	ident = model or group,
VOL=SER=ser. no.	identify specific volume,
SPACE=(unit,(quan.,incr.),RLSE)	required for direct access data sets,
DCB=(parameters)	parameters as in DCB macro instructions

This is not a complete list of possible operands, or a complete list of the options within each operand, but it should be enough machinery to use for some time.

12.6   Examples of Specific Data-Set Operations

The preceding section introduced operands of DD statements and explained in a general way when and how the individual parameters should be used. Now you will see how the operands and parameters are put together in specific situations.

CREATING DATA SETS ON DIRECT ACCESS VOLUMES

To create a data set to be used only in one job step is very simple; only UNIT and SPACE parameters need be given. The data set can be written, read, reread, and changed within a program, as required, by a program that needs more storage space than is available in main storage. Supposing that the data set is used under a ddname TEMPSTOR in the GO step of a catalogued procedure and that it requires space for approximately 250 blocks of 800 characters each, the DD statement could be

```
//GO.TEMPSTOR   DD   UNIT=SYSDA,SPACE=(8ØØ,(25Ø,25))
```

No DISP parameter is necessary, as (NEW,DELETE) is the default value supplied.

If a newly created data set is to be saved for use by later jobs, DISP and DSNAME parameters must be added. Besides, if the data set is to be kept, pay attention to where it is kept; a VOL specification may be appropriate. Usually, however, the policies of the installation, plus the operating system's classification of private and public volumes, keep you out of trouble if you neglect a VOL specification. A DD statement could be

```
//SKBLOC       DD   UNIT=SYSDA,SPACE=(8ØØØ,(25,5),RLSE),
//                  DISP=(,CATLG),DSN=SKBLOCK3
```

To use this particular data set in a later job is much easier; let the job scheduler find the data set through the catalogue, and space is already allocated. So the required DD statement is simply

```
//NOTHER       DD   DSNAME=SKBLOCK3,DISP=SHR
```

PASSING A DATA SET

Suppose that a data set, created during one step of a job, is to be kept only for use during one subsequent step of the same job and then abandoned. This is the situation for PASSing a data set. Assume you have a direct-access volume and a DD statement in a step named STEP1 of

```
//DNEXT     DD   DISP=(,PASS),UNIT=SYSDA,SPACE=(4000,(250,25))
```

As in other DISP operands, omit NEW, which is assumed by default. A dsname is not necessary, nor is a VOL designation.

Suppose now that STEP2 of the job does not refer to this data set, but STEP3 does, under a ddname of INTERMED. The DD statement in STEP3 could be

```
//INTERMED DD   DSNAME=*.STEP1.DNEXT,DISP=(OLD,DELETE)
```

Once the data set is identified as existing from the previous step, all the information about it is retrieved from the DD statement which guided the creation of the data set.

CREATING AND USING A DATA SET ON MAGNETIC TAPE

First, suppose that a data set is to be created and kept on magnetic tape for use in later jobs. Operands DISP, UNIT, and DSNAME must be specified. Optional operands include DCB and VOL. Supposing that the program creating the data set does it under a ddname of TAPOUT, observe that a possible DD statement is

```
//TAPOUT    DD   DISP=(NEW,KEEP),UNIT=TAPE62,DSN=TAP349
```

A disposition of KEEP is given to reserve the tape but not to catalog it. The class TAPE62 specifies a 6250-bpi tape drive, and the data set is given the unimaginative name of TAP349.

After the job is run and the tape is created, the user is informed of its serial number, which may be 101378. To use the tape in a later program, with a ddname of INTAP2, you may write a DD statement

```
//INTAP2    DD   DISP=OLD,UNIT=TAPE62,DSNAME=TAP349,VOL=SER=101378
```

The tape will be kept after this use too. I do not recommend a disposition of (OLD,DELETE) or even (OLD,DELETE,KEEP); wait to delete your tape until you are sure your program ran correctly and you are indeed through with it. Deletion can easily be done then by the operations staff. DCB operands could, of course, be added to either or both DD statements.

COMPLETE JOB CONTROL FOR A SIMPLE STEP

Now let us examine the job control for a complete but simple job step, execution of the record-blocking program of Fig. 12.6. An EXEC statement and two DD statements are required, one each for the DCBs

```
FILE1     DCB   DSORG=PS,RECFM=F,MACRF=GM,BLKSIZE=80,          X
                LRECL=80,DDNAME=SYSIN,EODAD=FINISH
FILE2     DCB   DSORG=PS,RECFM=FB,MACRF=PM,LRECL=80,           X
                DDNAME=BLKFILE
```

The second DCB left BLKSIZE to be specified in the DD statement, but other DCB parameters are complete. Let us suppose that the first data set is records in the job stream, and that the second is to be written to disk. Assuming that the program BLOCK is in a system library in load module format under the name BLOCK (the name would not *necessarily* be the same as the name on the CSECT statement), the complete job control for the step is

```
//BLKSTEP   EXEC   PGM=BLOCK
//BLKFILE   DD     UNIT=SYSDA,DISP=(NEW,KEEP,DELETE),DSN=QUEST215,
//                 DCB=(BLKSIZE=2ØØØ),SPACE=(2ØØØ,(2ØØ,5Ø),RLSE)
//SYSIN     DD     *
```

Records of first data set

```
/*
```

The definition of a data set in the main job stream is usually the last definition for the job step.

JOB CONTROL FOR A QUESTIONNAIRE ANALYSIS PROGRAM

As a further example, consider again the job control statements for a questionnaire analysis program that was outlined at the end of Section 12.4. This time, suppose that the program has been assembled and link-edited in the current job, and that it exists in a temporary data set whose ddname is SYSLMOD, which was created during a step named LKED. The data set of questionnaire data is that created in the example just given, which we now assume to be on the disk volume with serial number VSPKØ1. Though LRECL and BLKSIZE are not specified in the DCB macro instruction for the data set, the data-set label can supply them. We may direct the output to the printer, but because BLKSIZE was not specified in the DCB macro instruction, it must be supplied in the DD statement. The DCBs, themselves, from the previous section are

```
CONTROLC   DCB    DSORG=PS,RECFM=F,MACRF=GM,                          X
                  BLKSIZE=8Ø,LRECL=8Ø,DDNAME=SYSIN,EODAD=D
DATA       DCB    DSORG=PS,RECFM=FB,MACRF=GM,                         X
                  DDNAME=INDATA,EODAD=FIN
OUT        DCB    DSORG=PS,RECFM=FBA,MACRF=PM,LRECL=133,              X
                  DDNAME=SYSPRINT
```

The job control for the step is

```
//STEPGO    EXEC   PGM=*.LKED.SYSLMOD,COND=(5,LT,LKED)
//INDATA    DD     DISP=SHR,UNIT=SYSDA,DSNAME=QUEST215,
//                 VOL=SER=VSPKØ1
//SYSPRINT  DD     SYSOUT=A,DCB=(BLKSIZE=133)
//SYSIN     DD     *
```

Control records

```
/*
```

OVERRIDING AND ADDING DD STATEMENTS TO
CATALOGUED PROCEDURES

Each step within a catalogued procedure has a name called the *procstepname*.
All modifications to data-set definitions for each step must be identified by the
procstepname, and must come before modifications for the next step. Furthermore, modifications overriding DD statements in the procedure must appear in
the same order as the corresponding statements in the procedure itself, and before additional definitions for the step. For example, if a procedure step consists of the statements

```
//GO        EXEC  PGM=*.LKED.SYSLMOD,COND=((5,LT,FORT),(5,LT,LKED))
//FTØ3FØØ1 DD     SYSOUT=&PRNTCLS,DCB=(RECFM=VA,BLKSIZE=137)
//FTØ2FØØ1 DD     UNIT=SYSCP,DCB=(LRECL=8Ø,RECFM=F,BLKSIZE=8Ø)
//FTØ1FØØ1 DD     DDNAME=SYSIN
```

we may wish in executing this step, to redefine FTØ2FØØ1 to write to disk instead of punch cards, and add definitions for data sets SYSUDUMP and
FTØ9FØØ1, as well as including a data set, to be used as FTØ1FØØ1, in the main
job stream. The redefinition of FTØ2FØØ1 must be first, and the inclusion of the
data set in the job stream itself must be last. This data set is included under the
name SYSIN; the definition of FTØ1FØØ1 essentially *deferred* the definition of
FTØ1FØØ1 until a later statement; this avoids the conflicting requirements that
redefinition of FTØ1FØØ1 must come before definition of additional data sets,
and that it come last because it defines a data set in the main job stream. Job
control statements to accomplish the modifications and additions are

```
//GO.FTØ2FØØ1   DD    UNIT=SYSDA,DISP=(,CATLG),DSN=SPECTR21,
//                    SPACE=(8Ø,(6ØØ,1ØØ),RLSE),VOL=SER=VSPKØ2
//GO.SYSUDUMP   DD    SYSOUT=&PRNTCLS
//GO.FTØ9FØØ1   DD    DISP=SHR,UNIT=SYSDA,DSN=OBSERV47,
//                    VOL=SER=VSPKØ1
//GO.SYSIN      DD    *
```

Records in the job stream

```
/*
```


A CATALOGUED PROCEDURE FOR ASSEMBLE,
LINK-EDIT, AND EXECUTE

You are by now in a position to understand the catalogued procedure ASMFCLG,
which was introduced in Chapter 5. Each installation, in cataloguing its own
procedures, makes slight variations to adjust to local conditions, so the procedure we exhibit in Fig. 12.7 will not be identical in all parameters to the one at
any particular installation. It is very close to the procedure suggested by IBM,
however (in the manual *IBM System/360 Operating System Assembler F
Programmer's Guide*, GC 26-3756), so it should be close to any a user may encounter. Some features of job control language used but not yet explained will

FIGURE 12.7   The AMSFCLG procedure

```
   //ASMFCLG   PROC MAC='SYS1.MACLIB',MAC1='SYS1.MACLIB',PRNTCLS=A
1. //ASM       EXEC PGM=IFOX00,REGION=128K,PARM='NODECK,OBJ'
2. //SYSLIB    DD   DSN=&MAC,DISP=SHR
3. //          DD   DSN=&MAC1,DISP=SHR
4. //SYSUT1    DD   DSN=&&SYSUT1,UNIT=SYSDA,SPACE=(1700,(600,100))
   //SYSUT2    DD   DSN=&&SYSUT2,UNIT=SYSDA,SPACE=(1700,(300,50))
   //SYSUT3    DD   DSN=&&SYSUT3,UNIT=SYSDA,SPACE=(1700,(300,50))
   //SYSPRINT  DD   SYSOUT=&PRNTCLS,DCB=BLKSIZE=1089
5. //SYSPUNCH  DD   SYSOUT=B
6. //SYSGO     DD   DSN=&&OBJSET,UNIT=SYSDA,SPACE=(80,(200,50)),
   //              DISP=(MOD,PASS)
7. //LKED      EXEC PGM=IEWL,PARM=(XREF,LET,LIST,NCAL),REGION=128K,
   //              COND=(8,LT,ASM)
   //SYSLIN    DD   DSN=&&OBJSET,DISP=(OLD,DELETE)
   //          DD   DDNAME=SYSIN
   //SYSLMOD   DD   DSN=&&GOSET(GO),UNIT=SYSDA,SPACE=(1024,(50,20,1)),
   //              DISP=(MOD,PASS)
   //SYSUT1    DD   DSN=&&SYSUT1,UNIT=SYSDA,SPACE=(1024,(50,20))
   //SYSPRINT  DD   SYSOUT=&PRNTCLS
   //GO        EXEC PGM=*.LKED.SYSLMOD,COND=((8,LT,ASM),(4,LT,LKED))
```

Notes

1. IFOX00 is the name of the data set in the system library that contains the assembler. The REGION parameter establishes the amount of main storage allocated to a step.
2. SYS1.MACLIB holds the standard macros currently defined.
3. &MAC1 can be defined as a second library of macros to be used—the ASSIST macros, or the CMS macros, for example. Since this DD statement does not have a ddname, it is a continuation of the previous data set, SYSLIB.
4. &&SYSUT1, &&SYSUT2, &&SYSUT3 are all temporary data-set names.
5. In most systems, SYSOUT=B directs output to the card punch.
6. DISP=(MOD,PASS) defaults to (NEW,PASS) if the data set does not yet exist. MOD permits several assemblies or compilations to contribute to the same module.
7. IEWL is the name of the linkage editor. The PARM parameters invoke options in the linkage editor.

---

be discussed now (see also the notes to Fig. 12.7). First is the PROC statement itself, which declares that a procedure named ASMFCLG is defined here. The PROC statement also gives default values to three symbolic parameters, &MAC, &MAC1, and &PRNTCLS. If, as user, you assign values to any of these parameters in the EXEC statement that invokes the procedure, those values will be used, but if you do not, the values assigned in the PROC statement will be used.

The procedure contains three steps. The first assembles a program (input SYSIN, listing SYSPRINT, punched object deck SYSPUNCH, data set for linking and executing SYSGO). The second step calls the linkage editor, which puts the assembled program and any other object modules that may be needed into a ready-to-execute *load module*. The linkage editor takes as its input the data set produced by the assembler, with the DSN of &&OBJSET. This is one of several *temporary names* used in the procedure; the initial *two* ampersands distinguish

FIGURE 12.8   A complete job, using ASMFCLG

```
//QUESTNAR JOB (204121),MACRO.POLO,MSGLEVEL=1
//         EXEC ASMFCLG,MAC1=ASSTLIB
//ASM.SYSIN    DD *
                    program to be assembled
/*
//LKED.SYSIN    DD DSN=USERLIB,DISP=SHR
//GO.SYSPRINT   DD SYSOUT=A,DCB=(BLKSIZE=133)
//GO.INDATA     DD DISP=SHR,UNIT=SYSDA,DSNAME=QUEST215,
//              VOL=SER=VSPK01
//GO.SYSIN DD   *
                    control records
/*
```

them as temporary. The input to the linkage editor (ddname SYSLIN) is actually *two* concatenated data sets; whenever a DD statement does not have a ddname, it is treated as a continuation of the data set defined in the previous statement. In the case of linkage editor input, this permits a user to include an object module in the job stream or on disk, as well as the just-assembled module. The load module produced by the linkage editor, defined by the ddname SYSLMOD, is a member GO of a temporary partitioned data set &&GOSET. The third step of the procedure executes this program, defined by its stepname, procstepname, and ddname. *All* data-set definitions required during execution of the user's program are left to the user; none are provided by the catalogued procedure.

A possible complete job, including the ASMFCLG procedure but including reference to a routine in the data set USERLIB, is shown in Fig. 12.8. This example is drawn from the questionnaire analysis example discussed previously, and the GO step data sets are identical to those discussed earlier in that connection.

AN INVENTORY UPDATE PROGRAM

Let us now explore an entire problem or at least all input and output pertaining to it. Suppose that you have a data set (call it an *inventory master*), containing inventory data for a warehouseful of items. Each item has a part number, and the information in the data set is recorded in ascending order by part number. In the record for each item there is, of course, the number of pieces currently on hand, as well as other information such as perhaps number on order and bin location. Periodically, perhaps once or twice a day, the inventory file must be brought up to date. Each transaction, such as an order placed, order received, quantity shipped out, change of bin location, is in a record identified with the part number. The transactions are sorted into part number order (see the next section), and written into a data set that is called the transaction file. Now the two data sets must be compared and merged into a new inventory master. At the same time a printed listing of exceptional conditions, such as negative quantity on hand, will be printed for human attention because errors *will* creep in and they must be found and corrected. It is this program that we shall explore.

Suppose that a record on the inventory master or the transaction file, including the information on one item, is 60 characters, and that the part number is the first eight of the 60 characters. The records may be blocked, perhaps with 1200-character blocks in all data sets. If we had no transactions that could create new master records, it would be natural to use exchange buffering with substitute mode for reading and writing the inventory master records. Because we want to allow new master records to be created, we should use simple buffering and move mode for all files. Therefore the DCB macro instructions can be written

```
OLDMAST   DCB    DSORG=PS,RECFM=FB,BFTEK=S,MACRF=GM,BLKSIZE=1200,   X
                 LRECL=60,DDNAME=INVMASOL,EODAD=FINOLD
NEWMAST   DCB    DSORG=PS,RECFM=FB,BFTEK=S,MACRF=PM,BLKSIZE=1200,   X
                 LRECL=60,DDNAME=INVMASNW
TRANSACT  DCB    DSORG=PS,RECFM=FB,BFTEK=S,MACRF=GM,BLKSIZE=1200,   X
                 LRECL=60,DDNAME=SORTRANS,EODAD=FINTRAN
EXCEPT    DCB    DSORG=PS,RECFM=FA,MACRF=PM,BLKSIZE=133,LRECL=133, X
                 DDNAME=SYSPRINT
```

The inventory update program will be a standard program in the installation, so it will be kept in a library, perhaps under the name INVUPDAT. Supposing that the old inventory master has dsname INVMAS38 and is on disk volume INVSYS01, and that the sorted transaction file has dsname TRANS39 and is on disk volume VSPK01, we see that the complete job control for the job would be

```
//INVUP39    JOB    2136,E.SCROOGE
//           EXEC   PGM=INVUPDAT
//INVMASOL   DD     DISP = SHR,UNIT = SYSDA,DSNAME = INVMAS38,
//                  VOL = SER = INVSYS01
//INVMASNW   DD     DISP = ( ,KEEP),UNIT = SYSDA,DSNAME = INVMAS39
//SORTRANS   DD     DISP = SHR,UNIT = SYSDA,DSNAME = TRANS39,
//                  VOL = SER = VSPK01
//SYSPRINT   DD     SYSOUT = A
```

Neither old data set is deleted after use. Old inventory masters and transaction data sets should be kept for about four data sets back, so that if any mishap should destroy the most recent data set or even two data sets, the information could be recreated merely by running the update program a few more times. After a data set is more than five updates out of date, its space can be returned to reusable status by the operations staff.

It remains of interest to explore the logic and the input/output manipulations of the program itself. The logic is essentially that of a *merge*: always, the record with the lowest key (designated as *current key*) is processed. If there is a master record with the current key, consider that key *allocated*; then you can

FIGURE 12.9   Pseudo-code for the inventory update program

```
Open all files
Read master record
Read trans record
Current key = min(master key, trans key)
WHILE current key not = high-values
  IF master key = current key
    THEN   move master record to out record
           set allocated to true
           read master record
    ELSE   set allocated to false
  WHILE    trans key = current key
  IF       trans code = A
    THEN   IF allocated
             THEN   write error: key already exists
             ELSE   set allocated to true
                    move trans record fields to out record
                    move zeros to quantities in out record
    ELSE   IF   allocated
             THEN   apply trans record update to out record
             ELSE   write error:  key does not exist
    read trans record
  IF   allocated
    THEN   write out record
  Current key = min(current key, trans key)
Close all files
```

update the record but not add a new record with the same key. If there is no master record with that key, a transaction to *add* a record with that key to the file is permitted, and the key is then allocated, which means that further transactions can update the new master record. Your program should keep track of the fields master key (from the master record), and transaction key (from the transaction record) as well as current key. The tactic of setting the master key to high-values (hexadecimal FFs) is used when the program reaches the end of the master file, and similarly for the transaction file. This permits a sort of symmetry of treatment of the two files and means that you need not worry about which file runs out of records first. Keep the currently "allocated" master record in an area OUTREC, whether that record came from the master file or the transaction file.

Figure 12.9 shows a possible pseudo-code for the program. With this pseudo-code, transactions are permitted to add a record with a new key to the master file (include it in the new master file) and to update fields in the master record. It does not delete records, but to add that capability requires only logic to change the *allocated* switch from TRUE to FALSE.

Now let us examine a little of the coding. Just after the standard beginning instructions, the data sets are opened by

```
                    OPEN       (OLDMAST,INPUT,TRANSACT,INPUT)
                    OPEN       (NEWMAST,OUTPUT,EXCEPT,OUTPUT)
```

There are two places in the program where a record must be read from the OLDMAST file. For this purpose, define an internal subroutine, READOLD:

```
READOLD        GET        OLDMAST,OLDREC
               MVC        OLDKEY(8),OLDREC
               BR         R11
FINOLD         MVI        OLDKEY,X'FF'
               MVC        OLDKEY+1(7),OLDKEY
               BR         R11
```

In each place where the program needs to read an OLDMAST record, it calls this subroutine:

```
               BAL        R11,READOLD
```

A similar subroutine reads a transaction record.

12.7 Sorting by Merging

Sorting methods can be divided into two classes. One class is called *sequential*, because each file of items is treated only in a sequential manner. The other class uses items in nonsequential orders, effecting rearrangements or testing keys in various places. Since a method of this class is usually used in the internal storage of a computer, this class is called *internal*. Internal sorts can be most efficient if a fast direct-access storage of sufficient capacity for the entire file is available, but if the file is too large, sequential sorts are required. A sequential sort is described in this section partly to illustrate an important technique and partly to illustrate further input and output methods.

The procedure accepts an input file on a sequential device and assumes that records can be written as well as read there. In any one pass, however, records are read or written but not both. The sorted file is finally generated in the same data set, replacing the unsorted file, and three scratch data sets are used internal to the process. Each record is identified with a key; for brevity we speak of writing the key, when we mean of course writing a record identified with the key. We assume that the actual keys are composed of characters in the EBCDIC format, and order the file so that the keys, considered as unsigned integers, will be in ascending order. A quick glance at a table of EBCDIC representations will assure you that alphabetical order is thus preserved, with digits following the alphabet and other special characters sprinkled throughout.

We may speak of a *string* of records, meaning a sequence whose keys are in ascending order. In fact, we mean by "a string" a maximal sequence in ascending order, so that no larger sequence from the file, including the given string, is still a string. Obviously, the entire point of the sort is to merge the whole file into one string, and the procedure does that, in stages. If the entire

FIGURE 12.10   Sort illustration

Data set 1:   01, 27, 82, 34, 33, 69, 11, 87, 92
Data set 2:   19, 12, 74, 53, 58, 84, 95
     merge into
Data set 3:   01, 19, 27, 82, 33, 53, 58, 69, 84, 95
Data set 4:   12, 34, 74, 11, 87, 92
     merge into
Data set 1:   01, 12, 19, 27, 34, 74, 82
Data set 2:   11, 33, 53, 58, 69, 84, 87, 92, 95
     merge into
Data set 3:   01, 11, 12, 19, 27, 33, 34, 53, 58, 69, 74, 82, 84, 87, 92, 95
Data set 4:   ——

---

file is divided into two data sets, a string from one can be merged with a string from the other to form a single string: 04,13,27 and 10,11,16,32 can be merged to form a string 04,10,11,13,16,27,32. The mechanism is simple: two items, the first from each string, are compared, the one with smaller key is written, and so long as eligible items remain in both strings, another is read to replace in consideration the one just written. When one string is exhausted, the remainder of the other is written.

If there are n strings, approximately $n/2$ in each of two data sets, they can be merged to form $n/2$ strings, and if two output data sets are available, the output can be alternated so that each output data set contains only $n/4$ strings. Furthermore, the data sets are ready for another merge, using the previous output as input and the previous input data sets for output. Each merge pass of this kind is called a *phase*. The file containing n strings can be completely sorted in $[\log_2 n] + 1$ merge phases, where $[\log_2 n]$ represents the largest integer less than the logarithm to the base 2 of n. For example, a file of 300 strings can be sorted in nine phases and a file of 7000 strings in 13 phases. The process is illustrated in Fig. 12.10. The brackets show the strings but have no physical representation in the data sets.

Figure 12.11 shows a pseudo-code description of the program. The pseudo-code description is not specific to the IBM System/370, though it is followed shortly by an assembler language program. The keys KEY0, KEY1, and KEY2 are central to the process. KEY1 and KEY2 are keys (associated with records) from the current input data sets file1 and file2, respectively. The key of the record just written is KEY0, and output continues into the same output file as long as either KEY1 or KEY2 or both are greater than KEY0. The pseudo-code expresses this as three WHILE loops: as long as KEY1 is not less than KEY0, the data sets file1 and file2 are merged into the output file. Then records from file2 are copied into the same output file until KEY2 is less than KEY0. This ensures that each string will contain all the records that can possi-

FIGURE 12.11   Pseudo-code for SORT-BY-MERGE program

```
Set up the initial file D2 as an empty file

REPEAT
    Set sequence changes = 0
    Open files
    Get initial records from the two input files
    WHILE NOT (end-of-file1 AND end-of-file2)
        Set Last-record-written (KEY∅) to Low values (binary ∅)
        WHILE (NOT end-of-file1) AND (KEY∅ ≤ KEY1)
            WHILE KEY2 ≤ KEY1 AND KEY2 ≥ KEY∅
                Write record from file2
                Move KEY2 to KEY∅
                Read another record from file2
            ENDWHILE
            Write record from file1
            Move KEY1 to KEY∅
            Read another record from file1
        ENDWHILE
        WHILE (NOT end-of-file2) AND (KEY2 ≥ KEY∅)
            Write record from file2
            Move KEY2 to KEY∅
            Read another record from file2
        ENDWHILE
        Add 1 to sequence changes
        Switch to other current output file
    ENDWHILE
    Close files
    Exchange pairs of input, output files
UNTIL sequence changes = 1
ENDREPEAT
IF sorted file is in file D3
    COPY file to D1
```

---

bly be merged into it. Then the program switches its output to the other output file, and resets KEY∅ to the lowest possible number in preparation for merging another string of records from file1 and file2.

A program for the sort procedure of Fig. 12.11 is shown in Fig. 12.12. The program follows the pseudo-code slavishly. For most of the input and output macro instructions we use a form in which the DCB address is given in a register, whose number is enclosed in parentheses. This enables us to switch data sets between input and ouptut and to switch back and forth between the two current output data sets.

The program keeps in register 7 a count of the number of times a string is finished and the output file switches to the other one of the current pair. When end of both input files is reached, the count is checked; if it is more than 1, more merge passes are needed. When the count is 1, the whole file is in a single

FIGURE 12.12   A sort-by-merge program

```
*************************************************************************
*** SORT A FILE USING TWO-WAY SERIAL SORT TECHNIQUE
*** INITIAL FILE IS ON DATA SET D1
*** FINAL SORTED FILE IS PLACED IN D1 ALSO
*** DATA SETS D2, D3, AND D4 ARE USED TEMPORARILY
*** RECORDS ARE ASSUMED TO BE NOT MORE THAN 200 BYTES LONG,
*** WITH EBCDIC KEYS IN THE FIRST 9 BYTES OF EACH RECORD
*************************************************************************
SERSORT   CSECT
          XSAVE TR=NO
          EQUREGS
* SET UP INITIAL D2 AS EMPTY FILE
          OPEN  (D2,OUTPUT)
          MVC   REC2(9),HIVAL
          PUT   D2,REC2
          CLOSE D2
*************************************************************************
*** R2 HOLDS DCB-ADDRESS OF CURRENT FILE 1 TO READ FROM
*** R3 HOLDS DCB-ADDRESS OF CURRENT FILE 2 TO READ FROM
*** R4 HOLDS DCB-ADDRESS OF CURRENT FILE 3 TO WRITE FROM
*** R5 HOLDS DCB-ADDRESS OF CURRENT FILE 4 TO WRITE FROM
*** R6 HOLDS DCB-ADDRESS OF FILE 3 OR FILE 4. CURRENT DEST.
*** R7 HOLDS NO. OF SEQUENCE CHANGES IN CURRENT MERGE PASS
          LA    R2,D1
          LA    R3,D2
          LA    R4,D3
          LA    R5,D4
* REPEAT
MAINLOOP  SR    R7,R7
* . PREPARE FOR A MERGE PASS
          OPEN  ((R2),INPUT)
          OPEN  ((R3),INPUT)
          OPEN  ((R4),OUTPUT)
          OPEN  ((R5),OUTPUT)
          LR    R6,R4
          BAL   R11,GETREC1
          BAL   R11,GETREC2
* . WHILE NOT (END-OF-FILE1 AND END-OF-FILE2)
*** END-OF-FILE IS REPRESENTED BY HIVAL IN KEY FIELD OF RECORD
PHASELP   CLC   REC1(9),HIVAL
          BNE   WRSTR
          CLC   REC2(9),HIVAL
          BE    MERGEFIN
* . . SET LAST-RECORD-WRITTEN (KEY0) TO LOVAL
WRSTR     MVC   KEY0(9),=XL9'0'
* . . WRITE A SEQUENCE OF RECORDS WITH KEYS IN SEQUENCE
* . . WHILE ((NOT END-OF-FILE1) AND (KEY0 <= KEY1))
MERGE1    CLC   REC1(9),HIVAL
          BE    RUNOUT2
          CLC   KEY0(9),REC1
          BH    RUNOUT2
* . . . WHILE ((KEY2 <= KEY1) AND (KEY2 >= KEY0))
WRITE2    CLC   REC2(9),REC1
          BH    WRITE1
          CLC   REC2(9),KEY0
          BL    WRITE1
* . . . . WRITE RECORD FROM FILE2, READ ANOTHER
          PUT   (R6),REC2
          MVC   KEY0(9),REC2
          BAL   R11,GETREC2
          B     WRITE2
* . . . ENDWHILE ((KEY2 <= KEY1) AND (KEY2 >= KEY0))
WRITE1    PUT   (R6),REC1
* . . . WRITE RECORD FROM FILE1, READ ANOTHER
          MVC   KEY0(9),REC1
          BAL   R11,GETREC1
          B     MERGE1
* . . ENDWHILE ((NOT END-OF-FILE1) AND (KEY0 <= KEY1))
* . . WHILE ((NOT END-OF-FILE2) AND (KEY2 >= KEY0))
```

continued

```
RUNOUT2  CLC     REC2(9),HIVAL
         BE      SWITCHFI
         CLC     REC2(9),KEY0
         BL      SWITCHFI
* . . . WRITE RECORDS FROM FILE2 AS LONG AS KEYS ARE IN SEQUENCE
         PUT     (R6),REC2
         MVC     KEY0(9),REC2
         BAL     R11,GETREC2
         B       RUNOUT2
* . . ENDWHILE ((NOT END-OF-FILE2) AND (KEY2 >= KEY0))
* . . SWITCH TO OTHER OUTPUT FILE, BEGIN NEW SEQUENCE
SWITCHFI LA      R7,1(,R7)       ADD 1 TO SEQUENCE CHANGE COUNT
* . . IF R6 CONTAINS SAME DCB-ADDRESS AS R4
         CR      R6,R4
         BNE     SWITCHB
* . . . THEN SET IT TO DCB-ADDRESS IN R5
         LR      R6,R5
         B       PHASELP
* . . . ELSE SET IT TO DCB-ADDRESS IN R4
SWITCHB  LR      R6,R4
* . . ENDIF (R6 CONTAINS SAME DCB-ADDRESS AS R4)
         B       PHASELP
* . ENDWHILE (NOT (END-OF-FILE1 AND END-OF-FILE2))
* . CLOSE FILES, PREPARE TO MERGE THE OTHER DIRECTION
MERGEFIN CLOSE ((R2),,(R3),,(R4),,(R5))
         XR      R2,R4           SWITCH FIRST INPUT, OUTPUT FILES
         XR      R4,R2
         XR      R2,R4
         XR      R3,R5           SWITCH SECOND INPUT, OUTPUT FILES
         XR      R5,R3
         XR      R3,R5
* UNTIL SEQUENCE CHANGES = 1
         C       R7,=F'1'
         BH      MAINLOOP
* ENDREPEAT
* COPY SORTED FILE FROM FILE3 TO FILE1 IF NECESSARY
* IF R2 IS DCB-ADDRESS D3
         C       R2,=A(D3)
         BNE     PROGFIN
* . THEN COPY FROM D3 TO D1
         OPEN    (D3,INPUT)
         OPEN    (D1,OUTPUT)
         BAL     R11,GETREC1
* . WHILE NOT END-OF-FILE1
COPYLOOP CLC     REC1(9),HIVAL
         BE      CLOSECPY
* . . WRITE, THEN READ
         PUT     D1,REC1
         BAL     R11,GETREC1
         B       COPYLOOP
* . ENDWHILE (NOT END-OF-FILE1)
CLOSECPY CLOSE (D1,,D3)
* ENDIF (R2 IS DEB-ADDRESS D3)
PROGFIN  XRETURN SA=*,TR=NO
* SUBROUTINE TO READ RECORD FROM D1 OR D3
GETREC1  MVC     REC1(9),HIVAL
         GET     (R2),REC1
GETFIN1  BR      R11
* SUBROUTINE TO READ RECORD FROM D2 OR D4
GETREC2  MVC     REC2(9),HIVAL
         GET     (R3),REC2
GETFIN2  BR      R11
D1       DCB     DSORG=PS,RECFM=FB,MACRF=(GM,PM),DDNAME=INFILE,
                 EODAD=GETFIN1
D2       DCB     DSORG=PS,RECFM=FB,MACRF=(GM,PM),DDNAME=TEMP1,
                 EODAD=GETFIN2
D3       DCB     DSORG=PS,RECFM=FB,MACRF=(GM,PM),DDNAME=TEMP2,
                 EODAD=GETFIN1
D4       DCB     DSORG=PS,RECFM=FB,MACRF=(GM,PM),DDNAME=TEMP3,
                 EODAD=GETFIN2
REC1     DS      CL200
REC2     DS      CL200
HIVAL    DC      9X'FF'
KEY0     DS      CL9
         LTORG
         END     SERSORT
```

string (it was incremented to 1 as end of string was recognized, *before* the test at PHASELP recognizes the end of both files) and nothing remains but to copy the file back into the original data set if it has ended up in one of the scratch files.

The EODAD parameter in the DCB causes problems to our careful structuring of programs. End of file is a special case in merging; the program obviously cannot merge a record from an exhausted file. The solutions to both of these problems are incorporated into internal subroutines that are called whenever the program needs to read a record. The subroutines are named GETREC1 and GETREC2; they are called with return address stored in register 11, which is used for no other purpose in the program. Because the subroutines use none of the other registers (except 0, 1, 14, 15 changed by GET), no special register saving is needed. The key is set to the highest possible number (X'FF. . . .'), and that key remains if end of file is encountered. The EODAD address is the return instruction of the corresponding subroutine, so control structure problems are localized and minimized. The high-values (HIVAL) acts as an end-of-file indicator in the main program, and also forces in a very natural way the desired merge completion when one file is exhausted, because any real key will be less than HIVAL and therefore will be merged into the current string. The same tactic forces the split of the original file into two files that can be merged; the second file is immediately recognized as being at end of file, and the regular logic of the program takes care of everything else. The use of high-values to represent end of file is a common strategy in data processing, and simplifies programs enormously.

m   a   i   n   i   d   e   a   s

☐ A user's program requests input and output service from the *supervisor* through macro instructions written in assembler language. The supervisor honors the requests when possible, protecting data sets from depredations by other programs, finding desired data sets in collaboration with the job scheduler, and taking advantage of all concurrency possible in handling input and output.

☐ The supervisor builds a *data control block* for each data set in use. The skeleton is provided by the programmer's DCB macro instruction, which specifies, among other parameters, a ddname. A DD statement in job control language, identified with that ddname, helps complete the data control block and gives the job scheduler information to help locate or create the data set. If the data set already exists, its label may also help complete the data control block.

☐ Data sets can be organized as sequential, partitioned, or VSAM, and the IBM operating systems have access methods to handle each of these organizations.

☐ *Logical records* are records desired by the logic of the user's program, but logical records can be *blocked* into larger units for efficient processing. The operating system can deal simultaneously with the user in logical records and with the data set itself in blocks. Logical records in a data set may be of fixed or variable length.

☐ An operating system manages concurrency of operations partly by having more than one *buffer* for each data set. The supervisor, in reading a data set, can pull ahead of the program's use of records, storing records in buffers so that future requests can be met immediately. Options for the management of buffers include simple and exchange buffering.

☐ Under QSAM (queued sequential access method) the macro instructions requesting input and output actions are

OPEN	complete the data control block prepare for action
GET	retrieve a logical record
PUT	output a logical record
CLOSE	terminate processing

Each refers to a data control block through the name of a DCB macro instruction. GET and PUT operate in move and substitute mode, which extend the options for management of buffer segments.

☐ The DCB macro instruction contains specifications of many options available to the user, including data-set organization, record form, block size, logical record size, number of buffers allocated, macro forms used, and an address to branch to when a request for a record follows the end of the data set. The operands are summarized in Fig. 12.5.

☐ A user specifies in *job control statements* directions about what programs to use, locations of data sets, and other information about data sets that is particular to each run. A user submits a *job*, headed by a JOB statement, to the computer requesting execution in each *job step* with an EXEC statement of a program or a catalogued procedure. Data sets are defined by DD statements for use in each step.

☐ Important parameters in JOB statements are accounting information, programmer name, CLASS, MSGLEVEL, and COND. Important in EXEC statements are program or procedure name, COND, PARM, and specification of symbolic parameters. A checklist of DD parameters needed for the most common tasks is shown in Fig. 12.13.

☐ A *catalogued procedure* allows the user to request simply a standard sequence of programs and associated data sets. However, the user may modify and add data-set definitions.

☐ Sequential sorts are done by merging strings of records whose keys are already in order. When strings can be merged back and forth between two pairs of devices, the sort can be quite efficient.

FIGURE 12.13   Summary of DD parameters by task

Task	Always required	May be necessary
Creating a temporary data set:		
Unit record	UNIT	DCB
Output stream	SYSOUT	DCB,UNIT,SPACE
Tape	UNIT	DCB,VOL
Direct access	UNIT,SPACE	DCB,VOL
Creating a nontemporary data set:		
Tape	UNIT,DISP,DSN	DCB,VOL
Direct access	UNIT,DISP,DSN,SPACE	DCB,VOL
Retrieving a data set:		
Catalogued	DISP,DSN	DCB,UNIT
Noncatalogued tape	DISP,DSN,UNIT,VOL	DCB
Noncatalogued direct access	DISP,DSN,UNIT,VOL	DCB
Passed data set	DISP,DSN	DCB,UNIT,VOL

■ **PROBLEMS** FOR REVIEW AND IMAGINATION

12.1   Think of examples of data sets, preferably from problems in fields related to your own experience, and write DD statements to describe them.

12.2   A program library is a partitioned data set consisting of members (programs), each of which is a sequential data set. Think of other possible examples of partitioned data sets.

12.3   Think of data-set organizations you think might be useful that do not fit any of the patterns of organization of sequential, VSAM, or partitioned data sets.

12.4   This chapter showed blocking, in which the logical record is smaller than the block. The opposite case, where one logical record spans several blocks, is called *spanned records*. Try to imagine what kind of software facilities would be appropriate for handling spanned records. Then look up the actual options in the IBM manuals.

12.5   In addition to move and substitute mode, a *locate* mode is also provided. When input is done under locate mode, the address of the buffer area containing a record is placed by the supervisor in register 1; the program can use the record in place, and the time required to move the record to the user's own area is saved. When the next GET is executed, the supervisor automatically takes back the buffer area in which the previous record was given to the programmer. Output under locate mode requires the user's program to generate its output record in the buffer area given to it (in register 1) by the previous PUT macro instruction. Think of instances where locate-mode input, output, or both would be advantageous.

12.6 The order of filling items in a data control block could have been the reverse of the practice implemented in the IBM operating systems. Namely, items from the data set label would have first priority, items not specified there would be taken from the DD statement, and items not specified in either would be filled in from the DCB macro instruction. This would have the advantage that the DCB macro instruction could contain a full description of all parameters, which would be controlling unless overridden; any parameter could be overridden by specifications from the other sources. Think of other advantages, and disadvantages of this possible scheme.

12.7 In some computing systems no such thing as an EODAD is provided; if a request for a record is made after the data set is exhausted, the program is terminated. Review the stratagems necessary in place of the EODAD option, and evaluate the relative merits of EODAD and the other stratagems.

12.8 What would you expect to happen if your program declared register 15 as your implied base register and also used the input and output macros?

12.9 Construct a subroutine named PRINT that can be called from a user's program. It should accept a record to be sent to the printer (SYSOUT), and should include the necessary PUT and DCB macro instructions. Pay special attention to the need to OPEN the data set the first time PRINT is called, but not thereafter. What about closing the data set?

12.10 In what sense and under what conditions can a decision about simple or exchange buffering be meaningfully left for the DD statement?

12.11 In the program BLOCK in Fig. 12.6, no provision is made for anything except abnormal termination of the program in the event of an input or output error. Think of circumstances in which some other action would be preferable; what information would you need from the system in order to put your ideas into effect? Design an implementation of your ideas, making assumptions where necessary.

12.12 The COND parameter in the EXEC statement gives sharper control of continued executions than the COND parameter in the JOB statement. Is the provision for a COND parameter in the JOB statement superfluous, or what are its uses?

12.13 A data set put on tape at one IBM System/370 installation can be used at another with the same job control, as if it had been written at the same installation. A data set written on a direct access volume at one installation, however, is certainly not catalogued at another and so must be addressed differently from catalogued direct access data sets.

However, each direct access volume has a serial number and a *volume table of contents*, and if directed to the correct volume, the operating system can find any named data set on it. This makes the job control similar to that of a tape data set; write a DD statement for an uncatalogued data set named FOREIGN on a direct access volume whose serial number is ZAPHOD.

12.14   Trace the creation, passing, and deletion of the various data sets used by ASMFCLG. What advantages does PASSing a data set have over cataloguing and then deleting it?

12.15   Learn about the catalogued procedures available at your installation.

12.16   The blocking program of Fig. 12.6, the sort program of Fig. 12.12, and the inventory update program sketched in Section 12.6 are not completely compatible in their input and output assumptions, or at least not with the job control presented. Can the problems be taken care of by different job control? Of those that cannot, which would you fix by generalization of the existing programs, and how?

12.17   The sort program of Fig. 12.12 can benefit from the use of exchange buffering and substitute mode. Make this change to the program for use with all four data sets.

12.18   If the data sets used by the sort program in Fig. 12.12 are on direct access volumes, the CLOSE, OPEN sequence takes practically no time. If the data sets are on tape units, this sequence involves a rewind, which is time-consuming. Some tape units are capable of reading (but not writing) backward. This affords the opportunity to eliminate rewind time. Data sets are written forward, then *read backward;* the backward read can begin immediately, and the other tape drives, having just *been* read backward, are at the load points and ready to start writing immediately. Note that the *file* is read forward, then backward, alternately. Consider the changes in comparisons and branches that would have to be made, and do what you can toward changing the program to accommodate the backward read.

12.19   Examine or design internal sort procedures, and then consider hybrid methods. Hybrid methods can be especially valuable during the early phases of a sort; an internal sort can immediately develop strings of significant length, which can afterward be merged in a sequential sort.

12.20   A Key-Word-In-Context (KWIC) index of, say book titles, indexes each title by every nontrivial word in the title. The entire title is shown in each entry if it is short enough, but the title is shifted so that the key words, which are ordered, form a column. Thus the title *Indians in North America* would be listed three times, once each under "Indians," "North," and "America." The word "in" is a trivial word and nothing is listed under it. A segment of the index might be

```
              ENGLAND AFTER THE NORMAN CONQUEST
                 INDIANS IN NORTH AMERICA
                      NORTH FROM ALASKA
          JUMPING OVER THE NORTH POLE
```

When a title is shifted over either edge of the column for alignment, it is brought around the other edge, but with a slash to show the boundary, as in

```
   AND THE NATIVES OF NORTHERN RHODESIA      /CECIL RHODES
```

Outline, and program as much as seems interesting, the generation of a KWIC index. Pay special attention to data sets and their treatment. The usual procedure is to read items (title plus location information), then to generate all the lines that should appear for that title in the index. Each word must be compared to the "trivial word" list, to determine whether it should generate a line. Then the data set of all lines is sorted by a sequential method.

12.21   Suppose that transcripts of students at a university are to be kept in a data set which is accessible to a computer. Design an efficient representation or layout of the data set. Then consider the problem of updating the transcripts with a term's grades. Design procedures, DCB macro instructions, DD statements, and as much program as you like for taking a large mass of unsorted grade reports and updating the transcripts with them.

12.22   In many situations in which a file is updated, several reports are desired as a by-product. During transcript updating, for example, every student must get a report of his or her term's work; the dean's office wants a file of everybody's term grades, preferably broken down by sex; the financial aids office wants the grades of every student who has a scholarship or loan; somebody wants the honor roll; somebody else the list of students with grades low enough to flunk out; and so forth. A computer does not have enough printers to print all these lists simultaneously. Should the lists be put on direct-access data sets for later printing, one by one, or should the entire file be processed once for each list to be produced? Are there other alternatives? What considerations would guide your decisions on what approach to take?

12.23   IBM has a SORT utility program that is primarily a merge sort. Find the manual on this utility and study (1) the options to the program, and how the user specifies the options, and (2) the job control required by the utility. Compare the job control with what would be necessary to use the program of Fig. 12.12. Think how you might generalize the program of Fig. 12.12 to provide some of the options of the utility—for example, the options in number, location, and type of sort keys.

12.24   Find out about the input and output macro instructions available through the ASSIST system, and modify one or more of the programs in this chapter to run under ASSIST.

12.25   A data set with ddname VORD has unblocked, variable-length records. The logical records are 60 to 960 bytes long. In each block the record is preceded by a four-byte area:

           2 bytes   logical record length (binary integer)

           2 bytes   binary zeros

Thus the maximum block size is 964 bytes. The DCB describing the data set should include

           RECFM=V,LRECL=96Ø,BLKSIZE=964

Write a program that will read the data set, and construct a new data set with ddname FORDHEAD. Each record in the new data set is the first 60 bytes of a logical record of VORD; records are to be blocked, 20 records to a block.

■ REFERENCES

Aho, Alfred V., John E. Hopcroft, and Jeffrey D. Ullman, *Data Structures and Algorithms*, Addison-Wesley, Reading, Mass., 1983. A good discussion of sorting.

Deitel, Harvey M., *An Introduction to Operating Systems* (Revised First Edition), Addison-Wesley, Reading, Mass., 1983. A good discussion of the operating system's role in input and output.

Dwyer, B., "One more time—how to update a master file," *Communications of the Association for Computing Machinery* 24, 1 (January 1981), pp. 3–8. Structured programming of updating a file by file merging.

IBM OS/VS1 Data Management Macro Instructions, GC 26-3872, or *OS/VS2 MVS Data Management Macro Instructions*, GC 26-3873, IBM Corporation. Reference for the macros.

IBM OS/VS1 Data Management Services Guide, GC 26-3874, or *OS/VS2 MVS Data Management Services Guide*, GC 26-3875, IBM Corporation. Detailed narrative descriptions of input/output through the operating system.

IBM OS/VS1 Job Control Language Reference, GC 24-5099, IBM Corporation. Reference for the JCL statements and parameters.

IBM OS/VS1 Job Control Language Services, GC 24-5100, IBM Corporation. Description of the facilities available through JCL.

IBM OS/VS Linkage Editor and Loader, GC 26-3813, IBM Corporation. Reference for linking and loading programs.

IBM OS/VS and VM/370 Assembler Programmer's Guide, GC 33-4021, IBM Corporation. Catalogued procedures for assembler language programmers, and information about JCL related to the assembler.

IBM Systems Journal 18, 1 (1979). A special issue on VM/370, including CMS.

IBM Virtual Machine Facility/370: CMS Command and Macro Reference, GC 20-1818, IBM Corporation. Reference for the input/output macros in CMS.

IBM Virtual Machine Facility/370: CMS User's Guide, GC 20-1819, IBM Corporation. Description of the CMS facilities for input and output.

Knuth, Donald E., *The Art of Computer Programming, Vol. 1: Fundamental Algorithms (2nd ed.)*, Addison-Wesley, Reading, Mass., 1974. A good description of input and output techniques, especially buffering.

_____, *The Art of Computer Programming, Vol. 3: Sorting and Searching*, Addison-Wesley, Reading, Mass., 1973. A discussion in depth of external sorting and merging techniques.

Levy, Michael R., "Modularity and the Sequential File Update Problem," *Communications of the Association for Computing Machinery* 25, 6 (June 1982), pp. 362–367. A helpful paper on structuring a file update program.

Martin, William A., "Sorting," *Computing Surveys* 3, 4 (December 1971), pp. 147–174. A tutorial survey of sorting techniques.

Mealy, G. H., B. I. Witt, and W. A. Clark, "The Functional Structure of OS/360," *IBM Systems Journal* 5 (1966), pp. 2–51. A study of the then current philosophy of the operating system.

FLOATING-POINT ARITHMETIC

In Chapter 1 the concept of floating-point representation of numbers was introduced, and the floating-point registers and arithmetic capabilities were mentioned. Since then, the arithmetic used has been binary integer arithmetic.
Binary integer arithmetic is most useful for address computation and modification, for counting events (like repetitions of a loop) and for miscellaneous
computations involving fairly small integers. Execution of binary integer
arithmetic instructions is fast.

For computations in which numbers of widely varying magnitudes may
arise, integer arithmetic does not suffice; fractions and numbers larger than 2^{32}
must be recorded. In some instances it is possible to keep a portion of a number, remembering that this portion, represented as an integer, is really some
scale factor—a power of 2 or 10—times the true value of the number represented. Programming must then take account of the scale factors. This becomes quite burdensome. The floating-point representation is a major bless-
ing: In accord with the principle that the computer is to do as much of our
clerical work as possible, the floating-point representation allows the computer to keep a scale factor, called a *characteristic*, with the number, and automatically to take account of scale factors in all arithmetic operations,
attaching the correct scale factor to the result.

This chapter explains floating-point representation in System/370 in more
detail than in Chapter 1 and discusses the floating-point arithmetic instructions. Examples show conversions between integer and floating-point representations and the analysis of a regression problem.

13.1   Representations of Floating-Point Numbers

Floating-point quantities in IBM System/370 computers may occupy either 32, 64, or 128 bits. The 32-bit numbers are called *short*, or *single precision*; the 64-bit numbers are called *long*, or *double precision*. The 128-bit numbers are called *extended precision*. In any case the bit in position 0 represents the sign of the number: 0 for positive numbers, 1 for negative numbers. The bits in positions 1–7 are the *characteristic*; we shall return to an explanation of the characteristic shortly.

The remaining bits of the floating-point number, either in positions 8–31 in the case of a short floating-point number or in positions 8–63 in the case of a long floating-point number, contain what is called the *fraction*, or sometimes the *mantissa*. The fraction is always recorded as a positive number; negative floating-point numbers are *not* represented in complement form. The (binary) point of the fraction is understood to be just before bit position 8. That is to say, a digit 1 in bit position 8 represents 2^{-1}, a digit 1 in bit position 9 represents 2^{-2}, etc.

An extended-precision number is formed by two double-precision numbers. The first double-precision number contains the sign, characteristic, and the most significant 56 fraction bits; the second double-precision number contains another 56 fraction bits, in positions 8–63. Bits 0–7 of the second double-precision number are ignored in extended-precision calculations.

As you study this chapter, you should realize that extended-precision instructions are not available in all models of the IBM System/370 family.

A floating-point number is represented by its fraction times a power of 16, with its sign attached to the result. The exponent indicating the power of 16 by which the fraction is multiplied is coded in the characteristic. The characteristic, in bit positions 1–7 of the representation, can hold numbers ranging from 0 to (decimal) 127. The characteristic is coded in what is called *excess-64* notation, meaning that the characteristic is 64 greater than the exponent. Thus a characteristic of 66 represents an exponent of $66 - 64 = 2$, and the magnitude of the floating-point number is the fraction $\times 16^2$. Similarly, a characteristic of 61 represents an exponent of $61 - 64 = -3$, and the magnitude of the floating-point number with a characteristic of 61 is the fraction $\times 16^{-3}$. The excess-64 notation is used so that a wide range of magnitudes, roughly from 16^{-64} to 16^{63}, can be represented.

The quantity 64 (or hexadecimal 40) is also sometimes called a *bias quantity*. Another way of considering the characteristic is to say that the exponent is coded in 2's complement notation, except that a 0 in bit position 1, the sign position of the characteristic, represents a *minus* sign and a 1 represents a plus sign.

Some examples of System/370 floating-point numbers should help to clarify the representation. First are several examples of short floating-point numbers, shown in binary. The pattern

Ø   1ØØØØØØ   1ØØØØØØØ   ØØØØØØØØ   ØØØØØØØØ

sign   charac-   fraction
         teristic

includes a characteristic of 64 (2^6 or hexadecimal 40) and therefore an exponent of 0. The fraction is (binary) .1000 . . . , or 2^{-1}, or decimal 0.50. Therefore, since the sign bit of 0 denotes a positive number, the number represented is $+.5 \times 16^0 = 0.50$. The pattern

1   1ØØØØØ1   Ø1Ø1Ø1ØØ   ØØØØØØØØ   ØØØØØØØØ

includes a characteristic of 65 and thereby codes an exponent of 1. The fraction is $.010101 = 2^{-2} + 2^{-4} + 2^{-6}$. The sign bit of 1 denotes a negative number, so the quantity represented by this pattern is $-(2^{-2} + 2^{-4} + 2^{-6}) \times 16^1 = -(2^2 + 2^0 + 2^{-2}) = -(4 + 1 + 0.25) = -5.25$. The pattern

Ø   Ø111111   11ØØ11ØØ   11ØØ11ØØ   11ØØ11ØØ

includes a characteristic of 63 (hexadecimal 3F) and thereby codes an exponent of -1. Therefore the magnitude of the number is the fraction times 16^{-1}. As you can verify, the fraction is the first 24 bits of the binary representation of 0.8, which cannot be represented exactly by a finite binary expansion. The number represented by the pattern is thus an approximation to $+16^{-1} \times 0.8 = 0.05$.

System/370 computers can be called hexadecimal machines, and it is helpful to think of floating-point representation in this light. Because the exponent is a power of 16, adding one to the exponent multiplies the quantity represented by 16. Thus in some sense the numbers represented in floating point by the patterns (in hexadecimal)

4162EØAØ   and   42Ø62EØA

are the same.

Let us now examine some long floating-point representations, and do it in hexadecimal to avoid writing 64 binary bits. The pattern

436D1ØØØ   ØØØØØØØØ

includes a sign of 0, or plus, because the first hexadecimal digit is less than 8. The characteristic is hexadecimal 43 or decimal 67, so the exponent is +3. The fraction is (.)6D100000000000, so the entire quantity represented is (still in hexadecimal) 6D1.00000000000. The reader can verify that this number is the decimal number 1745. The pattern

BE34A2ØB   68F1998C

represents a negative number since the first hexadecimal digit is greater than 8. The characteristic is 3E, or decimal 62, and codes an exponent of $62 - 64 = -2$. The fraction is (.)34A20B68F1998C, so the quantity represented by the full pattern is, in hexadecimal, $-.0034A20B68F1998C$.

NORMALIZATION

The representation of a nonzero floating-point number is said to be *normalized* if the first (high-order) hexadecimal digit of its fraction is not zero. It is almost always to our advantage to keep and generate numbers in normalized form, since this gives us the most digits of precision in our numbers (the digits we keep may not all be correct, but we generally make less error by keeping inexact digits than by throwing them away). The number 4162E0A0 is normalized, because the first hexadecimal digit of its fraction, 6, is nonzero. The equivalent number 42062E0A is not normalized.

Normalized nonzero floating-point numbers in System/370 can represent quantities whose magnitudes are

$$16^{-65} \quad \text{to} \quad (1 - 16^{-6}) \cdot 16^{63} \quad \text{in short form}$$

and

$$16^{-65} \quad \text{to} \quad (1 - 16^{-14}) \cdot 16^{63} \quad \text{in long form.}$$

Magnitudes of nonnormalized floating-point numbers can range down to 16^{-70} in short form and to 16^{-78} in the long form. You should verify these assertions by writing representations of the smallest and largest numbers possible and finding the corresponding magnitudes.

In most other computers, floating-point binary representations include an exponent which is a power of 2. That is, adding 1 to the exponent multiplies the quantity represented by 2. In these computers, normalization means that the highest-order binary bit of the (nonzero) fraction is nonzero. Since the exponent in System/370 is a power of 16, it is not possible to represent every number in such a way that the high-order bit of its fraction is nonzero. Normalized representations of some numbers (1.0, for example) have three leading zeros in the fraction.

When a number has a zero fraction, zero characteristic, and plus sign, it is called a *true zero*. When a zero fraction results from most floating-point operations, a true zero is forced. In any case, when the fraction in the result is zero, the sign of the result will be set positive.

You are urged to refer to Section 5.2 at this point to refresh your memory of the definition of floating-point constants, types E and D, in assembler language.

13.2 Floating-Point Registers; Load and Store Instructions

There are four floating-point registers in System/370, as was mentioned in Chapter 1. The registers are each 64 bits long and thus are capable of holding and working with either short or long floating-point numbers. The addresses of the four registers are 0, 2, 4, and 6.

Let us now consider the floating-point instructions in detail. Because all floating-point arithmetic is done in registers, all the instructions are of RR or

RX type. But because floating-point numbers are stored in main storage as bit patterns just like any other information, any instructions can operate on floating-point numbers. The MVC instruction, for example, can move floating-point numbers from one place to another within main storage.

In all floating-point instructions to be introduced in this chapter, the registers specified are floating-point registers. This must be understood as part of the specification of the instructions.

Addresses of main storage operands (*S2*) are formed as in other RX-type instructions; the *general registers* contain *X2* and *B2*, which are used in the address computations. In assembler language, it is helpful to use FØ, F2, F4, and F6 to refer to the floating-point registers. The REGEQU macro in CMS equates FØ, F2, F4, and F6 to 0, 2, 4, and 6 respectively, as well as equating RØ–R15 to 0–15. The ASSIST macro instruction

$$\text{EQUREGS} \quad \text{L=F,DO=(Ø,6,2)}$$

equates the F registers; you can use this macro instruction *in addition* to the EQUREGS *without* parameters, which equates RØ–R15 to 0–15. If you have neither EQUREGS or REGEQU available, you will have to write your own EQU statements. The main advantage of using FØ, F2, F4, and F6 is in improved readability of programs: it makes clear the intended use of floating-point registers instead of general registers.

The floating-point load instructions are a group of four instructions that load a floating-point register but do not set a condition code. Two load a short floating-point number (32 bits) and two load a long floating-point number; two load from main storage and two from floating-point registers. The instructions are as follows, if we denote a floating-point register as *FPR1* when used as first operand and as *FPR2* when used as second operand.

Instruction	Type	Action	
LER	RR	*FPR1*	$\leftarrow c(FPR2)$
LE	RX	*FPR1*	$\leftarrow c(S2)$
LDR	RR	$FPR1_{0\text{-}63} \leftarrow c(FPR2)_{0\text{-}63}$	
LD	RX	$FPR1_{0\text{-}63} \leftarrow c(S2)_{0\text{-}63}$	

The LER and LDR instructions load a (floating-point) register from a (floating-point) register, and the LE and LD instructions load a register from main storage. The LER and LE instructions load a short floating-point number into the high-order 32 bits of the 64-bit floating-point register, *leaving the low-order 32 bits unchanged*. The LDR and LD instructions load all 64 bits of the register.

There are helpful consistencies in the naming of floating-point instructions. All the RR-type instructions have mnemonic assembler language names ending in R, but none of the RX-type instructions do. The short-precision instructions contain the letter E, and the corresponding long-precision instructions the letter D. Besides, the function of the instruction is suggested in the name: L for Load, ST for STore, A for Add, M for Multiply, etc.

If main storage locations and registers have initial contents (hexadecimal)

Location	BETA:	41100000 00000000	(on double-word boundary)
	GSQ:	3F3429E2 9B76C870	(on double-word boundary)
	GSQ+8:	C5113D6A BD473F88	
General register	3:	00000008	
Floating-point register	0:	42326EE4 00000000	
	2:	D0F63984 7B38C420	
	4:	BC98624B 8849CF01	
	6:	40CCCCCC 44444440	

before each of the following instructions, the instructions will have the effects indicated:

Instruction		Register	New contents
LE	F4,BETA	4	41100000 8849CF01
LD	F6,BETA	6	41100000 00000000
LER	F0,F2	0	D0F63984 00000000
LDR	F6,F2	6	D0F63984 7B38C420
LD	F2,GSQ(R3)	2	C5113D6A BD473F88
LE	F4,GSQ+4	0	9B76C870 8849CF01

Note that the first, third, and sixth of these instructions leave unchanged the low-order halves of their first operand registers.

Extended-precision arithmetic is performed in the floating-point registers. An address of 0 can specify the pair of floating-point registers 0 and 2, which can hold an extended-precision operand or result; similarly 4 can specify the floating-point register pair 4 and 6. There are no special extended-precision load and store instructions; extended-precision numbers must be loaded and stored by the LD, LDR, and STD instructions, each moving half of an extended-precision number. For example, to load an extended-precision number from MPR to the register pair 0,2:

```
        LD    F0,MPR
        LD    F2,MPR+8
```

The next group of load instructions are all of RR type, and set a condition code. There are short-precision and long-precision forms, and they correspond to the integer instructions LTR, LCR, LPR, and LNR. They can be described as follows:

Instruction	Type	Action	Condition code
LTER	RR	$FPR1 \leftarrow c(FPR2)$	Yes
LTDR	RR	$FPR1_{0-63} \leftarrow c(FPR2)_{0-63}$	Yes
LCER	RR	$FPR1 \leftarrow -c(FPR2)$	Yes
LCDR	RR	$FPR1_{0-63} \leftarrow -c(FPR2)_{0-63}$	Yes
LPER	RR	$FPR1 \leftarrow |c(FPR2)|$	Yes
LPDR	RR	$FPR1_{0-63} \leftarrow |c(FPR2)_{0-63}|$	Yes
LNER	RR	$FPR1 \leftarrow -|c(FPR2)|$	Yes
LNDR	RR	$FPR1_{0-63} \leftarrow -|c(FPR2)_{0-63}|$	Yes

The LTER and LTDR do exactly the same operations as the LER and LDR instructions, respectively, except that LTER and LTDR set the condition code. The other six instructions, LCER, LCDR, LPER, LPDR, LNER, and LNDR, all load a floating-point register from a (same or different) floating-point register but perform various operations on the sign of the result. Since the numbers are represented in sign-and-absolute-value form, changing the sign of a number results in complementing only the bit in position 0 of the result register. The LCER and LCDR instructions change the sign of the number; the LPER and LPDR instructions set the sign bit to 0 (making the number positive) regardless of its previous value; the LNER and LNDR instructions set the sign bit to 1, making the number negative regardless of its previous value. A true zero can be changed into a negative zero by the LCER, LCDR, LNER, or LNDR instructions; the sign bit is changed or set to 1 regardless of the value of the number.

After the instruction has loaded a register with its new contents, the sign and fraction of the number are tested, and the condition code is set accordingly. The same condition code, in PSW bits 18 and 19, is used for floating-point instructions as for any other. The settings of the condition code are also similar to the settings resulting from other instructions:

$CC = 0$ if the fraction is zero,

$CC = 1$ if the result is less than zero (fraction nonzero, sign = 1),

$CC = 2$ if the result is greater than zero (fraction nonzero, sign = 0),

$CC = 3$ is not used.

No overflow is possible in this set of instructions because the fraction is never changed. In the short-precision instructions, the low-order 32 bits of the floating-point result register are neither changed nor tested.

If the floating-point registers have initial contents

Floating-point register 0:   42326E24   00000000
                        2:   D0F63984   7B38C420
                        4:   BC98624B   8849CF01
                        6:   00000000   00000000

before *each* of the following instructions or instruction pairs, the results will be as shown:

	Instruction		Register	New contents		Cond. code
a)	LTER	FØ,F2	0	DØF63984	ØØØØØØØØ	1
b)	LTDR	F4,F6	4	ØØØØØØØØ	ØØØØØØØØ	0
c)	LCER	FØ,F4	0	3C98624B	ØØØØØØØØ	2
d)	LCDR	F2,FØ	2	C2326E24	ØØØØØØØØ	1
e)	LPER	F4,F6	4	ØØØØØØØØ	8849CFØ1	0
f)	LER	F4,F6				
	LPDR	F4,F4	4	ØØØØØØØØ	8849CFØ1	2
g)	LNER	F4,F6	4	8ØØØØØØØ	8849CFØ1	0
h)	LNDR	F4,F2	4	DØF63984	7B38C42Ø	1
i)	LNDR	F4,FØ	4	C2326E24	ØØØØØØØØ	1
j)	LPDR	F4,F2	4	5ØF63984	7B38C42Ø	2
k)	LCER	F2,F6	2	8ØØØØØØØ	7B38C42Ø	0
l)	LCDR	F4,F4	4	3C98624B	8849CFØ1	2

Note the settings of the condition code in the various cases: the single-precision instructions load *and test* only the high-order portions of their registers; tests can yield zeros when the sign is negative.

Finally, there are the two store instructions. They are of RX type, for storing either short-precision or long-precision floating-point numbers from the floating-point registers into main storage. The instructions are

Instruction	Type	Action	
STE	RX	$S2$	$\leftarrow c(FPR1)$
STD	RX	$S2_{0-63}$	$\leftarrow c(FPR1)_{0-63}$

Neither instruction affects the condition code. The first operand remains unchanged by either instruction. If floating-point register 2 contains DØF63984   7B38C42Ø,

STE   F2,GAMMA

will cause DØF63984 to be stored at GAMMA, and the instruction

STD   F2,ALPHA

will cause DØF63984   7B38C42Ø to be stored at ALPHA.

13.3   Floating-Point Add, Subtract, and Compare Instructions

This section discusses the normalized add and subtract instructions and the compare instructions; unnormalized addition and subtraction are left until Section 13.5. Normalized add, subtract, and compare instructions of RR and RX types permit the second operand to be either in a floating-point register or in main storage. Short-precision and long-precision forms are provided. The extended-precision instructions are discussed in Section 13.8. Given first is an overall description of the process.

If we understand that + and − denote floating-point operations, the instructions can be described as shown in Fig. 13.1.

The operations of addition and subtraction take account of sign, characteristic, and fraction in producing the result. The short-precision addition and subtraction operations AER, AE, SER, and SE change only the high-order 32 bits of the first operand register; the low-order 32 bits remain unchanged. Condition codes are set by the addition and subtraction operations as follows:

If the result fraction is 0, the condition code is set to 0.

If the result is less than 0, the condition code is set to 1.

If the result is greater than 0, the condition code is set to 2.

Condition code 3 is not used.

FIGURE 13.1   Action of floating-point add, subtract, and compare instructions

Instruction	Type	Action	Cond. code set
AER	RR	$FPR1 \leftarrow c(FPR1) + c(FPR2)$	Yes
AE	RX	$FPR1 \leftarrow c(FPR1) + c(S2)$	Yes
ADR	RR	$FPR1_{0-63} \leftarrow c(FPR1)_{0-63} + c(FPR2)_{0-63}$	Yes
AD	RX	$FPR1_{0-63} \leftarrow c(FPR1)_{0-63} + c(S2)_{0-63}$	Yes
SER	RR	$FPR1 \leftarrow c(FPR1) - c(FPR2)$	Yes
SE	RX	$FPR1 \leftarrow c(FPR1) - c(S2)$	Yes
SDR	RR	$FPR1_{0-63} \leftarrow c(FPR1)_{0-63} - c(FPR2)_{0-63}$	Yes
SD	RX	$FPR1_{0-63} \leftarrow c(FPR1)_{0-63} - c(S2)_{0-63}$	Yes
CER	RR	—	Yes
CE	RX	—	Yes
CDR	RR	—	Yes
CD	RX	—	Yes

The whole purpose of a compare instruction is to set a condition code. The result of the comparison is as if the two operands were subtracted; thus the condition codes set by the compare instructions are

If the first operand equals the second operand, the condition code is set to 0.

If the first operand is less than the second operand, the condition code is set to 1.

If the first operand is greater than the second operand, the condition code is set to 2.

Some examples will illustrate the behavior of the instructions. If contents of registers and storage locations are (hexadecimal)

Floating-point register	0:	41100000	00000000
	2:	BCCCCCCC	CCCCCCCC
	4:	C41362E5	23A97230
	6:	3E450000	4594FDC1
Main storage location	GRAD:	C41362E5	1347B8E0
	BSQ:	41484000	
	GBD:	441362E5	00000000
	GRAB:	BEC00000	00000123

before *each* of the following instructions, results will be as follows:

Instruction			Register	New contents		Condition code
a)	AE	F0,BSQ	0	41584000	00000000	2
b)	SE	F0,BSQ	0	C1384000	00000000	1
c)	ADR	F0,F6	0	41100450	0004594F	2
d)	AE	F4,GBD	4	00000000	23A97230	0
e)	AD	F4,GBD	4	BE23A972	30000000	1
f)	SD	F6,GRAB	6	3F105000	04594FEE	2
g)	AER	F2,F6	2	3E443333	CCCCCCCC	2
h)	SER	F2,F6	2	BE45CCCC	CCCCCCCC	1
i)	SER	F6,F2	6	3E45CCCC	4594FDC1	2
j)	SDR	F6,F2	6	3E45CCCD	1261CA8D	2
k)	CER	F0,F6				2
l)	CE	F4,GBD				1
m)	CE	F4,GRAD				0
n)	CD	F4,GRAD				1
o)	CDR	F2,F4				2

You are urged to verify, from the definition of the floating-point representation and the gross description of the instructions, the essential correctness of these results. If you are puzzled by the last digit or so of the result, the following description of the procedure used by the floating-point instructions should clear up most questions.

In more detail then, floating-point addition and subtraction are performed as follows. First the second operand is moved to a special nonaddressable working register; this improves access to the operand in subsequent steps of the process and allows the original operand to be left unchanged. Actually, both operands are moved to special registers, but this need not concern you. We shall ignore these special registers in all further discussion; they were mentioned only to show that the second operand is not changed in its original location. Next there is a comparison of characteristics; the fraction of the number with the smaller characteristic is shifted right a number of hexadecimal characters equal to the difference. We may call this an *alignment* step. Thus if the first operand has a characteristic of 42 and the second operand a characteristic of 45, the fraction of the first operand is shifted right 3 hexadecimal positions or 12 bits.

Next, addition or subtraction of the fractions takes place, depending in the usual way on the signs of the operands and whether an add or subtract instruction was ordered. The sum or difference is formed in the first operand register, and the larger characteristic of the two characteristics is inserted. The correct sign of the result is inserted.

Either of two special actions may be necessary to complete the second step. If the fraction is zero and the fourth bit of the program mask (more about that later) is 0, a zero characteristic and sign are inserted, leaving a true zero. The condition code is also set to zero. The second case is one in which addition of the two fractions produced a carry out of the high-order hexadecimal digit (or high-order bit, which amounts to the same thing). In this case all digits of the fraction are shifted right one hexadecimal position or four bit positions, truncating the number *without* rounding, and a hexadecimal 1 is inserted as the highest-order hexadecimal digit of the fraction. The characteristic is increased by 1 to record the shift, and this can cause an exponent overflow.

Thus, in the addition of the numbers 41C12345 and 41523456, the sum of the fractions is

$$C12345$$
$$\underline{523456}$$
$$113579B$$

where the first 1 of the sum represents a carry. The result cannot hold all these digits, so the result given is 42113579. The digit B is lost, and the preceding digit, 9, is *not* rounded up to A.

The third step, called *normalization*, consists of a loop of the following actions given that the fraction is nonzero. The high-order hexadecimal digit is examined; if it is nonzero, normalization is finished. If it is zero, all digits of the fraction are shifted *left* one hexadecimal position, and the characteristic is correspondingly *decreased* by 1. The process of examining digits, shifting the fraction left, and decreasing the characteristic is continued until the high-order hexadecimal digit of the fraction becomes nonzero. The condition code is set according to the sign of the result.

In the addition of 41C12345 and C1C10123 we see that the signs are different, so the fractions are subtracted. The result of the subtraction is

$$
\begin{array}{r}
C12345 \\
-C1\emptyset123 \\
\hline
\emptyset\emptyset2222
\end{array}
$$

to which the characteristic 41 is attached. The normalization process requires two shifts, and the final result is 3F222200.

In every short- or long-precision floating-point arithmetic operation, each operand is furnished with a *guard digit*. The guard digit is essentially a hexadecimal digit just after the regular (6 or 14) digits of the fraction. The guard digit for each operand is zero at the beginning of an operation, but during the alignment step, digits shifted right go through the guard-digit position. Therefore the last digit shifted out of the normal part of the register is saved as a guard digit. The guard digits participate in addition, subtraction, and comparison, and during the normalization step the guard digit may reappear into the regular part of the result register. Thus addition of 4210778A and C1112217 is done as follows, with the guard digit shown in brackets:

Alignment:	4210778A	[0]
	C1011221	[7]
Additional yields:	420F6568	[9]
Normalization:	41F65689	[0]

and the final result is 41F65689. The guard digit provides one more hexadecimal digit of accuracy than would be kept otherwise.

Action of the compare instructions can be thought of as being exactly like the action of the corresponding subtract instructions.

Addition, subtraction, or comparison of unnormalized operands follows all the steps described, including full normalization. The processes can yield some odd results, which is one more reason not to use unnormalized numbers except for very specific purposes.

13.4 Floating-Point Multiply and Divide

Multiplication and division instructions are provided for single-precision and double-precision floating-point numbers, four of each, which include all combinations of RR- and RX-type, single- and double-precision. There are also two Halve instructions. We may represent the instructions in tabular form as follows, but the table must be understood to be only an outline or point of departure for the necessary discussion of the features of the instructions.

Instruction	Type	Action	Cond. code set
MER	RR	$FPR1_{0-63} \leftarrow c(FPR1) \quad \times c(FPR2)$	No
ME	RX	$FPR1_{0-63} \leftarrow c(FPR1) \quad \times c(S2)$	No
MDR	RR	$FPR1_{0-63} \leftarrow c(FPR1)_{0-63} \times c(FPR2)_{0-63}$	No
MD	RX	$FPR1_{0-63} \leftarrow c(FPR1)_{0-63} \times c(S2)_{0-63}$	No
DER	RR	$FPR1 \quad \leftarrow c(FPR1) \quad / \ c(FPR2)$	No
DE	RX	$FPR1 \quad \leftarrow c(FPR1) \quad / \ c(S2)$	No
DDR	RR	$FPR1_{0-63} \leftarrow c(FPR1)_{0-63} / \ c(FPR2)_{0-63}$	No
DD	RX	$FPR1_{0-63} \leftarrow c(FPR1)_{0-63} / \ c(S2)_{0-63}$	No
HER	RR	$FPR1 \quad \leftarrow c(FPR2) \quad / \ 2$	No
HDR	RR	$FPR1_{0-63} \leftarrow c(FPR2)_{0-63} / \ 2$	No

Prior to multiplication, both operands are normalized; this step is called *prenormalization*. The multiplication step itself involves a characteristic addition (and subtraction of the bias quantity 64 or hexadecimal 40 from the sum) and a fraction multiplication. Only 24 bits of fraction from each operand take part in short-precision multiplication, but the full floating-point register is used for the product. The fraction product is 48 bits long, so the low-order eight bits of the full register will always be zero. In a double-precision multiply instruction, all 56 fraction bits of each operand take part. The product is truncated to 60 bits (including a guard digit). In either a short-precision or long-precision multiplication, postnormalization finishes the operation. The highest-order digit of the intermediate product may be zero (but not more than the highest-order digit unless the entire fraction is zero; why?), so one normalizing shift of four bits (including, in long-precision multiplication, shift of the guard digit into the four low-order bit positions of the register) and a corresponding reduction of the characteristic by 1 may be necessary. The ordinary rule of signs governs the result; in other words, an EXCLUSIVE OR is performed on the sign bits of the operands to yield the sign of the product. However, if all bits of the fraction of the result are zeros, a true zero is forced.

We illustrate this with a few examples. If floating-point register 0 contains 41200000 00000000 and CHI contains 42335421 23001632, execution of ME FØ,CHI will take place in the following steps:

Prenormalization:	none necessary
Multiplication:	200000 × 335421 = Ø66A8420000000000
Characteristic:	41 + 42 − 40 = 43
Sign:	Ø (EXCLUSIVE OR) Ø = Ø
Yielding a result:	43066A84 20000000
Postnormalization:	4266A842 00000000

With the same initial contents, execution of MD FØ,CHI will be:

Prenormalization:	none
Multiplication:	2ØØØØØ ØØØØØØØØ×335421 23ØØ1632=
	Ø66A84 246ØØ2C6 4ØØØØØØØ ØØØØØØ

Characteristic and sign as above, yielding
43Ø66A84 246ØØ2C6 [4]

Postnormalization:	4266A842 46ØØ2C64

Note the contribution of the guard digit. If floating-point register 4 contains AEØØØ9ØØ 12345678, execution of MER F4,FØ proceeds as follows:

Prenormalization:	register 4 (or special register) becomes AB9ØØØØØ 12345678
Multiplication:	9ØØØØØ×2ØØØØØ=12ØØØØ ØØØØØØØØ
Characteristic:	2B+41−4Ø=2C
Sign:	1 (EXCLUSIVE OR) Ø=1
Yielding:	AC12ØØØØ ØØØØØØØØ.

No postnormalization is necessary.

In the divide operations the first operand is divided by the second operand; the quotient replaces the first operand, and no remainder is preserved. In short-precision only the 24 bits of each short floating-point number participate, and the low-order half of the first operand register remains unchanged. The process of division involves first prenormalization of both operands, then division of the fractions and subtraction of the characteristics (and addition of the bias quantity to the difference; why?) and adjustment of the sign of the quotient. Postnormalization is never necessary, but a right shift of one hexadecimal digit may be necessary, as you will see.

Suppose floating-point register 0 contains 41400000 ØØØØØØØØ, and SIX contains 416ØØØØØ ØØØØØØØØ. Then execution of DE FØ,SIX will be as follows:

No prenormalization is necessary

Division:	4ØØØØØ/6ØØØØØ=AAAAAA
Characteristic:	41−41+4Ø=4Ø
Sign:	Ø (EXCLUSIVE OR) Ø=Ø

yielding a result of 4ØAAAAAA, an approximation to 2/3. Next, suppose that floating-point register 6 contains C43ØØØØØ ØØØØØØØØ. Execution of DDR FØ,F6 is as follows:

No prenormalization is needed

Division:	4ØØØØØ ØØØØØØØØ/3ØØØØØ ØØØØØØØØ
Yields:	1555555 55555555, where the 1, as normally developed, is in a carry position.

Characteristic: $41 - 44 + 40 = 3D$

Sign: $\emptyset$ (EXCLUSIVE OR) $1 = 1$

Yielding an intermediate result of
$$BD(1)555555\ 55555555.$$

A right shift to make room for the leading digit of quotient yields a final result of BE155555 55555555.

There are also "Halve" operations, HER and HDR, which divide a short or long, respectively, second operand by 2 and place the result in the first operand register. The result is always identical to that upon a regular division by 2.

13.5   Unnormalized Add and Subtract Operations

System/370 computers, like many other computers, have a set of instructions that perform addition and subtraction in exactly the same way as the ordinary add and subtract instructions except that no normalization step takes place after the intermediate sum is developed. A carry from the high-order digit in the addition causes a right shift, but if the fraction contains any leading zeros, they remain.

The instructions are as follows, where the lack of normalization is understood:

Instruction	Type	Action		Cond. code set
AUR	RR	$FPR1$	$\leftarrow c(FPR1) + c(FPR2)$	Yes
AU	RX	$FPR1$	$\leftarrow c(FPR1) + c(S2)$	Yes
AWR	RR	$FPR1_{0-63}$	$\leftarrow c(FPR1)_{0-63} + c(FPR2)_{0-63}$	Yes
AW	RX	$FPR1_{0-63}$	$\leftarrow c(FPR1)_{0-63} + c(S2)_{0-63}$	Yes
SUR	RR	$FPR1$	$\leftarrow c(FPR1) - c(FPR2)$	Yes
SU	RX	$FPR1$	$\leftarrow c(FPR1) - c(S2)$	Yes
SWR	RR	$FPR1_{0-63}$	$\leftarrow c(FPR1)_{0-63} - c(FPR2)_{0-63}$	Yes
SW	RX	$FPR1_{0-63}$	$\leftarrow c(FPR1)_{0-63} - c(S2)_{0-63}$	Yes

The mnemonic operation codes are designed to help the user remember the right instruction; U is inserted in place of E to stand for Unnormalized, and W is inserted as a convenient pun (DOUBLE-U) standing for Double-precision Unnormalized.

For example, if floating-point register 0 contains 44100022 3456789A and HP contains C3FFC834, the instruction AU F0,HP will proceed:

Alignment: second operand fraction becomes $\emptyset$FFC83[4]

Addition: $100022[\emptyset]$

$-\emptyset$FFC83[4]

$\emptyset\emptyset\emptyset39E[C]$

The insertion of sign and characteristic 44 leaves the result in floating-point register 0: 4400039E 3456789A, and the condition code is set to 2. All operations standard to floating-point addition have taken place except normalization. Note that the guard digit never has a chance to enter the result of an unnormalized operation.

Uses for the regular addition, subtraction, multiplication, and division instructions are reasonably evident. Uses for unnormalized numbers and unnormalized operations are more obscure, so some uses should be mentioned here.

One use for unnormalized numbers is the intentional truncation of numbers. For example, suppose that we have a short floating-point number TSUB in main storage, and we want its integer part. Its integer part can be put at TSUBINT by

```
      LE    FØ,UNFLZ      UNFLZ=X'47ØØØØØØ'
      AE    FØ,TSUB
      STE   FØ,TSUBINT
```

The constant X'47ØØØØØØ' is an unnormalized zero; if TSUB is, for example, 44345F9E, action of the addition instruction is

Alignment: the fraction of TSUB is shifted right $47-44=3$:
 ØØØ345[F]

Addition: ØØØØØØ[Ø]+ØØØ345[F]=ØØØ345[F]

Normalization: 44345FØØ.

The fraction digits representing negative powers of 16 (this is called the *fractional part*) are lost during the alignment step. If TSUB had been a negative number, the action of the fraction would be exactly the same; we say that rounding *toward zero* takes place. You can verify that the preceding sequence of three instructions will not affect a number that is too large to have digits representing negative powers of 16, and that it will completely annihilate any number whose magnitude is less than 1. Characteristics other than 47 with a zero fraction will have similar results, truncating numbers at different places. We may say that zeros with nonzero characteristics are "bigger" than a true zero.

Unnormalized numbers and arithmetic are useful in conversions between floating-point representation and printable characters, as we will see in Section 13.7.

Experiments have been made, and schemes developed for using unnormalized numbers and arithmetic to help keep track of the significance of the digits in floating-point computations. The idea is that significant digits are lost most quickly when an addition or subtraction results in leading zeros. Therefore if the leading zeros are kept instead of removed by normalization we have an estimate of the number of significant digits of our result. Because of the radix 16 used by System/370 floating-point representation, this measure is rather too coarse to be useful, and the complete normalization done by multiplication and division instructions makes it very difficult to keep the leading zeros one has developed in a series of computations. Therefore other techniques of keeping track of significance are to be preferred to use of unnormalized numbers in the IBM System/370.

13.6   Exceptions and Interrupts

A variety of exceptions arise from the attempted execution of floating-point instructions. Discussion of them has been postponed until this section in order to give a unified treatment.

First, if the floating-point feature is not installed on the particular model, an *operation* exception is taken, with resulting interrupt, on attempted execution of any floating-point instruction, including the load and store instructions. Second, access exceptions can be caused by reference to main storage for operands, according to the usual rules. A *specification* exception, the most common during the debugging of programs, is taken and results in interrupt if a floating-point register address, *FPR1* or *FPR2* in our instruction descriptions, is other than 0, 2, 4, or 6. These exceptions were all explained in Chapter 9, and it should be sufficient here to remark that they apply.

There are also four types of exceptions that are peculiar to floating-point instructions. First is the *exponent overflow*. An exponent overflow results whenever, by following the procedures described for each instruction, the final characteristic of the result would exceed 127 (hexadecimal 7F) and the fraction is nonzero. The overflow can occur as the result of a carry out of the high-order fraction position during normalized or unnormalized addition or subtraction and the following characteristic adjustment after a right shift, or during the characteristic computations in multiplication or division. An exponent overflow exception will always cause interrupt. The operation is completed first, however, and the result is correct except that the characteristic is 128 smaller than the correct characteristic.

An *exponent underflow* exception occurs when the final characteristic of the result of a floating-point instruction would be less than 0. The underflow could occur as a result of normalization during normalized addition or subtraction and either during computation of the intermediate characteristic during multiplication or during the postnormalization. An underflow during prenormalization does *not* cause an exponent underflow exception. An exponent underflow may result from division, but if the underflow is rectified by a right shift to give the final quotient, no exponent underflow results. No underflows are possible in unnormalized addition or subtraction.

Action on an exponent underflow depends on bit 2 of the program mask. If this bit is 0, the result of the operation is forced to a true zero, that is, sign, characteristic, and fraction all become zero, and interrupt does not take place. If the bit is 1, the operation is completed, with a result whose characteristic is 128 larger than the correct characteristic, and an interrupt takes place.

In addition or subtraction instructions, normalized or unnormalized, when the fraction of the result is zero, a *significance* exception occurs. The point is that all significant digits of the result have been lost, and it is possible that further computations will be meaningless. Interruption because of a significance exception is controlled by bit 3 of the program mask. If the bit is 0, a true zero is forced, the condition code is set to 0 and no interrupt takes place. If the bit is 1 when a significance exception occurs, the characteristic is left as it is, the condition code is set to 0, and an interrupt takes place.

The last of the special floating-point exceptions is the *floating-point divide* exception. This exception occurs when a floating-point division is attempted by a divisor whose fraction is zero. The condition is discovered during attempted prenormalization of the divisor, and the dividend is left unchanged while the operation is suppressed and interrupt takes place.

The exceptions and the instructions that may cause them are summarized in the unified instruction list in Fig. 13.10.

13.7   An Example: A Regression Calculation

One of the common problems in the analysis of data is the fitting of a line or curve to a set of observations, which can be called *regression*. In its simplest form, which is carried through here, this involves a set of observations—pairs of values—and the fitting of a straight line to the observations. Usually, a perfect fit is unobtainable; the data simply do not lie on a straight line. We need a measure of the deviation from a perfect fit, and a way of drawing the line that will minimize that measure.

Let us choose then to denote one variable as "independent" and the other as "dependent," which is natural in most cases: we choose a temperature independently and observe the pressure in a physical system. The pressure can properly be termed dependent on the temperature we choose. Or we can survey a group of people, denoting age as one variable and yearly medical bill as another; we can at least adopt the hypothesis that yearly medical bill is dependent on (among other things) age. For the mathematical statement of the procedures let us denote x as the independent variable and y as the dependent variable. If we have n observations, each observation can be represented as the pair x_i, y_i, and the equation for the line we seek will be $y = a + bx$.

We choose as our measure of goodness of fit the sum of squares of deviations of predicted values $a + bx_i$ from actual values y_i of the dependent variable:

$$E = \sum_{i=1}^{n} [y_i - (a + bx_i)]^2 \tag{13.1}$$

When we choose a and b so as to minimize this measure E, we are doing what is called fitting by *least squares*. One reason for choosing this particular measure is that it weights heavily any large deviations $y_i - (a + bx_i)$, so that minimization of E is an attempt to eliminate large deviations. Another reason is that the measure E has a number of very nice mathematical properties, and a large body of theory has grown around least-squares curve-fitting.

One of the nice properties of E is that the coefficients a and b of the regression line are easily shown, by taking partial derivatives of E with respect to a and b, to be the solutions of the equations

$$an + b \sum_1^n x_i = \sum_1^n y_i,$$

$$a \sum_1^n x_i + b \sum_1^n x_i^2 = \sum_1^n x_i y_i. \qquad (13.2)$$

This pair of equations, requiring only computation of the sums

$$\sum_1^n x_i, \quad \sum_1^n y_i, \quad \sum_1^n x_i^2 \text{ and } \sum_1^n x_i y_i,$$

is easily solved. Another of the nice properties of E is that after a and b have been computed according to Eqs. (13.2), E itself can be computed as

$$E = \sum_1^n y_i^2 - a \sum_1^n y_i - b \sum_1^n x_i y_i, \qquad (13.3)$$

which requires only the additional computation of $\sum_1^n y_i^2$.

Computation, then, can be divided into three parts. First is the computation of the necessary sums

$$\sum_1^n x_i, \quad \sum_1^n y_i, \quad \sum_1^n x_i^2, \quad \sum_1^n x_i y_i, \quad \text{and} \quad \sum_1^n y_i^2.$$

Second is the solution of Eqs. (13.2) for the coefficients a and b, and third is the computation of E, which can be done according to Eq. (13.3).

Let us now consider a program segment computing the necessary sums. Assume that the observations are all in main storage, and that the number n of observations is given in register 5. Assume further that each observation is in a record, and that the address of the beginning of one record is a quantity p greater than the address of the beginning of the previous record, and that p is in register 4. Finally, suppose that the address of the beginning of the first record is in register 3, and that x_i and y_i, both in short floating-point form, are at the beginning of each record.

We must do some address calculation and looping control as well as the floating-point calculations. We control looping with a BCT instruction, decrementing register 7, and let register 6 always contain the address of the beginning of the current record, namely, the address of the current x_i. We keep

$$\sum_1^n x_i \quad \text{and} \quad \sum_1^n y_i$$

in floating-point registers 4 and 6, but keep the other sums in main storage. All computations are in short precision. Figure 13.2 shows the segment, which is reasonably straightforward. At the very end, n is stored as a floating-point number because it is needed in that form in the next segment. It is stored

FIGURE 13.2   Calculation of sums

```
          LE    F4,=F'0'
          LER   F6,F4          SUM Y = 0
          STE   F4,SUMX2       _____  = 0
          STE   F4,SUMXY               = 0
          STE   F4,SUMY2               = 0
          LR    R7,R5          N
          LR    R6,R3          ADDR OF CURRENT RECORD
* DO FOR COUNT = N TO 1, INCR -1
* . ADD TO SUMS OF X, Y, XY, X**2, Y**2
SUMLOOP   LE    F0,0(,R6)      X
          AER   F4,F0          SUM X
          MER   F0,F0          X SQUARED
          AE    F0,SUMX2
          STE   F0,SUMX2       SUM X SQUARED
          LE    F0,4(,R6)      Y
          AER   F6,F0          SUM Y
          ME    F0,0(,R6)      X Y
          AE    F0,SUMXY
          STE   F0,SUMXY       SUM X Y
          LE    F0,4(,R6)      Y
          MER   F0,F0          Y SQUARED
          AE    F0,SUMY2
          STE   F0,SUMY2       SUM Y SQUARED
* . UPDATE ADDR. OF CURRENT RECORD
          AR    R6,R4
          BCT   R7,SUMLOOP
* ENDFOR
* STORE RESULTS
          STE   F4,SUMX
          STE   F6,SUMY
          LR    R7,R5
          A     R5,=X'46000000' UNNORMALIZED ZERO
          ST    R5,FLN          STORE N, UNNORM. FLOATING PT.
```

unnormalized, and because of prenormalization in multiplication and division, it can be used that way. Conversions like this are illustrated further in Section 13.9.

We now turn to the solution of the set of two equations in a and b. There are many schemes for solving a set of simultaneous linear equations, and we choose here an *elimination* scheme due to Gauss. This scheme is quite efficient and lends itself well to computer use; many other schemes are based on this one. We can describe the elimination procedure as follows. We start with two equations with more or less arbitrary coefficients that we denote by c's, which are subscripted for row and column of the array we can construct of the coefficients:

$$c_{11}a + c_{12}b = c_{13},$$
$$c_{21}a + c_{22}b = c_{23}.$$

First we divide the first equation by c_{11}, changing it to

$$a + c'_{12}b = c'_{13},$$

FIGURE 13.3 Program segment to compute regression coefficients

```
*** COMPUTE REGRESSION COEFFICIENTS A AND B
          DE      F4,FLN         SUMX / N = C12 PRIME
          DE      F6,FLN         SUMY / N = C13 PRIME
          LE      F0,SUMX2
          LE      F2,SUMX
          MER     F2,F4
          SER     F0,F2          C22 PRIME = C22 - (C12 PRIME) * C21
          STE     F0,C22
          LE      F0,SUMXY
          LE      F2,SUMX
          MER     F2,F6
          SER     F0,F2          C23 PRIME = C23 - (C13 PRIME) * C31
          DE      F0,C22         B = (C23 PRIME) / (C22 PRIME)
          STE     F0,B
          MER     F4,F0          (C12 PRIME) * B
          SER     F6,F4          A = (C13 PRIME) - (C12 PRIME) * B
          STE     F6,A
```

where $c'_{12} = c_{12}/c_{11}$, $c'_{13} = c_{13}/c_{11}$. Next we eliminate a from the second equation by subtracting c_{21} times the new first equation from the second, leaving

$$c'_{22}b = c'_{23},$$

where $c'_{22} = c_{22} - c_{21} \cdot c'_{12}$, $c'_{23} = c_{23} - c_{21} \cdot c'_{13}$. Now b is simply c'_{23}/c'_{22}, and with this value of b we can compute a from the new first equation. This procedure must be modified if c_{11} or c'_{22} turn out to be zero, and it can be extended to any number of equations in the same number of unknowns. With many equations the coefficients are kept in what is considered a two-dimensional array, as suggested by our subscripts, and the address calculation for an efficient program is a good exercise.

We show a segment in Fig. 13.3 that is specific to Eqs. (13.2) and is designed to follow Fig. 13.2 directly.

FIGURE 13.4 Computation of regression error according to Eq. (13.3)

```
*** COMPUTE THE REGRESSION ERROR E
          LE      F0,SUMY
          ME      F0,A
          LE      F2,SUMXY
          ME      F2,B
          AER     F2,F0
          LE      F4,SUMY2
          SER     F4,F2
          STE     F4,E
```

As the third phase of our calculation we compute E, the measure of goodness of fit. Figure 13.4 accomplishes the computation according to Eq. (13.3).

When this sequence of segments is executed with a data set comprised of the ten observations (values given in decimal),

Observation	x	y
1	−21.23	65.72
2	−11.80	37.45
3	−6.12	20.34
4	−1.68	7.07
5	0.01	1.99
6	0.42	0.73
7	1.00	−1.01
8	2.56	−5.72
9	4.99	−12.93
10	18.00	−52.00

results include (here decimal and hexadecimal values are given)

	Decimal	Hexadecimal
a	2.007661	2.01F61
b	−3.000979	−3.00403
E	−0.003906250	−0.010000

The fit seems successful, since E is quite small. However, E is defined to be a sum of squares, so it should *not* be negative! The mathematics of deriving Eq. (13.3) is correct, and there are no bugs in the program, so we are forced to think about accuracy and rounding errors. The fact that so few hexadecimal digits of E are nonzero is no accident; it is because the numbers that were subtracted to give E are large and of nearly equal magnitude:

$$\sum_{1}^{10} y_i^2 = 2386.\text{B9} \quad \text{(hexadecimal)};$$

$$a \sum_{1}^{10} y_i + b \sum_{1}^{10} x_i y_i = 2386.\text{BA} \quad \text{(hexadecimal)}.$$

Since each of these numbers can be expected to include some effect of rounding errors, their last hexadecimal digits are not to be trusted. Since their first five hexadecimal digits agree, their difference has *no* significant digits, and the

FIGURE 13.5   Computation of regression error according to Eq. (13.1)

```
*** COMPUTE SUM OF SQUARED DEVIATIONS E
          LR     R5,R7            R7 CONTAINS INTEGER N, R5 FLOATED N
          LR     R6,R3            ADDR. OF CURRENT RECORD
          LE     F2,=F'0'         SUM OF SQUARED DEVS.
* DO FOR COUNT = N TO 1, INCR -1
ELOOP     LE     F4,0(,R6)        X
          ME     F4,B
          AE     F4,A             A + B * X
          SE     F4,4(,R6)        A + B * X = Y = - DEV
          MER    F4,F4            SQUARE DEV.
          AER    F2,F4            ADD TO SUM
          AR     R6,R4
          BCT    R5,ELOOP
* ENDFOR
          STE    F2,E
```

computed estimate of E is pure rounding error! This scheme for computing E then, while involving very little computational labor, yields at most one hexadecimal digit of accuracy. Of course, we could do some or all of the computations in double precision, but the same kind of calamity would still happen in larger problems. The point is that the scheme of Eq. (13.3) is computationally poor from the standpoint of accuracy. The alternative is to compute E directly from its defining Eq. (13.1); the segment in Fig. 13.5 does this. The segment is intended to replace that in Fig. 13.4; the four instructions of Fig. 13.2 computing SUMY2 can also be deleted, since SUMY2 is used only in Fig. 13.4.

Computation of E by Fig. 13.5 yields 0.006762601 decimal or .01BB31A hexadecimal, of which roughly three digits are accurate. Approximately three significant digits remain in each deviation and in the square of each deviation, and during the summing process these digits are not lost.

Least-squares regression can be generalized to problems of finding coefficients in an equation involving several independent variables: $y = a_0 + a_1x_1 + a_2x_2 + \cdots + a_kx_k$, where the $x_1, \ldots, x_k$ are values of independent variables in one observation. It can also be generalized to problems involving more complicated functions than linear ones, such as $y = a_0 + a_1x + a_2x^2 + \cdots + a_mx^m$. The computational schemes are roughly the same. The work involved increases linearly in phase 1, generation of sums, with the number of coefficients to be determined, and increases as the cube of the number of coefficients in phase 2, solution of the simultaneous linear equations. The biggest increase in work, however, comes when there are too many observations to be kept in main storage, so that the records must be read and the information taken from them, not only in phase 1, but in phase 3, the computation of E according to Eq. (13.1).

13.8   Extended-Precision Instructions

There are seven instructions in the group of extended-precision instructions. They are now available in most of the IBM System/370 series. Included are two rounding instructions, an add, a subtract, and three multiply instructions.

The instruction Load and Round Double (LRDR) is of RR type; it rounds an extended-precision number (second operand) to a double-precision number that is placed in the first operand register. Similarly, Load and Round (LRER) rounds a double-precision number to single-precision form. The LRER instruction therefore has nothing to do with extended-precision numbers, and is included in the extended-precision feature because it was introduced at the same time as the extended-precision instructions, several years after the implementation of the ordinary floating-point instruction set.

The RR-type instructions AXR, SXR, and MXR, respectively, add, subtract, and multiply two extended-precision operands, and leave an extended-precision result. The operations are completely analogous to the single-precision and double-precision operations with respect to guard digit, normalization, condition code, and exceptions.

The instructions MXDR and MXD each multiply two double-precision operands, leaving an extended-precision product. MXDR is of RR type, and MXD of RX type.

Any double-precision number can be loaded as an extended-precision number merely by appending a second double-precision number, with zero fraction and any characteristic, in the second register of the pair. Thus

```
LD   F4,A
LD   F6,D'Ø'
```

loads an extended-precision number in the register pair 4,6; the extended-precision number has the same value as the double-precision number at A.

There is no extended-precision divide instruction implemented in hardware, but a macro named DXR is provided. Its accessibility to a program also depends on provision of an appropriate SPIE macro; you must consult systems programmers at your installation for detailed arrangements. Similar arrangements can be made for simulation through macros of the other extended-precision instructions in installations where the extended-precision feature is not implemented in hardware.

The use of extended-precision arithmetic can be illustrated by showing how the quotient of two extended-precision numbers can be formed without using a divide instruction. The Newton-Raphson iterative process solves approximately an equation $f(x) = 0$ by computing successively

$$x_1 = x_0 - \frac{f(x_0)}{f'(x_0)}, \qquad x_2 = x_1 - \frac{f(x_1)}{f'(x_1)}, \ldots.$$

Under certain conditions the sequence $x_0, x_1, x_2, \ldots$ converges nicely to the solution of the equation. If we take $f(x) = (1/x) - b$, the solution of $(1/x) - b = 0$ is obviously the inverse of b. The iteration

$$x_{i+1} = x_i - \frac{f(x_i)}{f'(x_i)}$$

becomes

$$x_{i+1} = x_i(2 - bx_i),$$

which has two happy properties:

1. Each iteration more or less doubles the number of accurate digits of the approximations.
2. The inverse of b is obtained without division.

It is easy to generate a good first approximation of $1/b$ using double-precision arithmetic, and just one iteration beyond that generates $1/b$ correct to about 27 hexadecimal digits. Multiplying this inverse by a gives a good approximation to an extended-precision a/b.

Suppose then that A and B are extended-precision numbers in main storage. The segment shown in Fig. 13.6 generates at X the quotient A/B correct to about 27 hexadecimal digits.

In summary, the instructions in the extended-precision feature are represented as shown in Fig. 13.10, with the other floating-point instructions.

FIGURE 13.6   Division of extended-precision numbers

```
LD      F0,=D'1'
DD      F0,B              DOUBLE-PRECISION 1. / B = X
STD     F0,X
LD      F4,B              EXTENDED B
LD      F6,B+8
LD      F2,=D'0.'         EXTEND X BY ZEROS
MXR     F4,F0             FORM B * X
LD      F0,=D'2.'
SXR     F0,F4             2. - B * X
LD      F4,X
LD      F6,=D'0.'
MXR     F0,F4             X * (2. - B * X)
LD      F4,A              = EXT. PREC. 1. / B
LD      F6,A+8
MXR     F0,F4             FORM A * (1. / B)
STD     F0,X
STD     F2,X+8            STORE A / B AT X
```

13.9   Conversions

For conversions between printable characters and binary integers, the IBM System/370 has the simple helpful instructions PACK, CVB, CVD, and UNPK, which were introduced in Chapter 6. For converting to floating-point, there are no correspondingly easy instructions. One reason is that the conversion requirements, involving a wide range of values of floating-point numbers and several different external forms desired, are too varied to be serviced by any simple instructions. Let us therefore examine some sample segments that perform some conversions between floating-point and other forms.

First, in Fig. 13.7 is a segment that converts a binary integer in register 3 into a short normalized floating-point number stored at NORMINT. Let us follow execution of this segment on a particular number. Suppose register 3 contains hexadecimal FC8Ø34A3. Since floating-point numbers are not stored in 2's complement form but in sign-and-absolute value form, the first thing to do is find the absolute value of the number. The absolute value, Ø37FCB5D, is put in register 5. An unnormalized zero is loaded into register 4; the characteristic is 4E, so the number whose floating-point representation is now in registers (general, not floating-point) 4 and 5 has its actual hexadecimal point at the far right of register 5. The number 4EØØØØØØØ37FCB5D is actually already a floating-point representation of the integer 37FCB5D. The instruction N R3,MSKSGN annihilates all 1-bits in register 3 except the sign bit; in the example the sign bit is 1, so the result is 8ØØØØØØØ. The next instruction attaches the sign to the floating-

FIGURE 13.7   Converting an integer to floating point

```
*** CONVERT AN INTEGER N REG. 3
*** TO SHORT NORMALIZED FLOATING POINT FORM
*** STORING THE RESULT AT NORMINT
          LPR    R5,R3           TAKE ABSOLUTE VALUE
          L      R4,UNZRO        CREATE UNNORMALIZED FLOATED NO.
          N      R3,MSKSGN       ISOLATE SIGN
          OR     R4,R3           ATTACH SIGN
          STM    R4,R5,UNNO      UNNORMALIZED SIGNED NUMBER
          LD     F0,UNNO
          AD     F0,=D'0'        NORMALIZE
          STE    F0,NORMINT


UNNO      DS     1D
NORMINT   DS     1F
UNZRO     DC     X'4E000000'
MSKSGN    DC     X'80000000'
```

FIGURE 13.8   Converting a fraction to floating point

```
*** FOLLOWING DIRECTLY THE SEGMENT OF FIG. 13.7,
*** CONVERTS 7 DIGITS OF FRACTION FROM EBCDIC FORM
*** AT DECFRAC INTO FLOATING-POINT FORM, ATTACHING
*** THE NUMBER TO THE PRECEDING RESULT
          PACK  DBL(8),DECFRAC(7)
          CVB   R7,DBL          ASSUME NO MINUS SIGN ON DECFRAC
          L     R6,UNZRO
          OR    R6,R3           ATTACH SAME SIGN AS TO INTEGER
          STM   R6,R7,UNNO
          LD    F2,UNNO
          DD    F2,=D'1.0E7'    MAKE INTO FRACTION, NORMALIZE
          ADR   F0,F2           COMBINE INTEGER AND FRACTION
          STD   F0,RESULT



DBL       DS    1D
RESULT    DS    1D
```

point number (XR would do just as well as OR), making it CE000000 037FCB5D. This number is stored at UNNO, then loaded into floating-point register 0. A zero is added; this is the easiest way to normalize the number, which then is C737FCB5 D0000000. The last instruction stores the upper half of the result. In this case one significant hexadecimal digit is lost in the truncation to short floating-point form; in the worst case, two may be lost. They can be retained, of course, by storing the double-precision instead of single-precision result.

As a second example, suppose that the number in the preceding example was merely the integer part of a number whose EBCDIC form also included seven decimal fraction digits. We now convert these digits to floating-point form and attach the result to the preceding one.

This segment, Fig. 13.8, assumes that no minus sign is coded in the digits of DECFRAC, but that the sign is to be taken as the sign of the integer. This simplifies the segment somewhat. The process of "floating" the fraction is the same as that for floating the integer. The division by 10^7 not only reduces the digits to fraction status but prenormalizes and leaves a normalized result.

As a last example, consider the converse process of converting a floating-point number to an integer. Suppose that we have a short-precision floating-point number FLT, whose integer part, if it will fit, is to be stored as an integer at INTGR.

In this example, Fig. 13.9, all adjustments are made in floating-point registers. First, note that in order to make the short floating-point word into a double-precision one, we must clear the lower half of the register. If the absolute value of the number is greater than 2^{31}, the number is too large to be represented as an integer in one general register, so the largest possible integer

FIGURE 13.9   Converting a floating-point number to an integer

```
*** CONVERT A SHORT NORMALIZED FLOATING-POINT
*** NUMBER AT FLT TO A BINARY INTEGER AT INTGR.
*** IF NUMBER IS TOO BIG, 7FFFFFFF IS STORED.
          LD    F0,=D'0'      CLEAR LOWER HALF OF REG.
          LE    F0,FLT
* IF NUMBER IS TOO LARGE
          LPER  F2,F0
          CE    F2,=X'48800000'
          BL    OK
* . THEN STORE 7FFFFFFF (LARGEST POSSIBLE INTEGER)
          MVC   INTGR(4),=X'7FFFFFFF'
          B     NEXT
* . ELSE CONVERT
OK        AW    F0,=X'4E00000100000000' UNNORMALIZE, COMPLEMENT
*                                   IF NECESSARY
          STD   F0,DINT
          MVC   INTGR(4),DINT+4
* ENDIF
NEXT      DS    0H


DINT      DS    1D
```

is stored. Let us suppose that the number in FLT is C553F049 as we follow the remainder of the segment. The instruction AW FØ,=X'4EØØØØØ1ØØØØØØØØ' accomplishes several things. First, the alignment phase unnormalizes the number so that the actual (hexadecimal) point is just to the right of the register. All digits representing a fraction less than 1 are eliminated, and the absolute value of the desired integer is in the lower half of the register. In our example, the register contains CEØØØØØØ ØØ53FØ4. Integer representation requires that negative numbers be represented in 2's complement form, so this low-order portion must be complemented if the number is negative. This is accomplished very cleverly by the instruction AW FØ,=X'4EØØØØØ1ØØØØØØØØ'. If the result is negative, as in our case, the addition is of

$$4EØØØØØ1 \qquad ØØØØØØØØ$$

and

$$CEØØØØØØ \qquad ØØØ53FØ4,$$

which is in effect a subtraction yielding 4EØØØØØØ FFFADØFC, whose low-order 32 bits are the desired complement. If, on the other hand, the original number were positive, say 4EØØØØØØ ØØØ53FØ4, the result would be 4EØØØØØ1 ØØØ53FØ4. In either case, the lower half is in correct 2's complement form. Finally, the whole number is stored (there is no way to store only the lower half of a floating-point register) and the desired portion moved to INTGR.

FIGURE 13.10 Summary of floating-point instructions

Instruction	Type	Action			Cond.[2] code	Exceptions[3]
LER	RR	$FPR1$	$\leftarrow$	$c(FPR2)$	—	S
LE	RX	$FPR1$	$\leftarrow$	$c(S2)$	—	A,S
LDR	RR	$FPR1_{0-63}$	$\leftarrow$	$c(FPR2)_{0-63}$	—	S
LD	RX	$FPR1_{0-63}$	$\leftarrow$	$c(S2)_{0-63}$	—	A,S
LTER	RR	$FPR1$	$\leftarrow$	$c(FPR2)$	(a)	S
LTDR	RR	$FPR1_{0-63}$	$\leftarrow$	$c(FPR2)_{0-63}$	(a)	S
LCER	RR	$FPR1$	$\leftarrow$	$-c(FPR2)$	(a)	S
LCDR	RR	$FPR1_{0-63}$	$\leftarrow$	$-c(FPR2)_{0-63}$	(a)	S
LPER	RR	$FPR1$	$\leftarrow$	$|c(FPR2)|$	(a)	S
LPDR	RR	$FPR1_{0-63}$	$\leftarrow$	$|c(FPR2)_{0-63}|$	(a)	S
LNER	RR	$FPR1$	$\leftarrow$	$-|c(FPR2)|$	(a)	S
LNDR	RR	$FPR1_{0-63}$	$\leftarrow$	$-|c(FPR2)_{0-63}|$	(a)	S
LRER	RR	$FPR1$	$\leftarrow$	rounded $c(FPR2)_{0-63}$	—	S, E
LRDR	RR	$FPR1_{0-63}$	$\leftarrow$	rounded $c(S2)_{0-127}$	—	S, E
STE	RX	$S2$	$\leftarrow$	$c(FPR1)$	—	A,S
STD	RX	$S2_{0-63}$	$\leftarrow$	$c(FPR1)_{0-63}$	—	A,S
AER	RR	$FPR1$	$\leftarrow$	$c(FPR1)$ $+ c(FPR2)$	(a)	S,U,E,LS
AE	RX	$FPR1$	$\leftarrow$	$c(FPR1)$ $+ c(FPR2)$	(a)	A,S,U,E,LS
ADR	RR	$FPR1_{0-63}$	$\leftarrow$	$c(FPR1)_{0-63}$ $+ c(FPR2)_{0-63}$	(a)	S,U,E,LS
AD	RX	$FPR1_{0-63}$	$\leftarrow$	$c(FPR1)_{0-63}$ $+ c(STR2)_{0-63}$	(a)	A,S,U,E,LS
AXR	RR	$FPR1_{0-127}$	$\leftarrow$	$c(FPR1)_{0-127}$ $+ c(FPR2)_{0-127}$	(a)	S,U,E,LS
SER	RR	$FPR1$	$\leftarrow$	$c(FPR1)$ $- c(FPR2)$	(a)	S,U,E,LS
SE	RX	$FPR1$	$\leftarrow$	$c(FPR1)_{0-63}$ $- c(S2)$	(a)	A,S,U,E,LS
SDR	RR	$FPR1_{0-63}$	$\leftarrow$	$c(FPR1)_{0-63}$ $- c(FPR2)_{0-63}$	(a)	S,U,E,LS
SD	RX	$FPR1_{0-63}$	$\leftarrow$	$c(FPR1)_{0-63}$ $- c(S2)_{0-63}$	(a)	A,S,U,E,LS
SXR	RR	$FPR1_{0-127}$	$\leftarrow$	$c(FPR1)_{0-127}$ $- c(FPR2)_{0-127}$	(a)	S,U,E,LS
CER	RR	—			(b)	S
CE	RX	—			(b)	A,S
CDR	RR	—			(b)	S
CD	RX	—			(b)	A,S
AUR[1]	RR	$FPR1$	$\leftarrow$	$c(FPR1)$ $+ c(FPR2)$	(a)	S, E,LS
AU[1]	RX	$FPR1$	$\leftarrow$	$c(FPR1)$ $+ c(S2)$	(a)	A,S, E,LS
AWR[1]	RR	$FPR1$	$\leftarrow$	$c(FPR1)_{0-63}$ $+ c(FPR2)_{0-63}$	(a)	S, E,LS
AW[1]	RX	$FPR1_{0-63}$	$\leftarrow$	$c(FPR1)_{0-63}$ $+ c(S2)_{0-63}$	(a)	A,S, E,LS
SUR[1]	RR	$FPR1$	$\leftarrow$	$c(FPR1)$ $- c(FPR2)$	(a)	S, E,LS
SU[1]	RX	$FPR1$	$\leftarrow$	$c(FPR1)$ $- c(S2)$	(a)	A,S, E,LS
SWR[1]	RR	$FPR1_{0-63}$	$\leftarrow$	$c(FPR1)_{0-63}$ $- c(FPR2)_{0-63}$	(a)	S, E,LS
SW[1]	RX	$FPR1_{0-63}$	$\leftarrow$	$c(FPR1)_{0-63}$ $- c(S2)_{0-63}$	(a)	A,S, E,LS
MER	RR	$FPR1_{0-63}$	$\leftarrow$	$c(FPR1)$ $\times c(FPR2)$	—	S,U,E

FIGURE 13.10 Continued

Instruction	Type	Action	Cond.[2] code	Exceptions[3]
ME	RX	$FPR1_{0-63} \leftarrow c(FPR1) \times c(S2)$	—	A,S,U,E
MDR	RR	$FPR1_{0-63} \leftarrow c(FPR1)_{0-63} \times c(FPR2)_{0-63}$	—	S,U,E
MD	RX	$FPR1_{0-63} \leftarrow c(FPR1)_{0-63} \times c(S2)_{0-63}$	—	A,S,U,E
MXR	RR	$FPR1_{0-127} \leftarrow c(FPR1)_{0-127} \times c(FPR2)_{0-127}$	—	S,U,E
MXDR	RR	$FPR1_{0-127} \leftarrow c(FPR1)_{0-63} \times c(FPR2)_{0-63}$	—	S,U,E
MXD	RX	$FPR1_{0-127} \leftarrow c(FPR1)_{0-63} \times c(S2)_{0-63}$	—	A,S,U,E
DER	RR	$FPR1 \leftarrow c(FPR1) \ / \ c(FPR2)$	—	S,U,E,FK
DE	RX	$FPR1 \leftarrow c(FPR1) \ / \ c(S2)$	—	A,S,U,E,FK
DDR	RR	$FPR1_{0-63} \leftarrow c(FPR1)_{0-63} \ / \ c(FPR2)_{0-63}$	—	S,U,E,FK
DD	RX	$FPR1_{0-63} \leftarrow c(FPR1)_{0-63} \ / \ c(S2)_{0-63}$	—	A,S,U,E,FK
HER	RR	$FPR1 \leftarrow c(FPR2) \ / \ 2$	—	S,U
HDR	RR	$FPR1_{0-63} \leftarrow c(FPR2)_{0-63} \ / \ 2$	—	S,U

Notes
1. Addition and subtraction in these operations are unnormalized.
2. Condition codes are set to
   a) 0 if result fraction = 0;
      1 if result less than 0;
      2 if result greater than 0.
   b) 0 if $Op_1 = Op_2$;
      1 if Op_1 less than Op_2;
      2 if Op_1 greater than Op_2.
3. Exception codes: A: Access;
                     S: Specification;
                     U: Exponent underflow;
                     E: Exponent overflow;
                     LS: Significance;
                     FK: Floating divide by zero.

m a i n   i d e a s

□ Floating-point numbers, in 32-, 64-, and 128-bit lengths, represent quantities of widely varying magnitudes. The representation uses a characteristic—indicating an exponent of 16—and a fraction. Nonzero numbers are normalized if the first hexadecimal digit of the fraction is nonzero. Normalization enables the preservation of a maximum number of significant digits in a series of computations.

□ Floating-point registers, each 64 bits long, are numbered 0, 2, 4, and 6. Floating-point instructions are of RR and RX types; all the register operands of these are in floating-point registers, but general registers are used in the usual way to specify addresses of main storage operands.

□ Floating-point instructions perform load, store, add, subtract, compare, multiply, and divide operations. Add and subtract instructions are available in both normalizing and unnormalizing forms; multiply and divide instructions always normalize. See Fig. 13.10 for a summary.

□ Action of addition or subtraction involves the comparison of characteristics and a right shift in the alignment step, then addition or subtraction, then normalization. Multiplication and division operations include a prenormalization step.

□ In addition to exceptions for specification, operation, and access, special exceptions for exponent overflow, exponent underflow, significance, and floating-point zero divide may occur. All except exponent underflow and significance always cause interrupt; interrupts on exponent underflow and significance are controlled by program mask bits 2 and 3.

□ Regression, the fitting of a linear equation to a set of data minimizing the squares of the deviations, is accomplished by accumulating sums and sums of squares and cross products, and then solving a set of linear equations.

■ P R O B L E M S   F O R   R E V I E W   A N D   I M A G I N A T I O N

13.1   Write short floating-point representations for the decimal numbers

3.0	12.0	−0.75
−3.0	24.0	−0.1875
6.0	4212.0	0.1
		0.3

13.2   What decimal numbers are represented by the following floating-point numbers?

4236ØØØØ	3F2ØØØØØ
C12FØØØØ	BF24ØØØØ
C31ØA68Ø	5EØØØØØØ

13.3   Show the normalized equivalents of the following:

41Ø1ØØØØ	Ø5ØØØØØ2
FFØØØØØ1	54ØØØ68E
CEØØ3CEØ	8ØØFØØØØ

13.4   In most binary computers, the characteristic is used as a power of 2. To get the same range of magnitudes that System/370 does, these computers need three more bits for their characteristics than are required by the System/370. System/370 thus gains three bits for significant digits; however, it loses some again because of the necessity of up to three leading zero bits in normalized numbers. Making the reasonable assumption that numbers with 0, 1, 2, and 3 leading zeros occur equally often, what is the net gain or loss in significant bits carried by the IBM System/370, compared to a binary 32-bit-word computer whose characteristics are powers of 2? What other advantages and disadvantages can you think of for the power-of-16 system?

13.5 Assuming that the contents of floating-point registers and storage locations are:

Floating-point register	0:	42345200	00000000
	2:	C01E0000	EC86904A
	4:	BE003456	00000000
	6:	3D2136E1	02D46A71
Main storage locations:	TT:	42439A72	
	UU:	00000000	
	VV:	46000000	
	WW:	FE200000	
	XX:	00200000	
	YY:	D8400000	
	ZZ:	BC345678	

prior to execution of *each* of the following instructions or segments, give results of each, including condition code and any exceptions generated.

a)	LPER	F0,F2	i)	AD	F4,=D'2'	q)	ME	F4,XX
b)	LCDR	F2,F6	j)	LE	F2,YY	r)	SE	F4,UU
c)	LNER	F2,F4		SDR	F0,F2	s)	ME	F4,UU
d)	CE	F4,ZZ	k)	AU	F4,ZZ	t)	DE	F4,UU
e)	LE	F0,ZZ	l)	ME	F2,YY	u)	DE	F4,XX
	CDR	F0,F4	m)	ME	F4,YY	v)	DE	F4,WW
f)	AE	F0,TT	n)	ME	F0,WW	w)	SE	F4,ZZ
g)	SE	F0,VV	o)	ME	F2,WW	x)	SU	F4,ZZ
h)	ADR	F0,F6	p)	ME	F2,XX	y)	LD	F4,=D'-8.0'
							MDR	F6,F4

13.6 The LCR instruction can produce an overflow; the LCER instruction cannot. Why?

13.7 If two numbers are compared by the C instruction and also by the CE instruction, will the results of the comparisons be the same? If the numbers are both positive, will the results be the same? If the numbers are both positive and, as floating-point numbers, normalized, will the results be the same? If the numbers are both negative and normalized, will the results be the same? If one number is positive and one negative, will the results be the same?

13.8   In what cases does the guard digit affect the result of a floating-point compare instruction?

13.9   When floating-point numbers are computed with rounding errors, a test for whether one number is equal to another should take account of the rounding errors and ask only whether they are *approximately* equal. For example, one may ask whether they agree to within some preassigned tolerance. Show several ways in which such a test can be programmed.

13.10 Show that the guard digit is necessary to ensure that multiplication of a number by 1 yields the original number.

13.11 In what cases does the guard digit affect the result of an unnormalized add or subtract instruction?

13.12 What principles would guide you in deciding, for a particular program or program segment, whether to allow interrupt on exponent underflow, and if so, what action should be taken by the interrupt processor? What actions might be taken, and under what circumstances, on an exponent overflow exception?

13.13 Put together and supplement the program segments of Figs. 13.7 and 13.8 so that a number in character form stored at main-storage locations INPUT to INPUT+14 as

INPUT: sign: + or −
INPUT+1 to INPUT+6:   integer
INPUT+7:   decimal point
INPUT+8 to INPUT+14:   fraction

is converted to floating-point form. Correct the segment to allow for a negative number whose integer part is zero.

13.14 Write a program segment that will convert the *fractional* part of a floating-point number to character form. You may assume that your segment is given a number whose magnitude is less than 1.

13.15 Derive the equations necessary to generate a least-squares regression function of the form $y = ax + bx^2$.

13.16 Derive the equations necessary to generate a least-squares regression function of the form $y = a_0 + a_1x_1 + a_2x_2$, where each observation consists of a measurement each of variables y, x_1, and x_2. Extend the Gaussian solution of linear equations to a set of three equations in three unknowns, and write a program segment to follow this procedure.

13.17 Suppose we have n linear equations in n unknowns, $x_1, \ldots, x_n$:

$$a_{11}x_1 + a_{12}x_2 + \cdots + a_{1n}x_n = c_1,$$
$$a_{21}x_1 + a_{22}x_2 + \cdots + a_{2n}x_n = c_2,$$

$$\cdots$$

$$a_{n1}x_1 + a_{n2}x_2 + \cdots + a_{nn}x_n = c_n.$$

The coefficients are stored consecutively as short floating-point numbers beginning at location COEF in the order $a_{11}, a_{12}, \ldots, a_{1n}, c_1, a_{21}, a_{22}, \ldots, a_{2n}, c_2, \ldots, a_{n1}, a_{n2}, \ldots, a_{nn}, c_n$, which is called storing the coefficient array row-wise. Use the Gaussian procedure to solve this set of equations, leaving the results $x_1, \ldots, x_n$ in consecutive locations starting at X. Assume during your first attempt that none of the diagonal coefficients are 0.

13.18 One of the time-honored procedures for finding the square root of a positive number A is the Newton-Raphson iterative scheme

$$x_{i+1} = x_i + \frac{1}{2}\left(\frac{A}{x_i} - x_i\right),$$

which from an initial estimate x_0 computes successive approximations $x_1, x_2, \ldots$ that converge to the square root of A. If the initial approximation is chosen as $x_0 = \frac{1}{2}(1 + A)$, which is greater than the square root of A, all the approximations are (theoretically, in the absence of round-off error) greater than the square root of A. Therefore a good criterion for stopping the iteration in a computer is that $x_{i+1} \geq x_i$. Program a segment that will use this procedure to compute a square root. Then, maintaining $x_0 > \sqrt{A}$, improve the procedure by computing an initial approximation x_0 whose exponent (characteristic -64) is approximately half that of A.

13.19 A reasonably efficient procedure for finding the natural antilog e^x of a number x is to use the Taylor series

$$e^x = 1 + x + \frac{x^2}{2!} + \frac{x^3}{3!} + \frac{x^4}{4!} + \cdots,$$

where $n!$ (read n factorial, where n is a positive integer) is the product of the integers from 1 to n. Computation can proceed by computing partial sums, adding on terms one at a time until the sum does not change any longer. Each term can be derived from the preceding one by

$$t_0 = 1, \quad t_i = \frac{xt_{i-1}}{i}, \quad i = 1, 2, \ldots$$

Program a segment that will compute e^x by this procedure for a given x. Then analyze the number of significant digits produced by the computation, considering both positive and negative values of x.

■ R E F E R E N C E S

Gear, C. W., "Numerical Software: Science or Alchemy?" in *Advances in Computers, Vol. 19*, edited by Marshall C. Yovits, Academic Press, New York, 1980. A thought-provoking paper on the problems of numerical computation.

IBM System/370 Principles of Operation, GA 22-7000, IBM Corporation. Reference on the floating-point instructions.

Johnston, Robert L., *Numerical Methods: A Software Approach*, Wiley, New York, 1982.

Knuth, Donald E., *The Art of Computer Programming, Vol 2: Seminumerical Algorithms (2nd ed.)*, Addison-Wesley, Reading, Mass., 1981. Chapter 4 includes a study of the properties of floating-point arithmetic.

14

DECIMAL ARITHMETIC

The IBM System/370 has three modes of arithmetic; it can perform arithmetic operations on integers represented in binary or in decimal, and on floating-point (binary) numbers. The decimal arithmetic seems at first superfluous, but as implemented in System/370 it offers a number of conveniences. First, the packed decimal representation, which allows fields of greatly varying sizes, is a very efficient one for storage of numbers. Also convenient are the conversions from character representations to binary integer and back, with packed decimal forms as intermediate.

But aside from the mere representation of numbers, the decimal arithmetic has advantages in a number of situations. First, if numbers to be treated exactly grow rather large, requiring more than 32 bits for an exact binary representation, yet are of foreseeably bounded size, decimal representation offers a precision greater than binary integer arithmetic and greater convenience, especially in conversions, than double-precision floating-point. Many accounting problems are of this type: numbers ranging into the millions of dollars must nevertheless remain exact to the penny.

There are other situations in which numbers must be computed and rounded to the nearest penny, and for which no other rounding rules will do. In these situations binary integer arithmetic could be used, but decimal arithmetic is more convenient and straightforward.

In still other situations either binary integer or decimal integer arithmetic would be satisfactory, but the fact that decimal arithmetic is storage-to-storage makes it more convenient than arithmetic in registers. One storage-to-storage addition can consume less space (but usually more time) than a load, add, store sequence.

Described in this chapter in more detail than previously are the packed decimal representation, the definition of decimal constants and symbols in assembler language, and the packed decimal instruction repertoire. Examples and a description of the possible exceptions close the chapter.

14.1 Packed Decimal Representations: Internal and Assembler Language

In the packed decimal form of a number, two decimal digits are packed into each byte, with the exception that the lower-order half of the low-order byte contains a sign code. The length of a number may be from 1 to 16 bytes, and therefore 1 to 31 decimal digits:

Each digit or sign is coded in four bits. The digits 0-9 are each coded into their natural binary representations 0000 to 1001; 1010 to 1111 are not permitted as digits. On the other hand, 1010 to 1111 are recognized as signs—1010, 1100, 1110, and 1111 as plus, and 1011 and 1101 as minus; 0000 to 1001 are invalid as signs. Thus

0001 1001	0110 1100

is recognized as +196,

1000 0000	0111 1101

is recognized as −807, but

0110 1100	1010 0001

has invalid representations of both digits and signs. Note that a negative zero is perfectly possible.

It is easier to show and understand packed representations if they are stated in hexadecimal. The valid digits are 0-9, the valid signs are A-F, with A, C, E, and F defined as +, B and D as −. So the two-byte field 196C represents +196, 807D represents −807, and 6CA1 has both signs and digits in inappropriate places. Though the codes A-F are all recognized as signs, the decimal arithmetic instructions produce only C for plus and D for minus.

The packed decimal constants in assembler language introduced in Chapter 6 are reviewed here. An operand of a DC statement defining a packed decimal constant is of the form P'decimal number' or PLn'decimal number'. The decimal number is a string of decimal digits, an optional decimal point, and an optional sign. The sign, if present, precedes the digits. The decimal point has no effect on the constant assembled and is allowed merely to help readability of the program. Thus P'3.25', P'+.325', P'325', and P'32.5' all define the same packed decimal constant, whose hexadecimal value is 325C. Signs C and D, the EBCDIC forms, are generated.

No boundary alignment is performed for packed decimal constants. If no length modifier is included, the number of digits given determines the length of the constant: 1 digit, 1 byte; 2 or 3 digits, 2 bytes; 4 or 5 digits, 3 bytes, etc., with an extra zero supplied as a high-order digit in the packed representation when necessary. When a length modifier (in bytes) is specified, the constant is further padded with high-order zeros or else loses high-order digits, depending on the specified length. Several constants can be defined in one DC operand, either by listing or by use of a duplication factor. The following statements generate the constants shown.

```
JONES   DC   PL4'-2.19'          0000219D
FZER    DC   6PL7'0'             six consecutive repetitions
                                 of 000000000000000C
TARIFF  DC   P'2.01,1.20,9.75'   201C120C975C
BG      DC   PL2'3296'           296C; note loss of digit
RT9     DC   P'-.21,.1474'       021D01474C
```

Decimal constants may also be defined in literals.

```
        MVC   RATE(2),=P'.26'
```

The DS statement used with a P-type operand will have the same syntax and define the same amount of space as the DC statement. In the absence of a specified value or length modifier, one byte will be reserved. Thus

```
GP3    DS   P        has length of one byte,
NXT1   DS   PL3      has length of three bytes, and
LAST   DS   P'4795'  has length of three bytes.
```

14.2 General Structure of the Decimal Instruction Set

All decimal arithmetic takes place in main storage, so all of the instructions are of SS type. The fields are of variable length, and the lengths of operands are not required to be equal, so the length field in each decimal instruction is split into $L1$, the length of the first operand (in bytes, not digits), and $L2$, the length of the second operand. The result always replaces the first operand, so the first operand field must be large enough to hold the result.

In assembler language, operands may be addressed as

$$D1(L1,B1)$$
$$D2(L2,B2)$$

where *D1*, *D2*, *L1*, *L2*, *B1*, and *B2* are absolute expressions, or as

$$E1(L1)$$
$$E2(L2)$$

where *E1* and *E2* are relocatable expressions, or as

$$E1$$
$$E2$$

where the lengths *L1* and *L2* may be supplied by the assembler. If *E1* or *E2* is a single relocatable symbol, the assembler would supply the length attribute of the symbol; if *E1* or *E2* is a more complicated relocatable expression, the assembler would supply the length attribute of the first symbol appearing in the expression. For example, if RECD is defined by

```
RECD      DC      P'-296'
```

an operand RECD in a decimal-arithmetic instruction is equivalent to RECD(2) since the symbol has a length attribute of 2.

As elsewhere, we speak of lengths *L1* and *L2* as actual lengths of the fields, as they would be specified in assembler language. Recall that in machine language instructions the length codes are each 1 less than actual operand lengths.

Arithmetic instructions are provided for addition, subtraction, multiplication, and division of packed decimal numbers. These instructions are supported by others for comparing numbers and moving numbers and parts of numbers. The add, subtract, compare instructions and an instruction equivalent to a load set condition codes; the values of the condition code have the same meanings as in other arithmetic modes. We shall now investigate the instructions in detail.

14.3   Add, Subtract, and Compare Instructions

The add, subtract, and compare instructions have assembler language mnemonics of

```
AP     Add Packed
SP     Subtract Packed
CP     Compare Packed
```

The add and subtract instructions place the sum and difference, respectively, of their two operands in the first operand field. For example, if locations and contents are

```
ACC          Ø1362C
RECD         296D
PAYB         181C
BALANCE      21347C
```

prior to execution of each of the following instructions, the results of the instructions will be as indicated.

AP	ACC(3),RECD(2)	ACC:	Ø1Ø66C
AP	BALANCE(3),PAYB(2)	BALANCE:	21528C
SP	BALANCE(3),PAYB(2)	BALANCE:	21166C
SP	ACC(3),BALANCE(3)	ACC:	19985D
SP	RECD(2),PAYB(2)	RECD:	477D
AP	RECD(2),ACC(3)	Overflow	

An overflow occurs if the result field cannot hold the result. In the last example, the second operand field was larger than the first, and an overflow resulted. If 842C is added to 258C, the result is also an overflow, since a three-byte field would be required to hold the sum. The second operand field may be larger than the first, however, if the result fits in the first operand field. For example, addition of Ø24C (first operand) and ØØØØ7Ø3C (second operand) results in a correct sum of 727C in the first operand field with no overflow; similarly 136D (first operand) added to Ø1Ø75C (second operand) yields a result of 939C, which fits nicely into the first operand field. In summary, an overflow occurs if for any reason the first operand field is too short to contain all the nonzero digits of the result.

The condition code is set by both AP and SP operations to

  0   if the result is zero,
  1   if the result is less than zero,
  2   if the result is greater than zero, and
  3   if an overflow occurs.

The sign of a zero is always set to + by the AP and SP instructions, except that when the zero is the residue of an overflow, the sign of the true result remains.

The compare instruction, CP, acts just like the subtract instruction except that it

- changes *no* bytes of main storage, and therefore
- cannot result in an overflow.

All digits of both fields are checked, and the shorter field is considered to be extended with high-order zeros if necessary. A negative zero is considered equal to a positive zero. Therefore the condition code, the sole result of the operation, is set to

  0   if the two operands are equal,
  1   if the first operand is less than the second operand, and
  2   if the first operand is greater than the second operand.

14.4   Moving a Packed Decimal Number

Moving a packed decimal number, as it is, from one main storage location to another is quite easy, but extending or reducing the field, especially on the right, is not so simple. Some instructions that help will be introduced in order.

The MVC instruction can obviously be used to move a packed decimal field just as it can move any string of bytes. The length of the field can remain fixed, or if only the last part of the field is moved, the field is effectively shortened, with several digits wholly abandoned.

The instruction ZAP (Zero and Add Packed) moves a number from the second operand location to the first operand location, filling high-order zeros in the first operand field if it is longer than the second operand field. The ZAP instruction is equivalent in function to a load instruction, but since lengths of first and second operands are specified separately, the instruction can expand or contract fields. The ZAP instruction also sets a condition code, exactly as though it had first placed a zero in the first operand location and then *added* the second operand to it, as with an AP instruction. Thus the condition code reports whether the number is zero, less than zero, or greater than zero, or whether an overflow occurred. For example, if

RECD	contains	296D
BALANCE	contains	21347C,
ZP	contains	ØØØØØC,

and

SLS	contains	ØØØ21C,

the following ZAP instructions will have the results indicated.

ZAP	RES(2),RECD(2)	RES:	296D	CC = 1
ZAP	RES(5),BALANCE(3)	RES:	ØØØØ21347C	CC = 2
ZAP	RES(2),ZP(3)	RES:	ØØØC	CC = 0
ZAP	RES(2),SLS(3)	RES:	Ø21C	CC = 2
ZAP	RES(2),BALANCE(3)	RES:	347C (overflow)	CC = 3

Observe how simple it is to move a number and possibly change its length by adding zeros or deleting digits on the left. To add zeros or delete digits on the right, the equivalent of a shift, use the SRP (Shift and Round Packed) instruction. This instruction did not exist in the older computers in the IBM System/360 and 370 family. Called Shift and round Decimal in the IBM manuals, this instruction has three operands.

Operand 1, with a four-bit length field, identifies the field to be manipulated. Operand 2 gives the shift count. The *B2* and *D2* are added as usual, and the last six bits are considered a signed integer. If positive (bit 26 is 0), bits 27–31 indicate the amount of left shift. If negative (bit 26 is 1), the 2's comple-

FIGURE 14.1 Examples of SRP

Instruction		Result in GROSS
SRP	GROSS(5),2,∅	∅43∅26500C
SRP	GROSS(5),∅(R11),5	∅43∅26500C
SRP	GROSS(5),1(R11),∅	43∅265∅∅∅C
SRP	GROSS(5),62,∅	∅∅∅∅∅43∅2C
SRP	GROSS(5),62,5	∅∅∅∅∅43∅3C
SRP	GROSS(5),58,5	∅∅∅∅∅∅∅∅∅C
SRP	GROSS(5),58(R11),5	∅∅∅∅∅∅∅43C

ment of bits 27–31 indicates the amount of shift to the right. Therefore a right shift of x positions is specified by a second operand of $64 - x$. In any case, shifting is by decimal digits, or half-bytes. Zeros are supplied for digit positions vacated by the shift.

The third operand, *I3*, which occupies the *L2* field in the usual SS format, specifies the rounding factor used in right shifts. The rounding factor is added, as a decimal digit, to the last digit shifted out of the field, and the carry, if any, is added to the rightmost digit kept; this addition is carried out disregarding the sign of the operand. The usual values to be coded in *I3* would be 0, in case no rounding is desired, and 5, which produces normal rounding.

Suppose field GROSS is a five-byte field containing (hex) ∅∅∅43∅265C, and register 11 contains ∅∅∅∅∅∅∅2. The instructions in Fig. 14.1 will have results indicated. Note that either the contents of register *B2* or the displacement *D2* or a combination of both can specify the shift count; in practice, most shift counts will be specified as decimal integers.

The rounding factor must be a valid decimal digit; if not, a data exception results. A decimal overflow exception results if significant digits are shifted left out of the field.

The condition code is set, even if a shift of zero positions is called for.

CC = 0   if the result is 0 (and a zero result is always made positive),

CC = 1   if the result is less than 0,

CC = 2   if the result is greater than 0,

CC = 3   if an overflow occurs.

A sequence of ZAP and SRP will accomplish any move of a decimal field, lengthening or shortening the field and positioning the number anywhere in the new field. For example,

```
        ZAP    GROSS(5),BAL(4)
        SRP    GROSS(5),63,5
```

will take a BAL field Ø43Ø265C, place it in a five-byte field GROSS, shift it right one position and round: ØØØØ43Ø27C.

14.5   Multiply and Divide Instructions

The packed decimal multiply and divide instructions have some slightly odd features that mostly result from the limitation of the results to the first operand location. The Multiply Packed (MP) instruction multiplies the numbers in the first and second operands, and places the result in the first operand field. The size of the second operand is limited: it may not be more than eight bytes (15 digits + sign), nor may it be larger than the first operand field, even if high-order zeros in the second operand would actually permit the product to fit. Since the length of the significant portion of a product is the sum of the lengths of the significant portions of the operands, the first operand field must contain high-order zeros equal to the length of the significant portion of the second operand. The restriction actually imposed is more stringent: the first operand is required to have high-order zeros equal to the field length, including all digits and signs, of the second operand. This guarantees at least one high-order zero in every product.

Suppose that we have the following contents of storage locations.

UNIT1	ØØ6ØØC
UNIT2	Ø3ØD
RATE1	ØØØØ411C
RATE2	ØØØØ2C
RATE3	ØØØ52D
TEN	Ø1ØC
FDC	ØØØØ791C

With these contents existing in storage prior to execution of each of the following instructions, the results will be as indicated.

MP	RATE2(3),UNIT2(2)	RATE2:ØØØ6ØD
MP	RATE3(3),UNIT2(2)	Invalid: only three high-order zeros
MP	RATE1(4),UNIT1(3)	Invalid
MP	RATE1(4),UNIT+1(2)	RATE1:Ø246600C
MP	FDC(4),TEN(2)	FDC:ØØØ791ØC

The ZAP instruction can be used to extend the first operand field with high-order zeros before a multiplication.

The first operand of the Divide Packed instruction (DP) is the dividend and the second operand is the divisor. The *quotient and remainder* replace the dividend in main storage. The quotient occupies the high-order portion of the first operand field, and the remainder occupies the low-order portion. The remainder will always have the same length as the divisor and, even when zero, the same sign as the dividend. Therefore the length of the quotient is $L1 - L2$. The sign of the quotient is determined algebraically from the signs of the dividend and divisor, even if the quotient is zero. The length of the divisor is restricted to be less than the length of the dividend, and in no case greater than eight bytes. If the quotient cannot be held in the space allotted to it, the result is a decimal divide exception, but we shall see more about exceptions in the next section.

For example, suppose that SUM contains Ø Ø34Ø75C, and that QT contains 2ØØC. The instruction

$$\text{DP} \quad \text{SUM(4),QT(2)}$$

will leave 17ØCØ75C in place of SUM. The quotient is 17ØC, which is addressed at SUM; its length is $4 - 2 = 2$. The remainder is Ø75C, which is addressed at SUM+2.

As further examples, consider the following contents of fields.

TOT1	Ø Ø34Ø75C
TOT2	Ø Ø ØØ64Ø1ØD
TOT3	Ø ØØØØØ ØØ316C
UNIT1	2ØØC
UNIT2	ØØ5D
UNIT3	ØØ32ØC
TEN	Ø1ØC

With these contents in storage prior to execution of *each* of the following instructions, the results will be as indicated, with quotient and remainder bracketed.

DP	TOT2(5),UNIT2(2)	TOT2: 128Ø2C ØØØD
DP	TOT2+1(4),UNIT2+1(1)	TOT2: ØØ 128Ø2C ØD
DP	TOT2+1(4),UNIT2(2)	Invalid
DP	TOT2(5),UNIT2+1(1)	TOT2: ØØ128Ø2C ØD
DP	TOT1(4),UNIT2+1(1)	TOT1: Ø6815D ØC
DP	TOT2(5),UNIT1(2)	TOT2: ØØ32ØD Ø1ØD
DP	TOT3(6),UNIT3(3)	TOT3: ØØØØØC ØØ316C
DP	TOT3+3(3),UNIT3(3)	Invalid: no space for quotient
DP	TOT2(5),TEN(2)	TOT2: Ø64Ø1D ØØØD

Note the treatment of signs and the lengths of the various results.

In general, one may say that the number of leading zeros required in the first operand must be two plus the number of leading zeros in the second operand, although if the leading nonzero digit of the dividend is less than the leading nonzero digit of the divisor it may in effect be counted as a leading zero. You are urged to test this rule in various examples.

The condition code is not affected by the DP instruction.

14.6   Exceptions

Decimal arithmetic instructions are liable to some of the same exceptions as are other instructions: *addressing*, *protection*, and to an *operation* exception if the decimal feature is not installed. When in a MP or DP instruction the length of the second operand is greater than 8, a specification exception with interrupt occurs. In these cases the operation is suppressed, so contents of storage are unchanged.

If the quotient in a DP instruction would be too large for the available space, or if the divisor is zero, a *decimal divide* exception occurs, the divide operation is suppressed, and an interrupt is taken.

A *data* exception can arise in any of the instructions AP, SP, ZAP, SRP, CP, MP, and DP (and also the CVB instruction introduced in Chapter 6). Each of these instructions checks every half-byte it processes for a proper sign or digit code. If a digit code 0–9 appears in a sign position or a sign code A–F in a position that should contain a digit, the result is a data exception. The data exception is also taken if the first operand of a multiply decimal instruction has too few high-order zeros. A third cause of a data exception is improper overlap of first and second operand fields; in each of these instructions it is permissible to have the rightmost bytes of the operands coincide (you can add a number to itself, for example), but any other overlap of fields is prohibited.

One last exception is *decimal overflow*. This exception occurs when the result of an AP, SP, SRP, or ZAP instruction cannot be held in the available field. The result is truncated on the left, but lower-order digits and sign are exactly as they would be in a longer field that was sufficient to hold the result. For example, addition of 360C (first operand) and 02713C (second operand) places 073C in the first operand field; this is the low-order portion of the correct sum.

On decimal overflow the condition code is set to 3. Interrupt depends on bit 1 of the program mask: if this bit is 0, no interruption occurs, but interrupt does take place if this bit is 1.

14.7   Examples

This section illustrates the use of the decimal arithmetic instructions and also some of the standard manipulations performed on packed decimal numbers.

First, suppose that you have a field of length 7 named EXTEN, in which there are assumed to be five decimal places (and therefore eight digits before the assumed decimal point). Suppose that you wish to *round* the number in this field to the nearest cent (or hundredth), placing the result with its two decimal digits at a six-byte field CHARGE. Since the field EXTEN is longer than CHARGE, you must shift and round *before* moving to CHARGE:

```
SRP    EXTEN(7),61,5
ZAP    CHARGE(6),EXTEN(7)
```

This has the possible disadvantage of losing the original contents of EXTEN. If the field CHARGE were seven bytes long, you would move first

```
MVC    CHARGE(7),EXTEN
SRP    CHARGE(7),61,5
```

Second, if you wish to set or change the sign of a packed decimal number whose sign is represented by A, B, C or D (not E or F), you can do the job easily with logical operations. If the sign of a number is at, say FIELD+6, you can

set the sign to +:	NI	FIELD+6,B'11111110'
set the sign to −:	OI	FIELD+6,B'00000001'
reverse the sign:	XI	FIELD+6,B'00000001'

If the sign could be E or F (a PACK instruction on an unsigned field would leave a sign code of F), as well as A, B, C or D, the situation is more complicated. The sign at FIELD+6 can be set to minus, for example, by

```
NI    FIELD+6,X'F0'
OI    FIELD+6,X'0D'
```

To set a sign to plus is even easier;

```
OI    FIELD+6,X'0F'
```

The easiest way to reverse a sign may be to multiply the number by −1.

```
MP    FIELD(6),P'-1'
```

However, as explained in Section 14.5, this requires that FIELD contain at least a high-order byte of zeros. Because the ZAP instruction always produces a sign code of C or D, you can use instead the sequence

```
ZAP    FIELD(7),FIELD(7)
XI     FIELD+6,B'1'
```

Consider the following billing problem. Suppose there is a list of items and that the count of items in the list is (a binary integer) in register 3. Each item consists of a four-byte packed decimal quantity (an integer) followed by a five-byte packed decimal unit price, with four decimal places. These fields occupy the first nine bytes of a 20-byte record for each item; the items start at location ITEM and follow each other immediately. The problem is to compute quantity times unit price for each item, then round the total to two decimal places (cents) and store the result in the 10th through 15th bytes of the record. Finally, keep a running sum of the totals, and keep the grand total in an eight-byte field GRANDTOT.

Addressing in this problem requires some attention. If the address of the current item record or block is kept in register 4, it can be used to address the

FIGURE 14.2   Accumulating quantity times price

```
ITEMBLK   DSECT
ITMQUANT  DS      PL4
ITMPRICE  DS      PL5'1.0000'
ITMPROD   DS      PL6'1.00'
          DS      CL5


FIG1402   CSECT


          ZAP     GRANDTOT(8),=P'0'
          LA      R4,ITEM
          USING   ITEMBLK,R4
          L       R3,NRITEMS
* REPEAT
ITEMLP    ZAP     PROD(9),ITMPRICE(5) UNIT PRICE TO PROD AREA
          MP      PROD(9),ITMQUANT(4) MULTIPLY BY QUANTITY
          SRP     PROD(9),62,5   ROUND TO CENTS
          MVC     ITMPROD(6),PROD+3 MOVE PRODUCT TO ITEM AREA
          AP      GRANDTOT(8),PROD+3(6) ADD TO GRAND TOTAL
* . INCREMENT ITEM ADDR. AND DECREMENT NO. OF ITEMS REMAINING
          LA      R4,20(,R4)     PASS TO NEXT ITEM
* UNTIL ITEMS REMAINING (R3) = 0
          BCT     R3,ITEMLP
* ENDREPEAT
```

fields of the block. The definition of the fields in an item block in a DSECT makes the programming much clearer than using, for example,

$$\text{MVC} \quad 9(6,R4),\text{PROD}+3$$

In the loop, register 4 can be increased by 20 and the REPEAT-UNTIL can be accomplished by a BCT on register 3.

Figure 14.2 shows a program segment for this task. The product is developed in a nine-byte area PROD and has four decimal places. The SRP instruction rounds the product to the nearest cent, and the MVC instruction moves the rounded product to the item area. Note that the multiplication requires a product area of nine bytes, but it is quite reasonable to dispense with the upper two bytes of the rounded product. (Why?)

The final example is a questionnaire analysis. Suppose that 80-byte records containing responses to questionnaires contain in bytes 20–39 single-digit answers to questions. The responses of interest are the digits 0–9; other characters may code uninteresting responses such as "no answer" or "question does not apply." For each of the 20 questions, we want the *average* (*mean*) of the responses made in the 0–9 range and the *mode*, which is the response of greatest frequency.

For each of the 20 questions we maintain a 30-byte area containing

- 10 two-byte counters, one each for the responses 0–9, in that order;
- a two-byte counter of digits 0–9;
- a two-byte counter of other responses;
- a three-byte sum of the responses;
- three bytes to contain mode and the two-byte average (two decimal places).

We keep each counter and sum as a packed decimal field.

The logic needed in the segment is extensive enough that it is a good idea to outline the procedure first. Shown in Fig. 14.3 is the procedure in a structured pseudo-code that is almost identical to the structure to be put in remarks statements in the program segment itself. Let us then examine the implementation strategy of the segment, which is shown in Fig. 14.4. As we move through the inner loop, starting at LOOP2039, we keep in register 4 the address of the beginning of the area of counters and sums pertaining to the current question, and in register 3 the address of the current character position. We use registers 6 and 7 for loop control—that is, testing the contents of register 3 for exit from the loop. We shall use the response itself, 0–9, to help us compute the address of the field in which it is to be counted. For this purpose the digit must be converted to binary and multiplied by 2 (with a SLA instruction), and the result added to the address of the counter for the digit 0. The outer loop (MAINLOOP) involves nothing particularly new except the setup of the areas of sums

FIGURE 14.3   Procedure for analyzing a questionnaire

```
Set sums and counters to zero
WHILE there are records to be read
   READ a record
   DO FOR each character position 20 to 39
      IF character is in the range 0–9
         Add 1 to counter of digits 0–9
         Add digit to SUM of digits 0–9
         Add 1 to one of the counters for individual digits 0–9
      ELSE Add 1 to counter of uninteresting characters
Compute average and mode for each question:
FOR each character position 20 to 39 DO
   IF counter of digits 0–9 ≠ 0
      Compute average
      Compute mode:
      Set largest counter to count of zeros
      DO FOR digit = 1 to 9
         IF count (digit) ≥ largest counter
            Set largest counter = count (digit)
      Store largest counter as the mode
```

FIGURE 14.4 Program segment for analyzing a questionnaire

```
********************************************************************
*** SEGMENT TO READ 80-CHAR. RECORDS,
*** COMPUTE AVERAGE AND MODE OF DIGITS 0-9
*** IN CHARS. 20 - 39 OF THE RECORDS
********************************************************************
*** INITIALIZE SUMS AND COUNTERS TO ZERO
          LA    R8,20
          LA    R9,CTAREA
* FOR INDEX = 20 TO 0, INCR -1, DO
* . SET A 30-BYTE AREA TO ZEROS
ZEROLOOP  MVC   0(30,R9),ZEROAREA
          LA    R9,30(,R9)
          BCT   R8,ZEROLOOP
* ENDFOR
********************************************************************
*** READ RECORDS, INCREMENT SUMS, COUNTS
********************************************************************
* WHILE THERE ARE RECORDS TO READ
* . READ A RECORD (EODAD TO AVCOMP IS EXIT FROM WHILE)
MAINLOOP  GET   IN,REC
* . INITIALIZE FOR LOOP
          LA    R3,REC+20      CHAR. POSITION 20
          LA    R6,1
          LA    R7,REC+39
          LA    R4,CTAREA      AREA FOR CHAR. POSITION 20
* . DO FOR CHAR. POSITION 20 TO 39
* . . IF CHAR. IS IN THE RANGE 0 - 9
LOOP2039  CLI   0(R3),C'0'
          BL    NOT09
          CLI   0(R3),C'9'
          BH    NOT09
* . . . THEN ADD TO COUNTERS OF 0 - 9
          AP    20(2,R4),=P'1' 0 - 9 COUNTER
          PACK  DBL(8),0(1,R3)
          AP    24(3,R4),DBL+7(1) ADD DIGIT TO SUM
          CVB   R5,DBL
          SLA   R5,1           COMUPUTE ADDR. OF APPROPRIATE
          AR    R5,R4            COUNTER OF INDIVIDUAL DIGITS,
          AP    0(2,R5),=P'1'   THEN COUNT THE DIGIT
          B     L2039INC
* . . . ELSE COUNT AS UNINTERESTING RESPONSE
NOT09     AP    22(2,R4),=P'1'
* . . ENDIF (CHAR. IS IN THE RANGE 0 - 9)
L2039INC  LA    R4,30(,R4)
          BXLE  R3,R6,LOOP2039
* . ENDFOR (CHAR. POSITIONS 20 TO 39)
          B     MAINLOOP
* ENDWHILE (THERE ARE RECORDS TO READ)
********************************************************************
*** COMPUTE AVERAGE AND MODE FOR EACH OF 20 POSITIONS
********************************************************************
AVCOMP    LA    R8,20
          LA    R9,CTAREA
* DO FOR CHAR. POSITIONS 20 TO 39
* . IF COUNTER OF DIGITS 0 - 9 NOT = 0
AVLOOP    CP    20(2,R9),=P'0'
          BNH   AVLOOPIN
```

continued

```
* . . THEN COMPUTE AVERAGE...
          ZAP    DIVD(4),24(3,R9)
          SRP    DIVD(4),2,0    DIVD HAS 2 TRAILING ZEROS
          DP     DIVD(4),20(2,R9) QUOT. IS 2-BYTE FIELD AT DIVD
          MVC    28(2,R9),DIVD
* . . ALSO COMPUTE MODE
          LA     R4,2(,R9)      R4 SET TO ADDR. OF COUNT(DIGIT), DIGIT = 1
          LR     R5,R9          ADDR. OF LARGEST COUNT, INIT. TO COUNT(0)
          LA     R6,2
          LA     R7,18(,R9)
* . . DO FOR DIGIT = 1 TO 9
* . . . IF COUNT(DIGIT) > LARGEST COUNT,
MODELP    CP     0(2,R4),0(2,R5)
          BL     MODELPIN
* . . . . THEN SET LARGEST COUNT TO COUNT(DIGIT)
          LR     R5,R4
* . . . ENDIF (COUNT(DIGIT) > LARGEST COUNT)
MODELPIN  BXLE   R4,R6,MODELP
* . . ENDFOR (DIGIT = 1 TO 9)
* . . CONVERT FROM ADDR. OF COUNTER OF LARGEST DIGIT TO DIGIT ITSELF
          SR     R5,R9
          SRA    R5,1
          CVD    R5,DBL
          MVC    27(1,R9),DBL+7 STORE IN PACKED FORM
* . ENDIF (COUNTER OF DIGITS 0 - 9 NOT = 0)
AVLOOPIN  LA     R9,30(,R9)
          BCT    R8,AVLOOP
* ENDFOR (CHAR. POSITIONS 20 TO 39)
* NOW READY FOR OUTPUT


* CONSTANTS AND STORAGE AREAS REQUIRED BY SEGMENT
DBL       DS     1D
CTAREA    DS     20CL30           AREAS FOR COUNTING 20 CHAR. POSITIONS
*                BYTES 0-19 : 2-BYTE AREAS FOR COUNTING EACH OF DIGITS 0 - 9
*                      20-21 : COUNTER OF DIGITS 0 - 9
*                      22-23 : COUNTER OF NOT 0 - 9
*                      24-26 : SUM OF DIGITS IN RANGE 0 - 9
*                         27 : THE MODE
*                      28-29 : THE AVERAGE
ZEROAREA  DC     12PL2'0'         INITIALIZE ZEROS FOR A CHARACTER POSITION
          DC     PL3'0',PL1'0',PL2'0'
REC       DS     CL80
DIVD      DS     PL4
```

and counters, which illustrates the definition of packed decimal storage and constants.

The closing portion of the segment, beginning at AVCOMP, provides an example first of a division. In order to obtain two decimal places in the quotient, the dividend is extended two places on the right, thus creating two decimal places in the dividend. Be sure to verify for yourself that the instructions do, in fact, produce an average and that they cannot result in overflow. The computation of the mode is of course merely a search for the largest of the ten counters. The addresses of next counter to be compared and largest counter found so far are kept in registers 4 and 5, respectively. After all ten counters are examined, the address of the counter is converted to a packed decimal number in the reverse of the process that earlier generated the address of a counter.

This example could have been done in binary arithmetic, but decimal arithmetic is convenient and reasonably efficient in the use of storage. In particular, an instruction like AP 2Ø(2,R4),=P'1' can take the place of the three instructions, load, add, and store. Some convenience is lost, however, by not being able to index fields.

m a i n   i d e a s

- □ The packed decimal representation allows expression of numbers of from 1 to 31 digits; the digits are packed two per byte, with the sign occupying the lowest-order half-byte.

- □ The packed decimal instructions are all of SS type, with separate length specifications for the two operands. All packed decimal arithmetic is performed in main storage, and it can sometimes be quite convenient.

- □ The instructions introduced for manipulation are summarized in Fig. 14.5.

FIGURE 14.5   Instructions for manipulation of packed decimal fields

Name	Type	Action	Cond.[3] code	Exceptions[4]
AP	SS[2]	$S1 \leftarrow c(S1) + c(S2)$	(a)	A, D,DF
SP	SS[2]	$S1 \leftarrow c(S1) - c(S2)$	(a)	A, D,DF
ZAP	SS[2]	$S1 \leftarrow c(S2)$	(a)	A, D,DF
CP	SS[2]		(b)	A, D
MP	SS[2]	$S1 \leftarrow c(S1) \times c(S2)$		A,S,D
DP	SS[2]	$S1 \leftarrow$ [quotient, remainder of $c(S1)/c(S2)$][5]		A,S,D,DK
SRP	SS[1]	$S1 \leftarrow c(S1)$[6]	(a)	OP,A, D,DF

Notes
1. SS with $L1$ specifying length of operand field, $S2$ is shift count, $I3$ is rounding factor. Operands written $S1(L1),S2,I3$.
2. SS with separate length specification for each operand.
3. Condition codes are set to
   a) 0 if result = 0   b) 0 if $Op_1 = Op_2$
       1 if result < 0   1 if $Op_1 < Op_2$
       2 if result > 0   2 if $Op_1 > Op_2$
       3 if overflow
4. Exception codes:
   OP: Operation (if System/360)   D: Data
     A: Access   DF: Decimal overflow
     S: Specification   DK: Decimal divide
5. Quotient occupies bytes 0 to $L1-L2-1$: remainder occupies bytes $L1-L2$ to $L1-1$.
6. Field shifted left by $S2$ or right by $64 - S2$; right shifts rounded by $I3$.

■ **PROBLEMS** FOR REVIEW AND IMAGINATION

14.1 Given that the contents of main storage locations are as follows *prior to the execution of each instruction*, show the result of each instruction:

Main storage locations	Contents		Instructions
GBS	21346C	ZAP	FERMAG+1(3),NLQC(2)
WHP	ØØ12ØD	AP	GBS(3),NLQC(2)
NLQC	9ØØC	SP	GBS(3),MPHY(4)
MPHY	ØØØØØ24D	CP	NLQC(2),MPHY(4)
FERMAG	223344556C	SP	NLQC(2),WHP(3)
DRGN	ØØØØ325ØØD	AP	NLQC(2),GBS(2)
		MP	MPHY(4),NLQC(2)
		MP	WHP(3),MPHY+2(2)
		MP	WHP(3),MPHY+3(1)
		DP	DRGN(5),NLQC(2)
		DP	DRGN(5),WHP(3)
		DP	DRGN(5),WHP+1(2)
		SRP	DRGN(5),61,5
		SRP	DRGN(5),61,Ø
		SRP	DRGN(5),3,5

14.2 There is an instruction MVN (MoVe Numerics), of SS type with single length, that moves the low-order four bits(!) of each byte of the second operand to corresponding positions in the first operand. Thus if GG contains 123456 and HH contains 789ABC, the instruction

MVN   GG(3),HH

will move the half-bytes 8, A, C from HH to corresponding positions in GG, which is thus changed to 183A5C. Show how this can be useful in moving the *sign* of a packed decimal number. What other uses can you think of for MVN?

14.3 There is an instruction similar to MVN that is named MVZ (MoVe Zones). It moves the *high-order* four bits of each byte from the second operand to the first operand field. The names of the MVN and MVZ instructions are derived from their possible use in moving numeric and zone parts of *zoned decimal* numbers. Can you think of any uses for the MVZ instruction in manipulating packed decimal numbers?

14.4 There is an ingenious instruction MVO (MoVe with Offset), of SS type with two length subfields. This instruction moves the second operand, starting at the rightmost half-byte, to the first operand location, *start-*

ing at the high-order half of the rightmost byte. No checking for digits or signs is performed. Zeros are filled on the left of the first operand, or high-order digits of the second operand are ignored. For example, if QUANT contains 36247D and NEWF contains 6093271C,

$$\text{MVO} \quad \text{NEWF(4),QUANT(2)}$$

will change NEWF to 0003624C. Show how MVO can be used (perhaps with MVN) in shifting a packed decimal number an odd number of places to the left or right. What other uses can you think of for MVO?

14.5 From your knowledge that multiplication is performed by repeated shifting and addition and that division is performed by repeated subtraction, figure out the logical mechanism by which the MP and DP instructions are performed. It helps to postulate a working register of up to eight bytes that holds the second operand during either operation and that conceptually is aligned in turn "under" various portions of the first operand. Make sure your mechanism explains all the rules by which the instructions operate.

14.6 Write a program segment to perform in packed decimal arithmetic a calculation of an employee's take-home pay. Suppose that available fields are

GROSS   4 bytes   gross earnings for the month in dollars and cents

EXEMPT 2 bytes   number of exemptions, an integer

FICA   4 bytes   earnings for the year to date that have been subject to FICA withholding in dollars and cents

DEDUCT 3 bytes   deductions for the month

Compute federal withholding, FED, as

$$14\% \quad \text{of} \quad (\text{GROSS}-(\text{EXEMPT}*\$50.00))$$

Compute FICA tax in a field FICATAX as

$$6.7\% \quad \text{of} \quad \text{GROSS}$$

but only until a total of \$36,000 for the year has been taxed. Update the field FICA by the amount taxed. Then compute take-home pay as

$$\text{GROSS-FED-FICATAX-DEDUCT}$$

Taxes withheld should be rounded *down*, that is, truncated; it hardly costs anything and makes somebody feel good.

14.7 Manufacture a small amount of sample data and simulate execution of the parts of the program segment in Fig. 14.4 in order to understand them better. Reprogram the entire segment using binary integer instead of packed decimal arithmetic. Compare the two segments as to space required, number of instructions to be executed, limitations to be placed on the data, and straightforwardness of programming (a useful concept this, since it is inversely proportional to debugging time).

14.8 Add to the program segment of Fig. 14.4 an additional section computing the *median* of the responses in any card column. Roughly speaking, the median is the middle number of the sorted set of data. More precisely, it is a number such that no more than half of the data are larger than the number and no more than half are smaller. This computation is a little more difficult than the computation of the mode; if the median, by the definition given, should be fractional, take the next larger integer.

14.9 Write a program that will produce a mortgage amortization table. Input a card containing principal of the mortgage, nominal annual interest rate (e.g., 0.0900 for 9%), and the monthly payment. The printed table should consist of a line for each month of the life of the mortgage. Each line should contain
   a) the time period: 1, 2, 3,...;
   b) the principal outstanding at the beginning of the month;
   c) the interest for the month, computed as principal at the beginning of the month times annual interest rate divided by 12, rounded to the nearest cent; and
   d) the portion of monthly payment applied to the reduction of the principal, computed as the difference between the monthly payment and the interest.

The principal outstanding at the beginning of the next month is obtained by the appropriate subtraction. In the last period the payment required may be less than a full regular payment; it should be printed and labeled.

   Printing the table with decimal points and without a sign appearing as part of the last digit of each number can be a major bother in this program. The next chapter shows how the ED instruction eases this burden.

■ REFERENCES ▬▬▬▬▬▬▬▬▬▬▬▬▬▬▬▬▬

Grauer, Robert T., and Marshal A. Crawford, *The COBOL Environment*, Prentice-Hall, Englewood Cliffs, N.J., 1979, or *Structured COBOL: A Pragmatic Approach*, Prentice-Hall, Englewood Cliffs, N.J., 1981. If you are going to study COBOL, which uses the decimal instruction set, these texts best relate COBOL to the computer structure and action of the System/370 instructions, and therefore will be very effective for you.

IBM System/370 Principles of Operation, GA 22-7000, IBM Corporation. Description of the decimal arithmetic instructions.

TRANSLATE, EDIT, AND EXECUTE INSTRUCTIONS

Some powerful special-purpose instructions representative of the sophistication found in instruction repertoires of modern computers are presented in this chapter. Just as early experience in numerical computation showed that keeping track of number magnitudes was a very common problem, leading to development of floating-point arithmetic instructions, more recent experience in nonnumeric problems has shown that certain tasks are widespread, leading to development of instructions that handle the problems well.

One of the instructions is a code translation instruction, and a second is a search instruction. Two others are designed for editing numbers into a nice form for printing; they are tailored to the problem and fairly simple to use but are among the most complex instructions in the IBM System/370 instruction repertoire. The fifth instruction has two functions: it permits execution of a single instruction outside the usual sequence of instructions, and it provides convenient modification of the length codes, register addresses or "immediate" operands that are specified in the second byte of an instruction.

15.1 Translate Instructions

This section introduces two similar instructions: TRanslate (TR) and TRanslate and Test (TRT). Each is an SS-type instruction, with a single length specification that refers to the first operand only.

The purpose of the TR instruction is to translate the codes in the bytes of the first operand into other codes. The second operand is a table of codes defining the translation. Each byte b of the first operand acts as an index to the table; the sum of the second operand address and this index addresses the byte that replaces the first operand byte: the byte b is thus replaced by $c(S2 + b)$. For example, if the second operand address is ØØF6Ø4, an argument byte C6 is replaced by the byte at location ØØF6Ø4+C6 = ØØF6CA.

Think of the table in the second operand as a table of function values of one byte each and the first operand as a string of arguments to the function. The TR instruction replaces each argument by its function value. The table used in the second operand is ordered by the possible argument values and is therefore normally 256 bytes long. The length of the first operand is specified in the instruction and may be from 1 to 256 bytes.

As an example, suppose that your task is to change a few codes in an 80-byte record produced by a particularly benighted text editor. Brackets are represented by hexadecimal 51 and 61, and are to be changed to parentheses, which are hexadecimal 4D and 5D. Also, a code of hexadecimal 69 must be translated into a semicolon (hexadecimal 5E). Therefore, bytes in the source string whose hexadecimal values are 51, 61, and 69 are to be translated into 4D, 5D, and 5E, respectively. All other codes are to remain unchanged.

A 256-byte table must be set up, perhaps at a location TRTAB1, to be the second operand of a TR instruction; the table will contain bytes ØØ, Ø1, Ø2, Ø3,..., FF, but 51 will be replaced in the table by 4D, 61 by 5D, and 69 by 5E. Thus each code except these three is translated into itself. If the 80-byte record is at location REC, the codes will be translated as desired by the instruction

```
        TR    REC(8Ø),TRTAB1
```

Suppose the first character of REC is a space, which is hexadecimal 4Ø. The number 4Ø is added to TRTAB1, and the function byte at TRTAB1+4Ø, which of course happens to be 4Ø, replaces the 4Ø at REC. Other bytes are translated similarly into copies of themselves, but when a 51, for example, is encountered, it is replaced by the function byte at TRTAB1+51, which is 4D. All data are considered valid, and the translation proceeds until all 80 bytes are translated. The second operand and the condition code are unchanged. If a segment of the string at REC before the TR instruction is

4Ø	C1	51	D1	61	7A	7E	F1	69	4Ø	4Ø
b	A	[	J	]	:	=	1	what	b	b

(using b to represent a space) then the same portion of the string after the TR instruction will be

4Ø	C1	4D	D1	5D	7A	7E	F1	5E	4Ø	4Ø
b	A	(	J	)	:	=	1	;	b	b

A second type of standard chore is also handled very nicely by the TR instruction. This is the rearrangement problem, in which a string of bytes is to be moved from one area in main storage to another but is to be rearranged in the process. The rearrangement is accomplished by letting the string to be moved serve as the table in the second operand of a TR instruction, while the first operand is a series of pointers into the table. For example, suppose a 20-byte string is stored at SOURCE, preceded by one blank at SOURCE-1. If we desire to have at RESULT

> 3 spaces,
> bytes 3–7 of the string at SOURCE,
> 1 space,
> bytes 17–19 from SOURCE,
> 2 spaces,
> bytes 8–11 from SOURCE,

we first store at RESULT the following pattern, where the division into lines is only for visual correspondence with the preceding specification.

```
ØØ ØØ ØØ
Ø4 Ø5 Ø6 Ø7 Ø8
ØØ
12 13 14
ØØ ØØ
Ø9 ØA ØB ØC
```

The move with rearrangement is accomplished by

```
TR    RESULT(18),SOURCE-1
```

Wherever it appears in the pattern at RESULT, the argument byte ØØ is translated into the function byte at (SOURCE-1)+ØØ, which is the space. The byte Ø4 is translated into the function byte at (SOURCE-1)+Ø4, which is byte 3 of the string at SOURCE. The translation process fetches and stores whatever characters we wish and also makes repetitions and deletions of the second operand string as we wish. Note that the original string in the second operand is left intact by the TR instruction, but the pattern is destroyed. To rearrange more than one source string according to the same pattern, define the pattern as a constant, perhaps named PATT, then do the rearrangement by

```
MVC    RESULT(18),PATT
TR     RESULT(18),SOURCE
```

The TRanslate and Test (TRT) instruction uses an argument string as first operand and refers to a table of function bytes in exactly the same way that the TR instruction does. However, the argument string is not changed; the TRT instruction is a *search* for the first argument byte whose corresponding function byte is nonzero. The address of the argument byte found is placed in bit positions 8–31 of register 1, without alteration of bits 0–7, and the corresponding nonzero function byte is inserted into bit positions 24–31 of register 2, without alteration of bits 0–23. The operation terminates either when a nonzero function byte is found or when the end of the argument string is reached, and the condition code is set:

CC = 0: All referenced function bytes are zero.

CC = 1: A nonzero function byte is found before the argument string is exhausted.

CC = 2: The last argument byte corresponds to a nonzero function byte.

Thus the condition code is set to 0 or 2 if the entire first operand is examined, and to 1 if the search produces a nonzero function byte without examining the entire string. If no nonzero function byte is found, registers 1 and 2 are not altered.

The TRT instruction can, for example, find the length of the word or symbol beginning in a given location and extending to the first space. Suppose that an 80-character string begins at STMT. A 256-byte table at SRCHBLNK consists entirely of zeros except for the byte at SRCHBLNK+64(64=X'40'=C' '). The instruction sequence

```
LA    R1,STMT+80
TRT   STMT(80),SRCHBLNK
S     R1,=A(STMT)
```

will leave in register 1 the length of the character string up to the first space, or 80 if there was no space (in this case the TRT instruction does not alter register 1, so the address STMT+80 remains). If the first character of the string is a space, the length will quite reasonably be reported as zero.

In combination with the EXecute instruction, the TRT instruction can be used to find addresses and lengths of all words delimited by spaces or other punctuation, as you will see in Section 15.3.

The TR and TRT instructions are liable only to protection and addressing exceptions.

15.2 Editing

One of the most common tasks in the use of a computer is generating the output in a readable format. The CVD and UNPK instructions help enormously and are reasonably sufficient for some output. However, in many cases more gracious formats are desired, with

■ leading zeros eliminated,

■ punctuation inserted,

■ forcing of zeros after the decimal point,

■ designation of negative numbers by a CR suffix or by a sign just before the first significant digit,

■ a dollar sign preceding the first significant digit.

The EDit (ED) instruction and the EDit and MarK (EDMK) instruction were designed to provide these features. The two instructions are quite similar but quite complex, so first the features of the EDit instruction are introduced here one by one, with examples.

The general structure of the ED instruction is somewhat like the TRanslate instruction, but it is also a generalization of the UNPK instruction. ED is an SS-type instruction with a single length; the length refers only to the first operand, called the *pattern*. Bytes of the second operand, which must be in packed decimal form and are called the *source*, are used as needed. Bytes of the pattern may be any of four kinds, with the definitions

Code	Name
20	Digit selector
21	Significance starter
22	Field separator
All others	Message characters

The first byte of the pattern, however, is called the *fill character*; it is usually a space, and during editing, it replaces other bytes before significance is established. A *significance indicator* is kept during execution of the instruction; this indicator keeps track of whether zeros or message characters are to be considered leading zeros, whether punctuation is to be replaced by the fill character, or whether significant zeros and punctuation are to be printed. The significance indicator is *off* at the beginning of the instruction.

In the simplest case, in which the pattern consists only of the fill character followed by digit selectors, the action of the ED instruction is as follows. The pattern is examined from left to right. For each digit selector encountered, a digit is fetched from the source. If the digit is nonzero, it is unpacked into a zoned decimal byte by the attachment of bits 1111 (therefore yielding a printable digit), to replace the digit selector byte; it also turns *on* the significance indicator. If the digit fetched is zero and the significance indicator is off, the digit selector in the pattern is replaced by the fill character. If the digit fetched is zero and the significance indicator is on, the zero is expanded into a zoned digit to replace the digit selector. These three cases are summarized in the following table.

Conditions on meeting digit selector		Result character	Significance indicator set
Nonzero digit	Significance indicator on or off	Zoned digit	On
Zero	Significance indicator on	Zoned digit	On
Zero	Significance indicator off	Fill character	Off

For example, if the pattern at RESLTA is 40202020 and the packed decimal number at PD is 020C (decimal 20), the instruction

$$\text{ED} \quad \text{RESLTA(4),PD}$$

will yield the result 4040F2F0 at RESLTA, which is the character representation of *bb*20, where *b* represents a space. In execution of the instruction, the fill character is 40 (space). The first digit selector byte in the pattern causes the first zero to be fetched from PD; the significance indicator is off so the fill character is stored. The second digit selector causes the 2 to be fetched and inserted in the pattern; it also causes the significance indicator to be turned on. Because the significance indicator is on when the second zero is fetched, the zero is inserted in the pattern. The action taken on the sign will be described below.

Message characters included in the pattern do not cause fetching of a digit from the source string. They are subject to the influence of the significance indicator, however: if the indicator is off, the message character is replaced by the fill character. This feature is designed to enable the insertion of commas and decimal points at the right time. For example, if RESLTB contains

40	20	6B	20	20	20	6B	20	20	20	4B	20	20
b	ds	,	ds	ds	ds	,	ds	ds	ds	.	ds	ds

and the packed decimal number at PDB is

00	23	07	90	6C

the instruction

$$\text{ED} \quad \text{RESLTB(13),PDB}$$

will transform the pattern into

40	40	40	40	F2	F3	6B	F0	F7	F9	4B	F0	F6
b	*b*	*b*	*b*	2	3	,	0	7	9	.	0	6

The first comma is replaced by the fill character because the significance indicator is not yet on; the second comma and the decimal point follow the digit 2, which turned on the indicator, so they remain unchanged in the pattern.

You may often want to force the decimal point and following zeros, for example, to print even if no previous digit is nonzero. Do this by means of the significance starter character. This character acts like a digit selector in fetching a digit, but even if the digit is zero, the significance indicator is turned on (to affect the *following* digits, not the current one). Therefore, whereas the pattern RESLTB above would produce the printed string *bbbbbbbbbbbb*6 if the source were 000000006C, the pattern RESLTC of

4Ø	2Ø	6B	2Ø	2Ø	2Ø	6B	2Ø	2Ø	21	4B	2Ø	2Ø
b	ds	,	ds	ds	ds	,	ds	ds	sig. st.	.	ds	ds

and a source PDC of

ØØ	ØØ	ØØ	ØØ	6C

under the instruction

$$\text{ED} \qquad \text{RESLTC(13),PDC}$$

would produce

4Ø	4Ø	4Ø	4Ø	4Ø	4Ø	4Ø	4Ø	4Ø	4Ø	4B	FØ	F6
b	*b*	*b*	*b*	*b*	*b*	*b*	*b*	*b*	*b*	.	0	6

Each time a digit is fetched from the high-order four bits of a source byte, the low-order four bits are searched for a sign code. If a minus sign is present, the next digit to be fetched (if any) will be from the next byte. If a *plus* sign is present, not only will the next digit to be fetched be taken from the next byte, but also the *significance indicator will be turned off*! Thus the signficance indicator plays a dual role. At the end of the instruction it becomes a sign indicator, on for minus and off for plus. Its function in controlling message characters is still important, as shown in the following example, in which the negative numbers are indicated by characters CR following the number. Let RESLTD be the pattern

4Ø	2Ø	2Ø	21	4B	2Ø	2Ø	4Ø	C3	D9
b	ds	ds	sig. st.	.	ds	ds	*b*	C	R

and PDD be

Ø1	34	8D

Then the instruction

$$\text{ED} \qquad \text{RESLTD(1Ø),PDD}$$

will yield

4Ø	4Ø	F1	F3	4B	F4	F8	4Ø	C3	D9
b	*b*	1	3	.	4	8	*b*	C	R

but if PDD is

Ø4	97	2C

the same instruction and pattern will yield

4Ø	4Ø	F4	F9	4B	F7	F2	4Ø	4Ø	4Ø
b	b	4	9	.	7	2	b	b	b

where the CR symbols in the pattern are replaced by the fill character because the plus sign at PDD+2 turned off the significance indicator.

The field separator symbol in a pattern is replaced by the fill character, but it turns the significance indicator off. This allows several numbers (fields) to be edited by one ED instruction.

The ED instruction sets a condition code:

CC = 0: last source field is all zeros;

CC = 1: last source field is less than zero;

CC = 2: last source field is greater than zero.

The EDit and MarK (EDMK) instruction is identical to the EDit instruction except that it also places in bits 8–31 of register 1 (leaving bits 0–7 unchanged) the address of a result character that is a zoned source digit fetched when the significance indicator was off—in other words, the address of the first significant digit of the result. We can use this address in placing a dollar sign or minus sign in front of the first significant digit. If the significance indicator is turned on by the significance starter byte, however, no address is loaded into register 1 by the EDMK instruction, so an appropriate address should be loaded *before* the EDMK instruction.

For example, suppose that the pattern RESLTE is

4Ø	2Ø	2Ø	21	4B	2Ø	2Ø	4Ø	C3	D9
b	ds	ds	sig.	.	ds	ds	b	C	R
			st.						

and the field PDE contains

Ø1	34	8D

The instruction sequence

```
LA      R1,RESLTE+4
EDMK    RESLTE(1Ø),PDE
BCTR    R1,Ø
MVI     Ø(R1),C'$'
```

produces

4Ø	5B	F1	F3	4B	F4	F8	4Ø	C3	D9
b	\$	1	3	.	4	8	b	C	R

as follows:

1. The address of the decimal point is placed in register 1, so that if significance is forced, the decimal point will be considered the "most significant digit."
2. The pattern is edited into bb13.48bCR, and the address RESLTE+2, the address of the digit 1, is placed in register 1.
3. BCTR R1,Ø subtracts 1 from the contents of register 1.
4. The dollar sign is moved to RESLTE+1, just before the most significant digit.

FIGURE 15.1   Action of ED and EDMK instructions

	Condition				Results		
Pattern character	Significance indicator	Source digit	Low-order half of source byte		Result character	New state of significance indicator	Address placed in reg. 1[3]
Digit selector	Off	0	[1]		Fill char.	Off	No
Digit selector	Off	1–9	Not plus		Source dig.	On	Yes
Digit selector	Off	1–9	Plus		Source dig.	Off	Yes
Digit selector	On	0–9	Not plus		Source dig.	On	No
Digit selector	On	0–9	Plus		Source dig.	Off	No
Message char.	Off	[2]	[2]		Fill char.	Off	No
Message char.	On	[2]	[2]		Message char.	On	No
Signif. starter	Off	0	Not plus		Fill char.	On	No
Signif. starter	Off	0	Plus		Fill char.	Off	No
Signif. starter	Off	1–9	Not plus		Source dig.	On	Yes
Signif. starter	Off	1–9	Plus		Source dig.	Off	Yes
Signif. starter	On	0–9	Not plus		Source dig.	On	No
Signif. starter	On	0–9	Plus		Source dig.	Off	No
Field separator	[1]	[2]	[2]		Fill char.	Off	No

Notes
1) Irrelevant to the result.
2) Source digit not examined.
3) EDMK instruction only.

If the source had been ØØØ76C, the printable result would be *bbb$.76bbb*.
The ED and EDMK instructions are liable to several exceptions:

Operation: if the decimal feature is not installed,

Protection: store or fetch violation,

Addressing: attempt to use nonexistent storage locations,

Data: sign code (A-F) in high-order half of source byte.

A summary of the rules for forming result characters and for turning on
and off the significance indicator is presented in Fig. 15.1.

15.3 The EXecute Instruction

The EXecute (EX) instruction is an RX-type instruction that directs the execution of an instruction called the *subject* instruction, which is addressed by the second operand. The EX instruction is unlike a branch instruction in that (unless the subject instruction is a branch) the next instruction to be executed is the one following the EXecute; the subject instruction is in effect a one-instruction subroutine. Furthermore, the subject instruction is modified before execution (though not altered at its main storage location): bits 8–15 of the instruction are ORed with bits 24–31 of register *R1* to form the second byte of the instruction actually executed. Bits 8–15 of the instruction are the length codes in some instructions, register addresses in others, immediate operand bytes in others; the EXecute instruction is the best way we have of varying these specifications.

Suppose that you want to move a string of characters from B to A, but the length (actually, you need 1 less than the true length) has been computed and is in, say, register 9. You may include the definition

```
VARMVC     MVC   A(Ø),B
```

in an area of constant and symbol definitions, and include the instruction

```
           EX    R9,VARMVC
```

whenever you want the MVC instruction, with length supplied by register 9, executed. The instruction to be executed after the MVC instruction will be the one following the EX instruction.

Any instruction other than another EX instruction may be a subject instruction for EXecute; an attempt to EXecute another EXecute causes an *Execute exception* and interrupt. Other exceptions possible are access, and specification, which occurs if the second operand address, the address of the subject instruction, is odd. Of course, any subject instruction is subject to the usual rules for its type.

If the subject instruction is a branch and the branch is taken, control does not return to the instruction after the EXecute but follows the branch.

As illustration consider the use of TRT and EX instructions together in finding addresses and lengths of "words" of text. Words are composed of *text symbols*, including letters, digits, and perhaps a few special characters, delimited by *punctuation symbols*, which include spaces and most of the special characters. Two tables are defined for TRT instructions: one, named TEXTSYM, has zeros corresponding to punctuation symbols and nonzero function bytes corresponding to text symbols; using it as the second operand of a TRT instruction enables search for the first text symbol in a string. The other table, named PUNCTSYM, enables search for the first punctuation symbol; it has zeros corresponding to text symbols, and nonzero function bytes corresponding to punctuation symbols. The two are used alternately in a segment that records the addresses and lengths of words in the 80-character string beginning at TEXT. Assume a space exists at TEXT+80, just after the string; it simplifies exit from the loop. The length and address of each word are to be stored together in that order in a four-byte area; these areas begin at location WORDADDR.

FIGURE 15.2   Finding lengths and addresses of words in text

```
************************************************************************
*** SEARCH THE 81 CHARACTERS OF TEXT
*** FOR STRINGS OF TEXT SYMBOLS, AND STORE
*** LENGTHS AND ADDRESSES STARTING AT WORDADDR
************************************************************************
          LA    R8,WORDADDR
          LA    R4,80          LENGTH-1 OF REMAINING TEXT
          LA    R5,TEXT        ADDR. OF REMAINING TEXT
* WHILE THERE ARE TEXT SYMBOLS REMAINING
TEXTLP    EX    R4,SRCHTEXT    SEARCH FOR TEXT SYMBOL
          BZ    TEXTEXIT
* . STORE ADDR. AND LENGTH OF STRING OF TEXT SYMBOL
          ST    R1,0(,R8)      ADDR. OF SUBSTRING
          AR    R4,R5
          SR    R4,R1          LENGTH OF REMAINING TEXT
          LR    R5,R1          POSITION NEXT SEARCH
          EX    R4,SRCHPUNC    SEARCH FOR NEXT PUNCTUATION SYMBOL
          SR    R1,R5          LENGTH OF SUBSTRING STORED IN
          STC   R1,0(,R8)         ONE BYTE IN WORD WITH ADDRESS
* . PREPARE TO LOOK FOR NEXT STRING
          SR    R4,R1          LENGTH OF REMAINING TEXT
          AR    R5,R1          ADDR. FOR NEXT SEARCH
          LA    R8,4(,R8)      UPDATE POINTER TO ADDRESS AREA
          B     TEXTLP
* ENDWHILE
TEXTEXIT  DS    0H



* CONSTANTS AND STORAGE DEFINITIONS INCLUDE
SRCHTEXT  TRT   0(0,R5),TEXTSYM
SRCHPUNC  TRT   0(0,R5),PUNCTSYS
```

A segment for the problem is shown in Fig. 15.2. Register 5 always contains the address of the byte to start the next search from, and register 4 the length of the portion of string remaining to be searched. It is this use of register 4 to vary the length of the string to be searched that necessitates use of the EX instructions. Register 4 is ORed with the length code in each of the TRT instructions, and since the length codes in main storage are zero, the contents of register 4 *becomes* the effective length code. If the string at TEXT began, for example, with *bb*NOW IS THE TIME, the first TRT would insert in register 1 the address of the N. This address is stored as the address of the first substring (word) and also becomes the starting point for the next search. The next TRT finds the blank between NOW and IS, and the length of the word NOW, which it stores. The next time through the loop, the address and length of IS are found and stored; the process continues until the search yields no more text symbols.

Since MVCL and CLCL are interruptible instructions, special care must be taken if they are to be subject instructions of EXecute. First, neither *R1*, *X2*, or *B2* used in the EXecute instruction should be among those modified by the MVCL or CLCL instruction. Second, the area containing the EXecute instruction itself should not lie within the first (destination) operand area of MVCL. The reason for these restrictions is that if the MVCL or CLCL is interrupted, the EXecute instruction and the registers it uses must remain intact for reinterpretation upon resumption of the program.

m a i n   i d e a s

- ☐ The TR instruction enables translation of a string from one set of eight-bit codes into another.

- ☐ The TRT instruction enables a search of a string for the first byte containing one of any desired set of codes.

- ☐ The ED and EDMK instructions enable the unpacking of decimal numbers into fields with leading zero suppression, commas, decimal points, and other characters, and sign control and floating currency symbol placement.

- ☐ The EX instruction permits the execution out of sequence of one instruction, whose second byte is modified by the contents of a register. This allows for convenient modification of lengths, masks, and register specifications.

- ☐ These five instructions illustrate the tailoring of highly specialized instructions to the convenient performance of common but complex tasks.

- ☐ Be careful in using TRT and EDMK, because they implicitly use register 1 and TRT also uses register 2. This can be inconvenient but is worse than that if you do not realize that these instructions change the contents of registers 1 and 2.

■ **PROBLEMS** F O R   R E V I E W   A N D   I M A G I N A T I O N

15.1 Suppose that each byte of a 16-byte string at SPREAD contains a number whose first four bits are zeros. Write a TR instruction and necessary function table to translate the hexadecimal digit in the low-order half of each byte into a character representation of the digits 0–9 or A–F.

15.2 Given a 32-bit word at Y, write a sequence of three TR instructions (and about three other instructions), and design tables to go with them, that will produce an eight-character string of printable characters representing the hexadecimal digits at Y. *Hint:* The first TR can translate the high-order hexadecimal digit of each byte; for example, all codes 00 to 0F would be translated into F0. The second TR can similarly translate the low-order digits, and the third TR can merge the two 4-character strings.

15.3 Write a TRT instruction (and table) that will determine whether the six-byte character string at U contains only the digits 0–9.

15.4 In addition to searching a field for the first space, as was illustrated in Section 15.1, a TRT instruction can test the character string for illegal symbols; if different function byte codes are used for illegal symbols than for the space, a test of register 2 after the TRT instruction will indicate what was actually found. Illustrate by designing an instruction sequence and function table that will test an assembler language statement for characters that are illegal in the name field.

15.5 A mailing address is stored in a 160-byte region, with a slash (/) marking the end of each line (the text is carefully edited, so this is the only way the slash occurs). Use the TRT instruction to move each line of the address to the beginning of a fixed area for printing, so that the address will be printed in its usual block format. The EX instruction helps too.

15.6 Write an edit instruction and pattern that will produce a six-byte field from a two-byte packed decimal number. The numbers are to be printed with two digits before and one after the decimal point and a minus sign, if any, following the last digit; if the number is less than 1.0, one leading zero is to be printed. Examples are

$$67.9$$
$$3.4-$$
$$\emptyset.4$$

15.7 Write a sequence of instructions to edit a field and insert a dollar sign before the first nonblank character, but use ED and then TRT instead of EDMK.

15.8 Write a sequence of instructions, including EDMK, that will edit a number into some pattern you choose, but indicate a negative number by a minus sign just before the first nonblank character.

15.9 In order to maintain sign control in an ED or EDMK instruction, one must have significance starters and digit selectors in the pattern equal to the number of digits in the packed decimal number being edited. This means that the number of digits allowed must always be odd. Is this a burdensome restriction? If not, why not? If so, why, and what can we do about it?

15.10 Write an edit instruction and pattern that will unpack a three-byte packed decimal field (guaranteed not to be negative) into a string of seven characters to appear as dollars and cents, but with asterisks preceding the first nonzero digit. This is useful when printing checks.

15.11 Write a TR instruction and a translation table that will convert all lowercase letters to uppercase.

15.12 Write a program segment that will convert all uppercase letters to lowercase *except* the first letter that immediately follows a period and one or more spaces.

15.13 Write a sequence of one or two instructions (*hint*: use TR) that will create a string exactly reversing the sequence of the characters of a 30-byte string.

15.14 An organization keeps a file that includes a person's name in each record. The name is stored as last name followed by an asterisk (*) and then the first name, and optional middle name or initial. The length of the name field is 30 characters. Write a program segment that will convert a name field into first–middle–last name format (perhaps for addressing envelopes). For example, STRUBLE*GEORGE W would be converted to GEORGE W STRUBLE. Perhaps the hardest part is to know how long the first and middle name portion is; Problem 15.13 may help.

15.15 This chapter has introduced several specialized instructions. There are rumors that still more specialized instructions will be added to newer computers; a possible list follows. The rumors are denied, but some people claim that these instructions are already in their computers' instruction repertoire. List evidence for and against the current existence of these, and add your own candidates to the list.

BRI	Branch to Random Instruction
BT	Break Tape
EMIF	Erase Most Important File
EPB	Execute Program Bug
EPI	Execute Programmer Immediate
FIIL	Fall Into Infinite Loop
HBWT	Hide Bug until Worst Time
HCF	Halt and Catch Fire

IB	Insert Bug
OBB	Overflow Bit Bucket
ROD	Roll Over and Die
RWD	ReWind Disk
RWP	ReWind Printer
RYT	Rotate Your Tires
ZSI	Zap Space Invader

■ REFERENCE

IBM System/370 Principles of Operation, GA22-7000, IBM Corporation. Complete description of the instructions.

16

MACRO DEFINITION AND CONDITIONAL ASSEMBLY

In earlier chapters several macros were introduced. The OS/VS assembler also gives programmers the opportunity to define their own macros and use them. Such macros can be included in a program to be assembled, or they can be kept in a macro library where the assembler can find them when they are needed. The ASSIST system also includes macro definition capabilities.

In using the macro definition capability, you have access to variables that can be set, changed, and tested *during assembly*; in testing these variables, you can direct the assembler to jump around and even loop through the same statements in the assembler language program. This powerful facility, called *conditional assembly*, is most useful in macro definitions, but it is available for use outside macro definitions too.

If you do a good deal of programming, you will find that there are certain instruction sequences that, with variations, are repeated often. The basic patterns of these sequences can be defined as macros, and the minor variations can be accomplished by use of parameters to the macros and by conditional assembly; once such a macro is defined, one of the sequences can be inserted into your program through a macro instruction with the appropriate parameters. Macros can be simple or complex, but you will be more than a casual programmer before you bother to define any macros at all.

This chapter is an introduction, but not a comprehensive one, to the marcro definition features. If your interest is piqued by this introduction, you will want to find more details in the IBM Assembler Language manual. You will also find it quite instructive to study the macro libraries at your disposal—the IBM-supplied system macros, the CMS macro library, the ASSIST macros, and whatever your installation has—to see how the features are used.

16.1 Outline of Facilities

The heart of the facilities for macro definition and conditional assembly is the provision for *variable symbols*, variables which are given values during assembly of the program. One important kind of variable symbol is the *symbolic parameter*, a dummy symbol used in the definition of a macro. During expansion of a macro instruction at its proper place in the assembler language program, actual parameters specified in the macro instruction are substituted for the symbolic parameters in the macro definition; this provides flexibility in the use of macros.

A second class of variable symbol is the SET *symbol*. There are SET symbols with *arithmetic* (integer) values, others with *character* values, and still others with logical values, which are 0 or 1 (the manual calls them *binary*, so henceforth we shall too). In each of these types there can be *local* SET symbols, which are specific to each macro expansion and *global* SET symbols, whose values can be set in one macro and used in another, or be set and used outside macros entirely. Any of the SET symbols can be set, changed, and tested, and therefore used in various ways to control assembly.

In addition to the symbolic parameters and SET symbols, you the programmer have certain *attributes* at your disposal. The attributes *type* and *length* of symbolic parameters can be used by the macro to adjust to specific types and lengths of the actual parameters used in a macro instruction. The attribute *number* refers to a parameter list, and enables the macro to determine how many parameters are actually supplied in a macro instruction. With this information the macro can adjust to variation in the number of parameters. The *count* attribute represents the number of characters in the value of a variable symbol; through the use of a *substring* notation, the programmer can select one or more characters of a variable symbol, and thus control activities of the assembler based on the detailed contents of variable symbols; the count attribute helps in making and controlling the substring selections.

A third type of variable symbol is called a *system variable symbol*; there are six of them, set by the assembler but available for use in macros. We will show the use of only the system variable symbol &SYSNDX.

Finally, in order to make effective use of attributes, symbolic parameters, and SET symbols, the assembler instructions AIF and AGO enable modification of the *sequence* of inclusion of statements in the source program. *Sequence symbols* can be attached to statements; AGO (unconditional) and AIF (conditional) are branch instructions that direct the assembler to consider next the statement with a certain sequence symbol rather than the physically next one in the source program or macro definition. Thus we can build control structures, including loops, for the *assembler* to follow during assembly! In the following sections each of these facilities is described in greater detail.

16.2   Definition and Use of a Macro

The specific form of any macro definition must include, in order,

1. a header statement,
2. a prototype,
3. model statements, and finally
4. a trailer statement.

The header and trailer statements are very simple: The header has no name and no operands, and the operation MACRO. The trailer may have a name, which can be any sequence symbol (sequence symbols will be defined in Section 16.4), the operation MEND (for Macro END), and no operands. Neither header nor trailer may have a remarks field.

The prototype follows the header statement. In the operation field is the name of the macro being defined. The name may be any symbol except the mnemonic operation code of any machine or assembler instruction or the name of another macro in the same program. A symbolic parameter may be placed in the name field, and a sequence of symbolic parameters, separated by commas, in the operands field.

A *symbolic parameter* is written as an ampersand (&) followed by one to seven letters and digits, of which the first must be a letter. Thus &N, &GZA, &ZABCDEF, and &Z123456 are valid symbolic parameters.

Valid forms of macro prototypes are therefore

```
          ADD    &A,&B,&C,&D
&NAME     MOVE   &TO,&FROM,&LENGTH
&N        ABORT
          FILL
```

Model statements follow the prototype statement. Model statements can be rather normal machine or assembler instructions, and they follow more or less the same rules. The name field may be blank, or it may contain a sequence symbol or a variable symbol. The operation field may contain any machine or assembler instruction abbreviation (with a few exceptions such as END), the name of another macro, or a variable symbol.

The operands field may be formed as an operands field for any instruction, and it may include ordinary symbols and variable symbols. Apostrophes must be paired; characters inside a pair of apostrophes form a quoted string, and only within quoted strings are blanks permitted in the operands field. To represent a single apostrophe within a quoted string you must write two apostrophes. Exceptions to apostrophe pairing rules are made for attributes, which are discussed in Section 16.3. The ampersand has special meaning as the first character of a variable symbol; any other use of an ampersand requires two of them. A comments field may be written after the operands field.

The model statements in a macro may include a variety of different kinds of statements. There may be ordinary instructions to be assembled, although they may include variable symbols. Constant and storage definitions may be included. The use of SET symbols and conditional assembly also means that model statements may include declarations of SET symbols, statements that give values to SET symbols, and the AIF and AGO statements. In the next two sections we will show how to use these statements.

To use a macro, a programmer writes a macro instruction. The macro instruction, as shown in Chapters 5 and 12, has the name of the macro in the operation field, an optional symbol in the name field, and usually some parameters in the operands field. Comments may be included after the operands field. Operands entries must conform to the rules covering the use of apostrophes, ampersands, and blanks as noted previously. In addition, equal signs are permitted only as the first character of an operand or in a quoted string or paired parentheses. Parentheses must be paired; that is, there must be an equal number of right and left parentheses, and they must be divisible into pairs in which the left parenthesis precedes the right parenthesis. (Parentheses in quoted strings are, of course, not subject to the pairing rule.)

Expansion of macro instructions precedes assignment of any addresses by the assembler. The macro instruction is replaced by an appropriate (depending on parameters and execution of conditional assembly statements) sequence of model statements of the macro named. The symbolic parameters in the model statements are replaced by corresponding parameters from the macro instruction; SET symbols are replaced by their current values, and sequence symbols are removed. The result is a sequence of ordinary machine and assembler instructions.

For example, consider the macro definition of HALFSWAP shown in Fig. 16.1. If one of the statements in a program is

```
SWAP5H  HALFSWAP  R5,FW
```

the macro instruction is expanded into a modified sequence of the model statements of the macro definition. The symbolic parameter &LABEL is replaced by SWAP5H, &REG by R5, and &SV by FW, as shown in Fig. 16.2. Statements produced by the expansion of macro instructions are flagged in the listing with a + preceding position 1.

FIGURE 16.1   Definition of the HALFSWAP macro

```
        MACRO
&LABEL  HALFSWAP  &REG,&SV
&LABEL  ST        &REG,&SV
        SLL       &REG,8
        IC        &REG,&SV
        SLL       &REG,8
        IC        &REG,&SV+1
        MEND
```

FIGURE 16.2   Expansion of the HALFSWAP macro

```
SWAP5H      HALFSWAP R5,FW
+SWAP5H     ST      R5,FW
+           SLL     R5,8
+           IC      R5,FW
+           SLL     R5,8
+           IC      R5,FW+1
```

Symbols and variable symbols can be concatenated to form single symbols. If the second of two symbols to be concatenated is a variable symbol, its name is merely appended to the first symbol, as in SYMBOL&VAR. If something beginning with a letter, digit, left parenthesis, or period is to follow another symbol, a period is placed between them, as in &VAR.SYMBOL. Values of variable symbols are concatenated with the other things (and the period removed) during expansion of the macro. The example shown in Fig. 16.3 illustrates a concatenation. The concatenation of &TYPE to the operation codes in each of the model instructions allows the same macro to be used for integer addition, or for single- or double-precision floating-point addition. For example, the macro instruction

```
        LPAC        ADD     E,T,DELTA,TPRIME
```

will be expanded into

```
        +LPAC       STE     R2,SAVE
        +           LE      R2,T
        +           AE      R2,DELTA
        +           STE     R2,TPRIME
        +           LE      R2,SAVE
```

FIGURE 16.3   An addition macro

```
        MACRO
&N      ADD         &TYPE,&A,&B,&C
&N      ST&TYPE     R2,SAVE
        L&TYPE      R2,&A
        A&TYPE      R2,&B
        ST&TYPE     R2,&C
        L&TYPE      R2,SAVE
        MEND
```

Note that not only must T, DELTA, and TPRIME be defined as symbols in the main program, but SAVE must also.

If a parameter is omitted in a macro instruction, a blank character value is assigned. Appropriate commas ensure that macro instruction parameters correspond to the desired symbolic parameters. For example, with the macro ADD defined as in Fig. 16.3, the macro instruction

```
        ADD     ,CT,=F'1',CT
```

is replaced by the expansion

```
        +       ST      R2,SAVE
        +       L       R2,CT
        +       A       R2,=F'1'
        +       ST      R2,CT
        +       L       R2,SAVE
```

Parameters corresponding to both &N and &TYPE are omitted, and therefore &N and &TYPE are replaced by blanks.

Operands in a macro instruction can be supplied in a *sublist*, which is enclosed in parentheses. Individual parameters in a sublist can be used individually in the macro definition; the name of the entire symbolic parameter is followed by a position index in parentheses: &A(2) refers to the second operand supplied in the sublist corresponding to the symbolic parameter &A. Figure 16.4 shows an example of the use of a sublist in the macro definition and macro instruction. The real value of having a sublist, however, appears when we can use conditional assembly features to accommodate sublists of varying length, as will be shown in Section 16.4.

FIGURE 16.4   An ADD macro using a sublist

```
        MACRO
&S      ADD     &TYPE,&A,&C                   ⎫
&S      ST&TYPE R2,SAVE                       ⎪
        L&TYPE  R2,&A(1)                      ⎪  Macro
        A&TYPE  R2,&A(2)                      ⎬  definition
        A&TYPE  R2,&A(3)                      ⎪
        ST&TYPE R2,&C                         ⎪
        L&TYPE  R2,SAVE                       ⎪
        MEND                                  ⎭


  LPAC  ADD     E,(Y,CORR1,CORR2),YP    Macro instruction
 +LPAC  STE     R2,SAVE                       ⎫
 +      LE      R2,Y                          ⎪
 +      AE      R2,CORR1                      ⎬  Expansion
 +      AE      R2,CORR2                      ⎪
 +      STE     R2,YP                         ⎪
 +      LE      R2,SAVE                       ⎭
```

Symbolic parameters may be *positional*, as the preceding macros illustrated, or they may be *keyword* parameters. The distinction is one we have seen in Job Control Language, and we have already seen it in macros; remember that in Chapter 12, parameters to GET, PUT, and OPEN were positional, but DCB macro instructions specified keyword parameters. Keyword parameters have some advantages:

- a macro instruction may give keyword parameters in any sequence;
- the keywords help document the macro instructions;
- the macro may give a default value to a keyword parameter; and
- the macro instruction may omit that parameter if the default value is the one desired.

Let us consider an example. The FOR-DO control structure initializes three registers and starts the loop with a BXH instruction. We might like to incorporate this chunk of code into a macro, as shown in Fig. 16.5. There are several assumptions: a set of three registers is available for looping control, beginning with an odd-numbered register—7 is the default. We assume that starting value and limit value are numbers that can be put in an A-type constant and that the increment is positive. The assumptions are included in macro remark statements. The period in position 1 makes them comments in the macro definition only; they will *not* be reproduced in the macro expansion, as they would be if position 1 contained an asterisk.

Figure 16.6 shows how two different macro instructions use the FORDO macro. In the first, START and INCR are not given, so the defaults are used. However, the first macro instruction supplies a value of REG, thus overriding the default. We are not used to seeing things like R3+2 used as register oper-

FIGURE 16.5 Definition of a macro to initiate a FOR-DO structure

```
          MACRO
&LABEL    FORDO &START=1,&LIMIT=,&INCR=1,&LOOPAD=,&NEXTAD=,&REG=R7
.****************************************************************
.*** SETS UP REGISTERS FOR A FOR-DO STRUCTURE USING BXH.
.*** STARTING VALUE AND LIMIT VALUE MUST BE APPROPRIATE
.***    FOR A-TYPE CONSTANTS. THEY WILL BE FIRST AND LAST
.***    CONTENTS OF REGISTERS &REG WHEN BODY OF LOOP IS
.***    EXECUTED.
.*** INCREMENT MUST BE POSITIVE.
.*** THREE REGISTERS MUST BE AVAILABLE, STARTING WITH
.***    AN ODD-NUMBERED REGISTER. DEFAULT IS REGISTERS 7 - 9.
.*** STRUCTURE WILL BE COMPLETED BY
.***       B      &LOOPAD
.*** FOLLOWED BY AN INSTRUCTION WITH LABEL &NEXTAD
.****************************************************************
&LABEL    L      &REG,=A(&START-&INCR)
          LA     &REG+1,&INCR
          L      &REG+2,=A(&LIMIT)
&LOOPAD   BXH    &REG,&REG+1,&NEXTAD
          MEND
```

FIGURE 16.6   Two expansions of the FORDO macro

```
           FORDO LIMIT=20,LOOPAD=STEP3FOR,NEXTAD=STEP4,REG=R3
+          L     R3,=A(1-1)
+          LA    R3+1,1
+          L     R3+2,=A(20)
+STEP3FOR  BXH   R3,R3+1,STEP4

           FORDO LOOPAD=STEP6FOR,NEXTAD=STEP7,START=BUF,INCR=4,
                 LIMIT=BUF+76
+          L     R7,=A(BUF-4)
+          LA    R7+1,4
+          L     R7+2,=A(BUF+76)
+STEP6FOR  BXH   R7,R7+1,STEP7
```

ands in instructions, but they are absolute expressions, and fully valid. In the second macro instruction, START and INCR are given values, but REG is allowed its default. The sequence of the parameters is different from that in the proto- types; this is one of the things that keyword parameters allow. What would happen if you neglected to give a value to NEXTAD? It would have a (default) null value, and produce an instruction like

```
+STEP6FOR    BXH    R7,R7+1,
```

The assembler would expand the macro instruction without complaint but in a later phase would not be able to assemble the expanded instruction.

There are several ways in which you will be able to improve the FORDO macro once you have learned about conditional assembly and a few other fea- tures; we will return to it.

16.3   Set Symbols, System Variable Symbols, and Attributes

This section introduces the properties of SET symbols, system variable sym- bols, and attributes, and shows how SET symbols are defined and changed. This is preliminary to Section 16.4, where SET symbols and attributes are used to control conditional assembly.

A SET symbol is a type of variable symbol; its name is written the same as the name of a symbolic parameter: an ampersand followed by one to seven let- ters and digits, the first of which must be a letter. The distinction between sym- bolic parameters and various types of SET symbols is made by the manner of introduction: symbolic parameters by listing in a prototype statement, SET symbols by explicit declaration.

There are local and global SET symbols. *Local* SET symbols are particular to the macro in which they are used, and moreover to the expansion of a par- ticular macro instruction. The use or value of a local SET symbol named

&VARSYM in one expansion of a particular macro instruction has no bearing on the use or value of &VARSYM in another expansion of the same macro or on the use or value of a variable symbol named &VARSYM in any other macro. *Global* SET symbols, on the other hand, are common to the entire assembly, and a value of the global SET symbol &GLOBAL in one macro is available to be used by another macro.

There are three types of both local and global SET symbols: arithmetic (SETA), binary (SETB), and character (SETC). A local or global SETA symbol has an arithmetic value of from -2^{31} to $2^{31} - 1$. Such a symbol must be declared in a macro in which it is used by

LCLA   symbol name

or

GBLA   symbol name,

which declares the symbol to be a local or global SETA symbol. The label portion of a LCLA or GBLA statement (or LCLB, LCLC, GBLB, or GBLC, for that matter) is left blank. The declaration LCLA or GBLA in a macro must come just after the prototype and before any model statements; in a main program LCLA or GBLA declarations come after all macro definitions and before all regular statements. In either a main program or a macro definition, all global SET symbol declarations precede all local SET symbol declarations.

The value of a SETA symbol is initially 0. It may be changed by the SETA statement, which has the form

Label	Operation	Operands
Name of SETA symbol	SETA	An expression

The expression defining the new value may include self-defining terms (see Chapter 6), SETA symbols, attributes L (Length) and N (Number), and symbolic parameters whose values are self-defining terms, connected by arithmetic operators +,−,*, and /. Ordinary symbols, or symbolic parameters whose values are ordinary symbols, are not permitted, since their values are not yet defined when the macro is expanded. Thus

&VARS   SETA   &CT+3

is a valid statement if &CT is another SETA symbol, but

&VARS   SETA   R3

is not.

A SETA symbol may be used in an arithmetic expression in any statement. It may also be used where characters are called for, as in the name of an operand; in this case the absolute value of the symbol is converted to an unsigned decimal integer, with leading zeros removed (the value 0 is converted to a single 0). Thus, if &VARS is a SETA symbol whose value is 7, and &A is a symbolic parameter to which a sublist corresponds, the model statement

```
A       R3,&A(&VARS)
```

will be expanded to an add instruction whose second operand is the seventh member of the sublist &A. On the other hand, if &B is a symbolic parameter whose value is AREG, then

```
A       R3,&B&VARS
```

will be expanded to

```
A       R3,AREG7
```

A SETB symbol has a value of 0 or 1, which can represent *false* or *true*, respectively. When a SETB symbol is declared by

```
GBLB  name of SETB symbol
```

or

```
LCLB  name of SETB symbol
```

the initial value is 0. A new value can be given by

Label	Operation	Operand
Name of SETB symbol	SETB	An expression

The expression may be 0, 1, another SETB symbol, or a logical expression in parentheses, such as (&REG   NE 1). The SETA and SETC symbols are more important, so we will concentrate on them.

The statements

```
LCLC  name of SETC symbol
```

and

```
GBLC  name of SETC symbol
```

declare SETC symbols in the same manner that LCLA and GBLA declare SETA symbols. A SETC symbol has a value that may be up to 255 characters long. The initial value is *no* characters. A SETC symbol may be assigned a new value by the statement

Label	Operation	Operand
Name of SETC symbol	SETC	Character expression

A character expression may consist of a type attribute alone or a concatenation of one or more quoted strings; each quoted string can include a variable symbol and other characters. For example, if &BCD has the value GPDX, the character expression '&BCD.(2)' has the value GPDX(2). The statement

```
&CHAR    SETC    'RST&BCD'
```

assigns the value RSTGPDX to the SETC symbol &CHAR.

SETC symbols may be used in name, operation, and operand fields of statements. If used in an arithmetic expression, a SETC symbol must have a value which is from one to eight decimal digits.

There are six attributes of a symbol or symbolic parameter: type, length, scaling, integer, count, and number. We shall examine type, length, count, and number but ignore scaling and integer.

The *type* attribute is generally used in a macro to determine the type of value given to a symbolic parameter. The type of a symbolic parameter &S is written T'&S; exceptions to rules about paired apostrophes are made to accommodate this notation for attributes. The value of a type attribute is a single character; some of the more important are

A   A-type address constant or symbol

C   character constant or symbol

D   long floating-point constant or symbol, implied length

E   short floating-point constant or symbol, implied length

F   full-word fixed-point constant or symbol with implied length

X   hexadecimal constant

I   machine instruction

M   macro instruction

N   self-defining term

O   omitted operand

P   packed decimal constant or symbol

For example, if the value of &S given in a macro instruction is LOOP, where LOOP is defined by the statement

```
LOOP     L      R4,GWS
```

then the value of T'&S is I.

The *length* attribute of a symbolic parameter &S is written L'&S. Its value is an arithmetic quantity that gives the length associated with the symbol, either through explicit definition in a length modifier of a constant or symbol, or through the implied length associated with constants or symbols of that type (see Fig. 5.1). The length attribute can be used in any arithmetic expression, including definition of a SET symbol.

The *count* attribute of a variable symbol is the number of characters in its value. The count attribute of a symbol &S is written K'&S. The count and length attributes can be confused; the following example illustrates the difference. Suppose a program includes

```
MSG2      DC          C'TOO MANY DIGITS'
```

We recognize that MSG2 has a length of 15. Then suppose a macro includes

```
          MACRO
          EXAMPLE     &CHARCON
          LCLA        &LEN,&COUNT
&LEN      SETA        L'&CHARCON
&COUNT    SETA        K'&CHARCON
```

If the program calls the macro with

```
          EXAMPLE     MSG2
```

the SETA symbol &LEN will be set to 15, the length of MSG2, but &COUNT will be set to 4 because there are four characters in the name MSG2.

The *number* attribute of a symbolic parameter &S is written N'&S. Its value is the number of operands in the sublist corresponding to &S. Actually, the value is 1 greater than the number of commas, so leading omitted operands are counted. If the operand is not a sublist, the value of the number attribute is 1, except that if the operand is omitted entirely, the number attribute is 0. For example, number attributes of the following operands are

```
(ACT,DELTA,CORR)     3
(ACT,,CORR)          3
ACT                  1
none                 0
```

The next section shows how the number attribute allows programmers to form a conditional assembly loop to treat sublist elements in turn.

There are six system variable symbols; they are automatically defined and given values by the assembler; you may use their values but not change them. We will describe only &SYSNDX.

&SYSNDX is a four-digit sequence number assigned to each macro instruction. During the expansion of the first macro instruction in a program, &SYSNDX has the value 0001; during the next its value is 0002, and so on. Because a macro may include a macro instruction as one of its model statements (even recursively(!)), &SYSNDX may be, say, 0014 during the first part of an expansion, then 0015 during expansion of an inner macro instruction, then revert to 0014 for the last part of the expansion of the outer macro instruction. The main use for &SYSNDX is in creating unique symbols for use in the expansions.

Let us use &SYSNDX and a SETC symbol to improve the FORDO macro of the last section. The symbolic parameters &LOOPAD and &NEXTAD are a nuisance to the user, and we can spare the user from having to specify them. Figure 16.7 shows not only a revised FORDO macro, but an ENDFOR that will complete the control structure. Global SETC symbols are used to hold symbols used in the

FIGURE 16.7 An improved `FORDO` and `ENDFOR` using `&SYSNDX`

```
          MACRO
&LABEL    FORDO &START=1,&LIMIT=,&INCR=1,&REG=R7
.*******************************************************************
.*** SETS UP REGISTERS FOR A FOR-DO STRUCTURE USING BXH.
.*** STARTING VALUE AND LIMIT MUST BE APPROPRIATE
.***    FOR A-TYPE CONSTANTS. THEY WILL BE FIRST AND LAST
.***    CONTENTS OF &REG WHEN BODY OF LOOP IS
.***    EXECUTED.
.*** INCREMENT MUST BE POSITIVE.
.*** DEFAULT VALUES OF STARTING VALUE AND INCREMENT ARE 1.
.*** THREE REGISTERS MUST BE AVAILABLE, STARTING WITH
.***    AN ODD-NUMBERED REGISTER. DEFAULT IS REGISTERS 7 - 9.
.*** STRUCTURE WILL BE COMPLETED BY
.***    ENDFOR
.*******************************************************************
          GBLC  &LOOPAD,&NEXTAD
&LOOPAD   SETC  'LP&SYSNDX'
&NEXTAD   SETC  'NX&SYSNDX'
&LABEL    L     &REG,=A(&START-&INCR)
          LA    &REG+1,&INCR
          L     &REG+2,=A(&LIMIT)
&LOOPAD   BXH   &REG,&REG+1,&NEXTAD
          MEND


          MACRO
&LABEL    ENDFOR
          GBLC  &LOOPAD,&NEXTAD
&LABEL    B     &LOOPAD
&NEXTAD   DS    0H
          MEND
```

expansion of a `FORDO` macro instruction, so they can be used in the `ENDFOR` expansion. Since the value of `&SYSNDX` will be unique for each macro expansion, there may be several `FORDO` structures in the program, and they will have unique symbols replacing `&LOOPAD` and `&NEXTAD`. You are invited to simulate the assembler in expanding the macro instructions in the segment

```
          FORDO     LIMIT=20,REG=R3
          IC        R2,AREA(R3)
          S         R2,=F'9'
          STC       R2,AREA(R3)
          ENDFOR
```

There is another problem to work on too. The pair of macros can work well if the FOR-DO structure is used several times in sequence. But what happens if one FOR-DO is used inside another? The values of `&LOOPAD` and `&NEXTAD` in the outer structure are replaced, and the outer `ENDFOR` will return instead to the inner `LOOP`. Stacks are needed for `&LOOPAD` and `&NEXTAD`. You can make such stacks; remember that symbolic parameters could have subparameters, making the symbolic parameter essentially a list or an array. You can make lists or arrays of SET symbols; declare their dimensions in statements like

```
GBLC    &LOOPAD(5),&NEXTAD(5)
GBLA    &NUMLIST(8)
LCLC    &NAMEN(3),&FRONT(7)
LCLA    &K(6),&ARRAY(13),&I
```

Individual elements of such lists are accessed just like the subparameters of symbolic parameters, in statements like

```
&K(1)          SETA    35
&LOOPAD(&I)    SETC    'LP&SYSNDX'
&NUMLIST(&I)   SETA    &NUMLIST(&I-1)+&NUMLIST(&I-2)
```

FIGURE 16.8   FORDO and ENDFOR using stacks of addresses

```
          MACRO
&LABEL    FORDO &START=1,&LIMIT=,&INCR=1,&REG=R7
.*******************************************************************
.*** SETS UP REGISTERS FOR A FOR-DO STRUCTURE USING BXH.
.*** STARTING VALUE AND LIMIT MUST BE APPROPRIATE
.***    FOR A-TYPE CONSTANTS. THEY WILL BE FIRST AND LAST
.***    CONTENTS OF &REG WHEN BODY OF LOOP IS
.***    EXECUTED.
.*** INCREMENT MUST BE POSITIVE.
.*** DEFAULT VALUES OF STARTING VALUE AND INCREMENT ARE 1.
.*** THREE REGISTERS MUST BE AVAILABLE, STARTING WITH
.***    AN ODD-NUMBERED REGISTER. DEFAULT IS REGISTERS 7 - 9.
.*** STRUCTURE WILL BE COMPLETED BY
.***    ENDFOR
.*******************************************************************
          GBLC   &LOOPAD(4),&NEXTAD(4)
          GBLA   &STACKP
&STACKP   SETA   &STACKP+1
&LOOPAD(&STACKP) SETC 'LP&SYSNDX'
&NEXTAD(&STACKP) SETC 'NX&SYSNDX'
&LABEL    L      &REG,=A(&START-&INCR)
          LA     &REG+1,&INCR
          L      &REG+2,=A(&LIMIT)
&LOOPAD(&STACKP) BXH &REG,&REG+1,&NEXTAD(&STACKP)
          MEND


          MACRO
&LABEL    ENDFOR
          GBLC   &LOOPAD(4),&NEXTAD(4)
          GBLA   &STACKP
&LABEL    B      &LOOPAD(&STACKP)
&NEXTAD(&STACKP) DS 0H
&STACKP   SETA   &STACKP-1
          MEND
```

What must be done to make FORDO accommodate nested FOR-DO structures? An array or list of &LOOPAD and &NEXTAD is needed, and a *stack pointer* that will tell at any time which cells of &LOOPAD and &NEXTAD are the top of the stack. The stack pointer must be a global SETA symbol. Figure 16.8 shows versions of FORDO and ENDFOR that carry out the idea. Each time FORDO is used, the stack pointer &STACKP is incremented, and address symbols are inserted in the &LOOPAD and &NEXTAD stacks, not disturbing current values already there. An expansion of ENDFOR uses the top symbols on the stacks and then reduces &STACKP so that the next ENDFOR will use a *previously* stored pair of address symbols. Try making up a small example of nested (and sequential) FOR-DO structures and trace the macro instruction expansion process.

Note that each FORDO gobbles up three more registers, so a limit of four nested FOR-DO structures should be a great plenty! But again using &SYSNDX to ensure uniqueness of symbols, you could set up a small register-save area in each expansion of FORDO. See what you can do with that idea!

16.4   Conditional Assembly

The assembler can be made to branch and loop among assembler language statements in much the same way that the computer branches and loops among machine language instructions. The necessary elements are present: conditional and unconditional branch instructions and labels on statements to branch to. The labels are called *sequence symbols*; a sequence symbol is written as a period followed by from one to seven letters and digits of which the first is a letter. Some valid sequence symbols are .A and .Z23C4PQ. Sequence symbols may be attached (starting in column 1) to a machine or assembler instruction with some obvious exceptions like MACRO and prototype statements.

The unconditional branch instruction is very simple.

Label	Operation	Operand
Sequence symbol or blank	AGO	Sequence symbol

It causes the assembler to assemble succeeding statements beginning at the one with the designated sequence symbol.

The conditional branch is written as

Label	Operation	Operand
Sequence symbol or blank	AIF	A logical expression enclosed in parentheses, followed immediately by a sequence symbol

The logical expression is composed of one or more relations or values of SETB symbols connected by the logical connectors AND, OR, AND NOT, and OR NOT. A relation consists of two arithmetic expressions or two character expressions connected by a relational operator.

EQ	equal to
NE	not equal to
LT	less than
LE	less than or equal
GT	greater than
GE	greater than or equal

A relation has the value true (1) or false (0), and these values are combined by the logical connectors in the obvious way. If the value of the entire expression is true, the assembler branches to the statement named in the AIF statement; if the expression is false, the next instruction in sequence is taken.

The logical connectors and relational operators are immediately preceded and followed by at least one blank. The following are valid logical expressions:

```
&NO GE N'&A        where &NO has an arithmetic value,
&CT LT &NO
&OFF+255 LT &LEN
T'&REG NE '0'
(T'&INC EQ 'N') OR (&NO EQ Ø)
&FSWITCH AND NOT ('&A(&NO)' EQ '')
    where &FSWITCH is a SETB symbol
```

Using parentheses around each piece of a compound condition improves readability and is easier than checking the precedence rules for the logical operators.

One more statement is necessary. AIF and AGO statements may not branch to statements named by regular or variable symbols; when such a branch is desired, the branch can be made to an ANOP statement, which is labeled with a sequence symbol and just precedes the desired statement. For example, an unconditional branch to

```
&N        DC      4F'Ø'
```

is accomplished by

```
          AGO     .STN
```

where the statement labeled .STN is

```
.STN      ANOP
```

and is placed just before the DC statement.

Figure 16.4 showed a simple version of an ADD macro. One of its shortcomings was that it required exactly three operands to add together; another was

FIGURE 16.9   A more flexible ADD macro

```
           MACRO
&LABEL     ADD    &TYPE,&A,&C,&REG
.**************************************************************
.*** ADD AN ARBITRARY NUMBER OF OPERANDS, STORE RESULT.
.*** TYPE MAY BE D,E, OR OMITTED (FOR BINARY INTEGER ADD).
.*** IF A REGISTER IS AVAILABLE, SPECIFY AND IT WILL BE USED,
.***    OTHERWISE R2 WILL BE USED, BUT SAVED AND RESTORED.
.**************************************************************
           LCLC   &N,&R
           LCLA   &NO
&NO        SETA   1
&R         SETC   '&REG'
&N         SETC   '&LABEL'
.* IF &REG IS OMITTED,
           AIF    (T'&REG NE 'O').G1
.* . SAVE AND USE REG. R2
&R         SETC   'R2'
&N         ST&TYPE &R,SA&SYSNDX
&N         SETC   ''
.* ENDIF
.G1        ANOP
&N         L&TYPE &R,&A(1)
.* WHILE &NO < NUMBER OF OPERANDS TO ADD
.B         AIF    (&NO GE N'&A).E
.* . ADD EACH OPERAND
&NO        SETA   &NO+1
           A&TYPE &R,&A(&NO)
           AGO    .B
.* ENDWHILE
.E         ST&TYPE &R,&C
.* IF &REG IS OMITTED
.* . RESTORE REG. R2, ALLOCATE SAVE AREA
           AIF    (T'&REG NE 'O').G2
           B      NX&SYSNDX
SA&SYSNDX DS     D
NX&SYSNDX L&TYPE &R,SA&SYSNDX
.* ENDIF
.G2        MEND
```

that it required the user to provide an area named SAVE in which register 2 was to be stored, whether or not register 2 or any other register was available with unimportant contents. Figure 16.9 shows improvements in both of these areas, using conditional assembly. First, the new macro allows the user to specify a register that can be used and need not be stored. At the beginning of the macro, an AIF tests whether that parameter is present; if not, it stores register 2, but in a save area that the macro provides. SETC symbols are used to make sure the label is attached to the first instruction in the expansion and to hold the number of the register in which the arithmetic will be done. At the end of the macro, a similar IF structure is implemented with AIF; it restores register 2 but also allocates the register save area and of course branches around it. The system variable symbol &SYSNDX is again used to ensure uniqueness of the save area address and the branch address.

FIGURE 16.10   Two expansions of the ADD macro of Fig. 16.9

```
   STEP7    ADD    ,(B,=F'4',CORR,DECR),DEV,R7
  +STEP7    L      R7,B
  +         A      R7,=F'4'
  +         A      R7,CORR
  +         A      R7,DECR
  +         ST     R7,DEV


   STEP9    ADD    D,(FRTEN,C(R5)),DD(R5)
  +STEP9    STD    R2,SA0006
  +         LD     R2,FRTEN
  +         AD     R2,C(R5)
  +         STD    R2,DD(R5)
  +         B      NX0006
  +SA0006   DS     D
  +NX0006   LD     R2,SA0006
```

Conditional assembly also implements a WHILE structure that permits an arbitrary number of operands in a parameter sublist to be added. Figure 16.10 shows two expansions of this ADD macro, to show the results of the conditional assembly. Note that in the second expansion, the default register R2 is used in floating-point operations: while this may be misleading, R2 is (presumably) equated to 2, and the context makes *floating-point* register 2 the one used.

Let us do one more example in this section. A macro may need to know whether a certain string, such as perhaps '*', has been given as any of its pa-

FIGURE 16.11   A macro that searches a set of parameters for a given character
string

```
        MACRO
        PSRCH  &PARAMS,&STRING
.*******************************************************************
.*** SEARCH THE SUBPARAMETERS OF &PARAMS
.*** IF ANY IS EQUAL TO &STRING,
.***    &FOUND IS SET TO 1. OTHERWISE, IT IS SET TO 0.
.*******************************************************************
.
        GBLB   &FOUND
        LCLA   &I
&FOUND  SETB   0
.* WHILE &I < NO. OF PARAMS AND NOT FOUND
.LP     AIF    ((&I GE N'&PARAMS) OR &FOUND).E
.* . INCREMENT &I, AND TEST
&I      SETA   &I+1
&FOUND  SETB   ('&PARAMS(&I)' EQ '&STRING')
        AGO    .LP
.* ENDWHILE
.E      MEND
```

rameters. It would be nice to have a macro that could be called to determine the answer. Let us design such a macro. It must have two parameters: the set of parameters to be searched and the string to search for. It must also be able to report its result. Note that a macro cannot *change* any of its parameters; the only way to communicate a result that can control further assembly is through a global variable. Figure 16.11 shows a macro that does the search. One more modification might be helpful. Can you change the macro so that its output will be the *position* in the sublist in which the searched-for string is found, instead of a simple yes-or-no binary value?

The use of conditional assembly is not restricted to macros. It can also be used in *open code*, the CSECTs and DSECTs in a program. The SET symbols may also be used; conditional assembly is not worth much without them. If you want to use such things, your source module must be in this sequence: first, any macro definitions; second, the declarations of any SET symbols to be used in open code; and third, the open code itself. Because conditional assembly is rarely used in open code, no examples are offered here; but it can be useful, for example, in defining tables to be used by TR or TRT instructions.

Be sure to keep straight which tests are made by the assembler and which are made by your program at execution time. SET symbols are available only during the assembly of your program, and AIF and AGO statements are executed by the assembler. Things like condition codes and registers are available at program execution time, and machine language instructions like Compare and Branch on Condition use them at program execution time. These are two different worlds; the only connection is that the assembler, using conditional assembly as directed, controls the assembly of the machine language instructions.

16.5   Substrings and Other Macro Features

Sometimes assembler language programmers need to be able to test a parameter in more detail than illustrated in Fig. 16.11. Any substring of a parameter, including single characters, can be examined. Specify the beginning character position (1-origin) of the selection and the number of characters to be selected as the substring. For example, '&ADDR'(1,2) selects the first two characters of &ADDR. Note the use of quotes around the string, and the parentheses *outside* the quotes. One main reason is that both sublist and substring notations may be needed; sublist selectors (subscripts, if you wish) are *inside* the quotes and substring selectors outside: '&LIST(&I)'(K'&LIST(&I),1) is the last character of the &Ith subparameter of &LIST.

As an example, consider some of the input/output macros. An area address for the input or output may be given either as a register number in parentheses, meaning that the register contains the address, or in a form suitable for use in an RX-type instruction, which could be a plain symbol, a symbol with index register, or an address in base, index, displacement form. The macro must determine in which of the two ways the area is supplied. The best

FIGURE 16.12   A macro that uses substring notation

```
        MACRO
        TEST    &AREA
        LCLC    &T
.* IF &AREA IS NOT PARENTHESIZED
        AIF     (('&AREA'(1,1) EQ '(') AND ('&AREA'(K'&AREA,1) EQ ')')).E
.* . THEN LOAD ADDRESS, STORE
        LA      R1,&AREA
        ST      R1,PB&SYSNDX+8
        AGO     .ENDIF
.* . ELSE STORE REGISTER
.*      ST      '&AREA'(2,K'&AREA-2),PB&SYSNDX+8
.E      ANOP
&T      SETC    '&AREA'(2,K'&AREA-2)
        ST      &T,PB&SYSNDX+8
.* ENDIF
.ENDIF  ANOP
        MEND
```

way to do this is to see whether the first and last characters of the area parameter are parentheses. Figure 16.12 shows an IF-THEN-ELSE structure that tests &AREA for beginning and ending parentheses. If &AREA is (R8), this segment of the macro will generate

```
        ST      R8,PBØØ21+8
```

in the expansion; if &AREA is BUFFER(R1Ø),

```
        LA      R1,BUFFER(R1Ø)
        ST      R1,PBØØ21+8
```

will be generated.

The substring notation can be used in character expressions, which in their most general forms are permitted in SETC statements and in relational expressions (in AIF and SETB statements). They are not permitted directly in model statements; this is why Fig. 16.12 needs the SETC symbol &T.

A few other features of the macro language are worth noting briefly. There is a statement

```
                MEXIT
```

that exits from, or finishes, the expansion of the current macro instruction. It is really the same thing as an AGO to the MEND statement.

More important is MNOTE, which allows a macro to generate error messages into the assembler listing. For example, the ADD macro of Fig. 16.9 depends on the validity of the &TYPE parameter; a more foolproof system would have the macro ensure the validity. The MNOTE can even assign a severity code that, with codes for other errors discovered by the assembler, may flag the object program produced as nonexecutable. The ADD macro could include, for example:

```
.*    IF &TYPE IS NOT VALID
         AIF   ((T'&TYPE EQ 'O') OR ('&TYPE' EQ 'E') OR
              ('&TYPE' EQ 'D')).VALID
.* .   THEN  ERROR MESSAGE
         MNOTE 12,'***TYPE NOT VALID IN ADD MACRO INSTRUCTION'
         MEXIT
.* .   ELSE EXPAND THE MACRO INSTRUCTION
```

This sequence could appear at the beginning of the macro, just after the LCLC and LCLA declarations.

It is instructive to compare a macro to a subroutine. A subroutine, sometimes called a *closed subroutine*, is a section of standard code to which the program branches when the functions of that section are desired. A macro expansion can be called an *open subroutine*; it is inserted bodily at each point where it is to be used. However, the macro definition has much of the appearance of a closed subroutine, and the macro instruction is quite similar to a subroutine call, with parameters and a transfer of control (in the assembler) to and from the macro. In a sense, a subroutine and a macro are examples of the same idea—a standard code segment available to be called upon whenever needed—and the main difference is that a subroutine is called during *execution* of your program, whereas the macro is called during *assembly* of your program.

m a i n   i d e a s

- □ A macro is defined by a sequence of a *header* statement, a *prototype*, *model* statements, and a *trailer* statement. The model statements, with suitable substitutions defined by the correspondence of macro instruction operands and symbolic parameters listed in the prototype, and by conditional assembly, replace a macro instruction as the *expansion* of the macro.

- □ Variable symbols, written with an ampersand (&) as first character, include symbolic parameters, system symbols, andlocal and global SETA (arithmetic), SETB (binary), and SETC (character) symbols. SET symbols are declared by GBLA, GBLB, GBLC, LCLA, LCLB, and LCLC statements, and their values are changed by SETA, SETB, and SETC statements.

- □ Attributes T' (type), L' (length), N' (number), and K' (count) permit the assembler to determine the nature of symbolic parameters and to adjust the expansion accordingly.

- □ Symbolic parameters to a macro can be both positional and keyword. They may contain subparameter lists, just as SET symbols may be lists, accessed by subscript. Substrings or individual characters of parameters can be accessed through a substring notation.

- □ Conditional assembly is a mechanism for transfer of control by the assembler among statements in a macro or in open code. Unconditional branch (AGO) and conditional branch (AIF) statements enable a programmer to build control structures in macros, to be executed by the assembler.

- □ The system variable symbol &SYSNDX is useful in generating unique symbols.

■ **PROBLEMS**

16.1 Make a chart showing the objects (regular symbols, character strings, symbolic parameters, SETA symbols, SETC symbols, attributes, etc.) that are allowed in various places, such as operands of SETA and SETC statements, logical, arithmetic, and character expressions, macro instruction operands, model statement operands; and list the operators that are allowed as connectors between the objects.

16.2 Learn more about partitioned data sets; then set up job control necessary to (a) create a private macro library and put a few macros in it, and (b) use these macros from the library in a program.

16.3 The macros of Figs. 16.3, 16.4, and 16.9 can be used to add full-word fixed-point numbers or single- or double-precision floating-point quantities. Why can they not add halfword integers with a macro instruction whose first operand is H? By using conditional assembly, can you remedy the flaw?

16.4 What would happen if a macro instruction using the macro of Fig. 16.3 omitted the second operand?

16.5 Why are ordinary symbols not permitted in the defining expression of a SETA statement?

16.6 Type and length attributes may be written of ordinary symbols as well as of symbolic parameters. When might this be useful?

16.7 Write a macro without SETC symbols that generates the same expansion from a macro instruction as does the macro of Fig. 16.9.

FIGURE 16.13 The INVOKE macro

```
           MACRO
&LABEL     INVOKE  &NAME,&PARMS
           LCLA    &ELEMENT
&LABEL     STM     R14,R15,IN&SYSNDX
           L       R15,=V(&NAME.)
           AIF     ('&PARMS' EQ '').NOPARM1
           LA      R1,PLST&SYSNDX
.NOPARM1   BALR    R14,R15
           LM      R14,R15,IN&SYSNDX
           B       LV&SYSNDX
IN&SYSNDX  DS      2F
           AIF     ('&PARMS' EQ '').NOPARM2
PLST&SYSNDX DS     0A
.GENLOOP   ANOP
&ELEMENT   SETA    &ELEMENT+1
           DC      A(&PARMS(&ELEMENT).)
           AIF     (&ELEMENT LT N'&PARMS).GENLOOP
.NOPARM2   ANOP
LV&SYSNDX  DS      0H
           MEND
```

16.8 Given the MACRO definition shown in Fig. 16.13, show the expansion of the macro instruction

```
INVOKE   SORT,(TABLE,2Ø),2
```

assuming the value of &SYSNDX to be ØØØ7. Then, assuming &SYSNDX to be ØØ15, expand

```
INVOKE   CLOSET
```

16.9 Now that you have studied macro definition features, explain why parameters in a CLOSE macro instruction must be enclosed in parentheses, but why the parentheses can be omitted if there is only one parameter.

16.10 Convert the macro of Fig. 16.9 to the use of keyword parameters. Is anything gained by this?

16.11 Convert the FORDO macro of Fig. 16.8 to using positional parameters. Include the same behavior of supplying default values that is in Fig. 16.8; it can be done with SETC symbols and conditional assembly.

16.12 Write a macro that defines a 256-byte area and places in it the binary integers 0 to 255, one per byte.

16.13 Write a macro that will move a string of characters, from 1 to, say, 4096 bytes long, from one location to another, not using the MVCL instruction. Have the expansion contain straight-line coding, i.e., no loops.

16.14 Modify the macro of Problem 16.13 so that a series of strings, which are defined by location and length (perhaps you can permit the length to be omitted sometimes, and get the length by using a length attribute), are moved so as to follow one another in a new location.

16.15 Write a macro that will add a series of fixed-point quantities that are a specified distance (perhaps &INC) apart, for example, at &A, &A+&INC, &A+2*&INC, etc. The number of quantities to be added is, of course, another parameter. Generate a straight-line expansion.

16.16 Write another macro for the same job as that in Problem 16.15, but that generates a loop to do the addition. It is interesting to note that to generate straight-line code, the programmer must create an assembler loop, but to generate a loop in the expansion, the assembler does not need to go through a loop.

16.17 Combine the macros of Problems 16.15 and 16.16 so that if, say, ten or fewer numbers are to be added, a straight-line expansion is generated (as in Problem 16.15), otherwise a loop is generated, as in Problem 16.16.

16.18 The extended-precision floating-point instructions do arithmetic, but there are no explicit instructions for loading, comparing, storing, etc. extended-precision numbers. By analogy with the regular floating-point instruction repertoire, design a set of macros that will supplement the extended-precision instructions and round out the repertoire.

16.19 Write a macro that will compute the address of a cell in a two-dimensional array. The prototype should be

&LABEL ARRLOC &ORIG,&LROW,&LCELL,&SROW,&SCOL

The parameters are

&LABEL   Label for the first instruction in the expansion

&ORIG   Address of the first cell in the array

&LROW   Length of each row, expressed as the number of cells

&LCELL   Length, in bytes, of each cell in the array

&SROW   Row subscript

&SCOL   Column subscript

The formula for the address to be computed is

addr = origin + ((row − 1)(row length) + column − 1)(cell length)

Your macro expansion should use only registers 0 and 1, leaving the resulting address in register 1.

Assume that &ORIG is an A-type address, and that the last four parameters are addresses of full words where the actual lengths and subscripts will be. How might you generalize this macro further?

16.20 The EQUREGS macro in the ASSIST system can EQUate symbols in a variety of ways. A plain

EQUREGS

macro instruction will equate RØ to 0, R1 to 1, ..., R15 to 15. A macro instruction

EQUREGS L=F,DO=(Ø,6,2)

will equate FØ to 0, F2 to 2, F4 to 4, F6 to 6. Try to write a macro that will have this kind of flexibility.

16.21 Macros that save and restore registers (e.g., SAVE, RETURN, XSAVE, XRETURN) permit the user to specify individual registers as (R14), for example, or a range of registers, as (R14−R12). Write a piece of a macro that recognizes the distinction and generates an appropriate LM instruction in either case. *Hint:* Use substring notation to search the parameter for '−'.

16.22 Write a macro that will take two 5-digit integers in character (zoned-decimal) form (their addresses in main storage are two parameters to the macro), and put the sum of the two numbers (again in character form) in six bytes at the location given by the third parameter. The sign should be placed as the character + or − in the 7th byte. Also show an example of a macro instruction using your macro.

16.23 Improve several of the earlier macros in the chapter by checking parameters for validity and reporting problems with MNOTE statements.

16.24 Write macros, similar to FORDO and ENDFOR of Fig. 16.8, for other control structures. You may have to use parameters for the type of compare instruction to be used and the extended mnemonic to be used in a branch statement. Can your several macros, and FORDO and ENDFOR, use the same set of stacks? If so, you may be able to build in some testing to ensure proper nesting of the control structures. This is not a trivial project.

■ REFERENCES ▬▬▬▬▬▬▬▬▬▬▬▬

Freeman, D. N., "Macro language design for SYSTEM/360," *IBM Systems Journal* **5** (1966), pp. 62–77.

OS/VS–DOS/VSE–VM/370 Assembler Language, GC 33-4010, IBM Corporation. Reference description of the macro definition and conditional assembly facilities.

Kent, William, "Assembler-Language Macroprogramming," *Computing Surveys* **1**, 4 (December 1969), pp. 183–196. A tutorial exposition of the System/360 macro definition and conditional assembly facilities.

SYSTEM CONTROL FUNCTIONS

Throughout the earlier chapters of this volume, reference was made to machine functions that are performed by the supervisor or by machine elements controlled only through the supervisor. Mentioned were the program status word, control registers, the protection system, dynamic address translation and virtual storage management, the interrupt system, and performance of input and output, with almost no hint of how such things are used. This chapter introduces the capabilities of the IBM System/370 that are usually reserved for use by the supervisor.

The features of the System/370 computer considered in this chapter can be divided into several groups. First is the dynamic address translation facility, which implements virtual storage in some models of the IBM System/370. Second are functions controlled through the program status word and control registers. These functions include the storage protection system and control over which interrupts are permitted and which are not. There are special instructions that manipulate the fields of the program status word and control registers.

As an important part of manipulation of the program status word, we will study the interrupt system: the nature and mechanism of interrupt, the various types, and some of the considerations involved in using the interrupt system.

The most complex of the topics considered in this chapter is the input and output system. The input and output instructions are simple enough, but the input and output channels are themselves programmed, and we shall study channel programming. States of the channels, subchannels, and devices must be explained, as well as the workings of the input and output interrupts and the means of providing information to the central processing unit on the status of the input and output processes.

When this chapter was written for the first edition, the architecture of the IBM System/360 was relatively simple, and there was almost total consistency among the models. Fifteen years later, the structure is much more complex. The increase in the complexity of all computers has been made possible by the steep decrease in the cost of electronics and by technical and theoretical developments in computer architecture generally. The increased complexity of the IBM computers has been made necessary by demands to increase the capabilities of the systems and to use the newer developments in computer design in solving some of the problems of the original IBM System/360 design.

Through all of this, a very high degree of compatibility among models has been maintained in the instructions that are executed in the problem state—those we have been studying until this chapter. A few instructions have been added to the repertoire: SRP, ICM, STCM, CLM, MVCL, CLCL, the extended-precision instructions and a few more. But the problem-state instructions of the original IBM System/360 repertoire do what they did in 1964 (with a few very minor exceptions, like addition of the guard digit to floating-point arithmetic operations).

The instructions and features used in the supervisor state have not been nearly as stable. Compatibility was much less necessary; if the Job Control Language and the programmers' interface to the supervisor were stable except where the users wanted to take advantage of new features, why would anyone complain? Many fundamental architecture parameters have of course remained, but IBM and manufacturers of plug-compatible mainframe computers have been much more willing to vary the supervisor-state details between models, and have made large improvements in the capabilities of the systems as a result.

One prime example is in the area of virtual storage. There was no virtual storage in the IBM System/360 models (except the model 67), or in several models of System/370. There are two very different implementations of virtual storage in the 4300 series. One is the *dynamic address translation* used in System/370, the 3000 series and in the 4300s. There is also a one-level addressing implementation incorporated in ECPS/VSE mode in the 4300s. Thus far the one-level addressing is used only in the DOS/VSE operating system, not in the OS versions that we have dealt with in this text.

No attempt has been made to be complete and definitive in this chapter. The goal is to introduce the features used by the supervisor, so that you will have a better understanding of what the supervisor does and how, and thus will be more effective in your use of supervisor services. Use of the interrupt system and of direct input and output commands is sometimes necessary, and the supervisor includes provision for accommodating such use; this chapter can serve as an introduction to the facilities that are available to you when you need them. Finally, since all sophisticated computers of the current gen-eration have complex facilities that parallel those of the IBM System/370, study of the 370's interrupt and input/output systems can serve as an introduc-tion to the kind of structure used by other computer systems as well.

17.1 Dynamic Address Translation and Virtual Storage

In earlier chapters it was presumed that each address refers to a particular and fixed location in main storage, though there were occasional hints that it was not necessarily so. Almost all of the models in the System/370 family in cur-rent use implement virtual storage, which dynamically allocates real storage blocks to the virtual storage of several programs, as required.

WHY VIRTUAL STORAGE?

There are several reasons for implementing virtual storage. In a multiprogram-ming environment, programs and service routines are continually called in, executed, and finished. They come in all sizes, and seldom is the next one needed the same size as the one just finished. Therefore storage assignments become fragmented, and it becomes difficult to find a contiguous block of storage, even though enough storage is available in pieces. Storage would be managed better if each program's required space could be broken into several areas of fixed size, not necessarily contiguously assigned. Each programmer can arrange this to some extent, but it would be better to have the operating system take over storage management, since the programmer cannot foresee what size blocks will be available. Second, programs include sections used for initialization and for treating various exceptional conditions and allowance for data storage space often in excess of that required during a particular run. In any small interval of time, only a subset of the program's entire program and data areas are in active use. This subset is called the *working set*; only the working set need be actually resident in main storage at any time, but the sys-tem must be able to bring in other pieces easily and automatically when they are needed. A quantity of main storage can serve many more programs if it need hold only their working sets than if it must hold their entire defined stor-age areas. Third, and by extension, a computer can execute a program whose total storage requirements exceed the actual main storage available.

These considerations lead to an implementation design with the following characteristics.

- division of main storage into blocks (called *page frames*), each assignable to a program independently of other blocks;
- a hardware-implemented means of translating logical addresses that the pro-gram thinks it is using into real addresses in the page frames assigned;
- a way of managing the assignment of page frames and keeping current copies of program and data portions when they are not in main storage.

FIGURE 17.1 Mapping virtual and real storage

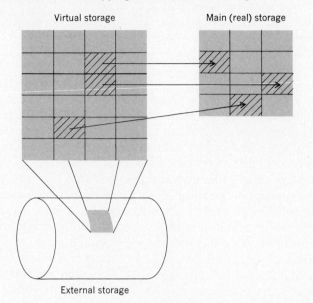

Figure 17.1 represents virtual and real storage and the mapping. The program assumes an area of contiguous pages, and the pages are actually kept in external storage, as shown. A few of the pages, the working set, reside in main storage in any blocks that may be available at the moment. An automatic translation is made so that addresses in virtual storage access the appropriate real storage and, when necessary, call for bringing a needed page from external storage to main storage for the use of the program.

THE DYNAMIC ADDRESS TRANSLATION FEATURE

As noted in the chapter introduction, there are two implementations of virtual storage in IBM systems. Only the dynamic address translation will be described because it is the implementation currently used in most of the computer models and in the versions of the OS operating system. One description is enough to illustrate virtual storage, anyway.

As we have used addresses in System/370, they are each 24 bits, and they define an *address space* of 16,777,216 (16,384 K or 16M) bytes. A recent introduction of *extended architecture* (XA) on some models increases address lengths, both for virtual and real storage, to 31 bits, and the operating systems are gradually allowing the use of addresses larger than 24 bits. But that is beyond the scope of this discussion.

A related new feature available in some newer models is *dual-address-space* (DAS), which permits a user to have *two* virtual address spaces. Control register 7 functions for the secondary address space as control register 1 func-

FIGURE 17.2 Fields of an address

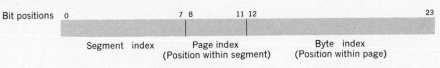

Segment index   Page index   Byte index
                (Position within segment)   (Position within page)

tions for the primary address space, and a program can control which address space is to be used at the moment. There are several special instructions related to using a secondary address space, such as one to move data from the primary space to the secondary space, and another instruction to move data the other way. The dual-address-space feature is beyond the scope of this text.

Restricting our attention to 24-bit addresses and one 16M byte address space, we have more than most programmers need. The range of addresses actually used by a program may be called its *virtual storage* space, and it may be assigned by relocation exactly as shown in earlier chapters. For management, the virtual storage is divided into a hierarchy of *segments* and *pages*. A *segment* is 64K bytes, and each segment is divided into 16 *pages* of 4K bytes each (in OS/VS1, a segment is divided into 32 pages of 2K bytes each, but this explanation will continue with the larger pages). The 24-bit address therefore is subdivided into fields as shown in Fig. 17.2. Note that the addition of base, index, and displacement is performed exactly as described heretofore, and the resulting address is a virtual address; it is the resulting virtual address that is interpreted in segment index, page index, and byte index.

Real storage is assigned in chunks of 4K bytes called *page frames*. Pages are the content of virtual storage, whereas page frames are physical portions of main storage assigned dynamically to hold pages. The assignment makes necessary a translation so that for every virtual storage address a program is directed to the page frame where that content is to be found.

SEGMENT AND PAGE TABLES

The segment index and page index are arranged so that translation from virtual into real addresses can follow a two-step process, referencing, in turn, a *segment table* and a *page table*. First, control register 1 gives the beginning address of the current segment table. For a given virtual address, the segment in-

FIGURE 17.3 Format of a segment table

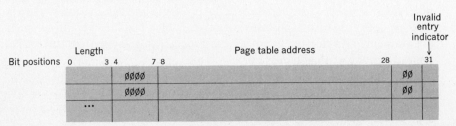

FIGURE 17.4   Format of a page table

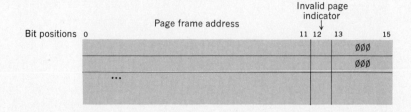

dex determines which entry in the segment table to use. The most important part of the entry is the address of the relevant page table. The page index determines which entry in the selected page table to use. The entry in the page table gives the upper twelve bits of the page frame address; the address is completed by concatenation with the byte index.

The format of a segment table is shown in Fig. 17.3. The length of a page table is given in bits 0–3, and the first 21 bits of the address of the page table are given in bits 8 to 28. The lower three bits of the page table address are supplied as zeros, which means that a page table always begins on a doubleword boundary. Bit 31 indicates whether there is a currently valid page table for the segment or not; if not, address translation must be suspended and the supervisor given control until the page table is made valid.

The format of a page table is shown in Fig. 17.4. Bit 12 indicates whether the desired page is currently in real storage (valid) or not (invalid). If it is not, translation must be suspended until the needed page is brought into main storage and the page table gives its correct page frame address. When translation can be carried out, bits 0–11 of the page-table entry hold the first twelve bits (page frame address) of the desired location in real storage.

THE TRANSLATION PROCESS

An example of use of the tables in the translation of an actual (virtual) address is shown in Fig. 17.5. The address generated by base, index, and displacement is Ø13A8C. Since each segment table entry is four bytes long, the segment index must be multiplied by 4; the result is added to the contents of control register 1 to give the proper address in the segment table. Similarly, since each page table entry is two bytes long, the page index is multiplied by 2 and the result added to the address found in the segment table. The result, ØØ4D56, indicates the address in the page table where we find the address of the real page frame containing the desired page. The combination of the page frame address and the byte index yields Ø3AA8C, the real address of the desired operand.

If the foregoing translation process had to be carried out for every reference to operands or instructions in main storage, execution of programs would be slowed significantly. A *translation look-aside buffer* (TLB) is provided to hold the page frame addresses of the most recently used pages. The translation process is carried out in parallel through the TLB and the segment and page

FIGURE 17.5   Example of address translation

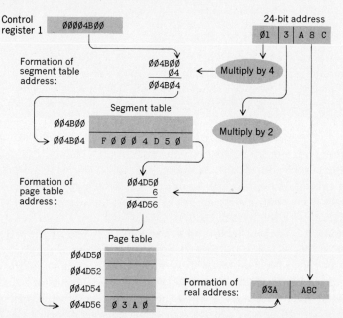

tables; in most cases the TLB will contain the desired entry, and operands can be addressed immediately while the translation process through segment and page tables is aborted. The TLB is an example of an *associative* or *content-addressable* memory. See Foster (reference at the end of the chapter) for a discussion of content-addressable memory techniques.

STORAGE MANAGEMENT

Outlined next are some other steps and considerations in the management of a virtual storage system. Most important is the dynamic change in assignment of page frames and the process of storing and retrieving contents of pages that are not currently in real page frames.

The supervisor must know what pages are in which page frames at any time. A *page frame table*, managed entirely through software (the supervisor) must contain

- page frame address,
- ID of the program to which the frame is assigned,
- segment and page index,
- status.

When a new page must be brought into main storage, the supervisor must find an available page frame and bring the proper page from external storage into the selected frame. This implies an *external page table*, with content like the page frame table, but instead of the page frame address it must contain the address in the external storage medium (drum or disk) used for the purpose.

SWAPPING

The working sets of active programs change, and more pages must be brought into main storage. Eventually, all page frames will contain pages for various programs. The next time a page is needed, one of the pages in main storage must be replaced. Replacement of one page in a page frame by another is called *swapping*. Which page will be replaced? The strategy adopted is that a page *least recently used* is most likely not to be needed again, at least for quite a while. To tell which page is least recently used, a *reference bit* is added to (essentially) the page frame table; every time the page in the frame is used by a program the bit is set to 1. If all reference bits are set to 0 every so often, those remaining at 0 when a page frame is needed have been used less recently than those whose reference bits have been set to 1.

The swapping entails the following. The operating system must be sure to keep the most recent version of each page, so if the page to be swapped out of main storage has been changed since it was last brought from external storage, the changed version must be moved back to external storage. How will the operating system know? A *change bit* is needed in (essentially) the page frame table, to be set to 1 every time the contents of the page are changed. The change bit must be tested when a page must be swapped out. You will learn in the next section that the reference and change bits are actually kept in special hardware locations where they are easy to set with no loss of time, not actually in the page frame table.

To swap pages, the following steps must occur.

1. By finding the *invalid* bit set to 1 in a page table, the hardware recognizes that a page must be brought from external storage. An interrupt passes control to the supervisor.
2. The supervisor scans the page frame table, searching for an available page frame. If one is available, it goes to step 9.
3. Otherwise, the supervisor examines the *reference bits* to pick a page that will be swapped out. A page whose reference bit is currently 0 will be chosen.
4. The invalid bit is set *on* in the page table for the page to be removed.
5. The page frame is marked *reserved* for swapping.
6. If the page to be swapped out has its change bit *off* (0), the supervisor goes to step 9.
7. Otherwise, it initiates transmission of the page from main storage to external storage.
8. Another program is activated until the transmission is completed.
9. After completion, transmission of the desired page is initiated from external storage into the assigned page frame.

10. Another program is activated until the transmission is completed.

11. The page table is updated to show the location of the new page.

12. The page frame table is updated to show use of the frame.

13. The program is reactivated, and will now be able to proceed with the instruction that was halted by the unavailability of the page just brought in.

This brief introduction to storage management can be supplemented by reference to the IBM text *Introduction to Virtual Storage in System/370*, GR 20-4260. The reference manuals *IBM System/370 Principles of Operation*, GA 22-7000, and *OS/VS Supervisor Services and Macro-Instructions*, GC 27-6979, provide more definitive information on the hardware and software, respectively.

17.2   The Program Status Word and Control Registers

There are two forms of the program status word (PSW). The first is *BC mode*; this is the form designed into the IBM System/360 and kept available in later models for compatibility. The second mode is *EC mode* (*Extended Control*), which we will study here.

The PSW is 64 bits long; it resides in a special part of the central processing unit, not a part of addressable main storage. It holds fields that are essentially parameters to the environment in which a program operates. As features were added to the computers in design of System/370, more parameters were necessary than would fit in a 64-bit PSW. The solution was to establish a set of 16 control registers and move some of the fields from the PSW to control registers, making possible a redefinition of the PSW.

The format of the PSW is shown in Fig. 17.6. Some of the fields of the PSW have been introduced in previous chapters, but some will have their first mention here. The condition code (bits 18–19) has been used extensively and needs no further discussion. The instruction address is the main storage address of the next instruction to be executed. It is usually increased by 2, 4, or 6, the length of the current instruction, in passing from one instruction to the next; execution of a branch is accomplished by loading the branch address into this portion of the PSW.

FIGURE 17.6   The format of the program status word in EC mode

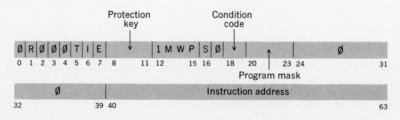

Bits 12–15 reflect the current status of the computer. Bit 12 controls the format of the PSW: 0 indicates BC mode, and 1 indicates EC mode. The W bit (position 14) is 1 when the central processing unit is in the *wait state*, and 0 when the CPU is in the running state. In the wait state no instructions are processed, but an interrupt is allowed; the interrupt can return the machine to the running state. The wait state differs from the *stop state* in that the stop state does not permit interruption, but is left (and entered) only by manual action. The P bit (position 15) denotes whether the CPU is in the *problem state* (when the bit is 1) or the *supervisor state* (when the bit is 0). Certain instructions, such as PSW manipulation and input and output manipulations, are executable only in the supervisor state; thus the status of the machine is protected against unwarranted change by a user.

Bit 5 of the PSW in EC mode specifies dynamic address translation. When the bit is 1, addresses are translated as described in Section 17.1; when the bit is 0, no translation takes place. Bit 16 specifies whether the primary address space (bit $16 = 0$) or secondary address space (bit $16 = 1$) is in use; the dual-address-space feature was mentioned briefly in Section 17.1

Bit 2 of the PSW controls program event recording, which was mentioned in Chapter 9 and will be treated in a little more detail below. Other bit positions are unused, but of course new features yet to be announced at this writing may find a new use for them!

The storage protection system was introduced in Chapter 9. A four-bit *storage key*, called *access-control bits* in some newer manuals, is associated with each block of 2048 bytes. A fifth bit, called the *fetch bit*, controls whether attempts to fetch information from the block are monitored as well as attempts to store information into the block; if the fetch bit is 1, fetch attempts are monitored, but if the fetch bit is 0 or if fetch protection is not implemented, fetch attempts are always permitted. The monitoring consists of comparison of the *protection key*, bits 8–11 of the PSW, called the *access key* in some newer manuals, with the storage key. If the two keys match or if the protection key is 0, access is permitted. A nonpermitted access attempt causes an interruption.

The reference bit and change bit, introduced in the previous section as an aid in the management of virtual storage, are in fact attached to the storage key, as shown in Fig. 17.7. This is a handy place to append the functions of reference and change bits because the storage keys are accessed for every reference and change anyway.

Two instructions enable the supervisor to manage the protection system. They are ISK, Insert Storage Key, which loads a storage key into a register for inspection, and SSK, Set Storage Key, which sets a storage key from the contents of a register. Both are RR-type instructions. In both, *R2* indicates to which block of storage the instruction pertains. The block is identified by bits 8–20 of the register; for example, if the register contains ØØØØB8ØØ, the storage key for the storage block ØØB8ØØ to ØØBFFF is accessed. Bits 0–7 and 21–27 are ignored, but bits 28–31 must be zero. Register *R1* bits 24–30 are stored as the

FIGURE 17.7   Storage keys

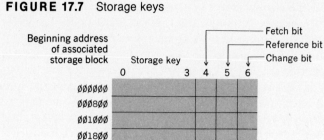

storage key by the SSK instruction; other bits are ignored. The ISK instruction inserts the storage key into bit positions 24–30. Position 31 is set to 0, but positions 0–23 are unchanged.

As an example, suppose that

$$\text{Register 8 contains } \emptyset\emptyset\emptyset\emptyset\emptyset\emptyset3\emptyset$$

$$\text{Register 9 contains } \emptyset\emptyset\emptyset\emptysetB8\emptyset\emptyset$$

The instruction SSK   R8,R9 will cause bit patterns $\emptyset\emptyset11\emptyset\emptyset\emptyset$ to be set as the storage key for the block of storage $\emptyset\emptyset$B8$\emptyset\emptyset$ to $\emptyset\emptyset$BFFF. Fetch access to the block will be permitted to any instruction but store access only if PSW bits 8–11 are $\emptyset\emptyset11$ or $\emptyset\emptyset\emptyset\emptyset$.

The ISK and SSK instructions are carried out without respect to segment and page tables, and accesses to the keys are not subject to the protection system itself. Both SSK and ISK are privileged, so they may be executed only in the supervisor state.

The other fields of the PSW are *mask* bits controlling (masking) whether certain conditions cause interrupts or not. The conditions are as shown in Fig. 17.8; a 1-bit permits interrupt on the condition, a 0-bit suppresses it. Bit 6 masks all input/output interrupts as a class; if the bit is 1, a further set of mask

FIGURE 17.8   PSW bits masking interrupts in EC mode

PSW bit	Interrupt condition
6	Input/output
7	External
13	Machine-check
20	Fixed-point overflow
21	Decimal overflow
22	Exponent underflow
23	Significance

bits in control register 2 controls whether an interrupt on each individual channel will cause an interrupt. Bit 7 similarly masks a class called *external* interrupts; control register 0 masks the individual interrupt types within the class. Bit 13 controls whether a machine-check condition (hardware error in the CPU) will cause interrupt or not. Bits 20–23 are the program mask, which is under control of the programmer as we shall see in the next section. All other interrupt masks may be set only by the supervisor.

There are up to 16 control registers. A summary of the functions controlled is shown in Fig. 17.9. To supplement the introduction to the features and functions presented here and in later sections, see the *IBM System/370 Principles of Operation* manual, GA 22-7000, and other manuals that set forth the software facilities built upon the hardware features.

Section 17.1 mentioned that there were choices of segment and page size in the virtual storage system; bits 8–12 of control register 0 specify the sizes. Con-

FIGURE 17.9 Summary of control register fields

Register	Bits	Name of field	Associated with
0	0–7	Control bits	Enable various features
	8–12	Translation format	Dynamic address translation
	13–31	Interrupt masks	External-class interrupts
1	0–7	Segment table length	⎫
	8–25	Segment table address	⎬ Dynamic address translation
	31	Space-switch-event control	⎭
2	0–31	Channel masks	Input/output interrupts
3–5			Dual-address space control
6			Extended facility and VM Assist
7	0–7	Secondary segment-table length	⎫ Dual address space control
	8–25	Secondary segment-table origin	⎬
8	16–31	Monitor masks	Monitor Call
9	0	Successful-branching event mask	⎫
	1	Instruction-fetching event mask	⎪
	2	Storage-alteration event mask	⎬ Program event recording (PER)
	3	General Register alteration event mask	⎪
	16–31	General register masks	⎭
10	8–31	PER starting address	Program event recording
11	8–31	PER ending address	Program event recording
14–15			Machine-check handling

trol register 1 is also associated with the virtual storage system; bits 0–7 specify the length of the segment table, in terms of four-byte entries. If only the first few segments of address space are assigned, only the first few lines of the segment table need be filled in, and the length specified prevents code beyond the actual entries from causing spurious address translations. Bits 8–31 are the address of the segment table, as shown in Section 17.1.

Control register 0 also contains a grand mixture of bits that control whether certain instructions (called *semiprivileged*) are to be allowed and whether certain conditions cause interrupts. We will discuss some of these in Section 17.4.

Control register 2 also controls interrupts—the mask bits in this register control input/output interrupts, which will be discussed in Section 17.8.

Control registers 3, 4, 5, and 7 are used by the dual-address space feature. Control register 6 is related to some of the special performance-enhancement features, such as VM (Virtual Machine) Assist, that may be installed.

Control register 8 contains monitor masks; an advanced programmer may set up to 16 mask bits, one for each of 16 varieties of events. A program may issue a Monitor Call (MC) instruction to indicate that a *monitor event* has occurred, and the operating system will store some information about the event. Monitoring is also beyond the scope of this text.

Control registers 9–11 are associated with program event recording. Program events such as a successful branch, fetching an instruction from a designated area, and alteration of specified general registers can cause interrupts and passage of control to a routine that will record the event, if the interrupts are not masked off. The monitored area of main storage is designated by addresses in control registers 10 and 11. Bits 0–7 of control register 9 mask those events that may cause interrupt. Bits 16–31 designate which general registers are monitored for change. Having a record of events of the sort indicated can provide a selective trace of program actions that can be very useful in debugging programs.

Control registers 12 and 13 are unused at this writing, and control registers 14 and 15 are used in the handling of machine-check conditions.

17.3   Instructions Pertaining to PSW and Advanced Features

Certain instructions change all or part of the PSW and also load and store control registers. Some of them are considered in this section, along with some of the special instructions that are used in managing a virtual-storage system.

First is the SI-type instruction Load PSW (LPSW). It has only one operand, a double word addressed by *D1* and *B1*. Bit positions 8–15, the *I2* portion of the instruction, are ignored. The double word from main storage addressed by *D1* and *B1* is loaded into the PSW, replacing the current PSW. Thus LPSW is a branch instruction, but it can also change all other status indications contained in the PSW. It is a privileged instruction, executable only from the supervisor state.

The program mask is accessible to the programmer in problem state, and it is the only part of the interrupt system that can be controlled by the user. The programmer can load a new program mask and condition code by the Set Program Mask (SPM) instruction, which is a nonprivileged instruction of RR type. The bits from positions 2 and 3 of register $R1$ are loaded into the condition code portion of the PSW, and the bits from positions 4–7 of register $R1$ are loaded into the program mask portion. The $R2$ field of SPM is ignored.

To gain access to the program mask, execute a BAL or BALR instruction. The register $R1$ is loaded with ILC (Instruction Length Code, a two-bit code that indicates the length of the current instruction), CC, the program mask, and the address of the next instruction, in that order. These fields are exactly bits 32–63 of the PSW in BC mode, but the same content is loaded regardless of current mode of the PSW. For example, if you wish at some stage in your program to enable interrupt on decimal overflow, the following instructions would do the job.

```
        BALR   R9,Ø
        O      R9,ENDECOV
        SPM    R9
        ⋮

ENDECOV DC     X'Ø4ØØØØØØ'
```

Another nonprivileged RR-type instruction is SuperVisor Call (SVC). Its format is actually different from that of other RR-type instructions; bits 8–15 are a byte of "immediate" data and not references to registers. The action of the SVC instruction is to force an interrupt of SVC type (more about the type in the next section) and to store the second byte of the instruction in the last eight bits of the interrupt code in the old PSW. The SVC is used by a programmer to request actions from the supervisor. The second byte of the instruction carries a message to the supervisor indicating what action is requested; for example,

```
        SVC    19
```

may request the opening of a data set (certain other parameters to the request are assumed to be in registers), and

```
        SVC    13
```

may request abnormal termination of the job step.

Three privileged instructions deal specifically with dynamic address translation. Load Real Address (LRA) is an RX-type instruction. The (virtual) address generated as the second operand (base, index, displacement) is translated into a real address, if possible, using the current segment and page tables; the resulting real address is loaded into register $R1$. The condition code is set to 0 if translation is successful; other condition code settings report various mishaps (e.g., encountering an *invalid* bit in one of the tables). The supervisor every now and then must generate a real address equivalent to a given virtual address; we shall see examples when we study input and output.

The instruction Purge Translation Lookaside Buffer (PTLB) must be executed whenever a page or segment table changes; otherwise the old entry would still be used through the Translation Lookaside Buffer. When the instruction is executed, the entire buffer is cleared; it will be reloaded automatically by the hardware, an entry at a time, as new pages are referenced. The instruction is of S type, with no operands.

The Reset Reference Bit (RRB) instruction is also of S type. It resets to 0 the reference bit associated with the block of storage designated by bits 8–20 of the operand address. The operand address itself is not subject to address translation. It is convenient to be able to reset the single reference bit without bothering any other portions of the storage key.

Two instructions provide for loading and storing control registers. They are Load ConTroL (LCTL) and STore ConTroL (STCTL). Both are of RS type, and load and store control registers as LM and STM load and store general registers. Two differences must be noted, however: LCTL and STCTL are privileged, and we are not promised what will be stored if we attempt to store a control register not implemented on the computer. No other manipulation (arithmetic,

FIGURE 17.10   System control instructions

Instruction	Format	Action	Exceptions
SSK	Ø8 | R1 | R2	Key for storage block addressed by $c(R2)_{8-20} \leftarrow c(R1)_{24-30}$	M,A,S
ISK	Ø9 | R1 | R2	$R1_{24-30} \leftarrow$ Key for storage block addressed by $c(R2)_{8-20}$	M,A,S
LPSW	82 ////// B1 | D1	$PSW_{0-63} \leftarrow c(S1)_{0-63}$	M,A,S
SPM	Ø4 | R1 //////	[CC, Prog. Mask] $\leftarrow c(R1)_{2-7}$	
SVC	ØA | I	$PSW_{24-31} \leftarrow I$; Interrupt	
LRA	B1 | R1 | X2 | B2 | D2	$R1 \leftarrow$ translated $S2$	M,A
PTLB	B2ØD //////////	$TLB \leftarrow 0$	M
RRB	B213 | B2 | D2	Stor. Key $(S2_{0-12})_5 \leftarrow 0$	M,A
LCTL	B7 | CR1 | CR3 | B2 | D2	$CR1, \ldots, CR3 \leftarrow c(S2), \ldots$	M,A,S
STCTL	B6 | CR1 | CR3 | B2 | D2	$S2, \ldots \leftarrow c(CR1), \ldots, c(CR3)$	M,A,S
STCK	B2Ø5 | B2 | D2	$S2_{0-63} \leftarrow$ time-of-day clock	A

logical instructions, shifts, etc.) can be done with control registers, so it is necessary to store their contents, perform any desired change, then reload the control registers.

One final instruction is introduced here because it was not convenient to do it elsewhere. The System/370 has several clocks with various functions. The *time-of-day clock* is a double-word binary integer whose value behaves as if 1 is added to position 51 every microsecond. Depending on model, a larger number may be added less often, but it is a fairly high-resolution clock. A user program operating in problem state can receive the value in this clock by executing the S-type instruction STCK. The double-word value is stored at the second-operand location. The value is arranged so that the *first word* of the clock (bit 31) is incremented every 1.048576 seconds, so often measurement of time intervals can be done accurately enough by computing the difference between two values of the first word of the clock. The condition code is set by STCK, to

0   if the clock is set,

1   if not set (but still running, so available for interval calculation),

2   error state,

3   not operational.

The instructions introduced in this chapter are summarized in Fig. 17.10. The formats are shown explicitly, since the instructions differ from other instructions of their respective types. Figure 17.11 shows by control field the instructions that deal with each control function.

A number of system control instructions have not been mentioned at all. They deal with yet more specialized control functions. Just a glimpse has been presented of some of the facilities with which the supervisor works. But you may well feel that too much has been covered already!

FIGURE 17.11   Instructions affecting system control features

Field	EC-mode PSW location	Instructions affecting the field
Storage key		ISK,SSK,RRB
Protection key	PSW_{8-11}	LPSW
Control mode	PSW_{12}	LPSW
MWP	PSW_{13-15}	LPSW
Condition code	PSW_{18-19}	SPM, LPSW, any instruction that sets condition code
Program mask	PSW_{20-23}	SPM, LPSW
Instruction address	PSW_{40-63}	LPSW, any branch instruction
Control register		LCTL, STCTL
Time-of-day clock		STCK

17.4 Interrupt Handling

The mechanism of interrupt is very simple. The current program status word, with appropriate instruction length code and interrupt code indicating the condition causing interrupt, is stored at a fixed location in main storage. A new program status word is loaded into the PSW from another fixed location (it is useful now to distinguish between PSW, the physical register, and a program status word, which is the information currently or formerly held in the PSW). Processing then resumes, according to directions and status given in the new program status word.

There are six classes of interrupts, and each class has its own set of fixed addresses for old and new program status words. The types and fixed addresses are shown in Fig. 17.12. A *restart* interrupt is caused by depressing the *restart* key at the operator's console. An *external* interrupt is caused by a signal from any of several clocks or timers, the interrupt key on the console, or external lines (perhaps attached to other computers—not to be confused with channels). The *supervisor call* interrupt is caused by execution of the SVC instruction. A *machine check* interrupt is caused by detection of a machine malfunction in the CPU; it can be masked by PSW bit 13 but should be masked only during processing of a machine check interrupt. An *input/output* interrupt is caused by conditions in the input/output system, as will be discussed further in Sections 17.5–17.8.

A *program* interrupt is caused by some condition, usually an invalid instruction or data for the instruction, arising from execution of the user's program. Fifteen program conditions were discussed in previous chapters; four of them can be masked by the program mask.

Three program conditions are associated with dynamic address translation. One is caused by a *segment fault*, in which the *invalid* bit for a needed entry in the segment table is found to be 1. A second is caused by a *page fault*, in which the *invalid* bit for a needed entry in the page table is found to be 1. Either of these is a signal that a needed page is not in main storage, and a swap-

FIGURE 17.12 Classes of interrupts and program status word addresses

Interrupt class	Old program status word stored at:	New program status word loaded from:
Restart	000008	000000
External	000018	000058
Supervisor call	000020	000060
Program	000028	000068
Machine check	000030	000070
Input/output	000038	000078

ping action must be taken, after which control is returned to the program. The third condition is a *translation specification* condition, caused by improper codes in control register 1 or in the segment and page tables.

A few more conditions are related to features not introduced here. All others are caused by a *program event*, to enable recording as mentioned in Section 17.2. One last program interrupt is caused by a *monitor call* instruction; the monitoring system is beyond the scope of the treatment of this chapter. A summary of interruption codes and actions is provided in Fig. 17.13.

Several interrupt conditions can arise simultaneously. When they do, interrupts occur in order of priority as follows:

1. machine check,
2. supervisor call,
3. program,
4. external,
5. input/output,
6. restart.

If conditions of, say, fixed-point overflow and input/output interrupt arise simultaneously, the fixed-point overflow interrupt is taken first. However, immediately afterward the input/output interrupt is taken, so it is really *processed before* the fixed-point overflow interrupt.

The program status word stored at each of the locations $\emptyset\emptyset\emptyset\emptyset\emptyset\emptyset$, $\emptyset\emptyset\emptyset\emptyset58$, $\emptyset\emptyset\emptyset\emptyset6\emptyset$, $\emptyset\emptyset\emptyset\emptyset68$, $\emptyset\emptyset\emptyset\emptyset7\emptyset$, and $\emptyset\emptyset\emptyset\emptyset78$ is obviously associated with the portion of the supervisor that is to handle the corresponding type of interrupt. Each of these program status words will contain a 0-bit in position 15 to put the CPU in the supervisor state. It will contain, in positions 40–63, the address of the routine that handles the particular type of interrupt. Finally, it will contain bits to mask out further interrupts of the type it is treating. For example, the program status word at location $\emptyset\emptyset\emptyset\emptyset58$ contains the address of the routine that handles external interrupts; it also contains a 1-bit in position 7 so that no further external interrupts may occur. The prohibition is necessary at least until the information in the old program status word from the current interrupt is safely stored; otherwise a new interrupt would put another program status word in location $\emptyset\emptyset\emptyset\emptyset18$, destroying the previous information. This is why masking provisions are necessary for external, input/output, and machine check interrupt conditions. Presumably, if the interrupt handling routines are written correctly, they will not *cause* program check or supervisor call interrupts, so masking provisions for these are not necessary.

If you want to handle interrupts of certain types resulting from your program, you can provide in a SPIE (Specify Program Interruption Exit) macro instruction the address of the interrupt-handling routine and the interrupt conditions under which you want it to operate. When one of these interrupts occurs, the supervisor will put register contents and program status word information, including the interrupt code, in a special region and give control (in the problem, not the supervisor state) to your own routine.

FIGURE 17.13   Interrupt action

Source	Inter-ruption code	PSW Mask bits	Mask bits in control register		Execution of instruction identified by old PSW
			Reg.:	Bits	
Machine check		13	14:	4– 7	completed if possible
Supervisor call	12				completed
External		7	0:	16–22 24–26	unaffected
Input/output		6	2:	0–31	unaffected
Restart					unaffected
Program:					
Operation	1				suppressed
Privileged operation	2				suppressed
Execute	3				suppressed
Protection	4				suppressed or terminated
Addressing	5				suppressed or terminated
Specification	6				suppressed
Data	7				suppressed or terminated
Fixed-point overflow	8	20			completed
Fixed-point divide	9				suppressed or completed
Decimal overflow	A	21			completed
Decimal divide	B				suppressed
Exponent overflow	C				completed
Exponent underflow	D	22			completed
Significance	E	23			completed
Floating-point divide	F				suppressed
Segment translation	10				nullified
Page translation	11				nullified
Translation specification	12				suppressed
Monitor event	40		8:	16–31	completed
Program event	80		9:	0–31	completed

17.5 The Basic Structure of Input and Output Processing

The structure of the input and output (we use the abbreviation I/O) system of System/370 is rather complex, designed for flexibility and the maximum decentralization of control possible consistent with standardized treatment wherever possible. There are ten I/O instructions in System/370, but only four major ones: Start I/O, Halt I/O, Test I/O, and Test Channel. The actual activity takes place in the channels, control units, and I/O devices under direction of programs executed by the channels. Channel programs consist of *commands*; a channel program is initiated by a Start I/O instruction, but is then executed independently of the CPU. The format of channel programs is standard for all devices, but a channel command may include a device-oriented code which will be translated by an I/O control unit into an *order* to a device.

A System/370 computer has several channels. The channels are of two types. A *byte-multiplexor* channel has several subchannels, and several subchannels may be active concurrently. They are expected to transmit data or status information in short segments, sometimes only one byte at a time (from which the channel gets its name). The devices attached to byte-multiplexor channels are usually slow-speed, and because the transmissions are broken into short segments, they can be serviced in turn, each operating at its full speed.

A *block-multiplexor* channel also has subchannels, and they are usually attached to higher-speed devices like disk storage drives or magnetic tape drives. Several channel programs may be active at the same time, but transmission is in larger blocks of data, and only one subchannel may be actually transmitting data at a time. We call the high-speed transmission of larger blocks of data *burst mode*, to distinguish it from *multiplex* mode; another multiplex-mode operation can be initiated when a multiplexor channel is operating in multiplex mode, but burst mode effectively prevents the beginning of another burst-mode operation.

Older systems also had *selector* channels, which are each capable of executing only one channel program at a time because each has only one subchannel.

Commands are kept in main storage, each in a double word. Information being transferred by the channel moves into or out of main storage; the use of main storage for both instructions in the CPU and for I/O operations causes the program in the CPU to slow slightly, but otherwise the CPU and the channels run independently. Communication is maintained, however; the CPU can halt an I/O operation with a Halt I/O instruction, and the channel can cause an interrupt of the CPU. At appropriate times information on the status of a channel is stored in a channel status world (CSW), which is accessible to the program in the CPU.

In the next three sections the I/O structure is examined in somewhat more detail.

▄▄▄▄▄

17.6   Input and Output Instructions and States of the System

All I/O instructions are of S type, with a two-byte operation code and a single operand. The instructions look normal enough in assembler language; for example

$$\text{SIO} \quad 19\emptyset$$

The sum of the displacement *D2* and the contents of the register *B2* is formed as usual, but it does not refer to a main storage location. The low-order half of the sum specifies a channel and a device on the channel as shown in Fig. 17.14. The channel and device addresses have nothing to do with addresses of main storage locations but are used to identify particular channels and devices attached to channels. For example,

$$\text{9C}\emptyset\emptyset\emptyset19\emptyset$$

is the hexadecimal code for a Start I/O instruction, addressing channel 1 and device 90 on the channel—*B2* is 0, so no register is used.

The four major I/O instructions are shown in Fig. 17.15. All four instructions set a condition code, as discussed subsequently. All are privileged. But before the actions of the individual instructions can be described in any detail, states of the I/O system must be described.

Each of the channels, subchannels, and control units and devices (let us consider the control unit and device to be merged into one unit) may be in one of the four states: *available, working, interrupt pending,* or *not operational.* A channel is in the *working* state if it is operating in the burst mode; a subchannel or device is in the working state if it is performing any operation. Devices, control units, subchannels, and channels are *not operational* mainly if not provided in the system, or if power is turned off. If a condition that can cause interrupt is present, the channel, subchannel, or device is said to be in the *interrupt-pending* state. If a channel, subchannel, or device is in either the working, not operational, or interrupt-pending state, it is said to be *not available;* the *available* state is the absence of the not-available states. Many combinations of states are possible, but fortunately only a few are detectable or significant; for example, if the channel is not operational, states of subchannels and devices on the channel are irrelevant. The condition codes set by the I/O instructions depend on these states. We can now study the instructions, one by one.

FIGURE 17.14   Addressing a channel and device

////////Ignored////////////	Channel address	Device address
0 15 16	23 24	31

FIGURE 17.15 Input/output instructions

Instruction	Type	Action	Cond. code[1]	Exceptions[2]
SIO	S	Start an I/O operation	Yes	M
HIO	S	Halt an I/O operation	Yes	M
TIO	S	Set condition code; perhaps store channel status word	Yes	M
TCH	S	Test a channel	Yes	M

Notes
1. Condition code settings partially explained in text.
2. M: Privileged operation.

The Start I/O (SIO) instruction starts an input or output operation: read, read backward, write, sense, or control, if the designated channel, subchannel, and device are available. A *channel address word* (CAW) at fixed location $\emptyset\emptyset\emptyset\emptyset 48$ gives to the channel the address of the channel program to be executed, and the protection key to be used by the channel in its main storage accesses. The information in the CAW is promptly stored in the channel itself, so location $\emptyset\emptyset\emptyset\emptyset 48$ can be used for other things. The SIO instruction takes very little time; the operation is initiated, if possible, and left to the channel. The condition code is set to reflect the result of the initiation attempt, as follows:

CC = 0: Operation is initiated and undergoing execution by the channel.

CC = 1: Some kind of exceptional condition exists, such as interrupt pending; information is stored in a channel status word (CSW).

CC = 2: Channel or subchannel is busy (in the working state).

CC = 3: Channel, subchannel, or device is not operational.

If the condition code is 1, 2, or 3, the operation is not initiated.

There is a variation of the SIO instruction: Start I/O Fast release (SIOF) has the same operands and the same function as SIO, but is willing to leave its channel operation pending in the subchannel and return control to the operation of further CPU instructions faster than SIO. Some validity checking of the operation is performed before completion of SIOF, but the actual I/O operation begins later. The condition code settings are the same as those set by SIO.

The Halt I/O (HIO) instruction terminates the operation in a device, subchannel, or channel; data transmission stops immediately, but the mechanical operation of the device usually continues until the end of the block of data. The condition code reports the result of the HIO instruction.

CC = 0: The subchannel was in an interrupt-pending state; no action taken.

CC = 1: A CSW is stored, giving details of the termination, which may or may not have been completed.

CC = 2: A burst-mode operation is terminated.

CC = 3: Channel, subchannel, or device is not operational.

The HIO instruction is not often used; normally, an operation is allowed to run to completion. However, if the user's program is being terminated, if the channel is desperately needed for another operation, or if it is found that the current operation is somehow erroneous, the HIO instruction is necessary.

The Test I/O (TIO) instruction tests the status of a designated channel, subchannel, and device. Status information is recorded in the condition code and sometimes in the CSW. An interrupt-pending condition is cleared. The condition code is set as follows:

CC = 0: Subchannel and device are available.

CC = 1: The device is busy, or the device or subchannel has an interrupt pending; the CSW gives the details.

CC = 2: Channel or subchannel is busy.

CC = 3: Channel, subchannel, or device is not operational.

An I/O-handling piece of the supervisor may well be carried out with I/O interrupts masked off. Before returning control to an interrupted program, it may test all operating devices to see if one has an interrupt-pending condition; the discovery of one enables the interrupt condition to be serviced without actually causing interrupt.

The Test Channel (TCH) instruction is very simple. The channel only is tested; subchannels and devices are not. The condition code is set as follows:

CC = 0: The channel is available.

CC = 1: The channel has an interrupt-pending condition.

CC = 2: The channel is operating in a burst mode.

CC = 3: The channel is not operational.

Because operations in the multiplex mode are not sensed, the channel is left available for still further multiplex-mode operations.

17.7 Channel Programming

If all goes well, the SIO instruction initiates execution of a channel program to carry out an operation or sequence of operations using a particular channel, subchannel, and device. The channel then proceeds until either the operation

FIGURE 17.16 Format of a channel address word (CAW)

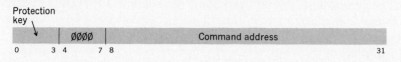

or sequence of operations is complete, a HIO instruction is given, or an exceptional condition, signaled by interrupt, makes completion impossible. We now study how operations are specified to the channel and how the channel executes its commands.

The sequence of operations to be performed by a channel program is defined by one or more *channel command words* (CCWs). The address of the first CCW in the channel program is given to the channel in the channel address word (CAW) at location Ø00048. The format of the CAW is as shown in Fig. 17.16. Bits 0–3 of the CAW contain a protection key that is compared to the storage key of any main storage location referenced, just as the protection key in the PSW is compared during instruction execution. The channel command words are double words that have the format shown in Fig. 17.17. The command code specifies the type of operation to be performed: Sense, Transfer in channel, Read backward, Write, Read, or Control. These types are described in more detail below. The data address is the address of the first byte to be used in information transfer (except when indirect data addressing is specified, as will be explained below); the count is the number of bytes to be transferred under control of the CCW. The flags in positions 32 to 38 carry further information about how the channel program is to proceed.

Two of the flags in the CCW control *chaining*. When the processing defined by one CCW is completed and the CCW indicates chaining, another CCW is fetched by the channel from main storage following the given CCW, and the channel program continues. If a CCW does not indicate chaining (and is not a transfer in channel command), it is the last CCW of the channel program. There are two types of chaining: *data chaining* and *command chaining*. Under data chaining, one operation—read, for example—is carried out using several main storage areas not necessarily contiguous. For instance, if a block contains three logical records of 80 bytes each, the block can be read in one op-

FIGURE 17.17 Format of a channel command word (CCW)

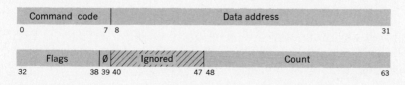

eration while the three logical records are placed in three buffer areas. Command chaining allows several operations, for example, the reading of several blocks in one channel program. Data chaining can take place within command chaining.

Sequences of CCWs in a channel program need not be contiguous in main storage. The *transfer-in-channel* command is an unconditional branch in a channel program, giving the location of a further sequence of CCWs. Thus a loop may be formed in a channel program!

When a block is being read or written, the count in the current CCW is decremented by 1 for each byte read or written. If the block is not completed when the count reaches zero, and data chaining is indicated, the next CCW is used for a continuation of the operation. If the count reaches zero before the block is completed and data chaining is *not* indicated, or if the block is completed before the count reaches zero, an incorrect length is indicated. The indication can be suppressed by the SLI (Suppress Length Indication) flag, but otherwise it causes the end of the channel program and generates an interrupt condition.

Another useful flag is the Program Controlled Interruption (PCI) flag, which generates an interrupt condition but allows the channel program to continue. The interrupt can be used by the supervisor to determine the current progress of the channel program. An interrupt could be generated after every block read, for example, so the user's program could start using the block while the channel program went on to read another block.

A *control* command causes the information sent to the device through the subchannel to be interpreted as control information instead of as data to be written. Control commands become *orders* to devices, causing rewinding of a magnetic tape, positioning of read-write heads to a particular cylinder of a magnetic disk pack, skipping the paper in a printer to a new page.

Although read and write commands are the most important commands, they are obvious. Only a few devices, such as some magnetic tape units, can read information backwards, but a separate command is necessary for *read backward*.

A *sense* command asks for detailed information on the status of the device and any unusual conditions detected in the last operation. The information is placed in main storage as though it came from a read operation, and it is often more extensive than information given in the CSW.

As an example, suppose that you want to read two blocks from a direct-access device, and that each block consists of two logical records which are to be read into noncontiguous buffer areas. The supervisor issues an SIO instruction after storing the address of your first CCW and an appropriate protection key (probably the same key used in your PSW) in location Ø0ØØ48 as a CAW. The SIO instruction designates the channel, let us suppose a block-multiplexor channel, and the device address; then the channel takes over. The CCWs required could be the following:

1. A *control* command to position the beginning of the read; a few bytes at a main storage location that contain the address of the desired area on the direct-access storage device are sent to the device as control information; the command chaining flag is on.

2. A *read* command, containing the address of the first buffer area and length of the logical record; the data chaining flag is on.

3. The command code is ignored, but the read operation continues, reading into the second buffer area; the command chaining flag is on.

4. Another *control* command, positioning the reading heads to read the second block; the command chaining flag is on, and so is the PCI flag; the PCI flag signals the supervisor that the first block has been read, but it does not affect execution of the channel program.

5. Another *read* command, including the data-chaining flag, and giving the address and length of the third buffer area.

6. The command code is ignored, but the address and length of the fourth buffer area enable continuation of the read operation; *no* flags are on, so the channel program ends here.

When the channel program is terminated, either by an HIO instruction, by detection of an error in the transmission or in the channel program, or by normal completion, an interrupt condition is generated; it causes an interrupt unless interrupts for the channel are masked off.

We have not yet considered the implications of virtual storage management on input and output in System/370. Two major implications are worthy of investigation.

1. Input and output are initiated and left to proceed while the CPU serves other tasks. Until the data transmission is completed, the main storage allocated for input/output areas must *not* be swapped out or made available for other uses; you can readily imagine the chaos that would result otherwise.

2. Main storage addressing for data transmission is *not* subject to dynamic address translation. This means that data addresses in channel programs must be real, not virtual addresses. It also means that a buffer that looks like one continuous block of main storage to the program may be, through paging, a set of several noncontiguous areas! While you get over your initial shock at this complication, let us think about why this design is necessary. First, data transmission is rapid and must not be hindered by address translation. Second, several input/output operations often proceed simultaneously, while several user programs and sections of the supervisor use the CPU in turn. One set of segment and page tables would be terribly strained trying to accommodate all users.

The remedy for point 1 is for the supervisor to "lock" the input/output areas into main storage and mark the page frames (in the page frame table) as not available for swapping.

For the second problem, the *indirect data addressing* feature, not available in older models, is helpful. If the IDA flag in the CCW is on, the data address portion of the CCW is interpreted as the address of a list of addresses of areas to be used in the actual information transmission. The count field of the CCW is still controlling; transmission begins with the address given in the first word of the IDA chain, and continues to the end of the 2048-byte block containing the first address (or until the count field is satisfied). If the count is not satisfied, transmission continues, starting at the second address in the chain (which will point to the beginning of a 2048-byte block), and it continues to the end of that block unless the count is satisfied first. Additional addresses in the chain are used similarly until the count is satisfied.

What then must the supervisor do when requested to execute a channel program in a virtual system? The channel program will be expressed in virtual addresses; the supervisor makes a copy that will be the one executed. The copy must then be modified. Each data address must be converted to a real address (this is where the LRA instruction comes in handy). The real address and count must be examined to see whether the data area crosses a page boundary. If so, the supervisor generates an IDA chain, puts its address in the CCW, and turns on the IDA flag. The appropriate page frames must be locked into main storage by changing their status in the page frame table. Then the supervisor may initiate execution of the channel program.

17.8   Interrupts and the Channel Status Word

The channel status word (CSW) occupies a double word at fixed main storage location ∅∅∅∅4∅; information is stored there regarding the status of an I/O device or conditions under which a channel program is terminated. The information is provided upon I/O interrupt or when a SIO, HIO, or TIO requires more information than can be given in the condition code. The general form of the CSW is as shown in Fig. 17.18. The channel, subchannel, or device whose status is given is indicated in the stored program status word in case of interrupt; for a CSW resulting from SIO, HIO, or TIO the channel, subchannel, and device are those addressed by the SIO, HIO, or TIO. The protection key that was sent to the channel through the CAW is included in the CSW, as well as the address of a CCW, usually the one beyond that producing the current condition. The residual count, that is, the number of bytes not yet processed under the current CCW, is given in bits 48–63; bits 32–47 indicate certain conditions, some of which are: busy, control-unit end, device end, channel end, unit check, unit exception, program-controlled interruption, incorrect length, program check, protection check, channel data check, and chaining check. You can gather from this list the general nature of the information conveyed even without detailed explanation of each of these conditions.

Detection of an error in any phase of an I/O operation will cause the channel program to be terminated and an interrupt generated. A parity error in the

FIGURE 17.18 Format of a channel status word (CSW)

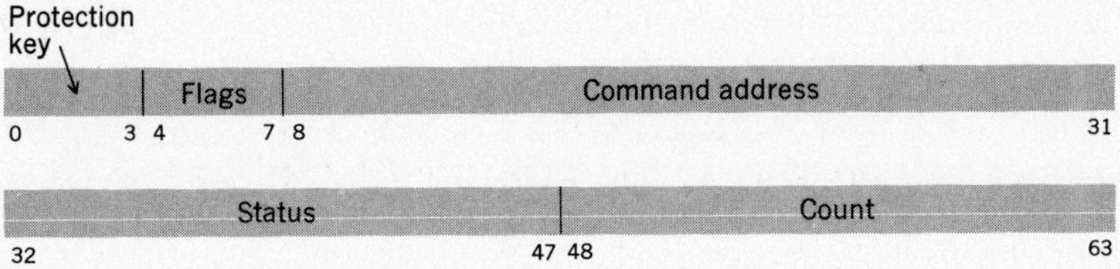

data read or written, which is reflected in a channel data check, does not cause interrupt until completion of the current I/O operation. Other errors actually caused by invalidities in the channel program are detected as a new CCW is being interpreted, and execution of the command is suppressed.

The example channel program described in Section 17.7 could be interrupted at any of several points. A channel data check in the execution of the second CCW does not terminate the channel program until after the read operation is completed, that is, at the end of the third CCW. However, an error in specification of the third CCW itself, called a program check, would terminate the program in the middle of the read operation. An exceptional condition in the device, such as equipment error or not-ready status, generates a unit-check and signals the program that more information can be obtained through execution of a sense command.

m a i n   i d e a s

□ Virtual storage systems assign page frames of main storage as needed to hold pages for a program, allowing more efficient use of main storage. The mapping of virtual to real storage requires dynamic address translation hardware, and segment table, page tables, page frame tables, and external page tables.

□ The program status word contains information about the state of the CPU and the program currently in execution, and about the categories of interrupts allowed. System/370 also keeps related information in control registers.

□ During execution of a program, instructions changing contents of main storage are monitored by the protection system. The protection key in the PSW must either be zero or match the storage key associated with the referenced storage block, or a protection interrupt occurs.

□ Some instructions, called privileged instructions, can be executed only when the computer is in the supervisor state. Among them are the protection-system instructions ISK and SSK described in Section 17.2, the PSW-manipulating instructions LPSW and LRA described in Section 17.3, and the I/O instructions SIO, HIO, TIO, and TCH described in Section 17.6.

□ An interrupt causes the contents of the PSW to be stored at a fixed location in main storage and causes another program status word, corresponding to an interrupt-handling routine, to be loaded from another fixed location. A pair of such locations is provided for each of the interrupt classes: external, supervisor call, program check, machine check, restart, and input/output.

□ Input and output operations are carried out through channels from the CPU to control units and devices. A byte-multiplexor channel may have several subchannels, all operating in the multiplex mode concurrently, thus handling several slow-speed devices. The block-multiplexor channel in System/370 allows several subchannels to execute programs concurrently, but only one at a time may transmit data, in burst mode.

□ An I/O instruction is initiated by the SIO instruction, which sends to the channel a channel address word (CAW). Thereafter the channel executes a channel program consisting of channel command words (CCWs) in main storage that specify the operations read, read backward, write, control, sense, and transfer in channel, as well as the address and length of the main-storage area to be used. Several CCWs may define several areas of main storage to be used in an I/O operation through data chaining. And through command chaining, several operations may be executed under control of one channel program. Since channels do not use dynamic address translation, the supervisor must map virtual addresses into real explicitly for channel programs, and often break virtual blocks into real discontiguous subblocks.

□ In addition to SIO, the instructions HIO, TIO, and TCH manipulate and get information from the channels. Each one sets a condition code that depends on whether the addressed channel, subchannel, and device are available, working, have interrupts pending, or are not operational; if necessary, more information is supplied in a channel status word (CSW).

□ An I/O interrupt can be generated as specified in a command or upon normal or abnormal termination of an I/O operation. The interrupt is always accompanied by further information about its cause in the CSW.

■ **PROBLEMS** FOR REVIEW AND IMAGINATION

17.1 Given the special meaning of a protection key of 0, what areas of main storage might have a storage key of 0?

17.2 Write sequences including SPM instructions that set the program mask to allow various combinations of the maskable program-check interrupts.

17.3 The LPSW instruction loads a new program status word; how can one store the current contents of the PSW for examination? Design an instruction sequence, including an interrupt-handling routine if necessary, that will change bit 13 of the current PSW to 1, not changing anything else except, of course, the instruction address.

17.4 An interrupt-handling routine should mask out interrupts of the type it is handling, but one can see problems of an interrupt of type x, followed by an interrupt of type y, followed by another interrupt of type x that wipes out information on the first x-type interrupt. The priority hierarchy given in Section 17.4 should therefore be consulted in determining which interrupt-handling routines should allow which other interrupts. Design such a scheme; would you make special provision for machine-check interrupts?

17.5   In a multiprogramming system, certain subroutines should be common to several jobs but cannot be in process at the same time. One example is a storage-allocation subroutine. When two routines each want a block of storage, we must arrange that one gets the first available block and the other gets the second available block. Some mechanism must be set up so that before the storage-allocation subroutine (or at least a certain critical section of it) is entered, the mechanism makes sure that the subroutine is not currently in use. Some indicator must therefore be set upon entrance to the subroutine and reset upon exit, but *tested before entrance*. Show that if testing and setting of the indicator are done by separate instructions, an interrupt *between* testing and setting would permit a second routine to enter the subroutine concurrently with the first.

There is an instruction Test and Set (TS) that helps us in this problem. This instruction is of SI type with one operand that is one byte in main storage. Test and Set first tests the leftmost bit of the first operand byte. The condition code is set to

0 if the leftmost bit is 0,
1 if the leftmost bit is 1.

Then, regardless of the outcome of the test, it sets the byte to (binary) 11111111. Show how an indicator byte can be tested and set by the TS instruction to try to gain entry to and reserve the subroutine. Should the TS instruction be used inside or outside the subroutine? What configuration of the indicator byte represents that the subroutine is in use? What configuration represents that the subroutine is available? How is the indicator reset, and when?

17.6   Think of as many different situations as possible that require different status indications in the page frame table, and outline some of the routines that would be required in managing page frame table, segment and page tables.

17.7   Design a program segment that will examine CCWs, translate virtual addresses to real addresses, and construct an indirect data addressing chain.

17.8   Design a program segment that will set reference bits for all page frames to 0.

17.9   Design a program segment that will add 2 to the number in bit positions 0–7 of control register 1.

17.10 Outline the routine that would handle a page fault interrupt and the swapping actions that must be taken. Either make assumptions about details left unspecified in this chapter or look up the actual conditions in appropriate manuals.

■ **REFERENCES** ▬▬▬▬▬▬▬▬▬▬▬▬▬▬▬▬▬▬▬▬▬

Auslander, M. A., and J. F. Jaffe, "Functional Structure of IBM Virtual Storage Operating Systems. Part I: Influences of Dynamic Address Translation on Operating System Technology," *IBM Systems Journal* **12**, 4 (1973), pp. 368–381.

Brown, D. T., R. L. Eibsen, and C. A. Thom, "Channel and Direct Access Device Architecture," *IBM Systems Journal* **11**, 3 (1972), pp. 186–199. The design of block-multiplexor channel and other System/370 input/output features.

Denning, Peter J., "Virtual Memory," *Computing Surveys* **2**, 3 (September 1970), pp. 153–189. A tutorial exposition of virtual storage techniques (not restricted to System/370).

Foster, Caxton C., *Computer Architecture*, Van Nostrand Reinhold, New York, 1970. A discussion of content-addressable memory and its uses, among other architectural features.

IBM System/370 Principles of Operation, GA 22-7000, IBM Corporation. A full description of the machine's facilities.

Introduction to Virtual Storage in System/370, GR 20-4260, IBM Corporation. A student text on virtual storage.

Morrison, J. E., "User Program Performance in Virtual Storage Systems," *IBM Systems Journal* **12**, 3 (1973), pp. 216–237.

Padegs, A., "The Structure of SYSTEM/360: Part IV—Channel Design Considerations," *IBM Systems Journal* **3** (1964), pp. 165–180. An explanation of the rationale of the input-output structure of System/360.

Scherr, A. L., "Functional Structure of IBM Virtual Storage Operating Systems. Part II: OS/VS2-2 Concepts and Philosophies," *IBM Systems Journal* **12**, 4 (1973), pp. 382–400.

REPRESENTATION OF CHARACTERS

8-bit code		Hexa-decimal	Decimal	Punched card code	EBCDIC characters
Ø1ØØ	ØØØØ	40	64	no punches	space
Ø1ØØ	1Ø1Ø	4A	74	12-8-2	¢
Ø1ØØ	1Ø11	4B	75	12-8-3	.
Ø1ØØ	11ØØ	4C	76	12-8-4	<
Ø1ØØ	11Ø1	4D	77	12-8-5	(
Ø1ØØ	111Ø	4E	78	12-8-6	+
Ø1ØØ	1111	4F	79	12-8-7	|
Ø1Ø1	ØØØØ	50	80	12	&
Ø1Ø1	1Ø1Ø	5A	90	11-8-2	!
Ø1Ø1	1Ø11	5B	91	11-8-3	$
Ø1Ø1	11ØØ	5C	92	11-8-4	*
Ø1Ø1	11Ø1	5D	93	11-8-5	)
Ø1Ø1	111Ø	5E	94	11-8-6	;
Ø1Ø1	1111	5F	95	11-8-7	¬
Ø11Ø	ØØØØ	60	96	11	_
Ø11Ø	ØØØ1	61	97	0-1	/
Ø11Ø	1Ø11	6B	107	0-8-3	,
Ø11Ø	11ØØ	6C	108	0-8-4	%
Ø11Ø	11Ø1	6D	109	0-8-5	—
Ø11Ø	111Ø	6E	110	0-8-6	>
Ø11Ø	1111	6F	111	0-8-7	?
Ø111	1Ø1Ø	7A	122	8-2	:
Ø111	1Ø11	7B	123	8-3	#
Ø111	11ØØ	7C	124	8-4	@
Ø111	11Ø1	7D	125	8-5	'
Ø111	111Ø	7E	126	8-6	=
Ø111	1111	7F	127	8-7	"
1ØØØ	ØØØ1	81	129	12-0-1	a
1ØØØ	ØØ1Ø	82	130	12-0-2	b
1ØØØ	ØØ11	83	131	12-0-3	c
1ØØØ	Ø1ØØ	84	132	12-0-4	d
1ØØØ	Ø1Ø1	85	133	12-0-5	e
1ØØØ	Ø11Ø	86	134	12-0-6	f
1ØØØ	Ø111	87	135	12-0-7	g
1ØØØ	1ØØØ	88	136	12-0-8	h
1ØØØ	1ØØ1	89	137	12-0-9	i
1ØØ1	ØØØ1	91	145	12-11-1	j
1ØØ1	ØØ1Ø	92	146	12-11-2	k

(continued)

REPRESENTATION OF CHARACTERS   [continued]

8-bit code	Hexa-decimal	Decimal	Punched card code	EBCDIC characters
1001 0011	93	147	12-11-3	l
1001 0100	94	148	12-11-4	m
1001 0101	95	149	12-11-5	n
1001 0110	96	150	12-11-6	o
1001 0111	97	151	12-11-7	p
1001 1000	98	152	12-11-8	q
1001 1001	99	153	12-11-9	r
1010 0001	A1	161	11-0-1	~
1010 0010	A2	162	11-0-2	s
1010 0011	A3	163	11-0-3	t
1010 0100	A4	164	11-0-4	u
1010 0101	A5	165	11-0-5	v
1010 0110	A6	166	11-0-6	w
1010 0111	A7	167	11-0-7	x
1010 1000	A8	168	11-0-8	y
1010 1001	A9	169	11-0-9	z
1100 0000	C0	192	12-0	{
1100 0001	C1	193	12-1	A
1100 0010	C2	194	12-2	B
1100 0011	C3	195	12-3	C
1100 0100	C4	196	12-4	D
1100 0101	C5	197	12-5	E
1100 0110	C6	198	12-6	F
1100 0111	C7	199	12-7	G
1100 1000	C8	200	12-8	H
1100 1001	C9	201	12-9	I
1101 0000	D0	208	11-0	}
1101 0001	D1	209	11-1	J
1101 0010	D2	210	11-2	K
1101 0011	D3	211	11-3	L
1101 0100	D4	212	11-4	M
1101 0101	D5	213	11-5	N
1101 0110	D6	214	11-6	O
1101 0111	D7	215	11-7	P
1101 1000	D8	216	11-8	Q
1101 1001	D9	217	11-9	R
1110 0000	E0	224	0-2-8	\

REPRESENTATION OF CHARACTERS   [continued]

8-bit code	Hexa-decimal	Decimal	Punched card code	EBCDIC characters
1110 0010	E2	226	0-2	S
1110 0011	E3	227	0-3	T
1110 0100	E4	228	0-4	U
1110 0101	E5	229	0-5	V
1110 0110	E6	230	0-6	W
1110 0111	E7	231	0-7	X
1110 1000	E8	232	0-8	Y
1110 1001	E9	233	0-9	Z
1111 0000	F0	240	0	0
1111 0001	F1	241	1	1
1111 0010	F2	242	2	2
1111 0011	F3	243	3	3
1111 0100	F4	244	4	4
1111 0101	F5	245	5	5
1111 0110	F6	246	6	6
1111 0111	F7	247	7	7
1111 1000	F8	248	8	8
1111 1001	F9	249	9	9

NOTATION FOR ACTION DESCRIPTION
OF INSTRUCTIONS

1. Entities

$R1$ General register specified as first operand
$R2$ General register specified as second operand
$R3$ General register specified as third operand
$FPR1$ Floating-point register specified as first operand
$FPR2$ Floating-point register specified as second operand
$CR1$ Control register specified as first operand
$CR3$ Control register specified as third operand
Reg. 1 General register 1; implied operand in certain instructions
Reg. 2 General register 2; implied operand in certain instructions
$S1$ First operand (specified by $D1$ and $B1$) in main storage
$S2$ Second operand (specified by $D2$, $B2$, and sometimes $X2$)
$c(R1)$ Contents of register $R1$
$c(R2)$, $c(R3)$, $c(FPR1)$, $c(FPR2)$, $c(S1)$, $c(S2)$ have similar meanings
$M1$ M1 portion of branch instruction
$M3$ M3 portion of masked character instruction
$I2$ I2 portion of SI instruction
$I3$ I3 portion of SRP instruction
cc Condition code
PSW Program status word

2. Lengths of Entities

a. Register and main storage operands are presumed to be 32 bits long unless otherwise noted.
$M1$ is always four bits and $I2$ always eight bits.

b. Bit positions of a portion of an entity are designated by subscripts:
Entity$_{a-b}$ designates bit positions a to b of an Entity.
$c(\text{Entity})_{a-b}$ designates contents of bit positions a to b of an Entity.
Bit positions are always numbered from 0 at the left (high-order) end.

c. Lengths of operands are also indicated in notes.

d. [Entity 1, Entity 2] indicates the concatenation of Entity 1 and Entity 2.

3. Actions on Entities

a. Operations $+ - * /$ AND OR Ex. OR and absolute value ($|\ \ |$) are shown. Mode of the operation—signed binary integer, unsigned binary integer (logical), floating point, decimal—is implied by the instruction name or notes. Mode of comparison is also implied in compare instructions.

b. Placement of a result is indicated by a left-pointing arrow: $R1 \leftarrow c(S2)$ designates placement of $c(S2)$ in register $R1$.

c. Branch is indicated by a right-pointing arrow: $\rightarrow S2$ designates a branch to the location $S2$.

IBM SYSTEM/370 INSTRUCTIONS

Mnemonic	Name	Type	Num. Op. Code	Operands	Cond. Code	Exceptions[44]	Action (See Appendix B)	Ref. Chapter and Sec.	Notes
A	Add	RX	5A	$R1,D2(X2,B2)$	(1)	A,S, IF	$R1 \leftarrow c(R1) + c(S2)$	4.3	
AR	Add Register	RR	1A	$R1,R2$	(1)	A,S, IF	$R1 \leftarrow c(R1) + c(R2)$	4.3	
AH	Add Half-word	RX	4A	$R1,D2(X2,B2)$	(1)	A,S, IF	$R1 \leftarrow c(R1) + c(S2)_{0-15}$	4.3	
AL	Add Logical	RX	5E	$R1,D2(X2,B2)$	(3)	A,S	$R1 \leftarrow c(R1) + c(S2)$	11.1	
ALR	Add Logical Register	RR	1E	$R1,R2$	(3)	A,S	$R1 \leftarrow c(R1) + c(R2)$	11.1	
AP	Add Decimal	SS	FA	$D1(L1,B1),D2(L2,B2)$	(1)	A, D, DF	$S1 \leftarrow c(S1) + c(S2)$	14.3	(20,26)
AD	Add Double	RX	6A	$R1,D2(X2,B2)$	(5)	A,S,U,E,LS	$FPR1 \leftarrow c(FPR1) + c(S2)$	13.3	(21,23)
ADR	Add Double Register	RR	2A	$R1,R2$	(5)	S,U,E,LS	$FPR1 \leftarrow c(FPR1) + c(FPR2)$	13.3	(21,23)
AE	Add Floating	RX	7A	$R1,D2(X2,B2)$	(5)	A,S,U,E,LS	$FPR1 \leftarrow c(FPR1) + c(S2)$	13.3	(21)
AER	Add Floating Register	RR	3A	$R1,R2$	(5)	S,U,E,LS	$FPR1 \leftarrow c(FPR1) + c(FPR2)$	13.3	(21)
AU	Add Unnormalized	RX	7E	$R1,D2(X2,B2)$	(5)	A,S, E,LS	$FPR1 \leftarrow c(FPR1) + c(S2)$	13.5	(21,24)
AUR	Add Unnormalized Register	RR	3E	$R1,R2$	(5)	S, E,LS	$FPR1 \leftarrow c(FPR1) + c(FPR2)$	13.5	(21,24)
AW	Add Double Unnormalized	RX	6E	$R1,D2(X2,B2)$	(5)	A,S, E,LS	$FPR1 \leftarrow c(FPR1) + c(S2)$	13.5	(21,23,24)
AWR	Add Double Unnormalized Register	RR	2E	$R1,R2$	(5)	S, E,LS	$FPR1 \leftarrow c(FPR1) + c(FPR2)$	13.5	(21,23,24)
AXR	Add eXtended	RR	36	$R1,R2$	(5)	S,U,E,LS	$FPR1_{0-127} \leftarrow c(FPR1)_{0-127} + c(FPR2)_{0-127}$	13.8	(39)
BAL	Branch And Link	RX	45	$R1,D2(X2,B2)$			$R1 \leftarrow [ILC,CC,Prog.Mask,c(PSW)_{40-63}];$ $\rightarrow S2$	Problem 6.2	
BALR	Branch And Link Register	RR	05	$R1,R2$			$R1 \leftarrow [ILC,CC,Prog.Mask,c(PSW)_{40-63}];$ $\rightarrow c(R2)$	6.1	(29)
BAS	Branch and Save	RX	4D	$R1,D2(X2,B2)$			$R1_{0-7} \leftarrow 0; R1_{8-31} \leftarrow c(PSW)_{40-63}; \rightarrow S2$		(35)

Mnemonic	Name	Format	Opcode	Operands			Operation	§	Notes
BASR	Branch and Save Register	RR	0D	R1,R2			$R1_{0-7} \leftarrow 0; R1_{8-31} \leftarrow c(PSW)_{40-63}; \rightarrow c(R2)$		(35)
BC	Branch on Condition	RX	47	M1,D2(X2,B2)			$\rightarrow S2$ if $(M1)_{cc}=1$	6.1,7.4	
BCR	Branch on Condition to Register	RR	07	M1,R2			$\rightarrow c(R2)$ if $(M1)_{cc}=1$	7.4	(29)
BCT	Branch on Count	RX	46	R1,D2(X2,B2)			$R1 \leftarrow c(R1)-1; \rightarrow S2$ if $c(R1) \neq 0$	8.6	
BCTR	Branch on Count to Register	RR	06	R1,R2			$R1 \leftarrow c(R1)-1; \rightarrow c(R2)$ if $c(R1) \neq 0$	8.6	(29)
BXH	Branch on Index High	RS	86	R1,R3,D2(B2)			$R1 \leftarrow c(R1)+c(R3)$; If $R3$ is even, $\rightarrow S2$ if $c(R1) > c(R3+1)$ If $R3$ is odd, $\rightarrow S2$ if $c(R1) > c(R3)$	8.4	
BXLE	Branch on Index Low or Equal	RS	87	R1,R3,D2(B2)			$R1 \leftarrow c(R1)+c(R3)$; If $R3$ is even, $\rightarrow S2$ if $c(R1) \leq c(R3+1)$ If $R3$ is odd, $\rightarrow S2$ if $c(R1) \leq c(R3)$	8.4	
C	Compare	RX	59	R1,D2(X2,B2)	(2)	A,S		7.3	
CR	Compare Register	RR	19	R1,R2	(2)			7.3	
CH	Compare Half-word	RX	49	R1,D2(X2,B2)	(2)	A,S		7.3	
CL	Compare Logical	RX	55	R1,D2(X2,B2)	(2)	A,S		11.1	
CLR	Compare Logical Register	RR	15	R1,R2	(2)			11.1	
CLC	Compare Logical Character	SS	D5	D1(L,B1),D2(B2)	(2)	A		10.2	(25)
CLI	Compare Logical Immediate	SI	95	D1(B1),I2	(2)	A		10.2	
CLM	Compare Logical under Mask	RS	BD	R1,M3,D2(B2)	(15)	A		10.2	(36,37)
CLCL	Compare Logical Characters Long	RR	0F	R1,R2	(2)	A,S		10.2	(36,38)
CP	Compare Decimal	SS	F9	D1(L1,B1),D2(L2,B2)	(2)	A, D		14.3	(20,26)
CD	Compare Double	RX	69	R1,D2(X2,B2)	(2)	A,S		13.3	(21,23)

(continued)

IBM SYSTEM/370 INSTRUCTIONS [continued]

Mnemonic	Name	Type	Num. Op. Code	Operands	Cond. Code	Exceptions[44]	Action (See Appendix B)	Ref. Chapter and Sec.	Notes
CDR	Compare Double Register	RR	29	R1,R2	(2)	S		13.3	(21,23)
CE	Compare Floating	RX	79	R1,D2(X2,B2)	(2)	A,S		13.3	(21)
CER	Compare Floating Register	RR	39	R1,R2	(2)	S		13.3	(21)
CS	Compare and Swap	RS	BA	R1,D2(B2)	(19)	A,S	If $c(R1) = c(S2),S2 \leftarrow c(R3)$ else $R1 \leftarrow c(S2)$		(43)
CDS	Compare Double and Swap	RS	BB	R1,D2(B2)	(19)	A,S	If $c(R1)_{0-63} = c(S2)_{0-63},S2_{0-63} \leftarrow c(R3)_{0-63}$ else $R1_{0-63} \leftarrow c(S2)_{0-63}$		(43)
CVB	Convert to Binary	RX	4F	R1,D2(X2,B2)		A,S,D, IK	$R1$ (binary)$\leftarrow c(S2)_{0-63}$(packed dec.)	6.5	
CVD	Convert to Decimal	RX	4E	R1,D2(X2,B2)		A,S	$S2_{0-63}$(packed dec.)$\leftarrow c(R1)$(binary)	6.5	
D	Divide	RX	5D	R1,D2(X2,B2)		A,S, IK	$R1 \leftarrow$ Rem. of $[c(R1),c(R1 + 1)]/c(S2)$ $R1 + 1 \leftarrow$ Quot. of $[c(R1),c(R1 + 1)]/c(S2)$	4.5	
DR	Divide Register	RR	1D	R1,R2		S, IK	$R1 \leftarrow$ Rem. of $[c(R1),c(R1 + 1)]/c(R2)$ $R1 + 1 \leftarrow$ Quot. of $[c(R1),c(R1 + 1)]/c(R2)$	4.5	
DP	Divide Decimal	SS	FD	D1(L1,B1),D2(L2,B2)		A,S,D, DK	$S1 \leftarrow$ [quot. of $c(S1)/c(S2)$, rem. of $c(S1)/c(S2)$]	14.5	(20,26)
DD	Divide Double	RX	6D	R1,D2(X2,B2)		A,S,U,E,FK	$FPR1 \leftarrow c(FPR1)/c(S2)$	13.4	(21,23)
DDR	Divide Double Register	RR	2D	R1,R2		S,U,E,FK	$FPR1 \leftarrow c(FPR1)/c(FPR2)$	13.4	(21,23)
DE	Divide Floating	RX	7D	R1,D2(X2,B2)		A,S,U,E,FK	$FPR1 \leftarrow c(FPR1)/c(S2)$	13.4	(21)
DER	Divide Floating Register	RR	3D	R1,R2		S,U,E,FK	$FPR1 \leftarrow c(FPR1)/c(FPR2)$	13.4	(21)
ED	Edit	SS	DE	D1(L,B1),D2(B2)	(1)	A, D	$S1 \leftarrow c(S2)$	15.2	(20,30)

Mnemonic	Name	Type	Code	Operands	Note	Flags	EX/IF	Operation	§	Ref
EDMK	Edit and Mark	SS	DF	D1(L,B1),D2(B2)	(1)	A, D		$S1 \leftarrow c(S2)$; Reg. $1_{8-31} \leftarrow$ Addr. of 1st sig. digit	15.2	(20,30)
EX	Execute	RX	44	R1,D2(X2,B2)		A,S	EX	Execute instr. $c(S2)$, mod. by $c(R1)_{24-31}$	15.3	(21)
HER	Halve	RR	34	R1,R2		S		$FPR1 \leftarrow c(FPR2)/2$	13.4	
HDR	Halve Double	RR	24	R1,R2		S		$FRP1 \leftarrow c(FPR2)/2$	13.4	(21,23)
HIO	Halt I/O	S	9E00	D2(B2)	(7)	M		Halt an I/O operation	17.6	
IC	Insert Character	RX	43	R1,D2(X2,B2)		A		$R1_{24-31} \leftarrow c(S2)_{0-7}$	10.1	
ICM	Insert Characters under Mask	RS	BF	R1,M3,D2(B2)	(16)	A		$R1 \leftarrow c(S2)$	10.1	(36,37)
ISK	Insert Storage Key	RR	09	R1,R2		M,A,S		$R1_{24-30} \leftarrow$ Storage key of $c(R2)_{8-20}$	17.2	(22)
L	Load	RX	58	R1,D2(X2,B2)		A,S		$R1 \leftarrow c(S2)$	4.2	
LH	Load Half-word	RX	48	R1,D2(X2,B2)		A,S		$R1_{16-31} \leftarrow c(S2)_{0-15}$; $R1_{0-15} \leftarrow c(S2)_0$	4.2	
LA	Load Address	RX	41	R1,D2(X2,B2)				$R1_{8-31} \leftarrow S2$; $R1_{0-7} \leftarrow 0$	4.7	
LM	Load Multiple	RS	98	R1,R3,D2(B2)		A,S		$R1,\ldots,R3 \leftarrow c(S2)\ldots$	4.6	(27)
LCTL	Load ConTroL registers	RS	B7	R1,R3,D2(B2)		M,A,S		$CR1,\ldots,CR3 \leftarrow c(S2)$	17.3	(27,36)
LR	Load Register	RR	18	R1,R2				$R1 \leftarrow c(R2)$	4.2	
LCR	Load Complement Register	RR	13	R1,R2	(1)		IF	$R1 \leftarrow -c(R2)$	4.2	
LNR	Load Negative Register	RR	11	R1,R2	(5)			$R1 \leftarrow -|c(R2)|$	4.2	
LPR	Load Positive Register	RR	10	R1,R2	(1)		IF	$R1 \leftarrow |c(R2)|$	4.2	
LTR	Load and Test Register	RR	12	R1,R2	(5)			$R1 \leftarrow c(R2)$	7.2	
LD	Load Double	RX	68	R1,D2(X2,B2)		A,S		$FPR1 \leftarrow c(S2)$	13.2	(21,23)
LDR	Load Double Register	RR	28	R1,R2		S		$FPR1 \leftarrow c(FPR2)$	13.2	(21,23)
LE	Load Floating	RX	78	R1,D2(X2,B2)		A,S		$FPR1 \leftarrow c(S2)$	13.2	(21)
LER	Load Floating Register	RR	38	R1,R2		S		$FPR1 \leftarrow c(FPR2)$	13.2	(21)
LCDR	Load Complement Double Register	RR	23	R1,R2	(5)	S		$FPR1 \leftarrow -c(FPR2)$	13.2	(21,23)

(continued)

IBM SYSTEM/370 INSTRUCTIONS [continued]

Mnemonic	Name	Type	Num. Op. Code	Operands	Cond. Code	Exceptions[44]	Action (See Appendix B)	Ref. Chapter and Sec.	Notes
LCER	Load Complement Floating Register	RR	33	R1,R2	(5)	S	$FPR1 \leftarrow -\,c(FPR2)$	13.2	(21)
LNDR	Load Negative Double Register	RR	21	R1,R2	(5)	S	$FPR1 \leftarrow -|c(FPR2)|$	13.2	(21,23)
LNER	Load Negative Floating Register	RR	31	R1,R2	(5)	S	$FPR1 \leftarrow -|c(FPR2)|$	13.2	(21)
LPDR	Load Positive Double Register	RR	20	R1,R2	(5)	S	$FPR1 \leftarrow |c(FPR2)|$	13.2	(21,23)
LPER	Load Positive Floating Register	RR	30	R1,R2	(5)	S	$FPR1 \leftarrow |c(FPR2)|$	13.2	(21)
LTDR	Load and Test Double Register	RR	22	R1,R2	(5)	S	$FPR1 \leftarrow c(FPR2)$	13.2	(21,23)
LTER	Load and Test Floating Register	RR	32	R1,R2	(5)	S	$FPR1 \leftarrow c(FPR2)$	13.2	(21)
LRA	Load Real Address	RX	B1	R1,D2(X2,B2)	(13)	M,A	$R1 \leftarrow$ Address translated from S2	17.3	(40)
LRDR	Load and Round Double	RR	25	R1,R2		S,E	$FPR1_{0-63} \leftarrow c(FPR2)_{0-127}$ rounded	13.8	(39)
LRER	Load and Round	RR	35	R1,R2		S,E	$FPR1 \leftarrow c(FPR2)_{0-63}$ rounded	13.8	(39)
LPSW	Load Program Status Word	SI	82	D1(B1)	(6)	M,A,S	$PSW \leftarrow c(S1)_{0-63}$	17.3	
MC	Monitor Call	SI	AF	D1(B1),I2		S	Interrupt if c(Control Reg. $8)_{16} + I2(0\text{-}3) = 1$; $148_{0-15} \leftarrow [0,I2]$; $157_{0-23} \leftarrow S1$	17.2	(36)
M	Multiply	RX	5C	R1,D2(X2,B2)		A,S	$[R1,R1+1] \leftarrow c(R1+1) \times c(S2)$	4.4	
MH	Multiply Half-word	RX	4C	R1,D2(X2,B2)		A,S	$R1 \leftarrow c(R1) \times c(S2)_{0-15,16-47}$	4.4	

Mnemonic	Name	Type	Op	Operands		Operation	CC	§	Ref
MR	Multiply Register	RR	1C	R1,R2		$[R1,R1+1] \leftarrow c(R1+1) \times c(R2)$	S	4.4	
MP	Multiply Decimal	SS	FC	D1(L1,B1),D2(L2,B2)		$S1 \leftarrow c(S1) \times c(S2)$	A,S,D	14.5	(20,26)
MD	Multiply Double	RX	6C	R1,D2(X2,B2)		$FPR1 \leftarrow c(FPR1) \times c(S2)$	A,S,U,E	13.4	(21,23)
MDR	Multiply Double Register	RR	2C	R1,R2		$FPR1 \leftarrow c(FPR1) \times c(FPR2)$	S,U,E	13.4	(21,23)
ME	Multiply Floating	RX	7C	R1,D2(X2,B2)		$FPR1 \leftarrow c(FPR1) \times c(S2)$	A,S,U,E	13.4	(21)
MER	Multiply Floating Register	RR	3C	R1,R2		$FPR1 \leftarrow c(FPR1) \times c(FPR2)$	S,U,E	13.4	(21)
MXR	Multiply eXtended Register	RR	26	R1,R2		$FPR1_{0-127} \leftarrow c(FPR1)_{0-127} \times c(FPR2)_{0-127}$	S,U,E	13.8	(39)
MXDR	Multiply eXtended from Double Registers	RR	27	R1,R2		$FPR1_{0-127} \leftarrow c(FPR1)_{0-63} \times c(FPR2)_{0-63}$	S,U,E	13.8	(39)
MXD	Multiply eXtended Double	RX	67	R1,D2(X2,B2)		$FPR1_{0-127} \leftarrow c(FPR1)_{0-63} \times c(S2)_{0-63}$	A,S,U,E	13.8	(39)
MVC	Move Character	SS	D2	D1(L,B1),D2(B2)		$S1 \leftarrow c(S2)$	A	4.2	(25)
MVCL	MoVe Characters Long	RR	0E	R1,R2	(17)	$c(R1) \leftarrow c(c(R2))$	A,S	10.1	(36,38)
MVCIN	Move Inverse	SS	E8	D1(L,B1),D2(B2)		$S1 \leftarrow c(S2)$	A	10.3 Problem	(25,41,42)
MVI	Move Immediate	SI	92	D1(B1),I2		$S1_{0-7} \leftarrow I2$	A	4.2 Problem	
MVN	Move Numerics	SS	D1	D1(L,B1),D2(B2)		$S1 \leftarrow c(S2)$	A	14.2 Problem	(25,31)
MVO	Move with Offset	SS	F1	D1(L1,B1),D2(L2,B2)		$S1 \leftarrow c(S2)$	A	14.4 Problem	(26,32)
MVZ	Move Zones	SS	D3	D1(L,B1),D2(B2)		$S1 \leftarrow c(S2)$	A	14.3 Problem	(25,33)
N	And	RX	54	R1,D2(X2,B2)	(4)	$R1 \leftarrow c(R1) \text{ AND } c(S2)$	A,S	11.4	
NC	And Character	SS	D4	D1(L,B1),D2(B2)	(4)	$S1 \leftarrow c(S1) \text{ AND } c(S2)$	A	11.4	(25)
NI	And Immediate	SI	94	D1(B1),I2	(4)	$S1_{0-7} \leftarrow c(S1)_{0-7} \text{ AND } I2$	A	11.4	
NR	And Register	RR	14	R1,R2	(4)	$R1 \leftarrow c(R1) \text{ AND } c(R2)$	A	11.4	
O	Or	RX	56	R1,D2(X2,B2)	(4)	$R1 \leftarrow c(R1) \text{ OR } c(S2)$	A,S	11.4	
OC	Or Character	SS	D6	D1(L,B1),D2(B2)	(4)	$S1 \leftarrow c(S1) \text{ OR } c(S2)$	A	11.4	(25)

(continued)

IBM SYSTEM/370 INSTRUCTIONS [continued]

Mnemonic	Name	Type	Num. Op. Code	Operands	Cond. Code	Exceptions[44]	Action (See Appendix B)	Ref. Chapter and Sec.	Notes
OI	Or Immediate	SI	96	D1(B1),I2	(4)	A	$S1_{0-7}\leftarrow c(S1)_{0-7}$ OR I2	11.4	
OR	Or Register	RR	16	R1,R2	(4)		$R1\leftarrow c(R1)$ OR $c(R2)$	11.4	
PACK	Pack	SS	F2	D1(L1,B1),D2(L2,B2)		A	$S1$ (packed dec.)$\leftarrow c(S2)$(zoned dec.)	6.5	(26)
PTLB	Purge Translation Lookaside Buffer	S	B20D	none		M	Clear translation lookaside buffer	17.3	(40)
RRB	Reset Reference Bit	S	B213	D2(B2)	(14)	M,A	Storage key $(S2)_5\leftarrow 0$	17.3	(40)
S	Subtract	RX	5B	R1,D2(X2,B2)	(1)	A,S, IF	$R1\leftarrow c(R1) - c(S2)$	4.3	
SR	Subtract Register	RR	1B	R1,R2	(1)	IF	$R1\leftarrow c(R1) - c(R2)$	4.3	
SH	Subtract Half-word	RX	4B	R1,D2(X2,B2)	(1)	A,S, IF	$R1\leftarrow c(R1) - c(S2)_{0-15}$	4.3	
SL	Subtract Logical	RX	5F	R1,D2(X2,B2)	(3)	A,S	$R1\leftarrow c(R1) - c(S2)$	11.1	
SLR	Subtract Logical Register	RR	1F	R1,R2	(3)		$R1\leftarrow c(R1) - c(R2)$	11.1	
SP	Subtract Decimal	SS	FB	D1(L1,B1),D2(L2,B2)	(1)	A, D, DF	$S1\leftarrow c(S1) - c(S2)$	14.3	(20,26)
SD	Subtract Double	RX	6B	R1,D2(X2,B2)	(5)	A,S,U,E,LS	$FPR1\leftarrow c(FPR1) - c(S2)$	13.3	(21,23)
SDR	Subtract Double Register	RR	2B	R1,R2	(5)	S,U,E,LS	$FPR1\leftarrow c(FPR1) - c(FPR2)$	13.3	(21,23)
SE	Subtract Floating	RX	7B	R1,D2(X2,B2)	(5)	A,S,U,E,LS	$FPR1\leftarrow c(FPR1) - c(S2)$	13.3	(21)
SER	Subtract Floating Register	RR	3B	R1,R2	(5)	S,U,E,LS	$FPR1\leftarrow c(FPR1) - c(FPR2)$	13.3	(21)
SU	Subtract Unnormalized	RX	6F	R1,D2(X2,B2)	(5)	A,S, E,LS	$FPR1\leftarrow c(FPR1) - c(S2)$	13.5	(21,24)
SUR	Subtract Unnormalized Register	RR	2F	R1,R2	(5)	S, E,LS	$FPR1\leftarrow c(FPR1) - c(FPR2)$	13.5	(21,24)
SW	Subtract Double Unnormalized	RX	7F	R1,D2(X2,B2)	(5)	A,S, E,LS	$FPR1\leftarrow c(FPR1) - c(S2)$	13.5	(21,23,24)

SWR	Subtract Double Unnormalized Register	RR	3F	R1,R2	(5)	S, E,LS	$FPR1 \leftarrow c(FPR1) - c(FPR2)$	13.5	(21,23,24)
SIO	Start I/O	S	9C00	D2(B2)	(8)	M	Start an I/O operation	17.6	
SIOF	Start I/O Fast Release	S	9C01	D2(B2)	(8)	M	Start an I/O operation	17.6	
SLA	Shift Left Arithmetic	RS	8B	R1,D2(B2)	(1)	IF	Left shift bits 1–31, fill (with) 0's	11.2	(28)
SLL	Shift Left Logical	RS	89	R1,D2(B2)			Left shift bits 0–31, fill 0's	11.2	(28)
SLDA	Shift Left Double Arithmetic	RS	8F	R1,D2(B2)	(1)	S, IF	Left shift bits 1–63, fill 0's	11.2	(28)
SLDL	Shift Left Double Logical	RS	8D	R1,D2(B2)		S	Left shift bits 0–63, fill 0's	11.2	(28)
SRA	Shift Right Arithmetic	RS	8A	R1,D2(B2)	(5)		Right shift bits 1–31, fill $c(R1)_0$	11.2	(28)
SRL	Shift Right Logical	RS	88	R1,D2(B2)			Right shift bits 0–31, fill 0's	11.2	(28)
SRDA	Shift Right Double Arithmetic	RS	8E	R1,D2(B2)	(5)	S	Right shift bits 1–63, fill $c(R1)_0$	11.2	(28)
SRDL	Shift Right Double Logical	RS	8C	R1,D2(B2)		S	Right shift bits 0–63, fill 0's	11.2	(28)
SRP	Shift and Round Packed	SS	F0	D1(L1,B1),D2(B2),I3	(1)	A,D,DF	c(S1) shifted S2 digits right or left, rounded by factor I3	14.4	(28,36)
SPM	Set Program Mask	RR	04	R1	(6)		$PSW_{34-39} \leftarrow c(R1)_{2-7}$	17.3	
SSK	Set Storage Key	RR	08	R1,R2		M,A,S	Storage key of $c(R2)_{8-20} \leftarrow c(R1)_{24-30}$	17.2	(22)
SSM	Set System Mask	SI	80	D1(B1)		M,A	$PSW_{0-7} \leftarrow c(S1)_{0-7}$	17.2	
STCK	STore ClocK	S	B205	D2(B2)	(18)	A	$S2_{0-63} \leftarrow c(\text{Clock})$	17.3	(36)
ST	STore	RX	50	R1,D2(X2,B2)		A,S	$S2 \leftarrow c(R1)$	4.2	
STH	STore Half-word	RX	40	R1,D2(X2,B2)		A,S	$S2_{0-15} \leftarrow c(R1)_{16-31}$	4.2	
STM	STore Multiple	RS	90	R1,R3,D2(B2)		A,S	$S2... \leftarrow c(R1),...,c(R3)$	4.6	(27)
STC	STore Character	RX	42	R1,D2(X2,B2)		A	$S2_{0-7} \leftarrow c(R1)_{24-31}$	10.1	
STCM	STore Characters under Mask	RS	BE	R1,M3,D2(B2)		A	$S2 \leftarrow c(R1)$	10.1	(36,37)
STCTL	STore ConTroL registers	RS	B6	R1,R3,D2(B2)		M,A,S	$S2... \leftarrow c(CR1),...,c(CR3)$	17.3	(27,36)

(continued)

IBM SYSTEM/370 INSTRUCTIONS [continued]

Mnemonic	Name	Type	Num. Op. Code	Operands	Cond. Code	Exceptions[44]	Action (See Appendix B)	Ref. Chapter and Sec.	Notes
STD	STore Double	RX	60	R1,D2(X2,B2)		A,S	$S2 \leftarrow c(FPR1)$	13.2	(21,23)
STE	STore Floating	RX	70	R1,D2(X2,B2)		A,S	$S2 \leftarrow c(FPR1)$	13.2	(21)
STNSM	STore then aNd System Mask	SI	AC	D1(B1),I2		M,A	$S1_{0-7} \leftarrow PSW_{0-7}$; $PSW_{0-7} \leftarrow PSW_{0-7}$ AND $I2$		(36)
STOSM	STore then Or System Mask	SI	AD	D1(B1),I2		M,A	$S1_{0-7} \leftarrow PSW_{0-7}$; $PSW_{0-7} \leftarrow PSW_{0-7}$ OR $I2$		(36)
SXR	Subtract EXtended	RR	37	R1,R2	(5)	S,U,E,LS	$FPR_{0-127} \leftarrow c(FPR1)_{0-127} - c(FPR2)_{0-127}$	13.8	(39)
SVC	Supervisor Call	RR	0A	I			Interrupt; $PSW(old)_{24-31} \leftarrow I$	17.3	
TCH	Test Channel	S	9F00	D2(B2)	(9)	M		17.6	
TIO	Test I/O	S	9D00	D2(B2)	(8)	M		17.6	
TM	Test Under Mask	SI	91	D1(B1),I2	(11)	A		Problem 11.26	
TR	Translate	SS	DC	D1(L,B1),D2(B2)		A	$S1 \leftarrow c(S2)$	15.1	(34)
TRT	Translate and Test	SS	DD	D1(L,B1),D2(B2)	(10)	A	Reg. $1_{8-31} \leftarrow$ Address of Argument byte; Reg. $2_{24-31} \leftarrow$ Function byte	15.1	
TS	Test and Set	SI	93	D1(B1)	(12)	A	$S1 \leftarrow FF$	Problem 17.5	
UNPK	Unpack	SS	F3	D1(L1,B1),D2(L2,B2)		A	$S1$(zoned dec.)$\leftarrow c(S2)$(packed dec.)	6.5	(26)
X	Exclusive Or	RX	57	R1,D2(X2,B2)	(4)	A,S	$R1 \leftarrow c(R1)$ Ex. OR $c(S2)$	11.4	
XC	Exclusive Or Character	SS	D7	D1(L,B1),D2(B2)	(4)	A	$S1 \leftarrow c(S1)$ Ex. OR $c(S2)$	11.4	(25)
XI	Exclusive OR Immediate	SI	97	D1(B1),I2	(4)	A	$S1_{0-7} \leftarrow c(S1)_{0-7}$ Ex. OR $I2$	11.4	
XR	Exclusive OR Register	RR	17	R1,R2	(4)		$R1 \leftarrow c(R1)$ Ex. OR $c(R2)$	11.4	
ZAP	Zero and Add Positive	SS	F8	D1(L1,B1),D2(L2,B2)	(1)	A, D, DF	$S1 \leftarrow c(S2)$	14.4	(20,26)

Notes

Condition code settings:

	0	1	2	3
1)	Result = 0	Result < 0	Result > 0	Overflow
2)	Op_1 = Op_2	Op_1 < Op_2	Op_1 > Op_2	—
3)	Result = 0, No carry	Result ≠ 0, No carry	Result = 0, Carry	Result ≠ 0, Carry
4)	Result = 0	Result ≠ 0	—	—
5)	Result = 0	Result < 0	Result > 0	—
6)	(Condition code loaded by instruction)			
7)	Interrupt in subchannel	CSW stored	Burst Op terminated	Not operational
8)	Available or Operation Proceeding	CSW stored	Channel or subchannel busy	Not operational
9)	Available	Interrupt in channel	Operating in burst mode	Not operational
10)	All function bytes are zero	Nonzero before 1st Op exhausted	Last function byte nonzero	—
11)	$S1_i$ = 0 for all i for which $I2_i$ = 1	For i such that $I2_i$ = 0, some $S1_i$ = 0, some $S1_i$ = 1	—	$S1_i$ = 1 for all i for which $I2_i$ = 1
12)	$S1_0$ = 0	$S1_0$ = 1		
13)	Translation available	Segment table entry invalid	Page-table entry invalid	Table length violation
14)	Ref bit = 0, change bit = 0	Ref bit = 0, change bit = 1	Ref bit = 1, Change bit = 0	Ref bit = 1, Change bit = 1
15)	Selected bytes equal, or mask = 0	Selected bytes of Op_1 low	Selected bytes of Op_1 high	—
16)	All inserted bits = 0, or mask = 0	First inserted bit = 1	First inserted bit = 0, but not all inserted bits are 0	—
17)	Lengths of operands equal	Op_1 shorter	Op_1 longer	Destructive overlap; no movement
18)	Clock in set state	Not-set state	Error state	Not-operational state
19)	Op_1 = Op_2	Op_1 ≠ Op_2	—	—

20) Instructions available only if decimal feature is installed; operands and results in packed decimal form.
21) Instructions available only if floating-point feature is installed; operands and results in floating-point form, normalized unless otherwise indicated by note (24).
22) Instructions available only if protection feature is installed.
23) Double-length floating-point instructions—each operand is 64 bits long.

(continued)

481

IBM SYSTEM/370 INSTRUCTIONS [continued]

Notes *(continued)*

24) Normalization not performed on result.

25) Length of each operand given by L.

26) Length of first operand given by $L1$; length of second operand given by $L2$.

27) Registers participate as follows, and bytes of main storage are correspondingly treated as shown:

   If $R1 < R3$, register $R1, R1 + 1, \ldots, R3,$ $4 \times (R3 - R1) + 4$ bytes.

   If $R1 = R3$, register $R1,$ 4 bytes.

   If $R1 > R3$, register $R1, R1 + 1, \ldots, 15, 0, \ldots, R3,$ $4 \times (16 + R3 - R1) + 4$ bytes.

28) Only the low-order six bits are used in defining the length of the shift.

29) No branch takes place if $R2 = 0$.

30) First operand is *pattern*, with length L; second operand is *source*, in packed decimal format, with length dictated by pattern.

31) Only the low-order four bits of each byte are moved.

32) Low-order four bits of rightmost byte of $S1$ are unchanged; move proceeds from right to left, thus offset by four bits.

33) Only the high-order four bits of each byte are moved.

34) Each byte of the first operand designates which byte from the second operand replaces it: $S1_{0-7} \leftarrow c(S2 + c(S1))_{0-7}$.

35) Instructions available only if Branch and Save feature is installed.

36) Not in System/360.

37) Op_1 = Concatenation of bytes $R1_{8i \text{ to } 8i+7}$ for which $M3_i = 1$, $i = 0,1,2,3$; $Op_2 = c(S2)$, of length equal to length of Op_1.

38) Length of Op_1 specified by $c(R1 + 1)$; length of Op_2 specified by $c(R2 + 1)_{8-31}$; fill character taken from $c(R2 + 1)_{0-7}$.

39) Instructions available only if extended-precision floating-point feature is installed; $FPR1_{0-127}$ is understood as abbreviation for $[(FPR1)_{0-63},$ $(FPR1 + 2)_{0-63}]$; $FPR2$ similarly.

40) Instructions available only if dynamic address translation feature is installed.

41) Bytes of first operand will be bytes from second operand in reverse order. Second operand address is of *rightmost* byte.

42) Instruction available only if Move Inverse feature is installed.

43) Instructions available only if Compare and Swap feature is installed.

44) Exceptions:

M	Privileged operation	D	Data	DF	Decimal overflow	FK	Floating-point divide
A	Access (Protection,	U	Exponent underflow	LS	Significance	EX	Execute
	Addressing, Translation)	E	Exponent overflow	IK	Fixed-point divide		
S	Specification	IF	Fixed-point overflow	DK	Decimal divide		

SELECTED PROBLEM SOLUTIONS

CHAPTER 1

1.5 Binary 10101 = Decimal 21
Binary 1110111 = Decimal 119

1.6 Hexadecimal A8 = Decimal 168
Hexadecimal 24D = Decimal 589

1.7 Hexadecimal 24D = Binary 1001001101
Binary 11011001110001 = Hexadecimal 3671

1.8 Decimal 18 = Binary 10010
32-bit 2's complement: 11111111111111111111111111Ø111Ø

1.9 Decimal 7:   ØØØØØØØØØØØØØØØØØØØØØØØØØØØØØ111
+Decimal −18:   11111111111111111111111111Ø111Ø
                11111111111111111111111111Ø1Ø1

which is the representation of decimal −11.

1.12 The break-even ratio is 1.0; if there are more decimal digits stored than characters, the eight-bit representations are more efficient than six-bit ones. Of course, this is only one component of the question of desirability of an eight-bit or six-bit scheme.

CHAPTER 2

2.2

Base	Index	Displacement	Effective address
2	–	1Ø4	ØØ25A6
3	–	ØØØ	ØØ531Ø
Ø	–	ØCE	ØØØØCE
1	3	1Ø1	ØØB624
2	Ø	233	ØØ26D5
Ø	2	233	ØØ26D5
Ø	Ø	FFF	ØØØFFF
3	1	1Ø1	ØØB624

2.3 Effective address desired: ØØ958A
Base   −ØØ9336
Displacement needed: 254

2.5   All RR-type instructions whose result is in a register and SS-type whose results are in main storage (there are a few exceptions) are defined so that the first operand is the destination or result. SI-type instructions can also be defined so that the first operand is the destination because you should never want the result to be put in the instruction itself.

CHAPTER 3

3.1   Valid symbols: A3, $3, GIH2J3K4, #34$Q

Invalid: (B9)   includes special characters ( )

       7X   does not begin with a letter

       GIH2J3K4L5 too long

       #@$&   includes special character &

3.2   Valid absolute expressions:

$$G, X'123F', X'123F'+G, *-P, Q-(P-K)+B'10100',$$
$$C'4578'-G-X'F4F23E4A'$$

Valid relocatable expressions:

$$P, =X'123F', X'123F'+P, P+4*X'CE', *, *-7,$$
$$*+X'123F', *+G, R+G+H, P+Q+R-W-(*+4)$$

Invalid: =X'123F'+G   expression including a literal

       G-(P-K)   pairing violated: (P-K) is subtracted

3.3   Invalid instructions:

L	19,19(H)	No register 19
L	R4,W(H,K)	W is relocatable, K is supplied as explicit base
L	W,4(R4)	Relocatable W may not be register address
L	4(4),W	4(4) is invalid *R1* specification
LR	R4,P	Relocatable P may not be *R2*
LM	K,W	Needs three operands
LM	3(R4),Q	3(R4) is invalid for *R1, R2*
LM	3,R4,Q(5)	No indexing of RS instructions
MVI	R,Q	*I2* must be absolute
MVC	W(8),P(8)	P is valid second operand, P(8) invalid
MVC	W(8,9),*+8	Explicit base with relocatable W

3.4   Second operand address: 009A48

3.5   Assuming that =F'24' has not been encountered in a previous statement, the assembler must put the constant F'24' in the word at relocatable 0003CC; note that the next available location in the literal pool is now 0003D0. The second operand of the current instruction will be assembled with base A, index 0, displacement 0003CC-00000C=3C0.

3.6

L	409452	
LM	569822	V-4=000828
AR	45	

```
A       6A9452      A is hexadecimal value of index G
MVI     FF982A
ST      4A9456
MVC     Ø79ØØC982B
```

3.7 Pairing rules ensure that any valid expression be either absolute or relocatable.

CHAPTER 4

4.1
```
LNR     R2,R7
LCR     R2,R2
```

4.2
```
LA      R5,Ø
L       R5, some location known to contain zero
```

4.4

Instruction		Result	
LPR	R7,R2	Reg. 7	ØØØØØØ4Ø
LNR	R8,R4	Reg. 8	CDEFØ123
AR	R1,R2	Reg. 1	FFFFFFEE
AR	R2,R1	Reg. 2	FFFFFFEE
SR	R1,R2	Reg. 1	ØØØØØØ6E
SR	R2,R1	Reg. 2	FFFFFF92
A	R1,K	Reg. 1	ØØØØØØ24
S	R1,K	Reg. 1	ØØØØØØ38
SH	R1,K	Reg. 1	ØØØØØØ2F
AH	R3,Q+2	Reg. 3	4567FFFF
MVI	Q+5,17	Q+5	11 (hexadecimal), replacing 1Ø
MVC	K+1(5),Q+2	K+1	76543210FE
STM	R2,R4,Q	Q	FFFFFFCØ
		Q+4	456789AB
		Q+8	CDEFØ123
LM	R5,R6,Q	Reg. 5	BA987654
		Reg. 6	321ØFEDC
LH	R7,Q+6	Reg. 7	FFFFFEDC
STH	R3,K	K	89AB
LA	R8,2(R3,R4)	Reg. 8	ØØ568ADØ
S	R2,Q	Reg. 2	4567896C

4.5 Both LR 5,4 and LA 5,Ø(4) load contents of register 4 into register 5. However, the latter strips off the first 8 bits and replaces them with zeros. LA 5,4 loads the number 4 into register 5. L 5,4 and L 5,Ø(4) both load register 5 from main-storage locations: the former from absolute locations ØØØØØ4 to ØØØØØ7; the latter from a full word whose address is in register 4.

4.6

Instruction		Result(Decimal)	
MR	R8,R9	Reg. 8	0
		Reg. 9	900
MR	R6,R9	Reg. 6	0
		Reg. 7	-360
M	R8,U	Reg. 8	0
		Reg. 9	-480
MH	R7,U+2	Reg. 7	192
DR	R2,R7	Reg. 2	1
		Reg. 3	4
DR	R4,R7	Reg. 4	0
		Reg. 5	-7
DR	R4,R9	Reg. 4	-24
		Reg. 5	2
D	R2,Y	Reg. 2	4
		Reg. 3	-9

```
4.7   L    R5,K
      M    R4,=F'1'
      D    R4,Q
      ST   R5,Z          QUOTIENT
```

4.10 Dividend: hexadecimal   8ØØØØØØØ
      Divisor: hexadecimal   FFFFFFFF

4.11 E=K+3:

```
              L    R2,K   ⎫ or ⎧ LA   R2,3
              A    R2,=F'3' ⎬    ⎨ A    R2,K
              ST   R2,E   ⎭    ⎩ ST   R2,E
```

E=(K+3)/Q

```
              L    R3,K
              A    R3,=F'3'
              LA   R2,Ø
              D    R2,Q
              ST   R3,E
```

E=(K+U)*R

```
              L    R3,K
              AR   R3,R6
              M    R2,R
              ST   R3,E
```

E=
(K-T+R*P)/(Y-5)

```
              L    R3,R
              M    R2,P
              SH   R3,T
              A    R3,K
              L    R4,Y
              S    R4,=F'5'
              DR   R2,R4
              ST   R3,E
```

CHAPTER 5

5.1 Statement   Bit pattern

DC	C'Ø'	1111ØØØØ
DC	CL4'Ø'	1111ØØØØØ1ØØØØØØØ1ØØØØØØØ1ØØØØØØ
DC	X'Ø'	ØØØØØØØØ
DC	XL4'Ø'	ØØØØØØØØØØØØØØØØØØØØØØØØØØØØØØØØ
DC	F'Ø'	ØØØØØØØØØØØØØØØØØØØØØØØØØØØØØØØØ
DC	E'Ø'	ØØØØØØØØØØØØØØØØØØØØØØØØØØØØØØØØ
DC	P'Ø'	ØØØØ11ØØ
DC	PL4'Ø'	ØØØØØØØØØØØØØØØØØØØØØØØØØØØØ11ØØ
DC	C'A'	11ØØØØØ1
DC	X'A'	ØØØØ1Ø1Ø
DC	F'19'	ØØØØØØØØØØØØØØØØØØØØØØØØØØ1ØØ11
DC	XL4'19'	ØØØØØØØØØØØØØØØØØØØØØØØØØ11ØØ1
DC	HL4'19'	ØØØØØØØØØØØØØØØØØØØØØØØØØØ1ØØ11

5.2 a) DC   F'-11,373,Ø'
    b) DC   1ØF'Ø'
    c) DS   ØH
       DC   B'11ØØ1ØØ1ØØ1ØØ1ØØ'
    d) DS   ØD
       DC   C'EGC123*$'
    e) DC   3X'E4'
    f) DC   4CL12Ø'RESULT ='

5.3 a)   ORG   X'1ØØ'
    b) PORG   EQU   256
    c) DEC3ØØ   DC   F'3ØØ'
    d) OUTBUF   DC   A(OUTSTR)
    e) OUTSTR   DS   CL132
    f)   END

5.5 The instruction LA R4,=A(TENNIS) loads register 4 with the address of a full word containing the address of TENNIS. Both LA R4,TENNIS and L R4,=A(TENNIS) load register 4 with the address of TENNIS. Finally, L R4,TENNIS loads register 4 with the contents of a full word *at* location TENNIS.

5.6 The difference in each case is in boundary alignment. If a length modifier is written, *no* alignment is done.

5.8 NAME   DS   CL3Ø
    NAME2   DS   CL3Ø
    ADDRESS   DS   CL3Ø
    CITYSTZP   DS   CL3Ø

```
XREAD    NAME,3Ø
XREAD    NAME2,3Ø
XREAD    ADDRESS,3Ø
XREAD    CITYSTZP,3Ø
```

5.9 Since RDTERM reads into a 130-byte area, we need an area to read into:

```
READAREA DS      CL130
```

```
WRTERM 'TYPE NAME ',EDIT=NO
RDTERM READAREA
MVC    NAME(30),READAREA
WRTERM 'TYPE SECOND LINE OF NAME ',EDIT=NO
RDTERM READAREA
MVC    NAME2(30),READAREA
WRTERM 'TYPE STREET ADDRESS ',EDIT=NO
RDTERM READAREA
MVC    ADDRESS(30),READAREA
WRTERM 'TYPE CITY, STATE, ZIP ',EDIT=NO
RDTERM READAREA
MVC    CITYSTZP(30),READAREA
```

CHAPTER 6

6.1 The branch address is determined *before* the address of the next instruction is stored. Since in BALR R12,R12 the *previous* contents of register 12 determines the branch address, the result will very rarely be the same as that of BALR R12,Ø.

6.3 The key fact is that only one subroutine is active and using the save area at a time.

6.4 *Hint:* The difficult part is restoring registers, because some base address must be used for addressing the save area. Subroutine *B* is presumably using all registers for its own purposes. But what about contents of register 14?

6.6 No difficulties would be encountered at all. But a save area trace (see Chapter 9) would be impossible.

6.7 Suppose subroutine *B* is interrupted while the address of the save area of the calling routine (the one that called *B*) is in register 13. If the supervisor stored register contents in that same area, it would destroy register contents belonging to the calling routine. Therefore the supervisor must save registers in its own area.

6.9 a) No good: The address of BBB is loaded into register 1 instead of the conventional address of the address.

   b) No good: Exactly like the previous case.

   c) Good.

   d) Confusing, but okay.

e) No good: The address of FF is loaded into register 1, which neither conforms to convention nor helps at all to make GG and HH accessible.

f) Okay.

g) Okay.

h) Okay. The address of the third parameter is stored in the block.

i) Okay, if the BAL statement is on a full-word boundary. This is known as an *in-line* parameter list. Note how the BAL instruction loads register 1 with the address of the parameter block and also jumps around the block. Problem 7.19 will show how to ensure proper alignment on a full-word boundary.

6.10 PACK overflows if there are more than $2d$-1 digits (leading zeros do not count) in the source field, where d is the length in bytes of the destination field.

UNPK overflows if there are more than d' significant (after leading zeros) digits in the packed decimal field, where d' is the length of the destination field.

CVB overflows if the number to be converted has a magnitude of over 2^{31}, or 2,147,483,648.

CVD can never overflow.

6.12
```
MVC   D(5),=XL5'Ø'      D IS ON A DOUBLE WORD BOUNDARY
MVC   D+5(3),N
CVB   R4,D
```

6.13
```
PACK  D(8),Q(1)    D: Hex.ØØØØØØØØØØØØØØ7C
CVB   R4,D         Reg. 4: Hex. ØØØØØØØ7
```

6.14
```
CVD   R7,D         D: ØØØØØØØØØØØØ1Ø7C
UNPK  U(3),D(8)    U: F1FØC7
```

The instruction UNPK U(3),D+5(3) would have the same effect.

6.17 Base C, Index Ø, Displacement ØØØ61C–ØØØ6Ø8=Ø14.

6.18 Reg. 4: ØØØØE844, as left by RDIGIT; irrelevant to RANDOM.

6.19 RANDOM returns 4ØØD2Ø19 = decimal 1,074,602,009.
RDIGIT returns ØØØØØØØ5.

6.21 The instruction

```
        LA    R15,RANDOM
```

could be substituted for

```
        L     R15,RANDAD
```

if RANDOM were assembled *after* RDIGIT (and within 4096 bytes after RDIGIT). Otherwise RANDOM could not be addressed in base + displacement form from RDIGIT.

```
6.24  CUBE     STM    R14,R12,12(R13)
               BALR   R12,0
               USING  *,R12
               L      R3,0(R1)      ADDRESS OF PARAMETER
               L      R5,0(R3)      PARAMETERS
               MR     R4,R5         SQUARE
               M      R4,0(R3)      CUBE
               LR     R0,R5         RESULT TO REG. 0
               LM     R1,R12,24(R13) RESTORE REGISTERS
               BR     R14
```

6.27 a) USING specifies register 11; we know because the base register used for the second operand is B.

b) The base register will hold ØØØDBC–CDE=ØØØØDE. The BALR instruction must be two bytes before that, at ØØØØDC.

c) BALR will load ØØØØ83AA.

d) The instruction will access ØØ83AA+CDE=ØØ9Ø88.

CHAPTER 7

7.3

Instruction		Condition code
SR	R3,R4	3
S	R3,W	2
SH	R2,W+2	2
A	R4,Q	1
C	R4,Q	1
CR	R4,R3	1
CR	R3,R4	2
C	R3,Y	2
LTR	R3,R3	2

7.4 1) $c(\text{Reg. 9}) \leq c(T)$ 2) $c(\text{Reg. 9}) < c(T)$
     3) $c(\text{Reg. 9}) + c(T) < 0$, or overflow
     4) Difference between $c(\text{Reg. 9})$ and $c(T)$ not 30 or -30

7.7 a)
```
      * IF C(AA) < C(BB)
                L      R2,BB
                C      R2,AA
                BNH    DONT
      * . THEN STORE C(BB) - C(AA) AT BB.
                S      R2,AA
                ST     R2,BB
      * ENDIF
      DONT      DS     0H
```

```
b)  * IF C(AA) = 15
            LA    R2,15
            C     R2,AA
            BNE   ELSE
     * . THEN LOAD C(BB) INTO REGISTER R8
            L     R8,BB
            B     ENDIF
     * . ELSE LOAD C(DD) INTO REGISTER R8
     ELSE   L     R8,DD
     * ENDIF
     ENDIF  DS    0H


c)          SR    R2,R2         ZERO R2
     * IF |C(AA)| < |C(BB)|
            L     R5,AA
            LPR   R5,R5
            L     R4,BB
            LPR   R4,R4
            CR    R5,R4
            BNL   ELSE2         |C(R3)| >= |C(R4)|
     * . THEN STORE THE REMAINDER OF |C(BB)| / |C(AA)| AT BB
            LR    R3,R4
            DR    R2,R5
            ST    R2,BB
            B     ENDIF2
     * . ELSE STORE THE REMAINDER OF |C(AA)| / |C(BB)| AT AA
     ELSE2  LR    R3,R5
            DR    R2,R4
            ST    R2,AA
     * ENDIF
     ENDIF2 DS    0H


d)  *** STORE THE MINIMUM OF C(AA) AND C(BB) IN DD
     * IF C(AA) <= C(BB)
            L     R2,AA
            L     R3,BB
            CR    R2,R3
            BH    BBISMIN
     * . THEN STORE C(AA) AT DD
            ST    R2,DD
            B     ENDIF3
     * . ELSE STORE C(BB) AT DD
     BBISMIN ST   R3,DD
     * ENDIF
     ENDIF3 DS    0H


e)  *** LOAD THE MINIMUM OF THE THREE NUMBERS INTO REGISTER R4
            L     R4,AA
     * IF C(R4) > C(BB)
            C     R4,BB
            BNH   AAISLE
     * . THEN LOAD BB INTO R4, PREPARE FOR FINAL COMPARISON
            L     R4,BB
     * ENDIF
     * IF C(R4) > C(CC)
     AAISLE C     R4,DD
            BNH   ENDIF4
     * . THEN LOAD C(CC) INTO REGISTER R4
            L     R4,DD
     * ENDIF
     ENDIF4 DS    0H
```

f)

```
* IF THE SUM OF EACH PAIR OF NUMBERS IS GREATER THAN THE THIRD
          L      R4,AA
          A      R4,BB
          C      R4,DD
          BNH    NOTVALID
          L      R4,AA
          A      R4,DD
          C      R4,BB
          BNH    NOTVALID
          L      R4,BB
          A      R4,DD
          C      R4,AA
          BNH    NOTVALID
* . THEN PRINT "VALID TRIANGLE"
          WRTERM 'VALID TRIANGLE'
          B      ENDIF5
NOTVALID DS      0H
* . ELSE PRINT "NOT SIDES OF A TRIANGLE"
          WRTERM 'NOT SIDES OF A TRIANGLE'
* ENDIF
ENDIF5   DS      0H
```

g)

```
          LA     R1,CARDIN
          LA     R7,0            SET SUM TO ZERO
* WHILE THERE ARE NUMBERS TO CONVERT
LOOP      XDECI R2,0(R1)         GET NEXT NUMBER, IF ANY
          BC     B'0001',ENDWHILE MAY BE AT END OF LIST
* . ADD THE LAST NUMBER CONVERTED TO SUM IN REGISTER R7
          AR     R7,R2           UPDATE SUM IN R7
          B      LOOP            GET ANOTHER NUMBER, IF ANY
* ENDWHILE
ENDWHILE DS      0H
```

h)

```
*** LOAD THE ABSOLUTE VALUE OF C(AA) INTO REGISTER R5.
          L      R5,AA
          LPR    R5,R5


*** LOAD THE ABSOLUTE VALUE OF C(AA) INTO REGISTER R5, DON'T USE LPR
          L      R5,AA
* IF C(AA) > 0
          LTR    R5,R5
          BH     DONE2
* . THEN CHANGE SIGN OF C(R5)
          LCR    R5,R5
* ENDIF
DONE2    DS      0H
```

7.7 *Hint:* What happens if the addition results in overflow?

7.8
```
          SR    R4,R4         SET TOTAL TO ZERO
* WHILE THERE ARE RECORDS TO BE READ
* . READ A RECORD
STEP2LP XREAD CARDIN,80
          BNZ   STEP3
* . CONVERT NUMBER, ADD TO TOTAL
          PACK  DBL(8),CARDIN(7)
          CVB   R3,DBL
          AR    R4,R3
          B     STEP2LP
* ENDWHILE
STEP3   DS    0H



CARDIN  DS    CL80
DBL     DS    1D
```

7.10
```
GUDDLE  CSECT
          EQUREGS
          XSAVE TR=NO
* WHILE THERE ARE RECORDS TO READ
* . READ A RECORD
NEXTREC XREAD CARDIN,80
          BNZ   OUT
* . CONVERT AND ADD 3 NUMBERS TO SUM
          XDECI R5,CARDIN
          XDECI R6,0(,R1)
          XDECI R7,0(,R1)
          LR    R8,F5         SUM
          AR    R8,R6
          AR    R8,R7
* . CONVERT TO OUTPUT AND PRINT
          XDECO R5,AREA+3
          XDECO R6,AREA+18
          XDECO R7,AREA+33
          XDECO R8,AREA+58
          XPRNT AREA,80
          B     NEXTREC
* ENDWHILE
OUT     XRETURN SA=*,TR=NO



CARDIN  DS    CL80
AREA    DC    CL52' '
        DC    CL28'SUM = '
        END   GUDDLE
```

7.13
```
     *****************************************************************
     *** PRINT DATA ITEM (4 PRINTABLE CHARACTERS)
     *** IN EACH CELL OF A LINKED LIST WHOSE ADDR. IS IN R2
     *** LAST CELL HAS 0 IN LINK
     *****************************************************************
     * WHILE THERE ARE STILL CELLS TO PRINT (R2 NOT = 0)
     TRAVERSE LTR   R2,R2
              BZ    OUT
     * . PRINT, GET NEXT CELL LINK
              MVC   AREA+3(4),4(R2)
              XPRNT AREA,7
              L     R2,0(,R2)
              B     TRAVERSE
     * ENDWHILE
     OUT      DS    0H
```

7.18   The list of parameters to the subroutine includes the address of the first cell
       in the list. If the list is empty, there is no first cell; the parameter must be
       zero. We can replace a zero with the address of the cell to be inserted, but
       how will the calling program know? The subroutine must leave (in *all*
       cases) the *new* address of the first cell of the list in register 0 as output from
       the subroutine.

```
     *****************************************************************
     *** SUBROUTINE INSERTS A CELL (THIRD PARAMETER)
     *** INTO A LINKED LIST (FIRST PARAMETER)
     *** AFTER THE CELL CONTAINING A GIVEN KEY (SECOND PARAMETER)
     *** IF THE KEY IS NOT IN THE LIST, THE NEW CELL IS INSERTED
     *** AT SUBROUTINE END, THE ADDR. OF THE FIRST CELL IN THE LIST
     *** IS LEFT IN REGISTER ZERO
     *****************************************************************
     LSTINSRT XSAVE TR=NO
              LM    R2,R4,0(R1)
              SR    R6,R6            ZERO FOR COMPARISONS
              LR    R0,R2
     * IF LIST IS EMPTY
              LTR   R2,R2
              BNZ   LISTINLP
     * . THEN PUT NEW CELL ADDR. IN R0 TO RETURN
              LR    R0,R4
              ST    R6,0(,R4)
              B     XRETURN
     * . ELSE INSERT CELL IN NONEMPTY LIST
     * . WHILE CURRENT CELL DOES NOT HAVE LINK = 0
     LSTINLP  C     R6,0(,R2)
              BZ    LSTIN2
     * . . IF DATA ITEM FOUND, CURRENT CELL = KEY
              L     R5,4(,R2)
              C     R5,0(,R3)
              BNE   LSTINLPA
     * . . . THEN WHILE COND. (KEY NOT FOUND) IS FALSE, EXIT WHILE
              B     LSTIN2
     * . . . ELSE GO TO NEXT CELL
     * . . ENDIF
     LSTINLPA L     R2,0(,R2)
              B     LSTINLP
     *** INSERT THE NEW CELL
     * . ENDWHILE (CURRENT CELL DOES NOT HAVE LINK = 0)
     LSTIN2   L     R7,0(,R2)        ADDR. OF NEXT CELL (OR ZERO)
              ST    R7,0(,R4)        STORE IN NEW CELL
              ST    R4,0(,R2)        STORE ADDR. OF NEW CELL
     * ENDIF (LIST IS EMPTY)
     XRETURN  XRETURN RGS=(R1-R12),SA=*,TR=NO
```

```
7.19            CNOP    Ø,4
                B       *+8
        A       DS      1F
                L       R3,A
```

Note that the CNOP statement must precede the branch instruction.

```
7.21            L       R2,4(,R1)       SECOND PARAMETER ADDRESS
                LTR     R2,R2
        * IF SECOND PARAMETER IS THE LAST
                BNM     NOTLAST
        * . THEN ...
                ...
                B       NEXTSTEP
        * . ELSE ...
        NOTLAST ...
```

CHAPTER 8

8.1 a)
```
                LA      R3,0
                LA      R6,4
                LA      R7,72
        * DO FOR I FROM 0 TO 18
        LP      L       R5,AA(R3)
        * . COMPUTE B(I) = A(I) - A(I+1)
                S       R5,AA+4(R3)
                ST      R5,BB(R3)
                BXLE    R3,R6,LP
        * ENDDO
```

b)
```
                LA      R3,0
        * DO FOR I FROM 0 TO 18
        LP      L       R5,AA(R3)
        * . COMPUTE B(I) = A(I) - A(I+1)
                S       R5,AA+4(R3)
                ST      R5,BB(R3)
                LA      R3,4(R3)
                C       R3,=F'72'
                BNH     LP
        * ENDDO
```

8.3 Blanks are stored from PRTAREA to PRTAREA+1999.

8.4 The second operand of the ST instruction is always on a full-word boundary; each time through the loop the S instruction subtracts 3 and the BCT instruction, 1. Copies of the contents of register 4 are stored at C+48, C+44, ... , C+4.

8.5 When the segment is completed, the half-word at LP+2 contains the address BB+4Ø in base + displacement form. Therefore initialization is not complete. It can be remedied by including

```
        MVC  LP+2(2),LPDUMMY+2
```

just before the loop, where the "constant" LPDUMMY is defined with other constants by

```
              LPDUMMY   A       R6,BB
```

Why and how?

```
8.6   LA    R6,FF+112
      LA    R7,BB
      LA    R8,4
      LA    R9,BB+112

      LA    R8,0
      LA    R9,112
      L     R7,=F'-4'
```

```
8.8           LA    R4,GG           K = ADDR. OF LARGEST
              LA    R5,GG+4         I = ADDR. OF NEXT NUMBER TO TEST
              L     R6,0(,R4)       LARGEST NUMBER YET
              LA    R8,4
              LA    R9,GG+64
      * DO FOR I FROM 2 TO 17
      LP      C     R6,0(,R5)
      * . IF NUMBER(I) IS LARGER
              BNL   TEXIT
      * . . THEN KEEP IT AND ITS ADDRESS
              LR    R4,R5
              L     R6,0(,R4)
      * . ENDIF
      TEXIT   BXLE  R5,R8,LP
      * ENDDO
      *** AT EXIT, R4 CONTAINS ADDR. OF LARGEST NUMBER
```

```
8.9   *******************************************************************
      *** SUBROUTINE TO EVALUATE A POLYNOMIAL BY HORNER'S METHOD
      *** ADAPTATION OF FIG. 8.12
      *** PARAMETERS ARE:
      ***    ADDRESS OF BEGINNING OF COEFFICIENT LIST
      ***    N, THE ORDER OF THE POLYNOMIAL
      ***    X, THE VALUE AT WHICH THE POLYNOMIAL IS TO BE EVALUATED
      *** THE COEFFICIENTS ARE PRESUMED STORED WITH COEF. OF HIGHEST-ORDER
      ***    TERM FIRST
      *** RESULT IS RETURNED IN REG. 0
      *******************************************************************
      POLEVAL CSECT
              XSAVE TR=NO
              LM    R2,R4,0(R1)
              L     R7,0(,R2)       ADDR. OF FIRST COEF.
              L     R11,0(,R3)      ORDER OF POLYNOMIAL
              L     R3,0(,R4)       VALUE X
              L     R5,0(,R7)       SUM = A(0)
              LA    R9,0            I = 0
              LA    R10,1
      * FOR I = 1 TO N DO
      LOOP    BXH   R9,R10,NEXT     ADD 1 TO I, COMPARE WITH N
              LA    R7,4(,R7)
      * . SUM = SUM * X + A(I)
              MR    R4,R3
              A     R5,0(,R7)
              B     LOOP
      * ENDFOR
      NEXT    LR    R0,R5
              XRETURN RGS=(R1-R12),SA=*,TR=NO
```

8.12 *Hint:* Change the structure from WHILE to REPEAT-UNTIL.

8.13
```
              SR    R8,R8         SUM = 0
              LA    R9,20         CARDS YET TO BE READ = 20
     * WHILE THERE ARE CARDS YET TO READ (UP TO 20)
     LOOP     LTR   R9,R9
              BNP   OUT
     * . READ A CARD
              XREAD CARDIN,80
              BNZ   OUT
     * . CONVERT A NUMBER
              XDECI R7,CARDIN
     * . IF A NUMBER HAS BEEN CONVERTED
              BO    COUNT
     * . . THEN ADD IT TO THE SUM
              AR    R8,R7
     * . ENDIF
     COUNT    BCTR  R9,0
              B     LOOP
     * ENDWHILE
     OUT      DS    0H
```

8.17
```
     *********************************************************************
     *** SUBROUTINE TO RETURN (IN REG. 0) THE LARGEST OF
     *** AN ARBITRARY (BUT AT LEAST ONE) NUMBER OF PARAMETERS
     *********************************************************************
     LARGEST  CSECT
              XSAVE TR=NO
              L     R2,0(,R1)      ADDR. OF PARAM
              L     R0,0(,R2)      LARGEST PARAM FOUND
     * WHILE THERE ARE MORE PARAMETERS
     LOOP     LTR   R2,R2
              BM    DONE
     * . GET NEXT ADDR.
              LA    R1,4(,R1)
              L     R2,0(,R1)
     * . IF NEXT PARAM IS LARGER
              C     R0,0(,R2)
              BNL   LOOP
     * . . THEN LOAD IT INTO REG. 0
              L     R0,0(,R2)
     * . ENDIF
              B     LOOP
     * ENDWHILE
     DONE     XRETURN RGS=(R1-R12),SA=*,TR=NO
```

CHAPTER 9

9.2 a) Just after the PACK instruction:

```
                CVB     R5,D
        * . IF CARD NUMBER IS IN RANGE -10 TO 9
                C       R5,=F'-10'
                BL      BADNUM
                C       R5,=F'9'
                BH      BADNUM
        * . . THEN MOVE IT INTO WORK AREA
                M       R4,=F'80'
                LA      R5,800(,R5)
                LA      R5,WORK(R5)
                MVC     0(80,R5),CARD
                B       BCTIN
        * . . ELSE PRINT ERROR MESSAGE
        BADNUM  XPRNT   =CL34' FOLLOWING CARD HAS INVALID NUMBER',34
                MVI     CARD-1,C' '
                XPRNT   CARD-1,81
        * . ENDIF
        BCTIN   BCT     R9,RDLOOP
```

b) Also just after the PACK instruction:

```
                CVB     R5,D
                M       R4,=F'80'
                LA      R5,800(,R5)
                LA      R5,WORK(R5)
        * . IF ADDRESS IS WITHIN WORK AREA
                C       R5,=A(WORK)
                BL      BADNUM
                C       R5,=A(WORK+20*80)
                BNL     BADNUM
        * . . THEN MOVE CARD TO WORK AREA
                MVC     0(80,R5),CARD
                B       BCTIN
        * . . ELSE PRINT ERROR MESSAGE
        BADNUM  XPRNT   =CL34' FOLLOWING CARD HAS INVALID NUMBER',34
                MVI     CARD-1,C' '
                XPRNT   CARD-1,81
        * . ENDIF
        BCTIN   BCT     R9,RDLOOP
```

   c) The second has an advantage. In checking the *address* for validity, it checks on the address computation as well as the data. It would have caught our program bug without crashing the program. There is also an advantage to an earlier validity check, but the first segment does not test early enough. If the contents of the last two card columns are not even numeric, neither of these tests prevents the program from blowing up.

CHAPTER 10

10.1 Substitute for IC R4,AB the segment

```
ST    R4,TP
MVC   TP+3(1),AB
L     R4,TP
```

Substitute for STC R6,G the segment

```
ST    R6,TP
MVC   G(1),TP+3
```

10.4 a)   MVCIN RESULT(8),SOURCE+7

     b)
```
                LA    R6,RESULT
                LA    R7,SOURCE+7
                LA    R8,1
                LA    R9,RESULT+7
* DO FOR R6 FROM RESULT TO RESULT+7
* . MOVE ONE CHARACTER
MVCINLP  MVC    0(1,R6),0(R7)
* . INCREASE R6, DECREASE R7
                BCTR  R7,0
                BXLE  R6,R8,MVCINLP
* ENDDO
```

10.5
```
       ******************************************************************
       *** SUBROUTINE TO REPLACE LOWERCASE (EBCDIC) LETTERS WITH UPPERCASE
       ***    EXCEPT AFTER ODD NO. OF QUOTES
       *** INPUT PARAMETERS ARE ADDRESS OF STRING AND LENGTH
       *** THE STRING IS CHANGED IN PLACE
       ******************************************************************
LCTOUPC  CSECT
         XSAVE SA=NO,TR=NO
         LM    R4,R5,0(R1)     ADDR. OF STRING IN R4
         L     R5,0(,R5)       LENGTH IN R5
         MVI   ODDQUOTE,X'0'   SET TO EVEN NO. OF QUOTES
* DO FOR R4 = ADDR. OF FIRST BYTE TO ADDR. OF LAST BYTE
         LA    R6,1
         LA    R7,0(R4,R5)
         SR    R7,R6           R7 = ADDR. OF LAST BYTE IN STRING
* . IF CHAR = QUOTE
LCTLOOP  CLI   0(R4),C''''
         BNE   NOTQ
* . . THEN CHANGE ODDQUOTE
         CLI   ODDQUOTE,X'0'
         BNE   SETEVEN
         MVI   ODDQUOTE,X'1'
         B     NOTLC
SETEVEN  MVI   ODDQUOTE,X'0'
         B     NOTLC
* . . ELSE IF EVEN QUOTES
NOTQ     CLI   ODDQUOTE,X'0'
         BNE   NOTLC
* . . . THEN IF CHAR IS LOWERCASE LETTER
         CLI   0(R4),X'80'
         BNH   NOTLC           BELOW LC RANGE
         CLI   0(R4),X'A9'
         BH    NOTLC           ABOVE LC RANGE
         CLI   0(R4),X'A1'
         BE    NOTLC           X'A1' IS NOT A LETTER
* . . . . THEN ADD X'40' TO CONVERT TO UPPERCASE
         IC    R8,0(,R4)
         LA    R8,X'40'(,R8)
         STC   R8,0(,R4)
* . . . ENDIF (CHAR IS LOWERCASE LETTER)
* . . ENDIF (EVEN QUOTES)
* . ENDIF (CHAR IS QUOTE)
NOTLC    BXLE  R4,R6,LCTLOOP
* ENDFOR (R4 = FIRST BYTE TO LAST)
         XRETURN SA=NO,TR=NO
ODDQUOTE DS    C
```

```
10.8            LA      R4,CON
                LA      R3,0            LENGTH
       * WHILE NEXT CHAR IS NOT A QUOTE (BUT 2 QUOTES DO NOT COUNT)
       LOOP     CLC     0(2,R2),=C''''''
                BE      CONTINUE
                CLC     0(1,R2),=C''''
                BE      DONE
       * . IF TWO AMPERSANDS OR TWO QUOTES
       CONTINUE CLC     0(2,R2),=C'&&&&'
                BE      TWO
                CLC     0(2,R2),=C''''''
                BNE     ONE
       * . . THEN INCREMENT R2 BY AN EXTRA 1
       TWO      LA      R2,1(,R2)
       * . ENDIF
       * . MOVE A CHAR., INCREMENT R2, R3, R4
                MVC     0(1,R4),0(R2)
                LA      R2,1(,R2)
                LA      R3,1(,R3)
                LA      R4,1(,R4)
                B       LOOP
       * ENDWHILE (NEXT NOT A SINGLE QUOTE)
       DONE     DS      0H
```

10.13 If the first division is by 509, the second could overflow.

```
10.14           MVI     ERIND,X'0'
                MVC     SYMBOL(8),=CL8' '
                LA      R4,STMT         SOURCE CHAR.
                LA      R5,SYMBOL       DEST. CHAR. (I = 0)
       * WHILE STMT(I) NOT = SPACE AND I < 8 DO
       FINDSLP  CLI     0(R4),C' '
                BE      FINDS2
                C       R5,=A(SYMBOL+8)
                BNL     FINDS2
       * . MOVE STMT(I) TO SYMBOL(I)
                MVC     0(1,R5),0(R4)
       * . INCREASE I BY 1
                LA      R4,1(,R4)
                LA      R5,1(,R5)
                B       FINDSLP
       * ENDWHILE
       * IF STMT(I) NOT = SPACE
       FINDS2   CLI     0(R4),C' '
                BE      NEXTSTEP
       * . THEN SET ERIND TO 1
                MVI     ERIND,X'1'
       * ENDIF
       NEXTSTEP DS      0H
```

10.17
```
              L      R4,=CL4' '      LOAD BLANKS
              LA     R5,HEAD         INITIALIZE ADDRESSES
              LA     R6,DHEAD
              LA     R8,4            LOOPING CONTROL
              LA     R9,DHEAD+76
     * DO FOR R6 FROM DHEAD TO DHEAD+76, INCR 4
     LP       ICM    R4,B'1010',0(R5) LOAD 2 BYTES
     * . SPREAD AND MOVE TWO CHARS.
     * . INCR. SOURCE ADDR. BY 2
              ST     R4,0(,R6)       STORE BYTES AND BLANKS
              LA     R5,2(,R5)
              BXLE   R6,R8,LP
     * ENDDO
```

10.18   Register 9 should contain the address of the last cell in the table; i.e., sub-
        tract register 6 from register 9 in the initialization. The increment in register
        8 should be initialized to be one cell length larger. This can be accom-
        plished by changing the initialization step SR R5,R6 to AR R5,R6. This kind
        of use of BXLE is not bad if commented well, but if not, it can drive a user
        up the wall.

10.19   CLCL needs two register pairs; we presume registers 0, 1, 10, and 11 are
        available, and for simplicity that the symbol length is in register 1 initially.
        Additional initialization needed are

```
              LA     RØ,SYMBOL
              LR     R11,R1
              ICM    R11,B'1ØØØ',=C' ' PADDING CHARACTER
```

The last is not really necessary because lengths of the two operands are the
same. Then replace the CLC instruction by

```
              LR     R1Ø,R4
              CLCL   RØ,R11
```

CHAPTER 11

11.2   This segment follows immediately the segment shown in Fig. 11.1.

```
              MVI    OVIND,X'0'    0 MEANS NO OVERFLOW
              L      R4,A            OVIND WILL BE CHANGED TO 1 LATER
              X      R4,B            IF OVERFLOW IS DETECTED
     * IF OPERAND SIGNS ARE THE SAME
              LTR    R4,R4
              BM     OUT
     * . THEN IF RESULT HAS DIFFERENT SIGN
              L      R4,A            IF RESULT SIGN IS SAME AS THE
              X      R4,C            OPERAND SIGNS, EX. OR GIVES
              LTR    R4,R4           NONNEG. NUMBER, SHOWING NO OVERFLOW
              BNM    OUT
     * . . THEN SUM HAS OVERFLOWED
              MVI    OVIND,X'1'    SET OVIND TO SHOW OVERFLOW
     * . ENDIF
     OUT      DS     0H
     * ENDIF
```

11.3 If the logical operand a is represented as $a = a_s + 2^{32}a_0$, where a_s is the same bit pattern considered as a signed number, and a_0 is the high-order bit, and similarly, $b = b_s + 2^{32}b_0$, then

$$ab = (a_s + 2^{32}a_0)(b_s + 2^{32}b_0) = a_sb_s + 2^{32}a_0b_s + 2^{32}b_0a_s + 2^{64}a_0b_0.$$

From this we can deduce that to the upper half of the ordinary arithmetic product a_sb_s we must add b if a appears negative and a if b appears negative. If the two numbers are in words at A and B, the logical product is stored at C by the segment

```
        L      R5,A
        M      R4,B
        CLI    A,X'80'
* IF A IS NEGATIVE
        BL     P1
* . THEN ADD B TO RESULT
        AL     R4,B
* ENDIF
P1      CLI    B,X'80'
* IF B IS NEGATIVE
        BL     P2
* . THEN ADD A TO RESULT
        AL     R4,A
* ENDIF
P2      STM    R4,R5,C
```

11.6
```
SLR   R4,R4    CLEAR REG. 4                  ⎫      ⎧ LR    R4,R5
SLDL  R4,7     SHIFT INTO REG. 4             ⎬ or ⎨
OR    R5,R4    BRING AROUND INTO REG. 5      ⎭      ⎩ SRDL  R4,25
```

11.7 The logic of the reversal is shown in the following diagram, assuming that the original word is loaded into register 7. Original contents of other registers are irrelevant.

```
        L      R7,FORWARD
        LA     R8,32
* DO FOR REG8 FROM 32 TO 1, INCR -1
LOOP    SLDL   R6,1
* . MOVE BITS FROM R7 TO R6 TO R4 TO R5
        LR     R4,R6
        SRDL   R4,1
        BCT    R8,LOOP
* ENDDO
        ST     R5,BACKWARD
```

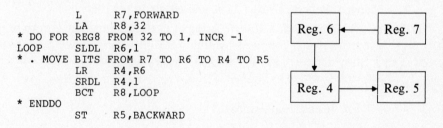

11.9 The following segment is shorter in time and space than that given in the text, but the difference is marginal. In most packing problems left and right shifts are equally efficient.

```
SRDL   R6,15
LR     R6,R5
SRDL   R6,15
LR     R6,R4
SRDL   R6,2
ST     R7,W
```

11.10   Unpacking is quite analogous to packing. To unpack the word at W, for example, returning IND, P, and Q to separate registers 4, 5, and 6, the following segment suffices.

```
L       R4,W
SRDL    R4,15
SRL     R5,17
LR      R6,R5            Q TO REG. 6
SRDL    R4,15            ISOLATE IND IN REG. 4
SRL     R5,17            P IN REG. 5
```

11.12
```
        LA      R6,0
        LA      R8,1
        LA      R9,31
* DO FOR REG. 6 FROM 0 TO 31
LOOP2   LA      R4,B'1111000' 1111000 ARE FIRST 7 BITS OF C'0' OR C'1'
* . GENERATE A CHARACTER, 0 OR 1, FROM A BIT
        SLDL    R4,1             ADD 0 OR 1, TO MAKE C'0' OR C'1'
        STC     R4,CHAR(6)       STORE
        BXLE    R6,R8,LOOP2
* ENDDO
```

11.14
```
        O       R4,MASK1
        N       R4,MASK2
        X       R4,MASK3
        ...
        DS      0F
MASK1   DC      X'00C00000'
MASK2   DC      X'FFCFFFFF'
MASK3   DC      X'0000FC00'
```

11.17   A NOT function changes all bits of the word; LCR   R6,R6 leaves unchanged the lowest-order 1-bit and all 0's below that.

11.21   a)   Assuming that a 20-byte string at BD2Ø contains four groups of 36-bit strings each followed by four zero bits, the following segment will transfer each 36-bit string to the beginning of a double word in an eight-word area BD32.

```
        MVC     BD32(32),=XL32'0'
        MVC     BD32(5),BD20
        MVC     BD32+8(5),BD20+5
        MVC     BD32+16(5),BD20+10
        MVC     BD32+24(5),BD20+15
```

   b)   If the 36-bit strings are packed into an 18-byte area BD18, the job is more complicated. The following segment will do the job, but the MVO (MoVe with Offset) instruction to be introduced in Problem 14.4 could do the job more easily.

```
MVC    BD32(5),BD18
NC     BD32+4(4),=X'F0000000' CLEAR LOW-ORDER 28 BITS
IC     R4,BD18+4
ICM    R5,X'F',BD18+5 BOUNDARY ALIGNMENT IRRELEVANT TO ICM
SLDL   R4,28
STM    R4,R5,BD32+8
MVC    BD32+16(5),BD18+9
NC     BD32+20(4),=X'F0000000'
IC     R4,BD18+13
ICM    R5,X'F',BD18+14
SLDL   R4,28
STM    R4,R5,BD32+24
```

The savings of the extra two bytes per board position do not seem worth the extra trouble.

11.22   The division strategy develops the units digit, then 10s, 100s, etc. Up to 11 digits may be needed; remaining digits must be set to $\emptyset$. The following segment collects digits in registers 2 and 3.

```
* IF NUMBER IS POSITIVE
          LTR    R1,R1
          BL     MINUS
* . THEN SET PACKED SIGN PLUS
          LA     R3,12          + SIGN
          B      ABS
* . ELSE SET PACKED SIGN MINUS
MINUS     LA     R3,13          - SIGN
* ENDIF
ABS       LPR    R1,R1          ABSOLUTE VALUE
          SLDL   R2,60          MOVE SIGN TO TOP OF REG. 2-3 PAIR
          LA     R4,15
* FOR R4 = 15 TO 1, INCR -1, DO
* . DEVELOP A REMAINDER DIGIT
LP        LA     R0,0
          D      R0,=F'10'      REMAINDER IN R0 IS OUR DIGIT
* . PUT DIGIT WITH OTHER DIGITS
          SLL    R0,28          MOVE TO BITS 0-3
          SRDL   R2,4           MAKE ROOM IN REG. 2
          OR     R2,R0          MOVE DIGIT TO TOP OF REG. 2
          BCT    R4,LP          GET 15 DIGITS
* ENDFOR
          STM    R2,R3,DBW
```

11.23   There are several strategies; the following represents one of the shortest.

```
            LA      R2,1
            LA      R3,0
*  REPEAT
SHIFT       SRDL    R2,1
            LR      R4,R3
*  .  SHIFT A BIT RIGHT ACROSS REG. 3
*  .  COMPARE IT WITH MULTJP
*  UNTIL RIGHT-SHIFTED BIT MATCHES ONE IN MULTJP
            N       R4,MULTJP
            BZ      SHIFT
*  ENDREPEAT
            ST      R4,MULTJP
```

CHAPTER 12

12.7   There are two other strategies in common use. One is to follow the last
"real" record with a record containing in some field a value that, by convention, means end of data; such a record is called a *sentinel record*. A second strategy is to require that the records be counted and the count fed to
the program before it starts reading the data. The count could be stored in
the program (if it is constant for all data sets to be used by the program),
kept in a record at the beginning of the data set, or given to the program
separately. Any of these is awkward.

12.8   Register 15 would be changed by execution of the macro instructions, and
from the point of return from the first macro instruction, addressing of
main storage would be completely haywire.

12.13   //YOURDD DD DISP=OLD,UNIT=3350,VOLUME=SER=ZAPHOD,DSN=FOREIGN

CHAPTER 13

13.1

Decimal	Hexadecimal floating point
3.0	41300000
−3.0	C1300000
6.0	41600000
12.0	41C00000
24.0	42180000
4212.0	44107400
−0.75	C0C00000
−0.1875	C0300000
0.1	4019999A
0.3	404CCCCD

13.2

Floating point	Decimal
42360000	54.0
C12F0000	−2.9375
C310A680	−266.40625
3F200000	.0078125
BF240000	−.0087890625
5E000000	0.0

13.4 The hexadecimal system permits, on the average, 1.5 more significant bits to be kept in a floating-point word.

13.7 a) If two normalized, positive floating-point numbers are compared by a C or a CE instruction, the results are the same.

b) If two unequal, normalized, negative floating-point numbers are compared by a C or a CE instruction, the results are opposite: the one that appears larger to a CE instruction appears smaller to the C instruction.

c) If one number is positive and one negative, C and CE give the same results.

d) If two floating-point numbers, at least one of which is unnormalized, are compared by CE and C instructions, the situation is more complicated.

13.8 The guard digit affects a compare instruction only when one number is unnormalized, and after shifting, the numbers agree except for the guard digit.

13.9 Several possible segments for testing approximate equality of two floating-point numbers involve high risk of a significance exception; the following does not.

```
* IF |A-B| > TOL
        LE    F2,A         COMPARE A AND B
        CE    F2,B            FOR AGREEMENT WITHIN TOL
        BE    APPEQ       BRANCH TO APPEQ IF EQUAL
        SE    F2,B
        LPER  F2,F2
        CE    F2,TOL
        BNH   APPEQ         ALSO IF DIFF LESS THAN TOL
* . THEN NOT APPROX. EQUAL
```

13.11 Never.

13.14 Suppose the fraction is stored in short floating-point form at FRAC and the character form, including sign, decimal point, and seven digits, is to be stored at CHAR.

```
              LE     F2,FRAC
              MVC    CHAR(2),=C'+.'
              LTER   F2,F2
        * IF NUMBER IS NEGATIVE
              BNM    P2
        * . THEN STORE '-'
              LPER   F2,F2                IF NEGATIVE,
              MVI    CHAR,C'-'              CHANGE SIGN BUT RECORD IT
        * ENDIF
        P2    AU     F2,UNZRO             UNZRO = X'40000000'
        *** UNNORMALIZE SO BINARY POINT IS JUST BEFORE BIT POSITION 8
              STE    F2,DT                DT IS A DOUBLE WORD
              MVI    DT,0                 CLEAR THE EXPONENT
              L      R5,DT
              M      R4,=F'10000000'
              SLDA   R4,8                 10000000 * NUMBER IN REG. 4
              CVD    R4,DT                CONVERT INTEGER PART
              UNPK   CHAR+2(7),DT(8)
              OI     CHAR+8,X'F0'
```

13.18 a)
```
              LE     F4,A
              LPER   F4,F4                IF NEGATIVE, TAKE ROOT OF ABS VALUE
              AE     F4,=E'1.0'
              ME     F4,=E'0.5'            FIRST APPROX.
        * REPEAT
        LP    LER    F2,F4                SAVE LAST APPROX.
        *** NEW APPROX. Y = X + .5 * (A / X - X)
              LE     F4,A
              DER    F4,F2
              SER    F4,F2
              ME     F4,=E'0.5'
              AER    F4,F2
        * UNTIL NEW APPROX. NOT < PREVIOUS
              CER    F4,F2
              BL     LP
        * ENDREPEAT
        DONE  STE    F2,X
```

b)
```
        LA     R6,0
        L      R7,A
        N      R7,=X'7FFFFFFF' ABS. VALUE OF FLT. PT. NO.
        SLDL   R6,8            EXPONENT INTO REG. 6
        LA     R6,66(,R6)
        SRA    R6,1            DIVIDE (EXP + 64) BY 2, ADD 1
        SRDL   R6,8            ATTACH NEW EXPONENT TO FRACTION
        ST     R7,X            THIS IS FIRST APPROX.
```

Then continue with loop, more or less as previously. In the worst case, the
first approximation is within a factor of 16 of the true square root. Can
you show that? Can you do better?

CHAPTER 14

14.1

Instruction		Result		Condition code
ZAP	FERMAG+1(3),NLQC(2)	FERMAG+1:	ØØ9ØØC	2
AP	GBS(3),NLQC(2)	GBS:	22246C	2
SP	GBS(3),MPHY(4)	GBS:	2137ØC	2
CP	NLQC(2),MPHY(4)			2
SP	NLQC(2),WHP(3)	NLQC:	Ø2ØC	3
AP	NLQC(2),GBS(2)	Data exception: 4 in sign position of second operand		
MP	MPHY(4),NLQC(2)	MPHY:	ØØ216ØØD	—
MP	WHP(3),MPHY+2(2)	Data exception: insufficient number of high-order zeros in first operand		
MP	WHP(3),MPHY+3(1)	WHP:	ØØ48ØC	—
DP	DRGN(5),NLQC(2)	DRGN:	ØØØ36D1ØØD	—
DP	DRGN(5),WHP(3)	DRGN:	27ØCØØ1ØØD	—
DP	DRGN(5),WHP+1(2)	DRGN:	ØØ27ØC1ØØD	—
SRP	DRGN(5),61,5	DRGN:	ØØØØØØØ33D	1
SRP	DRGN(5),61,Ø	DRGN:	ØØØØØØØ32D	1
SRP	DRGN(5),3,5	DRGN:	Ø325ØØØØD	1

14.4 For example, to shift a four-byte packed decimal number at ACCUM one digit to the right, we need a temporary four-byte area TEMP:

```
MVO    TEMP(4),ACCUM(3)
MVN    TEMP+3(1),ACCUM+3
MVC    ACCUM(4),TEMP
```

This segment does not round as it squeezes a digit out. The SRP instruction is easier to use and gives the option of rounding.

The MVO instruction can be useful in the problem (Problem 11.21) of unpacking 18-byte board positions.

```
14.6              ZAP    PROD(5),EXEMPT(2)
                  MP     PROD(5),=P'50.00' $50.00 EACH EXEMPTION
                  ZAP    PROD2(6),GROSS(4)
                  SP     PROD2(6),PROD(5) NET INCOME BASE FOR WITHHOLDING
      * IF GROSS < 50.00 * EXEMP
                  BP     FEDTAX
      * . THEN FED TAX = 0
                  ZAP    FED(4),=P'0'
                  B      FICACOMP
      * . ELSE WITHHOLD 14% OF DIFFERENCE
      FEDTAX      MP     PROD2(6),=P'.14'
                  SRP    PROD2(6),62,0 ROUND DOWN TO CENTS
                  ZAP    FED(4),PROD2+1(5)
      * ENDIF
      FICACOMP    ZAP    PROD2(6),GROSS(4)
                  AP     FICA(4),GROSS(4)
                  ZAP    PROD(4),=P'36000.00'
                  SP     PROD(4),FICA(4)
      * IF TOTAL FICA, INCL. GROSS, > 36000
                  BNM    FICAPCT
      * . THEN REDUCE FICA-TAXABLE BY EXCESS
                  AP     PROD2(6),PROD(4)
                  ZAP    FICA(4),=P'36000.00'
      * ENDIF
      FICAPCT     MP     PROD2(6),=P'.067' FICA TAX = 6.7% OF GROSS
                  SRP    PROD2(6),61,0       OR REMAINDER
                  ZAP    FICATAX(4),PROD2+1(5)
                  ZAP    TAKEHOME(4),GROSS(4)
                  SP     TAKEHOME(4),FEDTAX(4)
                  SP     TAKEHOME(4),FICATAX(4)
                  SP     TAKEHOME(4),DEDUCT(3)
```

14.8   The strategy is to add the counters of individual digits until the sum is more than half the total number of digits 0–9. The segment directly precedes AVLPCTRL, and puts the median in packed form in the 27th byte of the counter area.

```
      *** COMPUTE MEDIAN, STORE IN BYTE 27 OF AREA
                  LR     R5,R9
                  ZAP    DIVD(3),20(2,R9) GENERATE HALF THE TOTAL COUNT
                  DP     DIVD(3),=P'2'        AS A 2-BYTE QUOTIENT AT DIVD
                  ZAP    DBL(2),=P'0'
      * WHILE SUM OF COUNTS < HALF THE TOTAL, DO
      MEDLOOP     CP     DBL(2),DIVD(2)
                  BP     MEDST
      * . ADD COUNT, GO TO NEXT DIGIT
                  AP     DBL(2),0(2,R5)
                  LA     R5,2(,R5)
                  B      MEDLOOP
      * ENDWHILE
      MEDST       SR     R5,R9
                  SRA    R5,1               GENERATE DIGIT
                  BCTR   R5,0
                  CVD    R5,DBL             PUT IN PACKED FORM
                  MVC    26(1,R9),DBL+7
```

When you want the median of a set of numbers that can take on a great many different values, it becomes impractical to count frequencies of each different value. One approach then is to sort the set and find the "middle" number of the sorted set. Can you do better?

CHAPTER 15

15.1
```
TR      SPREAD(16),=C'0123456789ABCDEF'
```

15.2 Besides the solution suggested by the hint with the problem, the following slick solution presented by Tim Hagen takes much less space in tables.

```
        L       R2,Y
        L       R4,=X'0F0F0F0F'
        LR      R3,R2
        SRL     R3,4
        NR      R3,R4
        NR      R4,R2
        STM     R3,R4,WORKB
        TR      WORKB(8),=C'0123456789ABCDEF'
        MVC     WORKA(8),=X'0004010502060307'
        TR      WORKA(8),WORKB RESULT IN WORKA
        ...
WORKA   DS      2F
WORKB   DS      2F
```

15.3
```
        TRT     U(6),TABLE09
        BC      8,ALLDIGIT      COND. CODE = 0 IF ALL DIGITS ZERO
        B       BADDIGIT
TABLE09 DC      240X'01'
        DC      10X'00'
        DC      6X'01'
```

15.5 The essence of the following segment is that a TRT instruction finds the next slash, and from that is computed the length of the current line to be moved by an MVC instruction. Modification of the length in the MVC instruction is accomplished by an EX instruction; another EX is used to modify the length in the TRT instruction. We assume five printable lines of 50 bytes each. Be critical of this segment: it (and others) can be improved.

```
              MVC   LINE(250),=CL250' '
              LA    R4,160          161 CHARACTERS TO SCAN
              LA    R7,LINE
              LA    R5,ADDR         BEGINNING OF CURRENT STRING
     * WHILE THERE IS "/" BEFORE 161ST CHAR DO
     LOOP     EX    R4,ITRT         FIND A SLASH
              LA    R6,1(,R1)       ADDR. OF "/" + 1
              SR    R6,R5           LENGTH OF STRING INCLUDING "/"
              SR    R4,R6           NEW LENGTH FOR TRT
              BNH   OUT             EXIT IF LAST "/" REACHED
     * . IF TOO MANY LINES
              C     R7,=A(LINE+250)
     * . THEN ESCAPE TO ER42
              BNL   ER42            TOO MANY LINES
     * . . ELSE MOVE A LINE
              SH    R6,=H'2'        COMPUTE LENGTH FOR MVC
              EX    R6,IMVC
              LA    R5,1(,R1)
              LA    R7,50(,R7)
     * . ENDIF
              B     LOOP
     * ENDWHILE
     OUT      ...
     ITRT     TRT   0(0,R5),SLTAB
     IMVC     MVC   0(0,R7),0(R5)
     SLTAB    DC    97X'00'
              DC    X'01'           SLASH IS 98TH CHAR.
              DC    158X'00'
     LINE     DS    CL250
     ADDR     DS    CL160
              DC    C'/'
```

15.6

```
     MVC   CHAR(6),=X'4021204B2060'
     ED    CHAR(6),SOURCE
```

Pattern contains

Fill character:	40 (blank)	Decimal point:	4B
Sig. starter:	21	Digit selector:	20
Digit selector:	20	Minus sign:	60

15.7

```
              MVC   FIELD(8),PATT
              ED    FIELD(8),SOURCE SOURCE IS ONE WORD PACKED
              TRT   FIELD(8),BLTEST
     * IF THERE IS A NONBLANK CHAR.
              BZ    ALLZ
     * . THEN PUT $ IN PRECEDING BYTE
              S     R1,=F'1'
              MVI   0(R1),C'$'
     * ENDIF
     ALLZ     ...
              ...
     PATT     DC    XL8'4020202020202020'
     BLTEST   DC    64X'01'
              DC    X'00'
              DC    191X'01'
```

Except for the fill character, the content and length of the pattern are irrelevant and could be whatever is wanted to take care of other aspects of the problem.

CHAPTER 16

16.1 See Appendix VII, Summary of Macro Facility, of the *OS/VS-DOS/VSE-VM/370 Assembler Language* manual, GC33-4010.

16.4 Blanks would be used as the operand value, and a generated instruction

```
        L    R2,
```

would not be acceptable to the assembler.

16.5 Values of ordinary symbols are not yet defined at the time SETA symbols are set and used. The complete macro expansion is done before definition of the first ordinary symbol.

16.9 The parameters of CLOSE are actually subparameters of one parameter. But both a single subparameter and a simple parameter may be accessed by &PARAM(1).

16.12
```
              MACRO
&NAME         BYTASCEN
              LCLA    &N
&NAME         DS      0C
.* REPEAT
.*** DEVELOP 8 IN ONE LINE. WHO WANTS 256 LINES OF THIS?
.P            DC      AL1(&N,&N+1,&N+2,&N+3,&N+4,&N+5,&N+6,&N+7)
&N            SETA    &N+8
.* UNTIL &N >= 256
              AIF     (&N LT 256).P
.* ENDREPEAT
              MEND
```

16.13
```
              MACRO
&LABEL        MVCMAC &DEST,&LEN,&SOURCE
.*** &DEST AND &SOURCE ARE ASSUMED TO BE SYMBOLIC, NOT D(B)
              LCLA    &L
.* WHILE &L+256 <= &LEN
.LP           AIF     (&L+256 GT &LEN).TRAILER
.*** GENERATE A MVC FOR THE NEXT 256 BYTES
              MVC     &DEST+&L.(256),&SOURCE+&L
&L            SETA    &L+256
              AGO     .LP
.* ENDWHILE
.* IF &L < &LEN
.TRAILER AIF     (&L GE &LEN).E
.*** GENERATE ONE MORE MVC FOR ODD REMAINING BYTES
              MVC     &DEST+&L.(&LEN-&L),&SOURCE+&L
.* ENDIF
.E            MEND
```

If we want to allow source and destination addresses to be given in D(B) form, we need two registers, say 2 and 3, so the expansion can first load the addresses into registers, then generate MVC instructions like

```
        MVC     Ø(256,R2),Ø(R3)
        MVC     256(256,R2),256(R3)
```

16.19

```
        MACRO
&LABEL  ARRLOC &ORIG,&LROW,&LCELL,&SROW,&SCOL
.*      &ORIG   ADDR. OF FIRST CELL IN THE ARRAY (A-TYPE)
.*      &LROW   LENGTH OF EACH ROW, AS NO. OF CELLS
.*      &LCELL  LENGTH, IN BYTES, OF EACH ARRAY CELL
.*      &SROW   ROW SUBSCRIPT
.*      &SCOL   COLUMN SUBSCRIPT
.*      LAST 4 PARAMETERS ARE ADDRESSES OF WORDS CONTAINING THE NUMBERS
&LABEL  L       R1,&SROW
        BCTR    R1,0            ROW - 1
        M       R0,&LROW
        A       R1,&SCOL
        BCTR    R1,0
        M       R0,&LCELL
        A       R1,&ORIG
        MEND
```

16.21

```
        LCLA    &POS
        LCLB    &HYPHEN
        LCLC    &R1,&R2


        . . .


.* WHILE THERE ARE STILL CHARS. IN &REG UNTESTED (&POS+1 < K'&REG)
.*         AND HYPHEN NOT YET FOUND (&HYPHEN IS FALSE)
.LOOP   AIF     ((&POS+1 GE K'&REG) OR &HYPHEN).N
&POS    SETA    &POS+1
.* . IF NEXT CHARACTER IS A HYPHEN
        AIF     ('&REG'(&POS,1) NE '-').LOOP
.* . . THEN SET &HYPHEN TO TRUE
&HYPHEN SETB    (1)
.* . ENDIF
        AGO     .LOOP
.* ENDWHILE
.* IF THERE IS NO HYPHEN
.N      AIF     (&HYPHEN).ELSE
.* . THEN GENERATE LM FOR ONE REGISTER
&R1     SETC    '&REG'(2,K'&REG-2)
        LM      &R1,&R1,&AREA
        AGO     .NN
.* . ELSE GENERATE LM FOR RANGE OF REGISTERS
.ELSE   ANOP
&R1     SETC    '&REG'(2,&POS-2)
&R2     SETC    '&REG'(&POS+1,K'&REG-&POS-1)
        LM      &R1,&R2,&AREA
.* ENDIF
.NN     ANOP
```

CHAPTER 17

17.2 For example,
```
BALR   R3,Ø
N      R3,MPM     MPM=X'F5ØØØØØØ'
SPM    R3
```

set bits 36 and 38 of the PSW to 0's, thus preventing interrupt on fixed-point overflow and exponent underflow. Other mask bits are not affected.

17.3 The only way to store an entire program status word is to cause an interrupt. Suppose we decide the SVC 133 is to mean change bit 13 of the program status word to 1. The SVC interrupt-handling routine must include something like

```
         ORG    96
         CLI    39,133
         BE     P12T1
         ...
P12T1    OI     33,X'Ø4'
         LPSW   32
```

Note that if P12T1 is within the first 4096 main-storage locations, this requires *no* register contents; therefore none need be saved and restored. Of course, we users are not at liberty to write and insert code like this into the computer. However, we can define our own interrupt-handling routines; conventions are described in *OS/VS Supervisor Services and Macro-Instructions*, GC27-6979.

17.7 Suppose a CCW is in main storage, its address is in register 4, and it has already been determined that the command calls for data transfer and that the indirect data addressing flag is off. We will construct a new CCW at location NCCW, and if an indirect data addressing chain is necessary, it can start at location ADCHAIN.

```
              MVC    NCCW(8),0(R4)
              L      R5,NCCW           VIRTUAL STARTING ADDR.
              LRA    R6,0(,R5)
              STCM   R6,X'7',NCCW+1 STORE REAL ADDR.
              LA     R7,0
              ICM    R7,X'3',NCCW+6 BYTE COUNT
              LA     R8,0(,R5)
              AR     R8,R7             ENDING VIRTUAL ADDRESS
              N      R5,=X'00FFF800'
              LA     R5,2048(,R5)   STARTING ADDR. NEXT PAGE
       * IF BEGINNING OF NEXT PAGE > ENDING VIRTUAL ADDR,
              CR     R5,R8
              BNL    FIN
       * . THEN BUILD IDA CHAIN
       *** INITIALIZE CHAIN
              OI     NCCW+4,B'00000100' IDA FLAG ON
              MVC    ADCHAIN+1(3),NCCW+1 REAL ADDR. TO CHAIN
              MVC    NCCW+1(3),=AL3(ADCHAIN)
              LA     R9,ADCHAIN+4
       * . . REPEAT
       LPAD   LRA    R6,0(,R5)
              ST     R6,0(,R9)         STORE REAL ADDR. IN CHAIN
              LA     R9,4(,R9)         NEXT CHAIN ADDR.
              LA     R5,2048(,R5)   VIRTUAL ADDR. NEXT PAGE
       * . . UNTIL STARTING ADDR. NEXT PAGE > ENDING ADDR. OF I/O
              CR     R5,R8
              BL     LPAD
       * . . ENDREPEAT
       * ENDIF
       FIN    DS     0H
```

17.8
```
              LA     R9,0              ASSUME MAIN STORAGE
       BRR    RRB    0(R9)               SIZE OF 786432 BYTES
              LA     R9,2048(,R9)
              C      R9,=F'786432'
              BL     BRR
```

In practice, one would reset reference bits on a smaller subset of main storage, as some portions are not available for swapping pages.

17.9
```
       STCTL  C1,C1,B
       LA     R4,0
       IC     R4,B
       LA     R4,2(,R4)
       STC    R4,B
       LCTL   C1,C1,B
```